Language Assessment in Practice

Published in this series

BACHMAN: Fundamental Considerations in Language Testing
BACHMAN and PALMER: Language Testing in Practice
BRUMFIT: Individual Freedom and Language Teaching
BRUMFIT and CARTER (eds.): Literature and Language Teaching
CANAGARAJAH: Resisting Linguistic Imperialism in Language Teaching
COHEN and MACARO (eds.): Language Learner Strategies
COOK: Discourse and Literature
COOK: Language Play, Language Learning
COOK: Translation in Language Teaching
COOK and SEIDLHOFER (eds.): Principle and Practice in Applied Linguistics
DÖRNYEI: Research Methods in Applied Linguistics
DÖRNYEI: Psychology of Second Language Acquisition
ELLIS: SLA Research and Language Teaching
ELLIS: Task-based Language Learning and Teaching
ELLIS: The Study of Second Language Acquisition
ELLIS: Understanding Second Language Acquisition
ELLIS and BARKHUIZEN: Analysing Learner Language
FOTOS and NASSAJI (eds.): Form-focused Instruction and Teacher Education
HOLLIDAY: The Struggle to Teach English as an International Language
HOWATT: A History of English Language Teaching
JENKINS: English as a Lingua Franca
JENKINS: The Phonology of English as an International Language
KERN: Literacy and Language Teaching
KRAMSCH: Context and Culture in Language Teaching
KRAMSCH: The Multilingual Subject
LANTOLF (ed.): Sociocultural Theory and Second Language Learning
LANTOLF and THORNE: Sociocultural Theory and the Genesis of Second Language Development
LARSEN-FREEMAN and CAMERON: Complex Systems and Applied Linguistics
MACKEY (ed.): Conversational Interaction in SLA
MEINHOF: Language Learning in the Age of Satellite Television
NATTINGER and DECARRICO: Lexical Phrases and Language Teaching
PHILLIPSON: Linguistic Imperialism
SEIDLHOFER (ed.): Controversies in Applied Linguistics
SELIGER and SHOHAMY: Second Language Research Methods
SKEHAN: A Cognitive Approach to Language Learning
STERN: Fundamental Concepts of Language Teaching
STERN (eds. P. Allen and B. Harley): Issues and Options in Language Teaching
TARONE and YULE: Focus on the Language Learner
WIDDOWSON: Aspects of Language Teaching
WIDDOWSON: Defining Issues in English Language Teaching
WIDDOWSON: Practical Stylistics
WIDDOWSON: Teaching Language as Communication
WRAY: Formulaic Language

Language Assessment in Practice

Developing Language Assessments and Justifying their Use in the Real World

LYLE BACHMAN AND ADRIAN PALMER

UNIVERSITY PRESS

OXFORD
UNIVERSITY PRESS

Great Clarendon Street, Oxford OX2 6DP

Oxford University Press is a department of the University of Oxford.
It furthers the University's objective of excellence in research, scholarship, and education by publishing worldwide in

Oxford New York

Auckland Cape Town Dar es Salaam Hong Kong Karachi
Kuala Lumpur Madrid Melbourne Mexico City Nairobi
New Delhi Shanghai Taipei Toronto

With offices in

Argentina Austria Brazil Chile Czech Republic France Greece
Guatemala Hungary Italy Japan Poland Portugal Singapore
South Korea Switzerland Thailand Turkey Ukraine Vietnam

First published 2010

2019 2018 2017 2016 2015

10 9 8 7 6

ISBN: 978 0 19 442293 2

Printed in China

This book is printed on paper from certified and well-managed sources.

Contents

Acknowledgments

When we started work on *Language Assessment in Practice*, we thought of it as a revision of *Language Testing in Practice*, a general overhauling and updating by adding Lyle's work on the Assessment Use Argument to the existing frameworks. After struggling with this for a while, we realized that attempting to marry the old and the new in this way was leading to a book that looked more like a conglomeration than a unified work. So we decided to start with Lyle's Assessment Use Argument as the central organizing framework and see where that took us.

The process went through 90 versions of the Assessment Use Argument before it took on its final form, with each modification affecting and affected by the ever-changing shapes of other chapters in the book. Happily, it seemed to us that the more we worked with this process, the better the marriage between justification and the other frameworks in the book seemed to be. We hope you, the reader, feel the same.

Colleagues and their students

Helping us through the evolution of this book were many of our colleagues who have taken their students through the long progression of changes in the manuscript, struggling to make the ideas accessible. We thank them for their endurance, patience, and helpful feedback.

Nathan Carr: California State University, Fullerton, and his students
Carol Chapelle: Applied Linguistics Program, Department of English, Iowa State University
Fred Davidson: Division of English as an International Language (now Department of Linguistics), University of Illinois, Champaign-Urbana
Dan Douglas: Applied Linguistics Program, Department of English, Iowa State University
Antony Kunnan: Applied and Advanced Studies in Education, California State University, Los Angeles
Lorena Llosa: Department of Teaching and Learning at New York University's Steinhardt School of Education and her students
Jim Purpura: Applied Linguistics Program, Teachers College, Columbia University
Carolyn Turner: Integrated Studies in Education, McGill University, and especially Alison Crump, who put the students' comments together

Our own students

Among our many students over the years, we would particularly like to thank Lyle's students, Mikyung Kim, Yasuyo Sawaki, Sangkuen Shin, Sunyoung Shin, Youngsoon So, Viphavee Vongpumivitch, and Xiaming Xi from UCLA LA, and J. Lake, in the Graduate Program, Temple University, Japan. We'd also to thank in particular Adrian/Buzz's students, Jennifer Van Dyke and Vanessa Francis, for their extensive comments on a number of the chapters and for keeping the whole process entertaining. We need to give very special thanks to Gary Ockey. Gary has been through two books with us, an M.A. with Buzz, and a Ph.D. with Lyle, and still has the fortitude to give us proactive critical comments and to push us to make the vague clear, the abstruse transparent, and to discard the half-baked. Gary, we thank you.

So we are forever grateful to our students over these many years. Nothing helped us quite as much as trying to explain something to them. Their understanding—or lack thereof—and the resulting questions they posed were invaluable in helping us evaluate what we were doing and to fix what was needed.

Colleagues who gave us feedback

We'd like to acknowledge the many insightful and proactive criticisms and comments we've received from Bob Mislevy and Mike Kane. Their work has greatly influenced our thinking, and we believe that what we have arrived at here builds upon the solid foundation of their work.

We'd like to thank the following colleagues who read and commented on various chapters and versions of the book: Yutaka Kitamura, Institute of Foreign Language Education & Research, Kansai University, Penny McKay, School of Language and Literacy Education, Queensland University of Technology, and Andrea Sholl, who was a graduate student at the University of Washington when she sent us her comments.

Conference and workshop participants

We've presented many versions of the AUA and other frameworks in the book to participants in a wide variety of conferences, consultations, workshops, and short courses on language assessment around the world. The comments and questions from these participants have been very useful in helping us view our ideas from the perspective of their "real worlds," and in refining the ways in which we were communicating these.

Reviewers of the final manuscript

Carol Chapelle and Dan Douglas reviewed and provided us with extensive, honest, and proactively critical comments and suggestions on the final manuscript. Theirs was *exactly* the kind of feedback we wanted, and we thank them for the enormous amount of work they put into providing it.

Editors

First, we'd like to thank Cristina Whitecross, our editor at the beginning of this long journey. Cristina took what was a vague notion in our minds and nudged us along to turn it into a clear concept for a new book. We'd also like to thank Lynda Taylor for her careful and helpful content editing of the final draft. It was wonderful to have a person with professional knowledge of language assessment to work with at this stage of the editing. Finally, we'd like to thank Ann Hunter for her careful reading and editing as the book entered the final stage of production.

The women in our lives

I (Buzz) would like to give my *very* special thanks to my wife, MaryAnn Christison, who patiently sat through literally hundreds of presentations on various aspects of the book, co-presented workshops with me, and listened to my daily updates. She always let us know (very gently, of course) whether or not they made any sense at all and provided many concrete examples that helped bring both of us down to earth. I (Lyle) would like to thank Barbara Damböck, for bringing so much happiness to my life during the final writing stages, when I really needed her support to make it through. Her always-proactive insights and criticisms from a different, German, perspective on language teacher training, have also kept us in touch with that "real world".

Ourselves

Finally, these acknowledgements would not be complete if we didn't acknowledge each other. We've been the best of friends for nearly 40 years. Reflecting back on the richness of our experiences, we can honestly say that our friendship has been among the most rewarding and entertaining aspects of our lives. Bringing *Language Assessment in Practice* to life, with all the fun we've had along the way, has truly been the best of times.

Lyle and Buzz

The authors and publisher are grateful to those who have given permission to reproduce the following extracts and adaptations of copyright material:

p.27 Figure from *How can we link teaching with assessment when teaching English to young learners?* by Annie Hughes presented at the 'Learning and Assessment at Primary Schools' Conference, Cambridge, 2009. Reproduced by permission of Annie Hughes

p.53 Figure from Palmer, A. S., P. J. M. Groot, and G. A. Trosper (eds.). 1981. 'The construct validation of tests of communicative competence.' Washington, DC: TESOL. Reproduced by permission of Copyright Clearance Center

p.80 Table from Bachman, L. F. 1990. *Fundamental Considerations in Language Testing*. Oxford: Oxford University Press. Reproduced by permission of Oxford University Press

p.347 Figure from Christison, M. A. and A. Palmer. 2005. *Teaching Assistant's Handbook*. Salt Lake City: University of Utah. Reproduced by permission of University of Utah and M. A. Christison and A. Palmer

p.358 Breiner-Sanders, K. E., P. J. Lowe, J. Miles, and E. Swender (rev. 1999). The ACTFL Proficiency Guidelines—Speaking, from 2000 *Foreign Language Annals*, 33. Reproduced by permission of ACTFL

p.359 Figure from Weigle, S. C. 2002. *Assessing Writing*. Cambridge: Cambridge University Press. Reproduced by permission of Cambridge University Press

p.361 Figure from Weigle, S. C. 2002. *Assessing Writing*. Cambridge: Cambridge University Press. Reproduced by permission of Cambridge University Press

p.448 Extract from Coombe, C. A., and N. J. Hubley (eds.). 2003. 'Teachers of English to Speakers of Other Languages.' Alexandria, VA: TESOL. Reproduced by permission of Copyright Clearance Center

1

Objectives and expectations, or why we need another book about language testing

PEOPLE WHO DEVELOP AND USE LANGUAGE ASSESSMENTS

People use language assessments in the real world to collect information for making decisions, and these decisions have consequences, sometimes serious, for the individuals, programs, institutions, organizations, or societies that will be affected by the use of the assessment and the decisions made. The real world settings in which people develop and use language assessments are full of uncertainties and constraints, and these people vary greatly in their understanding of and experience in language assessment. Over the years we've worked with a wide range of people—language teachers who want to be able to use assessments as part of their classroom teaching, applied linguists interested in developing assessments for use as research instruments, people who are involved in large-scale language testing programs, and graduate students in fields such as applied linguistics, English as a second/foreign language, bilingual education, and foreign language education. Many who need to use a language assessment have had no training or experience in this. All around the world we have met individuals who may be required to use a particular language assessment, but feel that this is not very well suited to their situation. However, they lack the knowledge about language assessment that would enable them to articulate their concerns more clearly and convincingly. We also regularly work with people—language teachers, applied linguists, program administrators—who would like to develop and use a language assessment for their own particular situation, but have had no training or experience in this, and thus feel reluctant to embark on this activity. In all of these situations many of the people we meet feel that "language testing" is a highly specialized and technical discipline that is beyond their capability to master.

There are also people who are just beginning to develop and use language assessments who have had extensive education and training in the technical aspects of language assessment, but little practical experience in developing and using language assessments. These people often become frustrated with the uncertainties, changeability, and limitations of the real world settings in which they work, partly because their training has not included a means for relating their technical expertise to real world conditions, or for communicating the technical requirements of assessment with test users and other stakeholders.

Finally, there are people with extensive practical experience, but little education or training in the technical aspects of language assessment, who have been developing and using language assessments for years. Some of these people might not know or be able to determine what the consequences of using these assessments are for those who are affected. Some of these people may feel that simply asserting that their assessment "works" is sufficient to keep test users and other stakeholders satisfied.

We believe that despite the differences among people who use language assessments, what they all have in common is the need to be accountable for the uses for which their assessments are intended. In other words, they need to be able to demonstrate to stakeholders that the intended uses of their assessment are justified. This is particularly critical in situations where high-stakes decisions will be made at least in part on the basis of a language assessment. This professional responsibility needs to be exercised irrespective of the level of education, training, and experience in language testing of the language test developer and user.

Our aim in this book is to enable the reader to become competent in the development and use of language assessments. We believe that "being competent in language assessment" means being able demonstrate to stakeholders that the intended uses of their assessments are justified. Therefore, all of the various components of this book are tied in to a structure for justifying assessment use.

REAL WORLD CONDITIONS AND LIMITATIONS

Even when test developers follow the "best practice" in the field, as described in many textbooks on language testing, including the processes of assessment development and justification that we advocate in this book, the process itself does not always go as expected, and the assessments that are developed do not always turn out as intended. This is because language assessment development takes place in a real world that is often unpredictable and in which conditions and individuals who are involved in or affected by the assessment change over time. The setting in which assessment development takes place includes many uncertainties and conflicts, and is constantly changing. Test users or decision makers may change their minds, while new decision makers may have different values and priorities. Furthermore, the resources—people, materials, equipment, space, time—that are available for assessment development can change dramatically from the beginning of assessment development to the time the assessment is ready for operational use. Because of the uncertainties in the real world and the constant limitations on resources, even the most conscientious, well-intentioned, and competent test developer can sometimes feel overwhelmed. This is why we believe that an understanding of these real world conditions and limitations is just as important to your success as a language tester as is your understanding of the "best practice" in language testing. These real world conditions and limitations are discussed at length in Chapter 13.

SOME COMMON MISCONCEPTIONS AND UNREALISTIC EXPECTATIONS ABOUT LANGUAGE ASSESSMENT

We've found that many people who need to use language assessments in the real world have misconceptions and unrealistic expectations about what language assessments can do and what they should be like. These often prevent people from becoming competent in language assessment. Furthermore, there is often a belief that "language testers" have some almost magical procedures and formulae for creating the "best" test. These misconceptions and unrealistic expectations, and the mystique associated with language testing, constitute strong affective barriers to many people who want and need to be able to use language assessments in their professional work. Breaking down this affective barrier by dispelling and clarifying misconceptions, helping readers develop a sense of what can reasonably be expected of language assessments, and demystifying language testing is thus an important goal of this book.

An illustrative example

Perhaps the best way to illustrate these misconceptions and unrealistic expectations is with an example from our own experience with language testing. We first started working together in language testing nearly forty years ago, when we were in situations in which we needed to develop language tests for a particular use. We were both involved in developing tests for use in placing students into an appropriate level or group in English as a foreign language (EFL) courses in tertiary-level institutions in a country where, at that time, English was not the medium of instruction for education, and was not widely used in the society at large.

One of us was working in an English department at a major university in which all students were required to satisfy a foreign language requirement, and most students did so with English. English was taught non-intensively for three hours per week. It was taught primarily to prepare students to develop an ability to read material in English that would help them further their educational goals. The teachers consisted of both native and second language (L2) speakers of English who had extensive training in teaching EFL. The program was well funded and had the resources to hire a testing specialist to help them with assessment development.

The other was working at a national language center, where junior university faculty members were being trained in English, in preparation for studying for advanced degrees at institutions in countries where English was the medium of education. The English program was an intensive one, with students attending classes for eight hours per day, five days per week, for ten weeks. It was also partly English for specific purposes, with the classes in reading and writing focusing on differing disciplines, such as agriculture, economics, and education. The teachers were all native English speakers who had had extensive training, and were using what was considered to be the current "best" methodology. The center was well funded by an international educational foundation, so all kinds of learning materials—books, magazines, audio tapes—were readily available for the students to use.

We had come to the task with different backgrounds—one in theoretical linguistics and the other in English language and literature. One of us had had six years' practical experience working in a large-scale testing center at a university under the mentorship of one of the top language testers in the field at the time, while the other had had a brief encounter with assessment while helping to develop an achievement test for a large lecture course at a university. Neither of us, however, had had any formal training in either language testing or psychometrics. We had both had practical experience in teaching English as a second/foreign language, and considerable understanding of what was then known, in terms of theory and research, of second/foreign language learning and teaching. In addition, we shared a common concern: to develop the "best" test for our situations. We believed that there was a model language test and a set of straightforward procedures—a recipe, if you will—that we could follow to create a test that would be the best one for our intended uses and situations.

What we did, essentially, was to model our tests on the large-scale EFL tests that were widely used at that time, which included sections testing English grammar, vocabulary, reading, and listening comprehension. Following this model, we employed test development procedures that had been developed for psychological and educational tests to produce, rather mechanically, tests that both we and our colleagues believed were "state-of-the-art" EFL tests, and hence the "best" for our needs. We had started with the "best" models and had used sophisticated statistical techniques in test development, so that our tests were definitely state-of-the-art at that time, but now, in retrospect, we wonder whether they were the best for those situations. Indeed, we wonder if there is a single "best" test for any language testing situation.

In developing those tests, we believed that if we followed the model of a test that was widely recognized and used, it would automatically be useful for our own particular needs. These tests had been developed by the "experts" in the field, who were assumed to know more than we did. There were, however, several questions we did not ask. Were our situations similar enough to the ones for which these large-scale tests were developed to make them appropriate? Were our test takers like the ones who took those large-scale tests, and would the results of our tests be used to make the same kinds of decisions? We did not even ask whether the abilities tested in those tests were the ones we needed to test. Nor did we have any comprehensive, systematic way to think about the nature of language use.

Given what was known (and not known) about the nature of language use, of language learning, and of language testing at that time, these were questions that simply never occurred to us. Language ability was viewed as a set of finite components—grammar, vocabulary, pronunciation, spelling—that were realized as four skills—listening, speaking, reading, and writing. If we taught or tested these, we were teaching or testing everything that was needed. Language learners were viewed as organisms who all learned language by essentially the same processes—stimulus and response—as described by behaviorist psychology. Finally, it was assumed that the processes involved in language learning were more or less the same for all learners, for all situations, and for all uses. It is not surprising, then, that we believed that a single model would provide the best test for our particular test takers, for our particular uses, and for the areas of language ability that were of interest in our particular situation.

As it turned out, the two groups of test takers for whom we developed essentially the same kind of language test were quite different. The university group consisted of first-year students entering a university in which very little of their academic course work would involve the use of English. Most of them would be required to take at least one English course as part of their degree requirements. Though all of the students had had some exposure to English in their secondary school education, most had very little control of the language, and almost none of them had had any exposure to English outside of the EFL classroom. Few had ever spoken English with a native speaker or had had the opportunity to use English for any non-instructional purpose.

The other group consisted of university teachers from many different universities, and representing a wide range of academic disciplines, who had been selected as recipients of scholarships to continue work on advanced degrees in countries where English was the medium of instruction. They were much more highly specialized in their knowledge of their disciplines than were the first-year university students, were considerably older, on average, and were more experienced. They were also highly motivated to improve their English.

The programs into which these test takers would be placed by means of the tests were also quite different. The program into which the university students would be placed consisted of four levels of non-intensive (three hours per week) English instruction during their first and second years of university work. The program focused primarily on enabling the students to read academic reference works written in English. Students were placed in courses at one of the four levels by general ability level and not according to their area of academic specialization. Most of the English classes were taught by teachers who had learned English as a foreign language, and much of the classroom instruction was carried out in the students' native language.

The university teachers, on the other hand, would be placed into a ten-week intensive (forty hours per week) course at a national English language institute where they would be required to speak nothing but English between the hours of about eight and five every working day. They would take classes in all four skills, but would be divided into groups according to broad classifications of their academic disciplines, such as agriculture, engineering and sciences, medical sciences, and economics. Unlike the university English program, the teachers in this program were all native speakers of English, and all classroom instruction was carried out in English. This program was thus much more intensive than that of the university students: the curriculum was focused on English for specific purposes and involved a great deal more actual use of English.

Three common misconceptions

This example illustrates the most common misconception that we find among those who ask for advice about their specific testing needs. Many people believe, as we did, that there is an ideal of what a "good" language test is, and they want to know how to create tests on this ideal model for their own testing needs. Our answer is that there is no such thing as the one "best" test, even for a specific situation, and that the terms "good" and "bad" are not very useful for describing a language test. In any situation, there will be a number of alternatives, each with advantages and disadvantages. To understand why this is so, we must consider some of the problems that result from this misconception. If we assume that a single "best" test exists, and we attempt either to use this test itself, or to use it as a model for developing a test of our own, we are likely to end up with a test that will be inappropriate for at least some of our test takers. In the example above, the test we developed might have been appropriate for the university students, in terms of the areas of language ability measured (grammar, vocabulary, and reading comprehension) and topical content, since this was quite general and not specific to any particular discipline. However, the test was probably not particularly appropriate for the university teachers, since it did not include material related to the teachers' different disciplines or to the areas of English for Specific Purposes that were covered in the intensive course. This test was also of limited appropriateness for this group because it did not include an assessment of students' ability to perform listening and speaking tasks, which was heavily emphasized in the intensive program.

Because of these limitations, the test for the teachers did not meet all of the needs of the test users (the Director of and teachers in the intensive program). Specifically, teachers in the intensive course reported that students who were placed into levels on the basis of the test were quite homogeneous in terms of their reading, but that there were considerable differences among students within a given level in terms of their listening and speaking. These differences made it quite difficult for teachers to find and use listening and speaking activities that were appropriate for a given group. Teachers felt that the test should be able to accurately predict students' placement into the listening and speaking classes, as well as into the reading classes, and they urged the test developer to remedy this situation.

In an attempt to address this problem, a dictation task was added to the test. In this task, the test takers listened to a passage presented using a tape recorder, and were required to write down exactly what they heard. This particular task was added largely because it had been used previously, and was considered to be a "good" way to test listening. At the same time, the director of the intensive program agreed to group students homogeneously into listening and speaking groups on the basis of their scores on the dictation. This seemed to work well as a program modification, and teachers felt that it facilitated both their teaching and their students' learning.

It is not clear whether it was the dictation test or the program change that solved the problem with those classes. What is clear, however, is that adding a dictation task created another problem. Most of the listening tasks in the intensive course were interactive, conversational tasks, in which responses were generally oral, and quite different from the dictation test task, which involved no interaction and required only written responses. Thus, although the addition of the dictation did, perhaps, provide some general information about the students' ability to listen and understand spoken language, the test task itself was quite different from the kinds of listening tasks with which the students would be engaged in the intensive course, and both the test takers and the test users frequently complained about this. The final result was frustration on the part both of the teachers, whose expectations of the test tasks in terms of their use for placement and their match to the teaching activities were not met, and of the test developer, who felt he had done everything to make this the best test possible.

(Note: A number of approaches (e.g., s/he, he/she) can be used to deal with the fact that modern English no longer has non-gender specific forms in its singular personal pronouns. The approach we will use in this book is to alternate "he" and "she", more or less at random, but maintaining a given gender or combination of genders throughout a particular section or example.)

Table 1.1 on p. 8 summarizes some of the misconceptions and resulting problems that we have found to be very common among individuals who want to be able to use language tests in the real world but feel that they do not have the knowledge or competence to do so. The table also presents what we believe are some useful alternatives to these misconceptions.

Misconceptions	Resulting problems	Alternatives to misconception
1 Believing that there is one "best" way to test language ability for any given situation, and thus having unreasonable expectations about what language tests can do and what they should be.	(a) Continued use of a "favorite" test, even though it is inappropriate for the test takers or may not meet the specific needs of the test users. (b) Uninformed use of tests or testing methods simply because they have become popular. (c) Becoming frustrated when one is unable to find or develop the perfect test. (d) Being placed in a situation of trying to defend the indefensible, since many students, as well as administrators, may have unreasonable expectations about the infallibility of assessments and how they are used.	1 There is no perfect test for all situations. In any situation there are only alternatives, each with strengths and weaknesses.
2 Believing that language test development depends on highly technical procedures and should be left to experts.	(e) Loss of confidence in one's own capacity for developing and using tests appropriately, as well as a feeling that language testing is something that only "experts" can understand and do. (f) Test development is left to "experts" unfamiliar with the situation in which the test will be used.	2a Tests need to be developed by people who are competent in language testing and who are most familiar with the situation in which the test will be used. 2b Practitioners can become competent in language testing; they can learn procedures for developing and using language tests.
3 Believing that a test is either "good" or "bad," depending on whether it satisfies one particular quality.	(g) Focusing on a single quality of the test, and trying to maximize this, so that the test gets out of balance.	3 A "justifiable" test is one that has a clearly articulated Assessment Use Argument (AUA) and that is supported by backing. The AUA specifies a number of qualities, so to develop language assessments whose use we can justify, we must provide justification for multiple qualities.

Table 1.1 Some misconceptions, resulting problems, and alternatives to misconceptions

Misconception 1

Believing that there is a single best test for any particular situation, no matter how narrowly specified, can lead to testing practice that is indefensible and to frustration and loss of confidence on the part of the test developer. First, this misconception may lead people who need to use language tests either to stay with their favorite, safe "tried and true" tests, or to blindly use testing methods simply because they are widely used or are popular. In either case, the tests that get used may not be appropriate for the test takers, or they may not meet the needs of the test user. This is illustrated in the example above, where we unquestioningly modeled our tests on the kinds of tests that had been developed for large-scale EFL assessments, which were intended for very different uses and for very different populations of test takers from ours. Second, unrealistically expecting to be able to find or develop a perfect test for any situation will inevitably lead to frustration on the part of the test developer, as she discovers that whatever test she develops or uses will have some strengths and some weaknesses.

Misconception 2

The practice of using the same test year in and year out, simply because "it works," or of mimicking whatever test method is currently in widespread use, provides no basis for justifying test use if and when the developer is held accountable by stakeholders, including students, teachers, and administrators. When the test developer is placed in a situation of having to justify the indefensible, he is likely to lose confidence, as he realizes the shortcomings and inadequacies of the test he continues to use or has developed. Ultimately, the test developer may arrive at what he believes to be the answer to his problem: abandon any attempts to develop a test, and hope that a "language tester" can be found who will be able to develop the perfect test. This misconception, that language test design and development are too technical, and should be left to the experts, doesn't really address the problem of unjustifiable testing practice, since it merely places test development on hold. This misconception often leads to the practice of bringing in an outside "expert," who is likely to be unfamiliar with the situation, and expecting this person to develop a new test on her own, with little or no input from the test users. For example, it is very common for a language program or a publisher to develop a new set of course materials or textbook without giving any consideration to assessment. Then, after the course or textbook development team has been disbanded, the course director or publisher may realize that it would be useful to have some assessments that teachers can use for making decisions about achievement and progress. At that point, they typically ask a "language tester" to write, essentially from scratch, a set of classroom quizzes or achievement tests based on the content of the course materials or textbook.

Misconception 3

The third misconception, believing that a test is either good or bad, depending on whether it satisfies a single quality, can lead test developers to focus on a single quality of the test, and put all their efforts into maximizing this. In the previous example, the person who writes the quizzes and tests based on the course materials or textbook is most likely to focus on the match between the content of the materials and that of the tests. While content relevance is certainly an important consideration in this case, an equally important consideration is how test takers actually perform on the tests. If, for example, students studying in a course with the new materials or textbook actually perform very poorly on the tests, it wouldn't be clear whether this poor performance reflected inadequate learning, possibly due to ineffective teaching and materials, or whether the tests were simply too difficult for this particular group of students. In another situation, a classroom teacher might look at the technical qualities of many large-scale assessments and conclude that in order to be "good" his classroom quiz must be highly reliable. In order to achieve this, he may believe that he must use the same kinds of test tasks that are used in large-scale assessments, ignoring the fact that these tasks might be entirely unrelated to the kinds of teaching and learning tasks he uses with his students. In both of these examples, by focusing on a single quality, whether this be content relevance or reliability, the test developer ends up with a test that is out of balance, since it ignores other important qualities. In the first example, by ignoring how students perform on the test, the test developer risks not being able to justify her interpretations about students' learning and achievement in the course. In the second example, the test developer risks his students' perceiving the test tasks as not related in any way to their classroom language use.

Alternatives to misconceptions

The alternatives to the three misconceptions presented in Table 1.1 provide the rationale for the approach to language testing that we present in this book.

Alternative 1

The first alternative is to realize that looking for perfection in a language test is unrealistic. Rather what we should focus on is developing an assessment whose intended uses we can justify to stakeholders. For example, we could explain to stakeholders that students will know how well they performed and adjust study habits accordingly, and teachers will know how well students performed and adjust teaching accordingly.

Alternative 2a

Another alternative reflects our belief that the people who are closest to and most familiar with the assessment situation need to be directly involved in the assessment development process. These are the test stakeholders, the individuals who will be most directly affected by the way the test is used and by the consequences of using the test to make decisions. Equally important is our belief that people who design and develop the test need to be competent in language testing. Thus, in many cases, test development is a team effort, bringing together individuals with complementary skills, experience, and knowledge, such as content specialists, teachers, and specialists in language testing. However, there are many situations, such as the development of classroom language assessments, where individuals with expertise in language testing may not be available. In situations such as these, it is essential for the classroom teachers themselves to be competent in language testing.

Alternative 2b

Another alternative reflects our belief that practitioners can become competent in language testing. Ideally, language teachers and other applied linguists who need to use language tests will have access to formal training in language testing, either through courses or workshops. In many cases, however, this is not possible, either because courses or workshops are not available, or because practitioners may not have access to these due to limited time or resources. Self-instruction in language assessment is much more feasible now than it was even five years ago, as a wealth of materials, in addition to this book, is available for individuals who wish to become competent in language assessment. A list of some resource materials on language assessment is provided at the end of this chapter.

Alternative 3

The last alternative reflects our view that rather than thinking of assessments as "good" or "bad," it is more productive to consider the extent to which we can justify their intended uses by constructing an Assessment Use Argument (AUA) and providing backing to support this. This alternative also indicates that justifying the use of a particular assessment does not depend on a single quality, but is rather a function of many qualities that are articulated in an AUA. The ways in which these are stated in an AUA for a given assessment situation will determine the extent to which we can justify the intended uses of the assessment to stakeholders.

WHAT LANGUAGE TEST DEVELOPERS AND USERS NEED TO KNOW

In the real world of language assessment use, it is becoming increasingly important, and in many cases mandatory, for test developers and users to be accountable to stakeholders—those who may provide resources for developing and using the assessment, and who may be affected by the use of an assessment. Being accountable, or *accountability*, means being able to *demonstrate* to stakeholders that the intended uses of our assessment are justified. Thus *all* language test developers and users need to know how to go about justifying assessment development and use or, if they cannot do this themselves, what to look for and expect from other individuals who can help them out. Beyond this, the specifics of what test developers and users want to accomplish with their assessments will differ widely, as will the real world circumstances under which they are operating. Therefore, the details of what they will need to know will also vary widely.

For example, language assessments can be a valuable tool for providing information that is relevant to several concerns in language teaching. They can provide evidence of the results of learning and instruction, and hence feedback on the effectiveness of the teaching program itself. They can also provide information that is relevant to making decisions about individuals, such as determining what specific kinds of learning materials and activities should be provided to students, based on a diagnosis of their strengths and weaknesses, deciding whether individual students or an entire class are ready to move on to another unit of instruction, and assigning grades on the basis of students' achievement. Finally, assessment can also be used as a tool for clarifying instructional objectives and, in some cases, for evaluating the relevance of these objectives and the instructional materials and activities based on them to the language use needs of students following the program of instruction. For these reasons, virtually all language teaching programs involve some assessment, and hence language teachers need to be able either (1) to make informed judgments in selecting and justifying appropriate language assessment, or (2) to plan, develop, and justify appropriate assessments of their own.

Language assessments can also be valuable tools for providing information that is relevant to various kinds of research in applied linguistics. For example, we might use a variety of assessments to better understand the nature of the writing process and how this relates to the quality of writing. We might ask a number of individuals to provide verbal reports of the processes or strategies they employ while writing a term paper, analyze these verbal reports, and then prepare a detailed verbal description of the processes reported. We could also analyze the composition the individuals write, in terms of language use—e.g., grammar, vocabulary, cohesion, rhetorical organization—and write up detailed verbal descriptions of these analyses. We could then ask one or more trained raters to assign scores for grammatical accuracy, appropriate use of vocabulary, cohesive devices, and rhetorical organization, according to well-defined scoring rubrics. The results of all of these assessments—the analyses of the verbal reports and the language used in the compositions, and the ratings—could then be used to provide a fuller description of the relationships among writing processes and the characteristics and quality of the written products. Language assessments can also provide information about the outcomes of acquisition, and hence be used to investigate the relationships between these outcomes and various attributes of learners and the learning context that may be hypothesized to influence language acquisition. For these reasons, researchers in applied linguistics who want to use language assessments need to be able either (1) to make informed judgments in selecting and justifying appropriate language assessment, or (2) to plan, develop, and justify appropriate assessments of their own.

Despite the many differences in the details of what people who develop and use language assessments need to know, there is a systematic approach to developing and using language assessments that can guide test developers and users in thinking through the process of test development and use that will enable them to avoid problems associated with haphazard assessment development. The approach to language test development and use that we present in this book provides, in our view, a means for test developers to deal with these dilemmas and conflicts in a way that is systematic and rational and preserves one's sanity. More importantly, we believe that by following this approach, test developers and test users will be able to justify the uses that are made of language assessments.

INTENDED AUDIENCES

Because the needs of test developers and users vary widely, the intended audiences for this book are similarly wide. Some readers may be students just starting to learn about language teaching and assessment who are encountering this book in a course in language assessment. Some may be experienced teachers returning for additional training or recertification. Some may be teachers who realize they need to use a language assessment for some purpose and are looking for a reference work that can provide them with some guidance. Some may be applied linguists who need to use language assessments in their research projects and want to do so in an informed way. Finally, some may be professional language testers with many years of experience who may still be willing to learn a new trick or two and who may wonder just what we are up to and whether it makes any sense at all.

We've tried to make this book accessible for all of you. Because we anticipate that many readers will be individuals looking for practical solutions to their immediate assessment needs, we haven't written this book in the format of a scholarly research work, which could make it cumbersome to read and thus limit the accessibility of its contents. For example, we've minimized the use of "academic paraphernalia" such as extensive references to and citations of research in the body of the text. However, in doing so, we have not ignored important concepts just because they are challenging and would create a lot of work for us. Instead, we've tried to present them in as accessible a way as possible through the use of clearly defined terms used consistently and illustrated by means of numerous concrete examples. We've also tried to add a bit of humor here and there, although astute readers will quickly discover that we're challenged in this regard.

OVERVIEW OF THE BOOK

The book is organized into four main parts. Part I presents a conceptual foundation that provides the theoretical basis for developing and using language tests. This foundation includes three components: (1) a framework for thinking about language use and language ability, presented in Chapter 3, (2) a framework for describing assessment task characteristics, presented in Chapter 4, and (3) a set of principles and procedures for justifying the uses of language assessments, presented in Chapter 5. While this conceptual foundation is grounded in theoretical research in language testing, other areas of applied linguistics, and educational measurement, it is not simply theoretical, but is practical as well. Its primary purpose is to guide the development and use of language tests.

Part II describes the process of developing an Assessment Use Argument. In Chapter 6 we present an overview of the assessment development process. This is followed by a discussion of pre-development planning in Chapter 7, including several extended examples. In Chapter 8 we discuss how to go about articulating an Assessment Use Argument. Then in Chapters 9–12 we provide detailed discussions of the claims and warrants that constitute an Assessment Use Argument.

Part III describes the process of developing and using language assessments in the real world. This part begins with a discussion in Chapter 13 of the real world in which language assessment development and use take place. In Chapters 14–18 we discuss the procedures involved in assessment production: developing a design statement (Chapter 14), developing language assessment tasks (Chapter 15), recording performance on language assessments (Chapter 16), developing specifications ("Blueprints") for language assessments (Chapter 17), and preparing effective instructions (Chapter 18). In Chapter 19 we discuss procedures for collecting backing to support the claims and warrants in an AUA and for improving the quality of the assessment itself. In Chapter 20 we discuss the allocation and management of resources. Finally, in Chapter 21 we return to the real world and discuss issues and considerations in responsible language assessment use.

The last part of the book, which includes a number of illustrative assessment development projects that take the reader through the entire assessment development process, is available at http://www.oup.com/LAIP. These projects have been taken from our own work in developing language assessments over the years, as well as from projects that our students have completed in the language assessment courses we teach. They thus constitute genuine instances of assessment development which we hope will provide a rich source of activities that readers can pursue either as part of a class or on their own, so as to learn how to use and adapt our approach to their own language assessment development needs.

HOW TO USE THE BOOK AND THE PROJECTS

As with our previous book, *Language Testing in Practice*, this book is not a "cookbook" with recipes for developing every type of language assessment imaginable. It is also not intended to present a scholarly treatment of the field.

Finally, it is not intended to serve as a resource for individuals who may want to know what language assessments are out there that might be of use to them. (For references to such books, see the Suggested Readings.) Nevertheless, this book does contain a lot of information. Therefore, we cannot imagine anyone sitting down and reading it cover to cover. Perhaps one way to figure out how to use it (if you have a choice in the matter) is to start by looking the whole thing over quickly to get a sense of its scope. You might then peruse the many illustrative Projects (http://www.oup.com/LAIP) to see what ground we cover there. These Projects are designed to be used interactively with the material in the book. If you find a Project that addresses an assessment situation similar to one that you also have to deal with, this Project may provide you with a structure for thinking through your own assessment needs and a vehicle for personalizing some of the content of the book. Also, glance at the exercises at the end of most of the chapters and at the end of each Project. These are designed to help you work with the material in the book and projects. Then you might be in a good position to develop a strategy for working with the material that works for you.

Book

Each chapter of the book includes the following components:

- Exercises: These are intended to provide the opportunity for readers to apply the ideas that are introduced in the chapter to their own language assessment situations, or to work these through in practice by working with the Projects. (There are no Exercises in this chapter nor in Chapters 6, 7, and 8.)
- Suggested Readings: These are intended to provide additional information about content that is introduced in the chapter and that some readers may want to pursue in more detail.

In addition, throughout the book we refer to Projects as examples to illustrate a particular point or concept.

Projects

The Projects on the web page (http://www.oup.com/LAIP) are intended to provide extensive real-life illustrations of language assessment situations and how our approach can be applied to these. All of the Projects include exercises that are specific to that particular project. In addition, as noted above, the Projects also provide the basis for many of the Exercises in the book. The first three Projects are those we use throughout the book as examples: (1) The Kindergarten ESL assessment, (2) the University academic reading assessment, and (3) the University Chinese speaking assessment. These are included in their entirety to provide easy access for readers who may want to refer to specific parts of them. The rest of the Projects are intended to cover a wide range of assessment development situations. These Projects are not fully developed, in the sense that they are missing one or more parts of the assessment development documentation. It is our intention that this will give readers the opportunity to practice creating different parts of the assessment development documentation, e.g., AUA, Design Statement, Blueprint, or example assessment tasks, that are not included in these Projects.

SUGGESTED READINGS ON LANGUAGE ASSESSMENT

Alderson, J. C. and **L. F. Bachman** (eds.). 2000–6. Cambridge language assessment series. Cambridge: Cambridge University Press.

——, **Clapham, G.**, and **D. Wall.** 1995. *Language Test Construction and Evaluation.* Cambridge: Cambridge University Press.

Bachman, L. F. 1990. *Fundamental Considerations in Language Testing.* Oxford: Oxford University Press.

—— 2004. *Statistical Analyses for Language Assessment.* Cambridge: Cambridge University Press.

Brown, J. D. (ed.). 1998. *New Ways of Classroom Assessment.* Alexandria, Va: TESOL.

Coombe, C. A. and **Hubley, N. J.** (eds.). 2003. *Assessment Practices.* Arlington, Va: *Teachers of English to Speakers of Other Languages.*

O'Malley, J. M. and **L. V. Pierce.** 1996. *Authentic Assessment for English Language Learners.* New York: Addison-Wesley.

PART I
Conceptual foundations

In Part I we discuss the conceptual foundations of language assessment that provide the basis for the practical procedures discussed in the rest of the book.

In Chapter 2 we discuss a number of issues and considerations that underlie the development and use of language assessments. These include the nature of assessment and the uses that are made of language assessments. We provide an overview of the approach to language assessment that we develop in the rest of the book. In Chapter 3 we discuss the nature of language use and language ability. An understanding of language use, including the kinds of interactions involved in this, and the ways in which language use tasks engage participants, will inform the ways in which we view the particular setting to which we want our assessment results to generalize. An understanding of language ability is essential, since it is this ability, the capacity to engage in language use, that we want to assess. In Chapter 4 we present a framework for describing the characteristics of language use tasks. We believe that such a framework provides the basis for demonstrating the extent to which the tasks we use in language assessments correspond to the tasks that test takers need to perform in settings beyond the assessment itself. In Chapter 5 we discuss the need for language test developers and users to be able to justify the intended uses of a particular language assessment, and describe the process of assessment justification. This chapter is central to the whole book, as we believe that justifying assessment use to stakeholders is a fundamental responsibility of language test developers and users. We also believe that articulating what we will call an "Assessment Use Argument" (AUA) and providing evidence to support this provide the best means for responsibly discharging this responsibility.

2

Issues and considerations

INTRODUCTION

Language assessments are widely used in the real world to collect information that is used to make decisions. These uses of language assessments and the decisions that are made have consequences for stakeholders—the individuals, programs, institutions, organizations, or societies that will be affected by the assessment and the decisions made. As mentioned in Chapter 1, developers and users of language assessments need to be able to justify the uses for which their language assessments are intended. For this reason, test developers and users need to be familiar with some basic notions and issues in language assessment, including the nature of language assessment, and the uses of language assessments. We believe that it is also important for individuals who develop and use language assessments to have a theoretically grounded and systematic set of principles and procedures for developing and using language tests.

THE NATURE OF LANGUAGE ASSESSMENT

In our field, the terms "assessment," "measurement," "test," and "evaluation" are commonly used to refer to more or less the same activity: collecting information. However, there doesn't seem to be much agreement on the precise nature of the distinctions among the terms "assessment," "measurement," and "test." Some writers talk of "tests" as formal and "assessments" as informal, without clearly defining what this means. For others, there is a distinction between just plain tests and "alternative assessments," or "performance assessments," the latter of which are supposed to be more "authentic" or real-life-like than tests. Bachman (1990, 2004b) has suggested some clear distinctions among these terms, but in our view, such fine distinctions may be unnecessary for the purposes of developing and using language assessments. Bachman (2004b) defines "assessment" very broadly as the process of collecting information, and this definition suits our purpose well. However, because of the wide range of ways in which we can collect information (e.g., observation, self-report, questionnaire, interview, elicitation), and the variety of ways of recording this information (e.g., audio or video recording, verbal description, qualitative analysis, scoring, rating), we believe that precise distinctions among the terms "assessment," "measurement," and "test" are unnecessary. What *is* important, we believe, is that the test developer clearly and explicitly specifies the *conditions* under which the test taker's performance will be obtained and the *procedures* that will be followed for recording this performance. Thus, we view "assessment," "measurement," and "test" as simply variations of a single process, assessment, and will use the terms "test" and "assess" or "assessment" more or less synonymously throughout this book. However, simply for convenience, we will refer to the people involved in assessment as "test takers," "test developers," and "test users."

Assessment

Assessment is the process of collecting information about something that we're interested in, according to procedures that are systematic and substantively grounded (Bachman 2004b: 6–7).[1] The outcome of this process, such as a score or a verbal description, is referred to as "an assessment." In a *language* assessment, what we're interested in is making an interpretation about some aspect of the test taker's language ability. There are two qualities that distinguish assessments from other ways of collecting information, such as casual observations, hearsay, or rumors: **systematicity** and **substantive grounding**. First, assessments are **systematic**—they are designed and carried out according to clearly defined procedures that are methodical and open to scrutiny by other test developers and researchers, as well as by stakeholders in the assessment. This means that an assessment conducted by one person at one time could potentially be replicated by another person at another time. For example, if a researcher who had been trained in a particular observation method used this method for observing and describing the spoken language of students in a classroom, it should be possible for another researcher to follow the same method with students in another class. To the extent that the researchers followed the same method for observation and reporting, they have a basis for claiming that they have used the same assessment for both classes of students.

The second quality is that assessments are **substantively grounded**, which means that they are based on a recognized and verifiable area of content, such as a course syllabus, a widely accepted theory about the nature of language ability, prior research, including a needs analysis, or the currently accepted practice in the field. In the classroom speaking assessment example above, if the procedures were based on accepted methodology in the field, and the verbal reports were informed by current practice in research into the nature of oral interaction, then the assessments that are obtained could be interpreted meaningfully.

Evaluation

Bachman (1990, 2004b) describes evaluation as an activity that is different from assessment. He describes evaluation as "one possible use of assessment" (Bachman 2004b: 9). **Evaluation** involves making value judgments and decisions on the basis of information, and gathering information to inform such decisions is the *primary* purpose for which language assessments are used. We frequently use assessments for evaluation in educational programs, where we may use assessments to identify students' areas of strength and weakness to help them make decisions to improve or facilitate their learning, to select and place individuals into instructional programs, or to decide which students pass a course. In the classroom speaking assessment example, if the classroom teachers felt that researchers' oral tests would be useful for collecting information relevant in deciding which students pass the course, they might decide to administer these tests for this use. In this case, this use of the test scores would be an example of evaluation.

Sometimes assessments are used to provide a description of the attributes of individuals, such as language aptitude or cognitive style, or about language use activities, such as engaging in a conversation or writing a term paper. This use is particularly common in applied linguistics research, where the focus may be on describing the attributes of language users and the dynamics of group interactions, or investigating the relationships among language use, the language use situation, and language ability. The classroom speaking assessment above would be an example of the use of assessment for description. However, even in the research use of language assessments, decisions will also be made. The researcher may make decisions about the focus or methodology of further research based on the results of the study in which a language assessment has been used. Or, the results of the research may lead other researchers to change the way they view and understand the particular language phenomenon that is of interest to them.

The relationships among assessment, measurement, tests, and their uses are illustrated in Figure 2.1 on p. 22.

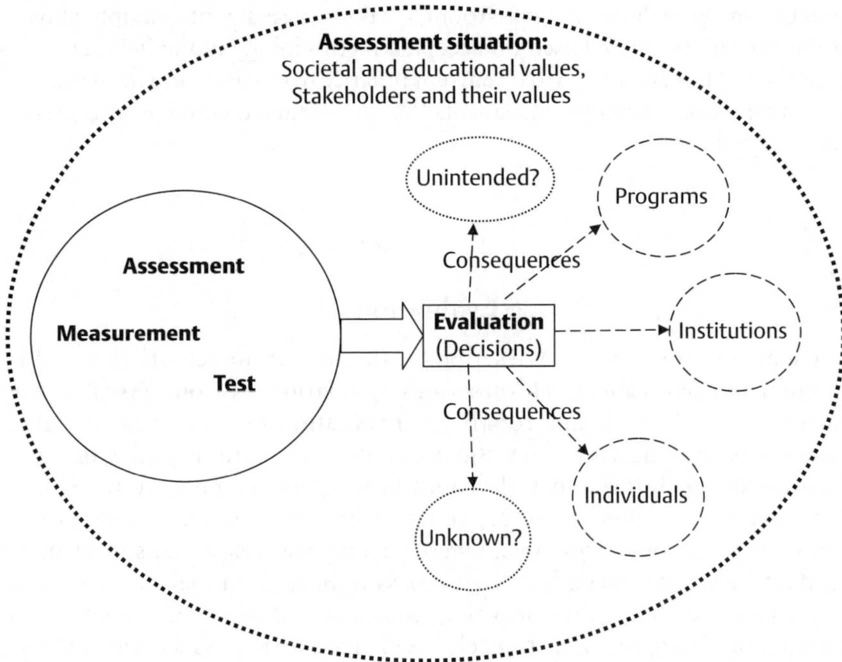

Figure 2.1 Relationship between assessments/measurements/tests, their use for evaluation, and the consequences of assessment use

USES OF LANGUAGE ASSESSMENTS

The primary use of any language assessment is to collect information for making decisions. Furthermore, the use of an assessment and the decisions made will have consequences for stakeholders, the individuals and programs in the educational and societal setting in which language assessment takes place. As we will argue in this book, the *intended* uses of language assessments are to help us make decisions that will ideally lead to *beneficial* consequences for stakeholders. One way to think of the use of a language assessment is as a series of inferences from the test taker's performance to the consequences. These links are illustrated in Figure 2.2.

For example, suppose an ESL writing teacher is teaching a lesson on markers of cohesion in academic writing. The teacher wants to give a short test to provide feedback to his students on their learning of the content of the lesson, to gather feedback on the effectiveness of his teaching, and to make decisions about modifying instruction. The test consists of a gap-filling test, that is, a written passage containing some blanks where markers of cohesion are needed. The students supply the appropriate markers of cohesion

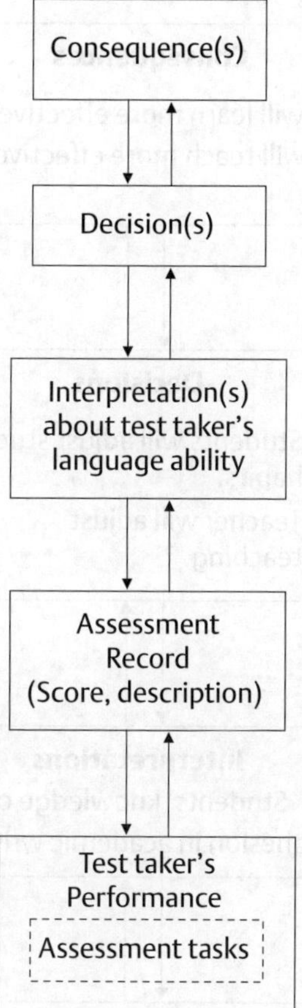

Figure 2.2 Links from test taker's performance to intended uses (decisions, consequences)

as needed. Scores consist of the total number of gaps that are filled with the appropriate markers of cohesion. The links from these students' performance to the intended uses in this example testing situation are illustrated in Figure 2.3 on p. 24.

Decisions

The decisions we make are generally about individuals or programs. Bachman (1990) provides extensive descriptions of the kinds of decisions that we typically make on the basis of assessments. Bachman (2004b) summarizes these as follows:

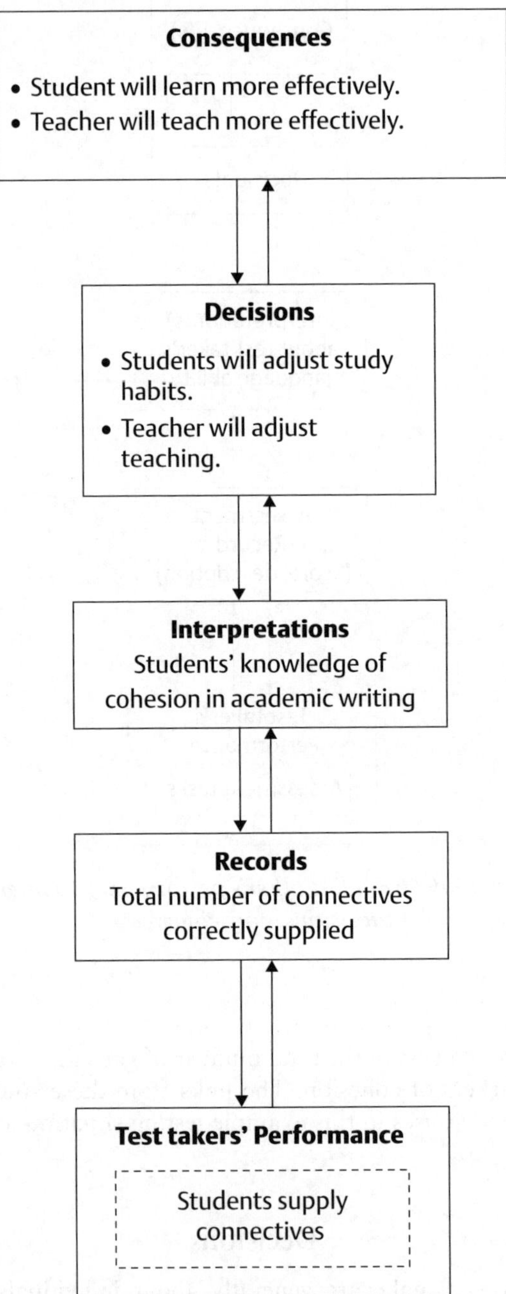

Figure 2.3 Links between test taker's performance and consequences: ESL writing example

1 Decisions about individuals (micro-evaluation), such as:

- Selection for admission or employment
- Placement into a course of study
- Making changes in instruction, or in teaching and learning activities
- Passing or failing students on a course on the basis of the progress or achievement of test takers
- Certification for professional employment
- Prediction of future performance.

2 Decisions about programs (macro-evaluation), such as:

- Formative, relating to making changes to improve an existing program
- Summative, relating to continuing an existing program or implementing a new program.

3 Decisions about research, such as:

- Deciding on new research questions or methodology for future research
- Changing our view of a particular language phenomenon
- Modifying our understanding of or explanation of a particular language phenomenon. (Bachman 2004b: 10.)

The way we justify these decisions is discussed in more detail in Chapters 5 and 8 through 12.

Consequences

As indicated in Figure 2.1 above, the assessments we use and the decisions we make are situated within educational and social settings, and will have consequences for individuals, programs, and institutions in these settings. Inherent in these will be the values of individuals, educational institutions, and communities, and of various stakeholder groups within the educational community or society, as well as laws, regulations, and policies that may govern the way we use an assessment and the decisions we may make. Thus, a central theme in this book is that test developers and test users need to take into consideration the potential consequences of using an assessment, and of the decisions to be made, for different stakeholders in the assessment situation. Related to this is our belief that test developers and test users use assessments, by and large, to help promote beneficial consequences for stakeholders in educational systems and society. Thus, it is essential for test developers and test users to carefully consider the extent to which using an assessment, making the intended decisions, and the consequences of these actions may be in conflict with existing educational and societal values. (See Project 12 for an example of an assessment in which the decisions and consequences are consistent with the values of one set of stakeholders but in conflict with those of another group.) In addition, as indicated in Figure 2.1, there may be consequences that are either unintended or unknown.

It is the responsibility of the test developer and decision maker to consult with all relevant stakeholders in order to identify as many unintended consequences as possible. It is of particular importance for the test developer and decision maker to try to anticipate any unintended detrimental consequences and attempt to implement procedures during assessment development and use to minimize the likelihood that these will happen. Nevertheless, in even the most well-planned assessment development, there are likely to be some consequences that are not known and that cannot be anticipated.

Language assessment in language instruction and learning

When we work with language teachers, they often ask us questions like, "*When* should we assess our students?," or "*How often* should we assess our students?," or "*How* should we assess our students?" They seldom ask us, "*What* should we assess?," because teachers usually have a pretty good idea of what learning objectives they hope to achieve, or what they want their students to learn. What teachers almost never ask us is, "*Why* should I assess my students?" This would seem to suggest that teachers either know why they should assess their students or that they seldom consider why they would want to do this.

For us, the "why" question is paramount, because without knowing the intended uses of the assessment, how can we know when or how often to assess? If the primary purpose of assessment is to collect information for making decisions, then it follows that if no decision is to be made, there is no need to assess. Similarly, whenever a teacher needs to make a decision, there is a potential need to assess.

To better understand the relationship between language assessment and language teaching, consider the relationships illustrated in Figure 2.4.

This figure indicates that the reason *why* we use an assessment is to collect information in order to make decisions. This information may be about our students' achievement of the learning objectives, about their perceptions, feelings, and attitudes towards language learning and the course of instruction. Or we may use an assessment to collect information about the effectiveness of our teaching. *When* we assess will be determined by when these decisions need to be made. Some of the decisions we make will occur continuously and instantaneously during instruction, as in on-line, dynamic assessment, discussed below. Other decisions may be more deliberate and occur only periodically at specified times during the course, or at the end of a course of instruction, as in "formal/explicit" assessment, discussed below. Similarly, our students may make continuous decisions during classroom interactions, as well as more considered decisions, both in and outside of the classroom.

Many of the decisions made will be formative ones that inform learning and instruction. We, as teachers, may decide to make changes in our instructional practice, or in the learning activities we present to our students, or in the way in which we present the "content" to be learned. The information

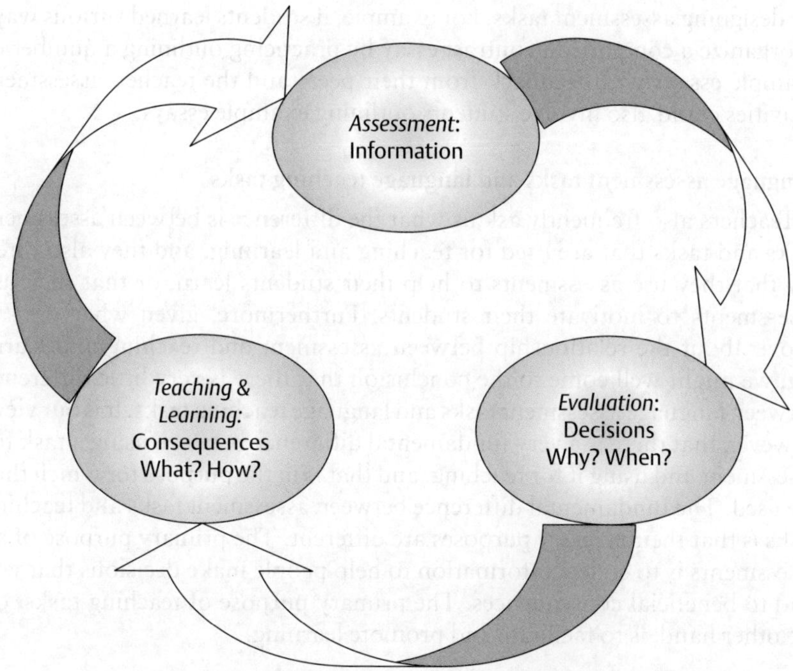

Figure 2.4 Assessment, evaluation, and teaching and learning[2]

from assessments may also provide formative feedback to our students, who can use this to make decisions about their own learning—what areas they need to focus on, how they can make better use of learning strategies, or how they can more effectively spend their time learning. Some of the decisions made are likely to be more summative, such as deciding which students will pass a course, or certifying their level of language ability.

The decisions we and our students make will hopefully have beneficial consequences for teaching and learning. We will become more effective at facilitating our students' learning, and they will become more effective learners. *What* we assess will be determined by "content" of the course: the learning objectives in the syllabus, the content of the teaching materials, and the content of the teaching and learning activities. In most cases the areas of language ability that the course is intended to cover will provide the basis for deciding what it is we want to assess. For example, if a course is intended to cover, among other things, various ways to organize a comparison/contrast essay, teachers would naturally want to be sure that students' mastery of this content was assessed in some way. *How* we go about assessing will be determined by the kinds of learning activities we use in the classroom. Similarly, the kinds of language use tasks we use in the classroom can provide a basis for designing assessment tasks. For example, if students learned various ways to organize a comparison/contrast essay by practicing outlining a number of example essays with feedback from their peers and the teacher, assessment activities could also involve students outlining example essays.

Language assessment tasks and language teaching tasks

Teachers also frequently ask us what the difference is between assessment tasks and tasks that are used for teaching and learning, and they also often say that they use assessments to help their students learn, or that they use assessments to motivate their students. Furthermore, given what we say above about the relationship between assessment and teaching and learning, we might well come to the conclusion that there is very little difference between language assessment tasks and language teaching tasks. It is our view, however, that there is a very fundamental difference between using a task for assessment and using it for teaching, and that is in the purpose for which they are used. The fundamental difference between assessment tasks and teaching tasks is that their *primary* purposes are different. The primary purpose of all assessments is to collect information to help people make decisions that will lead to beneficial consequences. The primary purpose of teaching tasks, on the other hand, is to facilitate and promote learning.

Modes of classroom language assessment

Although assessment tasks and teaching tasks typically serve different purposes, in much classroom assessment the same task serves both purposes, and this is where the distinction becomes blurry. Consider, for example, the kind of continuous "on-line," or "dynamic" assessment that a classroom teacher is constantly conducting during a class period. This mode of classroom assessment is instantaneous and cyclical: assessment—decision—instruction—assessment—decision—instruction. This mode of assessment is also **implicit**, in that learners are largely unaware that assessment is taking place. The teacher may be using this assessment to make decisions to facilitate his own minute-by-minute instruction by adjusting his presentation, rephrasing, repeating, moving from student to student, and so forth. In this case the teacher is constantly collecting feedback from his students in order to make decisions about his own instructional activity. At the same time, these assessments may also very well facilitate the students' learning, so that they are also performing the instructional function of teaching tasks. So, is the teacher really assessing or teaching? In this case, he's doing both.

In other situations, the distinction between teaching/learning and assessment is much clearer and explicit. This is the case when the teacher clearly indicates that an activity will be an assessment, or a test. In this mode of assessment, the assessment is clearly separate from teaching, and both the teacher and the students know that this is an assessment. They also generally know what the purpose of the assessment is. This **explicit** mode of assessment may be used for both formative and summative purposes. Consider, for example, a teacher who administers an in-class diagnostic writing assessment at the beginning of a writing course to help diagnose her students' areas of strength and weakness, so that she can more effectively tailor her instruction to their individual needs. Suppose she uses the students' writing samples to provide individual feedback to each student, so that the students can focus on the areas in which they are in greatest need of improvement. In this case, the diagnostic writing task is clearly an assessment, since the information from it will be used by both the teacher and the students to make decisions about their instruction and learning. The same teacher might use the explicit mode of assessment when she creates a final exam in which students write an essay that is rated on the main teaching points focused on during the course, such as rhetorical organization, paragraph unity, uses of markers of cohesion, and control of grammar and punctuation.

In summary, then, it is important to understand the difference between the *primary* purposes of assessment and teaching tasks, because this will lead to a better understanding of the role that assessment can play in support of teaching and learning. At the same time, it is important to recognize the role of assessment in teaching and learning, the purposes that assessment can serve, and the ways in which it occurs in the classroom. These relationships are illustrated in Table 2.1.

Mode	Characteristics	Purpose
Implicit	• Continuous • Instantaneous • Cyclical • Implicit: both teacher and students may be unaware that assessment is taking place	Formative decisions, e.g.: • Correct or not correct student's response • Change form of questioning • Call on another student • Produce a model utterance • Request a group response
Explicit	• Clearly distinct from teaching • Explicit: both teacher and learners are aware that assessment is taking place	Summative decisions, e.g.: • Decide who passes the course • Certify level of ability Formative decisions, e.g.: • *Teacher*: Move on to next lesson or review current lesson • *Teacher*: focus more on a specific area of content • *Student*: spend more time on particular area of language ability • *Student*: use a different learning strategy

Table 2.1 Role of assessment in teaching and learning

There are many, many times in the classroom when the same task or activity serves both purposes. In these cases, we would advise teachers not to concern themselves with whether they're teaching or assessing, but to do what they believe is most appropriate and effective for their students' learning.

AN APPROACH TO LANGUAGE ASSESSMENT

All assessments need to be developed and used according to explicitly stated procedures, and we believe that the approach to language test development and use we present comprises such a set of procedures. At the core of our approach is an **Assessment Use Argument** (AUA), which guides the assessment development process. The AUA consists of a set of claims that specify the conceptual links between a test taker's *performance* on an assessment, an *assessment record*, which is the score or qualitative description we obtain from the assessment, an *interpretation* about the ability we want to assess, the *decisions* that are to be made, and the *consequences* of using the assessment and of the decisions that are made. These are the links that are illustrated in Figure 2.2 above.

In addition, our approach goes beyond test development and provides a rationale and set of procedures for justifying the intended uses of the assessment, a process we refer to as assessment justification. **Assessment justification** consists of articulating an Assessment Use Argument (AUA) and collecting evidence to support this. The structure of an AUA and the process of justification are discussed in detail in Chapters 5 and 8–12. The process of assessment development is discussed in Chapters 14–20.

As stated in the Introduction, our aim in this book is to increase the reader's competence in developing and using language assessments. The approach to language assessment that we present in this book is not a "cookbook" approach, with a miscellany of templates for assessment tasks, along with a list of "recipes" for developing and using language assessments. Thus, it does not include examples of all types of items or tasks that have been used in language assessments. Nor is this is a book containing "everything you always wanted to know about language assessment but were afraid to ask." Thus, it does not include definitions for all the technical terms in the language assessment and measurement literature, though it suggests some useful resources where you can find these.

What our approach to language assessment *does* provide is the following:

- a theoretically grounded and systematic set of principles and procedures for developing and using language tests
- an understanding that will enable readers to make their own judgments and decisions about either selecting, modifying, or developing a language assessment whose use can be justified to stakeholders.

To facilitate this, we provide examples that clearly illustrate specific points, principles, and concepts that are important to our approach. We also have made every attempt to provide clear definitions of technical terms that are introduced and/or examples to make these terms clear to readers, and to use these terms consistently throughout the book. At the same time, we limit our use of technical terms to those that are essential to our approach.

Our approach to language test development and use is based on four fundamental principles:

1 The need for developers and users of language assessments to be able to *justify* to stakeholders the uses (decisions, consequences) that are made of assessments,
2 The need for *a clearly articulated and coherent Assessment Use Argument* (AUA), linking assessment performance to interpretations and to intended uses,
3 The *provision of evidence* to support the statements in the AUA,
4 The need for *collaboration among all stakeholders* during the process of assessment development and use.

Who can benefit from this approach to language assessment?

We believe that a wide range of individuals can benefit from our approach to language testing. This belief is based not only on our experience in teaching this approach to our students and practitioners, but also on having used it successfully in consulting with individuals and institutions in many parts of the world in the actual design and development of language tests. We have worked with language teachers who need to select, adapt, or develop tests for classroom use, with testing specialists developing tests for wider use within particular language teaching programs, and with material developers and textbook writers who need to include appropriate tests or suggestions for test development in the materials they produce. We have also worked with professional test developers in organizations that are responsible for producing high-stakes tests. Finally, we have worked with researchers in various areas of applied linguistics who need to select or develop language tests that are appropriate to their research needs.

EXERCISES

1 Think of a language assessment you may have developed or helped develop, or one that you have used. What were the intended consequences and decisions for this assessment? Use Figures 2.2 and 2.3 to help you.
2 What unintended consequences occurred or might have occurred with your use of the assessment in Exercise 1?
3 Recall your own classroom teaching and think of a five-minute sequence of continuous, *implicit* assessment. List the things you actually did in the assessment—decision—instruction cycle.

4 Compare your list of assessment—decision—instruction activities with another teacher's list.

How do you decide when to give an *explicit* assessment to your class? What "content" do you assess? What kinds of assessment tasks do you use?

NOTES

1 Another term that is sometimes used more or less synonymously with "assessment" is "appraisal"; if we use the term "appraisal" it will be in a non-technical, general sense.

2 This figure is an adaptation of a graphic in a presentation by Annie Hughes, "Which comes first? How can we link teaching with assessment when teaching English to young learners?," at the "Learning and assessment at primary schools" Conference, Cambridge, 12–14 June 2009.

3

Describing language use and language ability

INTRODUCTION

The primary purpose of a language assessment is to collect information to help us make decisions about test takers, and the attribute of test takers that is of primary interest in language assessment is language ability. In this chapter we describe **language ability** as a capacity that enables language users to create and interpret discourse. We define language ability as consisting of two components: language knowledge and strategic competence. Other attributes of language users or test takers that we also need to consider are personal attributes, topical knowledge, affective schemata, and cognitive strategies. We include these in our discussion for two reasons. First, these attributes can have important influences on both language use and assessment performance. Second, it is possible and desirable to design language assessments so that these attributes facilitate rather than impede test takers' performance.

When language users, including individuals who take language tests, engage in language use, they do this in a specific situation, and thus interact with the characteristics of this situation, which can also include other language users. In other words, language users exercise their language ability, or capacity for language use, in various kinds of interactions as they perform language use tasks in a target language use (TLU) situation, or domain. Thus, if we, as language test developers and users, want our interpretations of test takers' language ability to generalize to language use domains outside of the assessment itself, we also need to understand the nature of language use.

We begin this chapter by defining what we mean by language use in general. Next, we present a framework for describing some of the specific attributes of language users or potential test takers that we believe are involved in language use. We then describe the components of language ability in some detail, since assessing language ability is the primary focus of this book. Following this, we argue that the notion of "language skills" is problematic, and that what are commonly referred to as "listening," "speaking," "reading," and "writing" can more usefully be conceptualized as language use activities. We conclude with a practical application: using a language ability checklist in designing language assessments to help define the construct we want to measure.

Overview of a conceptual framework for language use

In the past twenty years, language use has been discussed from a number of different perspectives that emphasize its interactive[1] nature. (See, for example, the references in "Suggested Readings" for this chapter.) In general, **language use** can be defined as the creation or interpretation of intended meanings in discourse by an individual, or as the dynamic and interactive negotiation of intended meanings between two or more individuals in a particular situation. In using language to express, interpret, or negotiate intended meanings, language users create discourse. This discourse derives meaning not only from utterances or texts themselves, but, more importantly, from the ways in which characteristics of these utterances and texts interact with the characteristics of a particular language use situation. Language use, as we have defined it, involves two kinds of interactions: (1) those among the attributes of the individual language user, and (2) those between the language user and the characteristics of the language use situation, including other language users.

When using language, individual language users obviously need to employ their language ability. However, in addition to their language ability, a number of other attributes—their personal attributes, topical knowledge, affective schemata, and cognitive strategies—are engaged in language use. When an individual uses language to process utterances or texts to construct meaning or to produce utterances or texts, these attributes interact with each other. Language use is thus interactive, in the sense that it engages attributes within the language user, and these attributes interact with each other as the language user constructs meaning and discourse. We will use the term **internally interactive** to refer to these interactions among attributes within individual language users.

Language use also involves an interaction between a language user and the characteristics of the situation, which include, among other things, the language—written or spoken—that the language user is processing, the physical characteristics of the situation, and, in many cases, other language users. Language use is thus interactive in the sense that it involves the language user in interacting with characteristics in the language use situation. We will use the term **externally interactive** to refer to this aspect of language use. When more than one language user is involved directly in the interaction, we will refer to this as **reciprocal** language use. When only a single language user is involved, so that there is no give and take with other language users in the language use situation, we will refer to this as **non-reciprocal** language use. To illustrate the ways in which language use is both internally and externally interactive, we will provide three examples and two figures, below.

In these examples we refer to **strategic competence**, which we can think of as a set of metacognitive strategies that we use when we process language and respond with language in a particular language use situation. Sometimes these strategies are conscious, as when we think about how we will respond, and sometimes they are automatic, and are employed without our thinking about them. The output of these metacognitive strategies is a plan for how we will use language. We will also mention **cognitive strategies**, which we can think of as the ways in which we execute these plans in actual language use, as an interpretation or an utterance. We discuss these later in this chapter.

Example 1: Non-reciprocal language use

Our first example is of non-reciprocal language use. Think of someone reading the "apartments for rent" section of the newspaper in order to find an apartment. She knows which neighborhoods she'd like to live in and knows how much she can afford to pay. She decides to skim through the ads and circle only those that meet these specifications. Then she reads these ads more carefully and ranks them into three categories, excellent, good, and fair, depending upon other information provided in the ads. Figure 3.1 on p. 36 is a graphic organizer that shows the various parts of the interaction that we will be talking about. In the figure, the solid, bold circle (labeled "Attributes of the individual") represents the language user. The small ovals inside represent different attributes, including **topical knowledge, language knowledge, personal attributes**, strategic competence, and cognitive strategies. The area inside the two dashed circles represents the **affective schemata**. The large dotted oval outside represents the characteristics of the language use task and situation.

Now let's describe this example of non-reciprocal language use in more detail to see how it is both internally and externally interactive. The language use in the apartment search is externally interactive because it involves the language user in interacting with characteristics in the language use situation, including the way the newspaper is laid out, the location of the apartment ads, and the textual and perhaps graphic information in the ads.

In addition to being externally interactive, the language use in this example is also internally interactive because it engages attributes within the language user, and these attributes interact with each other as the language user constructs meaning and discourse. The apartment hunter uses her *strategic competence* when she sets her goal of reading newspaper ads in order to find an apartment, and when she plans to go about reading the list by first narrowing down the possibilities before reading the ads more carefully. She executes her plan by using *cognitive strategies* to focus her reading on the ads to find the specific information about location

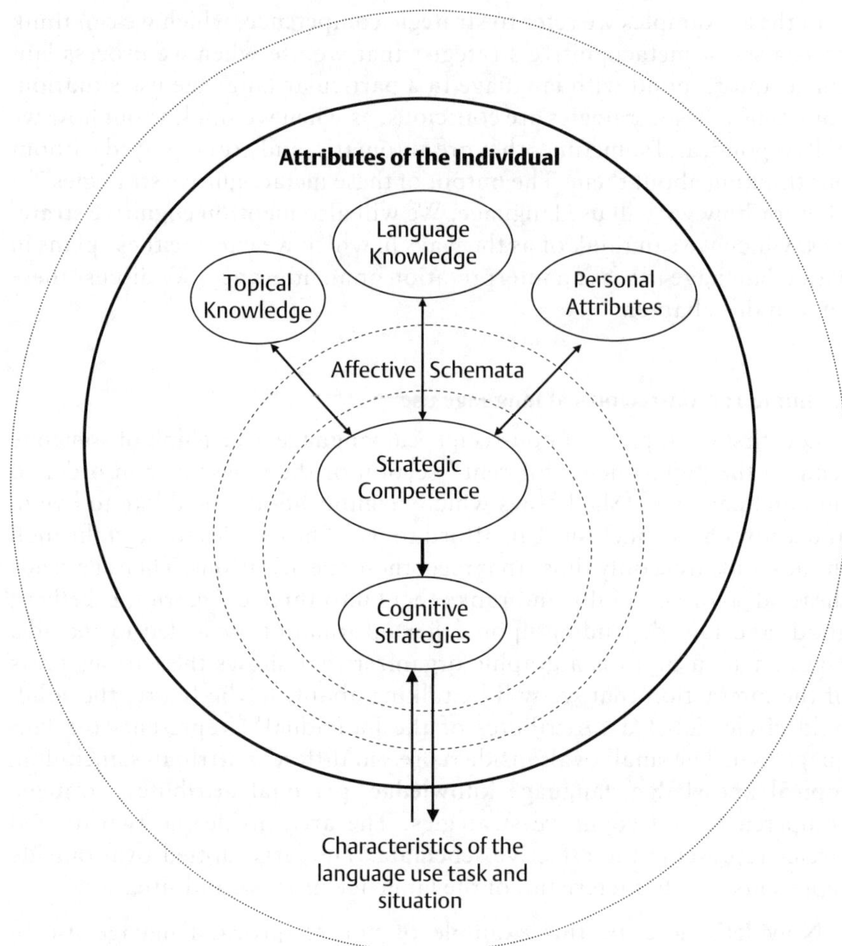

Figure 3.1 Non-reciprocal language use

and price. As part of her interaction with the text of the ads themselves, she creates a list of possible apartments, based on location and price, to narrow her search and to determine which ads she needs to read in detail. She uses her *topical knowledge* about the neighborhoods in the city and where they are located, and how expensive the housing is relative to the budget she has in mind. She also takes into account her *language knowledge*, such as how much grammar and vocabulary she knows, the organizational structure of the information in the ads, and her knowledge of abbreviations used in for-rent ads. In addition, she takes into account her *personal attributes* such as the fact that she prefers quiet environments in which she doesn't have to interact much with others unless she chooses to do so, and that she has to work within a limited budget.

Example 2: Non-reciprocal language use

Here is another example illustrating non-reciprocal language use involving a much less specific purpose. Think of someone turning on the TV with the very general goal of passing some time. The person might flip through the channels rather aimlessly looking for something that might attract more sustained attention, stopping now and then to watch a particular program.

The language use in this example is externally interactive because it involves the TV viewer interacting with the content of the TV programs that are on at the time he is channel surfing. Some of this content will include language, usually spoken, but in some cases, also written. In addition, the language use is internally interactive because it engages attributes within the TV viewer such as his *topical knowledge* (which influences what programs he would be interested in, as well as how much he will know, relate to, or potentially learn from the program he decides to watch), his *language knowledge* (needed to make sense of what he sees and hears), and his *personal attributes* (such as his preference for action and controversy). He uses his *strategic competence* when he sets his goal of watching TV to pass the time, when he plans in a very general way to spend thirty minutes channel surfing, and when he appraises what channels he actually subscribes to. He executes his plan by using *cognitive strategies* to compare the different programs and then select one to watch.

Example 3: Reciprocal language use

Our third example is of reciprocal language use. Imagine two individuals in a restaurant in Thailand: a customer who is a foreigner but who speaks Thai reasonably well and reads it to a limited extent, and a Thai waiter. The customer looks at the menu, finds it overwhelming (it's several pages long and lists almost 100 dishes), and decides that instead of reading through the menu and ordering from it, she'll simply ask the waiter what he recommends. In responding to the customer's question, the waiter figures that a good strategy would be to start with a suggestion about an appetizer, and recommends the steamed clams. The customer says that she really likes steamed clams and thanks the waiter for suggesting this.

Figure 3.2 on p. 38 is a graphic organizer that provides a visual representation of the various parts of the interaction that we'll be talking about. In the figure, the large oval on top (labeled "Attributes of the customer") represents the customer and the large oval on the bottom (labeled "Attributes of the waiter") represents the waiter. The rectangles between the large ovals represent the two utterances in the interchange.

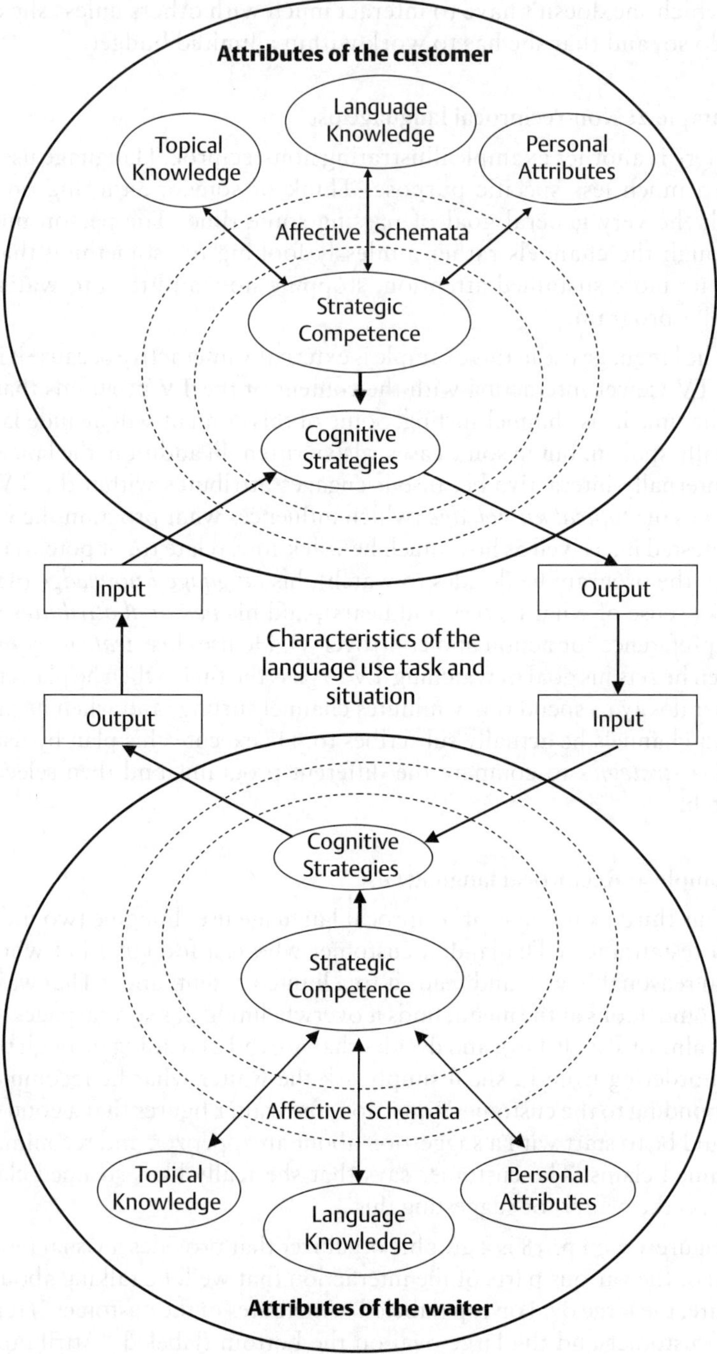

Figure 3.2 Reciprocal language use

Let's look at the conversational exchange in this example in more detail to see how it is both internally and externally interactive. (We'll focus primarily on the customer.) The language use in the restaurant is externally interactive because it involves the language user in interacting with characteristics in the language use situation, including the physical setting, which is a Thai restaurant, and the text of the menu, which is extremely long and contains mostly names of Thai and Chinese dishes. Also included in the characteristics of this language use situation are the waiter and his individual attributes. The customer engages the waiter's *topical knowledge* of the specialties of the restaurant when she questions him about these specialties. She engages his *language knowledge* (such as his knowledge of Thai grammar and vocabulary) when she tries to speak Thai with him. She engages his *personal attributes* when she notices that he appears to be open to some conversation about the food. She engages his *affective schemata* when she reacts to how he seems to be feeling about the conversation—he looks relaxed and not impatient about taking her order. And finally, she engages his output (utterance) when she structures what she says around what he has already said.

In addition to being externally interactive, the conversation is also internally interactive because it engages attributes within the language user, and these attributes interact with one another as the language user utilizes one or more grammatical forms to construct meaning and discourse. The customer organizes these internal interactions by using her *strategic competence,* by which we mean her ability to set goals, appraise what's going on within and around her, plan how to accomplish her goals, and to appraise the effectiveness of her communication. The customer's overall goal is to enjoy a delicious meal. In planning how to accomplish this goal, she draws on her *topical knowledge* of Thai customs—that menus are often completely ignored. She also takes into account her *language knowledge*—such as how much of the specialized vocabulary of Thai foods she knows and does not know, which influences how much she could actually understand of the names of the dishes in the menu. In addition, she takes into account her *personal attributes*, such as the fact that she enjoys free-wheeling conversations and doesn't need to think her whole meal out in advance before starting to order. She also takes into account her *affective schemata*—does she feel confident enough about her ability to speak Thai to participate in a conversation or is she so nervous that she only feels up to pointing to items on the menu? All of these combine to make up her planned utterance, which is simply to ask the waiter for his advice.

When the customer eventually replies to the waiter's recommendation, she uses her *strategic competence*, *cognitive strategies*, and *language knowledge* to process his utterance, she uses her *affective schemata* and *strategic competence* to appraise the extent to which she has achieved her communicative goal, and her *language knowledge* to formulate a plan for expressing agreement and thanks. Finally, she uses *cognitive strategies* to execute this plan as an utterance. We could use the same attributes to show how the language use of the waiter is also both externally and internally interactive.

How does this all relate to language assessment? According to our principle that we want to design a language assessment so that the performance corresponds to the way language is used in language use situations outside the assessment itself, then we need to have some way to organize our thinking about language use and the different characteristics—both the attributes within the language user and the characteristics of the language use situation—that may influence this. If we want our interpretations to generalize beyond the assessment itself, the same attributes—topical knowledge, language knowledge, affective schemata, personal attributes, strategic competence, and cognitive strategies—that enable language users to construct meaning in TLU tasks also need to be engaged when test takers process and respond to language assessment tasks. Similarly, the same characteristics of the language use situation that affect language use also need to be included in the kinds of assessment tasks that we design and present to test takers. (The characteristics of the language use situation are discussed in Chapter 4 below.)

In the remainder of this chapter, we provide a more extended discussion of personal attributes, topical knowledge, affective schemata, and cognitive strategies. We will then describe language ability as a combination of language knowledge and metacognitive strategies. We conclude with a reconceptualization of "language skills" that we believe provides a more useful basis for understanding language use and hence for the design and development of language assessments.

ATTRIBUTES OF INDIVIDUALS

As illustrated in the examples above, a large number of attributes of individuals may be engaged by language use in the real world. In this section we will discuss those attributes that are not part of language ability, namely personal attributes, topical knowledge, affective schemata, and cognitive strategies.

Personal attributes

Even though our focus in language assessment is on language ability, a number of personal attributes that are *not* part of test takers' language ability may still influence their performance on language assessments. A wide range of personal test taker attributes could be relevant to the decisions we make about assessment design and development, and extended discussions of these as they relate to second language learning and teaching can be found in Skehan (1989) and Brown (2000). Cohen (1994) discusses these in the context of language assessment, and provides a list of test taker attributes that includes age, foreign language aptitude, socio-psychological factors, personality, cognitive style, language use strategies, ethnolinguistic factors, and multilingual ability (Cohen 1994: 74).

In any assessment development project, the developer will need to develop a specific list of personal attributes that have to be considered in terms of their potential contribution to the usefulness of the assessment. For example, there is research indicating that some personal attributes, such as "age," "native language," "level and type of general education," or "type and amount of prior experience with a given assessment," may have an obvious influence on test takers' performance, and collecting information on these personal attributes may be quite valuable in designing assessment tasks that are optimally appropriate for different groups of test takers. The effect of other test taker attributes, such as extraversion/introversion, on the development of assessment tasks may be somewhat less obvious. Moreover, collecting information on these attributes may be less practical, in that this would require administering a separate assessment for each attribute that is of interest. Since the number of personal attributes that could potentially affect the assessment performance of any given test taker is very large, it is virtually impossible for us to provide a complete listing of all those that should be considered. Thus the following list of attributes is not intended to be exhaustive, but may provide a starting place for describing the characteristics of test takers. We discuss the specification of test takers' attributes in Chapter 11.

- Age
- Sex
- Nationality
- Resident status
- Length of residence
- Native language
- Level and type of general education
- Type and amount of preparation or prior experience with a given assessment.

Topical knowledge

What we will call topical knowledge (sometimes referred to as content knowledge, knowledge schemata, or real world knowledge) can be loosely thought of as knowledge structures in long-term memory. Individuals' topical knowledge needs to be considered in a description of language use because this provides the information base that enables them to use language with reference to the world in which they live, and hence is involved in all language use. Certain assessment tasks that presuppose cultural or topical knowledge on the part of test takers may be easier for those who have that knowledge and more difficult for those who do not. For example, we might expect students of economics or finance to bring relevant topical knowledge to a writing task that asks them to discuss the advantages and disadvantages of a liberal fiscal policy. By the same token, a reading passage that included a great deal of information specific to a particular culture might be more difficult for individuals who do not possess the relevant cultural knowledge than for those who do. In terms of an interactional model of language use, the topical knowledge of the individual (such as "knowledge of economics") interacts with the topical content of the assessment task (such as "fiscal policy"). (The relationship between the topical knowledge of test takers and the topical content of assessment tasks is discussed in detail in Chapter 11.)

Affective schemata

Affective schemata can be thought of as feelings we associate with specific kinds of topical knowledge. These affective schemata provide the basis on which language users appraise, consciously or unconsciously, the characteristics of the language use task and its setting in terms of past emotional experiences in similar contexts. The language user's affective schemata, in combination with the characteristics of the particular language use task, determine, to a large extent, his affective response to the task, and can either facilitate or inhibit how he uses the language in a given context. The affective responses of language users may thus influence not only whether they even attempt to use language in a given situation, but also how flexible they arc in adapting their language use to variations in the setting.

In a language assessment, test takers' affective schemata may influence the ways in which they process and attempt to complete the assessment tasks. If we ask test takers to deal with an emotionally charged topic, such as religion, abortion, gun control, or national sovereignty, their affective responses to this topic may limit their ability to utilize the full range of language knowledge and strategic competence available to them. This is not to say that we should avoid emotionally charged topics in language assessments, but simply to point out that we need to be aware that test takers' performance on tasks that include such topics may be affected as much by their affective schemata as by their language ability. Emotional responses can also facilitate language use, and we need to recognize that controversial topics may stimulate some individuals to perform at a high level, precisely because they feel strongly about the topic. Similarly, individuals who have positive feelings about interacting conversationally with others are likely to perform very well in a face-to-face oral interview. Assessment performance can thus be facilitated or inhibited by positive or negative affective responses, both to the topical content of assessment tasks and to a particular type of assessment task.

A number of language assessors have indicated that we should attempt to design our assessments to elicit test takers' best performance.[2] We believe that one way to do this is to design the characteristics of the assessment task so as to promote feelings of comfort or safety in test takers that will in turn facilitate their responding to the task. However, there needs to be a balance between what the test taker feels comfortable with and what we want to measure. For example, we may want to use a one-on-one oral interview because this most closely corresponds to a task in the TLU domain (see Chapter 4 below), even though we realize that some test takers may feel threatened by a face-to-face interaction. Realizing this, we could try to minimize this threat by building into the interview a warm-up phase, conducted at a level of language with which the test taker feels comfortable, and designed to put the test taker at ease.

Cognitive strategies[3]

Cognitive strategies are what language users employ when they execute plans, so as to realize these in language use, either in comprehending information in the discourse, or in co-constructing discourse with another interlocutor. (For further discussions of cognitive strategies, see Bialystok (1990), Oxford (1996), and Purpura (1999) in the Suggested Readings at the end of this chapter.)

We now turn from the more peripheral attributes of language users, in terms of their language use, to that attribute which is the main focus of this book: language ability.

LANGUAGE ABILITY[4]

If we are to make interpretations about language ability on the basis of performance on language assessments, we need to define this ability in sufficiently precise terms to distinguish it from other individual attributes that can affect assessment performance. We also need to define language ability in a way that is appropriate *for each particular assessment situation*. For example, for one particular assessment situation we may want to focus on test takers' knowledge of how to organize utterances to form texts, while in another we may be more interested in their knowledge of appropriate politeness markers. When we define an ability this way, for purposes of measurement, we are defining what we call a **construct**. For our purposes, we can consider a construct to be the specific definition of an ability that provides the basis for a given assessment or assessment task and for interpreting scores derived from this task. The construct definition for a particular assessment situation becomes the basis for the kinds of interpretations we can make from the assessment performance. In designing, developing, and using language assessments, we can define the construct from a number of perspectives, including everything from the content of a particular part of a language course to a needs analysis of the components of language ability that may be required to perform language use tasks in a target language use domain, to a theoretical model of language ability. (We discuss the process of defining the construct in detail in Chapter 11.)

In this section we present a framework for describing language ability that provides valuable guidance for defining the specific construct(s) that may be the focus in developing any language assessment. It is not our intention to suggest that all language assessments should be based on all or even specific parts of this particular framework. At the same time, however, we believe very strongly that the consideration of language ability in its totality needs to inform the development and use of any language assessment.

The framework of language ability proposed in this book is essentially that proposed by Bachman (1990), who describes this broadly as "the ability to use language communicatively" (p. 81). More specifically, Bachman defines this as comprising two components: language competence, which we will call language knowledge, and strategic competence, which we will describe as a set of metacognitive strategies that manage the ways in which language users utilize their different attributes (e.g., language knowledge, topical knowledge, affective schemata) to interact with the characteristics of the language use situation. It is this combination of language knowledge and strategic competence that provides language users with the ability, or capacity, to create and interpret discourse, either in responding to tasks on language assessments or in non-assessment language use.[5]

Language knowledge

Language knowledge can be thought of as a domain of information in memory that is available to the language user for creating and interpreting discourse in language use. Language knowledge includes two broad categories: organizational knowledge and pragmatic knowledge. Many of the language assessments we develop will focus on assessing only one or a few of these areas of language knowledge. That is, in most language assessments, the construct definition and scoring criteria will focus on one or more specific areas of language knowledge. Nevertheless, there is a need to be aware of the full range of areas of language knowledge as we design and develop language assessments and interpret the results from language assessments. For example, even though we may only be interested in assessing an individual's knowledge of vocabulary, the kinds of assessment tasks or texts that we include in the assessment need to be selected with an awareness of what other areas of language knowledge they may evoke. This is because other areas of language knowledge will inevitably be involved in language assessment performance, no matter how narrowly focused are the construct definition and scoring criteria. (We discuss ways to define constructs in Chapter 11 and scoring procedures in Chapter 16.) The design of every language assessment, no matter how narrow its focus, needs to be informed by a broad view of language knowledge. The areas of language knowledge are listed in outline format in Table 3.1.

Organizational knowledge

Organizational knowledge is involved in controlling the formal elements of language for producing or comprehending grammatically acceptable utterances or sentences, and for organizing these to form texts, both oral and written.[6]

Grammatical knowledge

Grammatical knowledge is involved in producing or comprehending formally accurate utterances or sentences.[7] This includes knowledge of syntax, vocabulary, phonology, and graphology.

I **Organizational Knowledge** (how utterances or sentences and texts are organized)
  A **Grammatical Knowledge** (how individual utterances or sentences are organized)
    1 Knowledge of vocabulary
    2 Knowledge of syntax
    3 Knowledge of phonology/graphology
  B **Textual Knowledge** (how utterances or sentences are organized to form texts)
    1 Knowledge of cohesion
    2 Knowledge of rhetorical or conversational organization
II **Pragmatic Knowledge** (how utterances or sentences and texts are related to the communicative goals of the language user and to the features of the language use setting)
  A **Functional Knowledge** (how utterances or sentences and texts are related to the communicative goals of language users)
    1 Knowledge of ideational functions
    2 Knowledge of manipulative functions
    3 Knowledge of heuristic functions
    4 Knowledge of imaginative functions
  B **Sociolinguistic Knowledge** (how utterances or sentences and texts are related to features of the language use setting)
    1 Knowledge of genres
    2 Knowledge of dialects/varieties
    3 Knowledge of registers
    4 Knowledge of natural or idiomatic expressions
    5 Knowledge of cultural references and figures of speech

Table 3.1 Areas of language knowledge

Textual knowledge

Textual knowledge is involved in producing or comprehending the sequence of units of informat ion in text (whether written or spoken). There are two areas of textual knowledge: knowledge of cohesion and rhetorical organization.

Knowledge of cohesion

Knowledge of cohesion is involved in producing or comprehending the explicitly marked relationships among sentences in written texts or among utterances in conversation. Some examples of the way cohesive relationships are marked in English include connecting words such as "therefore," "on the other hand," "however," and "because," pro-forms, ellipsis, and the use of synonyms and paraphrases. These are not limited to written English, but are also marked in interactive, conversational English with utterances such as "like I said before," "yeah, but," and "the next thing we need to discuss is."

Knowledge of rhetorical or conversational organization

Knowledge of rhetorical organization involves conventions for sequencing units of information in written texts. Some examples include narrative, description, argumentation, and comparison-contrast. Knowledge of conversational organization involves the ways in which interactants manage conversations. Examples include topic nomination, turn taking, pre-sequencing, and preference organization. (For a discussion of rhetorical organization language assessment, see Weigle 2002. For a discussion of conversational organization in language assessment, see Luoma 2004a.)

Pragmatic knowledge

Pragmatic knowledge enables us to create or interpret discourse by relating utterances or sentences and texts to their meanings, to the intentions of language users, and to relevant characteristics of the language use setting. There are two areas of pragmatic knowledge: functional knowledge and sociolinguistic knowledge.

Functional knowledge

Functional knowledge, or what Bachman (1990) calls "illocutionary competence," enables us to interpret relationships between utterances or sentences and texts and the intentions of language users. The utterance "Could you tell me how to get to the post office?," for example, most likely functions as a request for directions rather than request for a "yes" or "no" answer. The most appropriate responses are likely to be either a set of directions or, if the speaker does not know how to get to the post office, a statement to this effect. A verbal response such as "Yes, I could," while accurate in terms of the literal meaning of the question, is inappropriate, since it misinterprets the function of the question as a request for information. Quite frequently the appropriate interpretation of a given utterance also involves the language users' prior knowledge of the language use setting, including the characteristics of the participants. For example, to determine whether the comment "How many times have you tried to fix this lock yourself" should be interpreted as a compliment or as a criticism, we need to know whether or not the person who has tried to fix the lock is generally successful in completing tasks such as this, and whether the person making the remark is prone to indirect criticism. Functional knowledge includes knowledge of four categories of language functions: ideational, manipulative, heuristic, and imaginative. Although we have grouped functions into four general categories, these are by no means mutually exclusive. Furthermore, functions do not normally occur only in individual, isolated utterances. On the contrary, the majority of language use involves the performance of multiple functions in connected discourse.

Knowledge of ideational functions

Knowledge of ideational functions enables us to express or interpret meaning in terms of our experience of the real world. These functions include the use of language to inform, to express or exchange information about ideas, knowledge, or feelings. Descriptions, classifications, explanations, and expressions of sorrow or anger are examples of utterances that perform ideational functions.

Knowledge of manipulative functions

Knowledge of manipulative functions enables us to use language to affect the world around us. This includes knowledge of the following:

Instrumental functions, which are performed to get other people to do things for us (examples include requests, suggestions, commands, and warnings);

Regulatory functions, which are used to control what other people do (examples include rules, regulations, and laws); and

Interpersonal functions, which are used to establish, maintain, and change interpersonal relationships (examples include greetings and leave-takings, compliments, insults, and apologies).

Knowledge of heuristic functions

Knowledge of heuristic functions enables us to use language to extend our knowledge of the world around us, such as when we use language for teaching and learning, for problem solving, and for the retention of information.

Knowledge of imaginative functions

Knowledge of imaginative functions enables us to use language to create an imaginary world or extend the world around us for humorous or aesthetic purposes; examples include jokes and the use of figurative language and poetry.

Sociolinguistic knowledge

Sociolinguistic knowledge enables us to create or interpret language that is appropriate to a particular language use setting. This includes knowledge of the conventions that determine the appropriate use of genres, dialects or varieties, registers, natural or idiomatic expressions, cultural references, and figures of speech.

Knowledge of genres[8]

Swales (1990) defines genre as "a system for accomplishing social purposes by verbal means… [that is] valuably fundamental to the realization of goals and that acts as a determinant of linguistic choices" (pp. 41–2). Orlikowski and Yates (1994) describe genres as "socially recognized types of communicative actions—such as memos, meetings, expense forms, training seminars—that are habitually enacted by members of a community to realize particular social purposes" (p. 542). A genre established within a particular community serves as an institutionalized template for social action—an organizing structure—that shapes the ongoing communicative actions of community members through their use of it. Such genre usage, in turn reinforces that genre." As such, knowledge of genres involves knowledge of the conventions that shape communicative actions for particular social purposes.

Knowledge of dialects/varieties

Knowledge of dialects and varieties includes the characteristics of social and regional varieties of language.

Knowledge of register

Knowledge of register includes the characteristics of different levels of formality in language use.

Knowledge of natural or idiomatic expressions

Natural expressions include those expressions that are not only structurally accurate but also expressed in the same way as would the members of a specific speech community.[9] For example, the utterances "the street was very full of cars," and "I will be the one to go," are grammatically correct, and most likely fully understandable. However, members of the English speaking community in North America would be more likely to say, "the traffic was really bad," and "I'll go." Idiomatic expressions are phrases or utterances in a language that generally do not mean exactly what the words themselves mean. Knowledge of this component of sociolinguistic knowledge enables language users to distinguish between language use that sounds native-like and that which sounds like it has been translated from another language.

Knowledge of cultural references and figures of speech

Knowledge of cultural references includes extended meanings given by a specific culture to particular events, places, institutions, or people. For example, the utterances "We shall overcome," "Don't ask, don't tell," and "Yes, we can!" carry meanings beyond the specific individuals who first popularized them and the particular political contexts in which they were used. Knowledge of figures of speech includes figurative language such as metaphors (e.g., "his words were syrup"), similes (e.g., "her reply was like a cold blast of arctic air"), and hyperboles (e.g., "our team's victory tonight is the greatest moment in the annals of baseball").

Strategic competence

Strategic competence can be thought of as higher-order metacognitive strategies that provide a management function in language use, as well as in other cognitive activities.[10] We view strategic competence as a set of metacognitive strategies. This view is derived largely from Sternberg's description of the metacomponents in his model of intelligence (see, for example, Sternberg 1985, 1988). These strategies are involved in planning, monitoring, and evaluating individuals' problem solving. We would thus hypothesize that the metacognitive strategies we discuss here are involved not only in language use, but in virtually all cognitive activity. Skehan (1998) uses the term "ability for use" to capture essentially the same function, of linking areas of what he calls "underlying competence" to performance (p. 168). There is a growing research literature about the role of strategies in language learning and language use, where metacognitive strategies are generally seen to have the function of "planning, organizing and evaluating one's own learning" (Hsiao and Oxford 2002: 371). Purpura (1999), for example, defines metacognitive strategy use as "a set of conscious or unconscious mental activities which are directly or indirectly related to some specific stage of the overall process of language acquisition, use, or testing" (p. 6).

Using language involves the language user's topical knowledge and affective schemata, as well as all the areas of language knowledge discussed above. What makes language use possible is the integration of these attributes as language users create and interpret discourse in situationally appropriate ways. We identify three general areas in which metacognitive strategies operate: goal setting, appraising, and planning. The three areas of executive process use are illustrated in Table 3.2.

Goal setting (deciding what one is going to do)

- Identifying the language use or assessment tasks to be attempted
- Choosing one or more tasks from a set of possible tasks (sometimes by default, if only one task is understandable)
- Deciding whether or not to attempt to complete the task(s) selected.

Appraising (taking stock of what is needed, what one has to work with, and how well one has done)

- Appraising the characteristics of the language use or assessment task to determine the desirability and feasibility of successfully completing it and what resources are needed to complete it
- Appraising our own knowledge (topical, language) components to see if relevant areas of knowledge are available for successfully completing the language use or assessment task
- Appraising the degree to which the language use or assessment task has been successfully completed.

Planning (deciding how to use what one has)

- Selecting elements from the areas of topical knowledge and language knowledge for successfully completing the assessment task
- Formulating one or more plans for implementing these elements in a response to the assessment task
- Selecting one plan for initial implementation as a response to the assessment task.

Table 3.2 Areas of metacognitive strategy use

Goal setting (deciding what one is going to do)

Goal setting involves:

1 identifying the language use tasks or assessment tasks,
2 choosing, where given a choice, one or more tasks from a set of possible tasks, and
3 deciding whether or not to attempt to complete the task(s).

In language use, the purpose for using language is to accomplish a communicative goal. That communicative goal may range from maintaining a personal relationship (as in returning a friend's greeting in the morning), to explaining a difficult concept (as in teaching what a standard deviation is in statistics), to persuading someone to do something (as in trying to convince one's fellow teachers to adopt a particular textbook), to creating humor (as in telling a joke). We accomplish these communicative goals by using language, that is, by performing language use tasks. In virtually every language use setting, we have a choice. For example, we can choose whether or not to return our friend's morning greeting, knowing that whatever we choose—to greet or not to greet—will communicate meaning to our friend. In many language use settings we have several options, or possible language use tasks from which to choose. When we enter a room at a party, for example, we could choose to find a group of friends and go talk with them. Or, we could look around the room to find someone we don't know who looks interesting, and go and introduce ourselves to that person. Or, we could go get some snacks and a drink and find a spot along the wall away from people. We could also think of these choices in terms of different functions the language user may choose to perform. Thus, choosing to return your friend's greeting involves choosing to perform a manipulative function aimed at maintaining your friendship. Not returning the greeting would also perform a manipulative function, but with a possibly very different purpose.

In many assessments, the language user who is being assessed may have a range of choices, in terms of the language he uses. When a teacher assesses his students, based on their classroom language use, for example, what the students choose to say may affect the assessment as much as how they say it. Or, in a portfolio assessment for writing, the student may choose the specific samples of writing he wants to include. In a language assessment, however, the purpose is to elicit a specific sample of language use, so that we typically present the test taker with a limited range of tasks. Thus, the test taker's flexibility in setting goals for performance on assessment tasks is generally not as great as that enjoyed by language users in non-assessment language use. However, by allowing test takers to select among a set of tasks (such as different composition topics), some opportunity for goal setting may be provided.

Appraising (taking stock of what is needed, what one has to work with, and how well one has done)

Appraising provides a means by which the individual relates her internal topical knowledge and language knowledge to the external characteristics of the language use situation and tasks, or of the assessment situation and its tasks. Appraising also takes into consideration the individual's affective responses in the application of appraising strategies. For example, different degrees and kinds of appraising would be involved in responding to a discrete point grammar item and a task involving writing a composition on a technical topic.

Appraising the characteristics of the language use or assessment task

Appraising the characteristics of the language use or assessment task involves identifying the characteristics of the task, in order to determine (1) the desirability and feasibility of successfully completing the task, and (2) what elements of topical knowledge and language knowledge this is likely to require.

Appraising one's own topical knowledge and language knowledge

Appraising one's own topical knowledge and language knowledge involves determining the extent to which relevant topical knowledge and areas of language knowledge are available, and if available, which ones might be utilized for successfully completing the task. This aspect of appraising also considers the individual's available affective schemata for coping with the demands of the task.

Appraising the extent to which the communicative goal of the task has been successfully accomplished

In language use, appraising the success to which the communicative goal has been successfully accomplished involves appraising one's response to the task, in terms of one's own topical knowledge and affective schemata, the characteristics of the language use situation, and the discourse that is created. In reading a book, for example, the reader may appraise how well she has comprehended a particular part of the text by comparing this with what she already knows about the topic, or by continuing to read. In a conversational exchange, the language user can appraise the extent to which his communicative goal has been accomplished by the way his interlocutor responds, with language, with non-verbal communication, or with both. Depending on this appraisal, the language user might decide to continue with the task, or to revise the interpretation or rephrase the utterance, or he might choose to change the communicative goal entirely, either to repair a misunderstanding, or to abandon the communication entirely.

Appraising the correctness or appropriateness of the response to an assessment task involves appraising the individual's response to the task with respect to the perceived criteria for correctness or appropriateness. The relevant criteria pertain to the grammatical, textual, functional, and sociolinguistic characteristics of the response, as well as its topical content. In the event the response appears to be incorrect or inappropriate, this aspect of appraising enables the individual to diagnose the possible causes of the problem, which might lead to changing the communicative goal, the plan for implementing that goal, or both, depending on the situation. Affective schemata are involved in determining the extent to which failure was due to inadequate effort, to the difficulty of the task, or to random sources of interference.

Planning (deciding how to use what one has)

Planning involves deciding how to utilize language knowledge, topical knowledge, and affective schemata to complete the task successfully. Assuming that the appraisal strategies have determined which of these components are available for use, planning involves three aspects:

1 identifying a set of specific elements from topical knowledge and language knowledge (for example, concepts, words, structures, functions) that could be used in a plan,
2 formulating one or more mental plans whose realization will be a response (interpretation, utterance) to the task, and
3 mentally selecting one plan for execution as a response to the task.

Formulating a plan may involve an internal prioritization among the various elements that have been identified, as well as the consideration of how these can be most effectively combined to execute a response. The plan thus provides a set of mental or written specifications for how the various elements might be combined and ordered when realized in language use, as an interpretation or an utterance. The product of the planning strategy, then, is a plan whose realization is a response to the task.

Strategic competence, or the metacognitive strategies, along with language knowledge and topical knowledge, are involved in arriving at a plan for accomplishing the communicative goal, or for completing a language use or assessment task. Execution, or the implementation of this plan in language use, involves cognitive strategies.

Illustrative examples of the use of strategic competence

Strategic competence use in an assessment task

The following example illustrates the interactions among the metacognitive strategies of goal setting, appraisal, and planning. Palmer (1972, 1981) described an assessment in which the test taker was instructed to describe a picture as quickly as possible so that the examiner could distinguish this picture from three other similar pictures in a set of four pictures. Each of the four pictures in a given set included a stick figure of a person doing something, and each picture in the set differed from two of the other three by a single feature, and from the third by two features. One set of four pictures is reproduced in Figure 3.3.

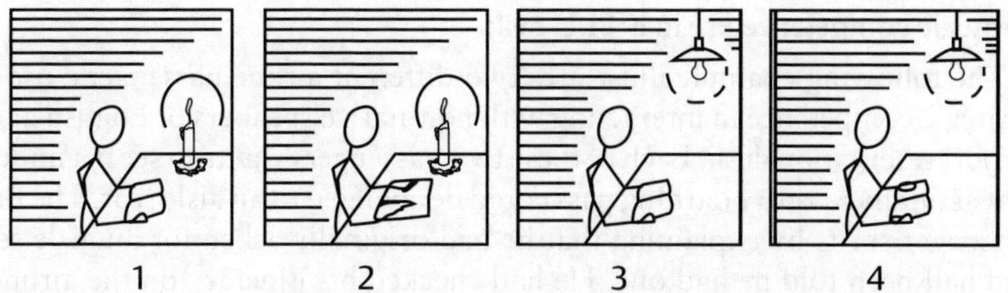

Figure 3.3 Example pictures from experimental speaking assessment (After Palmer 1981: 44)

Palmer reported that in responding to these tasks, the test takers appeared to have made different appraisals of what was required for accomplishing this task. We would further speculate that as a result of these different appraisals, test takers set different goals and formulated different types of plans for their responses. Some test takers, for example, may have set a goal of describing the entire picture, and of responding in complete sentences. These test takers formulated plans that were realized in grammatically accurate utterances that provided a great deal of descriptive information about the pictures. Other test takers may have set a goal of conveying only the critical information that was unique to the particular picture to be described, and formulated plans that were realized in responses that were often single words or short phrases. Still other test takers, whose lexical knowledge may not have included the words needed to describe the features of the objects in the particular picture, may have set as their goal describing the physical characteristics of the picture itself. These test takers formulated plans for responses that did not refer to the topical content of the pictures at all, but that described the pictures in terms of their placement on the page (e.g., "the one on the right") or their non-verbal visual information (e.g. lines and shapes, different shades of black and gray). All of the test takers used their strategic competence to arrive at plans for responding to the test tasks. Some arrived at plans for producing responses (short, telegraphic, or describing placement) that would be rewarded by the scoring system, while the others arrived plans for utterances (complete, grammatical sentences, full descriptions of the pictures) that were penalized by the scoring system. Given the instructions, in which the communicative goal was to describe the picture as quickly as possible, we might conclude that the test takers who paid very little attention to grammatical accuracy or completeness of description made the most effective use of their strategic competence in responding to the test task. On the other hand, those test takers who focused on producing grammatically accurate, complete descriptions of the pictures either appraised the goal of the task incorrectly or made ineffective use of planning and goal setting in responding to the test tasks.

Strategic competence use in a TLU task

The following example illustrates two different airline passengers' use of strategic competence in interacting with non-native speakers of English at an airport reservation desk. Each of these two passengers wants to see if a middle seat assignment on a boarding pass could be changed to an aisle seat. The first passenger starts by explaining that he had originally asked for an aisle seat and had been told he had one. He had checked his itinerary on the airline's website which indicated he had an aisle seat. His boarding pass had been issued back in an airport two flights prior to this one, and he hadn't taken the time to check the seat printed on the boarding pass. Now he just noticed that he had a window seat. He wonders if an aisle seat is available. In addition, he would like one near the front of the plane because he has a short connection at the end of this flight, and wants to be sure he can get off the plane as soon as possible in order to make his connection. The reservation agent's eyes start to glaze over as she struggles to follow the details of the conversation and figure out exactly what the passenger wants. When the agent actually figures out what the passenger wants and starts to check the computer for seat availability, the passenger continues to interrupt the agent with information about his frequent flier status and other assorted matters. Despite the fact that the agent is slowed down by all this conversation and this is obvious to anyone looking at the interaction, the passenger continues to talk on and on. Eventually, the problem is solved, but the whole process takes several minutes.

The second passenger also has the same goal of getting an aisle seat. She appraises the situation. Having heard the agent talking very slowly with the passenger in front of her and seen the agent frequently looking puzzled and asking for repetition, she realizes that the agent has some difficulty following spoken English, especially when spoken quickly and using unsimplified language. She also notices that the agent seems to be completely at home working with written English on the computer screen. She therefore plans to accomplish her goal by using as little spoken language as possible and using language likely to be most familiar to the ticket agent. She executes her plan by putting the ticket down in front of the agent and saying "Hi. Could I change my seat (pointing to it on the boarding pass) to an aisle seat near the front of the plane (pointing the front of the plane)?" She waits quietly until the agent provides an answer and hands the passenger a new boarding pass with an aisle seat. The passenger says, "thank you very much." This transaction takes less than a minute.

Both passengers accomplished their goals of getting their seats changed but did so in different ways. If the success of the communication were to be measured only in terms of whether or not the goal was accomplished, both interactions would be assessed as equally effective. However, if the success of the communication were to be measured in terms of how economical the use of time was, the second interaction would receive a higher score. (This measure of success is essentially the same as that used in the experimental speaking assessment described above.) The same would be true if what was measured was the effectiveness of use of available resources such as the existing boarding passes which provided most of the critical information for the interaction. The same would also be true if the success of the communication were to be measured in terms of affect, such as the amount of stress on the ticket agent. Discussing interactions of this sort both in assessment situations and in real life language use has helped to inform our thinking about the nature of strategic competence, as well as our thinking about different ways to define the construct to be measured and the evaluation criteria to be used.

LANGUAGE "SKILLS"

Language ability has traditionally been considered, by language teachers and language testers alike, to consist of four skills: listening, reading, speaking, and writing. Indeed, a model of language proficiency that has been very influential in language assessment since the second half of the last century describes language ability in terms of these four skills and several components (e.g., grammar, vocabulary, and pronunciation).[11] The four "skills" have traditionally been distinguished in terms of channel (audio, visual) and mode (productive, receptive). Thus, listening and speaking involve the audio channel, and receptive and productive modes, respectively, while reading and writing are in the visual channel, and receptive and productive modes, respectively. However, is it adequate to distinguish the four skills simply in terms of channel and mode? And does it make sense to define a construct simply as the name of a skill? If so, then all language use that involves the audio channel and the productive mode could be considered speaking, while any language use in the visual channel and receptive mode would be reading.

It takes very little reflection to discover the limitations of this approach. First, it would classify widely divergent language use tasks or activities together under a single "skill." Consider, for example, how different are activities such as participating in a face-to-face conversation and listening to a radio newscast, even though both involve listening. Similarly, engaging in an e-mail "chat" probably has more in common with an oral conversation than with either writing a letter or reading a newspaper, even though the e-mail chat, writing a letter, and reading a newspaper all involve the visual channel. Second, this approach fails to take into consideration the fact that language use is not simply a general phenomenon that takes place in a vacuum. We do not just "read"; we read about something specific, for some particular purpose, in a particular setting. That is, language use takes place, or is realized, in the performance of specific situated language use tasks.

It is this conception of language use as the performance of specific situated language use tasks that provides a much more useful means for characterizing what have traditionally been called language skills. We would thus conceptualize "language skills" as the contextualized realizations of the capacity for language use in the performance of specific language use tasks. We would therefore argue that it is not useful to think in terms of "skills," but rather to think in terms of specific activities or tasks in which language is used purposefully. Thus, rather than attempting to define "speaking" as an abstract skill, it is more useful to identify a specific language use task that involves the activity of speaking, and describe it in terms of its task characteristics and the areas of language ability it engages. We would thus argue that the concept that has been called "skill" can be much more usefully seen as a specific combination of language ability and task characteristics.[12] Furthermore, if we are to find this concept of "ability–task" to be useful in the development and use of language assessments, then we must define specific instances of it in terms of their task characteristics (setting, input, expected response, and relationship between input and response) and the components of language ability and areas of topical knowledge these tasks engage. We shall go on to consider how we can describe the characteristics of language use and language assessment tasks in Chapter 4.

EXERCISES

1 Think of your own example of non-reciprocal language use. Write a short paragraph to describe it using the graphic organizer in Figure 3.1.
2 Think of your own example of reciprocal language use. Use the graphic organizer in Figure 3.2 to write a short description of it.

SUGGESTED READINGS

Language use

Eckert, P. and **J. Rickford.** (2001). *Style and Sociolinguistic Variation.* Cambridge: Cambridge University Press.

Genre

Freedman, A. and P. **Medway.** (eds.). 1994. *Genre and the New Rhetoric.* London: Taylor & Francis.

Swales, J. M. 1990. *Genre Analysis: English in Academic and Research Settings.* Cambridge: Cambridge University Press.

——(2004). *Research Genres: Explorations and Applications*: Cambridge University Press.

Strategies

Bialystok, E. 1990. *Communication Strategies.* Cambridge, MA: Basil Blackwell.

Cohen, A. D. 1998. *Strategies in Learning and Using a Second Language.* New York: Addison-Wesley.

Oxford, R. 1996. *Language Learning Strategies around the World: Cross-cultural Perspectives.* Honolulu: University of Hawai'i Press.

Purpura, J. E. 1999. *Modeling the Relationships between Test Takers' Reported Cognitive and Metacognitive Strategy Use and Performance on Language Assessments*. Cambridge: University of Cambridge Local Examinations Syndicate and Cambridge University Press.

NOTES

1 The terms "interactive" and "interactional" are both used in the research literature to refer to the way individuals interact in the creation of discourse, whether this is for purposes of communication, socialization, or when creating discourse is part of learning a language. In order to avoid confusion, we will use the term "interactive."

2 Swain (1985) refers to this principle in designing assessments so as to "bias for best."

3 A discussion of cognitive strategies is beyond the scope of this book. Some references to this research literature are included in the "Suggested Readings" at the end of the chapter.

4 There is a long and complex history of terms, and perspectives represented in the terms, for what we are calling "language ability." Bachman (1990: 108) provides a discussion of these terms. The view and perspective we present here builds upon the work of Hymes (1972), Savignon (1972, 1983), Canale and Swain (1980), and Canale (1983), on "communicative competence," and Widdowson (1978, 1983) on language use. This view is quite different from that of "proficiency" which continues to inform much of the work on the assessment of foreign languages in the US (e.g., American Council on the Teaching of Foreign Languages 1983; Clark 1979; Lowe 1988).

5 This view of language ability is consistent with what Widdowson (1983) has called "communicative capacity," and Skehan (1998) has called "ability for use," as well as with research in applied linguistics that has increasingly come to view language ability as consisting of two components: (1) language knowledge, sometimes referred to as "competence," and (2) cognitive processes, or strategies, which implement that knowledge in language use (see, for example, Bachman 1990; Bialystok 1990; Widdowson 1983). It is also consistent with information processing, or cognitive models of mental abilities, which also distinguish processes or heuristics from domains of knowledge (see, for example, Sternberg, 1985, 1988).

6 Organizational knowledge includes those components that enable individuals to produce or comprehend instances of what Widdowson (1978) calls "usage."

7 We will follow Brown and Yule's (1983) distinction between "utterances," which are spoken, and "sentences," which are written. However, since we hypothesize that the areas of language knowledge are involved in both oral and written language use, we will use both terms, "utterance" and "sentence," in our discussion, unless we intend to specify either oral or written language.

8 A discussion of genre is beyond the scope of this book. Some references to this research literature are included in the "Suggested Readings" at the end of the chapter.

9 Pawley and Syder (1983) use the term "nativelike" to refer to such expressions.

10 Some researchers distinguish strategies from processes in terms of the extent to which they are "conscious." Cohen (1998), for example, argues that strategies are conscious, or controlled, while processes are unconscious, or automatic. It is our

view that metacognitive strategies may sometimes be controlled, and may sometimes operate automatically. We will thus use the term "strategy" to cover both.

11 Lado (1961) and Carroll (1961, 1968) provide examples of such "skills and components" models.

12 This concept that the activities of listening, speaking, reading, writing are realizations of the interaction between language ability and the characteristics of language use or assessment tasks is consistent with the measurement concept that assessment items can best be seen as combinations of constructs, or traits, and assessment methods. This view of assessment items as trait-method units provides the conceptual basis for one approach to construct validation. (See the discussion and references in Bachman 1990: Chapter 7.)

4

Describing characteristics of language use and language assessment tasks

INTRODUCTION

As indicated in Chapter 2, being able to describe the characteristics of language use tasks and assessment tasks is critical in order to demonstrate how performance on a given language assessment generalizes to language use in specific settings other than the language test itself. The characteristics of tasks are of interest for several reasons. First, these characteristics provide the link between tasks in different settings—that of the assessment and that of non-assessment language use—and permit us to select or design assessment tasks that correspond in specific ways to non-assessment language use tasks. Second, the characteristics of the assessment task will help determine the extent and ways in which the test taker's language ability is engaged, and this will determine, to a large extent, the meaningfulness of the inferences or interpretations about language ability that are made. Third, the degree of correspondence between the characteristics of a given assessment task and those of a particular language use task will determine, to a large extent, the generalizability of the interpretations to the setting of the target language use tasks. Finally, because a task is the fundamental element of an assessment, by controlling the characteristics of the assessment tasks the test developer can help assure that test takers' performance will generalize to settings beyond the test itself.

In order to utilize the notion of language use task in the development of language assessment tasks, we need to describe what we mean by this term. We can begin our discussion of language use tasks with a definition of **task** given by the psychologist John B. Carroll (1993) in discussing cognitive abilities: "a task [is] any activity in which a person engages, given an appropriate setting, in order to achieve a specifiable class of objectives" (p. 8). Applied linguists have discussed *language* tasks extensively, and there seems to be general agreement that these are (1) closely associated with, or situated in specific situations, (2) goal-oriented, and (3) involve the active participation of language users. (See the references in Suggested Readings.) Building upon these definitions, we define a **language use task** as an activity that involves individuals in using language for the purpose of achieving a particular goal or objective in a particular setting. This definition of language use task thus includes both the specific activity and the setting in which it takes place.

In this chapter we present a framework that can be used for describing language use tasks. The material in this chapter operationalizes the concepts presented in Bachman (1990: Chapter 5). In the chapters in Parts II and III, and in the Projects (http://www.oup.com/LAIP), we provide extensive discussions, along with examples, of how this framework can be applied to practical problems in designing and developing useful assessments of language ability.

TARGET LANGUAGE USE (TLU) DOMAINS

In language assessment, we are primarily interested in making interpretations about test takers' language ability. We also want those interpretations to generalize beyond the particular tasks in the assessment. However, we're not interested in generalizing to just any, or all, language use tasks in any or all settings. Rather, we want our interpretations to generalize to those specific language use tasks which test takers are likely to perform in specific settings. For our purposes, we define a **target language use (TLU) domain** as a specific setting outside of the test itself that requires the test taker to perform language use tasks. If a language use task is within a specific TLU domain, then we will call it a **target language use (TLU) task.** It is TLU tasks to which we want our interpretations about language ability to generalize.

Types of TLU domains

There are two general types of TLU domain that are of particular interest to the development of language assessment tasks. One type of TLU domain consists of a setting in which language is used for the purpose of language teaching and language learning. We will refer to this as a **language teaching domain.** The other type of TLU domain consists of settings in which language is used for purposes other than teaching and learning language. We will refer to these as **real life domains.**[1] If a language use task is within a specific TLU domain, then we will call it a **target language use task.** In developing an assessment, the test developer will identify and describe a specific TLU domain and select one or more TLU tasks as a basis for developing assessment tasks. For example, if the domain were a language teaching domain, the test developer would describe that particular domain and its TLU tasks in detail. Similarly if the domain were a real life domain, as in the "English for Business Communication" example discussed below, the test developer would describe that particular domain and its TLU tasks. (The processes of identifying TLU domains and selecting TLU tasks are discussed in Chapters 14 and 15.)

TLU domains and tasks and decisions to be made

Because we use the information we collect with language assessments to help us make decisions, it's necessary for the test developer to consider the decisions to be made in selecting TLU task(s) as a basis for a given assessment. That is, in addition to selecting a TLU domain and tasks to which we want our interpretations of ability to generalize, these TLU domains and tasks must also be relevant to the decisions to be made.

Situation 1: multiple TLU domains and tasks, only some of relevance to decisions

In some assessment situations there may be multiple TLU domains and tasks, only some of which are relevant to the decisions to be made. That is, any particular test taker or group of test takers might need to perform a variety of language use tasks in a variety of settings outside of the assessment itself. However, for the purpose of a particular assessment, not all of these will be of relevance to the decisions to be made. Suppose, for example, that the director of a study abroad program needed to decide whether to place students into a program of academic courses conducted entirely in a foreign language or into a course in which they would be given language support as part of the courses. When living abroad, these students will be performing language use tasks in a variety of settings, such as shopping, going to dinner, and making housing arrangements, as well as attending academic lectures, discussing course content with teachers and other students, and reading course materials in the foreign language. However, for the purpose of making the placement decisions, only the tasks in the academic setting are relevant. Thus, in this example, the test developer would identify the academic setting as the TLU domain and select tasks from this domain as a basis for developing assessment tasks.

Situation 2: same TLU domain, different decisions

In other assessment situations, there may be a single TLU domain, but different decisions, affecting different stakeholders, will be made on the basis of the assessment. Suppose that in the study abroad example, the assessment was used not only to place students into the appropriate study abroad program, but was also used to collect information about the effectiveness of the language courses and teachers that prepare students for study abroad. If an oral interview were part of the assessment, for example, teachers might use this to identify students' areas of weakness in oral interactions and make changes in the course or in their teaching. Or, the head of the department in which the courses are offered could use information from students' performance to make decisions about retaining teachers or letting them go, promoting them, or giving them raises in their salaries.

Situation 3: different TLU domains, different decisions

A very common situation is one in which there are several different TLU domains and different decisions to be made. Suppose, for example, that for the purpose of developing a given language assessment procedure, we might initially identify the TLU domain as "English for Business Communication," and within this TLU domain we might identify a number of different language use settings, such as the corporate office or out in the field, at a customer's place of business. Within each of these settings, it is possible to identify a number of specific language use tasks. In the office setting, for example, the language use tasks might include writing memos, preparing reports, answering and taking messages on the phone, and giving and following directions. Language use tasks involved out in the field, on the other hand, might include demonstrating products, diagnosing problems customers are having with their current products, writing proposals, responding to written offers, and oral interactions, both face to face and over the telephone. All of these tasks, which are within our defined TLU domain, are thus TLU tasks. When we consider the decisions to be made, however, we might find that different TLU domains and tasks are relevant to different decisions. If we were hiring people to perform tasks in the corporate office, then only those tasks would be of relevance to the decision, and hence could be used as a basis for developing assessment tasks. If, on the other hand, we were hiring people to sell or service our products, the tasks in the field domain would be relevant. Figure 4.1 illustrates the relationships among TLU domains and tasks.

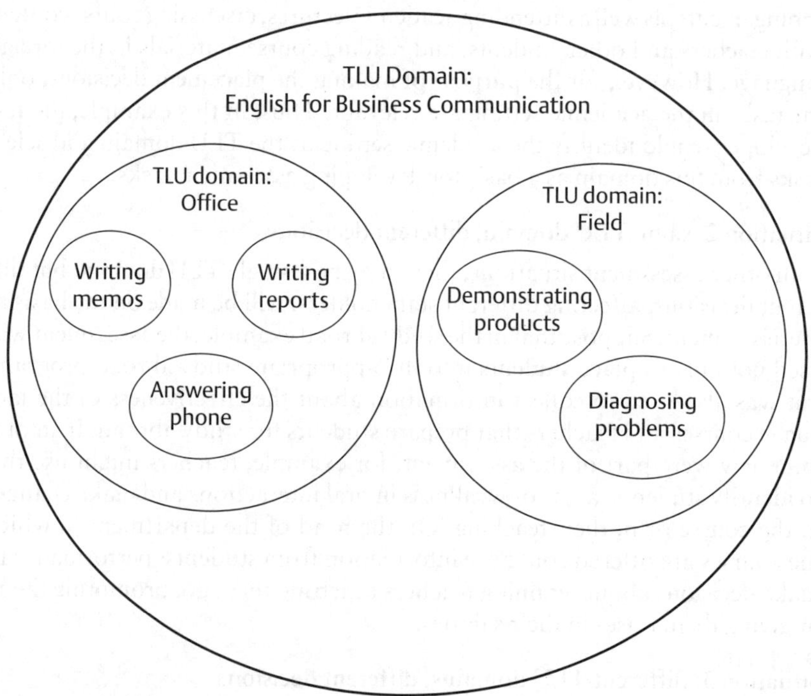

Figure 4.1 TLU domain and TLU tasks

RATIONALE FOR A FRAMEWORK FOR DESCRIBING ASSESSMENT TASK CHARACTERISTICS

Language use tasks can be thought of informally as constituting the elemental activities of language use. That is, language use can be viewed as the performance of a series of language use tasks that are interrelated, in terms of the setting, the communicative goal to be achieved, and the participants. A language assessment task can be thought of as a procedure for eliciting responses from which inferences can be made about an individual's language ability. It therefore follows that in order for such inferences to be made, a language assessment should consist of language use tasks. In designing language assessments whose use we can justify, it is important to include tasks whose characteristics correspond to those of TLU tasks. In order to accomplish this, we need a framework of task characteristics that will enable us to systematically describe both the TLU tasks and the tasks to be included in the assessment procedure.

Two issues we face when designing assessments are how to characterize tasks and how to distinguish one task from another with sufficient precision to inform assessment development. For example, consider two tasks carried out in the office domain in the example above, "writing memos" and "writing reports," which are, on the surface, at least, quite similar. At the same time, it is clear that they are not exactly the same. In order to describe these similarities and differences in more detail, we need to consider specific characteristics. These tasks have a number of characteristics in common. Both are written, both may include vocabulary items that are typical of the office setting and refer to individuals or parts of the corporation that are familiar to everyone in the office. However, these two tasks have characteristics in which they differ as well. Memos are generally shorter than reports, they do not need to follow the same rhetorical organization conventions as reports, and they are often written in a more informal register. The characteristics "channel" (written) and "topic" (corporate sales) are shared or common to both tasks while the characteristics "length" (short versus long) and "register" (informal versus formal) distinguishes the two tasks; this characteristic is different for these tasks.

Using these characteristics, we can also describe, with precision, why the tasks "writing memos" and "writing reports" are more similar than "writing reports" and "answering the phone." They clearly have very few characteristics in common, and differ in the channel (written versus audio), the type of organization (conversational versus formal written), the length (long versus short), the register (rather formal versus somewhat informal), and so forth.

In this section we provide a rationale for developing a framework for describing task characteristics. We will first discuss the effects of specific task characteristics on assessment performance. We will then discuss why we need to describe assessment tasks in terms of specific characteristics, rather than as holistic entities, and the need for greater precision in the way we characterize assessment tasks. We also provide a brief overview of some of the purposes that a framework of assessment task characteristics can serve.

Effects of task characteristics on assessment performance

Language teachers intuitively realize that the types of tasks that are included in language assessment procedures are important. Frequently one of the first questions asked in our classes on assessment is about our opinions of the "best" way to assess a particular area of language ability. These teachers may not yet have refined their thinking as to what specific characteristics might make one assessment procedure more appropriate for a given purpose than another. However, they are clearly aware that the way they assess language ability affects how their students perform on language assessments and hence the quality of the information obtained from their assessment.

There is also considerable research in language testing that demonstrates the effects of test method on test performance. (See, for example, the Suggested Readings for this chapter.) This research, and language teachers' intuitions, both lead to the same conclusion: the characteristics of the tasks used are always likely to affect assessment results to some degree, so that there is no assessment that yields only information about the ability we want to assess. The implication of this conclusion for the design, development, and use of language assessments is equally clear: since we cannot totally eliminate the effects of task characteristics, we must learn to understand them and to manage them so as to assure that the assessments we use will have the qualities we desire and are appropriate for the uses for which they are intended.

Precision in characterizing different assessment tasks

When we think about the different types of tasks that are commonly used for language assessment, we often tend to think of them as single entities. However, for the purpose of developing language assessments, it is useful to think about tasks as collections of characteristics. For example, the "multiple-choice item" is often discussed as a kind of test task, even though such items vary in a number of ways, such as in their length, syntactic complexity, level of vocabulary, topical content, and type of response required, to name but a few. Similarly, the "composition" task type encompasses a wide variety of prompts that can differ in characteristics such as the intended audience, purpose, and specific organizational pattern requested. We cannot characterize assessment tasks precisely if we think of them only as holistic types or think that simply naming a task provides enough information to characterize the nature of the task with any precision. Therefore we need a descriptive framework of task characteristics.

The following section provides a framework for describing the characteristics of assessment tasks in a way that enables test developers and test users to investigate the degree of correspondence between TLU tasks and assessment tasks. It is neither feasible nor necessary, for the purpose of developing language assessment tasks and assessment procedures, to provide an exhaustive discourse analysis of target language use. This is because we need to focus our assessment specifications on those characteristics that are relevant to the kinds of interpretations we want to make and the specific TLU domains to which we want these interpretations to generalize.

This framework also enables assessment developers to better understand *which* specific characteristics can be varied, and to suggest *how* these can be varied, thus providing a valuable tool for tailoring assessments appropriately for specific groups of test takers so they can perform at their best. Of the many factors that can affect assessment performance (for example, unexpected disturbances during the assessment administration, individual characteristics of test takers, or temporary changes in their physical or mental condition), the characteristics of the assessment task are the only factors directly under our control as assessment developers. Attempting to control the assessment task characteristics by design provides the most useful and practical means for maximizing the usefulness of our assessments for their intended purposes.

Task characteristics can be used for the following:

1 describing TLU tasks as a basis for designing language assessment tasks;
2 comparing the characteristics of TLU and assessment tasks to evaluate generalizability;
3 describing different assessment tasks in order to assure their comparability, and, thus, as one means for evaluating consistency.

In our own experience in assessment development, as well as in teaching courses in language assessment and consulting on assessment development projects, we have found these characteristics useful for describing not only the characteristics of assessment tasks, but also the characteristics of TLU tasks that are relevant to the design and development of assessment tasks. Thus, in the discussion below, we will use the term "task" to refer to both TLU tasks and assessment tasks.

Our purpose is not to prescribe any particular types of assessment tasks or combination of assessment task characteristics. On the contrary, the framework is a tool for achieving greater flexibility or adaptability in the development of assessment procedures, rather than as a recipe for developing assessment procedures in one particular way. In addition, we do not insist on using this particular set of characteristics for all assessment development situations. Indeed, we have found that, in many situations, assessment developers need to make some modifications in the specific characteristics they include for their own purposes, and we illustrate this in some of the Projects. Furthermore, the order in which the assessment task characteristics are specified in a given Project will not necessarily follow the order in which they are described in this framework. In fact, it is because of its adaptability that we believe the framework presented below provides a valuable tool for learning the process of analyzing tasks for purposes of assessment development and a starting place for task analysis in many practical assessment development projects. But above all, we believe that it is crucial that the assessment developer work with some set of task characteristics in developing assessment tasks.

A FRAMEWORK OF LANGUAGE TASK CHARACTERISTICS

The framework of task characteristics that we describe below builds on that proposed by Bachman (1990), and consists of a set of characteristics for describing five aspects of tasks: setting, assessment rubric, input, expected response, and relationship between input and expected response.[2] Our framework of task characteristics is presented first in outline form in Table 4.1. We provide this framework in the format of an outline to facilitate referencing of the levels in the examples of assessment task characteristics in later chapters back to the levels in this outline.

I CHARACTERISTICS OF THE SETTING
- A Physical characteristics
- B Participants
- C Time of task

II CHARACTERISTICS OF THE RUBRIC
- A Instructions
  - 1 Language (native, target, both)
  - 2 Channel (aural, visual)
  - 3 Specification of structure, procedures to be followed by test takers, and procedures for producing assessment records
- B Structure
  - 1 Number of parts/tasks
  - 2 Salience of parts/tasks
  - 3 Sequence of parts/tasks
  - 4 Relative importance of parts/tasks
  - 5 Number of tasks per part
- C Time allotment
- D Recording method
  - 1 Type of assessment record (score, description)
  - 2 Criteria for correctness (for scoring)
  - 3 Procedures for producing an assessment record
  - 4 Recorders (scorers/raters, describers)

III CHARACTERISTICS OF THE INPUT
- A Format
  - 1 Channel (aural, visual, both)

- 2 Form (language, non-language, both)
- 3 Language (native, target, both)
- 4 Length/time
- 5 Vehicle (live, reproduced, both)
- 6 Degree of speededness
- 7 Type (item, prompt, input for interpretation)

B Language of input

1 Language characteristics

a) Organizational characteristics (rhetorical or conversational)

(1) Grammatical

(a) Vocabulary

(b) Syntax

(c) Phonology/graphology

(2) Textual

(a) Cohesion

(b) Organization (rhetorical, conversational)

b) Pragmatic characteristics

(1) Functional (ideational, manipulative, heuristic, imaginative)

(2) Sociolinguistic (genre, dialect/variety, register, naturalness, cultural references, and figures of speech)

2 Topical characteristics

IV CHARACTERISTICS OF THE EXPECTED RESPONSE

A Format

- 1 Channel (oral, visual, both)
- 2 Form (language, non-language, both)
- 3 Language (native, target, both)
- 4 Length/time
- 5 Type (selected, limited production, extended production)
- 6 Degree of speededness

B Language of expected response

1 Language characteristics

a) Organizational characteristics

(1) Grammatical

(a) Vocabulary

(b) Syntax

(c) Phonology/graphology

(2) Textual

(a) Cohesion

(b) Organization (rhetorical, conversational)

b) Pragmatic characteristics

(1) Functional (ideational, manipulative, heuristic, imaginative)

(2) Sociolinguistic (genre, dialect/variety, register, naturalness, cultural references and figures of speech)

2 Topical characteristics

V RELATIONSHIP BETWEEN INPUT AND EXPECTED RESPONSE
- A Type of external interactiveness (type of interaction among participants and between participants and equipment and materials in the language use task): reciprocal, non-reciprocal, adaptive
- B Scope of relationship (broad, narrow)
- C Directness of relationship (direct, indirect)

Table 4.1 Task characteristics

Characteristics of the setting

The **setting** comprises the circumstances under which either language use or testing takes place. The characteristics of the setting include the physical characteristics, the participants, and the time of task.

Physical characteristics

Physical characteristics include the location, the noise level, temperature, humidity, seating conditions, and lighting. Also included are the degree of familiarity of the test takers or language user with the materials and equipment to be used. In an assessment setting, materials and equipment may be fairly specialized (for instance, pencils, paper, computers, audio-visual equipment, props). In a TLU setting such as in an office, for example, familiarity with files, a voice-mail system, or a computer for sending and receiving e-mail messages will clearly affect an individual's use of language.

Participants

Participants are the people who are involved in the task. In some language use tasks, such as a conversation, two or more participants actively engage with each other in the negotiation of meaning. In other tasks, such as reading a book, the participants may have quite different roles, with one (the reader) interpreting the discourse without the possibility of actively engaging the other (the writer) in the negotiation of meaning. In writing tasks, such as writing an essay, the participants will include not only the writer, but his or her intended audience. In this case, the characteristics of the intended audience (e.g., their familiarity with and relationship to the writer, their familiarity with and level of expertise in the topic) will be or can be used to characterize the intended audience. In an assessment setting, the participants include not only the test takers, but also those who are involved in administering the assessment, or in engaging in language use with the test takers. The characteristics of these participants are likely to affect the nature of the task, and the test taker's performance. What is their status and their relationship to the test takers? How familiar are they to the test takers?

Time of task

The **time of task** is the time at which the assessment is conducted or at which the TLU task takes place. For example, does the language use take place when the language users are fresh, or when they are fatigued? This characteristic is probably of the greatest use in evaluating the degree to which the time of an assessment influences the test takers' ability to perform at their best.

Characteristics of the rubric

What we will call the **rubric** provides the context in which TLU tasks *and* assessment tasks are performed. The rubric includes those characteristics that provide the purpose and structure for particular tasks and that indicate how language users or test takers are to proceed in accomplishing the tasks. The characteristics of rubric include the following:

1 the instructions,
2 the structure of the assessment: how the tasks are organized in the assessment,
3 the duration of the assessment as a whole and of the individual tasks, and
4 how a record will be produced from the test taker's response.

For assessment tasks, the characteristics of the rubric are likely to be fairly obvious, since we think through the organization of the assessment and how test takers' responses will be recorded when we go through the process of developing it. We also provide information of this type in the instructions and in the way the tasks are structured and organized.

In TLU tasks, on the other hand, the characteristics of the rubric may be less obvious, since we may not be used to thinking of TLU tasks as having a rubric in the same sense as do assessment tasks. However, if we think about it, we can see how TLU tasks can be thought of as having implicit instructions (the communicative goal the tasks are designed to accomplish) and a structure (e.g., characteristics of the genre within which the tasks fall, such as a memo, a report, an account of an important event, an evaluation, and so on). Similarly, the characteristics of the task duration can be described, as well as how the responses of other language users will be evaluated.

For example, consider the TLU task "describing a short vacation trip to a friend." The implicit instructions or communicative goal of this task might be to provide an account of the vacation and get the friend to empathize with its ups and downs as you describe them. The structure of the task might include a general thesis ("It had its ups and downs, but we survived it"), short accounts of each event during the vacation, and some sort of lesson we learned from the experience (e.g., whether or not to take such a trip again.) The duration would be contingent upon the patience of the friend to indulge your story telling. Your friend's evaluation might be that even though he isn't interested in every detail of your vacation, he does want to show some empathy for you. Your own evaluation might be whether or not you felt like you had been indulged to the extent you wanted to be and whether you succeeded in getting through the account without eliciting signals that your friend was bored by your account, and thought that your conclusions made sense, in the broader scheme of things.

Instructions

In language assessment, **instructions** are the means by which the test takers are informed about the procedures for taking the assessment, how it is structured (see "Structure" below), how it will be scored, and how the results will be used. The purpose of the instructions is to inform test takers how they are to respond to the input. Thus, instructions are not part of the input (see discussion of input below). As a result, instructions need to be explicit and comprehensible to the test takers. This is because of the need to base our interpretations on test taker's responses to assessment tasks, not on their ability to understand instructions. Well-prepared instructions should not, in and of themselves, constitute a problem for the test takers. (Instructions are discussed in detail in Chapter 14.)

In a TLU task, the instructions may or may not be explicitly stated. However, the purpose of performing a TLU task, how it is structured or organized, how one's performance will be evaluated, and how long the task will take or last are all determined, to a large extent implicitly, by the participants in the task, and the characteristics of the setting in which the task takes place. In the example in Chapter 3 of the customer in the Thai restaurant, for example, the implicit instructions include a purpose (to enjoy a delicious meal), and a structure (waiter invites the customer to sit down, gives her a menu, asks if she'd like something to drink, brings back the drink, discusses various options on the menu, and so forth).

Language of the instructions

The characteristics of **language in which the instructions are presented** include the following: native language, the target language, or both. As mentioned above, the instructions are not intended to be part of the assessment (i.e., they should not challenge the test takers' ability to understand them). Therefore, the instructions need to be presented either at a level of the target language that the test takers will be able to understand, or in their native language, where this is feasible.

Channel

The characteristics of the **channel** in which the instructions are presented include the following: aural, visual, or both.

Specification of structure of the assessment, the procedures to be followed by the test takers, and the procedures for producing an assessment record

The structure of the assessment, the procedures the test takers are expected to follow in taking the assessment, and the procedures for producing a record should be specified in the instructions. The structure and procedures can be specified very briefly as:

- lengthy or brief
- with or without examples
- provided one at a time, linked to particular parts of the assessment, or provided entirely in one location.

However, structure and procedures may be specified in greater detail and in a variety of ways, depending upon the situation in which the assessment is to be used. For example, in a composition test developed for use in a writing class, the specification of procedures might include information about the process the test takers are asked to follow (such as preparing an outline, a rough draft, and a final draft) as well as characteristics of the product (such as the purpose of the composition, the intended audience, the kinds of support, the kind of organization, the register).

An understanding of the type of assessment record that will be produced, as well as the criteria and procedures for producing the record, may well affect how test takers respond to the task. If, for example, test takers know that their responses to a composition test task will be scored only in terms of its organization and content, this may lead them to focus less on grammatical accuracy and more on how they organize the content of their composition. Thus, it is a matter of fairness to assure that the procedures for producing an assessment record are made explicit in the instructions.

Structure

An assessment can be structured to include several parts, and each part can include a number of tasks. The characteristics of the **structure** include how the parts of the assessment procedure are put together and presented to the test takers. These should be clearly described in the instructions. Characteristics of the structure include the following:

Number of parts and tasks

The **number of parts and tasks** consists of the main divisions, or parts, that are included in the assessment as a whole, and how many tasks there are in each part.

Salience of parts and tasks

The **salience of parts and tasks** consists of the extent to which the different parts and tasks of the assessment are clearly distinguishable from one another by the test takers. Are the divisions between the parts of the assessment clearly indicated to the test takers, and are the separate tasks clearly indicated?

Sequence of parts and tasks

The **sequence of parts and tasks** is the order of the parts or tasks of the assessment. The sequence can be either fixed or variable. For example, in some assessments, the test takers may be required to complete the parts of the test in a specific sequence in order to standardize the assessment procedure, while in other assessments test takers may be allowed to complete the tasks in any order they wish. In a computer adaptive test, the sequence of tasks is determined by the test taker's response and the computer.

Relative importance of parts and tasks

The **relative importance of parts and tasks** is the extent to which the parts or tasks of the assessment differ in importance. If some parts or tasks are considered to be more important than others, this may influence how the test takers allocate their time and focus their attention, so that they need to be informed of this.

Number of tasks/items per part

The **number of tasks/items per part** indicates how many different tasks or items are included in each part of the test. (Refer to Project 4 for an example of an assessment that consists of multiple parts, each consisting of differing numbers of tasks.)

Time allotment

The **time allotment** is the amount of time provided for individual assessment tasks, for the parts, and for the entire assessment, which is the score or verbal description we obtain from the assessment.

Recording method

One outcome of the assessment process is an assessment record, and this can be a score, a verbal description, or a combination of these. If the assessment record is a score, then the **criteria for correctness** and **procedures for producing an assessment record** need to be specified. Finally, the characteristics of the **recorders**, the individuals who will prepare the assessment record, need to be specified. (Procedures for producing an assessment record are discussed in detail in Chapter 16.)

Type of assessment record

The **type of assessment record** is a score or a description.

Criteria for correctness

For assessments in which the test taker's performance will be scored, the **criteria for correctness** specify (1) the components of language ability that will be scored and (2) the way scores will be assigned with respect to different levels on the components of language ability to be recorded. In an assessment task requiring students to write a composition, for example, the test takers' performance could be rated on several rating scales, one for each of the components of language ability to be assessed, with a rating (e.g., 1 to 4) assigned according to the criteria described in the rating scales. In a test consisting of multiple tasks or items, each of which is scored, the test taker's score on the test might consist of the total of all these different scores.

The criteria for judging or evaluating performance when a record is a description are essentially the same as the criteria described in rating scales, but instead of numerical ratings (scores) descriptive labels will be used. In many assessments, records contain both numerical ratings and descriptive labels or more extensive descriptions of the meanings of the numerical ratings. (See Chapter 16 for an example of an assessment that contains records consisting of both numerical ratings and descriptions of the meanings of these ratings.)

Procedures for producing an assessment record

The procedures for arriving at an assessment record include who will do the recording, when the recording will take place, where it will take place, and in what sequence the steps in recording will be followed. For example, in scoring a test in which students write a composition, the composition might be rated by a single rater or multiple raters, and the raters might be course instructors or individuals hired specifically to rate the compositions. The raters could also provide a verbal description of the test takers' performance, describing how well they have performed on the different components of language ability. In rating an oral interview test, the ratings might take place while the test is being administered or later. Scoring on a high-stakes test might take place where the test is administered or at the location of an agency where the test was developed. Ratings of a composition test might take place in a series of steps in which two raters rate the composition, and if their ratings differ by more than one level, a third rater would be called in. Additionally, the raters might be required to review the rating criteria and benchmark examples before each rating session. As with a composition assessment, raters could also be asked to record a verbal description of test takers' performance.

Recorders (scorers/raters, or describers)

In assessments that elicit either a limited or extended production response (see below), assessment records are arrived at by human beings. In addition, in some situations, scores are arrived at by computer scoring algorithms.[3] The characteristics of the recorders thus can have an effect on the assessment record that test takers receive. The characteristics that are of particular interest are those that might influence their ability to provide assessment records that are consistent and that can be interpreted as meaningful indicators of the ability to be measured. Particularly relevant in the recording of extended production responses are the amount of training or prior experience recorders have had in recording, their level of language ability, the background knowledge that they bring to the recording task, and any particular biases they may have. (See the references by Weigle and Luoma in the Suggested Readings below, for discussions of rater attributes and training for writing and speaking assessments, respectively.)

Characteristics of the input

Input consists of the material contained in the task which the test takers or language users are expected to process in some way and to which they are expected to respond. For example, in an assessment task in which test takers are presented with a reading passage, expected to read and answer questions about it, the input would include both the reading passage and the questions. If the assessment task consisted of an oral interview in which the test takers were interviewed by an examiner, the input would consist of everything the examiner might say. (Everything that the test taker might say would be part of the expected response.) In a TLU task such as ordering a meal, the input could consist of whatever the customer reads in the menu or hears from the server's promotional spiel.

In an assessment task, input is distinguished from "instructions" (see p. 70 above) in that input is considered part of the problem that the test takers are supposed to solve in responding to the assessment task. As such, the ability to process the input is expected to have an effect on assessment performance. Instructions, on the other hand, are intended to be so transparent that they have no effect on performance on assessment tasks. In other words, instructions are intended to facilitate performance on the assessment.

Note that the amount and type of input may vary considerably from one assessment task to another. In some assessment tasks, such as multiple-choice or short answer tasks, there may be relatively little input. Or, in a task involving writing a composition about the test takers' experiences (such as writing about their experience with a university's admission procedures, as illustrated in Project 8), there may be no input other than the prompt itself. In this case, the information which the test taker draws upon in writing the composition is in the test taker's mind, and not actually presented to the test taker as input. In other tasks, however, there may be extensive input. In most assessments of reading, for example, test takers need to process a reading passage in order to answer the questions. Similarly, many listening assessments require test takers to listen to a short segment of spoken discourse in order to answer questions.

Format

The **format** of the input consists of the way in which the input is presented, and includes the following characteristics: channel, form, language, length, vehicle, degree of speededness, and type.

Channel

The **channel** of the input can be aural, visual, or both. For example, if the test takers watch and listen to a video of a lecture before answering questions about the content, the channel characteristics would be aural and visual. In a TLU task such as answering questions about difficulties with computer software, the input could be both aural (what the language user hears over the phone) and visual (whatever reference material the language user might access via computer).

Form

The **form** of the input can be language-based, non-language-based (pictures, gestures, actions, etc.), or both.

Language of input

If the form of the input involves language, this **language** can be characterized as the native language(s) of the test takers, the language to be assessed, or both.

Length/time

The **length/time** of the input is the amount of language or non-language material that the test taker needs to process and the amount of time that is allotted for them to do so. If the input is language, the length of the input can vary from single words, to phrases, sentences, paragraphs, or extended discourse. If the input includes non-language material, it can vary from short (as with a single picture) to long (as with a videotape of a lecture).

The length of the input influences the amount of processing required. Input can be presented in very short chunks and thus require limited processing, or it can be presented in extended discourse requiring more extensive processing.

Vehicle

The **vehicle** of the input can be "live," "reproduced," or both, and this distinction applies to both audio and visual input. For example, in an assessment task consisting of a lecture for assessing listening comprehension, the input could be presented as a live lecture in front of the test takers or a reproduced lecture (via audio or videotape, CD, DVD, or MP3). A videotaped lecture would consist of both language and non-language input, and both would be reproduced.

Degree of speededness

The **degree of speededness** is essentially the rate at which the information in the input is presented.[4] For example, the input in a meeting where people are energetically exchanging views would be more speeded than the input in a language classroom where the teacher is more likely to adjust his speed of speaking to the rate his students can process. Similarly, in a reading test, if the test takers are given the same amount of time to process a long passage as opposed to a shorter passage, the longer passage would be more speeded than the shorter passage.

Type

Types of input consist of item, prompt, or input for interpretation.

Item

An **item** consists of a highly focused chunk of language or non-language information whose function is to elicit either a selected or a limited production response (see "Type of response" below). The input in many assessment tasks, such as multiple-choice or completion tasks for testing discrete areas of language knowledge, consists of items. In real life language use, the input in a telephone conversation in which we listen to short utterances and provide short, limited responses (e.g., "yes," "ummm," "really?") could be characterized as a series of items.

Prompt

A **prompt** is input in the form of a directive, the purpose of which is to elicit an extended production response. (See "Type of response" below.) An assessment task such as a directive to write a composition contains input of this type. In real life language use, a friend's request that you tell him about your vacation would be input in the form of a directive.

Even though the focus of the prompt is not on the test takers' understanding of it, their performance on the assessment task will nonetheless be affected by their understanding of the prompt. For example, in a task involving writing a composition, the prompt might well contain a specification of the purpose of the composition, the intended audience, the type of presentation, the kinds of evidence that need to be provided, and the register of the language to be used. If the test takers do not understand what these specifications mean, this lack of understanding could be expected to influence their performance on the task.

Input for interpretation

Input for interpretation consists of language, either written or oral, that the language user is presented with and must process in order to complete the task. The purpose of the input is to provide the substantive content that will be the focus of the language use task, or, in an assessment, of either items or prompts. In a reading assessment, for example, the test takers might be presented with a passage that they need to read and comprehend in order to respond to the items that follow it. Another example is a test that was developed for placing university students into an appropriate study abroad program (Bachman, Lynch, and Mason 1995). In this test, test takers watched and listened to a video clip of part of a lecture from an academic course and also read a passage from a textbook for the same academic course. Test takers then watched a video clip in which the lecturer presented them with a spoken prompt that required them to produce a short oral response integrating the information provided to them in the lecture with that provided in the reading passage. In this example, both the lecture and reading passage would be considered input for interpretation, which they needed to process in order to respond to the spoken prompt. In a real life language use task, students might attend a lecture presented by a professor. This input for interpretation could provide the substantive content that will be the focus items (specific questions about the input) or prompts (directives designed to elicit extended production responses) that could come up in a discussion section led by a teaching assistant.

Language of input

In tasks in which the form of the input is language, the characteristics of the **language of the input** relate to the nature of the language presented to the test takers or language users to which they respond. These characteristics can be described using the same categories used to describe the characteristics of language knowledge presented in Chapter 3. For this reason, we will simply list these characteristics here.

Language characteristics

Language characteristics include organizational and pragmatic characteristics.

Organizational characteristics

Organizational characteristics include grammatical characteristics (vocabulary, morphology, syntax, phonology, graphology) and textual characteristics (cohesion, rhetorical or conversational organization).

Pragmatic characteristics

Pragmatic characteristics include functional characteristics (ideational, manipulative, heuristic, and imaginative) and sociolinguistic characteristics (genre, dialect/variety, register, naturalness, cultural references, and figurative language). (Refer to the section on "Pragmatic knowledge" in Chapter 3 for a discussion of these.)

Topical characteristics

Topical characteristics refer to the type of information, such as personal, cultural, academic, or technical, that is contained in the input. For example, if a reading passage on transformer design is presented to test takers as part of an assessment task, the topical characteristics of the input might be "technical–electronics."

Characteristics of the expected response

In any language use situation, the participants will have certain expectations about the characteristics of their respective responses as the discourse evolves. In a language assessment, the **expected response** consists of the linguistic or non-linguistic behavior the assessment task is attempting to elicit by the way the instructions have been written, the rubric has been specified, and by the input provided. For example, in an assessment task that requires test takers to listen to a dictation and write down what they hear, the expected response is the test takers' written version of what they hear. The input is what they listen to. In a language use task such as asking for directions to a friend's house, the expected response would be a set of directions that one could follow to get to the friend's house.

In some assessment tasks, the entire expected response may be non-linguistic. For example, if the test takers are required to put a check next to the correct answer in a multiple-choice test task, the actual response (making a check mark) is non-linguistic. The written alternatives in such a task are part of the input, not the expected response. Similarly, in an assessment task that requires the test takers to draw a picture of a scene which they hear described, the expected response would be non-linguistic in nature. Because test takers do not always understand instructions, or may choose not to respond in the way intended, we distinguish the expected response, which is part of the test design, from the actual response, which may or may not be what was intended or expected.

The characteristics of the expected response are listed in outline form in Table 4.1 above. Since most of these characteristics are essentially the same as those for characteristics of the input described above, we will only address characteristics specific to the expected response and that are not already discussed above under "characteristics of input."

Format

Format of expected response has to do with the way in which the response is produced: the channel, form, language, and length (see p. 75 above).

Type

The **type of response** can be characterized as selected, limited production, and extended production. Measurement specialists traditionally distinguish two kinds of responses: a *selected* response in which the test taker must select one response from among several given choices, and a *constructed* response in which the test taker actually has to produce or construct a response. However, since constructed responses may vary considerably in length, we believe it is useful to distinguish two constructed response types, based on the notion of a sentence or utterance. Using the sentence or utterance as a means of distinguishing different types of constructed responses is not entirely arbitrary, since it is with texts consisting of multiple sentences or utterances that a wider range of areas of language knowledge, including knowledge of cohesion and rhetorical organization, comes into play.

Selected response

In a **selected response**, typified by multiple-choice and matching tasks, the test taker must select one response from among two or more that are provided.

Limited production response

A **limited production response** consists of a single word or phrase, and may be as long as a single sentence or utterance. This response type is typical of what are sometimes called short answer or completion items.

Extended production response

An **extended production response** is one that is longer than a single sentence or utterance, and can range from two sentences or utterances to much longer stretches of language. An extended production written response might consist of an essay, while an extended production oral response might consist of a speech, explanation, or lecture.

Degree of speededness

The **degree of speededness** is the amount of time that the language user or test taker has to plan and execute a response.[5] As in the example above for speededness of input, the speed of the expected response in a meeting where people are energetically exchanging views would be more speeded than the speed of the responses in a language classroom where students are given time to think through what they want to say in response to a teacher's questions.

Language of expected response

When the response type is either a limited or an extended production and the form of the response is language, we need to describe the language of the expected response. This can be done using the same characteristics as for the language of the input (organizational and pragmatic), as discussed above.

Relationship between input and expected response

In addition to describing the characteristics of the input and response separately, we can describe how these are related to each other, in terms of the interrelatedness, scope, and directness of the relationship.

Type of external interactiveness

Type of external interactiveness refers to the type of interaction among participants and between participants and equipment and materials in the language use task or an assessment task. (See Chapter 3 above for a discussion of external interactiveness.) This can be characterized in terms of the extent to which the input or the response directly affects subsequent input and responses. We will describe this in terms of three different types: reciprocal, non-reciprocal, or adaptive.

Reciprocal

Reciprocal tasks are those in which the test taker or language user engages in language use with another interlocutor. In reciprocal language use, the language user receives feedback on the relevance, appropriateness, and accuracy of the response, and the response in turn affects the input that is subsequently provided by the interlocutor. The feedback may be either explicit or implicit in the reactions (verbal or physical) of the interlocutor. Reciprocal language use and assessment tasks thus have two distinguishing features: (1) the presence of feedback, and (2) back-and-forth interplay between the two interlocutors, so that the language used by the participants at any given point in the exchange affects subsequent language use. A typical example of a reciprocal assessment task would be the give and take that occurs in a face-to-face oral interview. (See Chapter 3 for examples of reciprocal and non-reciprocal language use.)

Non-reciprocal

Non-reciprocal tasks are those in which there is neither feedback nor back-and-forth interplay between language users. Reading is an example of non-reciprocal language use since the language user's internal or external response to what is read does not change the form of subsequent material in the text. Typical examples of non-reciprocal assessment tasks are taking a dictation and writing a composition. (See Chapter 3 for examples of reciprocal and non-reciprocal language use.)

Adaptive

In an adaptive test, the particular tasks presented to the test taker are determined by the responses to previous tasks. Adaptive tests are typically administered with a computer, which enables tasks to be presented to individual test takers.[6] In an adaptively administered test the first task presented is expected to be of medium difficulty for most test takers. If the test taker responds to this task successfully, the next task presented will be slightly more difficult. If the test taker performs poorly on that task, the next one will be slightly easier, and so on. In most adaptive tests, test takers do not receive feedback on the correctness of their responses, and may not know that their responses determine which tasks will be presented subsequently. **Adaptive test tasks** thus do not involve the feedback that characterizes reciprocal language use, but they do involve an aspect of interaction, in the sense that their responses affect subsequent input. The differences among interactional, non-interactional, and adaptive types of external interactiveness are summarized in Table 4.2, from Bachman (1990).

Relationship between input and response	Feedback provided on relevance or correctness of response	Response affects subsequent input
Reciprocal	+ (present)	+ (present)
Adaptive	– (absent)	+ (present)
Non-reciprocal	– (absent)	– (absent)

Table 4.2 Distinguishing characteristics of types of external interactiveness (After Bachman 1990: 151)

Scope of relationship

Scope of relationship refers to the amount or range of input that must be processed in order for the test taker or language user to respond as expected. The scope may be relatively broad or relatively narrow.

Broad scope

Tasks that require the test taker or language user to process a lot of input can be characterized as **broad scope.** An example of a broad scope assessment task is a "main idea" reading comprehension question that deals with the content of an entire passage. A broad scope language use task might be listening to a conversation in a foreign language with the idea of getting the gist, without focusing on specific details.

Narrow scope

Tasks that require the processing of only a limited amount of input can be characterized as **narrow scope.** An example of a narrow scope test task is a short stand-alone multiple-choice grammar item, since the response is to be made on the basis of a relatively limited amount of input. Another example would be a reading comprehension question that focuses on a specific detail or a limited part of the reading passage. An example of a narrow scope language use task might be scanning the sale ads in the newspaper for a particular piece of furniture. Note that in this example, the scope of the relationship between input and expected response is narrow even though the input is relatively long.

Directness of relationship

Directness of relationship refers to the degree to which the task can be successfully completed by referring primarily to information that is included in the input, or whether the test taker or language user must also rely on information in the context or in her own topical knowledge.

Direct

A **direct relationship** is one in which a successful response can be based primarily upon information supplied in the input. An example of a relatively direct response to an assessment task would be a speaking assessment in which the test taker describes the content of a picture presented to the test taker at the time of assessment.

Indirect

An **indirect relationship** is one in which a successful response requires the test taker or language user to draw on information not supplied in the input of the assessment task itself; this information might be found in the language use setting, or come from the test taker's own topical knowledge. An example of a relatively indirect assessment task would be a speaking task in which the test taker gives his opinion of a recent event. Note that in this example, the information the test taker draws upon when giving his opinion is *not* part of the input.

It is fairly common for certain types of test tasks to include a direct relationship between input and response. A task that requires the test taker to read a piece of discourse and then answer comprehension questions that request information explicitly stated in the passage, for example, involves such a direct relationship. Many language use tasks, on the other hand, involve an indirect relationship between input and response. In a conversation, for example, the language users expect each other to respond with new rather than given information, the new information being supplied by the language users.

APPLICATIONS OF THE TASK CHARACTERISTICS FRAMEWORK

The task characteristics framework can be used in a variety of ways. Two of the most important are describing TLU tasks and comparing characteristics of TLU and assessment tasks in order to determine the degree of match between the two. These applications play a central role in the development of assessment tasks, which is described in Chapter 15, and in justifying their use.

EXERCISES

1 Think of an assessment you have used or are familiar with. What kinds of TLU domain seemed to have been used to select tasks as a basis for developing the assessment tasks: real life, language teaching, both? What kinds of decisions are made? How are these domains relevant to the decisions to be made?
2 Examine the descriptions of the characteristics of assessment tasks provided in the Projects on pp. 440–85. Notice that these are written at different levels of detail. What real world conditions or constraints do you think might influence the amount of detail provided in the descriptions of the task characteristics?
3 Select an assessment task with which you are familiar that is somewhat similar to one of the assessment tasks used in the Projects. Then describe the characteristics of your assessment task, using the framework of language task characteristics provided in this chapter. You may also find that the terms used to describe task characteristics in other projects may provide some terms that will help you get started in describing the characteristics of your own tasks.
4 Think of an assessment task with which you are familiar that is clearly patterned after some sort of TLU task from either a real life or language teaching domain. Describe the characteristics of the two tasks using a table

such as the one found in Chapter 15. Then identify the similarities and differences between the characteristics of the two tasks.

SUGGESTED READINGS

Language use and discourse

Brown, G. and **G. Yule.** 1983. *Discourse Analysis*. Cambridge: Cambridge University Press.

van Dijk, T. A. 1977. *Text and Context: Explorations in the Semantics and Pragmatics of Discourse*. London: Longman.

Widdowson, H. G. 1978. *Teaching Language as Communication*. Oxford: Oxford University Press.

Features of language use context

Hymes, D. H. 1972. 'On communicative competence', in J. B. Pride and J. Holmes (eds.). *Sociolinguistics* (pp. 269–93). Harmondsworth: Penguin.

Tasks and task characteristics

The following research studies illustrate the effects of various aspects of test methods on test performance:

Alderson, J. C. and **A. H. Urquhart.** 1985. 'The effect of students' academic discipline on their performance on ESP reading tests.' *Language Testing* 2 (2): 192–204.

Bachman, L. F. and **A. S. Palmer.** 1982. 'The construct validation of some components of communicative proficiency.' *TESOL Quarterly* 16 (4): 449–65.

Shohamy, E. 1984. 'Does the testing method make a difference? The case of reading comprehension.' *Language Testing* 1 (2): 147–70.

A detailed discussion of "test method facets" can be found in:

Bachman, L. F. 1990. *Fundamental Considerations in Language Testing*. Oxford: Oxford University Press, Chapter 5.

Carroll, J. B. 1993. *Human Cognitive Abilities: A Survey of Factor-Analytic Studies*. Cambridge: Cambridge University Press. (Provides a discussion of tasks from the perspective of cognitive psychology.)

Discussions of tasks in language learning can be found in the following collections of articles:

Bygate, M., P. Skehan, and **M. Swain** (eds.) 2001. *Researching Pedagogic Tasks: Second Language Learning, Teaching and Testing*. Harlow: Longman.

Crookes, G. V. and **S. Gass.** 1993a. *Tasks and Language Learning: Integrating Theory and Practice*. Clevedon: Multilingual Matters.

——, ——(1993b). *Tasks in a Pedagogical Context: Integrating Theory and Practice*. Clevedon: Multilingual Matters.

Computer adaptive language tests and scoring algorithms

Chalhoub-Deville, M. 1999. *Issues in Computer-Adaptive Testing of Reading Proficiency*. Cambridge: University of Cambridge Local Examinations Syndicate and Cambridge University Press.

Chapelle, C. A. and **D. Douglas.** 2006. *Assessing Language Ability by Computer*. Cambridge: Cambridge University Press.

Raters in writing and speaking

Extensive discussions of rater attributes and training for writing can be found in:
Weigle, S. C. 2002. *Assessing Writing*. Cambridge: Cambridge University Press.

and for speaking in:
Fulcher, G. 2003. *Testing Second Language Speaking*. London: Pearson Longman.
Luoma, S. 2004. *Assessing Speaking*. Cambridge: Cambridge University Press.

NOTES

1 These two domains are not necessarily distinct, since much of the research and thinking in language teaching methodology for at least the past 20 years has generally been aimed at creating teaching and learning tasks in which the purpose for using language is to communicate in the real world, and not simply to learn the target language. It is also true to say, of course, that real life domains are themselves contexts in which language learning can take place.

2 Bachman (1990) uses the terms "test method" and "facets" to refer to what we call here "tasks" and "characteristics." We prefer the term "task" for two reasons. First, this refers directly to what the test taker is actually presented with in a language test, rather than to an abstract entity. Second, the term "task" is more general, and relates more directly to the notion of task as it is currently used in the contexts of language acquisition and language teaching. We have found that the term "facets" is perceived by many practitioners as highly technical and inaccessible, while the term "characteristics" is much less of a problem.

3 A discussion of computer scoring is beyond the scope of this book. Some references to this literature are included in the Suggested Readings at the end of the chapter.

4 We would note that our definition of speededness is different from the definition in educational and psychological measurement. According to that definition, a "speeded" test is one in which all the tasks are of about equal difficulty, and not all test takers are expected to complete all the tasks. In this definition, speed of processing is the construct to be measured.

5 See previous note about the speededness of input.

6 A discussion of computer adaptive testing is beyond the scope of this book. Some references to this literature are included in the Suggested Readings at the end of the chapter.

5

Justifying the use of language assessments

INTRODUCTION

When we use a language assessment, we generally do so because we have some particular use in mind. The immediate use will typically involve making decisions about individuals, programs, institutions, or organizations. However, the act of using an assessment, as opposed to another means of collecting information, and the decisions we make on the basis of this assessment will have consequences for stakeholders. Therefore, when we think about the uses of language assessments, we need to clearly identify who the stakeholders are and how they will be affected by both the use of the assessment and the decisions we make. We also need to consider how we will justify the uses of a particular language assessment to these stakeholders. Thus, we need to be prepared to be held accountable to ourselves, as language testing professionals, to test users, or decision makers, and to other stakeholders.

In this chapter we first discuss the use of language assessments, beginning with the beneficial consequences that we, as test developers and test users, want to bring about, and the decisions we need to make to achieve these consequences. We need to base these decisions upon information about test takers' language ability, and these interpretations will be based on their performance on a language assessment. We discuss the use of language assessments as involving a set of inferential links from assessment performance to consequences. We then discuss accountability as an essential responsibility of everyone who is involved in the development and use of language assessments. This includes test developers and decision makers. We next discuss the process of assessment justification, which provides a basis for accountability. There are two foundational axioms in our approach to assessment development. The first is that test developers and decision makers need to be accountable to the individuals who are affected by the use of the assessment and the decisions that are made on the basis of the assessment. The second axiom is that in order to be accountable, test developers and decision makers must *demonstrate*, through argumentation and the collection of supporting evidence, that the use of a particular assessment is justified. We then discuss practical reasoning and the elements and structure of practical arguments, which provide the basis for articulating an Assessment Use Argument (AUA). The AUA provides the conceptual framework for guiding the development and use of a particular language assessment, including the interpretations and uses we make on the basis of the assessment. Next, we discuss the elements and structure of an AUA, specific kinds of statements in an AUA, and how these support the links between assessment performance and assessment use. Finally, we discuss fairness in the development and use of language assessments, and how issues of fairness are addressed in an Assessment Use Argument.

THE USE OF LANGUAGE ASSESSMENTS

Using a language assessment involves obtaining samples of individuals' language performance, recording their performance in some way, interpreting these records as indicators of some aspect of the test takers' language ability, and making decisions on the basis of these interpretations. Since assessment use will have consequences, when we develop a language assessment, we begin by considering the consequences of this use.

Consequences

We begin with the premise that people generally use language assessments in order to bring about some beneficial outcomes or consequences for stakeholders as a result of using the assessment and making decisions based on the assessment. We recognize that the consequences of language assessments are not always viewed as beneficial, particularly to test takers who may not perform well on them. However, we will argue that responsible test developers and test users consider the extent to which any detrimental consequences may offset the intended beneficial consequences. For example, many colleges and universities in English speaking countries require non-native English speaking applicants to take a test of English as a second or foreign language. It is not the intent of this requirement to keep people out of universities. Rather, the intent is to assure that students who are admitted have sufficient proficiency in English to be able to successfully participate in an academic program that is in English.

In general, **stakeholders** include (1) the test developer, (2) the test user,[1] or decision maker, who may also be the test developer, and (3) those individuals, programs, institutions, or organizations that the decision maker and/or test developer specifically targets or intends to be affected by or to benefit from the intended consequences. (As we will discuss in Chapters 8 and 9, for any particular assessment, we will identify and describe the specific stakeholders.) Individual stakeholders who are typically affected by the uses of language assessments include the test takers[2] themselves, as well as other students and teachers in an instructional program, potential employers and fellow employees, and recipients of professional services. Programs that may be affected by the uses of the assessment range from a specific class to a course to a whole educational program. Institutions that may be affected range from an entire educational system (specific class, grade, school, school district, state educational system, national system), to a small company, to a large multinational corporation, and potentially to society at large. If we were thinking of using a language assessment to place students into homogeneous ability groups, for example, an intended consequence might be that this will facilitate teaching and learning. Or, if we were to use a language assessment to certify language teachers, one intended consequence might be that this will help assure that only competent language teachers will provide instruction in language classes. There is, of course, always the possibility that using the assessment will not lead to the intended consequences, or that the assessment use will lead to unintended consequences that may be detrimental to stakeholders. Therefore, in addition to the beneficial consequences we intend to bring about, we will also need to consider potential unintended detrimental consequences.

Decisions

While an individual test user, or group of test users, may have in mind some specific beneficial consequences that they would like to see happen, they cannot just sit around and hope that somehow, by good luck, good intentions, or chance, the intended beneficial consequences will come about. In order to help bring about the intended consequences a test user needs to take action, and this involves making decisions. Decisions can thus be viewed as actions the test user takes to attain his ends—the intended beneficial consequences. Many of the decisions that are made will involve the classification of stakeholders into groups such as "pass/fail," "certified/not certified," "beginning/intermediated/advanced." For example, the director of an academic language program may use a language assessment to classify international students entering a university into two groups—those who need additional language instruction to pursue an academic program in the language that is the medium of instruction and those who do not. Or an assessment could be used to classify schools into groups—those whose students are meeting certain target levels of academic achievement and those whose students are not. Not all decisions will classify stakeholders into just two groups, as many of the examples below illustrate.

In language instructional domains, learners may use diagnostic information from language assessments to make formative decisions about their own learning. For example, in a language class that focused on writing, the teacher might give the students verbal descriptions of specific problems in their writing. The students might use these verbal reports to make decisions about what areas of writing they need to focus their study and practice on.

The decisions that are made are typically about individuals. In language programs, decisions may need to be made about selecting students for admission to the program, classifying them into homogeneous ability levels for instructional purposes, assessing their progress and achievement in the program, or assigning grades. Language assessments are also widely used in educational programs to assess the language ability of students who are not native speakers of the language of instruction.[3] In many countries where the primary language of instruction is English, for example, assessments of English proficiency are used to identify non-native English speaking students who might benefit from additional instruction in English to facilitate their performance in their academic courses. The results of language assessments are also sometimes used to evaluate the effectiveness of teachers or administrators in educational programs. Language assessments are also used to help select individuals for employment and to certify people's language ability for professional purposes, such as language teaching, translating, or providing medical or legal services.

In addition to using language assessments to make decisions about individuals, they are also sometimes used to make decisions about educational programs themselves, such as providing formative feedback to instructional and program staff about how to improve a program, or using assessments to try to evaluate the effects of a program on learners, teachers, and other stakeholders. In some cases, an instructor may need to make formative pedagogical decisions about how to most effectively sequence a set of learning objectives, or what types of learning tasks might be most effective for a particular type or group of learners. Decisions about program resourcing also need to be made: which applicants to hire as teachers, which teachers to promote or retain, or how to allocate resources in a school system.

Language assessments are also used in Applied Linguistics research to investigate a wide range of questions, such as the nature of language ability, how this enables language users and test takers to use language, the ways in which the characteristics of the assessment itself may affect performance, or the relationships between language ability and other factors that can affect assessment performance. For example, a researcher may be interested in investigating the extent to which different conditions for planning lead to differences in the amount and quality of spoken language that second language (L2) learners produce. In this case, she could present L2 learners with a task to perform, say, an oral narrative describing a video clip that they watch, and provide two different groups of learners with two different conditions of planning—time for pre-task planning and on-line planning, through repeating the task. The researcher could then provide a rich qualitative description of the participants' speaking performance, or she could devise a coding procedure for measuring specific qualities of the participants' speech, such as fluency, accuracy, and complexity.[4] The information collected through this assessment would enable the researcher to make decisions about accepting or rejecting her research hypotheses. Another researcher might want to investigate the extent to which L2 learners who differ in certain personal characteristics (e.g., native language and culture, level of formal education, prior exposure to the second language, motivation, aptitude) differ in the speed or effectiveness with which they acquire certain aspects of a second language. Or, he may want to investigate whether learners who are exposed to one approach to language teaching have acquired the L2 better than learners who are exposed to another approach. In these cases in which the researcher uses an assessment of L2 learners' language ability, information from this assessment will inform decisions about research hypotheses, as well as decisions about whether the study gets published, the researcher gets promoted, and so forth.

In all such situations, decision makers use language assessments to help them make decisions that they believe will help bring about some specific beneficial consequence to particular individuals or groups of individuals, and perhaps to an educational program and society at large. Researchers use language assessments with the intended beneficial consequence of expanding our knowledge about a whole range of language use phenomena in real world settings.

Interpretations about test takers' language ability

In order to make decisions, test users need to collect information about the stakeholders who will be affected by these decisions, and in the vast majority of situations, these stakeholders are the test takers themselves. One way to do this is to use an assessment, the results of which can be interpreted as an indicator of the construct in which they are interested. (See Chapter 3 for a discussion of constructs.) The reason a test user may choose to use a language assessment to help make a decision is because he may believe that some aspect of language ability is required in order for the test takers to successfully perform whatever tasks they may need to accomplish in a target language use domain outside of the assessment itself (see Chapter 4 for a discussion of target language use domain). If, for example, an employer wanted to hire people who could interact orally at a professional level in English with potential customers, then he might include an English test as part of the employment screening procedure. Or, if instructors in a language program believe that placing students into language classes of approximately the same levels of language ability will facilitate effective teaching and learning, they could administer a test to students as they enter the program and use the information about the students' language ability obtained from this test to place students into different levels of courses. Thus, when someone gives a language assessment, he intends to interpret the performance on this assessment as an indicator of some aspect of the individual's language ability.

Procedures for observing and recording test takers' language performance

If the test user needs to arrive at an interpretation of test takers' language ability, then she will need to develop procedures for observing their language performance and recording this. When test takers engage with the tasks in a language assessment, they respond to these tasks in some way. Different assessment tasks may require different kind of responses, such as by marking an "a," "b," "c," or "d" on an answer sheet, by writing their responses in a blank, by producing some language, either written or spoken, or by performing some physical activity. The test taker's performance—their responses to the test tasks—may then be assigned scores according to scoring criteria and procedures established by the test developer, or they can be analyzed to provide verbal descriptions of their performance. We will refer to these scores or verbal descriptions as **assessment records**. (Note that these are not the same as "assessment *reports*," which are sent to test takers and other stakeholders, as discussed below.) Test users, or decision makers, interpret assessment records as indicators of the particular aspect of language ability and then use these interpretations to make decisions, which will, they believe, lead to their intended consequences.

Inferential links from consequences to assessment performance

From this discussion we can see that there is a series of inferential links between the consequences we as test developers and users intend to bring about, on the one hand, and the test taker's performance, on the other. These links are illustrated in Figure 5.1.

This figure illustrates the links between the consequences, the decisions, the interpretations about the test taker's language ability, the assessment record (score, description), and the test taker's performance on the assessment tasks. These links provide a basis for both the development of language assessments (illustrated by the downward pointing arrow in Figure 5.1) and for interpreting and using assessment performance (illustrated by the upward pointing arrow in Figure 5.1).

Whether we are thinking about adopting an existing language assessment or developing a new one of our own, we begin by considering the beneficial consequences we want to bring about. Given these intended consequences, we then consider the decisions we need to make to help bring these about. Next, we determine what aspect of language ability (discussed in Chapter 3) is relevant to making this decision. We then determine what kind of information we need to collect (such as a score or verbal description of performance) that we can interpret as an indicator of that aspect of language ability, and whether we need to use an assessment to obtain information about this. Assuming that we decide to use an assessment, we then determine what kind of performance

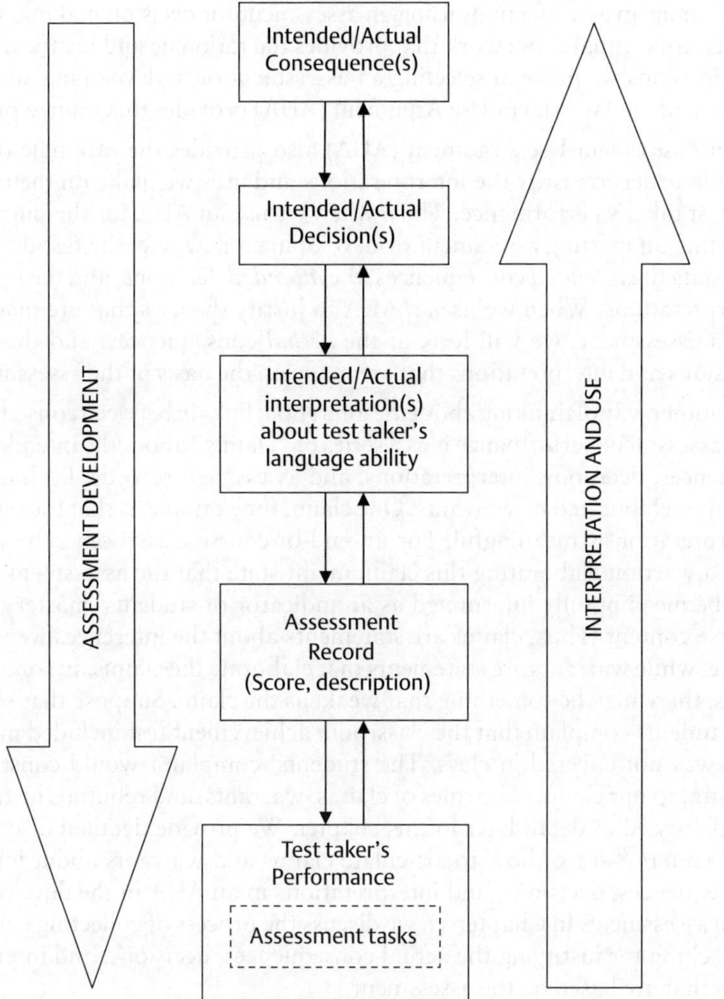

Figure 5.1 Inferential links from consequences to assessment performance

we need to obtain from test takers that can be observed and interpreted as an indicator of the aspect of language ability we want to assess. Finally we determine what kind of assessment tasks we need to use in order to elicit the performance we need, and how we will record this performance. This will involve a decision about whether to use an existing assessment or to develop a new assessment of our own. When we use performance on a language assessment to help us make a decision, the links go the other way, as we make a series of inferences from performance on the assessment task, to assessment records, to interpretations, to decisions, and to consequences. In either case, developing an assessment or using an assessment for decision making, we will need a conceptual framework that provides the rationale and justification for the decisions we make in selecting an assessment or in developing an assessment, and an Assessment Use Argument (AUA) provides this framework.

An Assessment Use Argument (AUA) also provides the rationale that we need in order to justify the interpretations and uses we make on the basis of the test taker's performance. Thus, when we use an AUA for the purpose of selecting an existing assessment or developing a new one, the test developer will state the *intended* consequences, the *intended* decisions, and the *intended* interpretations. When we use an AUA to justify the uses that are made of a given assessment, we will look at the *actual* consequences, and the *actual* decisions and interpretations that are made on the basis of the assessment.

Another way of thinking about the inferential links in between consequences and assessment performance is as a series of "claims" about the intended consequences, decisions, interpretations, and assessment records. Each of these claims is elaborated by warrants. One claim, for example, is that the intended interpretation is meaningful. For an end-of-course classroom achievement test, a warrant elaborating this claim might state that the assessment record can be meaningfully interpreted as an indicator of students' mastery of the course content. Thus, claims are statements about the inferences we wish to make, while warrants are statements that elaborate the claims. In some situations, there may be something that weakens the claim. Suppose that some of the students complain that the classroom achievement test included material that was not covered in class. The students' complaint would constitute a rebuttal to our claim. (The roles of claims, warrants, and rebuttals in an AUA are discussed in detail later in this chapter. We provide detailed discussions in Chapters 8–11 of how to articulate claims and warrants about intended consequences, decisions, and interpretations in an AUA in the development of an assessment. In Chapter 16 we discuss the process of collecting evidence, or backing for justifying the actual consequences, decisions, and interpretations that are based on the assessment.)

ACCOUNTABILITY

The uses of any given assessment will affect the lives of individual stakeholders, and may affect the institutions in which these individuals study or work. Any or all of the different stakeholders or stakeholder groups may hold us, as test developers and decision makers, accountable for the uses of a particular assessment. We thus need to be able to justify the uses—consequences and decisions—of a particular assessment so that we can be accountable to ourselves and to other stakeholders. Being accountable, or **accountability**, means being able to *demonstrate* to stakeholders that the intended uses of our assessment are justified. Another way to think about this is that we, as test developers and decision makers, need to convince stakeholders that the intended uses—decisions and consequences—of the assessment are justified. The process we follow in being accountable, or convincing stakeholders that our intended uses are justified, is that of justification, which is discussed below.

Accountability is essential for language assessment use, because without accountability, test developers and users, that is decision makers, can unquestioningly use language assessments for a wide range of purposes, affecting the lives of individuals in potentially important ways. Not all of the decisions made may be equitable, and not all of these consequences for stakeholders may be beneficial. Without accountability, even the most careful and conscientious test developer and user can inadvertently or unknowingly use an assessment inappropriately, and can be unaware of potentially negative consequences of the way his assessment is used.

Suppose that the classroom achievement test in the example above was intended to be used for the purpose of deciding which of their students would pass the course, and the students complained that the test was not fair because it included material that was not covered in class. In this case, an AUA that included statements, or warrants, that clearly stated (1) what was to be included in the test, and (2) that students would be notified in advance of what they would be responsible for, would elaborate the claim that scores on the test are meaningful indicators of students' achievement in the course. Evidence, or backing, in support of these warrants could be provided by (1) comparing the course syllabus with the test specifications, which would show which test tasks were based on which parts of the course content, and with the actual test itself, and (2) the teachers' class notes and handouts, indicating exactly when students were notified about the test and what it would cover. This backing would also serve to reject or weaken the students' rebuttal.

Or consider the case of a large-scale high-stakes language test in which a particular group of test takers claims that the content of the test is biased in favor of other groups of test takers. In this case, the test developer could provide a well-articulated AUA that included a warrant that the content of the test does not favor or disfavor any particular group of test takers. The test takers' statement about bias could be rejected or weakened by collecting backing through a careful analysis of test content, and empirical research demonstrating that there is no evidence of bias in the way different groups of test takers perform on the test. This AUA and relevant backing would therefore provide a basis for rejecting or discounting the rebuttal and thus strengthening the justification for this use of the test.

To whom do we need to be accountable?

The people to whom we, as test developers and users, need to be accountable are those stakeholders, individuals, or institutions that are most likely to be directly affected by the assessment and its use. The first person we need to convince, of course, is ourselves. If we lack confidence that we can justify the consequences of the assessment use, the decisions to be made, how we will interpret the assessment records, or how we will analyze or score test takers' performances, then we are in no position to be able to convince other stakeholders. An important step towards convincing ourselves is to articulate an AUA that will include claims and warrants about our intended uses. This process will lead us to systematically think through the links from assessment performance to intended consequences, and will help us anticipate possible alternative explanations, possible ways in which the assessment may be used other than as we intend, or possible unintended consequences of using the assessment in this way.

There are other stakeholders to whom we also need to be accountable. The stakeholders who are most directly affected by the assessment are the test takers. In the example above, the teachers need to be able to demonstrate to their students that the test covered only the material that was included in the course content. We may also need to be accountable to our fellow teachers. In the example above, suppose you were the person who took the lead in developing the achievement test. In this case, you would need to demonstrate to your fellow teachers that your ideas for the kind of test you need will lead to test use that can be justified. Another group of stakeholders who may be very interested in or concerned about test results are parents. We will need to demonstrate to them that the test is not biased against their children, that their children have been given adequate opportunities to learn the material on the test, and that they have been given an adequate opportunity to perform at their best on the test. In some situations, where assessments are used for school accountability, we may need to demonstrate to school administrators that the intended uses of the test are justified. Finally, there may be other individuals, such as potential employers, professionals who need to be certified, or directors of funding agencies, who may be interested in or be affected by the test results. The way we can be accountable is to convince stakeholders that the intended uses—decisions and consequences—of the assessment are justified. The factors that are involved in this, and the stakeholders who are primarily responsible, are discussed in the final section of this chapter.

JUSTIFICATION OF ASSESSMENT USE

In order to justify the intended uses of a particular assessment and hence to be accountable to stakeholders for the way it will be used, test developers and decision makers need to clearly articulate a rationale for the intended uses and provide evidence in support of this rationale. We believe that an Assessment Use Argument (AUA), which is described in detail below, provides the framework for doing this. An AUA will include statements about the intended uses of assessment performance, along wit h statements supporting these uses. The

AUA also will indicate the kinds of evidence that the test developer needs to collect to support these statements. An AUA thus provides a framework for investigating the extent to which the intended use of a particular assessment is, in fact, justified.

The process that test developers will follow to investigate the extent to which the intended uses of an assessment are justified is called **assessment justification**. This process is analogous to that of building a legal case to convince a judge or a jury. A lawyer presents her "case" to the court that, let us say, her client is innocent of any wrongdoing. This case consists of a clearly articulated argument and evidence that the lawyer submits to the court to support this argument. The lawyer's purpose in presenting her case is to convince the judge or jury that her client is innocent. Similarly, the process of assessment justification consists of building a "case" that the intended uses of the assessment are justified. This process includes two sets of interrelated activities:[5]

1 articulating specific statements in an Assessment Use Argument (AUA) that support the links between consequences and assessment performance, and
2 collecting relevant evidence, or backing, in support of the statements in the AUA.

The process of justification serves two essential purposes:

1 It guides the development and use of a given language assessment and provides the basis for quality control throughout the entire process of assessment development.
2 It provides the basis for test developers and decision makers to be held accountable to those who will be affected by the use of the assessment and the decisions that are made.

It is important for test developers and test users, or decision makers, to realize that they may be held accountable by any stakeholder at any time for the uses of an assessment they have developed and used. The interpretations and decisions that are made on the basis of assessment results can never be considered justified in any absolute sense. Test developers also need to recognize that because of the nature of the AUA and the uncertainties in any assessment situation, they can never "prove" that their intended uses of the assessment are "true," "valid," or "correct." What they can do is articulate a clear and coherent AUA and provide supporting evidence that stakeholders will find convincing and that will enable them to be held accountable for the intended uses of their assessment. Furthermore, the conditions in the assessment situation will vary from one specific assessment to another. The particular combination of intended uses, test takers, stakeholders, construct to be assessed, and target language use (TLU) domain is likely to be unique to any specific assessment situation. Because of this, an AUA is specific to a particular assessment situation and the process of assessment justification will be local and relevant to that situation. In addition, the conditions of the assessment situation can change over time, so that the AUA for any assessment should be regularly reviewed, and revised if necessary to reflect these changes. This is particularly important in situations where an assessment that was originally developed for one use may be considered for a different use, or where the characteristics of the test taker population change over time. Thus, assessment justification is ongoing, beginning with an AUA and assessment development, and continuing with the collection of relevant evidence as long as the assessment is used to make decisions. (In Chapters 8–12 we discuss how to construct an AUA, including specific questions that might be asked during the assessment development process. In Chapter 19 we discuss some ways for collecting and providing backing in support of the warrants in an AUA.)

PRACTICAL REASONING

Before we discuss the structure of an Assessment Use Argument, it will be helpful to provide a brief discussion of the framework of practical reasoning that underlies it. Bachman (2004a, 2006b) has proposed that we use Toulmin's (2003) approach to practical reasoning as a basis for articulating an AUA. For Toulmin, the primary function of a practical argument is to provide support for a statement or assertion, or what he calls a "claim." For example, if your friend says, "Jim's sick," this is a claim. If you don't accept your friend's claim outright, you might ask him how he knows this, to which he might reply, "He said he was going to the hospital." Your friend has now provided some "data" upon which his claim is based. Or, to put it another way, the claim is an inference that is based on data. Two elements of a Toulmin argument are thus a **claim**, which is "a conclusion whose merits we are seeking to establish," and some **data**, which consist of "the facts we appeal to as a foundation for the claim" (Toulmin 2003: 90). A claim consists of a proposition that identifies an **entity** and ascribes one or more **qualities** to that entity. In this example, "Jim" is the **entity** and "sick" is the **quality** that is ascribed to Jim in the claim. Your friend bases his claim on the fact that Jim is going to the hospital. But we might ask what the connection is between Jim's going to the hospital and his being sick. In this example, there is an implied statement that supports the inference, or inferential link, from data to claim: "People often go to the hospital when they are sick." Such general statements that provide the legitimacy of the inference from data to claim are called **warrants** (Toulmin 2003: 92). Warrants are thus propositions that we use to justify the claim. In an AUA, the warrants will help support the qualities of the claims. Warrants can be supported by evidence, or **backing**.

As we all know from our own experience in everyday reasoning, it is one thing to assert a claim, but it may be quite another to convince or persuade others of the credibility of our claim. In the example above, you might well say to your friend, "Just because Jim's going to the hospital doesn't mean he's sick. He could be going to visit someone there." Now you've challenged the claim your friend has made on the basis of his data by suggesting an alternative reason for someone's going to a hospital, namely, to visit a friend. In Toulmin's terminology, statements of conditions under which a warrant may not apply are called **rebuttals**. Such statements weaken or reject the original claim, and support alternative explanations, or **counterclaims** to the original claim.

Now suppose Jim calls you from the hospital and says, "I thought you'd like to know that Steve's in the hospital, and I'm here with him. I'm fine." This information supports, or provides backing for, your rebuttal, and rejects your friend's original claim. We now have an argument structure that includes more elements than a simple data–claim inferential link. The argument in this example can be stated as follows, with the implied warrant in parentheses:

> Jim is going to the hospital. (Since people often go to the hospital when they are sick) I can conclude that Jim is sick, unless he is visiting someone. Jim is visiting his partner in the hospital, so we can conclude that Jim is not sick.

Using Toulmin's terminology, we can identify the elements of this argument as follows:

DATA	Jim is going to the hospital.
CLAIM	Jim is sick.
WARRANT (Implicit)	People often go to the hospital when they are sick.
REBUTTAL	Jim could be visiting someone who is in the hospital.
REBUTTAL BACKING	Jim is visiting his partner in the hospital.
COUNTERCLAIM	Jim is not sick.

The structure of this argument can be illustrated as in Figure 5.2.

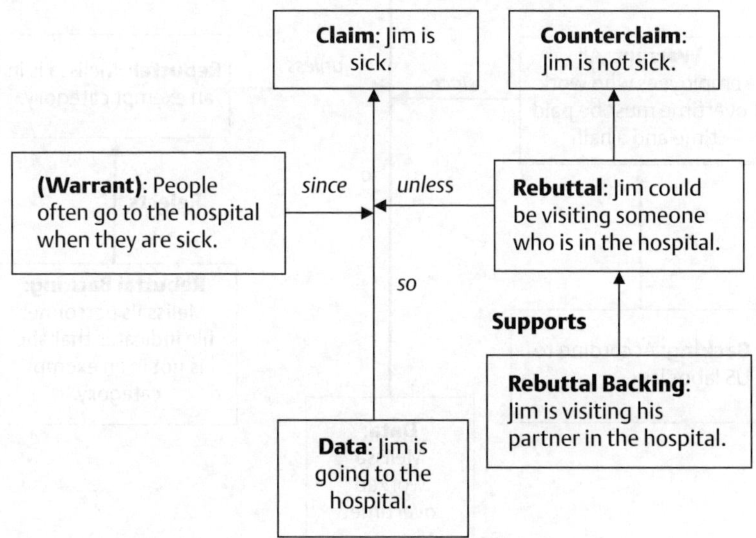

Figure 5.2 Structure of example practical argument

Here's another example of a Toulmin argument structure:

According to US labor law, all employees who work overtime must be paid time and a half. Since Melissa worked overtime, she should have been paid overtime, unless she is in an exempt category. Melissa's personnel file indicates that she is not in an exempt category, so we can conclude that she was paid time and a half.

The components of this argument are as follows:

DATA	Melissa worked overtime.
CLAIM	Melissa was paid time and a half.
WARRANT	All employees who work overtime must be paid time and a half.
BACKING	According to US labor law, all employees who work overtime must be paid time and a half.
REBUTTAL	Melissa is in an exempt category.
REBUTTAL BACKING	Melissa's personnel file indicates that she is not in an exempt category.

In this example, the rebuttal is rejected by the rebuttal backing, so we would accept the claim that Melissa was paid time and a half. If Melissa's personnel file indicated that she *was* in an exempt category, then this would support the rebuttal and lead to a different claim—that she was not paid time and a half.

The structure of this argument is illustrated in Figure 5.3.

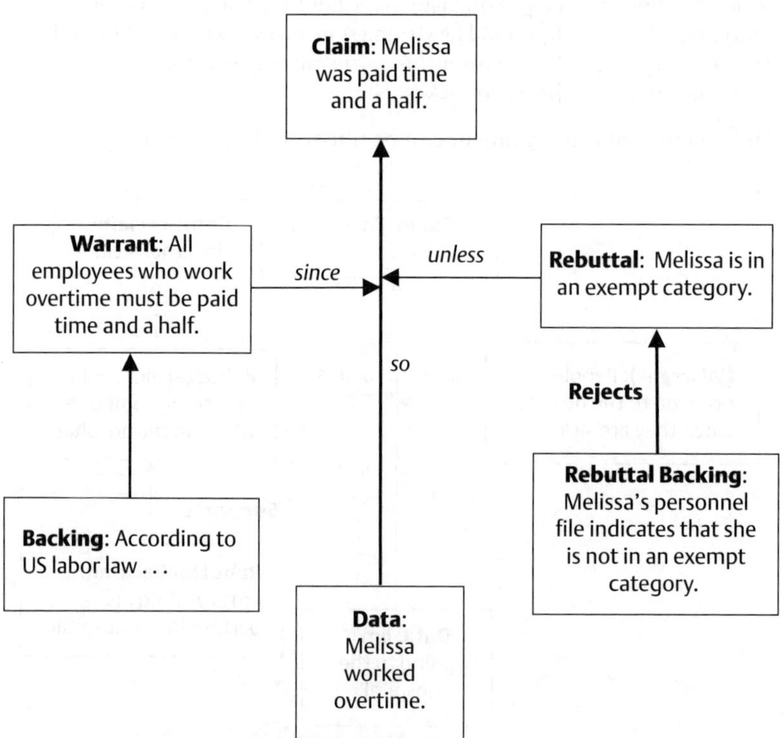

Figure 5.3 Toulmin diagram for example argument

ASSESSMENT USE ARGUMENTS

The Assessment Use Argument (AUA) is a conceptual framework for guiding the development and use of a particular language assessment, including the interpretations and uses we make on the basis of the assessment. Following Toulmin's structure of practical reasoning as in the example presented above, an AUA will include the following elements: data, claims, warrants, backing, rebuttals, and rebuttal backing.[6]

Data and claims

Two elements of an AUA are claims and data. **Claims** are statements about the inferences to be made on the basis of data and the qualities of those inferences. A claim thus includes two parts: (1) an **outcome** of the assessment process and (2) one or more **qualities** of that outcome. **Data** consist of the information on which a claim is based. Bachman (2006b) has proposed that the basic "building block" of an AUA is a data-claim inferential link that is structured as described by Toulmin (2003). In other words, the claim resulting from one inferential link becomes the data that serve as the basis for the next inference in the chain. We can apply this approach to the links illustrated in Figure 5.1 above, to show that an AUA includes several data-claim links, as illustrated in Figure 5.4 on p. 100.

In the lowermost pair in Figure 5.4, the "data" consist of the test taker's performance on the assessment, while the "claim" consists of an outcome, which is an assessment record (score, description), and the qualities that are claimed of that record. In this pair the assessment record is based on the test taker's performance on the assessment tasks, while the claimed qualities of the record will be supported by warrants in the argument. (The specific nature of these qualities and warrants is discussed in more detail below. See "Claims and warrants in an AUA," pp. 103–27. In this section we want to focus on the structure of the argument.) In the next pair in Figure 5.4, the assessment record is the "data," while the "claim" consists of an outcome, an interpretation, and the qualities that are claimed of that interpretation. In this pair the interpretation is based on the assessment record while the claimed qualities of the interpretation will be supported by warrants in the argument. The interpretation, in turn, is the "data" for the next pair in Figure 5.4, while the "claim" consists of the outcome, which is the decision to be made, and the qualities that are claimed of that decision. In this pair the decision to be made is based on the interpretation, while the claimed qualities of that decision will be supported by warrants in the argument. Finally, in the topmost pair in Figure 5.4, the "data" consist of the decision that is made, and the "claim" consists of an outcome, the consequences of using the assessment and of making this decision and the qualities claimed for these consequences. In this pair the consequences are based on the decision that is made, while the claimed quality of the consequences will be supported by warrants in the argument.

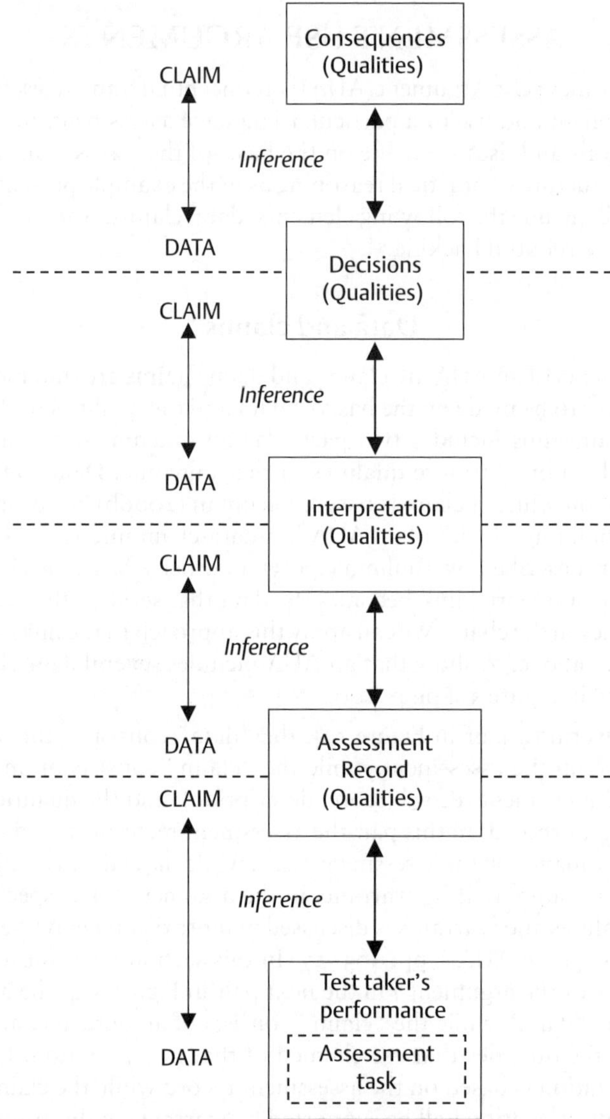

Figure 5.4 Data-claim inferential links in an Assessment Use Argument

To illustrate these inferential links in language assessment, let's consider the example that is described in more detail later in the book (Chapter 8), of a speaking test that is given in a university course in Modern Chinese. This test will be used to provide formative feedback to the instructors on the effectiveness of their teaching and to students about how to best focus their study time and effort. In this example, students are given a "mini-speech" task that requires them to give a short oral presentation, which is then rated by two instructors in the Chinese course. The student's rating is the average of these two ratings.

Following the links illustrated in Figure 5.4 for this example, the "data" in the lowermost data–claim pair consist of a student's performance on the mini-speech task, while the "claim" consists of the average of the two instructors' ratings of this performance, and the quality, consistency, that is claimed of that rating. In the next pair in Figure 5.4, the average rating is the "data," while the "claim" consists of an outcome, an interpretation about the student's level of Chinese speaking, and the qualities, e.g., meaningfulness, generalizability (see below), that are claimed of that interpretation. The interpretation of the student's level of Chinese speaking, in turn, is the "data" for the next pair in Figure 5.4, while the "claim" consists of the outcome, which are the decisions to be made—changes in the instructors' teaching, in the course syllabus, and in the student's study patterns—and the qualities, e.g., equitability, that are claimed of these decisions. Finally, in the topmost pair in Figure 5.4, the "data" consist of the formative decisions about instruction and learning that are made, and the "claim" consists of an outcome, the intended consequences of using the mini-speech test and of making the formative decisions and the qualities claimed for these consequences. In this example, the intended consequences are that students will take the course's learning objectives in speaking more seriously, the instructors will make adjustments to their teaching to make this more effective, and the course supervisor will make changes in the syllabus to improve the course as a whole. The claimed quality of these intended consequences is that they are beneficial for the students, the instructors, and for the course supervisor.

Warrants and rebuttals

If we want our AUA to be convincing to stakeholders, we cannot rely simply on stating our claims. We need to include additional elements in our AUA: warrants that articulate the qualities of our claims and as well as rebuttals that may potentially challenge or even reject our claims.

Warrants are explicit statements that elaborate one or more qualities of a claim specifically for the given assessment situation. Warrants provide specific justification for the qualities that are claimed of the intended consequences, of the decisions, of the interpretations, and of the assessment records. The specific nature of these warrants is discussed in more detail below (see "Claims and warrants in an AUA," pp. 103–127) and in Chapters 9–13.

Rebuttals are statements that challenge or reject the qualities of the claims. For every warrant that supports a claim there is an implied rebuttal. For example, two possible warrants to support the claim about the consistency of scores might be that the scores from the assessment are internally consistent, or that ratings by different raters are consistent. Implied rebuttals would be that the scores are *not* internally consistent and that the ratings by different raters are *not* consistent, respectively.

Backing

As we mentioned above, articulating specific statements (claims, warrants, and rebuttals) in an AUA constitutes one set of activities in the assessment justification process. The other activities involved in assessment justification include collecting evidence or backing, to support the warrants in the AUA and to weaken or reject rebuttals to these warrants. (See Chapter 19 for a detailed discussion of types of backing and procedures for collecting backing.)

Backing consists of the evidence that we need to provide to support the warrants in the AUA. The backing to support our warrants in language assessment generally comes from a variety of sources, including documents, regulations, legal requirements, theory, prior research or experience, the procedures we use to develop the assessment, the procedures we follow in administering the assessment and scoring the test takers' responses, and evidence collected specifically as part of the justification process. Because there is an implied rebuttal for every warrant in the AUA, the backing we collect to support the warrants also serves to reject or weaken rebuttals to the stated claims and warrants.

Backing can be collected from a wide range of sources and in a variety of ways. Some backing may be provided at the outset of assessment development, as we begin to articulate the warrants in an AUA. Other backing will be provided during assessment development itself, and will comprise the procedures we follow and the documents we produce, such as a Design Statement, a Blueprint, and the assessment itself. Finally, we will need to provide additional backing in the form of empirical evidence, and this will be collected specifically as part of the justification process, during the tryout and operational administration of the assessment. (We provide a detailed discussion of how to go about collecting backing in Chapter 19.)

In the process of assessment justification, the test developer and the decision maker are responsible for collecting backing for all the warrants in the particular AUA. This is not to say, however, that the process of justification is always conducted exclusively by the test developer or decision maker herself. In many situations, particularly where high-stakes decisions are to be made, other stakeholders are likely to be involved, taking the role of articulating rebuttals and then collecting evidence to determine if these are supported. If, for example, one stakeholder group believed that the decisions made were not equitable, this group might articulate this as a rebuttal and provide evidence or backing to support this. It is then the test developer's and decision maker's responsibility to review the decisions and decision rules to address the rebuttal. (See Chapter 21 for a discussion of the roles of the test developer, decision maker, and other stakeholders in the use of an assessment.)

CLAIMS AND WARRANTS IN AN AUA

We have argued that an Assessment Use Argument (AUA) provides the basis for justifying the intended uses of an assessment. The AUA is a conceptual framework consisting of a series of inferences that link the test taker's performance to a claim about assessment records, to a claim about interpretations, to a claim about decisions, and to a claim about intended consequences, along with warrants and backing to support these claims. In this section we discuss the types of claims and warrants that an Assessment Use Argument will include.

As mentioned above, in our approach to language assessment, the primary purposes of the AUA and the process of justification are to guide assessment development and to enable test developers and decision makers to be accountable to stakeholders for the intended uses of the assessment. For this reason, the claims and warrants are stated in terms that directly link them to these two purposes. We would also note that these claims and warrants are stated in general terms here, but that they will be stated in specific terms for any given assessment. In Chapters 8–12 we discuss how to articulate specific claims and warrants in the process of assessment development and provide examples of AUAs that include specific warrants and rebuttals. In Chapter 19 we discuss in greater detail the kinds of backing that can be provided to support the warrants in an AUA, and ways in which this backing can be collected.

An AUA will include four general claims, listed in Table 5.1.[7]

Claim 1	The *consequences* of using an assessment and of the decisions that are made are **beneficial** to stakeholders.
Claim 2	The *decisions* that are made on the basis of the interpretations: • take into consideration community **values** and relevant legal requirements and • are **equitable** for those stakeholders who are affected by the decision.
Claim 3	The *interpretations* about the ability to be assessed are: • **meaningful** with respect to a particular learning syllabus, an analysis of the abilities needed to perform tasks in the TLU domain, a general theory of language ability, or any combination of these, • **impartial** to all groups of test takers, • **generalizable** to the TLU domain in which the decision is to be made, • **relevant** to the decision to be made, and • **sufficient** for the decision to be made.
Claim 4	The *assessment records* (scores, descriptions) are **consistent** across different assessment tasks, different aspects of the assessment procedure (e.g., forms, occasions, raters), and across different groups of test takers.

Table 5.1 Four types of claims in an AUA

Each of these types of claims in an AUA will be elaborated by different types of warrants. The structure of the claims and warrants in an AUA is illustrated in Figure 5.5.

In this figure, the claims of the AUA are represented in rectangles and the warrants are represented in ovals. We will discuss the claims and warrants in an AUA, beginning with the claim about the intended consequences.

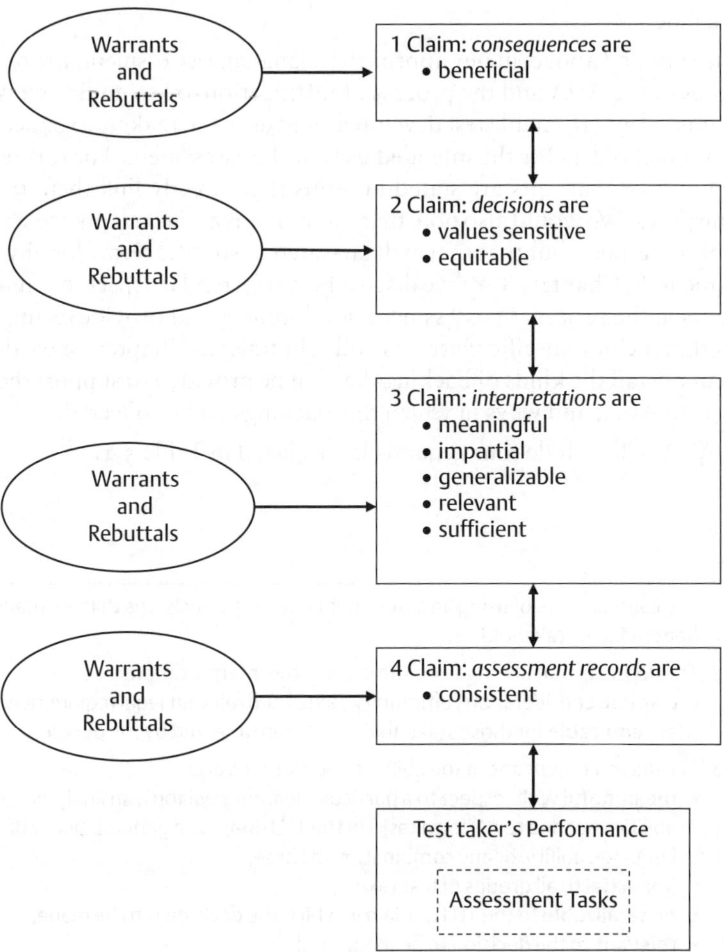

Figure 5.5 Claims and warrants in an Assessment Use Argument

Claim 1: intended consequences

The data for this claim consist of the use of the assessment and the decisions that are made. The claim is as follows:

Claim 1: The consequences of using an assessment and of the decisions that are made are **beneficial** to all stakeholders.

Beneficence

The very acts of administering and taking a test have consequences. Similarly, the decisions we make on the basis of assessment-based interpretations have consequences. These consequences will affect society and educational systems, as well as the individuals within those systems. Kunnan (2000a) has argued convincingly that test developers and users need to pay serious attention to the extent to which "testing programs contribute to social equity or not and in general, whether there are any pernicious effects due to them" (p. 4). Drawing on work in ethics, Kunnan (2004) articulates what he calls "the principle of beneficence":

> A test ought to bring about good in society; that is, it should not be harmful or detrimental to society.

Following Kunnan, we define **beneficence** as the degree to which the consequences of using an assessment and of the decisions that are made promote good and are not detrimental to stakeholders.

Consequences of assessment use

We must always consider the consequences both of *using* an assessment and of the *decisions made*, realizing that the use of a language assessment is likely to affect not only the individual stakeholders, as discussed above, but also the educational system and society. This is of particular concern with high-stakes assessments, which are used to make major decisions about individuals. Consider, for example, the potential impact on the language teaching practice and language programs in a given country of using a particular type of assessment task, such as the multiple-choice item or a specific type of oral interview, in widely used high-stakes assessments on a national level. Similarly, we need to consider the potential impact on society of using language assessments and making decisions based on them. For example, what might be the consequences for a school system of using language assessments to group schoolchildren into different instructional programs, or what might be the impact on society of using a language test to screen individuals applying for immigration, or as part of the licensing procedure for health care professionals? If assessment use reflects the values and goals of only a small segment of society, to what extent might this use exert a positive or a negative influence on the values and goals of the society as a whole?

Consequences for individuals

A variety of individual stakeholders may be affected by the use of a given test in any particular situation. Stakeholders who will be directly affected include the test takers themselves, and educational programs and teachers. In addition, a large number of individuals (e.g., test takers' future classmates or co-workers, future employers) may be indirectly affected. Finally, to the extent that the assessment has an impact on the educational system or society at large, it could be argued that virtually every member of the system is indirectly affected by its use. For example, widely used and expensive commercial tests have a considerable economic impact not only upon the test takers who take them, but also upon individuals in the organizations that develop them and in the communities within which these organizations are located. Rather than attempting to discuss the general systemic effect of assessment use or the potential indirect impact on all individuals, we will focus our attention here on the consequences for those individuals who are most often directly affected by assessment use: test takers and teachers.

Consequences for test takers

Test takers can be affected by three aspects of the assessment procedure:

1 the experience of preparing for and taking the assessment,
2 the feedback they receive about their performance on the assessment, and
3 the decisions that may be made about them on the basis of their assessment results.

The experiences of preparing for and taking the assessment have the potential for affecting those characteristics of test takers that are discussed in our description of language use in Chapter 3. In high-stakes tests such as public examinations or standardized tests for nationally or internationally recognized qualifications, test takers may spend weeks or months preparing for the test. In some countries, where high-stakes nationwide public examinations are used for selecting and placing individuals into higher levels of the school system or into universities, teaching may be focused on the syllabus of the test for several years before the actual examination, and the specific techniques for responding to examination tasks may be practiced in class.

The experience of taking the assessment itself can also have an effect on test takers. The test takers' affective response, or feelings, may be affected by the content of the assessment. For example, if the content of a reading passage is perceived as either threatening or otherwise emotionally disturbing to test takers, their responses to questions based on the passage might be adversely affected.[8] The test taker's topical knowledge might be affected if the assessment provides topical or cultural information that is new. We thus need to ask whether the topical content of the assessment task evokes negative emotional reactions from test takers or if it informs or misinforms the test takers. In addition, the test takers' perceptions of the characteristics of the TLU domain may be affected by the assessment, particularly in cases where the TLU domain may be unfamiliar (for example, an international student planning to enroll in a program of study at an American college or university). We thus need to ask whether the assessment informs or misleads the test takers as to various aspects of the TLU domain. Test takers' areas of language knowledge may also be affected by the assessment. For many test takers, the assessment can provide some confirmation or disconfirmation of their perceptions of their own language ability, and may affect their areas of language knowledge. For example, if something is presented as grammatically correct in the input, but is actually ungrammatical, this might be misleading. Conversely, the test taker may improve her language knowledge either while taking the assessment or from feedback received. Finally, the test taker's use of strategies may be affected by the characteristics of the assessment task. One way to promote the potential for positive consequences of assessment use is through involving test takers in the development of the assessment, as well as collecting information from them about their perceptions of the assessment and assessment tasks. If test takers are involved in this way, we would hypothesize that the assessment tasks are more likely to be perceived as authentic, and that test takers will have a more positive perception of the assessment, be more highly motivated, and probably perform better.

The types of feedback test takers receive about their assessment performance are also likely to affect them directly. We will refer to the feedback that is given to test takers and other stakeholders as an **assessment report**. This assessment report will include the assessment record (discussed below) plus an interpretation of the record, in terms of the ability to be assessed and the domain to which this interpretation generalizes. In some cases the assessment report may also include the decision that is made. The specific contents of this assessment report will vary, depending upon the situation in which the assessment is used. For example, when a test is used for research purposes, test takers may not expect or need much in the way of feedback. In other situations, much more information would be provided. An assessment report for a student who has taken a placement test, for example, would most likely include the course into which the student has been placed (decision), as well as the student's score (assessment record), and perhaps an interpretation of this score, in terms of the components of language ability that were assessed. Because of its potential impact on test takers, we need to consider how to make feedback as relevant, complete, and meaningful to the test taker as possible. When feedback is in the form of a score, we need to make sure that the scores we record are meaningful to test takers.[9] We also need to consider additional types of feedback, such as verbal descriptions to help interpret test scores, as well as verbal descriptions of the actual test tasks and the test taker's performance. The provision of rich verbal description, especially if given in a personal debriefing with the appropriate test administrator, can be very effective in developing a positive affective response toward the test on the part of test takers.[10] When the assessment results are presented as a verbal description, without a score, we need to make sure that this description is stated in language that the test taker will understand.

Finally, test takers will be directly affected by the decisions that are made about them on the basis of the assessment-based interpretations. Assessments are used to make a wide range of decisions that directly affect test takers. These decisions include relatively low-stakes ones such as formative decisions students may make about their own approaches to learning, or that teachers make about the kinds of learning tasks to present to students and how these will be sequenced in a course of instruction. The decisions also include high-stakes decisions such as selection for employment, university entrance, or professional certification.

Consequences for teachers

A second group of individuals who are often directly affected by assessments are teachers. The effect, or impact of assessment use on teachers as the implementers of a program of instruction has been referred to by language assessors as **washback**. (See also discussion of washback below.) Most teachers are familiar with the ways in which an externally mandated assessment can influence their instruction. Despite the fact that teachers may personally prefer to teach certain material in a specific way, if they find that they have to use a specified assessment they may find "teaching to the test" almost unavoidable. The term "teaching to the test" in this case implies doing something in teaching that may not be compatible with teachers' own values and goals, or with the values and goals of the instructional program. The notion of teaching to the test can be related to generalizability (discussed below) if we consider the instructional setting to be the TLU domain. From this perspective, if teachers feel that what they teach is not relevant to the test, or vice versa, this must be seen as an instance of low test generalizability, in which the test may have harmful washback, or negative impact on instruction. One way to minimize the potential for negative impact on instruction is to change the way we test so that the characteristics of the test and test tasks correspond to the characteristics of learning tasks in the instructional program. If the content of the assessment is thus aligned with the goals and objectives of instruction and with instructional activities, then "teaching to the test" may become an aspect of positive impact on instruction.

The opposite situation is where those responsible for the instructional program are not satisfied with the quality of that program and the results it produces. This dissatisfaction is often based on the results of tests, but it may also arise because various aspects of the program, such as the curriculum, materials, and types of learning activities, may be out of touch with what teachers currently believe promotes effective learning. A number of language testers have argued that, in situations such as this, one way to bring instructional practice in line with current thinking in the field is to develop an assessment procedure that reflects this thinking. That is, in this situation the hypothesis is that we should be able to bring about improvement in instructional practice through the use of assessments that incorporate or are compatible with what we believe to be principles of effective teaching and learning. However, we would reinforce Wall and Alderson's (1993) point that we cannot simply assume that imposing an "enlightened" assessment will automatically have an effect on instructional practice. Indeed, as their research and that of others (e.g., Cheng 1999; Cheng, Watanabe, and Curtis 2004) has demonstrated, the impact of assessment on instruction varies with respect to the particular aspects of instruction that are affected, and the extent of the impact can range from virtually nothing to quite a lot, and can be both positive and negative.

Finally, as with test takers, teachers may also be directly affected by the decisions that are made on the basis of assessment-based interpretations. In many countries, for example, large-scale standardized assessments of students' academic achievement are used to make decisions about resourcing, which may include the hiring and retention of teachers, their salaries, and the quality of the physical resources of the school in which they are teaching.

Consequences for education systems and society

Washback

While "washback" was discussed above in terms of the effect of assessment use on teachers' instructional practice, this term is also used to refer to the broad effects of an assessment on learning and instruction in an educational system. This aspect of impact has been of particular interest to both language assessment researchers and practitioners, and most discussions of this have focused on processes (learning and instruction).[11] These processes take place in and are implemented by individuals, as well as educational and societal systems, and they have effects on individuals, educational systems, and society at large. We thus feel washback can best be considered within the scope of consequences, and this is the perspective we will present here.[12]

Washback has been discussed in language assessment largely as the direct impact of testing on individuals, and it is widely assumed to exist. Hughes (2003), for example, defines what he refers to as "backwash" as "the effect of testing on teaching and learning" (p. 1), and asserts that testing can have either a beneficial or a harmful effect on teaching and learning. Cohen (1984) discusses the effects of washback more broadly, in terms of "how assessment instruments affect educational practices and beliefs" (p. 41). Wall and Alderson (1993), on the other hand, argue convincingly, on the basis of extensive empirical research, that test developers and users cannot simply assume that assessments will have an impact on teaching and learning, but must actually investigate the specific areas (such as content of teaching, teaching methodology, ways of assessing achievement), direction (positive, negative), and extent of the presumed impact. Their work also makes it clear that washback has potential for affecting not only individuals, but the educational system as well, which implies that language assessors need to investigate this aspect of washback also. Thus, in investigating washback, one must be prepared to find that it is far more complex and thorny than simply the effect of assessment on teaching.

The role of warrants and rebuttals about beneficence in an AUA

Warrants about beneficence in an AUA elaborate this quality of consequences specifically for the given assessment situation, as illustrated in the topmost oval on the left in Figure 5.5 above. Warrants about **beneficence** state that the consequences of using the assessment and making intended decisions will be beneficial to individuals, the educational program, company, institution, or system, or to society at large. With respect to the consequences of using the assessment, warrants will state that assessment records (scores, descriptions) of individual test takers are treated confidentially, are presented in ways that are clear and understandable to all stakeholder groups, and are distributed in a timely manner. In language instructional settings, a warrant will state that the assessment will help promote good instructional practice and effective learning. With respect to the decisions that are made, a warrant will state that the consequences of the decisions made will be beneficial to each group of stakeholders.

Rebuttals: unintended consequences

Just as there are warrants that support the beneficence of the intended consequences, there are also some possible rebuttals that may weaken this claim of beneficence. Specifically, there may be unintended negative consequences of using an assessment or of making the decision that the developer may need to anticipate. One specific possible unintended detrimental consequence of the decisions that are made may be due to classification errors.

For example, a paper and pencil multiple-choice test may be familiar to test takers and economical to administer. However, using such a test for assigning grades or evaluating the effectiveness of teachers in an oral communication course may have some negative consequences. For example, continued use of such tests may perpetuate the use of a curriculum and methods of instruction that focus on teaching tasks and ways of learning that will be counterproductive to the students' ability to perform those language use tasks necessary in the target language use domain for which they may be preparing. Or, the decision to terminate the contract of a highly experienced teacher on the basis of a single oral assessment may have the negative consequence of leaving the school without a teacher for the classes that need to be taught, not to mention the negative consequences for the teacher and his family.

Given the almost infinite range of possible unintended consequences of using a particular assessment and of making a decision based on this, even the most conscientious and diligent test developer cannot possibly anticipate or guard against all the potential unintended consequences of using a particular assessment. Thus, the real issue here is that of determining which, out of all the possible unintended consequences, need to be anticipated. In Chapters 9 and 10 we discuss unintended consequences of decision classification errors. The uncertainties of anticipating unintended consequences are discussed in Chapter 13.

Claim 2: decisions

The data for this claim consist of the assessment-based interpretation about the test taker's ability that is to be assessed. The claim is as follows:

Claim 2: The decisions that are made on the basis of the assessment-based interpretations:

- take into consideration existing community **values** and relevant legal requirements, and
- are **equitable** for those stakeholders who are affected by the decision.

Values sensitivity

The beneficial consequences that the test user hopes to bring about may be ones that virtually all stakeholders agree with. However, there may be a variety of decisions that will achieve these. These decisions, or the means by which the test users hope to achieve their ends, the intended beneficial consequences, thus need to be considered within the context of the educational and societal value systems, as well as legal requirements and regulations that may delimit the kinds of decisions that are either acceptable or possible. The consideration of these values is particularly complex in the context of second or foreign language assessment, since this situation inevitably leads us to the realization that the values and goals that inform assessment use may vary from one culture to the next. For example, one culture may place great value on individual effort and achievement, while in another culture group cooperation and respect for authority may be highly valued. Values and goals also change over time, so that issues such as access to information, privacy, and confidentiality, which are now considered by many to be basic rights of test takers, were at one time not even a matter of consideration.

The assessments we use and the decisions we make on the basis of these take place in a real world context that is typically full of complex and sometimes competing rules, regulations, laws, and values. This is true whether the decisions to be made are low stakes or high stakes. In low-stakes situations, such as a teacher-based assessment for instructional purposes, the procedures used for the assessment and the instructional decisions made must be consistent with the teacher's own values about teaching and learning and about how he regards his students. They must also be consistent with any school regulations or legal requirements that may govern this particular instructional setting. Finally, these decisions need to be sensitive to, or take into consideration, the educational values of the community in which the school is located, particularly the values of parents and other community members who are interested in the well-being of the students and the school. Needless to say, the values of these different stakeholders may not always be the same. In a high-stakes setting, in which assessment-based decisions may affect teachers and schools as well as local and state school districts, the value systems, laws, and regulations are even more likely to differ, and sometimes to clash. Consider, for example, the use of large-scale standardized tests for making decisions about the allocation of resources to schools, districts, and states. While in many countries such assessment-based decisions are mandated by law, their use is almost always fraught with conflicting values and priorities. Students may feel that because the decisions based on these assessments will not directly affect their progress through school or their grades, they do not need to take the assessments seriously. Teachers, whose jobs may be in jeopardy if their students do not perform well, may feel they must give up precious instructional time in order to prepare their students for the test. Similarly, school administrators may either encourage or pressure teachers and students to focus on what is being tested, sometimes at the expense of what teachers believe should be taught in the course syllabus.

Because of the complexity of different regulations and differing values of different stakeholder groups, we cannot expect that the decisions we make will be consistent with all of them. Our decisions must at least be sensitive to, or take into consideration these regulations and values. We thus define **values sensitivity** as the degree to which the use of an assessment and the decisions that are made take into consideration existing educational and community values and relevant legal requirements. Bachman (1990) observed that "tests are not developed and used in a values-free psychometric test tube; they are virtually always intended to serve the needs of an educational system or of society at large" (p. 279). If we do not take these needs and values into consideration, we risk the danger of making decisions that may alienate the very stakeholders our assessments are intended to serve.

Values sensitivity does not necessarily mean agreeing with or accepting existing community values. The history of language testing is full of examples of tests used to make decisions that reflected existing community values, but which were nevertheless detrimental to large segments of the communities in which they took place (e.g., McNamara and Roever 2006; Shohamy 2001). Rather, values sensitivity means taking the time and effort to understand educational and community values and existing legal requirements. It means engaging with stakeholders to understand their values. Thus, even if we make a decision that is consistent with one stakeholder group's values but not another's, we need to acknowledge the other group's values in the argument. By doing so it is more likely that the other group will be able to "hear" the first group's position, and they will feel heard and acknowledged. Finally, values sensitivity also means critically analyzing community values to assure that the decisions we make are fair and equitable.

The role of the warrant about values sensitivity in an AUA

Warrants that existing educational and community values and relevant legal requirements are carefully and critically considered in the decisions are explicit articulations of this quality of the decisions. As with the warrants discussed below, about relevance and sufficiency, articulating these warrants requires the test developer and decision maker to work closely with stakeholders who will be affected by the use of the assessment and the decisions that will be made.

Equitability

We define **equitability** as the degree to which different test takers who are at equivalent levels of the ability to be assessed have equivalent chances of being classified into the same group. When we use assessment-based interpretations to make classification decisions, such as admission to a program, advancement from one grade to the next, selection for employment, or professional certification, we want to be sure that test takers who are at the same level of ability have equivalent chances of being classified into the same groups. Another way to think about equitability is that we want to make sure that the decisions we make are not biased for or against any particular group of test takers. In many situations the person who administers the assessment may also be the decision maker, so that personal attributes may affect the relationship between the test taker and the assessor/decision maker, and hence the equitability of the decision. This is of particular concern when test takers may differ from the assessor in attributes such as ethnicity, gender, age, or socioeconomic status.

In situations where we want to assess students' achievement or mastery of material covered in a course of instruction, equitability also has to do with equal opportunity to learn. If students do not have equal opportunity to learn the material that is being assessed, they may perform more poorly than students who have had ample opportunity to learn. This is not because of any impartiality (see below) in the interpretation, because the assessment-based interpretation of ability may meaningfully reflect their lack of achievement. However, the decisions that are based on this interpretation will be inequitable because these students do not have the same chance of being classified as "pass," or "proficient," as do other students. This is because they have not had equal opportunity to learn what is being assessed.

Suppose, for example, that in a particular country all the students who are not native speakers (NNSs) of the language that is the medium of instruction are required to pass a test of that language before they can pass on to the next grade. Suppose further that some of the NNSs have been in the school in the country for several years, and so have had many years' instruction in the language, while other NNSs have just arrived in the country, and have had very little instruction in the language. If these latter students performed poorly on the test and were not passed on to the next grade because of this, then this decision would not be equitable because these students have not had an equal opportunity to learn the language.

The role of the warrant about equitability in an AUA

Warrants that assessment-based decisions are equitable are explicit statements that elaborate this quality of the decisions to be made. Warrants about **equitability** state that test takers are classified *only* according to the cut scores and decision rules, and not according to any other considerations, and that they are fully informed about how the decisions will be made and whether decisions are actually made in the way described to them. Another equitability warrant also states that for achievement and certification decisions, test takers have equal opportunity to learn the ability that will be assessed.

Claim 3: interpretations

The data for this claim consist of the test taker's assessment record. The claim is as follows:

Claim 3: The interpretations about the ability to be assessed are:
- **meaningful** with respect to a particular learning syllabus, an analysis of the abilities needed to perform tasks in the TLU domain, a general theory of language ability, or any combination of these;
- **impartial** to all groups of test takers;
- **generalizable** to the TLU domain in which the decision is to be made;
- **relevant** to the decision to be made; and
- **sufficient** for the decision to be made.

Meaningfulness

We use the term **meaningfulness** to refer to the extent to which a given assessment record (1) provides stakeholders with information about the ability to be assessed, and (2) conveys this information in terms that they can understand and relate to. The meaningfulness of the interpretations that we make on the basis of assessment results derives from the way in which we have defined the ability construct to be assessed and the way in which we communicate this to stakeholders. In most language assessment settings, constructs are defined on the basis of a specific language learning syllabus, a needs analysis of the abilities required to perform TLU tasks, a general theory of language ability, or any combination of these. (See Chapter 11 for a discussion of defining constructs.)

When a test taker interacts with an assessment task, this will engage a number of individual attributes, such as her topical knowledge, her affective schemata (e.g., her anxiety or level of comfort), her cognitive style, and so forth. In addition, attributes such as gender, age, or cultural background may also affect the way she performs. (See the discussion of the interactions between the test taker and the assessment task in Chapter 3.) However, in language assessment, the constructs in which we are most interested are aspects of language ability.[13] (See the discussion of language ability in Chapter 3.) Thus, in order for us to be able to make interpretations about language ability, the test taker's response must engage her language ability. We can think of many types of assessment tasks, such as those involving mathematical calculation or responding to visual, non-verbal information, that might involve a great deal of interaction between the test taker and the assessment task. However, unless this interaction requires the use of language ability, we would not be able to make interpretations about language ability on the basis of the test taker's performance. For example, an assessment task of geometry that requires the test taker to utilize graphic and numeric information in a diagram to solve the problem presented may be very engaging, but we would not attempt to interpret performance on this task as an indication of language ability.

The labels or descriptions we use for the constructs to be assessed also play an important role in meaningfulness. In defining the construct, the test developer may use terminology from a course syllabus, or from a general theory of language ability. These terms may be needed to help the test developers, including individuals who create assessment tasks, to clearly understand the ability to be assessed. However, these terms may be technical, and may not be meaningful to other stakeholders. It is thus the test developer's responsibility to work with relevant stakeholders to assure that the labels used to describe the ability to be assessed are understandable.

The role of warrants about meaningfulness in an AUA

In order to argue that an interpretation is meaningful, we need to articulate specific warrants that elaborate the meaningfulness of the interpretation for a given assessment situation. One meaningfulness warrant will state the basis, such as a course syllabus, a needs analysis of language use in a TLU domain, or a general theory of language ability, on which the construct has been defined. Other meaningfulness warrants will state that the assessment tasks will elicit performance from which we can make inferences about the construct to be assessed, that the recording procedure focuses on those aspects of performance that are relevant to the construct definition, that the assessment tasks engage the ability defined in the construct definition, that the assessment records can be interpreted as indicators of the ability to be assessed, and that the test developer communicates the definition of the construct to be assessed in terms that are clearly understandable to the stakeholders.

Impartiality

We define **impartiality** as the degree to which the format and content of the assessment tasks and all aspects of the administration of the assessment are free from bias that may favor or disfavor some test takers. Bias in the assessment may cause takers who are at the same ability level to perform differently on the assessment. It is quite possible, for example, that both the format of assessment tasks and their content can affect test takers' performance. Differences in performance that are not due to differences in language ability are potential sources of bias. If the way the assessment is administered is not familiar to some test takers, they may perform poorly on the test even though their language ability might be quite high. When computer- or web-based tests were first introduced in large-scale language assessments, for example, test developers went to considerable lengths to research the extent to which lack of computer familiarity might affect test takers' performance. Another potential source of bias is when students with disabilities may not be able to either access the input of an assessment task, or respond to it appropriately. Students who are hearing impaired or who have a visual disability, for example, may not be able to process auditory or visual input, respectively, and hence perform poorly on the assessment. In such cases, specific alterations in either the test format or in the way it is administered may help reduce this potential source of bias (Koenig 2002; Koenig and Bachman 2004). The assessment might also be biased if test takers do not have equal access to information about the assessment, or to the assessment itself. For example, when computer-based language assessments were first introduced in large-scale assessments, there was considerable concern about the availability of places where test takers could take these in many countries around the world (e.g., Taylor et al. 1999).

The role of warrants about impartiality in an AUA

Warrants that the interpretation is impartial elaborate this quality of the interpretation. All of these warrants are related to the fairness of assessment-based interpretations. Some warrants will state that the assessment tasks do not include response formats or content that may either favor or disfavor some test takers, and do not include content that may be offensive, that is, topically, culturally, or linguistically inappropriate, to some test takers. Other warrants will state that individuals have equal access to information about the assessment content and assessment procedures, as well as to the assessment itself, have equal opportunity to prepare for the assessment, and, for achievement and certification decisions, test takers have equal opportunity to learn or acquire the ability to be assessed.

Generalizability

In most language assessment situations, we are not interested so much in how test takers perform on the assessment itself, but rather in the information this performance provides us about test takers' language ability that applies beyond their performance on the test itself. That is, we want our interpretations about language ability to generalize beyond the assessment itself to a particular TLU domain and its associated TLU tasks. When we identify a particular TLU domain for considering the relative generalizability of a given assessment task, we are, in effect, defining the language use domain to which we want our interpretation to generalize. We define a **domain of generalization** as a set of language use tasks in the TLU domain to which the assessment tasks correspond. We define **generalizability** as the degree of correspondence between a given language assessment task and a TLU task in their task characteristics.

Characteristics of assessment and TLU tasks

Generalizability has to do with the characteristics of the assessment tasks themselves. In addressing this issue, we need to consider all of the relevant characteristics of the assessment tasks and the TLU tasks. (See Chapter 4 for a discussion of a framework of task characteristics.) We need to consider the extent to which the characteristics of the task itself, such as the complexity of the language (e.g., grammar, vocabulary, cohesion) or the area and specificity of the topical content of the input, correspond to those of a TLU task. We also need to consider the correspondence between the way the test taker responds to the assessment task and how he would be likely to respond to a corresponding TLU task. We also need to consider the correspondence between the way the test taker's response to the assessment task is evaluated and how his response to similar tasks would likely be evaluated in the TLU domain (e.g., Goodwin and Goodwin 1992; Jacoby and McNamara 1999). For example, if the assessment task were part of a group oral interview, then the aspects of generalizability that would need to be considered include the context or setting of the interview, the number and personal attributes of the other participants, the topics that are being discussed, the kinds of input and prompts the test taker receives from the interviewer and the other participants, the way the test taker responds to these, and the kinds of feedback the test taker receives from the interviewer and other participants, as the interview unfolds. In other words, generalizability includes the whole range of characteristics that can be used to describe a particular instance of language use. (See Chapter 3 for a discussion of language use and Chapter 4 for a discussion of the characteristics of language use tasks and assessment tasks.)

Because of the way in which we have defined the TLU domain, our definition of generalizability can apply to a wide variety of language use settings, including language classrooms in which the teacher's approach to teaching may range from "focus on form," to "communicative," to "content-based" or "task-based." This view of generalizability thus allows us to consider the relevance of assessment content and tasks to classroom teaching and learning activities that may themselves be related to a specific TLU domain beyond the language classroom.

The role of warrants about generalizability in an AUA

Warrants that an interpretation is generalizable to the TLU domain of the assessment elaborate this quality of the interpretation. Warrants of generalizability state that the characteristics of the assessment tasks, including the kinds of interactions these engage, the responses of the test takers to the assessment task, and how these are evaluated, correspond to the characteristics, interactions, responses, and evaluations of tasks in the TLU domain.

The following example illustrates what we mean by generalizability. Imagine an eighth grade science class, a TLU domain in which the tasks to be performed require language ability, such as reading about science in a textbook and discussing this with fellow students and the teacher. Suppose that the teacher wanted to collect information about students' achievement for the purpose of providing them with formative feedback on their learning, and he defined the construct to be assessed as "knowledge of science at the eighth grade level." Suppose the teacher developed an assessment task that consisted of a diagram of an apparatus used in science and that required students to choose the correct use of this apparatus from among five pictures of students using the apparatus in different ways. Interpretations of students' performance on this task might be considered meaningful, in terms of the construct definition. However, since neither the input of the assessment task nor the students' response to it requires the use of language, this task might be considered to be of low generalizability, with respect to performing tasks in the TLU domain. In this case, it would appear that the teacher has not adequately taken into consideration the language ability required to perform TLU tasks when he defined the construct. Thus, even though the students' performance on the assessment tasks may tell him something about their knowledge of science, it tells him little, if anything, about their ability to use language to perform classroom tasks.

Relevance

In order to be useful for making the intended decisions, the assessment-based interpretations must provide information that is relevant to the decision. We define **relevance** as the degree to which the interpretation provides the information the decision maker needs to make a decision.

The role of the warrant about relevance in an AUA

The warrant that our interpretation is relevant to the decision to be made elaborates this quality of the interpretation. The warrant refers to the relationship between the interpretation and the decisions to be made. This warrant underscores the importance of carefully discussing the needs of the test users, or the decision makers, as well as carefully analyzing the language use demands of the TLU domain, in the development of an assessment. In some cases, the decision maker may have a very clear idea of what she needs to know about test takers to make decisions. In many situations, however, the decision maker's view of what areas of language knowledge are relevant to the decision may not correspond to the demands of the language use in the domain of generalization. In such cases, test developers may need to take greater responsibility for identifying what information about test takers is relevant to making the decision. This can be done through a needs analysis, the results of which can be used to help the decision maker better understand the information about test takers that will be relevant to the decisions to be made.

Sufficiency

We define **sufficiency** as the degree to which the interpretation provides enough information for the decision maker to make a decision. Sufficiency can be seen as an extension of relevance, in that it addresses the question of *how much* relevant information is needed for the decision maker to feel comfortable that she is able to make correct decisions based on the interpretation derived from the assessment record. In some cases an interpretation from a single assessment may provide sufficient information, while in others, several complementary interpretations may be needed in order for the decision maker to feel she has sufficient information to make the correct decisions. We can also view sufficiency from the perspective of decision errors, and say that it has to do with providing enough information so that the decision maker is comfortable with the number or proportion of decision errors that result in using the assessment-based interpretations.

The key to sufficiency, then, is understanding the decision maker's **comfort zone**, or her level of tolerance for making classification errors: the greater the tolerance, the larger the comfort zone. Although we may define this comfort zone as the proportion of decision errors the decision maker is comfortable with, it is very seldom possible to know this with any degree of accuracy. Often, the decision maker herself may not have thought this through. In addition, it is seldom possible to obtain complete information about classification errors, especially false negatives, as discussed in Chapter 9. Furthermore, the decision maker's comfort zone may vary, depending on a number of real world factors that are very difficult to predict. These include the factors that are discussed in Chapter 9, with respect to the level of importance, or the stakes of the decision, and the relative ease or difficulty of correcting decision errors. In addition, the comfort zone may vary according to the availability of the resources that will be allocated on the basis of the decision, and what other competing demands for these resources there may be. Finally, the comfort zone will depend on a whole host of personality factors, so that in essentially the same decision setting, different decision makers might have very different levels of tolerance for decision errors.

The role of the warrant about sufficiency in an AUA

The warrant that an interpretation is sufficient states that the assessment-based interpretation, by itself, provides sufficient information for making the intended decision. This warrant elaborates this quality of the intended interpretations and refers to the relationship between the interpretation and the decisions to be made.

In many situations the decisions that we need to make depend on information about several different aspects of language ability, so that a single assessment-based interpretation may not provide sufficient information for making the intended decision. In a situation such as this, if we were to define the construct very narrowly, or assess only one aspect of the ability required for the decision, this might negatively impact individuals who are weak in that area, but who may be strong in other areas. Similarly, if we were to select individuals who are strong only in the area assessed, then this might negatively impact other stakeholders. Suppose, for example, that we needed to develop an assessment for use in determining whether the English language ability of international teaching assistants (ITAs) is sufficient to teach university courses in English. If we were to define the construct for this assessment solely in terms of pronunciation accuracy, we might exclude some ITAs from teaching assignments even though they may have other abilities, such as the ability to organize their instructional material or to relate to their students, that more than compensate for weaknesses in their pronunciation.

As with relevance, this warrant emphasizes how important it is for the test developer to work with the decision maker and to understand the decision maker's "comfort zone," or tolerance for decision errors. The possibility of making decision errors because of insufficient information is one rebuttal to the sufficiency warrant. Another is the possibility that the cut score for classifying test takers has been set in the wrong place.

Generalizability, relevance, and sufficiency

In order to better understand generalizability, relevance, and sufficiency, we provide three examples: (1) in which decisions about employment are to be made, (2) in which decisions about students in an instructional program are to be made, and (3) in which decisions about revising a language program are to be made.

Example 1: phone company employees selection test

Suppose the manager of a phone company calls to ask our advice in selecting an assessment that would provide her with the information she needed to select phone company employees. She tells us that she wants employees with "good pronunciation and grammar" in English. One of her colleagues suggested that she use a standardized multiple-choice test of general English proficiency that included a section on speaking. Following this suggestion, she found such a test that was commercially available and tried using scores from this test to select which applicants to hire. However, she is now very unhappy with this test. She tells us that the people she has hired are not able to perform their jobs because of what she calls "inadequate speaking skills." We discuss this problem, and conclude that this might be due to a number of reasons. The multiple-choice tasks may not correspond at all to the tasks in the TLU domain, and hence are of low generalizability to that domain. Another reason might be that the standardized test does not measure grammar and pronunciation specifically, in which case the information it is providing is not relevant to what the manager has said she needs to make the decisions. Or, the manager may not understand what components of language ability are required for successful job performance, in which case the components of language ability she has identified may not be relevant or not sufficient for making the decisions.

Suppose the manager still believes that grammar and pronunciation are the components of language ability she needs to assess, and so we decide that the lack of generalizability of the standardized test is the main problem. She asks us to develop a new test, and we suggest that we do a needs analysis to better understand the ways in which the employees need to use English in their jobs. We discover that the jobs require employees to listen to and respond to customer complaints, largely over the phone. We thus develop an oral assessment that simulates an actual phone conversation with a customer who has a complaint. We score test takers' performance on this task using rating scales for pronunciation and grammar. These ratings are recorded separately and also added together for a total score.

Again, after a period of time the manager calls and says that she is not happy. Although the new test is more useful for selecting new employees than was the standardized English proficiency test, there are still too many false positives, which are very costly because the procedure for firing employees is very complex legally. In addition, she tells us that when she has to fire someone, she loses that position and has to go back to her manager to get it back. We reply that we developed the test based on what she said she wanted, employees with good pronunciation and grammar. Going back to our needs analysis, and following this up with current employees and customers who have called to complain about their service, we discover that what seems to be most important is good listening comprehension and conversational management. We thus develop rating scales for conversational management and listening comprehension, and add these to the existing scales for grammar and pronunciation, and score test takers' performance on all four scales. After a period of time, the manager calls to tell us that she is very happy with the usefulness of information from this oral assessment for selecting new employees, as she's hired only one person in that time who did not have sufficient speaking ability to perform his job.

By developing and redeveloping the test the way we did, we were able to increase both the generalizability and the sufficiency of the interpretations. By developing tasks that simulated the phone conversation, the test tasks themselves corresponded more closely to those in the TLU domain. By adding rating scales for listening comprehension and conversational management, we gained generalizability, since the scoring procedures corresponded more closely to the way employees' telephone conversations were being evaluated by customers. In addition, we gained sufficiency, in that these two additional ratings provided sufficient information for the decision maker to tolerate the relatively small number of employment decision errors she was making.

Suppose that in this example the manager had been able to fire unqualified new employees very easily, or could have placed them in other departments where they did not need to use English. Suppose, too, that her supervisor had told her she could hire as many new employees as she needed. In this case, the manager's comfort zone might have been much larger, and she might have been comfortable with the information provided by the first test we developed, despite the apparently low generalizability of the items in that test to the TLU domain. In this case, the manager clearly valued relevance and sufficiency over generalizability. But we, as test developers, might not be satisfied with this because of our concern that performance on assessment tasks generalize to performance on TLU tasks.

Example 2: eighth grade science test

The second example that illustrates the interactions among generalizability, relevance, and sufficiency is from an educational setting, in which the decision to be made is that of advancement to the next grade on the basis of an assessment of achievement. In the eighth grade science class example above, the TLU domain is one in which the instructional tasks that students need to perform, such as reading about science and discussing this with fellow students and the teacher, require language ability in addition to topical knowledge about science. Based on state standards for eighth grade science, the construct to be assessed was defined as "knowledge of science at the eighth grade level." Suppose that the assessment-based interpretations from this assessment were going to be used to make decisions about students' advancement to ninth grade. One possible assessment would be the task discussed above, in which students are presented with a diagram of an apparatus used in science and then have to choose the correct use of this apparatus from among five pictures of students using the apparatus in different ways. As noted above, the scores obtained from this task might be of low generalizability, with respect to the TLU domain of the eighth grade science class. Nevertheless, the score-based interpretations from this test might be meaningful, with respect to the construct to be tested, and highly relevant to making decisions about advancement. But would they be sufficient? If the ninth grade science teachers felt that the students who were advanced to ninth grade science on the basis of this test were not, in fact, ready for ninth grade science, then one might conclude that the assessment-based interpretations are too narrow, and are not sufficient. However, if the ninth grade teachers were generally able to deal with, perhaps through tutorials, the small number of students who were not ready for ninth grade science, then the interpretation could be considered to be sufficient.

Now suppose that eighth and ninth grade science teachers wanted information from an assessment to help them diagnose students' areas of strength and weakness in learning science, to help them better tailor their instruction to their students' needs. In this case, the score-based interpretations from the multiple-choice test of science knowledge might be considered to be relevant to the decisions to be made. But are they sufficient? The instructional tasks in the TLU domain, in this case eighth and ninth grade science classes, require considerable language knowledge for students to complete successfully. Thus one might well question whether an interpretation solely about knowledge of science is sufficient for making these instructional decisions. In order to address this limitation, the teachers might decide to develop their own assessment. Rather than presenting students with pictures of science apparatuses, the assessment tasks might be reading passages that describe such apparatuses. Students might then be asked to explain, either orally or in writing, how the apparatus works, and perhaps how it might be used in a science experiment. Students' responses could be scored both for language and for knowledge of science. In addition, they could be analyzed qualitatively, in order to provide richer feedback to the students. In this case, what the teachers hope to have achieved is score-based interpretations that provide sufficient information for them to make instructional decisions. In the process, they may have also arrived at scores that are more generalizable to the domain of the science classroom.

Example 3: university foreign language program

Our third example illustrates a different situation, one in which the interpretations may be meaningful, in terms of the way the construct has been defined, and generalizable to the TLU domain, but are not sufficient for the decisions to be made. The coordinator for a foreign language program at a university needs to collect information to help inform a revision of a conversation course. This is an advanced-level course aimed at enabling students who have already learned sufficient grammar, vocabulary, register markers, and cohesive devices to consolidate these and develop fluency in conversational discourse. The course coordinator decides to use an oral interview test that is widely used in the field, and for which there is a version for her language. The kinds of tasks and interactions that are included in the interview correspond very closely to kinds of interactions in which students are expected to engage in their conversation classes, as well as when they use the language to converse with speakers of the language outside of class. The students' oral performances on the interview are scored on a single scale from 0 to 5, and a verbal description of what students can be expected to be able to do with their language ability is provided for each scale point. In choosing this particular test, the course coordinator implicitly, perhaps without realizing it, defined the construct very broadly as "language proficiency," or "the language ability needed to successfully engage in face-to-face conversations."

The coordinator hires officially certified oral examiners to test all the students in the course at the end of the term. When the coordinator and instructors look at the results, they are rather disappointed that the students did not perform better. Furthermore, the single ratings and verbal descriptions of the scale levels provide little information about what specific components of language ability their students need to work on in order to improve. Hence, the assessment did not provide the coordinator the information she needed to make decisions about how to revise the course, curriculum, and learning activities so that these will more effectively enable students to meet the stated course objectives. In this case, the characteristics of the oral assessment correspond closely to those of conversations both in and outside of the classroom, so the interpretations could be considered to have high generalizability. However, the information provided by the ratings on the oral assessment is not sufficient for the course coordinator and instructors to make the decisions they need to make.

These three examples illustrate a couple of things. First, they illustrate the importance of considering all of the qualities of the claims when developing and using an assessment. Focusing on only one or two, or ignoring some, will almost always lead to problems. They also illustrate the fact that there are always some uncertainties with the development and use of any language assessment. Some of these uncertainties have to do with our inability either to anticipate all possible eventualities or to obtain the information we need to resolve the uncertainties. These uncertainties are discussed in more detail in Chapter 13.

Claim 4: assessment records

The data for this claim consist of the test taker's performance on an assessment task. The claim is as follows:

> Claim 4: Assessment records are **consistent** across different assessment tasks, different aspects of the assessment procedure, and across different groups of test takers.

Consistency

In our conceptualization, consistency is a quality that is claimed for assessment records (scores, verbal descriptions).[14] **Consistency** is the extent to which test takers' performances on different assessments of the same construct yield essentially the same assessment records. A consistent assessment record will provide essentially the same information about the ability to be assessed across different aspects of the assessment procedure, such as different tasks, different times, or different raters or recorders.

What constitutes "essentially the same" for any given assessment situation will depend on the importance of the decisions to be made. By "essentially the same," we mean that the assessment records are consistent enough for the test developer, test user, and other stakeholders to be comfortable with the degree of consistency, or convinced that this is acceptable. What stakeholders are comfortable with will depend on the importance of the decisions to be made and their comfort zones. As discussed above, decision makers' comfort zones will depend on a number of real world factors, such as their flexibility in making decisions, the availability of resources, and the competing demands for these resources, as well as the decision maker's personal attributes.

Consistency of scores

When a test taker takes a test, his score should not be affected by which specific set of tasks he takes, which test form he takes, or when he takes it. If his performance is rated by a human rater, it should not matter which of a number of qualified raters rate it; his score should be the same. To put it another way, if the same test were to be administered to the same group of individuals on two different occasions, in two different settings, their scores should be the same.[15] It should not make any difference to a particular test taker whether he takes the test on one occasion and administration or the other. Or suppose that we had developed two forms of a test that were intended to be used interchangeably. It should not make any difference to a particular test taker which form of the test he takes; he should obtain the same score on both forms. Thus, in a test intended to rank order individuals from highest to lowest, if the scores obtained on the different forms do not rank individuals in essentially the same order, then these scores would not be considered to be consistent indicators of the ability we want to measure. Similarly, in a test intended to distinguish individuals who are at or above a particular mastery level of ability from those who are below it, if the scores obtained from the two forms do not identify the same individuals as "masters" and "non-masters," then the scores from these two forms of the test would not be consistent for making such classification decisions. Another example would be if we used several different raters to rate a large number of compositions. In this case, a given composition should receive the same score irrespective of which particular rater scored it. If some raters rate more severely than others, then the ratings obtained could not be considered to be very consistent.

Consistency of scores is clearly essential, for unless these are relatively consistent, they cannot provide us with very much information at all about the ability we want to assess. At the same time, we need to recognize that it is not possible to eliminate inconsistencies entirely. Test takers' performance, and hence their scores, will always be affected to some extent by **random** factors, such as temporary conditions of the test takers themselves (e.g., health, motivation, concentration), or unexpected interruptions or variations in the way the test is administered. While we cannot control random sources of inconsistency such as these, we can try to minimize the effects of those potential sources of inconsistency that are to some extent under our control. We do this by the way we develop and administer the assessment.

Consistency of verbal descriptions

When assessment records consist of verbal descriptions, then the quality of consistency is conceived of in a slightly different way and needs to be considered along with meaningfulness. With qualitative assessment records, we need to consider what constitutes consistency, and to what extent this is desirable. Bachman (2006a, 2009) discusses consistency of verbal reports in terms of the purposes for which these are intended. If the purpose of the verbal report is to provide a rich description, such as might be of interest for giving feedback to learners, then consistency between two recorders' reports may be less important than the complementarity of the information they provide. In an oral interview, for example, two different recorders, using essentially the same procedures, might still differ in the specific information they include, and what they emphasize, while at the same time providing information that will be helpful to learners. Similarly in the literature on writing assessment, some researchers view different "readings" of a composition by different raters as a positive outcome (Weigle 2002). Building up a rich description on the basis of multiple observers' reports may enable the teacher and learner to benefit from both commonalities and differences in the reports.

If the purpose of the assessment is to *interpret* the verbal report in a way that gives it meaning within a particular language use domain, the recorders will need to consider both the consistency of the verbal reports and the meaningfulness of their interpretations. In situations like this, consistency has to do with the extent to which any given observation report provides essentially the same information, or generalizes, across different aspects of the observation and reporting procedure (e.g., instances, events, observers, ethnographers, categorizers, analysts, raters). That is, in order to provide a basis for a common interpretation, we would expect descriptions that are recorded by different recorders to be consistent in the information they provide. That is, we would expect these descriptions to include essentially the same information, presented in essentially the same way.

So whether consistency is viewed as desirable or necessary will reflect the purpose of the assessment. If the test user's purpose is to describe the test taker's performance in all its richness, as might be the case in formative classroom assessments, then variations in reports may be viewed as adding to and enhancing the description of the phenomenon.[16] If, however, the purpose is to interpret different observation reports as descriptions of essentially the same construct, as is the case with language assessment, then consistency among reports is essential.

The role of warrants about consistency in an AUA

Warrants that our assessment is consistent elaborate this quality of the assessment record for a specific assessment. These warrants will refer to both the way the assessment is administered and to the assessment records themselves. They thus support a quality of the assessment records. Consistency warrants state that the *assessment records* are consistent across different characteristics of the assessment situation, such as different assessment tasks, different forms of the assessment, different assessors, or different times of assessment. Some consistency warrants will state that the procedures for administering and scoring the assessment are consistent, and that raters are trained to rate consistently. Other warrants will state that test takers' assessment records are consistent across different aspects of the assessment procedure, e.g., tasks or items, assessors, forms, and over time. Finally, a consistency warrant may also state that the assessment records are consistent across different groups of test takers. We would note that in addition to elaborating consistency, this warrant also pertains to the fairness of the assessment records across different groups of test takers. This warrant is one of many in the AUA that are related to fairness. In our conceptualization, we operationalize issues of fairness as warrants throughout the AUA. (See the discussion of fairness below.)

We cannot control all the factors mentioned above that are unrelated to the construct we want to assess and that may lead to inconsistencies in test takers' scores. However, of the many factors that can affect assessment performance, the various aspects of the assessment procedure itself are at least partly under our control. We can also try to minimize inconsistencies in the way the test is administered and scored. Some of the warrants for consistency, therefore, will refer to consistencies in administrative procedures and the ways in which the test takers' performances are scored. These warrants will state, for example, that the procedures for administering the assessment and the method for recording test takers' performance are consistent. All of these warrants elaborate the quality of consistency by stating that the test developer has carefully followed accepted procedures in the development and administration of the assessment.

FAIRNESS

According to the *Standards for Educational and Psychological Testing* (American Educational Research Association, American Psychological Association, and National Council on Measurement in Education 1999), "concern for fairness in testing is pervasive" (p. 71). In addition, there has been considerable discussion of fairness in the field of language assessment (e.g., Elder 1997; Kunnan 2004, 2000b). Although specialists in educational measurement and language testing agree that fairness is a fundamental concern, defining this has proven elusive. The *Standards for Educational and Psychological Testing* (American Educational Research Association, American Psychological Association, and National Council on Measurement in Education 1999), for example, avoids defining the term entirely, stating, "a full consideration of fairness would explore the many functions of testing in relation to its many goals, including the broad goal of achieving equality of opportunity in our society" (p. 73). Nevertheless, the *Standards* discuss several different characteristics that comprise fairness: absence of bias, equitable treatment of test takers in the testing process, equality of testing outcomes for different groups of test takers, and equity in opportunity to learn the content that is measured in an achievement test. Similarly, Kunnan (2004) does not define fairness, but discusses it in terms of different qualities: validity, absence of bias, equity of access, administration, and social consequences. From this, it is clear that fairness is not a single quality, but is a function of many different aspects of not only the assessment process itself, but also the use of assessments.

Because of the significance that is attached to fairness in both language assessment and educational measurement, we feel that it is important to discuss how fairness issues are addressed in the claims and warrants in an AUA. Both the assessment process and the decisions that are made about stakeholders (e.g., students, teachers, schools, potential employees, individuals seeking professional certification) on the basis of assessment results will directly affect them in a number of ways. It is thus essential that we consider the fairness of the assessment process both in the decisions we make on the basis of the assessment, and in the consequences of assessment use.

Fairness in the assessment process

Fairness in assessment has to do with two aspects of assessment:

1 equitable treatment of individuals in the assessment process, and
2 absence of bias in the assessment process, assessment records and in the interpretations that are made on the basis of these records.

Equitability of treatment

Equitability of treatment in the assessment process has to do with access, test administration, and recording of results. Equitability of treatment requires that:

- All test takers have equal access to information about the assessment and the assessment procedures.
- All test takers have equal opportunity to prepare for the assessment. For example, giving an achievement test that is based on the content of a specific course to students who have not been taught this content would not be fair.
- All test takers have equal access to the assessment, in terms of location, cost, and familiarity with the procedures and equipment used.
- All test takers are given comparable opportunities to demonstrate their ability.
- All test takers are given the assessment under equivalent and appropriate conditions.
- The results of the assessment are reported in a timely manner, in ways that are clearly understandable to all stakeholder groups, that assure confidentiality to individuals.

Equitability of treatment in an AUA

These requirements are addressed in several places in the AUA. Consistency warrants state that the assessment is given under the same conditions to all test takers, while impartiality warrants state that the assessment tasks do not include response formats or content that may either favor or disfavor some test takers, do not include content that may be offensive, that individuals have equal access to information about the assessment content and assessment procedures, as well as to the assessment itself, and have equal opportunity to prepare for the assessment and for achievement and certification decisions. Equitability warrants state that test takers are classified *only* according to the cut scores and decision rules, and not according to any other considerations, that test takers and other stakeholders are fully informed about how the decision will be made and whether decisions are actually made in the way described to them, and that test takers have equal opportunity to learn or acquire the ability to be assessed. Finally, beneficence warrants state that assessment reports of individual test takers are treated confidentially, that they are reported in a timely manner, and in ways that are clearly understandable.

Absence of bias in the assessment process

Bias can be defined as a difference in the meanings of assessment records for individuals from different identifiable groups (e.g., by gender, ethnicity, religion, native language) that is not related to the ability that is assessed. In other words, bias results in interpretations that are not equally meaningful, relevant, or generalizable for individuals in different groups. The most obvious instance of bias is when members of a particular group perform better or worse on an assessment due to factors that are not related to the ability being assessed.

Bias can arise from a number of different sources. One potential source of bias is the format of the intended response. For example, consider a test intended to measure how well test takers can comprehend a spoken conversation, in which they are required to write their responses. Those test takers who are better writers may receive higher scores, so that the scores could not be interpreted as valid indicators of listening. Another potential source of bias is the content of assessment itself (e.g., cultural content, specialized topical content). For example, if a test that is intended to measure ability in a foreign language contains specialized topical content that is familiar to some groups of test takers and unfamiliar to others, then this might be a source of bias. In this case, test takers who are familiar with the specialized content might perform better because of this, and not because of their higher language ability, but because of their knowledge of the topical content. The test scores could not be interpreted as meaningful indicators of language ability. Inconsistent scoring can also be a source of bias. For example, if different raters score the compositions of one group of test takers more severely than others, then this will result in biased, inconsistent scoring, and the meaningfulness of the intended interpretations of these scores would consequently be compromised.

Absence of bias in an AUA

Issues of potential bias in the assessment process, assessment records, and interpretations are also addressed in several places in the AUA. Impartiality warrants state that the assessment tasks do not include response formats or specialized content that may either favor or disfavor some test takers. Potential bias in the scoring method and differential consistency of assessment records across different groups of test takers are addressed in consistency warrants.

The evaluation of bias in the assessment process is complex and requires both technical, statistical analysis and expert judgment. What makes this particularly difficult is that differences in assessment performance across groups are not sufficient to demonstrate bias. We must also demonstrate that these differences are not due to differences in the ability we want to assess. (See the Additional Readings at the end of the chapter for some references on bias.)

Fairness in assessment use

While it is important to investigate the different sources of bias that can lead to different interpretations of assessment results, we also need to consider fairness in the decisions we make using assessment results and the consequences of these decisions. Acceptance or non-acceptance into an instructional program, advancement or non-advancement from one course to another, or in a career, employment or non-employment, are all decisions that can have serious consequences for individuals.

Fair decisions are those that are equally appropriate, regardless of an individual's group membership. We need to ask whether the decision procedures and criteria are applied uniformly to all groups of individuals. Fair test use also has to do with the relevance and sufficiency of the assessment results to the decision. Thus we need to consider the various kinds of information, including the assessment results, that could be used in making the decisions, as well as their relative importance and the criteria that will be used. Is it fair, for example, to make a life-affecting decision solely on the basis of a single test score?

Finally, fair test use has to do with whether and by what means individuals are fully informed about how the decision will be made and whether decisions are actually made in the way described to them. For example, if test takers are told that acceptance into a program will be based on their test scores and grades, but acceptance is actually based primarily on letters of reference, we might question the fairness of the decision procedure. Or, if teachers are not told that raises in their salaries will be made primarily on the basis of their students' standardized test scores, and then some teachers are denied raises because their students performed poorly on the standardized test, we would most likely feel that this is not a fair decision. We need to ask if the intended consequences of using the assessment and of the decisions made are beneficial to all groups of stakeholders.

Fairness of assessment use in an AUA

Issues related to the fairness of assessment use are addressed in an AUA in the warrants that support the beneficence of the consequences, the equitability of the decisions, and the relevance and sufficiency of the interpretations for the decisions to be made.

Fairness in assessment use is a fundamental consideration in the development and use of language assessments. It is for this reason that warrants specifically addressing fairness issues are central to the AUA. If the assessment procedure does not provide assessment records that are *consistent* across different groups of individuals, it is not fair. If the interpretations that we make of assessment records for individuals who are members of different groups are differentially *meaningful* or are not *impartial*, then they are not fair. If the interpretations are not *generalizable* beyond the assessment itself, or are not *relevant* and *sufficient*, then the decisions we make may not be fair. If the decisions we make ignore existing community *values* and legal requirements and are not *equitable* for individuals in different groups, they will not be fair. If the consequences of using the assessment and of the decisions made are not *beneficial*, then these will not be fair.

It is particularly important for developers and users of assessments to address these issues of fairness in high-stakes assessments, where major, life-affecting decisions are made. However, even in low-stakes assessments, because the assessment will have some consequences for individuals, fairness should always be a consideration. The considerations and procedures that we discuss in the later chapters of this book are aimed at enabling us to develop and use language assessments that will be justified—that will yield assessment records that are consistent, interpretations that are meaningful and impartial, that generalize beyond the assessment, and that are relevant and sufficient for the decisions to be made, decisions that are values sensitive and equitable, and that have consequences that are beneficial in ways that are fair to all test takers.

CONCLUSION

We believe the approach to assessment justification developed here makes a contribution to the field of language testing for a number of reasons. This approach provides a conceptual framework, an Assessment Use Argument (AUA), that can guide the development and use of language assessments. The AUA consists of a series of statements (claims, warrants, rebuttals) about the outcomes (consequences, decisions, interpretations, assessment records) of a given assessment and about the qualities of these outcomes. It thus provides a *principled* means for clearly describing how these outcomes are related to each other for any given assessment. In addition, the AUA provides a means both for defining the qualities that are associated with specific assessment outcomes, as well as for understanding the relationships among these qualities. Thus, unlike previous frameworks which consist essentially of unordered lists of qualities such as reliability, validity, authenticity, and impact, in an AUA, the qualities of consistency, meaningfulness, impartiality, generalizability, relevance, sufficiency, values sensitivity, equitability, and beneficence are associated with specific claims and warrants in an AUA, and are linked conceptually by the structure of the AUA itself. In other words, the value of an AUA for assessment use is not simply in the relabeling of the qualities, but in the way these are clearly related to specific outcomes and to each other.

The AUA ties the process of assessment justification to the specific testing situation. That is, it links considerations of beneficence, values sensitivity, equitability, meaningfulness, impartiality, generalizability, relevance, sufficiency, and consistency to the specific consequences that are intended, the specific decisions to be made, to a specific TLU domain, and to specific groups of test takers and test users. This approach to assessment justification thus makes two requirements of test developers and test users. First, we must consider the construction of an AUA with respect to specific assessments, and not just in terms of abstract theories and statistical formulae. Second, we must consider the AUA from the very beginning of the test planning and development process, and rather than relying solely on *ex post facto* analyses.

We believe that the process of assessment justification is essential to the development and use of any language assessment. Without this process, the test developer cannot be held accountable to stakeholders. An AUA guides the test developer through the process of justification, and so we would argue that articulating an AUA is also essential to the development and use of any language assessment. As many readers will note, the qualities that are associated with the claims and warrants in an AUA look very much like an expanded list of "technical qualities" of measurements (e.g., reliability, validity), or the qualities of usefulness. As such, they might be viewed as a prescriptive set of qualities that need to be demonstrated for the claims in every language assessment. Viewed this way, an AUA and the qualities associated with its claims could be seen as constituting a set of standards to which test developers and test users need to adhere. While this is certainly something to be considered, it is not our intention here to prescribe standards for language assessment. Rather, our purpose is to provide test developers and test users with a framework and tools that will enable them to develop language assessments and justify their uses to stakeholders.

The AUA and the necessity for justifying the intended uses of language assessments are the bedrocks of our approach to language assessment use. However, the development and use of language assessments always takes place in a real world setting that is full of uncertainties, where stakeholders behave as real people, that is to say, often unpredictably, and where the resources that are available for assessment development and use are almost always limited. The nature of these real world conditions and constraints and how our approach to language assessment use can help us deal with these in a rational and principled manner are dealt with in Part III of this book.

EXERCISES

1 Describe all the stakeholders that are likely to be affected by each of the following uses of language assessments:
Using a language assessment to:
   (a) certify that health care professionals have sufficient language ability to practice their professions;
   (b) certify that language teachers have sufficient language ability to teach effectively;
   (c) decide if non-native English speaking students need additional English language instruction;
   (d) decide if non-native English speaking students have sufficient language ability to take academic achievement tests in science and mathematics that are given in English;
   (e) decide if individuals who are seeking political asylum in a country are legitimately eligible for this;
   (f) decide if individuals who want to immigrate to a country should be given an immigrant visa to do so;
   (g) decide if citizens of a country are eligible to vote in an election.

2 Describe the intended beneficial consequences and possible detrimental consequences of the decisions made in Exercise 1.

3 Describe how the test developer and/or decision maker would convince stakeholders that the decisions made in Exercise 1 are values sensitive and equitable.

4 For the Modern Chinese speaking test example above (pp. 100–1), draw a figure with stacked boxes like Figure 5.5 to show the different claims in the AUA.

5 Read over Project 10 on the web, which illustrates how rebuttals to selected warrants in the AUA are affected by changing values of stakeholders. Think of an assessment situation that you are familiar with in which values of stakeholders may be changing. How might these changing values cause you to rethink the use of the assessment?

6 Read over "setting" for Project 12 on the web (http://www.oup.com/LAIP), in which an assessment is used in a situation in which two sets of stakeholders have differing values and perceive the usefulness of the test quite differently. This is a situation we have encountered many times in our discussions with language testers around the world. Have you encountered such a situation? If so, describe it briefly and explain the major areas in which differing values of stakeholders affect their perceptions of the usefulness of the assessment.

SUGGESTED READINGS

1 Sources of bias in item format and content: Alderson and Urquhardt 1985; Shohamy 1984.

2 *Standards for Educational and Psychological Testing* (American Educational Research Association et al. 1999) provides an extensive and authoritative discussion of reliability and validity, as well as standards for test use. The standards described in this publication are widely accepted by the measurement profession, as well as by test developers and test users.

3 ILTA *Code of Ethics* (International Language Testing Association 2000) and Guidelines for Practice (International Language Testing Association 2005) provide a set of principles intended to guide good professional conduct in language testing. These are both available at http://www.iltaonline.com/code.pdf. Codes of practice for other language assessment associations and language testing organizations can be found at the following web pages:

- www.alte.org/cop/index.php (ALTE, The Association of Language Testers in Europe)
- www.ealta.eu.org/guidelines.htm (EALTA, The European Association for Language Testing and Assessment
- www.avis.ne.jp/~youichi/COP.html (JLTA, the Japan Language Testing Association)

4 Bachman (2005) provides a detailed discussion of an Assessment Use Argument in the context of language testing.

5 Bachman (1990) discusses reliability and validity conceptually, while Bachman (2004b) provides detailed discussions of statistical procedures for estimating reliability, and discusses statistical approaches to investigating validity. Discussions of reliability and validity in non-measurement assessments can be found in Kirk and Miller (1999) and Denzin and Lincoln (2005).

6 Discussions of test qualities in the context of educational performance assessment can be found in Moss (1992), Wiggins (1993), Messick (1994a), Linn (1994), Baker, O'Neil, and Linn (1993), and Linn, Baker, and Dunbar (1991).

7 Bachman (1990: Chapter 8) provides an extensive discussion of authenticity in language tests.

8 Canale (1988) discusses the importance of providing rich feedback to test takers.

9 Swain (1985) speaks of developing test tasks that "bias for the best," or that provide test takers with opportunities to perform at their highest level of ability.

10 For an overview discussion of washback, see Wall (1997). For recent research studies into washback, see Alderson and Wall (1996) and Cheng, Watanabe, and Curtis (2004).

11 For discussions of impact, consequences, fairness, and ethics in language testing, see Davies (1997) and Kunnan (2004, 2000b).
12 For discussions of test bias, see Bond (1995), Hamp-Lyons and Davies (2008), and Elder (1997).

NOTES

1 For convenience we will use the term "test developer" to refer to individuals who design and develop assessments, and "test user" to those who make decisions based on the assessment, whether these are tests or other kinds of assessments. We will use the singular form, even though in many situations these may constitute groups of individuals.
2 For convenience we will use the term "test taker" to refer to individuals who take assessments, whether these are tests or other kinds of assessments.
3 Different terms are used to refer to such students, e.g., bilingual learners, foreign language learners, or second language learners (McKay 2006). In countries where English is the language of instruction, different terms are also used. In the United States, for example, the most commonly used term is "English language learners" (ELLs), while in Australia, the term "English as a second language (ESL) learners" is used, and in the United Kingdom, the term "English as an additional language (EAL) learners" is used.
4 This example is from Wang (2008).
5 We would note that we are using the term "justification," rather than "validation." "Validation" is the term that is used in many references in language testing to refer specifically to collecting evidence to support the link between the assessment record and the interpretation. We use the term "justification" because we believe this captures the notion that what we investigate in this process is not simply the assessment-based interpretation, but the extent to which the intended uses of the assessment are justified.
6 Our conceptualization of an Assessment Use Argument builds on the work of Michael Kane on validity and validation (Kane 2002, 2006; Kane, Crooks, and Cohen 1999).
7 We would note that way we conceptualize qualities in our AUA and the terms we use for these are quite different from either the "qualities of usefulness" discussed in Bachman and Palmer (1996) or in current textbooks and standards in language assessment and educational measurement.
8 See Norton and Stein (1998) for an example of this kind of response.
9 Bachman (2004b) discusses a number of ways for reporting scores in ways that are appropriate for different stakeholders.
10 Canale (1988) discusses the need to "humanize" the experience of testing, and includes the provision of rich feedback about performance in this.
11 Another term that has also been used is "backwash" (for example, Hughes 2003; Weir 1990). The term "washback," however, seems to be more prevalent in both language testing and applied linguistics, and so we will use this term.
12 Considering washback within the scope of consequences appears to be consistent with current research in language testing (e.g., Alderson and Wall 1993; Cheng, Watanabe, and Curtis 2004; Hawkey 2006; Wall 1996; Wall and Alderson 1993), who use the term "impact study" to refer to their research into washback.

13 We would note that language testers, teachers, and researchers are also sometimes interested in assessing other attributes of individuals such as motivation, anxiety, learning style, and language aptitude.

14 In current formulations in language testing and educational measurement, consistency is defined as reliability, or consistency of *measurement*, and is a quality of test scores. Because we define assessment more broadly, to include other kinds of score reports, we define consistency more broadly.

15 According to most measurement models, their scores would be within a certain range of each other. This range is determined by the amount of measurement error and the level of confidence the test user feels comfortable with. (See Additional Readings in Chapter 19 for relevant references.)

16 See Heider (1988) for a discussion of different ways of interpreting differences among ethnographies, and factors that may contribute to these.

PART II
Constructing an Assessment Use Argument

When a decision maker needs to make decisions that will promote beneficial consequences for stakeholders, he may consider using a language assessment to collect the information needed to help us make these decisions. If he decides that he does need language assessment for this purpose, the decision maker then must decide whether to use an existing assessment that might be available or to develop one of his own. In either case, there are a number of considerations that must be made and procedures that need to be followed in order to assure that he will be able to justify the intended uses of this assessment. In Part I (Chapters 2–5), we described some conceptual frameworks that will guide the process of assessment development and use. In this part of the book, Part II, we begin the discussion of this process. We describe the pre-development planning that needs to be done in order to decide whether the test developer needs to use an assessment. We then describe in detail the issues and considerations in the articulation of an Assessment Use Argument (AUA), which guides the process of assessment development and use.

Chapter 6 provides an overview of the process of language assessment development and use, and serves as a pre-organizer to the other chapters in Part II. Chapter 7 discusses the considerations in initial planning that will help us decide whether to use an existing assessment or to develop one of our own. In Chapter 7 we also introduce two example language assessment settings which we will use to illustrate the construction of an AUA, as well as the procedures discussed in Part III. We chose these two examples because they illustrate the usability of an AUA for two very different, but common, language assessment situations. One example is of a low-stakes kindergarten classroom formative assessment, while the other is of a high-stakes university summative assessment. Using only two examples reduces the amount of processing needed to follow the new content that is introduced. If we provided a wide variety of examples, the reader would continually have to shift gears and grapple with new material. We have added exercises that guide the reader to those Projects on the web in which relevant issues are discussed in the context of different examples. In Chapter 8 we discuss a set of "generic" claims and warrants that need to be articulated in an Assessment Use Argument for any given assessment, along with a list of questions that language test developers can ask to guide their articulation of these claims and warrants. Chapters 9–12 describe in detail the considerations and procedures for articulating the claims and warrants in an AUA for a specific assessment, illustrating these with two examples of assessment development and use. Chapter 9 discusses intended consequences, Chapter 10 decisions, Chapter 11 interpretations, and Chapter 12 discusses assessment records.

6

Overview of assessment development and use

INTRODUCTION: PROCEDURES IN ASSESSMENT DEVELOPMENT AND USE

This chapter serves as a general pre-organizer for the chapters in Parts II and III. Here we provide a general overview of the procedures in assessment development and use that will be discussed in greater detail in later chapters. Readers thus might want to read this chapter now as a general preview of material to come and then review it prior to reading each of the remaining chapters in order to reacquaint themselves with the whole process of assessment development and use before considering the details of each part of the process.

We define the process of **assessment development and use** as a series of activities that include: initial planning; articulating an Assessment Use Argument (AUA); selecting or producing an assessment; trialing this assessment to collect feedback that will help the test developer modify or revise it and provide backing to support the warrants in the AUA; administering the assessment to the intended test takers to obtain assessment records; interpreting these records as indicators of test takers' language ability; and using these interpretations to make decisions. These activities can be viewed conceptually as occurring in five stages: (1) Initial Planning, (2) Design, (3) Operationalization, (4) Trialing, and (5) Assessment Use. **Assessment development** begins with initial planning, or the initial consideration by a decision maker of whether she needs to use an assessment for a particular use (decisions, consequences), and continues through to the selection or production of one or more assessments, in Stage 4, Trialing. **Assessment use** involves administering these assessments to test takers, and using their performance to make interpretations and decisions. Both assessment development and assessment use involve the ongoing collection of backing to support the justification of the assessment for its intended use. Assessment development and use consist of a number of activities which serve two purposes and yield two products. **Assessment justification**, which was discussed in Chapter 5, yields an AUA that is supported by relevant backing. **Assessment production** is aimed at creating the assessment itself. Thus all the activities that we discuss below, that are involved in assessment development and use, serve two purposes: (1) the justification of the assessment for its intended uses and (2) the production and use of the assessment itself.

We say that the activities involved in assessment development and use are "conceptually" ordered into five stages, because these activities are not implemented in a strictly sequential order. In practice, although assessment development and use is generally a linear process, progressing from one stage to the next, the process is also an iterative one, in which the decisions that are made and procedures that are completed at any stage may lead the test developer to reconsider and revise decisions that have been made at another stage and then repeat procedures that have been followed before, but that are now informed by the revised decision. While there are many ways in which one might organize the activities involved in assessment development and use, we have come to believe over the years that the type of organization we describe in this book provides an effective way of monitoring the process of assessment development and use and hence increases the likelihood of being able to justify the intended uses for any given assessment. These five stages or activities are illustrated in Figure 6.1.

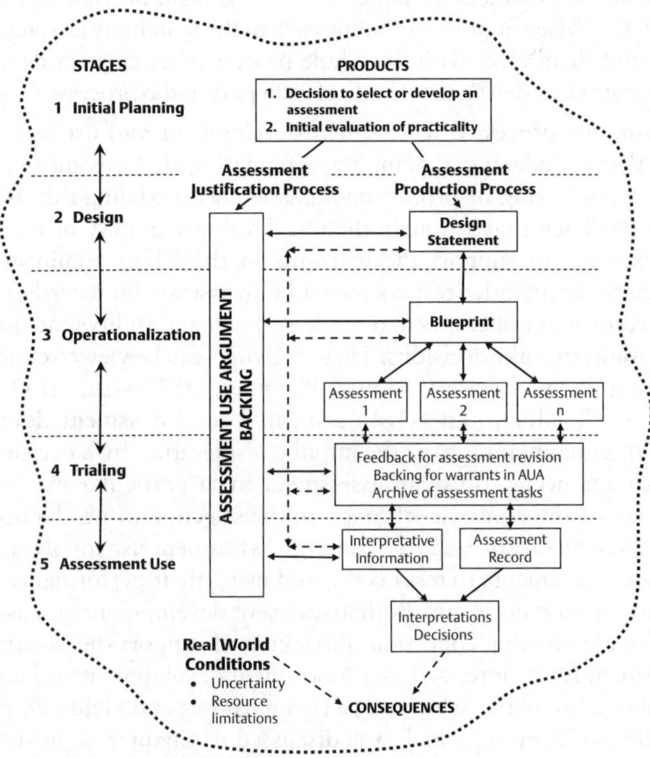

Figure 6.1 Assessment development and use, Stages 1–5

There are two columns in Figure 6.1 labeled "Stages" and "Products." Under "Stages" there are five headings, each of which represents a set of activities that are conducted during each stage in the assessment development and use process. Under "Products" are listed the tangible outcomes of the activities conducted at the different stages of assessment development and use.

As discussed in Chapter 7 below, the activities conducted during Stage 1, Initial Planning, lead to a decision by the test developer whether to use an assessment at all to provide information for the intended decisions. If the decision is to use an assessment, the initial planning activities will produce an initial evaluation of practicality. If the decision is to *select* a particular assessment, then the test developer needs to articulate the claims and warrants in the AUA that justify the use of this existing assessment for the intended uses. The test developer then proceeds to Trialing and Assessment use, which will provide backing for the warrants in the AUA, actual assessments, assessment records, and interpretive information for test users.

If the decision is to *develop* an assessment, then the test developer proceeds to Stage 2, the Design stage. Activities conducted during the Design stage produce a "Design Statement," along with warrants in the AUA. Operationalization activities produce a "Blueprint," one or more "Assessments," and some of the interpretive information for test users, along with additional warrants in the AUA. Trialing activities produce feedback, backing for the warrants in the AUA, an archive of assessment tasks, and additional interpretive information for test users. Assessment use activities produce assessment records, additional interpretive information for test users, interpretations, and decisions. The cumulative **interpretive information** that is produced during the process will include a description of the construct to be assessed, along with a description of the assessment tasks that were presented to test takers and how the assessment records were produced. This information will be provided by the test developer to test users and other stakeholders in terms and a form that will be useful for them. The decisions that are based on the interpretations will have consequences in the real world, consequences which will also be determined by real world conditions. An overarching "product" of assessment development is the AUA itself, as different specific warrants are articulated and backing is collected during different stages of assessment development and use.

The area within the outer border (dotted curved line) represents the "real world," which includes the uncertainty of real world conditions and the resourcing constraints that are discussed in Chapter 13. The justification process provides quality control over the various activities of assessment development and use, while real world considerations provide the "bottom-line" reality check at every stage of assessment development and use. That is, process of assessment development and real world conditions will interact with each other and evolve as the test developer makes adjustments to the AUA and the justification process to reflect changes and uncertainties and resourcing limitations in the real world, or as she reallocates resources to meet the requirements of the justification process.

While the AUA informs the development and use of the assessment, the AUA itself also gets elaborated and revised throughout the process of assessment development and use. Similarly, while real world conditions will influence the kinds of decisions that are made during assessment development and use, these conditions may evolve as the test developer makes changes and adjustments to the activities in the process of assessment development and use. Thus, both justification and real world conditions guide and inform all decisions and procedures involved in assessment development and use, so as to assure that the intended uses of the assessment can be justified and that the assessment will be practical to use.

The amount of time and effort we put into the processes of assessment justification and production will, of course, vary, depending upon the situation. At one extreme, with low-stakes assessments, these processes might be quite informal, and require very few resources, as might be the case if one teacher were preparing a short classroom assessment to be used to collect feedback on his students' learning. With a medium-stakes decision, such as placing students into levels in a language program, we might decide to develop an assessment of our own, with moderate resources required, or to use an existing assessment. At the other extreme, with high-stakes assessments, the process of developing a language assessment will be much more complex, involving extensive planning, trialing, and revision, as well as coordinating the efforts of a large assessment development team, and requiring a large amount of resources. This will be particularly necessary if the assessment is intended for use in making high-stakes decisions that will have a major impact on the lives of people. These people may include not only the test takers themselves, but other stakeholders, such as teachers, schools, parents, and the public at large. Although the amount of resources—time, effort, materials—that goes into assessment development may vary, depending on the use for which the assessment is intended, the same considerations will need to be carefully addressed, in both low-stakes and high-stakes situations.

Whatever the situation might be, careful planning and implementation of the assessment development process in all language assessment situations is crucial. This is because careful planning and implementation will enable the test developer to justify the intended uses of the assessment and hence, to be accountable to stakeholders. As discussed in Chapter 5, the test developer must expect that some stakeholders (e.g., students, teachers, parents, administrators, researchers) will question or challenge the intended uses of the assessment or some of the other claims in the Assessment Use Argument (AUA). Careful planning and implementation thus include the articulation of an AUA and the collection of relevant backing for justifying the warrants in the AUA.

STAGE 1: INITIAL PLANNING

The Initial Planning stage needs to take place before any decision has been made about whether or not to proceed with assessment development. This is because in this stage the test developer will provide answers to key questions that will determine whether he needs to use an assessment at all, and if so, whether to use an existing assessment or to develop one of his own. In the Initial Planning stage, the decision maker and test developer ask themselves a series of questions regarding the following: the intended beneficial consequences; the decisions that need to be made to help promote these; the information that is needed to help make these decisions; whether she needs to use an assessment to collect this information; whether to adopt an existing assessment or to develop a new one; and the resources that will be needed and that will be available for adopting or developing and using an assessment (including justifying the intended uses of the assessment). Although many of these considerations will need to be addressed in greater detail in an AUA, should we decide to develop our own assessment, the initial planning provides us with a principled basis for selecting an existing assessment, or for developing a new one. The Initial Planning stage is discussed in detail in Chapter 7.

STAGE 2: DESIGN

In the Design stage the test developer will implement specific activities that will produce the beginnings of an Assessment Use Argument (AUA) and a Design Statement. The **Design Statement** is a document that states what one needs to know before actually creating an assessment. This document serves several purposes. Its primary purpose is to guide the test developer in the last three stages—Operationalization, Trialing, and Assessment Use—in the process of assessment development and use. This document also provides information that will serve as backing for several warrants in the AUA. Finally, the Design Statement will be used to provide interpretive information about the assessment to test users and other stakeholders in terms that they can understand. The Design stage begins with the articulation of an AUA for the particular assessment. One purpose of this AUA is to guide the test developer in assessment development and use and in the collection of backing. Another purpose of the AUA is to communicate to stakeholders the specific claims and warrants that underlie the intended assessment use and the backing that the test developer has collected to justify this use. The AUA and the backing that is provided to support it thus serves as the basis for a public document that is intended to provide enough information to justify the assessment use to stakeholders. (We discuss the process of articulating an AUA in greater detail in Chapters 8–12. We discuss the activities of the Design stage in Chapter 14.)

STAGE 3: OPERATIONALIZATION

Operationalization involves developing a Blueprint, developing actual assessment tasks, and then organizing the assessment tasks into an overall assessment, following the Blueprint. A **Blueprint** is a set of specifications for the assessment as a whole and for the individual tasks within the assessment. The primary purpose of the Blueprint is to guide the test developer in the process of creating assessment tasks and actual assessments. As with the Design Statement, the Blueprint also serves as a basis for providing interpretive information to test users and other stakeholders. The Blueprint includes a description of the overall structure of the assessment and the specifications for each type of task to be included in the assessment. The other products of operationalization are the individual assessment tasks and assessment as a whole, including multiple forms of this, all of which are based upon the Blueprint, and interpretive information for test users and other stakeholders.

STAGE 4: TRIALING

The Trialing stage of assessment development involves trying out the assessment with a group of individuals, collecting information, and analyzing this information for the purpose of improving the assessment. The products of these activities include feedback, backing, an archive of assessment tasks, and additional interpretive information for test users. The test developer uses the information collected during trialing to provide backing to support the warrants in the AUA, or to revise the specific warrants in the AUA. She also uses this information to guide her in the revision of assessment tasks or the assessment as a whole, so that she is able to provide stronger backing for the warrants in the AUA.

The revisions that are made on the basis of feedback obtained from a tryout might be fairly local, and might consist of minor editing. Analyses of the results of the tryout might indicate that a more global revision is required, perhaps involving returning to and rethinking some of the components in the Design Statement or warrants in the AUA. In major assessment efforts, assessments or assessment tasks are almost always tried out before they are actually used. In classroom assessments, tryouts are often omitted, although we strongly recommend giving the assessment to selected students or fellow teachers in advance, since this can provide the assessment developer with useful information for improving the assessment and assessment tasks *before* the assessment is used operationally to make decisions.

Since it is the assessment itself that is being evaluated and refined in this stage, the results of tryout assessments are not used to make decisions about test takers or other stakeholders. Once the test developer and other stakeholders are convinced that the assessment and its intended uses are as justifiable as the available resources enable them to make it, the test developer proceeds to assessment use. Trialing of assessments and collecting feedback and backing is discussed in Chapter 19.

STAGE 5: ASSESSMENT USE

Assessment Use, or, as it is sometimes called, "operational use," involves administering the assessment to collect information about test takers' language ability in order to make the intended decisions. That is, in assessment use test users interpret the assessment records as indicators of the abilities they want to assess, and use these to make the decisions for which the assessment was intended. In addition, assessment use will be used for continuing to collect information as part of the process of assessment justification. This also provides additional interpretive information for test users. These activities are discussed in Chapter 21.

7

Initial planning

INTRODUCTION

There are a number of situations in which a decision maker may think she needs to use a language assessment, such as deciding at what level to place students in a language program, deciding whether individuals should be certified as professionals, or selecting individuals for admission to an academic program or for employment. In situations such as these, the decision maker needs to do some initial thinking about the kinds of decisions she needs to make, who will be affected by these decisions, what kind of information she will need to make these decisions, how best to collect that information, and how to assure that the information she collects is useful for making the decision.

The test developer also needs to address questions about costs and availability of resources for collecting this information. Thus, before she even gets to the point of selecting an existing assessment or developing a new one, she needs to address a number of questions. By addressing these questions, she can assure that she has systematically considered the whole range of issues that will influence her decision about whether or not she needs an assessment, and if so, whether she should select an existing assessment or develop a new one. In addition, by addressing these questions, she will have laid the groundwork for many of the decisions that she will have to make should she proceed to select an existing assessment or to develop a new one.

The initial planning stage accomplishes two very important functions. First, it leads the decision maker to consider the essential issues that will inform her decision about whether to rely upon non-assessment sources of information, to select an existing assessment, or develop a new assessment. Second, it provides the test developer with an initial evaluation of the resources that will be required, and the resources that will potentially be available, should she undertake the development of a new assessment. By evaluating these resources, initial planning includes an initial evaluation of whether the assessment will be practical.

Without doing some initial planning, the test developer may create two problems. First, she may begin developing the assessment without having adequately considered basic assessment development issues such as the decisions that she intends to make on the basis of the assessment, or the specific aspects of language ability she will need to assess. Second, she may end up investing considerable resources in a project that may be doomed to failure in the long run because of inadequate resources, or whose goals could have been accomplished in a far more economical way. These functions and problems are illustrated in Table 7.1.

Initial planning function	Potential problems created by not planning
1 Consideration of basic issues of the intended assessment use	Assessment selected or assessment development begins without clear sense of direction
2 Evaluation of resources that will be required	Resources wasted on ill-conceived efforts to develop assessment

Table 7.1 Planning functions and potential problems

In this chapter we will discuss the questions that need to be answered in the first stage of assessment development, Initial Planning. As will be seen in the next chapter, addressing some of these questions will lay the groundwork for articulating an Assessment Use Argument (AUA). We will illustrate the points in our discussion with examples of two very different assessment situations: one involving very low-stakes decisions about instruction by a kindergarten teacher that are based on his continuous assessment as part of learning activities, and another involving fairly high-stakes decisions about placement into a university ESL program.

INITIAL PLANNING CONSIDERATIONS

There are two considerations that the test developer needs to address in the Initial Planning stage: (1) the amount of resources that will be required for initial planning, and (2) the questions that he needs to answer to determine whether an assessment is needed, and whether assessment development will be needed.

Amount of resources to expend

Since one of the objectives of Initial Planning is to determine whether using an assessment is practical, one consideration in initial planning is the amount of resources the test developer should expend in this process itself. The amount of resources the potential test developer puts into initial planning will depend upon the importance of the consequences that are to be achieved, the decisions that are to be made, and the numbers of stakeholders that will be affected. For a very low-stakes decision such as the need to collect information about students' learning for formative diagnostic purposes, initial planning might take only a few minutes and involve only the teacher. This is not to undervalue the importance of initial planning for classroom formative assessment, but simply to point out that planning in such situations will typically require relatively few resources. In situations where high-stakes decisions will be made, on the other hand, initial planning might involve a considerable amount of time and involve a number of individuals.

Determining whether an assessment is needed

In order to make the intended decisions, the decision maker will most likely want to collect some information about the individuals who will be most directly affected by these decisions. He will need to determine what kind of information will be the most helpful in reaching his decisions, and how he can most effectively obtain this information. To guide the decision maker in making this determination, there are a number of questions that can be raised and answered.

Initial planning questions

The questions that the decision maker and test developer need to answer in Stage I, Initial Planning, are listed in Table 7.2.

Stage 1: Initial Planning questions

1 What beneficial consequences do we want to happen? Who are the stakeholders? Who will be directly affected by the use of the assessment?
  (a) Who are the intended test takers? How will they be affected?
  (b) Who else will be affected? How will they be affected?
2 What specific decisions do we need to make to help promote the intended consequences?
3 What do we need to know about the test takers' language ability in order to make the intended decisions?
4 What sources could we use or are available for obtaining this information?
5 Do we need to use an assessment to obtain this information?
6 Is an existing assessment available?
  (a) Is an existing assessment available that provides the information that is needed for the decisions we need to make?
  (b) Is this assessment appropriate for our intended test takers?
  (c) Do the assessment tasks correspond to TLU tasks?
  (d) Does the test developer provide evidence justifying our intended uses of the assessment?
  (e) Can we afford it?
7 Do we need to develop our own assessment? (If the answer is "yes," then the developer needs to answer the following questions.)
  (a) How will the test developer assure that the intended uses (i.e., decisions and consequences) of the assessment can be justified with an AUA and backing?
  (b) What resources will we need for the development and use of the assessment (including justifying the intended uses of the assessment)?
  (c) What resources do we have or can we obtain?

Table 7.2 Stage 1: Initial Planning questions

The assessment user who is considering the need to use a language assessment will typically answer these questions in the order listed. However, for Question 6, there are several sub-questions. If the answer to any of these sub-questions is "no," then the assessment user will skip ahead to Question 7.

EXAMPLES OF INITIAL ASSESSMENT PLANNING

The following examples illustrate the Stage 1 Initial Planning process for two different language assessment situations. These situations are illustrative of two different levels of importance, in terms of the consequences of using an assessment. The first example is a low-stakes situation: a classroom assessment that is used primarily by one teacher for providing feedback to his students and for making formative decisions about how to improve his own teaching. The second example is higher stakes: an incomplete outline test that is used either to place non-native English speaking students at a university into an ESL reading class or to exempt them from further ESL instruction. In addition, the test developers for the two projects are very different. In this chapter we discuss only the Initial Planning Questions. (The articulation of the specific claims, warrants, and rebuttals in the AUAs for these examples is discussed in Chapters 9–12, while the assessment development process for each of the examples is discussed in Chapters 13–18.)

Example 1 Kindergarten ELL speaking and writing assessment in support of instruction and learning (adapted from Frey and Fisher 2003)

Setting

The setting is several kindergarten classes in a large urban elementary school with about 1,500 students who come from a wide variety of cultures and backgrounds; most are English Language Learners (ELLs) with a wide variety of first languages. The teacher of these classes would like to collect information about students' performance that will help guide his instructional practice, that is, to help him set the pace of instruction for these students, and to help him improve his instruction for the future. He believes that continuous assessment as part of regular learning activities will provide the best opportunity for him to collect the information he needs. In addition, such assessment will not be intrusive, and will not require additional time. In this example, the classroom teacher is both the test developer and the test user, or decision maker.

Initial planning questions and answers

(The answers to the questions are shown in *italics*.)

1 What beneficial consequences does the teacher want to happen? Who are the stakeholders? Who will be directly affected by the use of the assessment?

(a) Who are the intended test takers? How will they be affected?

The students: students will be positively motivated by the feedback the teacher provides.

(b) Who else will be affected? How will they be affected?

i The kindergarten teacher, whose instruction will become more effective

ii Possibly other kindergarten teachers, who may adopt the teacher's assessment and teaching methods

iii Possibly the first grade teachers, who will teach his students the following year.

2 What specific decisions does the teacher need to make to help promote the intended consequences?

Formative decisions: The teacher will use the results of the assessment to pace his own instruction with this class of students, as well as to make adjustments in the way he conducts this instructional activity in the future.

3 What does the teacher need to know about students' language ability in order to make the intended decisions?

The teacher needs to collect information about how well students can perform on a particular set of speaking and writing activities that are related to learning objectives specified in the syllabus.

4 What sources does he have for obtaining this information?

(a) *Implicit (continuous, on-going, dynamic) assessments.* (See Chapter 2 for a discussion of this.)

(b) *Explicit assessments.* (See Chapter 2 for a discussion of this.)

5 Does he need to use an assessment to obtain this information? *Yes, an informal assessment.*

6 Is an existing assessment available?

(a) Is an existing assessment available that provides the information the teacher needs for the decisions he needs to make? *No*

7 Does the teacher need to develop his own assessment? *Yes*

(a) How will the teacher assure that the intended uses (i.e., decisions and consequences) of the assessment can be justified with an AUA and backing?

The teacher is familiar with justification procedures and will construct an AUA and collect backing at a level of detail suitable for this low-stakes assessment.

(b) What resources will he need for the development and use of the assessment (including justifying the intended uses of the assessment)?

The teacher's own time and efforts in developing the observation checklist, which can be developed as part of his lesson planning. No additional class time will be needed for the observation and assessment.

(c) What resources does the teacher have? *His own time and effort; class time, in addition to his own experience and knowledge of the syllabus and the test takers.*

As a result of this initial planning, the teacher decides to develop his own classroom assessment.

Example 2 University ESL reading test for making placement/exemption decisions

Setting

The director of an ESL program at a large research university in which English is the medium of instruction needs to collect information to make decisions about placing non-native English speaking students who have been admitted to the university into an ESL reading course or exempting them from study in these courses. For the past several years, she has been using a fairly traditional multiple-choice reading test, administered in a paper and pencil format, for collecting this information. However, the costs of producing copies of the test, of administering it to large groups of students, and of producing test reports and sending these to the students and university administrators have escalated at a time when the university is facing a budget crisis. She is thus under pressure from the administration to find a way to cut the costs of administering this test. In addition, the teachers in the ESL reading course have become increasingly dissatisfied with the test itself. They feel that the test items do not reflect what students actually do in their academic reading courses, and they believe the test does not really measure what students need in order to successfully complete these courses.

Based on their many years of experience, the ESL director, the ESL reading teachers, and the teachers of the academic course agree that placing students who need developmental instruction in English academic reading into an ESL reading course greatly facilitates their academic coursework and reduces their time to degree. They also know that exempting students who do not need additional instruction will conserve resources for both teachers and students. Finally, they all agree that the most effective way to obtain the information they need is to give students a placement test. Thus, the question is not whether to eliminate the test, but whether to adapt an existing one or develop a new one.

Since the placement/exemption decisions the ESL Program Director needs to make are relatively high stakes, she is willing to allocate considerable resources for assessment development, if it is determined that this is needed. The "test developer" consists of a team of individuals, the ESL Program Director, the ESL instructors, and a Visiting Assistant Professor, as Project Director, with all members of the team assuming a collective responsibility for the test development, use, and justification. While the ESL Program Director is the decision maker, the ESL instructors and academic course instructors can also be considered to be test users.

Initial planning questions and answers

1 What beneficial consequences does the ESL Program Director want to happen? Who are the stakeholders? Who will be directly affected by the use of the assessment?

(a) Who are the intended test takers? How will they be affected?

Intended test takers: Non-native English speaking students. ESL reading instruction will be appropriate to students' level of reading ability and, therefore, more effective and less frustrating; students who take the ESL reading course will have improved chances of succeeding in their academic courses.

(b) Who else will be affected? How will they be affected?

i ESL course instructors: more knowledge of students' reading ability will enable instructors to better tailor their instruction appropriately; their teaching will be more effective and they will feel more rewarded when they teach classes with students at about the same level of ability.

ii ESL Program Director: fewer student complaints about inappropriate instruction or about their inability to pass reading courses; fewer complaints from ESL teachers about difficulty in teaching students of widely varying abilities.

iii Instructors in academic courses: L2 students will be better able to handle the reading demands of academic courses.

2 What specific decisions does the ESL Program Director need to make to help promote the intended consequences?

Decisions to place non-native English speaking students into ESL reading classes or exempt them from these classes.

3 What do we need to know about the test takers' language ability in order to make the intended decisions?

The Program Director needs to collect information about students' reading ability relevant to making the decisions listed above. Consultation with the teachers in the program indicates the specific information needed is the ability to recognize the rhetorical structure of academic reading passages.

4 What sources could the ESL Program Director use or are available for obtaining this information?
   (a) *Student self-placements into or exemptions from the program,*
   (b) *Existing scores from the standardized tests of EFL that the university requires international students applying for admission to the university to provide,*
   (c) *Develop her own assessment.*

5 Does the ESL Program Director need to use an assessment to obtain this information?

   Yes. Years of experience on the part of the ESL Program Director and the teachers in the program indicate that self-assessments are not likely to provide the needed information. Some students may over-report their language ability in order to avoid having to take ESL classes. Others may under-report it in order to take courses they don't need, in order to raise their Grade Point Averages (GPAs).

6 Is an existing assessment available?

   Yes. The Test of English as a Foreign Language (TOEFL) or the International English Language Testing System (IELTS), either of which is required of all international students applying to the university. (The ESL Program Director searched the information available on the web pages for these two tests. She also consulted with the University Admissions Office to see if this information would be available for all students.)

   (a) Does either of these tests provide the information needed for the decisions the ESL Program Director needs to make?

      No. Although both the TOEFL and IELTS include sections that test reading, neither of these tests focuses on the specific area of language ability that the stakeholders have identified.

   (b) Are the assessments appropriate for the intended test takers? Yes.
   (c) Do the assessment tasks correspond to TLU tasks?

      Not closely. Tasks on these tests do not involve the same language use activities, such as outlining, as do tasks in the TLU domain.

   (d) Do the test developers provide evidence justifying our intended uses of the assessments?

      No. These tests are intended primarily for making admissions decisions and not placement decisions.

(e) Can we afford it?

Yes. Most L2 speakers of English will already have taken one of these tests.

7 Does the program need to develop its own assessment? *Yes*

(a) How will the ESL Program Director assure that the intended uses (i.e., decisions and consequences) of the assessment can be justified with an AUA and backing?

The ESL Program Director will assign this task to the Visiting Assistant Professor with expertise in language assessment, who will, in turn, assign the task of producing portions of the AUA and backing to Ph.D. students on the test development committee and will oversee their work. The Visiting Assistant Professor will put a template on line in which members of the committee can enter their justification and review material entered by other members of the committee. Thus, an evolving document will be continually available to all members of the committee.

(b) What resources will the Program Director need for the development and use of the assessment (including justifying the intended uses of the assessment)?

i Human: (Administrator to direct and monitor the progress of the test development effort, people with expertise in reading to provide input into the selection of reading passages, creation of test tasks, the creation and implementation of the scoring procedures; someone with expertise in language assessment to provide guidance in the development of the speaking tasks and scoring procedures, and with analyses of the test results; project staff; support staff)

ii Material: (e.g., copies of academic reading texts, paper, personal computers, statistical analysis software, space for administering the reading test)

iii Time: Two years for the development of the test; one hour per student for administering the test, several hours for scoring the test and reporting the results to test takers and relevant university officials; one month for analyzing data and improving the test.

(c) What resources does the program have or is able to obtain?

i Human: The instructors in the ESL program will serve as members of the test development team. The ESL Director will use funds from the Dean to hire a full-time Visiting Assistant Professor with expertise in language assessment to oversee the development of the test, as well as several Ph.D. students in language testing as part-time Research Assistants.

ii Material: Some will be made available from the ESL Program, and some will be purchased from the grant from the Dean. The Department of Applied Linguistics will provide space for the test development team to meet, and space for administering the test can be scheduled regularly with the campus Office of Space Management.

iii Time: The ESL Director has received a grant from the Dean for two years for developing and administering this placement test. The Chair of the Department of Applied Linguistics has also made a commitment of clerical support and space for an indefinite period of time.

Discussion

Because of the cost of personnel for administering the test, including proctors for the large lecture rooms in which it is administered, the ESL Program Director is looking for ways to reduce this expense. In addition, she needs to find a way to cut the costs of reproducing copies of the test, scoring it, and of printing test reports. During the initial planning it thus becomes clear to the ESL Program Director and instructors that administering the placement test in a paper and pencil format to large groups of test takers will no longer be feasible, given the increased costs of this and the reduced resources that are available. One way that is suggested to make the test feasible is to administer it via computers. Therefore, as a result of this planning, the Program Director decides to develop a new computer-administered placement test for the program.

Having decided to go ahead with assessment development, the test developers now need to continue the process of articulating an AUA. This process is described in detail in Chapter 8 and illustrated via examples in Chapters 9–12.

8

Constructing an Assessment Use Argument for developing and justifying a language assessment

INTRODUCTION

Assuming that the decision maker answers the initial planning questions discussed in Chapter 7 and decides there is a need to develop a language assessment to meet her specific needs, how does she go about developing such an assessment, and how does she justify using it to make the intended decisions? The answers to these questions are to be found in the assessment development process. This chapter will focus on the construction of an Assessment Use Argument (AUA) that will guide both assessment justification and assessment production.

As we argued in Chapter 5, we need to demonstrate that the uses of our assessments are justified so that we can be accountable to stakeholders. Furthermore, we have argued that the assessment justification process provides the most effective means for accomplishing this. The process of justifying the use of a particular assessment includes the following:

1 articulating the claims, warrants, and rebuttals in an AUA for the specific assessment, and
2 providing backing to support the warrants and weaken the rebuttals in the AUA.

An AUA provides the conceptual framework for linking a claim about a particular set of consequences to the performance of individuals on a language assessment. In this chapter we apply the concepts that we introduced in Chapter 4 to the process of articulating the claims, warrants, and rebuttals in an AUA for any particular language assessment. We discuss this process from the perspective of assessment development. We first discuss the different audiences for whom any given AUA might be intended. We then provide a table listing the "generic" claims, warrants, and rebuttals that make up an AUA. Next, we discuss the dynamic and iterative nature of the AUA and the assessment development process. We then present a list of questions that can be used to guide the construction of an AUA. Finally, we illustrate the points in this discussion with the example of a Chinese mini-speech test.

Who is the audience for the AUA?

When a test developer constructs an AUA, he needs to consider how best to communicate this to different "audiences" of stakeholders. One audience is the test developer himself, or, in some cases, a whole test development team. These individuals will articulate the AUA to clarify their own thinking and to guide assessment development. Another audience will be the test user, or decision maker, for whom the assessment is being developed. Still another audience will include those who will be most directly affected by the use of the assessment and the decisions that are made. This audience will include the test takers, and other stakeholders such as teachers, administrators, certifying agencies, and employers. In some cases, particularly with large-scale, high-stakes assessments, the audience may include individuals who are not directly affected by the assessment, such as politicians, regulatory agencies, government officials, and the general public. Thus, the test developer may need to articulate the AUA in different versions for different audiences. For example, the test developer or development team might utilize relatively technical terms in the AUA to achieve the precision they need for assessment development. For a wider audience, the claims and warrants in the AUA might be incorporated into interpretive information, with technical terms paraphrased using more general phraseology. Or, interpretive information that is produced for potential test takers might provide more detail in some areas, while interpretive information that is intended for decision makers might focus on other areas. Whoever the audience might be, the specific claims, warrants, and rebuttals in the AUA will be the same. Only the form in which it is presented, the language, and the amount of explanation and detail will differ.

The primary audience for the AUA of the Kindergarten example presented in Chapter 7 is the teacher himself. At some later point in time, if the teacher's supervisor or other teachers became interested in the assessment, they might be included in the audience. In the University example that we presented in Chapter 7 the audiences for the AUA are the program administrator, the ESL instructors on the test development team, and the academic instructors. In this example, the terminology that is used to describe the specific aspect of reading that is to be assessed might be expressed using technical terms from linguistics for the test developers, while this might be expressed in more general terms for the academic instructors or for the students who are required to take the test. The audience for this AUA might be extended to include other ESL instructors who will not have been involved in the test development but need to know how it was developed and what it is intended to measure. The AUA might also eventually be adapted for presentation to an accrediting agency that is reviewing the ESL program. It could even conceivably be used in adapted form by the program administrator or the ESL instructors on the development team in conference presentations or academic papers.

In this chapter we will only refer in passing to some of the backing that could be collected to support warrants or weaken rebuttals, reserving a detailed discussion of this to the later chapters in the book. Much of the backing for an AUA will come from the procedures that we follow during assessment development and from the documents (Design Statement, Blueprint) this produces. Backing from assessment development and related documents is discussed in Chapters 9–12. Other backing to be collected as part of the justification process is discussed in Chapter 19.

ELEMENTS OF AN ASSESSMENT USE ARGUMENT

Once we have embarked on the path of assessment development, the first, critical step is to articulate an Assessment Use Argument (AUA). The claims, warrants and rebuttals in an AUA are listed in Table 8.1. We do not include the backing for these warrants here, as we want to focus on the claims and warrants. The elements listed in this table are "generic" in the sense that they are general, and not specific to any given assessment situation. In constructing an AUA for a particular assessment, the test developer will adapt, or restate each claim, warrant, and rebuttal in specific terms that relate to his specific assessment situation. Because we need to begin the process of assessment development with a consideration of consequences, we begin with this as the first claim in an AUA.

Claim 1: CONSEQUENCES: The consequences of using an assessment and of the decisions that are made are beneficial to stakeholders.

A Warrants about the **beneficence** of the consequences of *using the assessment*:

1 The consequences of using the assessment that are *specific to each stakeholder group* will be beneficial.

2 Assessment reports of individual test takers are treated confidentially. (See discussion of assessment reports in Chapter 5.)

3 Assessment reports are presented in ways that are clear and understandable to all stakeholder groups.

4 Assessment reports are distributed to stake holders in a timely manner.

5 In language instructional settings, the assessment helps promote good instructional practice and effective learning, and the use of the assessment is thus beneficial to students, instructors, supervisors, the program, etc.

B Warrant and rebuttal about the **beneficence** of the consequences of the *decisions that are made*:

1 Warrant: The consequences of the decisions will be beneficial for *each group* of stakeholders.

2 Rebuttal: Either false *positive* classification errors or false *negative* classification errors, or both, will have detrimental consequences for the stakeholders who are affected.

NB: For a particular assessment, the adapted Rebuttal B2 includes:

(a) a list of the possible detrimental consequences of decision classification errors

(b) a list of possible ways of mitigating the detrimental consequences of decision classification errors if they occur.

Claim 2: DECISIONS. The decisions that are made on the basis of the interpretations:

i take into consideration existing educational and societal **values** and relevant laws, rules, and regulations and

ii are **equitable** for those stake holders who are affected by the decision.

A Warrants about the **values sensitivity** of the decisions that are made:

1 Existing educational and societal values and relevant legal requirements are carefully and critically considered in the kinds of decisions that are to be made.

2 Existing educational and societal values and relevant legal requirements are carefully and critically considered in determining the relative seriousness of false positive and false negative classification errors.

3 Cut scores are set so as to minimize the most serious classification errors.

B Warrants about the **equitability** of the decisions that are made:

1 Test takers are classified *only* according to the cut scores and decision rules, and not according to any other considerations.

2 Test takers and other affected stakeholders are fully informed about how the decision will be made and whether decisions are actually made in the way described to them.

3 For achievement and certification decisions, test takers have equal opportunity to learn or acquire the ability to be assessed.

Claim 3: INTERPRETATIONS. The interpretations about the ability to be assessed are:

i **meaningful** with respect to a particular learning syllabus, an analysis of the abilities needed to perform tasks in the TLU domain, a general theory of language ability, or any combination of these,

ii **impartial** to all groups of test takers,

iii **generalizable** to the TLU domain in which the decision is to be made,

iv **relevant** to the decision to be made, and

v **sufficient** for the decision to be made.

Claim 3 for a particular assessment includes a descriptive label for the construct to be assessed.

A Warrants about the **meaningfulness** of the interpretations:

1 The definition of the construct is based on a frame of reference such as a course, syllabus, a needs analysis or a current research and/or theory, and clearly distinguishes the construct from other, related constructs.

2 The assessment task specifications clearly specify the conditions under which we will observe or elicit performance from which we can make inferences about the construct we intend to assess.

3 The procedures for administering the assessment enable test takers to perform at their highest level on the ability to be assessed.

4 The procedures for producing an assessment record focus on those aspects of the performance that are relevant to the construct we intend to assess.

5 Assessment tasks engage the ability defined in the construct definition.
6 Assessment records can be interpreted as indicators of the ability to be assessed.
7 The test developer communicates the definition of the construct to be assessed in terms that are clearly understandable to all stakeholders.

B Warrants about the **impartiality** of the interpretations:

1 The assessment tasks do not include response formats or content that may either favor or disfavor some test takers.
2 The assessment tasks do not include content that may be offensive (topically, culturally, or linguistically inappropriate) to some test takers.
3 The procedures for producing an assessment record are clearly described in terms that are understandable to all test takers.
4 Individuals are treated impartially during all aspects of the administration of the assessment: registering for the assessment, taking the assessment.
   (a) Individuals have equal access to information about the assessment content and assessment procedures, and for achievement and certification decisions have equal opportunity to prepare.
   (b) Individuals have equal access to the assessment, in terms of cost, location, and familiarity with conditions and equipment.
   (c) Individuals have equal opportunity to demonstrate the ability to be assessed.
5 Interpretations of the ability to be assessed are equally meaningful across different groups of test takers.

C Warrants about the **generalizability** of the interpretations:

1 The characteristics of the assessment tasks (i.e., setting, input, expected response, types of external interactions) correspond closely to those of TLU tasks.
2 The criteria and procedures for recording the responses to the assessment tasks correspond closely to those that are typically used by language users in assessing performance in TLU tasks.

D Warrant about the **relevance** of the interpretation:
The assessment-based interpretations provide information that is relevant to the decision. That is, the information provided in the interpretation is helpful for the decision makers to make decisions.

E Warrant about the **sufficiency** of the interpretation:
The assessment-based interpretation provides sufficient information to make the required decisions. That is, there is enough information in the interpretation for the decision makers to make the decision.

Claim 4: **ASSESSMENT RECORDS.** Assessment records (scores, descriptions) are **consistent** across different assessment tasks, different aspects of the assessment procedure, and across different groups of test takers.

NB: The output part of this claim is an "assessment record", which is reported to the relevant stakeholders, along with the interpretation from Claim 3 above.

Warrants about the **consistency** of the assessment records:

1 Administrative procedures are followed consistently across different occasions, and for all test taker groups.
2 Procedures for producing the assessment records are well specified and are adhered to.
3 Raters undergo training and must be certified.
4 Raters are trained to avoid bias for or against different groups of test takers.

5 Scores on different tasks in the assessment are internally consistent (internal consistency reliability).
6 Ratings of different raters are consistent (inter-rater reliability).
7 Different ratings by the same rater are consistent (intra-rater reliability).
8 Scores from different forms of the test are consistent (equivalence, or equivalent forms reliability).
9 Scores from different administrations of the test are consistent (stability, or test-retest reliability).
10 Assessment records are of comparable consistency across different groups of test takers.

Data: Observed performance on assessment tasks

Table 8.1 Assessment Use Argument Claims, Warrants, and Rebuttal

We would make several points about the elements of an AUA in Table 8.1. The first has to do with the nature of warrants and rebuttals. As described in Chapter 5, warrants are statements that elaborate the qualities of a claim, while rebuttals are statements that weaken or refute the claim, and support a counterclaim. Recall also from Chapter 5 that for every warrant that we articulate in an AUA there is an implied rebuttal. Furthermore, the backing that we collect to *support* a particular warrant could also serve as rebuttal backing to *weaken* its corresponding implied rebuttal. For example, for the warrant about the consistency of the ratings of different raters (Claim 4, Warrant 8 in Table 8.1), the implied rebuttal is that ratings of different raters are *in*consistent. The backing that we might collect to support the warrant (e.g., intra-rater correlations) would also serve to weaken the implied rebuttal of rater *in*consistency. Thus, rather than articulating warrants that elaborate the qualities of the claims in an AUA, we could articulate the implied rebuttals. However, it generally makes more sense for test developers to argue for the consistency of assessment reports, meaningfulness of interpretations, beneficence of consequence, and so forth, and to provide backing that supports these warrants, rather than to state these as implied rebuttals of *in*consistency, meaning*less*-ness, *malevol*ence, and so forth.

A second point, which is mentioned above, and that we want to reiterate, is that the claims, warrants, and rebuttals that are included in Table 8.1 are stated in generic terms. As we will see in the examples below and in the chapters that follow, the claims, warrants, and rebuttals in the AUA for a particular assessment will be stated in terms that apply specifically to that assessment. The claims, warrants, and rebuttals that are included in Table 8.1 are also intended to be illustrative rather than prescriptive. However, each assessment situation is unique, so that different specific warrants and rebuttals may be required in the AUA for any given assessment.

A third point is that not all of the warrants and rebuttals we list in Table 8.1 will necessarily be required in the AUA for any given assessment. An example of this is the Kindergarten example that is discussed in the following chapters The final point is that the list in Table 8.1 may not be exhaustive. It presents the warrants and rebuttals that we have so far found to be needed in at least some of the research and development projects in which we, our students, and our colleagues—all those people who think like us and believe in the salvation we have to offer—have been involved. It may be that additional claims and warrants will be discovered in the future.

AN EVOLVING ASSESSMENT USE ARGUMENT

For any particular assessment situation, a specific AUA provides the conceptual framework that informs all of the decisions the test developer makes during the process of assessment development. An AUA thus guides the assessment development process. Since any specific AUA will include warrants and specify the backing that will be required to support these, this AUA also serves as a basis for ongoing quality control during the assessment development process. However, as assessment development moves though the four Stages and on to assessment use, the test developer will constantly be reconsidering the details of the AUA—the claims he wants to make, the warrants that will elaborate the qualities of these claims, and the rebuttals that may weaken these claims. Furthermore, as discussed in Chapter 6, the real world is an ever-changing kaleidoscope of strange and wondrous realities, all of which contribute to our well-being, the discovery of our inner selves, and the true path to oneness with existence, in which the availability of or demand for resources may change during the course of assessment development and use. Thus, the test developer will also be constantly monitoring the resources that will be required not only for test development itself, but also for collecting the backing he needs to support the warrants and weaken the rebuttals in the AUA.

It is thus important to view the AUA for any particular assessment not as a static, rigid structure. An AUA should be seen as a flexible, dynamic, and malleable form that is sensitive to changing real world conditions and resourcing demands, and can evolve over the course of assessment development and use. It is this adaptivity, flexibility, capacity for constant, iterative, ongoing revision that enables an AUA to adjust to changes in real world conditions, so as to continue to function as a guide to assessment development and quality control. While the AUA may need to be adjusted during the process of assessment development, just as we need to provide a sound rationale for articulating an AUA, so we will need to provide a rationale for every adjustment in the AUA we make. As discussed in Chapter 6, real world conditions and resourcing constraints can lead to trade-offs, or having to choose one development option over another, or to limiting the development options to one rather than many. For example, consider a program for teaching a foreign language via the internet. The developer of the program wants to include learning activities that require students to respond in speaking.

Their responses will be used to provide formative diagnostic feedback to the students and their on-line instructors. In addition, the program developer would like to score these spoken responses in order to track students' progress through the program, and eventually to inform decisions about certifying students' levels of speaking. The program developer is planning to use a computerized speech recognition system to do the scoring. Now, suppose it turns out that the speech recognition system is able to provide consistent scores, but, because of the extreme limitations on the input and response formats this requires, these scores cannot provide the basis for meaningful interpretations of students' responses to these tasks. In this case, the developer will need to reconsider the decisions to be made (awarding certificates) on the basis of this particular activity, as well as the intended consequences. The lack of an adequate computerized speech recognition system may require that students' responses be scored by human raters, so that different warrants about consistency of scores and meaningfulness of interpretations may need to be articulated and supported with backing.

In another situation, the test developer may need to make a choice between two different types of assessment tasks for assessing listening comprehension, for example, multiple-choice tasks and tasks that require short spoken answers. While the former can be scored very efficiently by machine, the tasks may not correspond very well to TLU tasks, so that the scores may not generalize to the TLU domain. The short answer tasks, on the other hand, may correspond more closely to TLU tasks, but are more costly to score, as they must be scored by trained human raters. In this situation, there may be a trade-off: the assessment developer may need to choose between scoring efficiency and generalizability. To make matters more complex, the developer may also need to consider whether marking answers on an answer sheet and speaking an answer measure the same construct, and the extent to which either is relevant to the decision to be made. Thus, any alteration in a particular part of the AUA may lead us to reconsider other elements of the AUA. Since the primary purpose of the justification process—articulating an AUA and providing backing for this—is to be able to be accountable to stakeholders, decisions about altering the AUA need to take into consideration the kinds of warrants and backing that stakeholders are likely to be most concerned about, rather than simply making these decisions on the basis of ease or personal preference.

CONSTRUCTING AN AUA

In constructing an AUA, there are a number of ways in which we could proceed. We could articulate each specific claim we want to make, starting with intended consequences, list the warrants that we believe elaborate the qualities of this claim and any potential rebuttals, consider the backing we need to provide, and then move to the next claim. Or, we could start by listing all the claims in the AUA, from intended consequences to assessment record, and then consider the warrants and rebuttals that we need to include. Then, once these elements of the AUA are in place, we could begin thinking about the backing we need to provide and the resources that will be needed for this. Or, we could start by asking a series of questions about the claims we want to make and the warrants that elaborate these, and then state the answers to these questions as claims and warrants in the AUA. Whichever way we decide to proceed in articulating an AUA for a particular assessment, it is likely that as we address some questions, we will be thinking of others in other parts of the AUA. For example, when we address the question of how we will assure that the interpretation about language ability will generalize beyond the assessment to a particular TLU domain, we will most likely begin to think about possible assessment tasks that may correspond to TLU tasks. In whatever way we decide to proceed in articulating an AUA, it is critical that we consider the assessment use—intended consequences and decisions—early in the process, and that we eventually end up with a complete AUA with claims, warrants, rebuttals, and the backing needed.

Guide questions for articulating and developing an AUA assessment development

The procedural option for articulating an AUA that we will follow in this chapter and those that follow is to begin by asking questions and then stating the answers to these as claims and warrants in an AUA. Several of these questions will already have been addressed in more general terms in the Initial Planning stage, as discussed in Chapter 7. The questions for guiding the articulation of an AUA and assessment development are listed in Table 8.2.

AUA articulation and assessment development guide questions

Consequences (Claim 1)

1 What beneficial consequences do we intend to promote by using the assessment and making decisions based on it, and whom do we intend to benefit from these consequences?
Answer: *Articulate Claim 1, describe the stakeholders who will be affected by the use of the assessment and by the decisions that are made, and list the intended consequences.*

2 How can we assure that the consequences of *using* the assessment will be beneficial to each stakeholder group that is affected?
Answer: *Articulate beneficence Warrants A1–A5 for each stakeholder group.*

3 How can we assure that the consequences of *the decisions that are made* will be beneficial to each stakeholder group that is affected?
Answer: *Articulate beneficence Warrant B1 for each stakeholder group.*

4 What are the potential detrimental consequences of false positive and negative classification decisions, and how might we mitigate these?
Answer: *Articulate Rebuttal B2 and list:*
(a) *possible detrimental consequences of classification decision errors*
(b) *possible ways of mitigating these consequences.*

Decisions (Claim 2)

5 What specific decisions need to be made to promote the intended consequences, and who will be responsible for making these decisions?
Answer: *Articulate Claim 2 and list*:
(a) *the specific decisions to be made*
(b) *which stakeholder groups will be affected by which decisions*
(c) *who will be responsible for making these decisions.*

6 How can we assure that these decisions take into consideration existing educational and societal values and relevant legal requirements?
Answer: *Articulate Warrants A1–A3 about values sensitivity.*
Warrant A2 will specify *the relative seriousness of false positive and false negative decisions.*
Warrant A3 will specify:
(a) *the policy-level procedures for setting standards*
(b) *the level of ability needed to meet or exceed the standards.*

7 How can we assure that these decisions will be equitable?
Answer: *Articulate Warrants B1–B3 about equitability.*

Interpretations (Claim 3)

8 What do we need to know about the test takers' language ability in order to make these decisions?
Answer: *Articulate Claim 3, providing a descriptive label for the construct to be assessed.*

9 How can we assure that the interpretations of ability are *meaningful*?
Answer:
Articulate Warrant A1 about meaningfulness; including:
(a) *a descriptive label and definition of the construct*
(b) *the specific source(s) of the construct definition.*
Articulate Warrant A2 about meaningfulness; including:
(a) *the setting in which the assessment will be administered*
(b) *the characteristics of the rubric, input, expected response, and relationship between input and expected response for each assessment task type.*
Articulate Warrant A3
Articulate Warrant A4, and specify the following:
(a) *the specific points to be included in a verbal report*
(b) *the scoring method (criteria for correctness, scoring procedures) for a measure.*
Articulate Warrants A5–A7.

10 How can we assure that the interpretations about test takers' language ability are *impartial* for all groups of stakeholders?
Answer: *Articulate Warrants B1–B5 about impartiality.*

11 How can we assure that the interpretation of language ability *generalizes* to the TLU domain of the decision?
Answer:
Articulate Warrant C1, and provide a description of the task characteristics of the TLU tasks that have been selected as a basis for assessment tasks.
Articulate Warrant C2, including a description of the ways in which language users assess performance on the TLU tasks that have been selected as a basis for assessment tasks.

12 How can we assure that our interpretations about test takers' language ability are *relevant* to the decision?
Answer: *Articulate Warrant D about relevance.*

13 How can we assure that our interpretation about test takers' language ability provides *sufficient* information to make the decisions?
Answer: *Articulate Warrant E about sufficiency.*

Assessment records (Claim 4)

14 How will we assure that these assessment records are consistent?
Answer: *Articulate Warrants 1–9 about consistency.*

15 How will we assure that assessment records are of comparable consistency across different groups of test takers?
Answer: *Articulate Warrant 10 about comparable consistency.*

Table 8.2 Assessment development questions

Illustrative example: Chinese mini-speech test

In the discussion below, we illustrate the use of the guide questions for constructing an AUA with an example of a Chinese mini-speech test that forms part of course assessment in a university elementary Modern Chinese speaking course. (Adapted from materials supplied by Michelle Fu and Hongyin Tao.) In this example we demonstrate how we can adapt the "generic" claims and warrants of the AUA to the specific language assessment situation.

Audiences

The primary audiences for an AUA for the Chinese mini-speech test are the course supervisor and the course instructors. Over time, the audience will likely be extended to include other Chinese instructors who will not have been involved in the test development but need to know how it was developed and what it is intended to measure.

Setting

Native English speaking students at a large US university are studying Elementary Modern Chinese, where the focus is on speaking Chinese. There are multiple sections of this course, and multiple TAs as instructors. The instructors in the course are native Chinese speaking graduate students in the Departments of Asian Languages and Literatures and Applied Linguistics. The course supervisor is a native speaker of Modern Chinese, an experienced language teacher and supervisor, and has a Ph.D. in Chinese linguistics. She would like the instructors to test their students' ability to speak Chinese in order to assign course grades and provide feedback to students on their achievement of course objectives.

The supervisor believes that a formal speaking test administered on a program-wide basis several times each term will provide the program with a way to obtain this information systematically in all sections of the course. This information will be used for several purposes. The supervisor will use this information to make decisions about the curriculum and staffing. The course instructors will use this information to make instructional decisions about their teaching and to provide formative feedback to inform their students' decisions about their learning. They will also use the scores, along with other assessments in the course, to make decisions about which students will progress to the next higher course.

As with the elements of an AUA listed above, assessment development begins with the questions about consequences. We will discuss this example from the perspective of the Chinese course supervisor, who is the head of the test development team.

Consequences

The initial set of questions (1–4) concerns consequences. The first question the course supervisor needs to address in articulating an AUA for a particular assessment is:

1 What beneficial consequences do we intend to promote by using the assessment and making decisions based on it, and whom do we intend to benefit from these consequences?

The Chinese course supervisor will begin answering this question by articulating her claim regarding the intended consequences.

> **Claim 1**: The consequences of using the mini-speech test and of the decisions that are made based on them will be beneficial for students, the instructors, and the course supervisor.

Since there are multiple stakeholders, the course supervisor will need to specify the claim in more detail by listing and describing the stakeholders who she believes will be directly affected. In this setting, these stakeholders are:

(i) Native English speaking students at a large university who are studying Elementary Modern Chinese.
(ii) Instructors in the course, who are native Chinese speaking graduate students in the Departments of Asian Languages and Literatures and Applied Linguistics.
(iii) The course supervisor, who is a native speaker of Modern Chinese, an experienced language teacher and supervisor, and has a Ph.D. in Chinese linguistics.

The next two questions require the course supervisor to consider the nature of the consequences.

2 How can we assure that the consequences of *using the assessment* will be beneficial to each stakeholder group that is affected?

In answering this question the course supervisor articulates warrants to elaborate her claim that the consequences of using the test will be beneficial. Here are the warrants (A1–A5) elaborating this claim:

A1 The consequences of using the assessment that are specific to each stakeholder group will be beneficial.

The course supervisor will need to specify how each stakeholder group will be affected by using the assessment. Here are the intended consequences of using the assessment for each stakeholder group:

(i) Students: The Chinese speaking of students in Elementary Modern Chinese classes will improve.
(ii) Instructors: The classroom teaching of the instructors will improve.
(iii) Course supervisor: The overall effectiveness of the course will improve.

A2 The scores from the mini-speech tests and the course grades of individual students are treated confidentially.
A3 The scores from the mini-speech tests and the decisions made are reported in ways that are clear and understandable to students, teachers, and the course supervisor.
A4 Scores from the mini-speech tests and the decisions made are reported in a timely manner.

Another warrant that is part of the AUA for this test is that the use of the test will promote good teaching practice and effective learning (See "impact on instruction" or "washback" in Chapter 5, p. 109).

A5 The mini-speech test helps promote good instructional practice and effective learning, and the use of this is thus beneficial to students, instructors, the course supervisor, and the program. Because the mini-speech test requires students to speak Chinese;

(i) *students* will take the course's learning objectives in speaking seriously and organize their study accordingly, so as to optimize the time and effort spent learning to speak Chinese;
(ii) *instructors* will devote more time to activities that engage students in speaking Chinese. Instructors will use the experience of giving the mini-speech test and the students' performance on this to make adjustments in their teaching, and hence make this more effective;
(iii) the *course supervisor* will observe greater attention to speaking in the classes. The course supervisor will use scores to make decisions about retaining and hiring of instructors, and about changes in the syllabus that will improve the course as a whole.

3 How can we assure that the consequences of the decisions that are made will be beneficial to each stakeholder group who are affected?

In answering this question the course supervisor will articulate warrants to elaborate her claim that the consequences of the decisions that are made will be beneficial. Here are the warrants elaborating this claim:

B1 The consequences of using scores from the mini-speech test to make progress/not progress decisions about students in the course are beneficial to students, instructors, and the course supervisor.

The course supervisor will need to specify how each stakeholder group would be affected by the decisions that are made. Here are the intended consequences of the decisions that are made for each stakeholder group:

(i) Because the scores from the mini-speech test will be used to determine whether they progress to the next higher course, students will take the learning objectives of the course seriously and organize their study accordingly, so as to optimize the time and effort spent studying Chinese, and hence mastering the course objectives and improving their spoken Chinese.

(ii) Because the scores from the mini-speech test will be part of their own evaluation, instructors will make adjustments in their teaching, and hence make this more effective.

(iii) Because the scores from the mini-speech test will be part of the instructors' evaluations, the course supervisor will give greater attention to speaking in the classes.

In instructional settings such as this, where promoting positive washback is an intended consequence, it may not always be possible to clearly determine whether good instructional practice and effective learning is a consequence of *using* the assessment or of the decisions to be made. In this example, the fact that the mini-speech test requires students to speak is intended to encourage teachers to spend more class time in speaking activities, and students to work more on improving their speaking. The fact that scores from this test will be part of information used to make decisions about progress is intended to make both students and teachers take speaking Chinese seriously. Thus, the type of response (extended production of speaking) that is required by the test is intended to focus the washback on this area of language use, while the seriousness of the decision to be made (progress/not progress) is intended to increase the probability that the intended washback will occur.

Because there is a possibility that not all the consequences of our decisions will benefit all stakeholders, we need to consider the next question.

4 What are the potential detrimental consequences of false positive and negative classification decisions and how might we mitigate these?

In order to address this question, the course supervisor will first articulate, as rebuttals, some of the possible unintended detrimental consequences of decision classification errors. (See Chapter 10 for a discussion of decision errors.)

Rebuttal B2: The consequences of making progress/not progress decisions about students will be detrimental for students who are erroneously misclassified as progress or not progress.

(i) False *positives* (allowing students who should not progress to progress) can result in students receiving unrealistic feedback on their abilities; students may move on to courses for which they are unprepared.
(ii) False *negatives* (not letting students progress who should progress) can result in students feeling demotivated.

The course supervisor and the instructors will then need to list some possible ways of mitigating these detrimental consequences, should there be any classification decision errors:

(i) Possible remedies for false *positives*:
  - Use additional information, such as class participation and other speaking assignments, to assign grades.
  - Provide additional tutoring or small group work to help students practice their speaking.

(ii) Possible remedies for false *negatives*:
  - Use additional information, such as class participation and other speaking assignments, to decide which students progress.

Decisions

The next set of questions (5–7) has to do with the decisions that we intend to make on the basis of our assessment-based interpretations.

5 What specific decisions need to be made to promote the intended consequences, and who will be responsible for making these decisions?

To answer this question the course supervisor will first articulate her claim regarding the specific decisions to be made, and who will be responsible for making these. In this setting, the claim is as follows:

Claim 2: The decisions to be made reflect the university's regulations and values, and the common practice and values of the academic community, including students, teachers, and administrators, and are equitable to all students in the course.

Since different stakeholders in this case may make different decisions, these need to be listed, as in Table 8.3.

The next question requires us to consider the context in which these decisions are made.

6 How can we assure that these decisions take into consideration existing educational and societal values and relevant legal requirements?

Decision	Individual(s) responsible for making the decision	Stakeholders who will be affected by the decision
Decide which students progress to the next course partly on the basis of scores on the mini-speech test	1 Instructors 2 Course supervisor	Students
Adjust individual learning activities to focus on speaking	1 Students 2 Instructors	Students, instructors
Adjust teaching style, focus, and activities	Classroom instructors	Instructors, students
Revise curriculum	1 Course supervisor 2 Instructors	Instructors, students
Maintain or change instructional staff	Course supervisor	Course supervisor, instructors, students

Table 8.3 List of decisions, decision makers, and stakeholders

In answering this question, the course supervisor will articulate the following warrants A1–A3:

A1 University and departmental regulations, "customary practice" among the faculty in the Department, and the opinions of students were carefully and critically considered in the kinds of decisions that are to be made.

A2 University and departmental regulations, "customary practice" among the faculty in the Department, and the opinions of students were carefully and critically considered in determining the relative seriousness of false positive and false negative classification errors.

A3 Because the scores on the mini-speech tests comprise just one part of students' course grades, no cut scores are needed.

The next question leads us to consider the nature of these decisions.

7 How can we assure that these decisions will be equitable?

In answering this question, the course supervisor will articulate equitability Warrants B1–B3 to elaborate her claim that the decisions made will be equitable. In this setting, the warrants of equitability are as follows:

B1 Decisions about which students will progress to the next course are awarded only according to the procedures that have been established, and not on the basis of other considerations.

B2 Students and instructors are fully informed of the procedures for making decisions about which students will progress to the next course whether these procedures are actually followed making these decisions.

B3 Students have equal opportunities to learn or acquire speaking ability in Modern Chinese.

We would note that equitability warrants B1–B3 don't apply to the instructors' decisions to modify instruction or to the students' decisions to change their study patterns. This is because these decisions do not involve classifying students into groups.

Interpretations

Since we need to be sure that our decisions are based on interpretations that generalize to the TLU domain of the decision, and that the interpretation about language ability is relevant to the decision to be made, the next set of questions (8–13) have to do with the link between the interpretations and the decisions to be made. The first question is about the interpretations that we intend to make on the basis of our assessment records.

8 What do we need to know about the test takers' language ability in order to make these decisions?

The course supervisor will answer this question by stating the claim, including a descriptive label for the construct, the area of language ability, to be assessed. In this setting, this claim is as follows:

Claim 3: The interpretations about language ability in Modern Chinese are:

(i) meaningful with respect to the course syllabus,
(ii) impartial to the students in the course,
(iii) generalizable to tasks in the language instructional domain,
(iv) relevant to the different kinds of decisions to be made, and
(v) sufficient for the different kinds of decisions to be made.

The next question has to do with the *meaningfulness* of the claimed interpretations. We answer this question by articulating warrants to elaborate the meaningfulness of the intended interpretation.

9 How can we assure that the interpretation of ability is meaningful?

The course supervisor will answer this question by stating warrants that elaborate the meaningfulness of the intended interpretation. For this test, these warrants are as follows:

A1 The definition of the construct includes (1) freedom from grammatical and pronunciation errors, (2) organization, (3) spontaneity, creativity, and fluency, (4) vocabulary and sentence patterns used, and (5) ability to stay within allotted time. These abilities differ from other possible construct definitions, such as knowledge of the Chinese writing system. This definition of the construct is based on the course syllabus.

A2 The test task specifications clearly specify the mini-speech test procedure that will elicit speaking performance from which we can make inferences about (1) freedom from grammatical and pronunciation errors, (2) organization, (3) spontaneity, creativity, and fluency, (4) vocabulary and sentence patterns used, and (5) ability to stay within allotted time.

A3 The procedures for administering the mini-speech test are followed consistently across classes and different occasions.

A4 The rating scales that are used to score the students' performance on the mini-speech test reflect the five parts of the definition of language ability in Chinese articulated in Warrant A2.

A5 The mini-speech test tasks engage the students in speaking Chinese.

A6 The scores from the mini-speech test can be interpreted as indicators of the students' language ability in Chinese.

A7 The instructors communicate the definition of language ability in Chinese articulated in Warrant A2 in terms that are clearly understandable to the students.

The next question addresses the *impartiality* of the interpretations:

10 How can we assure that the interpretations about the test takers' language ability are impartial to all groups of test takers?

The test developer will answer this question by stating Warrants B1–B5 that elaborate the impartiality of the intended interpretation. In this setting, these warrants are as follows:

B1 The mini-speech test tasks do not include response formats or content that may either favor or disfavor some students.

B2 The mini-speech tasks do not include content that may be offensive (topically, culturally, or linguistically inappropriate) to some test takers.

B3 Students are treated impartially during all aspects of the administration of the mini-speech tests.

B4a Students have equal access to information about the test content and procedures, and have equal opportunity to prepare for the mini-speech test.

B4b Students have equal access to the test. It is given as part of the course at no extra cost, in the Chinese classrooms, under conditions with which the students are familiar.

B4c Students have equal opportunity to demonstrate their Chinese speaking.

B5 Interpretations of language ability in Chinese based on the mini-speech tests are equally meaningful across different classes in the Modern Chinese course.

The next question addresses the *generalizability* of the interpretations:

11 How can we assure that the interpretation of language ability generalizes to the TLU domain of the decision?

To answer this question the course supervisor will describe the TLU domain to which she wants the interpretations of speaking based on the scores from the mini-speech tasks to generalize. In this setting, the primary TLU domain is the language instructional domain of the elementary Modern Chinese classes at this university.

Next, the course supervisor will articulate Warrants C1 and C2 elaborating the generalizability of the interpretation to the TLU domain. Because of the wide variety of future TLU domains in which different students in the course might find themselves, the claim of generalizability will be limited to that of the Modern Chinese classes at the university. In this setting these warrants are as follows:

C1 The characteristics (e.g., input, expected response, type of external interaction) of the mini-speech test tasks correspond closely to those of instructional tasks.

C2 The criteria and procedures for evaluating the responses to the mini-speech test tasks correspond closely to those that instructors have identified as important for assessing performance in speaking tasks in the instructional setting.

The next question has to do with the *relevance* of the interpretations about language ability to the decisions to be made:

12 How can we assure that that our interpretations about test takers' language ability are relevant to the decisions?

To answer this question the course supervisor will articulate Warrant D elaborating the relevance of the interpretation to the decision to be made. In this setting, this warrant is:

D The interpretations of speaking based on the mini-speech tests provide information that is needed by the course director, instructors, and students to make the decisions articulated in Table 8.3.

The last question about interpretations has to do with the *sufficiency* of the interpretations about language ability to the decisions to be made:

13 How can we assure that our interpretation about test takers' language ability provides sufficient information to make the decisions?

The answer to this question is an articulation of Warrant E elaborating the sufficiency of the interpretation to the decision to be made. In this example, this warrant is:

E The interpretation of language ability in Chinese based on the mini-speech test scores, is *not* sufficient to make the decisions listed in Table

8.3. That is, this interpretation needs to be supplemented with other information gathered by the class instructors.

Assessment records

The last two questions have to do with the link from the test takers' performance to the assessment records.

14 How will we assure that these assessment records are consistent?

The course supervisor will answer this question by articulating Claim 4. In this setting, this claim is as follows:

Claim 4: Scores obtained from students' performance on the mini-speech tests are consistent across different tasks, administrations, instructors/raters, and classes of students.

In answering this question, the course supervisor will articulate warrants to elaborate the consistency of the assessment records, taking into account the aspects of the assessment procedure that are indicated in the claim. The consistency warrants for the Chinese mini-speech test are as follows:

1 Administrative procedures are followed consistently across different occasions, and for all classes and students.
2 The criteria and procedures for rating students' performance on the mini-speech task are well specified and adhered to.
3 Instructors undergo training at the beginning of each school term.
4 Instructors are trained to avoid bias for or against different groups of students.
5 (Not relevant to this test, since the mini-speech test is essentially a single task.)
6 Ratings of different instructors are consistent.
7 Different ratings by the same instructor are consistent.
8 Scores from different forms of the mini-speech test are consistent.
9 Scores from different administrations of the test are consistent.

The last question has to do with an issue of fairness, namely, the degree to which assessment records are consistent across different groups of test takers.

15 How will we assure that assessment records are of comparable consistency across different groups of test takers?

In answering this question, the course supervisor will articulate Warrant 10:

10 Ratings of students' performance on the mini-speech test are of comparable consistency across different classes and subgroups of students in the elementary Modern Chinese course.

SUMMARY

In this chapter we have provided an overview of the elements of an Assessment Use Argument. There are four claims in an AUA, as follows:

Claim 1: The *consequences* of using an assessment and of the decisions that are made are **beneficial** to all stakeholders.

Claim 2: The *decisions* that are made on the basis of the assessment-based interpretations take into consideration existing educational and societal **values** and relevant legal requirements and are **equitable** for those stakeholders who are affected by the decision.

Claim 3: The *interpretations* about the ability to be assessed are **meaningful, impartial, generalizable, relevant,** and **sufficient.**

Claim 4: The *assessment records* (scores, descriptions) are consistent across different assessment tasks, different aspects of the assessment procedure, and across different groups of test takers.

The qualities of each of these claims will be elaborated in warrants and these will be supported by backing that is appropriate for the specific language assessment situation. We have also provided a list of questions that can guide assessment development and illustrated this from an example of an actual assessment.

In the subsequent chapters in this part of the book we will provide more detailed discussions for articulating each of the four claims in an AUA and for stating the warrants that elaborate the qualities of these claims. We shall illustrate this process using the example assessments that we introduced in Chapter 7—the Kindergarten ELL speaking and writing assessment, and the University ESL reading placement test. In Chapter 9 we discuss Claim 1, about the intended consequences of language assessment use and of the decisions that are made. In Chapter 10 we discuss Claim 2, about the decisions we intend to make on the basis of language assessments. In Chapter 11 we discuss Claim 3, about the intended interpretations, which include considerations and options in defining the components of language ability we want to assess and the TLU domain to which we want our assessment to generalize. In Chapter 12 we discuss Claim 4, about the assessment records.

9

The intended consequences of using language assessments

INTRODUCTION

In this chapter we discuss the process of articulating specific claims and warrants in an Assessment Use Argument about the intended consequences of using the assessment and of the decisions that are made. During the initial planning process described in Chapter 7, the test developers will have decided whether to continue with a test development project or not, and gathered some important information that will be used in the AUA itself. Having done this, they will need to start to articulate an AUA, which will inform and be informed by the rest of the process of assessment development and use.

We illustrate this process for the two Projects introduced in Chapter 7: the Kindergarten and University examples. The settings and initial planning processes for these two Projects are provided in Chapter 7, and you might want to review them before working through the examples in this chapter.

For each example, we first provide the "generic" claim or warrant, as these are stated in Chapter 8. We then restate the claim or warrant in an "adapted" form that is specific to the example. This will illustrate how we can use the generic claims and warrants as a basis for stating claims and warrants for a specific AUA for any given assessment. In doing so, we provide two types of discussions. In "Backing from the design and development procedures," we outline the specific procedures the assessment developers followed during the Design and Operationalization stages of the assessment development process that provide backing for each warrant. In "Discussion" we provide a general discussion or commentary on that part of the AUA and related considerations. In presenting the two examples, we work through Questions 1 to 4 presented in Table 8.2 in Chapter 8 to show how the process of articulating the claims and warrants and providing backing addresses these questions.

QUESTION 1

"What beneficial consequences do we intend to promote by using the assessment and making decisions based on it, and whom do we intend to benefit from these consequences?"

We answer Question 1 by articulating Claim 1, which has two parts: one pertaining to the intended consequences, and the second to the stakeholders who will be affected by these consequences. Claim 1 will thus include (1) a list and description of the intended consequences, and (2) a list of the stakeholders whom we intend to be affected by the use of the assessment and by the decisions made.

> *Generic version of Claim 1:* The consequences of using an assessment and of the decisions that are made are beneficial to stakeholders.
>
> *Adapted Claim 1 for the Kindergarten example:* The consequences of using the checklist and of the formative decisions that the teacher makes to improve his instruction are beneficial to the students (test takers), the kindergarten teacher, and other teachers who will teach these students in first grade.
>
> *Adapted Claim 1 for the University example:* The consequences of using the reading assessment and of the placement/exemption decisions that are made are beneficial to the test takers, teachers in the ESL reading courses, the ESL Program Director, and instructors in academic courses at the university who will encounter ESL students in their classes.

Discussion

Here we discuss two kinds of considerations: describing the intended beneficial consequences and identifying and listing the stakeholders.

Intended beneficial consequences

The first consequence stated in Claim 1 is that the *act of using the assessment* will be beneficial to stakeholders. One group of stakeholders who will always be affected by the use of the test is the test takers. They may have either positive or negative perceptions of the process of preparing for the test, of taking it, and of waiting for the results. For example, they may have positive perceptions if the scores are reported promptly and in an easily understood way, and negative perceptions if score reports are delayed or confusing, regardless of what decisions are made on the basis of these reports. In addition, test takers may learn something from the content of the test and feedback on how they performed on it (including various types of grades), and what they learn may have either positive or negative consequences. Other potential stakeholder groups who may be affected by the test use include individuals who administer the test, individuals who debrief students who have taken the test, individuals who may have to deal with complaints about the test or challenges to the results, etc.

The second consequence stated in Claim 1 is that consequences of the *decisions that are made* will be beneficial to stakeholders. These consequences can affect a variety of possible stakeholders, such as the test takers themselves, teachers, instructors, program directors, universities to which students are admitted, employers who hire the test takers, and so on (see Chapter 5).

Stakeholders

Identifying and listing the test takers and other stakeholders guides the steps in assessment development. Moreover, knowing who the test takers and other stakeholders are helps us articulate the warrants used to argue for the beneficial consequences of using an assessment and of the decisions that are made.

In the Kindergarten example the primary stakeholders include only the teacher and the students in his kindergarten classes. Although other stakeholders are not specifically mentioned in this claim, it is possible that other teachers who teach his students, and the school as a whole, will also benefit indirectly from his assessment and the decisions that are made.

In the University example, the primary stakeholders include the test takers, the ESL reading teachers, teachers in regular introductory university courses, and the ESL program administrator. Other stakeholders less directly affected might include family members of test takers who might need to remain in the university longer in order to complete an extra course or might have to pay more for said course.

Which stakeholders to include

A variety of individuals will be affected by and thus have an interest, or hold a "stake," in the use of a given assessment in any particular situation. Test takers and test administrators will always be affected in some way by the use of the assessment. However, stakeholders that are affected by the decisions that are made may or may not include the test takers. For example, if an assessment were used to make decisions about the future of funding for an ESL program, the students tested might not be affected at all by these decisions, although future students might be affected. The teachers giving assessment may only be affected if they remain teachers long enough to be affected by the future funding decisions. The stakeholders primarily affected would be the program itself and those associated with it after the decision has been made. Similarly, if an assessment is used to make decisions about teachers (retain, dismiss, promote, etc.) the test takers might not be affected to any great extent.

In addition, a large number of individuals (e.g., test takers' future classmates or co-workers, future employers) will be indirectly affected. Finally, to the extent that the assessment has consequences for the societal or educational system at large, it can be argued that virtually every member of the system is indirectly affected by its use. For example, widely used and expensive commercial tests have a considerable economic impact not only upon the test takers who take them, but also upon individuals in the organizations that develop them and in the communities within which these organizations are located. Rather than attempting to discuss the general systemic consequences of assessment use or the potential indirect consequences for individuals, we will focus our attention here on the consequences for those stakeholders who are most directly affected by assessment use: test takers and teachers.

Source of information about stakeholders

We will base our list of stakeholders' attributes on a wide variety of sources and kinds of information. We may begin informally, using our own knowledge, talking with others who are familiar with the test takers, etc., and this knowledge may be sufficient in low-stakes assessment situations, such as the Kindergarten example. In higher-stakes situations such as the University example, even where the assessment developer may be quite familiar with the test takers, we believe it is important to refine these initial informal approaches with a more systematic approach. This is even more important where the assessment developer is not at all familiar with the test takers. What we recommend is to use a combination of interviews, observations, self- reports, and questionnaires.

QUESTION 2

"How can we assure that the consequences of *using* the assessment will be beneficial to each stakeholder group that is affected?"

We answer this question by articulating the beneficence Warrants A1–A5 and specifying the backing.

Warrant A1 for Kindergarten and University examples

Generic version of Warrant A1: The consequences of using the assessment *that are specific to each stakeholder group* will be beneficial.

Adapted Warrant A1 for the Kindergarten example: The consequences of using the checklist that are specific to the students (test takers), the kindergarten teacher, and other teachers who will teach these students in first grade will be beneficial.

Adapted Warrant A1 for the University example: The consequences of using the incomplete outline test that are specific to the test takers, teachers in the ESL reading courses, the ESL Program Director, and instructors in academic courses at the University who will encounter ESL students in their classes will be beneficial.

Backing from design and development process for Kindergarten and University examples

The kindergarten teacher is the test developer. He has used his professional knowledge and teaching experience to develop the assessment to be useful to him, his students, and other kindergarten teachers teaching the same material to the same kinds of students. He has also carefully followed the assessment procedure, using the same rubric for recording students' performance.

The incomplete outline test was developed in consultation with teachers in the ESL reading courses, the ESL Program Director, and instructors in academic courses at the university who will encounter ESL students in their classes, all of whom had input into the development of the test. Thus, the beneficial consequences to each group of stakeholders were taken into consideration.

Discussion

In articulating Warrant A1, the test developer helps to assure that the needs of all principal stakeholders influence the development of the assessment and the beneficial consequences of assessment use. In some test development situations, an assessment is designed and developed by individuals who are not in touch with principal stakeholders. For example, assessments developed by a central authority may not involve consulting principal stakeholders and may not involve them in the development process. In other situations, an assessment might be developed by only some of the principal stakeholders, who do not take into consideration the needs of other stakeholders. Thus, Warrant A1 is needed to assure that the consequences for all principal stakeholders are dealt with systematically.

In some situations, just articulating Warrant A1 may be convincing to the primary stakeholders without the need for extensive backing. In the Kindergarten example, the test developer is also the primary test user and stakeholder, so he will most likely not need to provide extensive backing to support his warrant of intended consequences. In low-stakes situations such as this one, the backing may consist of the instructor/developer's own intuitions/experience.

In many situations, however, just claiming and articulating warrants that the intended consequences will be beneficial may not be convincing to all stakeholders, in which case more extensive backing will need to be provided. For example, stakeholders in the higher-stakes University example may require more backing to be convinced than do the stakeholders in the Kindergarten example.

Furthermore, different stakeholder groups may be concerned about different kinds of consequences and hence require different kinds of backing to be convinced. In the University example, the ESL reading instructors are likely to be convinced by the claim that placing students into the ESL reading class on the basis of a placement test will facilitate their teaching and help their students learn more effectively. Indeed, it may be their own experience that provides the backing they need to be convinced.

However, if the Department Chair were asked to provide resources for test development, she may need more backing to be convinced. She may be interested in trimming budgets by eliminating unnecessary activities and perhaps increasing class size, and so may question the need for homogeneous grouping. She may also question the need for what she may perceive as an expensive placement exam and procedure. She may therefore ask the ESL Program Director to cite research results that support the efficacy of homogeneous grouping on language learning. Other stakeholders, such as the students themselves and their academic advisors, may be less concerned about the efficacy of homogeneous ability grouping, than they are about other consequences related to fairness, such as that the placement reports are treated confidentially, that these are clear and understandable, and that they receive the reports in time to act upon them, in terms of arranging their own class schedules.

Finally, in the University example, one can imagine a long chain of possible consequences, for example, that because of the decision to place students in homogeneous ability groups, one particular international student excelled in English, which greatly facilitated his performance in his courses in economics, which led to his finding a job in the government when he returned to his native country, which in turn eventually led to his becoming Prime Minister. Can the ESL Program Director thus claim that an intended consequence of the placement exam is to help students become high government officials in their home countries?

In this example, clearly some consequences more directly affect specific stakeholders who need to be convinced than others, some consequences will require more resources to provide backing for than others, and regardless of how many consequences the test developer chooses to list, uncertainty surrounding the choice of consequences will remain. Thus, the decisions to list some consequences rather than others will depend upon how we choose to balance these various considerations.

From these examples, it should be clear that the test developer should only claim as intended consequences those that he believes will be directly affected by the use of the assessment.

Warrant A2 for Kindergarten and University examples

Generic version of Warrant A2: Assessment reports of individual test takers are treated confidentially.

Adapted Warrant A2 for the Kindergarten example: The checklist that the teacher completes for each student is kept confidential.

Adapted Warrant A2 for the University example: Assessment reports, which include (1) the scores from the incomplete outline test and (2) the placement decisions made on the basis of them, are treated confidentially.

Backing from design and development process for Kindergarten and University examples

The kindergarten teacher is the test developer, and he is sensitive to the need to treat reports of individual test takers confidentially.

In the University example, the scores from the incomplete outline test will be kept confidential and given only to the test takers themselves and to university officials, such as their academic advisors who need to know that information. The course supervisor monitors the process and students may complain if process is not followed, and complaints will be considered and, where justified, acted upon.

Discussion

It is a fundamental fairness requirement that assessment reports need to be kept confidential in order to protect the rights of the test takers. These rights are discussed in various standards for our field (e.g., American Educational Research Association, American Psychological Association, and National Council on Measurement in Education 1999; International Language Testing Association 2005), and are also discussed in Chapter 5. Implementing this warrant in practice means that assessment records can be provided only to the test takers themselves and individuals who are authorized to receive them. The particular individuals who are authorized to see test takers' assessment records will, of course, be a local decision for any particular assessment, and will be generally guided largely by existing laws, regulations, and accepted practice.

Warrant A3 for Kindergarten and University examples

Generic version of Warrant A3: Assessment reports are presented in ways that are clear and understandable to all stakeholder groups.

Adapted Warrant A3 for the Kindergarten example: The information in the checklist that may help the students in their learning is presented in ways that are clear and understandable to the students.

Adapted Warrant A3 for the University example: Assessment reports, which include (1) the scores from the incomplete outline test and (2) the placement decisions made on the basis of them are presented in ways that are clear and understandable to all the test takers.

Backing from design and development process for Kindergarten and University examples

The kindergarten teacher has had years of experience in working with students and providing feedback and encouragement. There is no negative feedback on his ability to do so in any of his teaching evaluations.

In the University example assessment reports are presented as the percentage of correct answers to the incomplete outline test. As a result of their previous educational experiences, test takers are familiar with this type of feedback.

Discussion

The types of feedback test takers receive about their assessment performance are likely to affect them directly. We thus need to consider how to make feedback as relevant, complete, and meaningful to the test taker as possible. When feedback is in the form of a score or a grade, we need to make sure that the scores we report are meaningful to test takers.[1] We also need to consider additional types of feedback, such as verbal descriptions to help interpret assessment scores, as well as verbal descriptions of the actual assessment tasks and the test taker's performance. The provision of rich verbal description, especially if given in a personal debriefing with the appropriate test administrator, can be very effective in developing a positive affective response toward the assessment on the part of test takers.[2] When the assessment results are presented as a verbal description, without a score, we need to make sure that this report is stated in language that the test taker will understand.

Warrant A4 for Kindergarten and University examples

Generic version of Warrant A4: Assessment reports are distributed to stakeholders in a timely manner.

Adapted Warrant A4 for the Kindergarten example: Not needed, because the teacher does not distribute his checklists to anyone else, including the students.

Adapted Warrant A3 for the University example: The ESL Program Director distributes the assessment reports to test takers and authorized university faculty and officials in time for them to be used for the intended decisions.

Backing from design and development process for Kindergarten and University examples

Since the warrant is not needed, no backing is needed for the Kindergarten example.

Assessment reports are provided within two days of completion of the incomplete outline test.

Discussion

Assessment reports need to be distributed to stakeholders in a timely manner so that decisions based upon these reports can also be made expeditiously and the beneficial consequences of these decisions realized without undue delay.

Warrant A5 for Kindergarten and University examples

Generic version of Warrant A5: In language instructional settings, the use of the assessment helps promote good instructional practice and effective learning, and the use of the assessment is thus beneficial to students, instructors, the program, etc.

Adapted Warrant A5 for the Kindergarten example: The use of the checklist will help the teacher improve his instructional practice and will facilitate effective learning by his students.

Adapted Warrant A5 for the University example: Use of the incomplete outline test helps promote good instructional practice and effective learning by linking the assessment task specifications to one of the performance objectives in the ESL reading course into which students are placed.

Backing from design and development process for Kindergarten and University examples

The checklist was developed specifically to provide formative feedback on the attainment of instructional objectives and promote good instructional practices. The kindergarten teacher uses the checklist for ongoing feedback on the attainment of the instructional objectives, and he uses this feedback to make adjustments in his instruction.

ESL reading teachers were involved in the design of the incomplete outline test, and they had been taught to think of assessment as a starting point for developing performance objectives. In this view, they defined the construct to be measured so as to be identical to one of the performance objectives in the reading course. Both the construct definition and performance objectives for the ESL reading course consisted of two parts: (1) a knowledge component and (2) a task component. The knowledge component consisted of "knowledge of rhetorical organization of academic prose." The task component consisted of "a task involving completing an outline of an academic reading passage." The reading teachers were taught to reflect on the fact that their students had been placed in their classes based on their lacking the ability to complete exactly the same tasks as those they were supposed to focus on in their instruction. This was intended to help the teachers keep their instruction on task. Past experience has suggested if the teaching assistants (TAs) do not think that their students will be assessed on a specific performance objective, they may decide to focus their instruction elsewhere.

Discussion

Warrant A5 is used only in language instructional settings, in which the beneficial consequences of using the test specifically include the promotion of good instructional practice and effective learning. (See discussion of impact on instruction, or "washback," in Chapter 5.) Good instructional practice and effective learning benefit all stakeholders in educational settings, whereas the consequences of decisions (see below) benefit different stakeholders in different ways. In non-instructional settings, such as the use of an assessment to make hiring decisions, no instruction is involved, so Warrant A4 would not be relevant. Both the Kindergarten and University examples are situated in instructional settings, so this warrant is relevant to both examples.

QUESTION 3

"How can we assure that the consequences of *the decisions that are made* will be beneficial to each group of stakeholders that is affected?"

We answer Question 3 by articulating the beneficence Warrant B and specifying the backing. This information also becomes part of the Design Statement for the assessment.

Warrant B for Kindergarten and University examples

Generic version of Warrant B: The consequences of the decisions will be beneficial for *each group* of stakeholders.

Adapted Warrant B for the Kindergarten example:

1 The consequences of the kindergarten teacher's changes in his instructional practice will be beneficial to the teacher.
2 The consequences of the kindergarten teacher's changes in his instructional practice will be beneficial for his students.
3 The consequences of the teacher's changes in his instructional practice, and of the students learning pre-literacy skills, will be beneficial for the teachers in first grade, who will teach these students to read.

Adapted Warrant B for the University example:

1 The consequences of the placement and exemption decisions that are made will be beneficial for the students.
2 The consequences of the placement and exemption decisions that are made will be beneficial for the teachers in the ESL reading course.
3 The consequences of the placement and exemption decisions that are made will be beneficial for the teachers in academic university courses.
4 The consequences of the placement and exemption decisions that are made will be beneficial for the ESL program administrator.

Backing from design and development process: Kindergarten example

In the Kindergarten example there are multiple stakeholders, with different consequences of the decisions that are made for each. The teacher will be able to improve his instruction, the students will learn pre-literacy skills more effectively, and the first grade teachers will be able to teach these students to read more easily.

The experience of the kindergarten teacher indicates the value of using formative assessment to make decisions about appropriate modification of instruction. The experience of the teacher and his colleagues indicates the value of using interpretations of the test takers' language ability to make placement/exemption decisions, and that there are positive effects on students of formative assessment and appropriate modification of instruction. Experience of first grade teachers indicates that they can do a better job of teaching their students to read if they have had quality instruction in pre-literacy skills.

Backing from design and development process: University example, Warrants B1–3

Warrant B1: One of the main reasons for using a test to exempt students from the ESL reading course is the collective experience of the TAs in which they have experienced problems with placements in courses they do not need. They also do not want students to waste their time and money on unnecessary coursework.

Warrant B2: Teachers repeatedly express frustration when they cannot teach in such a way as to engage the majority of the students in their classes. Teaching to a relatively homogeneous group of students will avoid this problem. Since the primary audience for this AUA consists of teachers who have students without the benefit of some sort of placement procedures, their experience is all that is needed to justify the use of a placement/exemption test.

The intended audience for this AUA includes the Project Director, the members of the test development team, and ESL reading teachers, who use the AUA to organize their thinking and document their justification for the use of the test. Suppose, however, external reviewers, who would then comprise another audience, were reviewing this program. In this case, the external reviewers might question the validity of teachers' experience and ask for backing from the research into the learning benefits of homogeneous classes.

Warrant B3: Instructors in university academic courses in which the placed or exempted students will eventually enroll are also stakeholders. The ESL reading course is designed to help students read academic texts more efficiently, so the test users hope that the results of the placement test and subsequent instruction will facilitate this. The passages used in the incomplete outline test are drawn from examples of the introductory texts used in non-ESL university courses into which many of the students will eventually enroll. If students learn more as a result of these decisions, stakeholders relying on students' ability to read these texts will benefit from their students being well prepared to do so.

Warrant B4: The program administrator's years of experience administering programs with and without some sort of placement experience constitute one source of backing for using this test to make placement decisions.

Discussion

When there are different consequences for different stakeholders, we need to state this warrant. For the Kindergarten example, consequences of the teacher's decisions to adjust instruction are limited to the students and the teacher, and the adapted warrant reflects this. For the incomplete outline test, consequences are far more wide ranging and extend also to the program administrator and instructors in the non-ESL university courses. When consequences affect a variety of stakeholders, it is often convenient to state them in a table, as we have done for the University example (see Table 8.3 in Chapter 8).

Finally, in some cases, the decisions might benefit one group of stakeholders but might be neutral or detrimental to another. If this is the case, this needs to be noted in the warrant and backing.

QUESTION 4

"What are the potential detrimental consequences of false positive and negative classification decisions and how might we mitigate these?"

We answer Question 4 by articulating the unintended detrimental consequences (rebuttals) and specifying the backing needed to weaken the rebuttals.

Generic version of rebuttal: Either false *positive* classification errors or false *negative* classification errors, or both, will have detrimental consequences for the stakeholders who are affected.

For Kindergarten example there is no rebuttal because students are not classified on the basis of assessment results. The only decisions made are to modify instruction on basis feedback from formative assessment.

Adapted rebuttal for University example: The consequences of false positive and false negative classification errors will be different, as follows:

1 *False positive classification errors*. Exempting students from the ESL reading course who actually need the course will have detrimental consequences for students because they will feel overwhelmed, frustrated, may get low grades in their academic courses, and may even be dropped from the university. Furthermore, even though these students may have to struggle in their academic courses, they may not report this, and so there is little chance of helping them. Instructors in academic courses may also feel frustrated because their students are not able to keep up with the reading assignments. These instructors may complain to the ESL program administrator, who will have to deal with complaints. In this example, therefore, false positive classification errors are regarded as very serious.
2 *False negative classification errors*. Placing students in the ESL reading course who do not need it will have detrimental consequences for students. Students may feel bored with the coursework and resent what they may perceive as time and money wasted for the course. They may also suffer because taking an ESL class prevents them from taking an additional academic course, which may delay their progress toward their degree. In this example, therefore, false negative classification errors are regarded as moderately serious.

Possible ways of mitigating the detrimental consequences of decision classification errors if they occur

1 *False positive classification errors*. Teachers in regular university courses will be notified of the existence of the ESL reading courses and asked to be alert for students who seem to be struggling with the reading assignments. They will be asked to advise students to consider taking the ESL reading course even though they were exempted from it on the basis of the ESL reading test.
2 *False negative classification errors*. ESL reading teachers will be alerted to be on the lookout for misplaced students, to collect additional information about the students' reading ability during the first week of class, and to make recommendations to the Program Director for exempting those students who they feel do not need the class.

Discussion

Any time a decision maker makes classification decisions, there is the possibility that some of these will be in error; some of these errors may be false positives, and some may be false negatives. Furthermore, as discussed above, the consequences of false positive and false negative classification errors can be quite different and not equally serious. In order to minimize these detrimental consequences, the test developer and decision maker, in consultation with all relevant stakeholders, will need to establish procedures for setting cut scores so as to minimize those classification errors whose consequences are the most serious. These procedures will be specified during the Design Stage, in the Design Statement (discussed in Chapter 14), and during the Operationalization Stage, in the Blueprint (discussed in Chapter 17).

In addition to establishing procedures to minimize classification errors, the test developer, decision maker, and other stakeholders will need to anticipate the unintended consequences that may result from classification decision errors and consider the steps that could be taken to mitigate the consequences of classification errors, if they occur. The following steps can be taken to provide backing from design and development process to weaken rebuttals:

1 Identify the detrimental consequences of decision errors if they happen.
2 Determine what can be done to minimize detrimental consequences.
3 Indicate what resources will be required to do this, e.g., who is responsible for doing this, time, space, etc.

Identifying detrimental consequences of decision errors if they happen

Identifying detrimental consequences of decision errors involves listing each possible decision error and thinking through what could happen in the event that such an error occurs.

Determining what can be done to minimize detrimental consequences

The following are some general strategies for minimizing detrimental consequences of decision errors.

Find ways to reclassify stakeholders after they have been misclassified on the basis of the assessment itself

After the assessment has been used to classify stakeholders and classification errors have been found, it may be possible to reclassify stakeholders who have been misclassified on the basis of the assessment itself. In the University example, after the initial classification decisions have been made, we know that a number of students will still be placed in ESL reading courses that they may not need. In this situation, a procedure for easily re-placing students who are misplaced can be instituted. We can alert the teachers to be on the lookout for misplaced students. We can require the teachers to collect additional information about the students' reading ability during the first week of class and make recommendations to the Program Director for exempting those students who they feel do not need the class. This reclassification procedure can then be included as the backing in the AUA to weaken the rebuttal of classification errors, as has been done in the University example.

Find ways to "repair"/mitigate the consequences of errors that do not rely on reclassification strategies and decide which of these we can put into effect

Other ways can often be found to "repair" classification errors that do not involve reclassifying stakeholders or changing the assessment or cut scores. In the case of the University example, these might include providing tutorials for students exempted from the ESL reading course or providing a content-based adjunct to help students exempted from the ESL reading course who still seem to be struggling.

Indicate what resources will be required to do this, e.g., who is responsible for doing this, time, space, etc.

Identifying who is responsible for making sure that the consequences are beneficial is surely a complicated issue without easy, all-purpose answers. At one level, this is an issue of professionalism, which requires both test developers and test users to adhere to a professional code of ethics (e.g. International Language Testing Association 2000). At the same time, this is a critical issue that needs to be dealt with in every practical assessment development situation. A reasonably clear-cut case is when a decision maker decides to use an assessment for a different use from the one for which it was originally developed. In this case, the decision maker would be responsible for justifying this new use of the assessment. For example, suppose an achievement test were developed by ESL teachers to assess the mastery of course content, and a college admissions officer later decided to use this test to make admissions decisions because of its availability and low cost of use. In this example, it would seem to us that the admissions officer would be responsible for justifying this new use of this test. She might go back to the ESL teachers to seek their assistance in providing warrants and backing for new assessment, in which case they would then also share responsibility. If the admissions officer contacted a different group to do this, then the admissions officer and that group would share responsibility, and the ESL teachers would not.

Practicality considerations will influence our choice of strategies to deal with false positive and false negative classification errors. Sometimes the resources required to prevent one type of error (such as a false positive) or to repair its consequences may be much greater than the cost of doing the same with another type of error (such as a false negative). Ultimately, however, we are unlikely to arrive at a perfect solution to all possible problems that may arise, whether anticipated, unanticipated, known, or unknown. As discussed in Chapter 5, the decision maker's comfort zone, or tolerance for decision errors, will depend on a whole host of personality factors, so that in essentially the same decision setting, different decision makers might have very different levels of tolerance of decision errors.

In this chapter we have discussed the process of articulating specific claim and warrants in an Assessment Use Argument about the intended consequences of using the assessment and of the decisions that are made. In the next chapter, we discuss the process of articulating the claim and warrants about the decisions to be made on the basis of language assessments.

EXERCISES

1 Think of an assessment you have used. What were some of the intended beneficial consequences of assessment use in this situation? What were some of the intended beneficial consequences of the decisions that were made?
2 Read through some of the Projects, paying particular attention to the distinction between consequences of assessment use and decisions that are made. Then think of an assessment use situation with which you are familiar. What were some of the intended beneficial consequences of (a) using the assessment and (b) the decisions that were made?
3 Think of an assessment development situation with which you are familiar in which essentially no thought seemed to have been given to consequences; i.e., the assessment development started with the kinds of tasks, and consequences were only addressed as an afterthought. What problems came up as a result of this approach to assessment development?
4 Think of an assessment use situation with which you are familiar. If you were to justify assessment use in this situation, who would the audience be for the AUA and backing? How would you take this audience into consideration in constructing the AUA?
5 Think of an assessment use situation with which you are familiar. Make a list of the principal stakeholders for this situation.
6 Think of an assessment use situation with which you are familiar. What steps are taken to assure that assessment reports of individual test takers are treated confidentially? Can you think of a situation in which this warrant might not be needed? This might be a very low-stakes test in which the distinction between assessment and instruction is blurred.
7 Think of an assessment use situation with which you are familiar. How were assessment reports presented to stakeholders? Would you be able to justify this using Warrant A3? Why or why not?
8 Can you think of an assessment use situation in which use of the assessment or the decisions that were made did not promote good instructional practice and effective learning? How did this situation come to pass?
9 Think of an assessment use situation with which you are familiar. Describe the false positive and negative classification errors and list some potential detrimental consequences of these errors. What steps might be taken to minimize these consequences after the errors have been found?

NOTES

1 Bachman (2004) discusses a number of methods for reporting scores in ways that are appropriate for different stakeholders.
2 Canale (1988) discusses the need to "humanize" the experience of testing, and includes the provision of rich feedback about performance in this.

10

The decisions to be made on the basis of language assessments

INTRODUCTION

In order to help bring about the intended consequences a test user needs to take some action and this entails making decisions. Many of these decisions will involve the classification of stakeholders into groups. Other kinds of decisions, such as focusing on a particular area of language ability to be studied, will be made by test takers themselves. In this chapter we organize the discussion of decisions as we did with consequences in Chapter 9. We work through the same two examples: the Kindergarten and University examples. In presenting these two examples, we work through Questions 5–7 provided in Chapter 8 and show how the process of articulating the claims and warrants and providing backing addresses these questions.

QUESTION 5

"What specific decisions need to be made to promote the intended consequences and who will be responsible for making these decisions?"

We answer Question 5 by articulating Claim 2 for a particular assessment. This adapted claim will list:

(a) the specific decisions that are to be made,
(b) which stakeholder groups will be affected by which decisions, and
(c) who will be responsible for making these decisions.

Generic and adapted versions of Claim 2 for Kindergarten and University examples

The following are generic and adapted versions of Claim 2 for the Kindergarten and University examples:

Generic version of Claim 2: The decisions that are made on the basis of the interpretation take into consideration existing educational and societal **values** and relevant laws, rules, and regulations and are **equitable** for those stakeholders who are affected by the decisions.

Adapted Claim 2 for the Kindergarten example: The formative decisions that are made in support of instruction and learning take into consideration existing educational and societal **values** and relevant legal requirements and school regulations and are **equitable** for the kindergarten students. These decisions will be made by the classroom teacher.

Adapted Claim 2 for the University example: The decisions to place students in or exempt students from the ESL reading course reflect relevant existing educational and societal **values** and relevant university regulations and are **equitable** for those students who are placed or exempted. These decisions are made by the ESL Program Director.

The decisions, stakeholders affected by decisions, and individuals responsible for making the decisions are provided in Table 10.1.

Decision	Stakeholders who will be affected by the decision	Individual(s) responsible for making the decision
Place students in ESL reading course	Students, instructors in ESL reading course, teachers in students' academic courses	ESL Program Director
Exempt students from ESL reading course	Students, instructors in ESL reading course, teachers in students' academic courses	ESL Program Director
Adjust instruction in ESL reading course	Instructors in ESL reading course, students in ESL reading course	Instructors in ESL reading course

Table 10.1 The decisions, stakeholders affected by decisions, and individuals responsible for making the decisions

Discussion: types of decisions

The decisions that are most commonly made on the basis of a language assessment are about the test takers, teachers, instruction, and programs. The decision makers will typically include a wide range of individuals, such as test takers, teachers, administrators, and employers, as well as various groups of individuals, such as district school boards, state boards of education, and the boards of directors of companies.

High- and low-stakes decisions

High-stakes decisions are those that are likely to have major consequences for the lives of individuals, or on programs. Examples of high-stakes decisions about individuals include decisions about admission to academic programs, the awarding of scholarships, and about the employment and retention of teachers. An example of a high-stakes decision about programs is the allocation of resources, teachers, funds, and materials to schools in a given state or district. In addition to having major consequences for individuals or programs, high-stakes decisions are not easily reversed, so that decision errors cannot be easily corrected. (See the discussion of decision errors on p. 201 below.) For example, if an applicant performs poorly on a job interview because of nervousness or lack of specific preparation, he may not be offered a job, even though he is well qualified for it. And once the job is filled, there may not be another opening for a long time. Similarly, if a language program is eliminated from a school system, it may be extremely difficult to reinstate it at a later time.

Low-stakes decisions are those that have relatively minor consequences for the individuals, or programs, and that can generally be reversed quite easily. For example, a teacher might use an assessment to diagnose students' strengths and weaknesses, in order to assign them to specific learning activities. If the teacher misdiagnoses some students' areas of weakness and then assigns them to inappropriate learning activities, relatively few individuals are affected, and he can correct the errors as soon as they are discovered. Similarly, if the teacher uses a classroom quiz to help gather feedback on the effectiveness of a particular unit of materials or set of learning activities, and then decides, on the basis of scores on the quiz, to continue with these materials and activities, he can easily change this if he finds, from subsequent feedback from his classes, that the materials and activities really are not working effectively.

It is important to understand that a given assessment may have different consequences, and thus represents different "stakes" for different groups of stakeholders. For example, in many countries, large-scale tests of students' academic achievement, and, in many cases, language ability, are used for accountability, that is, for allocating resources such as teachers, funds, and materials, to schools. These resourcing decisions are thus high stakes for the schools. However, the results of these tests are not typically used to make decisions about individual students, such as assigning grades or promotion to the next grade. Thus, they are no or low stakes for the students who take them.

Decisions about test takers: selection and certification

Selection decisions involve determining which individuals should be admitted to a particular educational program or offered a particular job. For example, teachers or administrators may need to decide which international students are most likely to succeed in a college-level program, and may want to use performance on language assessments to help make these admission decisions. In other situations, employers may want to use a language assessment as part of a procedure for hiring an applicant for a job. Language tests are also widely used for certifying professionals, such as teachers, doctors, nurses, air traffic control officers, pilots, business people, and interpreters. In some language instructional domains, students may be given an assessment at the end of the course, and their score or grade may be used to certify their level of achievement or their level of language ability (see discussion of grading below).

Decisions about test takers: placement

Placement decisions involve determining which of several different levels of instruction would be most appropriate in which to place the test taker. For example, if high school students who have studied a foreign language would like to be considered for placement into advanced level foreign language courses in college, they might be required to take a language assessment to determine the appropriate level of course for them. Based on the results of this assessment, the language department head and teachers will decide which applicants to accept. Decisions to place students in or exempt them from a course or courses presumably take place in the context of a well-thought-through instructional program, which begins with a needs assessment. If this is the case, the AUA for the test can refer to this existing needs analysis and doesn't need to create it.

Decisions about test takers: learning and instruction

Information from an assessment can provide a basis for making decisions about learning and instruction. When we interpret assessment records as indicting specific areas of strength or weakness in language ability, this is typically referred to as **diagnosis**, or **diagnostic assessment**. This diagnosis can be used to make decisions that the teacher or students may believe will facilitate their learning. Some of these decisions will be made by the teacher. One kind of teacher decision will involve a change in the teachers' syllabus or instructional activities. This is illustrated in the Kindergarten example, where the teacher uses the results of his in-class assessments primarily to fine-tune the learning activities in which he engages his students. Another kind of teacher decision will involve directing students to different kinds of learning activities. For example, if a language program included three different courses, one focused on the editing of sentence-level grammar and punctuation errors, a second focused on revising the organization of essays, and a third focused on logic of argumentation in writing, a teacher might use an assessment that included all these different language use activities as a basis for deciding which course would be most appropriate for students to take. Finally, some decisions may be made by the students. For example, the teacher may provide diagnostic feedback to students based on their performance on the assessment, and suggest that they focus on specific areas of language ability in which they need to improve. The students may then decide to follow the teacher's suggestions. Or, if one objective of the course is to promote learner autonomy, the teacher may simply provide the diagnostic feedback to the students and then let them decide what learning activities will be most appropriate and effective for them.

Decisions about test takers: progress

In most instructional programs, both students and teachers are interested in receiving feedback on students' progress. Information from language assessments can be useful for the purpose of **formative decisions**, which are intended to help students guide their own subsequent learning, or for helping teachers modify their teaching methods and materials so as to make them more appropriate for their students' needs, interests, and capabilities. Language assessments can also provide useful information for **summative decisions** based on information about students' achievement or progress at the end of a course of study. Summative decisions will involve determining what students will do after the end of a course, such as passing students to the next course of study, or requiring them to repeat the course.

Decisions about students' progress are often associated with the assigning of grades: A, B, C, and so on. In many settings, for example, grades of "A," "B," "C," and "D" are considered "passing," while a grade of "E" or "F" is not passing. With respect to assigning grades, it is important to clearly distinguish between arriving at an assessment record and making a decision based on that assessment record. When a teacher assigns grades for a course, whether these are expressed in percentages, rankings, or as letters, these are essentially *assessment records*. In some situations such grades will also include interpretations, which make the grades more meaningful, such as the following:

A = Analytic, critical understanding of concepts and principles, and their creative application to issues and problems in language assessment.
B = Thorough understanding of concepts and principles, and their appropriate application to issues and problems in language assessment.
C = Accurate recall or recognition of concepts and principles, with some application to issues and problems in language assessment.
D = Inaccurate recall or recognition of concepts and principles, with little application to issues and problems in language assessment.
F = No evidence of recall or recognition of concepts and principles, or of their application to issues and problems in language assessment.

Even though assigning grades may be viewed as classifying students into groups according to their grades, these grades, in themselves, do not necessarily entail a classification *decision*. In many situations, the difference between some grades may have little or no consequence for students, while the difference between other grades will result in a specific, highly predictable decision, such as a pass or fail decision, with potentially serious consequences. Thus, giving a student a "B" or a "C," which are both passing grades, may have very different, idiosyncratic, and therefore unpredictable consequences for different students. Giving an "F," or failing grade, as opposed to a "D," or minimally passing grade, however, will most likely have predictable consequences, such as students being placed on academic probation, or having to take the course again, as opposed to being given credit for the course and then being able to take other courses. Thus, assigning grades at just above or below the pass/fail cut point, will result in a *decision* with specific consequences. In summary, assigning grades does not constitute making decisions about stakeholders. Nevertheless, test developers and decision makers need to understand that grades are ways of reporting levels of performance that are almost always highly value-laden.

Decisions about teachers or administrators

Inferences about students' language ability can be used to evaluate the effectiveness of teachers and administrators, and this evaluation might subsequently be used as a basis for making decisions about hiring, salaries, retention, and promotion.

Decisions about teachers or programs

Finally, inferences about students' language ability can be used to make decisions about programs. For example, a teacher, or school principal, or state board of education might use students' language assessment scores to determine the effectiveness of various levels of instructional programs in meeting their objectives. Such decisions could be used further to determine whether to continue a given program as is, to modify it, or to eliminate it.

Multiple decisions

The scores from a given language assessment can be used for multiple as well as single purposes. For example, a test such as that described in the ESL Writing example in Project 8 can be used not only to select students for entrance into ESL writing the program or to exempt students from study in the program, but also to determine the level at which they would be placed within a series of courses in the program. And if administered both before and after instruction, the test could also be used to make decisions about the effectiveness of instruction. Brown (1989) provides a discussion of an actual example of a similar multi-use test in the context of a university writing program.

Due to the cost of developing and administering language assessments, it makes good sense to make as much use of them as is appropriate. However, what constitutes an "appropriate" use of an assessment needs to be clearly demonstrated as part of the process of assessment justification, as discussed in Chapters 5–8. That is, each use that is made of a given assessment needs to be justified with appropriate evidence supporting its use. It is therefore important for the assessment developer to carefully consider whether the amounts and types of resources that are saved through multiple uses offset the additional resources that will be required to justify those additional uses.

QUESTION 6

"How can we assure that these decisions take into consideration existing educational and societal values and relevant legal requirements?"

We answer this question by articulating warrants about values sensitivity and specifying the backing that is needed to support these: Warrants A1–A3.

Warrant A1 for Kindergarten and University examples

Generic version of Warrant A1: Existing educational and societal values and relevant legal requirements are carefully and critically considered in the kinds of decisions that are to be made.

Adapted Warrant A1 for the Kindergarten example: Relevant educational values of the kindergarten teacher and his colleagues, and school regulations, are carefully considered in the decisions to modify instruction as needed.

Adapted Warrant A1 for the University example: Relevant educational values of the university community and legal requirements of the university itself as an institution are carefully considered in the placement and exemption decisions that are made.

Backing from design and development process for Kindergarten and University examples

The kindergarten teacher's own educational values, as well as those of his colleagues and the school, indicate that formative feedback is needed in order to make decisions to maximize the effectiveness of instruction. Societal values that need to be taken into consideration include parents' expectations that their children's teachers will do their best to monitor the effects of their instruction and adapt it as needed.

For the University example, the test developers consulted widely with members of the faculty, the university administration, international student advisors, and international students themselves about the advisability of the use of the assessment and about the decisions to be made. All the stakeholders consulted felt that the decisions to be made were appropriate. The ESL Program Director also checked with the university's legal affairs office to make sure that there were no legal prohibitions of this kind of assessment. The test developers' notes and records of these conversations and discussions are part of the documentation of the project and provide backing for this warrant.

Discussion

Assessments are almost always developed for use in a specific educational system or segment of society and the values specific to that context. In addition, they are sometimes developed under the auspices of organizations, both educational and governmental, whose values, laws, or regulations can affect different aspects of assessment use. In some cases, the laws or regulations and educational and societal values may be consistent with one another, so it may be possible to design an assessment that is consistent with all. In other cases, the laws or regulations may not be entirely consistent with educational and societal values. Or, there may be competing values of different stakeholder groups. In such cases, the assessment developer will have to work with the different groups involved to reach the best solution possible. (See discussion of this situation in Chapter 6.) In still other cases, the assessment developer may have reasons for using the assessment to make decisions that are not consistent with laws or educational values because the assessment developer wants the assessment to lead the way in affecting change.

For example, consider a situation in which an educational program has had a long tradition of having well-qualified, experienced teachers who could be left pretty much on their own as far as their teaching is concerned. Now, however, suppose the program has expanded dramatically, and has had to hire a large number of new teachers, many of whom have very little training and experience in language teaching. In addition, many of these new teachers leave after only a short time in the program. In this case, the institutional value of "teacher independence" is leading to a great deal of ineffective teaching. If the Program Director wanted to implement a procedure to help new teachers be more effective, she might implement a policy of having the experienced and well-trained teachers regularly observe new teachers, assess their performance with an observation checklist, and then give them feedback. This use of assessments contradicts the institution's traditional educational values, but does so for a specific, well-thought-out, and well-documented purpose.

Regardless of what course of action the assessment developer decides to take, it is important that she provide evidence of awareness of relevant educational and societal values, laws, and regulations, and that these have been taken into consideration. In very low-stakes assessment, simply citing the educational values, laws, and regulation that were considered may suffice. In higher-stakes situations, a more extensive argument will be needed.

For example, suppose one is developing an assessment to make decisions about programs funded under the auspices of a governmental grant. Considerable documentation may need to be provided to indicate that the decisions are in compliance with the grant regulations as well as state laws affecting modifications to educational programs. In addition, there may be teachers' unions that have negotiated specific agreements that may affect the kinds of decisions made, and that also need to be considered.

Warrant A2 for Kindergarten and University examples

Generic version of Warrant A2: Existing educational and societal values and relevant legal requirements are carefully and critically considered in determining the relative seriousness of false positive and false negative classification errors.

Adapted Warrant A2 for the Kindergarten example: Since students are not classified on the basis of this assessment, this warrant is not needed.

Adapted Warrant A2 for the University example: Existing educational values of the ESL teachers and academic instructors, as well as relevant university regulations, are carefully considered in determining the relative seriousness of false positive and false negative classification errors.

Backing from design and development process for Kindergarten and University examples

This warrant is not needed for the Kindergarten example, so no backing is required.

For the University example, based on consultations with members of the faculty, the university administration, international student advisors, and international students themselves, the ESL Program Director determined that false positive classification errors were more serious than false negatives. This was because students who were mistakenly exempted from the courses would be placed in jeopardy of failing their academic courses. Furthermore, it was very difficult to move these students out of their academic courses and into the ESL reading program once the school term had started. Students who were mistakenly placed into the reading course (i.e., false negatives), on the other hand, could be identified quite easily by the ESL instructors during the first week of classes, and be permitted to enroll in academic courses.

Discussion on determining the relative seriousness of classification errors

Determining the relative seriousness of the classification errors is a policy decision that needs to be based on a consideration of the educational and societal values of the stakeholders, as well as existing legal requirements, rules, and regulations. It is clearly helpful if the test developer is involved in the process of making this decision. However, in many situations, this decision has already been made, or may be part of an institutionalized value set, even before the development of an assessment for this purpose begins.

In general, the seriousness of the *unintended* consequences will be related to the seriousness of the *intended* consequences. In high-stakes situations, where the decisions to be made are intended to have major life-affecting *beneficial* consequences for those affected, the seriousness of an unintended *detrimental* consequence can be equally or more serious. For example, the decision whether or not to promote employees to higher-paying positions will have relatively serious beneficial consequences for those who are promoted, in terms of their income and ability to meet expenses. At the same time, it may have equally detrimental consequences for those employees who are not promoted. In low-stakes decisions, on the other hand, where the decisions to be made will have relatively minor consequences for those affected, the seriousness of an unintended consequence is likely to be relatively low as well. For example, decisions to award students pass or fail on a quiz may have relatively minor consequences for the students, particularly if the quiz is used primarily to provide formative feedback to the students so they can make decisions about how to structure their learning activities, and if the pass/fail decision has only a small influence on their final grade in the course.

Warrant A3 for Kindergarten and University examples

Generic version of Warrant A3: Cut scores are set so as to minimize the most serious classification errors.

Adapted Warrant A3 for the Kindergarten example: Since students are not classified on the basis of this assessment, and the information the teacher obtains from the assessment is not in the form of scores, this warrant is not needed.

Adapted Warrant A3 for the University example:

- **Policy-level procedures for setting standards**: The standard for exemption from the ESL reading course was set by the ESL course director in consultation with ESL reading course instructors and academic course instructors.
- **Standard for exemption from the ESL reading course**: Students must demonstrate that they have sufficient knowledge of multilevel rhetorical organization of introductory academic texts to enable them to successfully participate in introductory level academic courses.

Backing from design and development process for Kindergarten and University examples

This warrant is not needed for the Kindergarten example, so no backing is required.

In making decisions to exempt university students or place them in an ESL reading course, the more serious misclassification error is a false positive. Students who are exempted from the ESL reading course may not be able to read well enough to cope with the readings in their academic course work. As a consequence, they may run the risk of doing poorly in a variety of courses and possibly not being able to complete their program of study at all. The less serious misclassification error is a false negative. Students who are required to take an ESL reading course they do not need will not be put at risk in their other academic courses. They will only suffer to the extent that they perceive this as a waste of their time and money for one academic term. Thus, cut scores are set relatively high to minimize false positive errors.

Discussion on using cut scores for decision making

There are two types of considerations in using cut scores for making decisions: the *kinds* of classification decision errors that might be made, and the *procedures* that are used to establish the cut score. Whenever the decision maker makes a classification decision, there is always the possibility that she will make false positive classification errors or false negative classification errors. (See the discussion of classification decision errors in Chapter 9, pp. 189–91.) In any given assessment situation, the number of test takers who are erroneously misclassified and the numbers of false negatives and false positives will depend on two things: where the cut score is set and on the dependability of the classification decisions at that cut score.

There are two steps involved in setting cut scores: specifying a performance standard and identifying a cut score. A "performance standard" defines a minimum level of the ability to be assessed that will be acceptable to be classified as a "master," "proficient," or "certified," depending on the specific situation. Performance standards are typically in the form of verbal descriptions of levels of language ability, or language use activities that individuals who are at or above the performance standard can perform. A "cut score" is a score (e.g., a number or grade) on a particular assessment that corresponds to the performance standard. Performance standards for specific decisions will be specified during the Design stage, in the Design Statement. Procedures for doing this are discussed in Chapter 14. Cut scores for a particular test will be set during the Operationalization stage, and will be specified in the Blueprint. Procedures for doing this are discussed in Chapter 17.

Dealing with decision classification errors

During the Trialing stage, the test developer will want to collect feedback on the numbers and types of decision classification errors that would be made on the basis of one or more possible cut scores. One way to do this is to include, as part of the trialing sample, test takers whose levels on the ability to be assessed are already known. If this contrasting groups method has already been used in the initial standard-setting procedure, then this will constitute a cross-validation of this procedure. Another way is to conduct a follow-up study in which relevant stakeholders are asked to indicate which, if any, test takers were misclassified. In the University example, the ESL Program Director could ask the ESL reading course instructors about false negatives, and the academic course instructor about false positives.

Irrespective of where the cut score has been set, it is likely that some decision errors will still occur. On the basis of analyzing scores from the trialing with different cut scores, the test developer and decision maker may determine that the numbers of decision errors are acceptably low, and stay with that cut score. However, if the number of decision errors is not acceptable, they need to be prepared to implement additional procedures to minimize these. There are two strategies that the test developer can use to further reduce the likelihood of decision errors. These involve making changes to the assessment itself and changing the cut scores used to make decisions.

Make changes to the assessment itself

The test developer may be able to reduce likelihood of serious classification errors by changing the assessment itself. One way to do this is by selecting test tasks that have higher correlations with the rest of the tasks in the assessment. This will tend to make the test more internally consistent, and also reduce the measurement error. Another way is to select test tasks that best discriminate masters from non-masters at the level of ability represented by the cut score. (A discussion of these procedures is beyond the scope of this book. Interested readers are referred to Bachman 2004b and Brown and Hudson 2002.) In some cases, classification decision errors may be a result of having defined the ability to be assessed too narrowly. In this case, the test developer may want to add some additional task types to the assessment that will provide additional kinds of information about the construct to be assessed. In the University example, it might turn out that the ESL Program Director could reduce the number of false positive errors by adding another section to the assessment in order to make interpretations about the test takers' ability to draw inferences from the reading passage.

Change the cut scores

Another way to lessen the likelihood of serious classification errors is to change the cut scores. In the University example, the Program Director could minimize false positives by setting the cut score relatively high so that few students will be classified as exempt from taking the ESL reading course. If few students are classified as exempt, then few students will be put at risk of failing academic courses they are not prepared for. At the same time, this will result in more students being placed at risk of spending time in an ESL reading course they don't think they need. If there is an unacceptably high number of false positives, based on feedback from instructors in academic courses, the Program Director could raise the cut score. However, it is important to understand that there is a limit to how high or low we can set the cut score. At the extreme, if she were to set the cut score at 100 per cent, for example, no students would be exempted. Similarly, if she set the cut score at 0 per cent, no students would be placed into the reading course. If either of these cut scores were used there would, in effect, be no reason for using an assessment to make the decision. Another important point to keep in mind is that the test scores we use to make decisions are not perfectly consistent. Because of this, wherever we set the cut score, there will always be some classification errors.

QUESTION 7

"How can we assure that these decisions will be equitable?"

We answer this question by articulating Warrants B1–B3 and specifying backing:

Warrant B1 for Kindergarten and University examples

Generic version of Warrant B1: Test takers are classified only according to the cut scores and decision rules, and not according to any other considerations.

Adapted Warrant 1 for the Kindergarten example: The primary decisions to be made are instructional ones, by the teacher, and students are not classified into groups, so this warrant does not apply.

Adapted Warrant B1 for the University example: The same cut score is used to classify all students taking the ESL incomplete outline test, and no other considerations are used.

Backing from design and development procedures for Kindergarten and University examples

Since this warrant is not needed for the Kindergarten example, backing is not needed.

For the University example, identical cut scores for placement/exemption are used for all test takers, and no other considerations are used. In addition, test takers are identified only by student ID number, so there is no possibility of test takers with equivalent levels of ability (as measured by test scores) being classified in different groups.

Discussion

We want to be sure that test takers who are at the same level of ability on the construct to be assessed have the same chances of being classified into the same groups. That is, we want to make sure that decisions we make are not inequitable for any particular group of test takers. The best way to accomplish this is to make sure that classification decisions are based on the same cut score, and that these decisions are made on the basis of the test takers' scores, and not on the basis of other considerations. Inequitability is a problem if the decision maker takes into account attributes of the test taker not included in the construct, such as ethnicity, gender, age, or socioeconomic status. For example, two test takers achieving the same score that would qualify them for "exemption" on the incomplete outline test should both be classified as "exempt." The individuals doing the classification should not, for some other reason such as prior experience with the students, classify one student as "exempt" and the other as "placed." Note that equitability is strictly a classification issue; it isn't related to predicting whether the two students achieving the same score will perform equally well in university academic courses involving the ability to read academic prose. Two students with the same score on the test could perform very differently in their academic courses because of differences in their personal attributes.

Finally, in some situations, the stakeholders classified on the basis of scores might not be the test takers. For example, if several teachers in a program are being evaluated for the purpose of promotion on the basis of their students' scores on some assessment, equitable decisions might require that equivalent scores of the students in several classes would each result in the same promotion decisions being made about the teachers of those classes.

Warrant B2 for Kindergarten and University examples

Generic version of Warrant B2: Test takers and other affected stakeholders are fully informed about how the decision will be made and whether decisions are actually made in the way described to them.

Adapted Warrant B2 for the Kindergarten example: Because decisions are made only about the learning and teaching tasks the instructor uses, and not about specific students, this warrant is not needed.

Adapted Warrant B2 for the University example: Test takers, ESL reading teachers, and other individuals within the university community are fully informed about how the decision will be made and whether decisions are actually made in the way described to them.

Backing from design and development procedures for Kindergarten and University examples

This warrant is not needed for the Kindergarten example, so no backing is required.

For the University example, the criterion for making placement/exemption decisions (i.e., the cut score on reading test) is published on the web, as are the procedures for making placement decisions anonymously with students identified only by student ID numbers.

Discussion

One aspect of fair test use is whether and by what means individuals are fully informed about how decisions will be made and whether decisions are actually made in the way described to them (see Chapter 5). This warrant provides justification that the appropriate procedures have been followed to inform test takers about criteria for making decisions and the procedures for doing so.

Warrant B3 for Kindergarten and University examples

Generic version of Warrant B3: For achievement and certification decisions, test takers have equal opportunity to learn or acquire the ability to be assessed.

Adapted Warrant B3 for the Kindergarten example: No decisions are made involving achievement and certification. The decisions are only formative decisions that are made in support of instruction and learning. Therefore, this warrant is not needed.

Adapted Warrant B3 for the University example: No decisions are made involving progress or certification. The only decisions made are "placed" or "exempt." Therefore, this warrant is not needed.

Backing from design and development procedures for Kindergarten and University examples

Since this warrant is not needed for either the Kindergarten or the University example, no backing is needed.

Discussion

In situations where we want to assess students' achievement or mastery of material covered in a course of instruction, if students do not have equal opportunity to learn this material, then the assessment may be biased. (See the discussion of equitability in Chapter 5.)

In summary, in order to help bring about the intended consequences we typically need to make decisions to classify stakeholders into groups. These decisions are typically made about individuals, such as students or teachers, but they can also be used to make decisions about programs or about the potential of assessments for use in a wide variety of settings. Whatever the case may be, these decisions are justified on the basis of three warrants about values sensitivity and their backing, as well as three warrants about equitability and their backing.

EXERCISES

1 Think of an assessment development situation with which you are familiar. Make a list of some of the educational values that were taken into consideration with respect to the decisions that were made on the basis of the assessment. Were any values overlooked that should have been taken into consideration?
2 Think of some legal requirements that must be taken into consideration when making decisions on the basis of assessments in your country. Are you familiar with any important legal precedents that brought these requirements to public awareness? What were they?
3 Are you working within an institution in which decisions to pass or fail students are made? If so, what educational values come to mind when you think about making these decisions?
4 Are you aware of any societal values that are considered when assessments are used making decisions in your country? What are they? Are they fairly stable, or do they tend to change over time? How might you anticipate them changing in the future?
5 Have you used assessments in educational settings in two different countries? If so, what differences in cultural and educational values were taken into consideration in making decisions on the basis of language assessments? Did you learn about any of these differences in the school of hard knocks? Are you wiser as a result?
6 Go through the Projects on the web (http://www.oup.com/LAIP). Make a list of some of the different kinds of decisions that are made on the basis

of language assessments. What kinds of decisions have you made on the basis of language assessments that you have used?

7 Look over Project 11 on the web, in which multiple tests are used to make multiple decisions. Are you familiar with any language teaching programs faced with the need to make similar decisions? If so, what were these decisions, and how were they made?

8 Think of an assessment use situation with which you are familiar that involved the use of a cut score to classify test takers. Describe the false positive and false negative decision errors for this situation. In this situation, what kind of classification decision error was the most serious: false positives or false negatives? Were any steps taken to reduce the likelihood of serious classification errors? If so, what were these steps?

9 Think of a situation in which an assessment is used to make decisions about test takers. To what extent were steps taken to justify the equitability of the decisions using Equitability Warrants B1–B3?

11
Interpretations

INTRODUCTION

Once we have articulated the intended beneficial consequences of using an assessment and the decisions that we need to make in order to realize these consequences, we need to specify the information about test takers' language ability we will need to make the decisions. In this chapter we go through the process of articulating Claim 3 and its associated warrants about assessment-based interpretations.

We will follow the same procedures as used in Chapter 10 to work through the Kindergarten ELL speaking and writing assessment and the University reading test examples to illustrate this process. In presenting these examples we work through Questions 8–13 given in Table 8.2 in Chapter 8 and show how the process of stating the claims, warrants, and backing provides answers to these questions.

In Chapter 3 we defined language ability as the capacity for creating and interpreting discourse. Language ability includes two components: language knowledge and strategic competence, or metacognitive strategies. We described language use as involving the interaction of the language user's language knowledge and topical knowledge with the context (the language use task), mediated by the metacognitive strategies and affective schemata. In most situations in which we may want to develop a language assessment, inferences are likely to be about the components of language ability or, more commonly, different areas of language knowledge. However, there are situations in which the test developer may wish or be asked to make broader inferences pertaining to individuals' future performance on tasks or in jobs that may involve language use. That is, the language test developer may be asked to provide predictions, on the basis of a language assessment, about individuals' capability to successfully perform future tasks or jobs that involve language use.

QUESTION 8

"What do we need to know about the test takers' language ability in order to make the intended decisions?"

We start to answer Question 8 by articulating Claim 3.

Claim 3

Generic version of Claim 3: The interpretations about the ability to be assessed are:

- **meaningful** with respect to a particular learning syllabus, a needs analysis of the abilities needed to perform tasks in the TLU domain, or a general theory of language ability or any combination of these,
- **impartial** to all groups of test takers,
- **generalizable** to the TLU domain in which the decision is be made,
- **relevant** to the decision to be made, and
- **sufficient** for the decision to be made.

Adapted Claim 3 for the Kindergarten example: The interpretations about the students' knowledge of letter formation and concepts of print, and their oral language, are **meaningful** with respect to the teaching syllabus and the teaching/learning activities in the class, **generalizable** to subsequent learning activities in the class, and **relevant** to and **sufficient** for the formative decisions that are to be made.

Adapted Claim 3 for the University example: The interpretations about the students' "knowledge of multilevel rhetorical organization of written texts" are **meaningful** in terms of an analysis of texts used in introductory level academic university courses, **impartial** to all groups of test takers, **generalizable** to reading tasks in texts used in introductory level university courses, and **relevant** to and **sufficient** for the placement decisions that are to be made.

QUESTION 9

"How can we assure that the interpretations of language ability are meaningful?"

To answer this question, we articulate seven warrants (A1–A7) about the meaningfulness of interpretations.

Warrant A1

Generic version of Warrant A1: The definition of the construct is based on a frame of reference such as course syllabus, a needs analysis, or current research and/or theory of language use, and clearly distinguishes the construct from other, related constructs.

Adapted Warrant A1 for the Kindergarten example: The constructs to be assessed include (a) letter formation, (b) concepts of print, and (c) oral language. These construct definitions are based on the teaching syllabus and clearly distinguish the constructs from other related constructs, such as knowledge of numbers.

Adapted Warrant A1 for the University example: The construct to be assessed is "knowledge of multilevel rhetorical organization of written texts." This definition is based on a needs analysis that included input from instructors in introductory level academic university courses, students who had completed these courses, and teachers in the ESL courses. It clearly distinguishes the construct from other related constructs, such as ability to draw inferences, ability to read critically, or knowledge of figures of speech.

Backing from the assessment development process for Kindergarten and University examples

Multiple constructs are measured in the Kindergarten example, including (a) letter formation, (b) concepts of print, and (c) oral language, because the teacher needs information about performance in each area as a basis for making instructional decisions. Backing for meaningfulness is based on the teacher's knowledge of students, the demands of the assessment activity, and the teacher's judgment about the meaningfulness of the descriptions. A more formal needs analysis was not needed because of the low-stakes nature of this assessment.

A single construct, "knowledge of multilevel rhetorical organization of written texts," is measured in the University example. In order to define the construct, the test development team conducted a needs analysis. This involved meeting with ESL reading instructors, the subject matter teachers in the university, and students. Surveys of students and academic instructors were also used. (See Chapter 14 for a detailed discussion of this needs analysis.) On the basis of this information, the development team decided that only one construct "knowledge of multilevel rhetorical organization of written texts" is needed to make placement/exemption decisions. However, the team is open to measuring more constructs if it turns out that more than one is needed to make the placement/exemption decisions. (See discussion of "sufficiency" below.)

Discussion: defining the construct to be assessed

When we articulate Claim 3, we name the construct to be assessed, and in Warrant A1, we define this construct and describe the specific source(s) of the construct definition. These sources provide the frame of reference for the meaningfulness of the interpretation. (See discussion below.) In defining the construct, we need to make a conscious and deliberate choice to specify particular components of the ability or abilities to be assessed in a way that is appropriate to a particular testing situation. Specific definitions of the constructs, or abilities to be assessed, are needed for two purposes:

1 to guide test development efforts,
2 to provide justification for the intended assessment-based interpretations.

We thus need to decide what abilities to include and not include in the construct definition(s), based on the kinds of interpretations that are needed to make the intended decisions.

What this means is that we cannot simply accept, without question, the construct labels that other test developers have used (particularly those that are used without being defined), as either corresponding to the construct to be measured, or as being appropriate for a particular testing situation of interest to us. Instead, we need to decide what construct label and definition is needed on the basis of what is needed for a particular test development project. In addition, we need to be able to explain why we chose that particular construct label and definition and not others. To do this, we need to understand what the options are as well as the strengths and weaknesses of each option.

It is important to keep in mind that the way we define the construct will have clear implications for the recording method to be used. Specifically, we need to keep in mind that whatever interpretation we want to make about a construct needs to be based on an observable "product" or "output," which will consist of an assessment record (a score or a verbal description). Thus, the more interpretations we include in our construct definitions, the more separate assessment records we will need to produce from test performance and, potentially, to report to test users. We are not suggesting that the recording method should determine how we define constructs. We are simply noting that the way we define the construct will have consequences, in terms of the numbers and types of assessment records we produce.

Defining the construct of "language ability"

When we define the construct "language ability" for a particular assessment, we need to go about this systematically with a clear understanding of a variety of options at our disposal. Our understanding of these options and when it is appropriate to use one or another will inform the way we state Warrant A1 and its associated backing for any given assessment. The specific options we discuss below include (1) the frame of reference for the construct definition, (2) strategic competence as a construct, (3) topical knowledge as a construct, and (4) performance (skills or tasks) as constructs.

Frame of reference for the construct definition

One of the first considerations we need to take into account is the need to provide a frame of reference for our construct definition that is meaningful to all stakeholders, including ourselves as test developers. In virtually all language assessment situations, this frame of reference will be a course syllabus, a needs analysis of TLU tasks, a theory of language ability, or some combination of these. Whichever frame of reference we use, the definition of the construct should be stated in terms that the stakeholders reading the AUA can relate to and understand. As indicated in Chapter 8, there may be different versions of the AUA for different audiences. Thus, the construct definition may be defined in technical terms for the test developers, as part of the Design Statement or Blueprint, while it will typically be stated in more general language for other stakeholder groups.

Construct definitions based on a language instructional syllabus

If an assessment is to be used in an instructional setting to diagnose areas of strength and weakness or to assess the achievement of specific syllabus objectives, we will then most likely base the construct definition on the specific components of language ability that are included in the course syllabus. This course syllabus, in turn, is likely to be based, at least implicitly and in part, on a theory of language ability. For example, suppose we were teaching a set of specific grammatical structures, and wanted to develop an achievement test to measure students' ability to use them, so as to provide feedback on mastery of these specific teaching points. We might prepare a definition of the construct "ability to use grammatical structures accurately," which included a list of the structures we had taught, such as article usage, use of the past tense, subject-verb agreement, and so forth. (See Projects 5, 6, and 7 for examples of syllabus-based construct definitions.)

Syllabus-based construct definitions can be written at different degrees of technicality, depending upon the audiences for whom the AUA is written. For example, if an AUA is written for experienced language teachers, a construct definition might be stated in quite technical terms, such as "knowledge of the tense-aspect-modal system in English." For other stakeholders, the definition might be stated in more general terms, such as "knowledge of English verbs."

Construct definitions based on a needs analysis

In other cases, such as the use of assessments for determining admission into an academic program, or for making decisions about employment, where there may not be a language instructional syllabus, we will most likely base the definition of the construct on a needs analysis of the language that is required to perform TLU tasks. In general, needs analysis, or needs assessment, involves the systematic gathering of specific information about the language use needs of learners and the analysis of this information for purposes of language syllabus design. The procedures of needs analysis can be adapted for the purposes of assessment development. (A discussion of needs analysis is provided in Chapter 14. See Projects 4, 5, and 13 on web for examples of construct definitions based on a needs analysis.)

Construct definitions based on a theory of language ability

In some situations, there is either no common syllabus upon which to base a construct definition, or the target language use domain may be too broad and varied to conduct a needs analysis. In such situations, we may base our construct definition solely on a theory of language ability. Large-scale language tests such as the TOEFL and the IELTS, for example, are intended to be taken by prospective college and university students from all over the world, so they cannot be based on a course syllabus. Furthermore, scores from these assessments are used by a wide variety of tertiary institutions in many different countries to make admissions decisions, so that the results of a needs analysis can provide only general guidelines for defining the constructs to be assessed. Tests that are based on a theory of language ability are commonly referred to as "proficiency" tests.

Another situation in which construct definition may be informed entirely by a theory of language is that of research settings, such as studies investigating the nature of language ability and how it can be measured. For example, in a series of research studies conducted in the early 1980s, researchers used complex research designs and statistical analyses to investigate whether or not tests could be developed whose scores were capable of distinguishing among different hypothesized components of language ability. (See, for example the papers in Oller (1983), and in Palmer, Groot, and Trosper (1981), and studies by Bachman and Palmer (1980, 1981).) The constructs in these studies were informed entirely by theories of language ability similar to the one described in Chapter 3. Another example would be in studies investigating the nature of second language acquisition or learning, in which tests based on a theory of language ability may be used as indicators of learners' levels of acquisition in different areas of language knowledge.

Components of language ability to be included

In all language assessment situations, the construct definition will include one or more specific components of language ability. There are situations in which we may want to make interpretations about specific components of *strategic competence*, in which case these will also need to be specified in the construct definition. (See Project 9, which illustrates how strategic competence can be specified in a construct definition and measured in a test.) There may also be situations, particularly where we need to develop tests of language for specific purposes or for content-based instruction, in which *topical knowledge* may be defined either as part of the construct, or as a separate construct. Thus, the way in which the construct is defined for any given test development situation will need to be tailored to the needs of that particular situation.

The role of strategic competence (metacognitive strategies) in construct definitions

Engaging with and responding to any language assessment task will always involve test takers' language ability to some degree. This is because when language use tasks are performed, both language knowledge and strategic competence, or metacognitive strategies, are always involved. (See Chapter 3 for discussion of these.) In assessments such as writing an essay or engaging in an oral interview, the involvement of both language knowledge and the metacognitive strategies is obvious; the test taker's knowledge of grammar, vocabulary, rhetorical organization, and so forth are involved, along with the test taker's ability to set goals for the essay, to appraise the demands of the task and the test taker's internal resources (including language knowledge), and to plan how to structure the essay. However, even tasks that do not require the production of language, such as selecting the correct synonym for a vocabulary item, involve the test taker's metacognitive strategies, albeit to a lesser extent. For example, in performing the vocabulary synonym task, the metacognitive strategy "appraising" (see Chapter 3) is involved when the test taker's internal knowledge of vocabulary is appraised. However, even though the metacognitive strategies will be engaged by virtually any language assessment task, these are not part of the construct to be assessed unless we include them explicitly in the definition of the construct.

This being said, there are two options for dealing with the metacognitive strategies in the way we define the construct to be assessed:

1 define the construct as language knowledge only, with the possibility of multiple constructs for different areas of language knowledge, and
2 define language knowledge and strategic competence as separate constructs.

The way we choose to define the construct, with respect to these two options, will guide the assessment development process, and also the way in which we will interpret the assessment records.

Option 1: construct definition: language knowledge only. In many language assessment situations we will want to make interpretations only about language knowledge, whether this is a single area or several areas. This is particularly common in language courses that focus on specific areas of language knowledge. For example, if we needed to use an assessment to determine the achievement of students over a lesson whose purpose was to review cohesive markers in English, we would define the construct in terms of the knowledge of these markers and score performance using the appropriate usage of these as a criterion. If we needed more fine-tuned information, we could define multiple constructs such as "knowledge of lexical cohesion," "knowledge of grammatical cohesion," "knowledge of ellipsis," and so on. In situations such as this, interpretations about test takers' strategic competence would not be needed. We would thus try to develop assessment tasks that would require very little strategic competence to perform by reducing the influence of the test taker's goal setting, appraisal, and planning in performing the assessment tasks.

Option 2: construct definition: language knowledge and strategic competence as separate constructs. We can define strategic competence as a separate construct from language knowledge when we need specific interpretations about test takers' strategic competence in order to make decisions. For example, suppose we wanted to assess students' ability to write a research paper in order to provide formative feedback to them and wanted to assess their control of the writing process. We might write separate construct definitions for the metacognitive strategies of "goal setting" (e.g., limiting the topic and scope of the paper), "appraisal" (e.g., determining what the writing task required, gathering information from source material, and eliciting and responding to feedback on the manuscript periodically during the revision process), and "planning" (e.g., working with and editing multiple versions of outlines and drafts). Rather than developing a test for this purpose, we might use an assessment that required students to submit a portfolio providing evidence of their use of the metacognitive strategies in their writing process. We might create assessment records consisting of separate qualitative descriptions of the material submitted that would allow us to make interpretations about each of the constructs. If we also needed interpretations about the quality of the students' writing product, that is, the final version of the paper, we might also include constructs covering various areas of language knowledge, such as knowledge of rhetorical structure and knowledge of cohesion. If we did so, separate definitions would be needed for each of these constructs.

The role of topical knowledge in construct definitions

Any language assessment will, by definition, be aimed at yielding interpretations about components of language ability. In real life settings, language use is also affected by attributes of individuals that are not associated with language ability. In our framework for language use (Chapter 3), we enumerate several of these, including topical knowledge, personal attributes, and affective schemata, and there is nothing in principle that would prevent us from trying to measure multiple constructs involving these, or other attributes in addition to language ability. However, we believe that the measurement of some of these attributes, such as personal attributes or affective schemata, lies outside the scope of this book, so we will not address the use of these attributes as a basis for defining constructs.

Information about test takers' topical knowledge, however, may be relevant to the decisions to be made, and this may influence the ways in which we define the construct to be assessed. In Chapter 3 we argued that the topical knowledge of language users is always involved in language use. It follows that if language assessment tasks engage test takers in language use, test takers' topical knowledge will always be a factor in their assessment performance. Historically, language testers have viewed topical knowledge almost exclusively as a potential source of test bias, or in our terms, as a rebuttal to the meaningfulness of interpretations about *language ability*. That is, if the assessment records are influenced by test takers' topical knowledge, then this weakens our claim that we can interpret these solely as indicators of language ability. The traditional practice in developing language tests has been to develop assessment tasks that will minimize, control, or at least manage the effect of test takers' topical knowledge on assessment performance. We take a slightly different view and argue that the way in which we deal with topical knowledge when we define the construct to be assessed will depend upon the information that is needed to make the intended decisions. Thus, in some situations, it may be appropriate to exclude topical knowledge from the construct definition, while there may be other situations in which topical knowledge may be included in the definition of the construct the test developer wants to measure. The crucial questions that need to be asked are "How does the test developer determine the role of topical knowledge in the construct definition?" and "What are the possible consequences of defining the construct in a particular way, with respect to topical knowledge?"

There are essentially three options for defining the construct to be measured with respect to topical knowledge:

1 define the construct solely in terms of language ability
2 define language ability and topical knowledge as a single construct
3 define language ability and topical knowledge as separate constructs.

Here we will discuss these three options for defining the construct, along with the interpretations that can be made on the basis of each option. In this regard, the issue is not whether topical knowledge affects test takers' performance, since, as we've argued earlier, it will do so in virtually all situations. The issue is whether we will obtain a separate assessment record, either a score or a description, for the test takers' topical knowledge.

Option 1: construct definition: language ability only. In the first option, the construct is defined solely in terms of language ability, and the intended interpretation is of components of language ability only. This option is appropriate for situations in which the decisions to be made involve language ability only. For example, suppose we were developing an assessment to be used to make decisions regarding the assignment of grades in a course focusing on English pronunciation. We would likely define the construct solely in terms of "knowledge of English pronunciation." We would want to obtain, therefore, a single assessment record that we could interpret as an indicator of students' knowledge of English pronunciation. Another example of Option 1 would be a situation in which we were hiring individuals to edit a variety of manuscripts for grammar and punctuation. We would likely define the construct solely in terms of knowledge of English grammar and punctuation.

Option 2: construct definition: language ability and topical knowledge defined as a single construct. In the second option, language ability and topical knowledge are defined as a single construct, and the intended interpretation is something like "the ability to use language to process topical information."[1] Decisions to be made require information about both language ability and topical knowledge, but the two cannot or do not need to be separated. For example, suppose we were developing an assessment to be used to make decisions to place students into a course for non-native English speaking students focusing on the technical vocabulary of agricultural engineering. (As students of agriculture, they will already be familiar with the technical content from agriculture classes taught in their L1.) We might have the students name the parts of a variety of machines used in farming, and we might define the construct as "knowledge of the technical vocabulary of agricultural equipment."

Option 3: construct definition: language ability and topical knowledge defined as separate constructs. In the third option, language ability and topical knowledge are defined as separate constructs, and the intended interpretations are components of language ability *and* areas of topical knowledge. Decisions to be made require distinct information about both language ability and topical knowledge. An example of Option 3 would be an essay test used in a content-based instruction class in which students are being taught language and topical content at the same time. For example, suppose the content objective for the class included "knowledge of the water cycle" and a language objective for the class included "knowledge of the rhetorical organization of descriptive essays." Students write an essay describing the water cycle. Their essays are scored on (1) range and accuracy of their knowledge of the water cycle and (2) their knowledge of the rhetorical organization of a description essay on a scientific topic. Scores on each of these constructs would be used to make the placement decisions.

Another example of Option 3 would be a situation in which we wanted to make decisions to hire individuals to take airline reservations over the telephone. Individuals might participate in simulated role-play telephone conversations, and the constructs might be defined as (1) knowledge of pronunciation and (2) knowledge of standard procedures for taking airline reservations. Their responses to the assessment tasks would receive two scores: one for pronunciation and one for knowledge of standard procedures for taking airline reservations.

As with the options for dealing with strategic competence in defining the construct, the option we choose in defining the construct, with respect to topical knowledge, will guide the assessment development process, and also the way in which we will interpret the assessment records.

"Performance on tasks" as the construct

An alternative to defining the construct in terms of language ability is to define it as "performance on assessment tasks." This approach has gone under the labels of "direct," "performance," or "task-based" assessment. (See Suggested Readings at the end of this chapter for references to these approaches.) In such an approach to language assessment, the test developer defines the TLU domain and identifies language use tasks in that domain. She then develops assessment tasks to be representative of these TLU tasks. Assessment records are interpreted as indicators of how well test takers perform an assessment task, and the purpose is to predict what test takers can do in the TLU domain, or how well they will be able to perform on TLU tasks. Since the primary use of this approach is to predict future performance, and not to infer interpretations about test takers' ability, constructs of language ability or specific areas of language knowledge are irrelevant.

How do we score an assessment in which "performance on tasks" is the construct?

In a task-based approach to language assessment, test takers' performance is typically given a single score in terms of task completion, that is, the degree to which they have successfully completed the assessment task. Since successful completion of the task presumably involves both language ability and topical content knowledge, this approach implies Option 2 above, with respect to the role of topical content knowledge. For example, suppose we developed a test to measure test takers' ability to perform a task such as "taking airplane reservations over the phone." We might develop a test task involving a simulated phone conversation in which the test taker interacts with a make-believe customer and then records the information obtained as a plane reservation, either on a written form or on a computer terminal. We ask raters to rate test takers as either "successfully completed the task" or "did not successfully complete the task," using a checklist of all the information that needs to be collected in taking the reservation. For test takers who successfully complete the task, it should be clear that they have the language ability, knowledge of procedures for taking a reservation over the phone, knowledge of the information that is required, and so forth, that is required. However, if the test taker does not successfully complete the task, we are not sure whether his areas of weakness are in language ability or in topical knowledge. Thus, without defining the construct in terms of one or more areas of language knowledge and topical knowledge, and using ratings based upon these construct definitions, we will not know how to interpret ratings of the test takers' performance on the designated task. In the example above, we won't know why "Job applicant A" got a 3 and not a 4.

Which TLU tasks do we select as a basis for developing assessment tasks?

In many real life TLU domains, a number of tasks may be identified by stakeholders as relatively important and representative of the TLU domain. In such cases, what criteria can we use as a basis for selecting some tasks and not others from the TLU domain? For example, consider a test used to certify flight attendants' ability to use English to perform their jobs. Suppose a needs analysis indicates that, among others, the following three tasks are relevant to the TLU domain and equally important: (1) giving flight safety announcements, (2) guiding passengers to an exit and getting them out of the plane in an emergency, and (3) interacting with passengers in responding to complaints. Suppose also that we only have resources for using one of these task types in our test to certify flight attendants. How do we decide which of these tasks to use as a basis for developing a test task without some specific criteria for selecting one task instead of another? (See Chapter 14 for a discussion of selecting TLU tasks for use as assessment tasks.)

How do we use interpretations of "performance on tasks" to gather information on the achievement in L2 teaching classrooms or provide feedback in classroom assessments?

In many classroom assessments, we want to provide test takers with feedback, or assess their achievement in areas of language knowledge that have been covered in the course, such as their knowledge of vocabulary, rhetorical organization, and cohesion. For example, in a writing class we might want to use an essay task to get students to provide a writing sample that can be used to diagnose errors in the areas of language knowledge mentioned above. In a task-based assessment, we could only provide feedback on something like "how well the student wrote an essay." Thus, there is no way we could use such interpretations to provide specific diagnostic information or make decisions based on students' achievement of learning objectives.

In summary, we believe that interpretations simply of how well task takers have performed on assessment tasks that closely resemble TLU tasks are of very limited use for making predictions. Scores from such assessments cannot be interpreted as indicators of what test takers know and bring to their performance on the task. Without such interpretations, we cannot make inferences about test takers' capacity for using their knowledge or abilities to performance on other tasks.

"Skills" as the construct

We have taken the position, in Chapter 3 above, that the familiar "language skills" (listening, reading, speaking, and writing) are not the constructs to be assessed. Rather, we consider them to be language use activities. Here's why. If we distinguish among the language skills only in terms of mode (productive or receptive) and channel (audio or visual), we end up with skill definitions that miss many of the other important distinctions between language used in particular tasks. For example, suppose we have two tasks. In one, test takers prepare and deliver a speech in which they compare and contrast the positions taken by two news commentators in two different commentaries on the same current event. In the second task, test takers write a two-line note to the mail carrier. Nominally, the first task is a speaking task, while the second is a writing task. Yet these two tasks differ in many other ways as well. In the first task, the length of the response is long, the language of the input is long and complex, the language of the expected response is highly organized rhetorically and in a formal register, and the scope of relationship between input and response is broad. In the second task, the length of the response is short, there is no input in language form, the language of the response is not highly organized, and it is in informal register, and the scope of relationship between input and response is narrow. Thus, focusing only on the difference between the so-called "skills" (speaking versus writing) misses much that goes into distinguishing between these two language use tasks. That is, it suggests that the names of skills alone are insufficient to define the critical characteristics of language use tasks.

Another reason for not including a specific "skill" in the construct definition is that many language use tasks involve more than one "skill." For example, what Widdowson (1978) calls the communicative ability of "conversation" involves listening and speaking, while what he calls "correspondence" involves reading and writing. Therefore, rather than defining a construct in terms of "skills," we suggest that the construct definition include only the relevant components of language ability, and that the "skill" elements be specified as characteristics of the tasks in which language ability is demonstrated.

Finally, on a practical level, when we define a construct as a skill, such as "speaking ability," and raters are told to rate test takers' speaking ability, the raters almost always ask, "What are we to look for in the speaking?" (This is the same problem we face when rating performance solely on ability to perform tasks, as discussed above.) Our answers to their questions take us immediately back to areas of language knowledge, such as "knowledge of grammar" (in speaking), or "knowledge of formal register" (in speaking), or "knowledge of instrumental function" (in speaking), or "knowledge of the sound system" (in speaking). We have, therefore, decided that construct definitions stated in terms of skills only are not useful for the purposes of language assessment.

In summary, if we define constructs either as performance on tasks or as "skills," we create problems with both scoring and interpretations. Our approach is to define all constructs in terms of the components of language ability, as we have defined these in Chapter 3. Such construct definitions form the basis for producing a record from the test taker's performance, from which interpretations of ability can be made.

An illustrative example: airline passengers' performance on a task

The following example illustrates the differences among two different approaches to defining the construct to be assessed: defining it in terms of language knowledge, language knowledge and strategic competence, language ability, and performance of tasks, as these were described above. In this example, we contrast the performances of four types of language users in completing a single language use task. The task is one of checking in at an airport ticket counter and changing their seat assignment, if possible. All four types are eventually able to complete the task. The following are descriptions of the four types of passenger and the four approaches to defining the constructs used to assess the passengers' performance.

Types of passenger

Passenger 1:	Native speaker: speaks a lot, but inefficiently; overloads employee with information that employee cannot process.
Passenger 2:	Non-native speaker: speaks a lot but inefficiently; overloads employee with information that employee cannot process, numerous errors in grammar.
Passenger 3:	Native speaker: speaks little but highly efficiently; provides only information needed to accomplish task
Passenger 4:	Non-native speaker: speaks little but highly efficiently; provides only information needed to accomplish task; numerous errors in grammar.

Approaches to construct definition

Construct definition A:	*Language knowledge and strategic competence* (two constructs)
Construct definition B:	*Language ability*: language knowledge and strategic competence (single construct)
Construct definition C:	*Language knowledge only*: knowledge of grammar is used for this example (single construct)
Construct definition D:	*Effectiveness in performing the task* (single construct)

In Table 11.1 we illustrate how the four types of passenger would be rated on scales developed in light of the four approaches to construct definition listed above.

	Type of construct definition			
	Single construct: Language knowledge (LK) (e.g., knowledge of grammar)	*Two constructs*: 1 Language knowledge (LK) 2 Strategic competence (SC)	*Single construct*: Language ability (language knowledge and strategic competence)	*Single construct*: Efficiency in completing the task
	Scales			
	Scale: grammar (low, mid, high)	Scales Grammar: (low, mid, high) SC: (low, mid, high)	low mid high	low mid high
	Ratings and interpretations			
Passenger 1	high	LK: high SC: low	mid	low
Passenger 2	low	LK: low SC: low	low	low
Passenger 3	high	LK: high SC: high	high	high
Passenger 4	low	LK: mid SC: high	mid	high

Table 11.1 Ratings of performance on scales consistent with four approaches to construct definitions

When we examine the possible ratings using the four approaches to construct definition, we see that the more narrowly the construct or constructs are defined (as is the case with Approaches A and B), the easier it is for the test user to interpret the reported ratings. The reported ratings for Approach C are subject to multiple interpretations because the test user cannot distinguish between the performance of passenger Types 2 and 4. Reported ratings for Approach D cannot be used to provide any information about what abilities the test takers bring to their performance on the assessment task.

Backing from the assessment development process for Kindergarten and University examples

For the Kindergarten example, the conditions under which performance is elicited, from which the teacher can make interpretations about letter formation, concepts of print, and oral language, are described in the course text and teacher's lesson plan. They consist of the instructions and materials for conducting the instructional tasks, which are also used for assessment purposes.

Warrant A2

Generic version of Warrant A2: The assessment task specifications clearly specify the conditions under which we will observe or elicit performance from which we can make inferences about the construct we intend to assess.

Adapted Warrant A2 for the Kindergarten example: The assessment task specifications clearly specify that the instructor will observe performance of selected students during the interactive writing activity and will record this in a checklist, from which the instructor can make interpretations about letter formation, concepts of print, and oral language.

Adapted Warrant A2 for the University example: The assessment task specifications clearly specify that the test takers will read a passage taken from an introductory academic text and then complete an incomplete outline that represents the rhetorical organization of this passage.

Discussion

This warrant states that conditions under which performance is observed or elicited need to be explicitly described in terms of assessment task specifications (the setting, input, expected response, relationship between input and response) and the recording method. This explicit description is needed for several reasons. First, "knowledge" (as defined in construct definitions such as "knowledge of multilevel rhetorical organization of introductory university academic reading passages") is not directly observable. We cannot look inside the brain and observe "knowledge of rhetorical organization." We can only *infer* interpretations about test takers' knowledge from our observance of their performance on assessment tasks. Since test takers' performance will depend not only on what they know but also on what they do to provide evidence of this knowledge, it is essential that these characteristics of assessment tasks be explicitly described. Second, during the Operationalization stage, a number of different assessment tasks could be developed to assess a given construct; so task specifications are needed to specify which of the many possible alternatives will be included in the assessment. In the University example, a number of different tasks, such as an outline completion task, a composition revision task, or a self-rating, could be developed to measure the construct "knowledge of multilevel rhetorical organization of written texts." Thus, the task specifications provided in the University example distinguish the outline completion task from other possible tasks.

In summary, unless the conditions under which performance is to be observed or elicited are clearly specified, there is no way we can begin to argue for the meaningfulness of the interpretations about components of language ability that are based on performance on assessment tasks.

Warrant A3

Generic version of Warrant A3: The procedures for administering the assessment enable test takers to perform at their highest level on the ability to be assessed.

Adapted Warrant A3 for the Kindergarten example: Not needed, because the assessment is not administered. Performance on an instructional task is simply observed.

Adapted Warrant A3 for the University example: The procedures for administering the incomplete outline test enable the test takers to perform at their highest level on the ability "knowledge of multilevel rhetorical organization of written texts."

Backing from the assessment development process for Kindergarten and University examples

For the Kindergarten example backing is not needed, since the warrant itself is not needed.

For the University example the procedures for administering the outline reading test include providing an opportunity for the test takers to work with a practice version of the test. The administrative procedures were developed to provide the test takers with ample time to complete the task. The testing environment is one with which the test takers are familiar and feel comfortable. Every attempt is made to eliminate possible sources of distraction.

Discussion

When we use a language assessment we are not interested in how test takers perform on the assessment, but rather in what their assessment performance tells us about their language ability. In most language testing situations, we are interested in knowing test takers' capacity for language use, that is, what their highest level of ability is. For this reason, we want to develop assessment tasks that will enable test takers to perform at their highest level of ability.[2]

Warrant A4

Generic version of Warrant A4: The procedures for producing an assessment record focus on those aspects of the performance that are relevant to the construct we intend to assess.

Adapted Warrant A4 for the Kindergarten example: The observation checklist and procedures for using it focus on letter formation, concepts of print, and oral language. These aspects of the performance are identical to the knowledge component of the learning objectives for this lesson in the syllabus.

Adapted Warrant A4 for the University example: The scoring key and procedures for using the key focus on elements of multilevel outline structure that, in essence, define the construct "knowledge of multilevel rhetorical organization of written texts."

Backing from the assessment development process for Kindergarten and University examples

The kindergarten teacher was trained in procedures for producing observation checklists, including the one in this lesson that focuses on components of constructs emphasized in language lessons. He used his training and experience in producing the observation focusing on letter formation, concepts of print, and oral language checklist and using it.

For the University example, the scoring key consists of ways of filling in the gaps in the incomplete outline considered to be consistent with good outlining practice. The procedures for scoring the test involve mechanically comparing the test takers' responses with the responses on the scoring key. In case a test taker response appears to be correct even though not included in the key, the members of the scoring team discuss whether or not it should be added to the scoring key. We would note that even if automated scoring procedures were used, some sort of scoring key would have to be developed. All these procedures and the rest of the detail in the task specifications provide backing for the warrant.

Discussion

Test developers must also be able to demonstrate that the way performance is recorded (the recording method) will yield information relevant to interpreting the construct. Both the recording method and, if the record is a score, the criteria for correctness must be appropriate for obtaining the desired information. This is because even if the test taker's performance could provide evidence of the ability to be assessed, the recording method might not focus on this, and thus might not be sensitive to this.

For example, suppose we wanted to assess the construct "knowledge of rhetorical organization," and have access to test takers' scores on a commercially available writing test used to admit students to a university. The rating procedures (e.g., multiple trained raters using a rubric) might be appropriate, but the rating criteria (e.g., "control of grammar") might not be relevant to the construct.

Backing for this warrant might consist of evidence that the scoring criteria and procedures were reviewed by experts and found to be appropriate for making interpretations about the construct. In the backing for Warrant A4, we should try to anticipate rebuttals to the effect that the scoring criteria and procedures do not focus on those aspects of the performance that are relevant to the construct we intend to assess. If we think that such rebuttals are likely to be made by stakeholders, we need to invest more resources in providing backing than would be the case if we do not anticipate such rebuttals.

Warrant A5

Generic version of Warrant A5: Assessment tasks engage the ability defined in the construct definition.

Adapted Warrant A5 for the Kindergarten example: The assessment tasks engage the "knowledge of (a) letter formation, (b) concepts of print, and (c) oral language."

Adapted Warrant A5 for the University example: The incomplete outline task engages the "knowledge of multilevel rhetorical organization in written texts."

Backing from the assessment development process for Kindergarten and University examples

For the Kindergarten example the instructor used instructional tasks as assessment tasks to elicit the abilities described in the construct definitions. The instructor also carefully monitored students' responses to the assessment tasks in order to assure that these were engaging the abilities he wanted to assess.

During the development and trialing of the incomplete outline task for the University reading test, test developers and instructors observed test takers as they completed the task. In addition, test developers elicited verbal protocols ("think-aloud") from test takers while they were completing the task.

Discussion

When we select a task to measure one or more components of language ability, it is important to consider the potential of the task for engaging the specific components of language ability we want to assess. We start with a construct definition as a component of language ability and then try to develop a task that we believe is likely to engage this construct. The University reading test is a good example of this because the task was developed specifically to engage the construct "knowledge of multilevel rhetorical organization in written texts." Since the task requires test takers to complete an outline of the rhetorical structure of the reading passage, the test developer believed that this task had a high potential for engaging the construct to be measured.

However, just believing that an assessment task engages the ability to be assessed is not enough evidence to support this warrant. In addition, the test developer needs to collect evidence that the task actually engages the ability to be assessed. This can be done in a variety of ways, such as observing test takers as they complete the task, and eliciting verbal protocols from test takers, either as they complete the task, or shortly after they have completed the task. (The use of verbal protocols is discussed in detail in Chapter 16.)

Warrant A6

Generic version of Warrant A6: Assessment records can be interpreted as indicators of the ability to be assessed.

Adapted Warrant A6 for the Kindergarten example: The instructor's notes on student performance on instructional tasks are interpreted as indicators of "knowledge of (a) letter formation, (b) concepts of print, and (c) oral language."

Adapted Warrant A6 for the University example: Scores on the incomplete outline test are interpreted as "knowledge of multilevel rhetorical organization of written texts."

Backing from the assessment development process : Kindergarten and University examples

The Kindergarten teacher has a great deal of experience observing his students' performance and making notes that he can interpret as indicators of his students' abilities.

Instructors in introductory university classes examined preliminary versions of the test and interpretations of records for students who took the test during the development process. These instructors indicated that test-based interpretations of the construct "knowledge of multilevel rhetorical structure" generally agreed with their own appraisal of students' knowledge of this construct. They also indicated that these interpretations differed from their impressions of other aspects of language ability for the students in question.

Discussion

Even if we can argue that an assessment task engages the ability we want to assess, we are not yet home free, for we still have to be able to support the claim that the assessment reports based on test takers' performance can be interpreted as indicators of the ability to be assessed. Backing from the development process can be obtained fairly easily. One way to do so is to ask stakeholders, such as teachers who are familiar with the test takers, whether their impressions of the test takers' language ability is consistent with interpretations made on the basis of the assessment under development (evidence of convergence). Similarly, the same stakeholders could be asked whether interpretations made on the basis of the assessment under development provide information different from other information they may have about other aspects of the test takers' language ability. If records of test takers' performance on the assessments are available, interpretations from these records can be compared with those from the assessment under development to see if they appear to provide different information.

Additional backing for this warrant could be obtained from statistical analyses of test takers' performance that are conducted as a part of the justification process. This kind of evidence is obtained from fairly complex studies that require fairly extensive resources, and is likely to be limited to high-stakes assessments or assessments used in research studies. (See Chapter 16 and the Suggested Readings there for a discussion of some of these analyses.)

Warrant A7

Generic version of Warrant A7: The test developer communicates the definition of the construct to be assessed in terms that are clearly understandable to all stakeholders.

Adapted Warrant A7 for the Kindergarten example: The teacher provides informal verbal feedback to students in terms they will understand.

Adapted Warrant A7 for the University example: The ESL Program Director communicates the definition of the construct in non-technical language via the instructions for the outline completion task and examples of multilevel outlines. The construct definition is also included in non-technical language in the assessment report for test takers and other stakeholders.

Backing from the assessment development process for Kindergarten and University examples

For the Kindergarten example, the teacher who developed this assessment has had a lot of experience providing feedback to students at this level. For the University example, the definition of the construct and illustrative examples were developed in consultation with several test takers and incorporated into the instructions for the test. In addition, the tests themselves show how the construct is defined and how this definition is communicated to the test takers.

QUESTION 10

"How can we assure that the interpretations of ability are impartial for all groups of stakeholders?"

The argument for impartiality of interpretations is established on the basis of five warrants: B1–B5.

> **Warrant B1**
>
> *Generic version of Warrant B1*: The assessment tasks do not include response formats or content that may either favor or disfavor some test takers.
>
> *Adapted Warrant B1 for the Kindergarten example*: The interactive writing activity is a task that the teacher uses for instruction, and does not include response formats or content that may either favor or disfavor some kindergarten students.
>
> *Adapted Warrant B1 for the University example*: The outline completion task does not include response formats or content that may either favor or disfavor some test takers.

Backing from the assessment development process for Kindergarten and University examples

For the Kindergarten example, the response formats and content for the interactive writing task are taken directly from the instructional tasks, which have been developed specifically for the kinds of students in the kindergarten class.

For the University example, the response format (filling in the blanks in a incomplete outline) may not be familiar to all students. Therefore, a tutorial is used to familiarize all test takers with this format prior to their taking the test. The content of the reading passage upon which the incomplete outline task is based is taken from texts in introductory level courses in the university, and is thus deemed not to be unduly technical, abstruse, or recondite for test takers.

Discussion

Response formats that are not familiar to some test takers may disfavor these test takers and perhaps result in poor performance that is not due to lack of the ability being measured. If this is the case, poor performance on the assessments will be difficult to interpret. Similarly, if the topical content of the assessment is familiar to some test takers, they may be advantaged, while test takers not familiar with the topical content may be disadvantaged.

If test developers have reason to believe that the format of the assessment may favor or disfavor some test takers, they need to provide test takers with an opportunity to develop enough familiarity with the formats to demonstrate whatever ability is being measured. The test developers also need to consult with content specialists and course instructors to assure that the topical content of the assessment does not favor or disfavor some test takers. (See the discussion of topical content below, under warrants of generalizability.)

Warrant B2

Generic version of Warrant B2: The assessment tasks do not include content that may be offensive (topically, culturally, or linguistically inappropriate) to some test takers.

Adapted Warrant B2 for the Kindergarten example: The interactive writing activity does not include content that may be offensive to some kindergarten students.

Adapted Warrant B2 for the University example: The outline completion task does not include content that may be offensive to some test takers.

Backing from the assessment development process for Kindergarten and University examples

The instructional tasks used for assessment purposes are taken from instructional materials developed for kindergarten students and involve content appropriate to these students.

The reading passages in the University assessment tasks are taken from introductory university texts, which contain content considered appropriate for students by the publishers of these texts.

Discussion

Assessment tasks that include content that is offensive to test takers may disfavor these test takers and perhaps result in poor performance not attributable to lack of the ability being measured, in which case poor performance on the assessments will be difficult to interpret. For example, test takers asked to write an essay about a civil war taking place in their country of origin might find it difficult to prevent their emotions from overwhelming their ability to write as well as they might otherwise be able to do. Test developers need to be sensitive to this possibility and take steps to determine whether this is, in fact, a problem that needs to be addressed. Test developers can ask teams of relevant stakeholders to conduct bias reviews of assessment tasks to help assure that the content is appropriate for all test takers.

Warrant B3

Generic version of Warrant B3: The procedures for producing an assessment record are clearly described in terms that are understandable to all test takers.

Adapted Warrant B3 for the Kindergarten example: This warrant is not needed because the assessment record is not made available to the test takers.

Adapted Warrant B3 for the University example: The procedures for producing an assessment record for the incomplete outline test are clearly described in terms that are understandable to all test takers.

Backing from the assessment development process for Kindergarten and University examples

For the Kindergarten example, backing is not needed, since this warrant is not needed.

For the University example, the procedures for producing an assessment record, including the scoring procedures, are described on the website. The wording of the description of the procedures was reviewed by a number of test takers, as well as members of the test development team.

Discussion

In many assessment situations, test takers will expect to be informed of how a record of their performance will be produced. A description of these procedures would typically be included either in the assessment report or in an interpretive manual for assessment users. This would describe how test takers' performance is scored or described and, possibly, how decisions are made on the basis of these scores or descriptions. The language of this description needs to be appropriate for the test takers to whom it is addressed.

Warrant B4

Generic version of Warrant B4: Individuals are treated impartially during all aspects of the administration of the assessment: registering for the assessment and taking the assessment.

(a) Individuals have equal access to information about the assessment content and assessment procedures, and for achievement and certification decisions have equal opportunity to prepare.
(b) Individuals have equal access to the assessment, in terms of cost, location, and familiarity with conditions and equipment.
(c) Individuals have equal opportunity to demonstrate the ability to be assessed.

Adapted Warrant B4 for the Kindergarten example: Kindergarten students are treated impartially while the teacher observes their performance on the interactive writing activity.

(a–c) Not needed. Only minimal documentation is required for this very low-stakes assessment, and the teacher's reputation for fair concern for his students and fair play will suffice.

Adapted Warrant B4 for the University example:

(a) Test takers have equal access to information about the incomplete outline test content and assessment procedures.
(b) Test takers have equal access to the university reading test, in terms of cost, location, and familiarity with conditions and equipment.
(c) Test takers have equal opportunity to demonstrate their knowledge of multilevel rhetorical organization in written texts.

Backing from the assessment development process for Kindergarten and University examples

For the low-stakes Kindergarten example, the students are simply observed performing learning tasks, and there is no opportunity to treat them differently, so sub-warrants (a–c) do not need to be stated.

For the higher-stakes University example, backing for sub-warrants (a–c) is needed.

(a) A description of the assessment content and procedures, as well as an assessment tutorial, are posted on the ESL program website and appropriate links to this website provided. Academic advisors are instructed to provide this information to students needing to take the exam. Achievement and certification decisions are not involved, so opportunity to prepare is not relevant.

(b) The assessment is given on multiple occasions prior to registering for the ESL reading course. The test is administered by computer at the University Testing Center under familiar conditions at no cost to test takers.

(c) The test is always measured to all test takers under similar conditions.

Discussion

Warrant B4 addresses three considerations that affect the impartiality of interpretations: comparability of access to information about the assessment, comparability of access to the assessment itself, and comparable opportunity to demonstrate the ability to be assessed. In the real world, completely equal access to information about the assessment is often very difficult to achieve, particularly in large-scale assessments that may be administered in many different countries and under conditions that may also be very different. Even in assessments that are administered in a single setting, there may be some concern among stakeholders about the considerations addressed in Warrant B4. In the University example, the ESL reading instructors may want assurance that the exam will be offered at times and places that are convenient for the students, and that it not be too long as to be burdensome.

Warrant B5

Generic version of Warrant B5: Interpretations of the ability to be assessed are equally meaningful across different groups of test takers.

Adapted Warrant B5 for the Kindergarten example: Interpretations of the test takers' "knowledge of (a) letter formation, (b) concepts of print, and (c) their oral language" are equally meaningful across students from different linguistic/ethnic groups.

Adapted Warrant B5 for the University example: Interpretations of the test takers' "knowledge of multilevel rhetorical organization of written texts" are equally meaningful across students from different first language backgrounds and academic disciplines.

Backing from the assessment development process for Kindergarten and University examples

None. The only backing for this warrant comes from the statistical analysis of test scores based on trialing and use of the tests. (See Chapter 19 for a discussion of collecting backing during trialing and use of tests.)

QUESTION 11: GENERALIZABILITY

"How can we assure that the interpretation of language ability *generalizes* to the TLU domain of the decision?"

The test developer articulates two warrants—C1 and C2—to elaborate the claim that the interpretation generalizes to the TLU domain.

Warrant C1

Generic version of Warrant C1: The characteristics of the setting, rubric, input, expected response, and relationship between input and expected response of the assessment tasks correspond closely to those of TLU tasks.

Adapted Warrant C1 for the Kindergarten example: Not needed.

Adapted Warrant C1 for the University example: The characteristics of the outline completion task correspond closely to those of tasks of reading introductory academic texts both in the academic domain (introductory level university courses) and in the language teaching domain (the ESL reading course).

Backing from the assessment development process for Kindergarten and University examples

For the Kindergarten example, backing for Warrant C1 is not needed because the TLU and assessment tasks are identical. The students are assessed while they are being taught.

For the incomplete outline test, the reading passages were taken directly from actual reading passages used in introductory level course texts that were judged by faculty and teachers to be appropriate for university students. Thus, the characteristics of this part of the input corresponded very closely with characteristics of the input in relevant TLU tasks. Characteristics of the incomplete outline correspond to characteristics of an outline that the test takers might see when provided with such outlines in their academic courses, except for the fact that portions of the outline are replaced by blanks. Characteristics of the expected response (completing an outline that one has started) correspond to one common way of studying a reading passage (by outlining it).

Discussion

As we discussed in Chapter 5, the domain of generalization is a set of language use tasks in the TLU domain to which the assessment tasks correspond. In Chapter 4, we noted there are two general types of TLU domains that are relevant to the development of language assessment tasks: language teaching domains and real life domains. Thus, in specifying the TLU domain, the test developers and stakeholders will need to decide which of these domains to focus on. When the test takers are not participating in any language classes, the real life domain will obviously be the only one of interest. However, when test takers are students in a language course while also needing to use the language to perform language use tasks in the real world, a major consideration is that of determining the relevance of these two domains to students' target language use needs.

In one type of situation, the tasks in the language-teaching domain may correspond closely to those in the relevant real life domain, in which case the test developer can use tasks in either the language teaching domain or the real life domain, or both, as a basis for developing assessment tasks. For example, suppose you were asked to develop classroom achievement tests for a course in "survival English" for immigrants. Suppose further that the teaching and learning tasks in this course included practicing dialogs, the content of which was based upon tasks in the real life domain: "survival" situations in the community. In this situation, the characteristics of test tasks patterned after characteristics of the instructional dialog tasks in the language teaching domain could also closely resemble the characteristics of the tasks in the real life domain.

In another type of situation, there may be a lack of clear correspondence between the characteristics of tasks in the language teaching and real life domains. Suppose, for example, that you were asked to develop an achievement test for a course in which instructional tasks do not correspond at all to tasks in the relevant real life domain. In situations such as this, it might be useful to discuss this lack of correspondence with various stakeholders, including the Program Director, teachers, and students, in order to determine what the relevant TLU domain for the achievement test should be.

When the test developer articulates warrants for the generalizability of assessment-based interpretations of language ability to the TLU domain, she does so by listing the specific characteristics of the TLU tasks and assessment tasks. She then compares these to determine which they have in common, and which ones differ. This comparison shows how similar the assessment and TLU tasks are. Backing for the generalizability Warrant (C1) thus consists of evidence of the degree to which characteristics of the assessment task correspond to characteristics of tasks in the TLU domain. (The process of examining the characteristics of TLU tasks and different approaches to developing assessment tasks with similar characteristics is discussed in detail in Chapters 14 and 15.)

Warrant C2

Generic version of Warrant C2: The criteria and procedures for recording the responses to the assessment tasks correspond closely to those that are typically used by language users in assessing performance in TLU tasks

Adapted Warrant C2 for the Kindergarten example: The way the assessment record is obtained is the same for the assessment tasks and instructional tasks.

Adapted Warrant C2 for the University example: The criteria and procedures for evaluating the responses to the outline completion task correspond closely to those that are typically used by teachers in assessing performance in reading introductory academic texts.

Backing from the assessment development process for Kindergarten and University examples

The kindergarten teacher follows the same procedure for both the assessment and instructional tasks.

University instructors in introductory level courses were consulted, and they stated that they evaluated test takers' ability to read introductory academic texts by means of a variety of traditional assessments, as well as observation of instructional tasks such as in-class discussions of material introduced in texts. They also agreed that the use of an incomplete outline to assess ability to read and understand academic texts made sense.

Discussion

Criteria

The focus here is on the criteria for evaluating responses to assessment tasks, such as grammatical correctness, meaningfulness, phonological accuracy, and accuracy of vocabulary use. The backing consists of a comparison of the criteria that are used for the assessment tasks with the criteria that stakeholders use for assessing performance in TLU tasks. For example, suppose an assessment is used to make hiring decisions for a job in which the individuals doing the hiring tell us that control of formal register in writing is important and they look for evidence of this in their employees' writing. We would want the criteria used to evaluate responses to a writing assessment to include "control of formal register in writing." If, for some reason, performance on the assessment task were rated only on grammatical accuracy, the criteria for evaluating responses on the assessment task would not reflect the concerns of the individuals making the hiring decisions.

Procedures for producing an assessment record

The focus here is on the correspondence of the procedures used to record responses to assessment tasks: when the recording will take place, where it will take place, and in what sequence the steps in recording will be followed. Backing consists of a demonstration that the procedures followed are those that stakeholders have identified as important for assessing performance in TLU tasks. In the same example as used above, employee supervisors typically evaluate employees' correspondence by reading samples of correspondence on a regular basis and discussing potential problems with a second supervisor. If, for some reason, the procedures for evaluating responses to the assessment task involve having someone unfamiliar with company expectations reviewing responses to assessment tasks on his own and counting the number of errors, the procedures for evaluating responses on the assessment task would be quite different from those used by supervisors evaluating employees' performance on TLU tasks.

QUESTION 12

"How can we assure that our interpretations about test takers' language are *relevant* to the decision?"

We answer this question by articulating warrant D.

Warrant D

Generic version of Warrant D: The assessment-based interpretations provide information that is relevant to the decisions to be made. That is, the information provided in the interpretation is helpful for the decision makers to make decisions.

Adapted Warrant D for the Kindergarten example: Interpretations about (a) letter formation, (b) concepts of print, and (c) oral language provide information that is relevant to the teacher's decisions about instruction.

Adapted Warrant D for the University example: The interpretation "knowledge of multilevel rhetorical organization in written texts" provides the information that is relevant to the ESL program director's decisions about placement or exemption.

Backing from the assessment development process for Kindergarten and University examples

The instructional objectives for the Kindergarten assessment include knowledge of (a) letter formation, (b) concepts of print, and (c) oral language. The teacher, who is the decision maker in this case, states that interpretations of these areas of language knowledge are relevant to making decisions about instruction.

For the University example the needs analysis referred to above identified "knowledge of multilevel rhetorical organization in written texts" as relevant to student success in their courses. The course director, who is the decision maker in this case, finds scores on the assessment to be useful for making decisions about placement or exemption.

Discussion

As we discussed in Chapter 5, relevance is the degree to which the interpretation provides the information the decision maker needs to make a decision. Some ways to establish this include discussions with major stakeholders (especially the decision makers), consultation with experts with training in making similar decisions, and reviews of publications dealing with decision making in similar situations. Moreover, assessment developers should expect rebuttals to the effect that the interpretations are not relevant to the decisions and be prepared to defend their choice of interpretations.

For example, suppose the manager of a department store wanted to make decisions about whether or not to hire clerks to interact with customers and wanted to use a test of language ability to obtain some of the information needed to make this decision. The manager might have a sample of customers, other clerks, and supervisors view videotaped examples of L2 speaking clerks interacting with customers. These stakeholders might be asked to comment on those areas of language ability that would be relevant to hiring decisions, and the assessment developers could include these in an assessment used to help make these decisions.

QUESTION 13

"How can we assure that our interpretation about test takers' language ability provides sufficient information to make the decisions?"

We answer this question by articulating Warrant E—the sufficiency warrant—and the associated rebuttals.

Warrant E

Generic version of Warrant E: The assessment-based interpretation provides sufficient information to make the required decisions. That is, there is enough information in the interpretation for the decision makers to make the decision.

Adapted Warrant E for the Kindergarten example: Interpretations about (a) letter formation, (b) concepts of print, and (c) oral language provide enough information for the teacher to make decisions about instruction.

Adapted Warrant E for the University example: The assessment-based interpretation of "knowledge of multilevel rhetorical organization of written texts" provides sufficient information to make the placement/exemption decisions.

Backing from the assessment development process for Kindergarten and University examples

The kindergarten teacher is highly experienced and knows what information he needs to make his decisions about instruction.

As part of the University assessment development process, the test developers consulted with the ESL teachers and teachers in introductory level academic courses as to what interpretations(s) about the test takers' language ability would provide sufficient information to make the placement/exemption decisions. Three different abilities were proposed and defined: knowledge of multilevel rhetorical organization of written texts, ability to draw interpretations from academic prose, and ability to read academic prose critically.

Of these constructs, most of the teachers agreed that knowledge of multilevel rhetorical organization of written texts was crucial, for without this knowledge students would not be able to organize the information in their readings, and without being able to organize it, they wouldn't be able to remember it. In addition, the teachers thought that outlining was an important study tool for students in their courses, so measuring knowledge of multilevel rhetorical organization of written texts would, as a measure of reading comprehension, also provide information about the students knowledge of strategy for studying.

A few of the teachers also thought that information about students' ability to read critically and ability to draw inferences would be necessary to make the placement/exemption decisions, but others thought that this was something that students would learn in the introductory level courses and that it did not need to be measured prior to registering in these courses. As a result, the test developers decided to start by measuring only knowledge of multilevel rhetorical organization of written texts and collect information to see whether additional information was needed or not.

Plans for collecting this information included tracking students exempted from the ESL reading course and asking their teachers in introductory level academic courses to rate and comment on these students' readiness to do the readings in their courses. Plans also included sending questionnaires to exempted students asking them to comment on their preparedness.

Discussion: sufficiency

As we indicated in Chapter 5, the information is sufficient (1) when the decisions that are made on the basis of this information fall within the decision maker's tolerance for classification errors (false positives and negatives) and (2) when the coherence of the AUA and the quality of the backing is convincing to major stakeholders. There is no "objective" way to determine when information is sufficient or insufficient to make decisions. However, a number of different considerations will affect the extent to which stakeholders may believe that the information used to make decisions is sufficient or insufficient. These include the scope of the construct, the stakeholders, limitations on resources, and the decision makers' tolerance for uncertainty. The nature of the stakeholders, limitations on resources, and uncertainty in the assessment situation are all discussed in Chapter 6 above. Here we will discuss the scope of the construct.

Deciding that information is sufficient means, in effect, that the scope of the construct is sufficiently wide to make the needed decisions. If information is insufficient, the scope of the construct measured is too narrow and must be widened. In the University example, suppose the test developers had decided that measuring the construct defined as "knowledge of multilevel rhetorical organization of written texts" did not provide sufficient information to make placement/exemption decisions, since there were too many false positives, that is, students who were exempted from the reading course but later had difficulties in their academic courses because of poor reading. The stakeholders and decision makers may have reason to believe that if "knowledge of ability to draw inferences from introductory university academic reading passages" were also measured, this additional information would reduce the number of false positives and thus be sufficient for making the decision. This could be accomplished by widening the scope of the construct to define it as "knowledge of multilevel rhetorical organization of *and* ability to draw inferences from introductory university academic reading passages" and then measuring this construct with a single score or rating.

Widening the scope of the construct can also be accomplished by increasing the *number* of constructs measured. In the University example, the scope of the construct could have been widened by defining two constructs (organizational knowledge and knowledge of inferences). A separate report could then have been obtained for each of these constructs, and both reports could have been used in some specified way to make the needed placement/exemption decisions.

EXERCISES

1 Find manuals for some language tests on-line. Locate the construct definitions and characterize these definitions in terms of the following considerations: frame of reference, role of strategic competence, role of topical knowledge, performance on tasks, "skills" as the construct.
2 Think of some tests you have developed or used. Characterize these definitions in terms of the following considerations: frame of reference, role of strategic competence, role of topical knowledge, performance on tasks, "skills" as the construct.
3 Look through the construct definitions in the example Projects on the web (http://www.oup.com/LAIP). Classify each of these construct definitions in terms of the considerations listed in Exercise 1 above.
4 Read through the manuals for some published tests or tests available on-line. In what cases do the manuals specify the conditions under which one will observe or elicit performance from which one can make inferences about the construct one intends to assess?

5 Think of a test you have developed or used. Go through each of the *meaningfulness* warrants that could be articulated for this test and evaluate the degree to which each of these warrants could be used to justify the use of the test. Do you find anything that might lead you to question the meaningfulness of the interpretations?
6 Think of a test you have developed or used. Go through each of the *impartiality* warrants that could be articulated for this test and evaluate the degree to which each of these warrants could be used to justify the use of the test. Do you find anything that might lead you to question the impartiality of the interpretations?
7 Think of a test you have developed or used. Go through each of the *generalizability* warrants that could be articulated for this test and evaluate the degree to which each of these warrants could be used to justify the use of the test. Do you find anything that might lead you to question the generalizability of the interpretations?
8 Think of a test you have developed or used. Go through each of the *relevance* warrants that could be articulated for this test and evaluate the degree to which each of these warrants could be used to justify the use of the test. Do you find anything that might lead you to question the relevance of the interpretations?
9 Think of a test you have developed or used. Go through each of the *sufficiency* warrants that could be articulated for this test and evaluate the degree to which each of these warrants could be used to justify the use of the test. Do you find anything that might lead you to question the sufficiency of the interpretations for making the intended decisions?

SUGGESTED READINGS

Brown, J. D., T. Hudson, J. M. Norris, and W. J. Bonk. 2002. *An investigation of second language task-based performance assessments* (Vol. SLTCC Technical Report 24). Honolulu: Second Language Teaching & Curriculum Center, University of Hawai'i at Manoa.

Douglas, D. 2000. *Assessing Language for Specific Purposes: Theory and Practice*. Cambridge: Cambridge University Press.

Hudson, T. and **J. D. Brown** (eds.). 2001. *A focus on language test development*. Honolulu: Second Language Teaching & Curriculum Center, University of Hawai'i at Manoa.

McNamara, T. F. 1996. *Measuring Second Language Performance*. London: Longman.

Norris, J. M., J. D. Brown, T. Hudson, and **J. Yoshioka.** 1998. *Designing second language performance assessments* (Vol. SLTCC Technical Report #18). Honolulu: Second Language Teaching & Curriculum Center, University of Hawai'i at Manoa.

NOTES

1 Douglas (2000) defines "specific purpose language ability" as a combination of language ability and topical knowledge.
2 Swain (1985) referred to this as "bias for the best."

12

Assessment records

INTRODUCTION

In Chapters 9–11 we described the claims and warrants that pertain to the intended beneficial consequences of using the assessment, the decisions that we need to make in order to realize these beneficial consequences, and the components of language ability that we intend to assess. Some of the information that we articulate in Claims 1, 2, and 3 and their supporting warrants will become part of the Design Statement, and some of this information will become part of the Blueprint. The last claim in the AUA is Claim 4 and it has to do with the assessment records and the quality, *consistency*, that we will claim of those records. In this chapter we go through the process of articulating Claim 4 and its associated warrants about the assessment records that we obtain on the basis of test takers' performance on the assessment.

Using the same approach we used in Chapters 9–11, we will work through the Kindergarten and University examples to illustrate this process. In presenting these examples we work through Questions 14 and 15 of Table 8.2 in Chapter 8 and show how the process of articulating the claims and warrants providing backing addresses these two final questions.

In articulating Claim 4 and its accompanying warrants, we will draw on the information provided in the warrants supporting Claim 3. In particular, we will draw on the definition of the construct to be assessed that is articulated in Warrant A1, the assessment task specifications in Warrant 2, and the recording procedures specified in Warrant A3.

QUESTION 14
"How will we assure that the assessment records are consistent?"

We begin answering Question 14 by articulating Claim 4 and Warrants 1–9.

Claim 4

Generic version of Claim 4: Assessment records (scores, descriptions) are **consistent** across different assessment tasks, different aspects of the assessment procedure, and across different groups of test takers.

Adapted version of Claim 4 for Kindergarten example: The teacher's notes in his observation checklist are consistent across different lessons and different students, and across different classes of students.

Adapted version of Claim 4 for University example: The scores from the incomplete outline test are consistent across different forms and administrations of the test, across students from different academic disciplines, and across different groups of international students entering the university.

Discussion

When a test developer adapts Claim 4 to her specific assessment, she will state the specific procedures that will be used to elicit or observe test takers' performance. As we indicated above, these procedures will have been articulated in Claim 3, Warrants A2 and A3, and in the Blueprint, as well. The adapted claim will also specify the aspects of the particular assessment procedure and identify the particular groups of test takers that will be taking the assessment.

Warrants to Support Claim 4

Generic versions of Warrants 1–9:

1 Administrative procedures are followed consistently across different occasions, and for all test taker groups.
2 Procedures for producing the assessment records are well specified and are adhered to.
3 Raters undergo training and must be certified.
4 Raters are trained to avoid bias for or against different groups of test takers.
5 Scores on different tasks in the assessment are internally consistent (internal consistency reliability).

(*continued*)

6 Ratings of different raters are consistent (inter-rater reliability).
7 Different ratings by the same rater are consistent (intra-rater reliability).
8 Scores from different forms of the test are consistent (equivalence, or equivalent forms reliability).
9 Scores from different administrations of the test are consistent (stability, or test-retest reliability).

Adapted Warrants 1–9 for the Kindergarten example:

1 The teacher elicits students' performance consistently across different administrations of the interactive writing task, across different sections of the class, for all students.
2 Procedures for recording students' performances in the checklist are well specified and are adhered to.

Since the teacher does not assign scores, and since he is the only person who produces assessment reports, Warrants 3–9 are not relevant in the Kindergarten example.

Adapted Warrants 1–9 for the University example:

1 The incomplete outline test is administered in a standard way every time it is offered.
2 The scoring criteria and procedures for the computer scoring algorithm are well specified and are adhered to.
3 The computer scoring algorithm was developed through extensive trialing and comparison with multiple human ratings.
4 The computer scoring algorithm was developed through trialing with several different groups of test takers.
5 Scores on different items in the incomplete outline test are internally consistent.
6 Not needed, since performance is not rated.
7 Not needed, since performance is not rated.
8 Scores from different forms of the incomplete outline test are consistent.
9 Scores from different administrations of the incomplete outline test are consistent.

Backing from the assessment development process for Kindergarten and University examples, Warrants 1–2

Backing for Warrants 1 and 2 will be collected during the use of the assessment. This is discussed in Chapter 19.

Backing from the assessment development process for University example, Warrants 1–4

For the University example the backing will be in the form of project documentation, including the Design Statement, scoring criteria, and procedures. The same Blueprint is used to create multiple forms of the test. All parts of the Blueprint are specified, and have been followed in creating multiple forms of the test. Each item consists of a deleted portion of an outline. The reading passages used as input are selected according to specified criteria. The same procedures are used to create the scoring key for each form. The test is administered by computer, which never does anything differently. The scoring criteria are specified in an algorithm. The same algorithm is used to score all tests.

Backing for Warrants 5, 8, and 9 will be obtained from data collected as part of the tryout and use of the test. This is discussed in Chapter 19.

Discussion

As was discussed in Chapter 4, consistency is a quality of the assessment records (scores, verbal descriptions). **Consistency** is the extent to which test takers' performance on different assessments of the same construct yields essentially the same assessment records. A consistent assessment record will provide essentially the same information about the ability to be assessed across different aspects of the assessment procedure, such as different tasks, different times, or different raters or recorders. Warrants 1–4 pertain to procedures that the test development team follow as they develop the assessment. These procedures are aimed at achieving consistency in the administration of the assessment and in recording test takers' performance. Documentation that these procedures were followed provides backing for these warrants. Warrants 5–9 pertain to the consistency of score reports, and the backing to support these is collected during the trialing and assessment use stages of assessment development.

QUESTION 15

"How will we assure that the assessment records are of comparable consistency across different groups of test takers?"

The claim of consistency of assessment reports across different groups of test takers is supported by Warrant 10.

> **Warrant 10**
>
> *Generic version of Warrant 10*: Assessment records are of comparable consistency across different groups of test takers.
>
> *Adapted Warrant 10 for the Kindergarten example*: The teacher's notes on his observation sheet and checklist are consistent across different groups of students and across different classes.
>
> *Adapted Warrant 10 for the University example*: Scores on incomplete outline test are consistent across different groups of students.

Backing from design and development procedures for Kindergarten and University examples

Backing for Warrant 10 will be collected during the use of the assessment. This is discussed in Chapter 19.

For the University test backing for Warrant 10 will be obtained from data collected as part of the tryout and use of the test. This is discussed in Chapter 19.

Discussion

Warrant 10 addresses a fairness issue, because if assessment records are not equally consistent for different groups of test takers, then this raises serious questions about the comparability of these records for different groups of test takers. For example, suppose the scores on a test of lexical cohesion in a second language were found to be highly consistent for speakers of one native language. This might occur if the topical content of the test was very familiar to speakers of Language A, but unfamiliar to speakers of Language B, resulting in the latter group's guessing at many of the assessment tasks. The inconsistency of scores from speakers of Language B would suggest that their scores are due to factors other than their knowledge of lexical cohesion. This would thus provide evidence that rebuts Warrant 12. Since scores that are not consistent cannot be meaningful, then the lack of consistency of the scores for the second group also rebuts the warrants about the meaningfulness of the score-based interpretations.

With the end of this chapter, we conclude Part II of the book, in which we have described the process of constructing an Assessment Use Argument. We now move to Part III of the book, where we describe the process of developing and using language assessments in the real world.

EXERCISES

1 Think of an assessment you have taken or used. Go through consistency Warrants 1–4. To what extent do you think the test developers had each of these warrants in mind when developing the assessment? In what ways might the assessment be modified to increase the consistency of assessment records?

2 Think of an assessment you have taken or used. Articulate the adapted consistency claim and warrants for this assessment. Note which warrants may not apply to your assessment.

PART III

Developing and using language assessments in the real world

In this part of the book, we describe the process of assessment development and use as it takes place in the real world. The conceptual foundations we discussed in Part I and the Assessment Use Argument (AUA) that we discussed in Part II guide the activities of assessment development and use. In Part I (Chapters 2–5) we described some general considerations and frameworks that will guide the process of assessment development. In Part II (Chapters 6–12) we used these conceptual foundations to construct an AUA. In Part III we build on the conceptual foundations of Part I and the AUA of Part II to delineate some specific procedures for selecting or developing language assessments and for justifying their use. Because of the real world conditions and constraints within which we must work, we will inevitably be faced with trade-offs among the values that inform our particular test development and use. We believe that the procedures we describe in this part of the book provide the most effective way of making decisions and choices as we design assessments for the real world.

In Chapter 13 we discuss the uncertainties of the real world contexts in which language assessments are developed and used, and the kinds of constraints we face in the resources that we have at our disposal for developing and using language assessments. The remaining chapters in Part III are organized, in a very general way, according to the process of assessment development and use. Chapter 14 describes the activities that are conducted during the Design Stage, including the development of a Design Statement and the interaction between this and the articulation of an AUA. Chapters 15–18 describe the activities that are conducted during the Operationalization stage.

Chapter 15 discusses the activities involved in developing assessment tasks, Chapter 16 discusses the issues and considerations in developing procedures for recording assessment performance, Chapter 17 describes developing a Blueprint, or assessment specifications, and Chapter 18 describes preparing effective instructions. Chapter 19 provides an overview of activities conducted during the Trialing and Use stages for collecting feedback to modify the assessment and for providing backing to support the warrants in an AUA. Chapter 20 discusses considerations and procedures for identifying and managing resources. Finally, in Chapter 21 we discuss the responsibilities of test developers and test users for assuring that the ways in which assessments are used, the decisions that are made, and the consequences of these are fair for stakeholders.

13

Real world conditions and constraints on language assessment

INTRODUCTION: WELCOME TO THE REAL WORLD

Many textbooks on language assessment, including one we wrote ourselves (Bachman and Palmer 1996), provide guidance for how to go about developing language assessments. These textbooks include lots of excellent advice and examples of good assessment development practice. Readers of such textbooks may feel that if they merely follow the advice and procedures described when they develop a language assessment of their own, everything will turn out just right: the assessment will have all those good qualities that language testers and other measurement specialists have told us about—reliability, validity, authenticity, positive washback, fairness, and so forth.

But this ideal world of language assessment textbooks and the world in which language assessment development takes place are quite different. Those of you who have been involved in developing a language assessment know all too well that, to paraphrase the words of the Scottish poet Robert Burns, the best-laid plans and development procedures "gang aft agley" (often go amiss).[1] We two authors also know, even from our relatively short experience in the field of developing and using language assessments, that lots can go wrong for even the most conscientious and well-intentioned test developer. Bachman (1990: 279) said that language testing does not take place "in a values-free psychometric test tube," and we would expand upon this by saying that language assessment development does not take in a predictable and unchanging world where everyone else knows and understands what we language testers think we know and understand about language assessment. The real world of language assessment development is one in which the other players may not know the "rules of the game" that we've been taught in language assessment courses. Or, they may choose not to play by those rules. Stakeholders change: test users or decision makers change their minds; new decision makers have different values, views, or priorities, with respect to the assessment. Thus, the test developer often needs to convince new stakeholders that the intended uses are justified, or reconsider how the uses may change as the players change. Furthermore, the setting in which the assessment development takes place includes many uncertainties and conflicts, and is constantly changing. The values and priorities of different levels in an educational system, such as the classroom, the school, the district, the state, and the nation, as well as those of different subgroups of stakeholders in the society, may differ and change over time. Resources that are available for assessment development can change dramatically from feast to famine, or may dry up entirely by the time the assessment is ready for operational use. Thus, even the most frugal and management savvy test developer may find himself unable to continue the enterprise without seriously compromising his professional standards.

The purpose of this chapter is not to overwhelm you, our gentle reader, with the near impossibility of ever producing an assessment whose use you can justify. Rather, our intent here is to prepare you for some of the eventualities that you may encounter as you toil in the fields of language assessment practice, on your quest for the perfect assessment, which, as we mentioned in Chapter 1, does not exist. The real world we discuss in this chapter is something your language testing teacher most likely never told you about; what we discuss in this chapter is a distillation of our experience as language test developers and test users over the past few years. Hopefully what we say in this chapter will provide some insights into, if not answers to, the questions you may have thought too mundane to ask. But the real world in which language assessment takes place is anything but humdrum. It's vibrant and exciting and at the same time challenging and at times frustrating. Thus, it's immensely rewarding when we do occasionally manage not only to "do language assessment" right, but also to get lucky and see some beneficial consequences come out of our efforts. For all of these reasons, we believe that an understanding of these real world conditions and constraints is every bit as vital to your success as a language tester as your understanding of the concepts and procedures that we discuss in the rest of the book. We think it is also essential for keeping your sanity.

To illustrate the importance of considering real world constraints from the very beginning, let us share an experience with you.

> Many years ago, in a far off land, I was working for a national language center as the language testing specialist. One day a young man called me and introduced himself as the person responsible for developing a new test for placing incoming university students into an academic English program. He said he was from one of the new open universities. I said I'd be happy to discuss this with him and we made an appointment to meet. From this short conversation, I could tell that this person had very little knowledge of or experience in language testing, so I was excited about the possibility of helping him develop what was obviously going to be a fairly high-stakes and large-scale test, as the university enrolled approximately 10,000 students each year.

When the young man arrived at my office, I had several handouts and references about language testing ready for him: lists, flow charts, definitions; I had everything I thought he would need to get started. For the next two hours we discussed the nature of the ESL program at the university, what the ESL teachers expected, what the members of the faculty and the university administration expected students to be able to do in English, what aspects of English ability they wanted to test, and a variety of ways in which these could be tested. At the end of our meeting, we'd come up with a rough design for a placement test that would include a written composition, a face-to-face oral interview, and multiple-choice tests of grammar and vocabulary. We both felt quite satisfied as we wrapped up our meeting.

As he was going out the door, I asked him, "How many people will be working with you on the development of this test?"

"It's only me," he replied.

I was almost speechless. He could see the shock on my face, but didn't say anything. What should I, the "language testing expert" say? I had to come clean.

"Forget everything we've talked about," I said. "We need to start all over."

This was one of my first encounters with the real world of language assessment practice.

We begin this chapter with a discussion of the uncertainties that language test developers face and must learn to deal with in the real world. Next, we discuss several sources of uncertainties. We then discuss briefly the test developer's need to be able to deal with these uncertainties, and we suggest that the justification process, as discussed in other chapters in this book, provides the most effective way to do this. We then discuss practicality as a relationship between the kinds of resources that are required in assessment development and use and those that are available. We discuss the kinds of resources that are typically required for the development and use of language assessments. Finally, we consider the choices test developers need to make in developing and using an assessment and the kinds of trade-offs that are associated with these choices.

DEALING WITH UNCERTAINTIES[2]

The enterprise of developing and using a language assessment is fraught with uncertainties. Or to put it another way, in language assessment we do not deal in certainties. This should not be surprising, since life itself is full of uncertainties. There are always factors in the assessment situation that are either entirely unexpected and unpredictable or that we cannot control. Stakeholders, being human, frequently act in ways that we may not expect, and their views and perceptions of the assessment may vary from one situation to another, and may change over time. The test developer and decision maker, also being human, are of course prone to error and cannot possibly address or even anticipate all of these uncertainties.

We would argue that the best means for minimizing errors and dealing with uncertainties is the Assessment Use Argument (AUA) and the assessment justification process that is described in Chapter 5 and that is discussed in detail in Chapters 8–12 of this book. We would hasten to point out, however, that the AUA itself has uncertainty built into it, and is thus *not* a magic formula for solving all the language tester's problems. Rather the AUA serves as a guide for the assessment developer as she negotiates "the changing winds and shifting sands"[3] of the real world to go about the systematic processes of assessment development and use, and of justification. The backing that is provided to support the warrants in the AUA gives the stakeholders the information they need to judge the degree of certainty in the AUA, and to decide if this is sufficient to convince them that the intended uses of the assessment are justified. The factors in the assessment situation that are sources of potential uncertainty include: (1) the qualities of the claimed assessment outcomes (assessment record, interpretation, decision, consequences) in the AUA itself; (2) the stakeholders and consequences; (3) the assessment situation; and (4) interpretations. (Refer to Project 7 (grammar achievement example) for an example of trade-offs in assessment development.)

Qualities of the claimed assessment outcomes

When someone asks, "Is such and such quality an attribute of something?" he is essentially presupposing that the answer is a certainty: yes or no. If we answer the question "Are all swans white?" with the reply "Yes, all swans are white," we are, in effect, claiming with certainty that all swans are white. "All dogs have four legs," "All mammals have hair," "No pigs can breathe underwater," and "No horses have horns" are all examples of such claims of certainty. This not to say, of course, that such claims can be accepted merely at face value. Each of the claims above can be falsified through empirical observation. Thus, if we were to find a red swan, a five-legged dog, or a mammal with scales or smooth skin instead of hair or fur, or see a pig skin diving without a snorkel or scuba gear, or a horse with a horn, this would reject, with certainty, each of these respective claims. When we ask the question, "*To what degree* is X an attribute of Y?," however, we are immediately inviting *un*certainty, since if something is an attribute of something else only to a certain degree, and not absolutely, we have to wonder when and under what conditions it is an attribute and when it is not.

When we look at the way the claims are stated in the AUA, all involve *relative* rather than *absolute* certainty because the qualities of the assessment outcomes in the claims are defined in terms of "the degree to which."

Claim 1: consequences

beneficence: the degree to which the consequences of using an assessment and of the decisions that are made promote good and are not detrimental to stakeholders;

Claim 2: decisions

equitability: the degree to which different test takers who are at equivalent levels on the construct to be assessed have equivalent chances of being classified into the same group;

values sensitivity: the degree to which the use of an assessment and the decisions that are made take into consideration relevant legal requirements and existing community values;

Claim 3: interpretations

meaningfulness: the degree to which a given assessment record (1) provides stakeholders with information about the ability or construct to be assessed, and (2) conveys this information in terms that they can understand and relate to;

impartiality: the degree to which the format and content of the assessment tasks and all aspects of the administration of the assessment are free from bias that may favor or disfavor some takers;

generalizability: the degree of correspondence between a given language assessment task and a TLU task in their task characteristics and the components of language ability that are engaged;

relevance: the degree to which the interpretation provides the relevant information the decision maker needs to make the decision;

sufficiency: the degree to which the interpretation provides enough information for decision makers to make a decision;

Claim 4: assessment reports

consistency: the degree to which test takers' performance on different assessments of the same construct yields essentially the same assessment records.

Even though Claim 1, for example, states that the consequences of the assessment and the decisions made are beneficial to all stakeholders, the *quality* of beneficence is defined as *the degree to which* the consequences of using an assessment and of the decisions that are made promote good and are not detrimental to stakeholders. Similarly, Claim 4 states that the assessment records are consistent across different assessment tasks, different aspects of the assessment procedure, and across different groups of test takers. However, the *quality*, consistency, is defined in a way that clearly indicates that this is not absolute: consistency is the degree to which test takers' performance on different assessments of the same construct yields essentially the same assessment records. In other words, all of the qualities that are claimed of outcomes in the AUA are relative or limited to specific conditions in the assessment situation.

The uncertainty that is built into these qualities reflects the uncertainty of the assessment process itself. Such uncertainty is due in part to the fact that the abilities we are interested in assessing cannot be observed directly, but can only be *inferred* on the basis of test takers' performance. The uncertainty of the assessment process is also due to the limitations in the ways in which we are able to observe and record this performance. Bachman (1990) discusses these limitations in terms of *incompleteness*, *imprecision*, *subjectivity*, and *relativeness*. He argues that all observations of performance in an assessment are *incomplete* samples of an individual's total or possible performance at any given point in time. Records of our observations are *imprecise* because of the lack of perfect comparability of the various assessment tasks we present to test takers. In addition, if we are assigning numbers to test takers' performances, these will be imprecise because of the potential lack of comparability of the scales that are used to assign these numbers. As Bachman (2006a) points out, records as verbal descriptions may also lack precision, depending on the purpose of the description and the training of the persons preparing the descriptions. Assessment records are also *subjective*. All of the decisions we make in the process of designing, developing, and using an assessment are based on the subjective judgments of the test developer. These subjective decisions also determine the way in which we choose to record our observations, whether this is as scores or as descriptions. Finally, assessment records are *relative*, in the sense that the test developer must provide an appropriate frame of reference in order for them to be meaningful. Records could be interpreted in either a norm-referenced or a criterion-referenced way. In the former, scores are interpreted as indicating the test taker's standing relative to that of other similar individuals who have taken the test, while in the latter, the score would be interpreted relative to some criterion independent of the test takers who took the test. With descriptions, labels such as "excellent," "good," or "fair," must also be clarified with fuller descriptions of what they mean, and whether these labels refer to a test taker's performance relative to others, or to criteria or standards of performance that are set independently of the particular individuals who have taken the assessment.

The function of the warrants and the backing that is collected to support them is to make clear to stakeholders the specific conditions under which the claimed qualities of the assessment outcome hold, and the degree to which they hold. Warrants about the consistency of assessment records, for example, will address the potential sources of inconsistency that are relevant to a particular assessment, and the test developer will provide backing to convince stakeholders that the assessment records are sufficiently consistent for the intended uses of the assessment. In an assessment that involves several raters rating a sample of spoken language, for example, the specific condition that the warrant would identify is the consistency among these raters. The backing that is provided might include correlations among the ratings of different raters, as an indication of the degree to which these are consistent. Warrants about the meaningfulness of the interpretations will address the potential effects of attributes that are not relevant to the ability to be assessed on test takers' performance. To support these warrants, the test developer will provide backing to convince stakeholders that these effects are either negligible or have been minimized. Suppose, for example, that test takers' topical knowledge might affect their performance on an assessment of their control of rhetorical structure in writing. In this case, the test developer would warrant that this condition does not hold, that is, that topical knowledge is not an important factor in test takers' performance. She could collect backing, in the form of a statistical analysis of the effects of test takers' knowledge on their scores, or through collecting verbal protocols from test takers to determine whether they felt that their topical knowledge helped them with the test. This backing would hopefully convince stakeholders that the degree to which topical knowledge is a factor in test takers' performance is very small and unimportant. Similarly, warrants and rebuttals, along with the relevant backing, about the beneficence of the consequences of the assessment, are intended to convince stakeholders that the consequences of the assessment are sufficiently beneficial for the assessment to be used. Thus, although the AUA has uncertainty built in, it is also the AUA that delineates the precise sources and limits of this uncertainty and builds the case that there is sufficient certainty for the intended uses of the assessment to be justified.

Stakeholders and consequences

In Claim 1 we identify the stakeholders—all the individuals and institutions that we believe may be directly affected by the use of the assessment and by the decisions that are made. We also state the intended beneficial consequences, supporting these with warrants and backing. In addition, we state rebuttals about possible unintended consequences that may be detrimental to some stakeholders, providing backing that we believe will weaken these rebuttals. With relatively low-stakes assessments such as a classroom assessment for formative purposes, the number of stakeholders may be quite small, including essentially the teacher and his students. With high-stakes assessments, on the other hand, the number of stakeholders is likely to be very large, and they are likely to be very diverse. Test takers may constitute different subgroups that vary according to characteristics such as gender, age, socioeconomic status, race, or ethnicity. In addition, in high-stakes assessments, it is always possible that some individuals may be indirectly affected by the assessment and the decisions that are made. For example, a decision not to admit an applicant to a university will directly affect the applicant, as well as his immediate family. But to what extent will the decision affect other members of the community in which the applicant lives? How can the test developer possibly know? A decision to admit an applicant is also likely to affect the university community, including the student's classmates and the instructors with whom he takes courses. But to what extent will this admissions decision affect the broader university community?

One uncertainty with respect to stakeholders, therefore, is that the test developer cannot identify every possible individual or institution who might conceivably be affected in some way indirectly by the assessment and the decisions that are made. What she can do is clearly identify, in Claim 1, the stakeholders that she believes are most likely to be directly affected by the assessment and the decisions to be made, and the likely consequences for these individuals. In addition, the test developer can articulate, in Claim 1, rebuttals that identify potential detrimental consequences, and the stakeholders who might be affected by these. She can then provide this information to stakeholders, inviting their feedback about individuals or institutions or potential detrimental consequences that may have been omitted. The test developer can then take this feedback into account to expand the list of stakeholders and the number of rebuttals, if warranted, and then make sure that the relevant backing to weaken these rebuttals is collected during the justification process. Nevertheless, even if the test developer has provided backing to support the claim that the consequences are beneficial, and to reject rebuttals about detrimental consequences, it is always possible that some stakeholders may not agree, or be convinced by this.

Another area of uncertainty is the diversity and changeability of the stakeholders. The more diverse the stakeholder groups, the greater the likelihood that they will have different perceptions of and responses to the assessment as well as to the decisions that are made and consequences of these decisions. Differences in stakeholders' perceptions and reactions can be seen as reflecting two sets of differences: differences in their value systems and differences in the kinds of warrants they require and the amount of evidence they need in order to be convinced by the AUA and its backing. Stakeholders' perceptions and responses to the assessment may also change over time or as conditions change. Stakeholders' perceptions of the assessment will reflect the value systems of the communities in which they live, and as these societal, community, or educational values change, so will those of the stakeholders. Stakeholders' perceptions of the assessment may also change as they become better informed about the nature of the assessment process and the limitations under which the test developer typically works. In this regard, we would again point out the importance of the test developer working closely with all relevant stakeholder groups in the design and development of the assessment, and of "educating" stakeholders about the rationale for and procedures followed in developing and using the assessment.

Decision makers, as one stakeholder group, will vary in terms of their "comfort zone," or their tolerance for decision errors, as discussed in Chapter 5 (pp. 116–17), under "Sufficiency." In situations where the resources that can be allocated are very limited or inflexible, the decision maker may have a very low tolerance for decision errors.

In the phone company example in Chapter 5 (pp. 119–20), the manager's tolerance for false positive decision errors depended on a number of factors, including the complexity of the company's procedures for firing employees, and the effect of doing this on her ability to hire new people. In the eighth grade science example, also in Chapter 5, the ninth grade teachers' tolerance for false positive decision errors—students who were erroneously identified as being ready for ninth grade science—depended on the number of students who were so classified, as well as on the teachers' resources for providing individual support for these students so that they could manage ninth grade science. What these two examples illustrate is that any decision maker's tolerance for decision errors may vary, depending on a number of factors that are very difficult to predict. Some of these factors include the level of importance, or the stakes of the decision, and the relative ease or difficulty of correcting decision errors, which are discussed in detail in Chapter 9. The decision maker's tolerance for decision errors will also depend on the availability of the resources, along with individual differences in personal characteristics. Because of these uncertainties, the test developer needs to work closely with the decision makers to determine how much relevant information they need to feel comfortable that they can make correct decisions based on the interpretation derived from the assessment record.

The assessment situation

The context in which the test is developed and will be used is also varied and complex. Not only may differing stakeholder groups have different values, but in many contexts assessments are subject to a variety of different laws and regulations. These often operate at different levels (e.g., school, district, state, nation), and are sometimes in conflict with each other and with societal or educational values. In some situations, it may be that making the decision implied by the assessment-based interpretation conflicts with institutional, educational, or socio-cultural values. Suppose, for example, that students from a particular group regularly achieve low scores on a university admissions test, as compared with students from other groups. If such differential performance is due to bias in test content, format, or the way it is administered, then not admitting such students would be considered unfair, and this might be a reason for not denying them university admissions.

In some situations, different warrants in the AUA may be in conflict. For example, if an assessment is based on material that students are expected to have learned in an educational program, the decision maker might feel it is justified to fail students who do poorly on this assessment. However, if some students have not had the opportunity to learn this material, not passing them could be considered unfair, and thus constitute a reason for not failing them on the basis of low test scores. In this case, a warrant supporting the equitability of decisions is in conflict with a warrant supporting the impartiality of interpretations.

The assessment situation can also be complicated by unpredictable idiosyncratic circumstances, or by "hidden agendas" of decision makers. Suppose, for example, that an assessment is being used for making decisions about employing people in a company, and one of the test takers is the company owner's son, who is going to be employed no matter how he does on the assessment. In such a case, the test developer might well question why this particular individual is even taking the assessment. Shohamy (2001) provides numerous examples of tests that are publicly claimed to promote beneficial consequences for stakeholders, but which are in fact intended to promote very different consequences for different stakeholder groups, some of whom will clearly be harmed by the decisions that are made.

If there are circumstances (e.g., one of the test takers is the owner's son) that override the decision that would be made on the basis of the assessment, then using an assessment for making a decision could be seen at the very least as a waste of resources. If there are hidden, unstated, and highly questionable alternative intended consequences, then this use of the assessment may constitute an unethical practice. Unfortunately, no matter how closely the test developer works with decision makers and other stakeholders, it is often not possible to discover such anomalies in assessment use until after the fact. In such cases, what the test developer may be able to do is to meet with other concerned stakeholders and look carefully at the AUA and evidence that was provided to support this. If the possible detrimental consequences to some groups of test takers have not been clearly articulated in the AUA, then this could constitute a reason to reverse any decisions that may have been made on the basis of the assessment.

Given the diversity of societal and community values in many assessment situations, along with differing legal requirements, the test developer cannot address all possible rebuttals about the values sensitivity and equitability of the decisions that are made. Likewise, the decision maker cannot expect that the decisions that are made will be consistent with all regulations and seen as equitable by all stakeholder groups. What the test developer can do is clearly identify, in Claim 2, the specific societal and community values and legal requirements that have been considered in the decisions to be made, and provide backing to support these warrants. She can then provide this information to stakeholders, inviting their feedback about relevant community values or regulations that may not have been considered in the AUA. The test developer can then take this feedback into account to expand the warrants about community values and regulations, and then make sure that the relevant backing to support these warrants is collected during the justification process. Nevertheless, even if the test developer has provided backing to support the claims that the decisions made are generally equitable, and that the consequences are beneficent, it is always possible that some stakeholders may not agree, or be convinced by this.

Interpretations

Uncertainty can also arise in the way the test developer identifies and defines, in Claim 3, the areas of language ability to be assessed. The test developer will do her best to identify the abilities that are relevant to the decisions to be made and that will generalize to the TLU domain. Nevertheless, it is virtually impossible for her to know with certainty all of the abilities that may be needed to perform the relevant TLU tasks, or how a high level in one ability may compensate for a low level in another. For example, being a successful language teacher requires a wide range of abilities, knowledge, and attitudes, including language ability, knowledge of language pedagogy, knowing how to present the language and content in a way that makes it understandable to students, skills in classroom management, a positive attitude toward learning and teaching, and respect for students. If one were to develop an assessment to certify language teachers, it would most likely be either impossible or unfeasible to assess all of these attributes. Thus, only a subset of these would be assessed, and the test developer may not know exactly which subset will provide sufficient information for making certification decisions. Furthermore, she might make different decisions, depending on the particular combination of abilities she decided to assess. Suppose, for example, the test developer included only the components of *language ability* needed to perform teaching tasks. In this case, test takers who excelled in these components would most likely be certified. Other test takers, who might be weak in language ability but who might excel in the other attributes that are not measured, might not be certified, unless having a high level of ability in these other areas enables test takers to compensate for weaknesses in language ability. The opposite outcome might be expected if we were to include in this test knowledge of language pedagogy, skills in classroom management, and a positive attitude toward learning and teaching. In either case, the uncertainty of not knowing exactly which combination of constructs will provide sufficient information may result in an inequitability in the certification decision that is due to the particular combination of attributes that we were able to measure.

Given the wide range of possible language use tasks that are in any TLU domain, and the impossibility of knowing exactly which areas of language ability are needed to successfully perform these tasks, the test developer cannot address all possible rebuttals about meaningfulness, impartiality, generalizability, relevance, and sufficiency. What the test developer can do is clearly identify, in Claim 3, the specific areas of language ability that are to be assessed, and articulate warrants for the qualities of the intended interpretations. She can then provide this information to stakeholders, inviting their feedback about any areas of language ability that may not have been articulated in the AUA. The test developer can then take this feedback into account to expand the definition of the ability to be assessed, along with the necessary warrants to support this, and then make sure that the relevant backing to support these warrants is collected during the justification process. Nevertheless, even if the test developer has provided backing to support the intended interpretations, it is always possible that some areas of the ability that are relevant to the decisions or that are required for TLU tasks may not be assessed.

The need to deal with uncertainty

The reason we raise these issues of uncertainty is that they occur frequently enough in the real world to warrant the test developer's consideration. Because of the complexity of factors in the assessment situation, many of which the test developer cannot anticipate or control, there is always the possibility that the use of the assessment and the decisions made will lead to consequences that are detrimental to some stakeholders. It is always possible that the construct to be assessed will be defined in a way that is at least in part irrelevant to the decisions that are to be made, or that does not adequately represent the full range of abilities that are needed to perform TLU tasks. In other words, there is always the possibility that an unanticipated rebuttal could weaken any of the claims in an AUA.

An awareness, on the part of the test developer, that such uncertainties may affect the intended interpretations, decisions, and consequences can help avoid a great deal of misunderstanding and frustration. In evaluating the need to address various unanticipated rebuttals, the test developer will need to determine (1) how serious the rebuttal is to the particular claim or warrant, (2) how likely the outcome of the rebuttal is to occur, and (3) what resources will be required to minimize the alternative assessment outcome that is implied in the rebuttal.

As we have noted, the AUA itself provides the most effective means for dealing with the numerous uncertainties in any given assessment situation. This is accomplished in the AUA by clearly identifying the specific factors in the assessment situation that are addressed and providing evidence to support the degree to which these have been adequately addressed. In addition, addressing the many factors that can affect the assessment and its outcomes requires that the test developer work in close consultation with relevant stakeholders, listening to their concerns and soliciting their feedback. The test developer needs to take an active, critical role in dealing with uncertainties of any particular assessment situation. That is, while the test developer must consult with stakeholders, and consider the relevant value systems and regulations that apply to the assessment, she cannot simply accept uncritically everything stakeholders tell her, or what standards or regulations may dictate. Rather, she must perform a balancing act as she navigates the shifting currents and drifting sands of assessment development and use.

It is a well-worn cliché that "assessment is the art of the possible,"[4] and, as stated in Chapter 2, there is no such thing as a perfect assessment, or even the "best" assessment for a particular use. Another cliché is that of the three qualities of an assessment that decision makers or those who provide resources for assessment development would like to have—fast, cheap, and good. However, only two of these are attainable. If you want a "good" test fast, then it won't be cheap. If you want a "good" test cheap, it won't be fast. And, if you want a fast, cheap test—don't even go there. Thus, there is no "best" assessment, and to develop an assessment whose intended uses can be justified requires resources. So what we are left with is "the best the test developer could do, given the constraints and conditions under which he had to operate." Having said this, it is still the test developer's professional responsibility to be able to demonstrate to the stakeholders that the assessment she has produced is, in fact, justifiable for its intended uses.

We have argued that a well-constructed and coherent AUA, supported by appropriate backing, provides a principled and justifiable approach to dealing with the uncertainties of the real world in which language assessment takes place. However, neither an AUA itself nor the backing that is provided to support it can provide a "scientific" or "logical" proof that any given test is perfect or the best. What the AUA and its supporting backing can do, however, is give stakeholders the information they need in order to determine for themselves that the intended uses of the assessment are justified. Thus, in our view, what the test developer can and should do is make the AUA and its supporting backing available to stakeholders as a public document. Making such information readily available can accomplish two things. It can provide a framework within which stakeholders can articulate any objections or rebuttals they may have. Second, it can go a long way toward helping stakeholders understand the rationale for why the assessment is the way it is, as well as the time and effort that goes into assessment development. In this regard, this document—the AUA and its supporting backing—becomes the interface between the test developer and the uncertainties of the real world.

PRACTICALITY AND RESOURCES

Developing and using an assessment requires resources. Every claim and warrant in an AUA has implications for costs. Resources are needed for assessment justification, assessment production, and assessment use. The claims and warrants in the AUA define qualities such as consistency, meaningfulness, generalizability, equitability, and beneficence that the test users expect to see as they interpret and use the assessment. These qualities pertain to the assessment records, the interpretations, decisions, and consequences that are claims in the AUA. Practicality, on the other hand, is not a quality of the assessment itself, but rather of the entire process of assessment development and use. Thus, developing an assessment task that corresponds to tasks in a TLU domain beyond the test itself will involve costs. Developing a task that engages the ability we want to assess will involve costs. In addition, collecting backing to support the warrants of meaningfulness and generalizability will cost resources.

In assessment development and use we need to consider *both* the quality control that the AUA and the justification process provide *and* the practicality of assessment development, given the resourcing constraints that are imposed by the real world. We need to articulate the warrants in the AUA for our particular testing situation. We need to determine the focus—which of these warrants will require the most backing in order for the AUA to provide convincing justification to stakeholders for the intended assessment use. We also need to produce the Design Statement, Blueprint, and actual assessments that are products of assessment production. Finally, we need to specify the administrative procedures we will follow to collect the information we need to provide assessment reports and to collect feedback on the assessment itself. All along the way, we need to keep track of the resources that will be required to collect backing for these warrants, in relationship to the resources that are available.

Thus, determining the practicality of a given assessment involves (1) determining the resources that will be required to develop and use an operational assessment and to collect the backing needed for the warrants in its AUA, and (2) allocating and managing the resources that are available. The allocation and management of resources is discussed and illustrated in detail in Chapter 20. In this chapter we will simply define practicality, describe the kinds of resources that need to be available for assessment development, and introduce the notion of trade-offs.

Practicality

We define **practicality** as the difference between the resources that will be *required* in the development and use of an assessment and the resources that will be *available* for these activities. This relationship can be represented as in Figure 13.1.

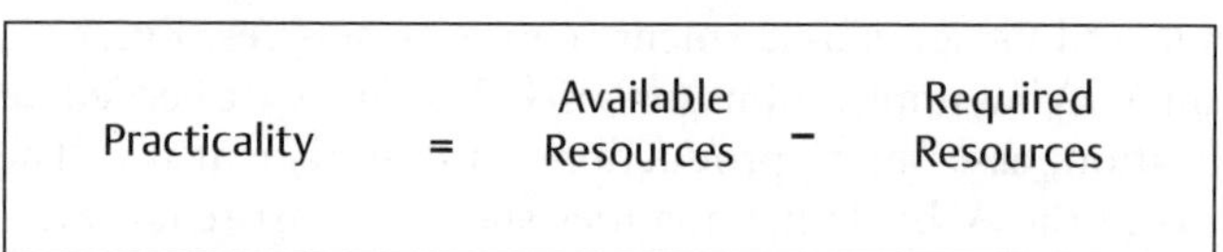

- If Available resources ≥ Required resources, then Practicality is *positive*, and the assessment is practical.
- If Available resources < Required resources, then Practicality is *negative*, and the assessment is not practical.

Figure 13.1 Practicality

From this relationship, we can derive a definition for a **practical assessment**: an assessment whose development and use do not require more resources than are available. For any given situation, if the resources required for developing and using the assessment exceed the resources available, the assessment will be impractical. In such a situation, the assessment will either not be used at all, or will not be sustainable in the long term, unless resources can be managed more efficiently, or additional resources can be allocated. Practicality thus pertains primarily to the ways in which the test will be developed and used, and, to a large degree, whether it will be developed and used at all. We believe this view of practicality is useful because it enables us to define a "threshold level" for practicality in any given assessment development and use. If the development process, including justification, requires extensive resources and the developer has only limited resources and is not able to manage these to meet the resource requirement, the assessment simply will not get developed. If it requires more resources than are available to administer and score, it will not get used.

Although the consideration of practicality is not a part of the AUA or a quality of the *products* of assessment production—the Initial Plan, Design Statement, Blueprint, and the assessment itself—this does not imply that practicality is any less important. On the contrary, in the development of an assessment, the processes of justification and production process are cyclical, so that considerations of practicality are likely to affect the test developer's decisions at every stage along the way, and may lead her to reconsider and perhaps revise some of the earlier specifications for the assessment. For example, suppose that members of the faculty in a large university system want to make sure that students will be able to write effective academic papers before they graduate. These faculty members assume that a composition test would be too costly to score, so they decide that they need to develop a multiple-choice test instead. They discuss this with the directors of the academic writing programs at the different campuses of the university, who agree to help develop an exit exam to test students' writing. They spend several months working with writing instructors to develop a sufficient number of multiple-choice items for the exit test. After trialing this test with a relatively large sample of students and obtaining the statistical analyses of the test items, the writing program directors find that very few, only about 20 per cent, of the items they have written are acceptable in terms of their measurement properties (e.g., how difficult they are or how well they discriminate students of high ability from those of low ability).[5] Furthermore, follow-up questionnaires from the test takers indicate that students did not think the test was a fair measure of their writing ability. The directors discuss these results with the writing instructors, who are obviously disappointed, but not surprised, as none of them had ever written multiple-choice items to test writing before this. What they are very experienced at, of course, is creating prompts for essay exams and at rating these. The directors realize that asking these instructors to write multiple-choice items is a misuse of their time and expertise, and probably an exercise in futility, given the poor results from the trial administration of the test. They then count the number of writing instructors in the university, estimate the number of essays that would need to be rated in any given year, and decide that the amount of the writing instructors' time and effort spent rating these essays would be more or less the same as required in the unsuccessful attempt to write multiple-choice items. They submit a proposal for a composition exam to the faculty members, who agree to this. The happy ending, of course, is that the composition exam is a huge hit with the faculty members, students feel that it is a reasonable measure of their writing ability, and the writing instructors feel validated.

The test user will need to consider practicality with respect to both *developing* an assessment and *using* an assessment for a given purpose. For example, suppose that a test user, such as a government language school, a state department of education, a school district, or a school, was considering the possibility of using a language assessment as part of the certification of teachers' credentials. This test user would need to evaluate the practicality of using an assessment for this purpose. They might, for example, consider if it is practical to administer and use an assessment, as opposed to using other sources of information that might be available. If the test user decides that it is potentially practical to use an assessment, then an AUA could be constructed and an assessment design developed following this AUA. Whether the assessment itself gets developed and used is then a matter of practicality. In this case, if the test user does not have the resources needed, the test user might send out a request for proposals from individuals, private companies, or other organizations to develop an assessment that meets the requirements of the AUA and design specifications. Proposals from potential test developers might be evaluated in terms of how well their plans adhere to the AUA and assessment design. In addition, proposals would most likely also be evaluated in terms of the resources that the developer brings to the development project, in terms of the developer's expertise, experience, and reputation, and the resources that the developer proposes will be required, in terms of budget and time line.

Resources for assessment development and use

In order to determine the practicality of an assessment, the test developer needs to specify what she means by resources. We classify resources into three general types. *Human resources* include, for example, the test developer, assessment task creators, scorers or raters, and assessment administrators, as well as clerical and technical support personnel. *Material resources* include space (such as rooms for assessment development and assessment administration), equipment (computers, audio and video (CD, DVD) recorders), and materials (such as paper, pictures, library resources, computer software). *Time* consists of development time (time from the beginning of the assessment development process to the use of assessment for making decisions about test takers in the first operational administration) and time for specific tasks: collecting backing to support warrants in the AUA, and assessment production tasks (for example, designing, creating, administering, scoring, analyzing). In considering the different types of resources, it is also essential to estimate the monetary costs that may be associated with each, since in many assessment situations the total amount of resources available is essentially a function of budget. These different types of resources are listed in Table 13.1.

1 **Human Resources**: (e.g., assessment task creators, scorers or raters, test administrators, and clerical support)

2 **Material Resources**:

- Space (e.g., rooms for assessment development and assessment administration)
- Equipment (e.g., tape, video, DVD recorders, computers)
- Materials (e.g., paper, pictures, library resources, computer software)

3 **Time**

- Development time (time from the beginning of the assessment development process to the recording of scores from the first operational administration)
- Time for specific tasks (e.g., designing, creating, administering, scoring, analyzing).

Table 13.1 Types of resources

Different types of resources, and their associated costs, will be required in varying degrees at different stages of assessment development and use. Furthermore, the specific types and amounts of resources required will vary according to the design and AUA of the specific assessment, and available resources will differ from one situation to another. For these reasons, practicality can only be determined for a specific assessment situation; an assessment that is practical in one situation may not be practical in another. It thus makes little sense to say in general terms that a given assessment or assessment task is more or less practical than another; this can only be determined for a specific assessment situation. What we can probably say in general, however, is that some assessments or assessment tasks, and some AUAs, are relatively more or less demanding of different types of resources, or at different stages in the assessment process. We discuss resource allocation and management in detail in Chapter 20.

Trade-offs

As stated above, practicality is a matter of the extent to which the resource demands of the particular assessment development process can be met within the limits of available resources. An unpleasant fact of assessment development is that in the real world resources are always limited, sometimes in ways that make assessment development extremely challenging. If available resources are exceeded, then the assessment is not practical and the developer faces four choices: (1) find additional resources, (2) manage the available resources so that they can be utilized more efficiently, (3) modify the AUA, the Design Statement, and Blueprint to reduce the resources required for assessment production and justification, or (4) abandon or not begin assessment development. In our experience, the most typical scenario is for the test developer to use a combination of efficient resource management and modifying the AUA, Design Statement, or Blueprint. That is, in most real world assessment situations, effectively managing limited resources requires the test developer to make choices, and these will inevitably involve trade-offs. A **trade-off** involves reducing the importance of one or more qualities of a claim in order to maintain or increase the qualities of another claim, either in response to competing values of different stakeholders, or in order to make the assessment practical. For example, in the eighth grade science assessment discussed in Chapter 5 (pp. 122–3), suppose that the school district wanted to develop an eighth grade science assessment that engaged students in the processes that they value as part of their knowledge of science, and that will correspond highly to learning tasks that students perform in the science classrooms. They might develop assessment tasks that require students to look at an apparatus that is used in science experiments, and then explain, either orally or in writing, how the apparatus works, and perhaps how it might be used in a science experiment. Students' responses could be scored both for language and for knowledge of science. The interpretations from this assessment might be very meaningful, in that it engages the areas of ability—language ability and knowledge of science—that the school district wants to assess. It could also be seen as highly generalizable, in that the characteristics of this assessment tasks correspond closely to instructional tasks in the science classroom. Finally, since this assessment will be used to decide if students are ready to go on to ninth grade, the interpretations could be seen as highly relevant to that decision.

Now suppose that the school district contracts with a test developer to develop this test, and that it turns out to be much more costly to develop, administer, and score than the school district can afford. What do they do? If they followed our approach, they would go back to the stakeholders and re-evaluate the importance of the generalizability, meaningfulness, and relevance of the interpretations. They may find that some stakeholders—ninth grade science teachers, school administrators—place the highest premium on relevance, with meaningfulness second, and generalizability not much of a concern. The students say simply that they would prefer a shorter test, and their parents indicate no real preference. The school district then goes back to the AUA and decides to focus their resources on providing backing for the warrant about relevance. They then meet with the test developer and revise the Design Statement, Blueprint, and test task specifications. The assessment task they end up with includes a picture of a science apparatus followed by multiple-choice questions about the names of parts of the apparatus, what functions the parts perform, the purpose of the apparatus, and how it is used in a science experiment. It is much less costly to produce multiple tasks like this, and these can be scored by computer. So what was the trade-off? There's clearly a loss in generalizability, since students work with actual apparatuses in their science classes and discuss these with the teacher and among themselves. However, given the nature of the input and the kinds of questions asked, the interpretations might be sufficiently meaningful for stakeholders. If the assessment-based interpretations help the teachers make correct decisions about which students are ready for ninth grade science, then they can be considered to be relevant.

While inadequate resources and trade-offs are an almost unavoidable reality in assessment development and use, we would point out that there are no "automatic" or "universal" trade-offs. That is, allocating more resources to supporting warrants for consistency, for example, does not automatically mean that support for warrants of meaningfulness or generalizability will be weakened. Rather, the specific trade-offs in any assessment development situation will be the result of conscious decisions, or choices, on the part of the test developer or test user, or both, in consultation with stakeholders.

EXERCISES

1. Think about your own experience with assessment development. If you have developed a test or been part of a development team, what trade-offs among the qualities of outcomes of claims did you make during the process of assessment design and development?
2. Look through the example Projects and find one that, for some reason, you find intriguing. Examine the assessment tasks or imagine what they would actually look like (in case example tasks are not actually provided). Then think about ways you might "improve" these tasks by changing some of their characteristics. What characteristics would you change? What qualities of outcomes of claims might be strengthened? What qualities of outcomes of claims might be weakened? How might the allocation of resources need to be modified? What trade-offs might be involved?
3. Think about your experience using assessments. Before reading this book, what did you think about the uncertainties involved in assessment development and use? What might you have claimed about the usefulness of the assessment at this point in time? How might your claims differ now that you've been walked through the forest of uncertainty?
4. Suppose you have put a lot of effort into developing an assessment, including providing extensive justification. Suppose someone else has come up

with many rebuttals, all of which you have patiently responded to. But the person won't stop. You face a never ending stream of "Yes, but…"s. What could you say to this individual to put an end to this process in one way or another?

5 Think of an assessment you have taken or used. Go through consistency Warrants 1–4. To what extent do you think the test developers had each of these warrants in mind when developing the assessment? In what ways might the assessment be modified to increase the consistency of assessment records?

6 Look through the example Projects. Find one that interests you, and imagine you were in the position of having to bring this project to fruition. Make a list of human resources, material resources, and time that you would have to find to achieve the project.

NOTES

1 Robert Burns, "To a Mouse, on Turning her up in her Nest with the Plough."

2 We acknowledge, in the heading of this section, our debt to the work of Alan Davies, which has been characterized in the title of a festschrift in his honor: *Experimenting with uncertainty* (Elder et al. 2001).

3 Markwardt, Albert D. (1972). 'Changing winds and shifting sands.' *MST English Quarterly* 21, p. 5.

4 Although Widdowson uses this phrase in the title of his paper "Communicative language testing: the art of the possible" (2001), this had long before become a cliché among those who dwell in the trenches of measurement and assessment.

5 See the discussion of the measurement properties of test items in Bachman (2004).

14

Developing a Design Statement

INTRODUCTION

In the Design stage the test developer will implement specific activities that will produce the beginnings of an Assessment Use Argument (AUA) along with a Design Statement. It is in this interaction between the articulation of an AUA and the development of a Design Statement that we can see the two parallel processes of assessment justification and assessment production that were described in Chapter 5. The articulation of an AUA was discussed in Part II. In this chapter, we discuss systematic procedures for developing a Design Statement.

During the Design stage, the test developer will also prepare a plan for collecting backing to support the AUA, make a detailed inventory of resources that will be required and that will be available for the development and use of the assessment, and prepare a plan for acquiring, allocating, and managing resources. Although these activities are generally implemented in a linear fashion, they are also likely to be performed iteratively, or be repeated a number of times. For example, there are certain activities, such as constructing the AUA, and planning for the allocation and management of resources, that may need to be revised as assessment development proceeds or as real world conditions change.

The **Design Statement** is a document that serves several purposes. Its primary purpose is to guide the test developer in the last three stages—Operationalization, Trialing, and Assessment Use—in the process of assessment development and use. This document also provides information that will serve as backing for several warrants in the AUA. Finally, the Design Statement can provide interpretive information about the assessment to test users and other stakeholders. The parts in the Design Statement are given in Table 14.1. Asterisks indicate the parts of the Design Statement that are also articulated in the AUA.

Design Statement
1 *Description of the test takers and other stakeholders (Claim 1)
2 *Intended beneficial consequences (Claim 1)
3 *Descriptions of the decisions to be made, stakeholders affected by the decisions, and individuals responsible for making the decisions (Claim 2)
4 *The relative seriousness of classification errors, policy-level decisions about standards, the standards themselves (Claim 2, Warrants A2 and A3)
5 *Definition of the construct(s) (Claim 3, Warrant A1)
6 *Description of the TLU domain (Claim 3, Warrant C1)
7 Tasks selected as a basis for developing assessment tasks
8 Description of the characteristics of TLU tasks that have been selected as a basis for assessment tasks
9 Plan for collecting feedback and backing
10 Plan for acquiring, allocating, and managing resources

Table 14.1 Design Statement

The activities that are conducted during the Design stage are discussed in the rest of this chapter. The sections of the chapter are numbered for easy reference to the parts in the Design Statement listed in Table 14.1. For each part of the Design Statement, we will discuss some general considerations to be kept in mind, and will then illustrate how this part can be developed with a discussion of the relevant part of the Design Statement for the University example, an incomplete outline test, which was introduced in Chapter 7 and used in Chapters 8–12 of Part II of this book. (Since the Kindergarten example is a very low-stakes assessment and since a TLU task is used as the assessment task, its Design Statement will contain very little detail, and so would not illustrate the points to be made in this chapter.)

1 DESCRIBING THE TEST TAKERS AND OTHER STAKEHOLDERS

General considerations

Stakeholders include a variety of individuals and institutions (e.g., schools, colleges, and universities, companies, professional associations) who will be affected by and thus have an interest in the use of a given assessment in any particular situation. Individual stakeholders include both the test takers and other individuals, such as teachers, program administrators, parents, and employers, who may be affected by decisions made on the basis of assessment results.

In the AUA, the test developer will identify and list the stakeholders whom she expects to be affected by the use of the test and the decisions made. These will be described in Claim 1 of the AUA. She will also list the intended consequences for these stakeholders, also describing these in Claim 1 of the AUA. In the Design Statement, the test developer will describe the attributes of the different stakeholders in as much detail as needed to guide assessment development. The descriptions of the attributes of the test takers provide one basis for designing assessment tasks in the Operationalization stage that are appropriate to the test takers.

Describing the attributes of test takers and other stakeholders guides subsequent stages (Operationalization, Trialing, Use) in the assessment development process. By making explicit those test taker attributes that may affect their assessment performance, we must, therefore, consider the characteristics of the assessment tasks. Knowing the attributes of the test takers helps us design assessment tasks that will be appropriate for them.

Knowing the attributes of other stakeholders helps us articulate the warrants used to argue for the beneficial consequences of using an assessment and of the decisions that are made on the basis of this. This information about other stakeholders also guides the ways in which we report assessment records, the kinds of information about the assessment that we provide, and the kinds of backing we will collect to support the warrants in the AUA. For all of these reasons, we need to describe the attributes of the test takers and other stakeholders in enough detail to guide assessment design and development. Furthermore, it is always important to base our descriptions upon the best information available and not to proceed on the basis of mere assumptions.

What kind of information to provide about attributes of stakeholders

The kind of information provided about stakeholders in the AUA depends upon what kind of information is needed to formulate the claims, warrants, and backing. For example, in stating the Warrant A6 in support of Claim 2 (i.e., knowledge of multilevel rhetorical organization of written texts to enable them to successfully participate in introductory level academic courses), the test developer warrants that the definition of the construct is communicated in terms that are clearly understandable to all stakeholders. Therefore, information about the stakeholders to whom the definition of the construct is to be communicated must be provided that can be used in the backing for this warrant. If the test takers include individuals who are not literate in the language in which they are being tested, this information would be important in providing backing to the effect that assessment results are provided orally. Exactly what information about stakeholders is needed may not be obvious at first but may emerge during the process of articulating the claims, warrants, and backing for the entire AUA. Since the purpose of an AUA is to justify the use of an assessment to stakeholders, the amount of detail to provide will depend upon how much is needed to accomplish this purpose.

Sources of information about attributes of stakeholders

We will base our description of test taker attributes on a wide variety of sources and kinds of information. We may be able to form an initial description informally, using our own knowledge, talking with others who are familiar with the test takers, etc., and this knowledge may be sufficient in low-stakes assessment situations, such as the Kindergarten example. In higher-stakes situations such as the University example, even where the assessment developer may be quite familiar with the test takers, we believe it is important to refine these initial informal approaches with a more systematic approach. This is even more important where the assessment developer is not at all familiar with the test takers. What we recommend is to use a combination of interviews, observations, self-reports, and questionnaires.

How much detail to provide

The amount of detail to provide depends upon the background knowledge of the particular audiences for the AUA. If the audience is highly familiar with the assessment situation, little detail may be needed, for the readers can provide this information from their own experience. If the audience is unfamiliar, more detailed information may be needed. For example, in the Kindergarten example, the teacher is the primary audience and knows enough about the stakeholders that almost no detail is needed. If the AUA for the University example is to be read by an external reviewer, more detail will be needed simply to make the AUA understandable and convincing.

Where to provide the detail

How much of this detail about the stakeholders to include in the AUA itself and how much to put in the Design Statement depends upon the purpose of and the audience for each document. Since the purpose of the AUA is to convince the audience (stakeholders) that the intended use of the assessment is justified, there is no reason to provide more detail in an AUA than is needed to accomplish this. The purpose of the Design Statement, on the other hand, is to guide assessment developers in their assessment development activities, so enough detail about the attributes of the stakeholders will need to be provided to accomplish this purpose.

General kinds of information about test takers

The attributes of test takers that are particularly relevant to assessment development can be divided into four categories:

1 personal attributes,
2 topical knowledge,
3 general level and profile of language ability, and
4 potential affective responses to different types of assessment tasks.

Personal attributes of test takers

In Chapter 3 we described personal attributes of test takers as individual attributes that are not part of test takers' language ability but which may still influence performance on language assessments. These include age, sex, and native language(s), level of general education, and amount and type of preparation for or prior experience with a given assessment. Clearly these attributes will affect the usefulness of specific assessment tasks for the purposes for which we are designing the assessment. As long as we have in mind a specific TLU domain and set of language users when we start to develop our assessment, we are unlikely to get very far off track. In most cases inappropriate assessment tasks result from trying to develop an assessment without a specific TLU domain or specific test takers in mind.

The number of personal attributes that could potentially affect the assessment performance of any given test taker is very large. Thus, rather than attempting to provide an exhaustive list, we will list the personal attributes we have included in our various Projects for illustrative purposes, namely those which have an obvious impact on our choice of assessment task characteristics in the context of the specific example Project. The following are some attributes that might be relevant to include in your description of test takers. The specific attributes that need to be included will depend, of course, on the particular assessment setting and will most likely vary from one assessment to another.

1 Age
2 Sex
3 Nationalities
4 Immigrant status
5 Native languages
6 Level and type of general education
7 Type and amount of preparation or prior experience with a given assessment

Topical knowledge of test takers

As we discussed in Chapter 3, language use is always about some topic or other, and thus all instances of language use engage language users' topical knowledge. Although individual test takers vary and may be at many different levels, for purposes of assessment design we can group them into two general categories, in terms of the topical knowledge that we presuppose they bring to the assessment: those with homogeneous specific topical knowledge, and those with widely varied topical knowledge. Information about topical knowledge will be needed to state warrants and provide backing for Claim 3.

A homogeneous group of test takers with relatively specific topical knowledge can use that knowledge as the information base with which they can demonstrate their language ability. In designing an assessment for this type of test taker, one possible source of information about their topical knowledge would be content area specialists. For example, if we were developing an English for academic purposes assessment for students intending to study English literature, we might ask literature instructors to help develop a description of relevant topical knowledge. Or suppose we wanted to assess the English speaking ability of experienced automobile mechanics in order to make decisions about employing them for jobs involving interaction with English speaking customers. Test takers would, as a group, know a lot about auto repair and could be expected to talk about it. When designing an assessment for them, we might want to consult with automobile mechanics to develop a suitable description of their topical knowledge. (See Chapter 11 for an extensive discussion of the potential role of topical knowledge in construct definitions.)

In other assessment situations, test takers as a group may not have a high level of control of a single area of topical knowledge in common. This might be the case if we were designing an assessment to develop profiles of English language learners' English ability, or if we were designing a speaking assessment to be administered to a very diverse population of test takers. In cases such as these, we may need to look for and describe a number of different areas of these test takers' topical knowledge to guide our subsequent development of assessment tasks.

Levels and profiles of language ability of test takers

In addition to describing the test takers' personal attributes and topical knowledge, we also need to describe their general level of language ability in performing different types of language use tasks, such as listening to lectures, asking directions, reading newspapers, or writing business memos. This information will be useful in helping us tailor the assessment tasks to the test takers' specific levels of ability and types of language use tasks, thus maximizing the usefulness of the assessment.

We might also want to develop a preliminary profile of test takers' levels of language ability in specific areas, such as grammatical knowledge, textual knowledge, and sociolinguistic knowledge. Suppose, for example, that we wanted to develop an achievement test to measure students' mastery of specific grammatical structures taught in a class designed to prepare them for entrance into an English medium university. And suppose we knew that these students had a fairly high level of control of reading but were quite weak in listening. We might use this information to develop assessment tasks that relied primarily upon written input that would be comprehensible to the test takers and not compromise their ability to respond to the assessment task.

Potential affective responses of test takers to assessment tasks

As noted in Chapter 5, the test takers' affective responses to the characteristics of the assessment environment and tasks can potentially inhibit or facilitate optimum performance. For this reason, we need to consider carefully and describe as specifically as possible our expectations about how test takers are likely to respond to various kinds of assessment tasks that might be considered for use in the testing situation, given what we know about their personal attributes, including their familiarity with the assessment environment, their topical knowledge, and their level of language ability.

Test takers' degree of familiarity with the assessment environment may determine, in part, their affective responses to the assessment tasks. When there is a high level of correspondence between characteristics of the TLU domain and tasks and the assessment environment and tasks, we may be able to assume that test takers will have a generally positive affective response to the assessment and assessment tasks. For example, suppose our TLU domain is that of a bilingual manager in an employment agency in Montreal, where both French and English are widely used. If we wanted to assess the bilingual ability of applicants for this kind of job, we could ask the test takers to perform the same kinds of tasks that bilingual managers perform, in each language, and assume that they will react positively to such tasks.

The level and specificity of topical knowledge presupposed or required of test takers can also influence their affective responses to the assessment. We would generally expect that test takers who have the relevant topical knowledge would have positive affective responses to assessment tasks that require such knowledge, while those who do not may have negative affective responses. Suppose, for example, that we were testing applicants to an English medium university to determine whether they should be exempted from classes designed to prepare them for academic writing in English. Since students already enrolled in university classes are able to apply their topical knowledge in completing academic writing tasks specific to a given course, tasks appropriate for these students might not be appropriate for students who are applying for admission. Including or presupposing highly specific topical content in the writing prompts in the admissions assessment might therefore be expected to induce negative affective responses on the part of these test takers.

Finally, test takers' general levels and profiles of language ability can influence their affective responses. Test takers who have high levels of language ability are likely to feel positive about taking a language assessment, while less proficient test takers may feel threatened.

Relevant part of the Design Statement for the University example

To illustrate these considerations, the descriptions of the attributes of the stakeholders for the University example are given in Table 14.2.

Stakeholders	Attributes
1 **Test takers**	ELLs; varied languages and cultures; upper level ESL proficiency, adults (ages mostly in upper teens and early 20s, with some older students)
2 **ESL reading teachers**	TAs in MA and Ph.D. Applied Linguistics Program, many with several years' experience teaching in university ESL program, some with many years of experience teaching ESL prior to involvement in the graduate program in Applied Linguistics
3 **Teachers in university academic classes**	Regular faculty teaching introductory General Educations courses
4 **ESL Program Director**	Professor of Linguistics, 25 years' experience directing the ESL program in a large US university; extensive experience in language test design and development

Table 14.2 Attributes of stakeholders for University example

2 DESCRIBING THE INTENDED BENEFICIAL CONSEQUENCES

General considerations

In Claim 1 of the AUA the test developer will articulate the intended beneficial consequences for the stakeholders listed in part 1 of the Design Statement. As indicated in Chapter 8, there are consequences of both using an assessment and of the decisions that are made. The description of these consequences in Claim 1 of the AUA provides a basis for evaluating the consequences of using the assessment and of decisions that are made. However, in order for these intended beneficial consequences to guide assessment development and use, they need to be stated in greater detail in the Design Statement. This is particularly important when there are multiple groups of stakeholders, and multiple consequences, so that each intended consequence is associated specifically with each group of stakeholders.

Relevant part of the Design Statement for the University example

In the University example there were four stakeholder groups: the test takers (students), the ESL reading teachers, the university academic courses, and the ESL Program Director. The intended consequences for these stakeholders are presented in Table 14.3.

Stakeholders	Intended beneficial consequences Of using the assessment	Of the decisions that are made
1 **Test takers**	Test takers placed in the ESL reading class will realize that the test tasks are similar to instructional tasks, and thus relevant to their target language use needs. Test takers placed in the ESL reading class will benefit from using the test by being tested in a way that is consistent with ways in which their performance in the ESL reading course is being evaluated.	Test takers who are exempted from the ESL reading course will benefit from not having to take a course they don't need. Test takers who are placed in the ESL reading course will benefit from being placed in a course they do need.
2 **ESL reading teachers**	ESL reading teachers will benefit from using a test in which the criteria for making placement decisions are similar to those used in making decisions about the effectiveness of their instruction.	ESL reading teachers will benefit from being able to focus their instruction on a group of students who are relatively homogeneous in their reading ability.
3 **Teachers in introductory level university academic classes**	Teachers in introductory level academic courses will be aware of the fact that students placed in their class, by virtue of their having taken the test, will have been sensitized to the need to pay attention to the rhetorical organization of material they read.	Teachers in introductory level university courses will benefit from having students in their classes who are prepared to read and understand the rhetorical structure of texts used in these courses.
4 **ESL program administrator**	The ESL program administrator will benefit from using a test whose scoring criteria are consistent with the performance objectives for the course they supervise.	The ESL program administrator will have to deal with fewer complaints from bored or frustrated students and frustrated teachers.

Table 14.3 Intended consequences for stakeholders for University example

3 DESCRIBING THE DECISIONS TO BE MADE AND INDIVIDUALS RESPONSIBLE FOR MAKING THESE

General considerations

As we noted in Chapters 5 and 10, decisions are the means by which decision makers hope to achieve the beneficial consequences that are articulated in Claim 1. However, even though the ends—the intended beneficial consequences—may be adequately supported by warrants and backing, the test user also needs to justify the means—decisions—by which he believes he can achieve those ends. The decisions that are to be made, the stakeholder groups who will be affected by these decisions, and the individuals who will make these decisions are described in Claim 2 of the AUA. These will also be included in the Design Statement, in Item 3, and will guide subsequent assessment development and use. Knowledge of the specific decisions to be made, and the relative importance of these will help the test development team keep these in mind as they develop assessment specifications and create assessment tasks. Specifying the individuals who will be responsible for making these decisions will clearly delineate this role and will thus guide assessment use.

Relevant part of the Design Statement for the University example

The decisions, the stakeholders affected by decisions, and the individuals responsible for making the decisions are provided in Table 14.4.

Decision	Stakeholders who will be affected by the decision	Individual(s) responsible for making the decision
Place students in ESL reading course	Students, instructors in ESL reading course, teachers in students' academic courses	ESL Program Director
Exempt students from ESL reading course	Students, instructors in ESL reading course, teachers in students' academic courses	ESL Program Director
Adjust instruction in ESL reading course	Instructors in ESL reading course, students in ESL reading course	Instructors in ESL reading course

Table 14.4 The decisions, stakeholders affected by decisions, and individuals responsible for making the decisions

4 DETERMINING THE RELATIVE SERIOUSNESS OF CLASSIFICATION ERRORS AND POLICY-LEVEL DECISIONS ABOUT STANDARDS

General considerations

As we discussed in Chapter 5, making decisions typically involves classifying test takers and sometimes other stakeholders into categories. Whenever we classify individuals, there is a possibility that the decision maker will make a classification error. When the test developer articulates Warrant A2 of Claim 2, in consultation with decision makers and other stakeholders, she determines which, if either, of the two possible decision classification errors—false positives or false negatives—is potentially more serious, or is likely to have the most detrimental consequences for test takers and other affected stakeholders. Then, in Warrant A3a of Claim 2, the test developer and decision maker, again in consultation with other stakeholders, determine the policy-level procedures for setting cut scores that will minimize the most serious classification errors.

In order to use an assessment to make decisions, the test developer and decision maker need to decide on the level of ability that they consider appropriate to classify individuals into groups. This level of ability, referred to as a **performance standard**,[1] will typically be stated in terms of the construct definition. A performance standard for exemption from taking an academic ESL writing course, for example, might be something like "extensive evidence of the accurate use of a variety of syntactic structures, appropriate use of cohesive devices and rhetorical organization, as demonstrated in a written composition." This performance standard identifies the minimum level of language knowledge that is considered necessary for participation in academic courses, and hence identifies the level of knowledge that will be used to classify test takers who are exempt from the academic ESL writing course. Test takers who are below this level will be placed into the writing course.

Deciding on a performance standard, or level of ability, that will be used as a minimum level or levels for classifying test takers into two or more groups is a policy decision, and will involve a sound understanding and careful analysis of the specific components of language ability to be assessed and of the language demands of language use tasks in the TLU domain. Once this performance standard has been set by the appropriate stakeholders, it will need to be operationalized as an assessment record, most typically a score. Such a score is called a "cut score," which Bachman (2004b) defines as a "predefined observed score that will be used as a minimal criterion for categorizing individuals" (Bachman 2004b: 198). Procedures for setting cut scores are discussed in Chapter 16.

Relevant part of the Design Statement for the University example

- *Relative seriousness of classification errors*: False positive classification decisions are relatively more serious than false negative classification decisions.
- *Policy-level procedures for setting standards*: The standard for exemption from the ESL reading course was set by the ESL course director in consultation with ESL reading course instructors and academic course instructors.
- *Standard for exemption from the ESL reading course*: Students must demonstrate that they have sufficient knowledge of multilevel rhetorical organization of introductory academic texts to enable them to successfully participate in introductory level academic courses.

Discussion of the example

In the University example, there are serious consequences of decision classification errors. If students are erroneously placed in the ESL reading course when they do not need it, then they may be bored, and become frustrated and discouraged. If, on the other hand, students are erroneously exempted from the reading course even though they are not, in fact, ready to take an academic course, then they may do poorly in the course, and may even fail, thus losing confidence in their ability. In this situation, there is a remedy in place for the false negatives, in that the reading teachers will conduct an additional diagnostic test during the first week of class, and if they identify students whom they feel do not need the course, they will recommend to the ESL Program Director that they be exempted from the course. False positives, however, may be much more difficult to identify, and so this decision classification error is more difficult to correct. For this reason, in this example, false positive errors are considered the more serious.

The ESL course director consulted with relevant stakeholders, in this case, the instructors in the introductory level academic courses and the ESL reading course, to set the standard for exemption from the ESL reading course. While this standard, "sufficient knowledge of multilevel rhetorical organization of introductory academic texts to enable them to successfully participate in introductory level academic courses," may appear to be quite vague,[2] it will nevertheless serve as the basis for a standard-setting procedure to set the cut score on the reading test. This is discussed in Chapter 17.

5 DEFINING THE CONSTRUCT TO BE ASSESSED

General considerations

The test developer will define the constructs, or abilities to be assessed, by articulating Claim 3 and Warrant A1 in the AUA. In Claim 3 the test developer will provide a descriptive label for the construct that will be understandable to stakeholders. In Warrant A1, the test developer will explicitly define the ability or abilities he wants to assess, also in terms that will be understandable to stakeholders. In addition, in Warrant A1 under Claim 3, the test developer describes the source of the construct definition. As discussed in Chapter 11, this source is typically from a course syllabus, a needs analysis, or a theoretical framework of language ability. The product of this activity is a definition of the construct(s), which provides the basis for the interpretations that will be made of the assessment record. This construct definition, which will be elaborated in the Design Statement, in part 5, will provide a basis for the development, in the Operationalization Stage, of assessment tasks. The definition of the construct that is provided in the Design Statement will thus be described in more detail than in the AUA, and may use technical terminology that will be sufficiently precise for the individuals who will develop the Blueprint and create assessment tasks.

Relevant part of the Design Statement for the University example

The definition of the construct for the University example is "knowledge of multilevel rhetorical organization of written texts."

This definition of the construct to be assessed is based upon a needs analysis of reading tasks in courses fulfilling students' general education requirement, and this is the domain within which the construct is meaningful.

Discussion of the example

In this example, the source of the construct definition was a needs analysis that was conducted by the test development team. In Chapter 11, "Construct definitions based on a needs analysis," (pp. 213–14) we point out that we can use a needs analysis to arrive at a definition of the ability to be assessed. In general, needs analysis, or needs assessment, involves the systematic gathering of specific information about the language use needs of learners and the analysis of this information for purposes of language syllabus design. The procedures of needs analysis can be adapted for the purposes of assessment development, and involve the following activities, with respect to defining the construct to be assessed:[3]

1 *identifying the stakeholders* who are familiar with the language use demands of tasks in the TLU domain, who can help in defining the construct(s) to be assessed;
2 *developing procedures* to be followed in working with stakeholders to define the construct to be assessed;
3 *carrying out the procedures* to obtain a definition of the construct to be assessed.

These activities will produce a definition of the construct to be assessed. In addition, as discussed below, under section 6, this needs analysis will provide a list of the TLU tasks that will be the basis for developing assessment tasks.

To illustrate the steps in this process, we will first describe each step of the needs analysis in general and then illustrate the step in the process using the University example.

1 Identifying the stakeholders who are familiar with the language demands of tasks in the TLU domain

As we have noted in previous chapters, when developing an assessment, the test developer needs to clearly identify who the stakeholders are and how they will be affected by both the use of the assessment and the decisions that are made. These stakeholders will also be able to help the test developers define the construct(s) to be assessed.

University example

In the University example, the test development team consisted of the ESL Program Director, a visiting professor, and a small group of Ph.D. students who had already taken a course in L2 assessment design. The team was highly familiar with the assessment situation and was able to identify the primary stakeholders in a short meeting. These stakeholders included the test takers, ESL reading instructors, the members of the test development team, and faculty members teaching regular introductory level academic courses in a variety of disciplines.

2 Developing procedures to be followed in working with stakeholders to develop a construct definition

A variety of procedures, such as focus groups, surveys, and interviews, can be used for gathering information about the TLU domain. Deciding which procedures to use involves real world considerations such as the cost of implementing the needs analysis and the time involved in carrying it out, as well as the amount and quality of the information needed. Assessment development projects for high-stakes decisions will require more sophisticated and resource intensive procedures than those required in low-stakes decisions.

In some cases, the test developer may be quite familiar with the language use demands of tasks in the TLU domain, and may be able to use her own knowledge to come up with an initial construct definition. However, in most situations, the test developer will need to work with other stakeholders to refine his initial definition. Furthermore, even in cases where the test developer is quite familiar with the TLU domain, we believe it is essential for her to employ a systematic approach to defining the construct to be assessed. Involving other stakeholders and using a systematic approach is particularly critical in cases where the test developer is not at all familiar with the language use demands of tasks in the TLU domain.

University example

In the University example, the test development team decided upon three procedures for creating a construct definition. The first procedure involved talking with the stakeholders identified in (1) above, both individually and in focus groups. The second involved reviewing data from a research study carried out in the preceding year in which the language use needs of L2 students in the University were surveyed. Third, since the team consisted of Ph.D. students who were currently studying in the university, the members of the team could also rely to a considerable extent upon their recollections of their collective experiences of their strategies for understanding the rhetorical organization of reading material. Of particular interest was the input from those Ph.D. students who spoke English as a second/foreign language.

3 Following the procedures to develop a construct definition

Once the test developer and other stakeholders have decided on the procedures to be used for arriving at a construct definition, they can then follow these procedures to define the construct to be assessed.

University example

The stakeholders provided a number of possible construct definitions, such as knowledge of general and special purpose vocabulary, textual cohesion, grammar, academic register, implicatures, and characteristics of genres used in texts for introductory undergraduate courses. While the stakeholders had various opinions about the relative importance of these different areas of language knowledge, they generally agreed that knowledge of the way material in written texts was organized was essential to understanding them. Many of the students who were interviewed were very conscious of how they had used their knowledge of rhetorical organization to make sense of texts they had read. Many of the teachers expected their students to understand the organization of texts they read as well. As a result, the test development team decided to define the construct as "knowledge of multilevel rhetorical organization of written texts."

6 IDENTIFYING AND DESCRIBING THE TLU DOMAIN

General considerations

In order to justify the use of an assessment, the test developer and decision maker must be able to support warrants that the interpretations about the ability to be assessed are generalizable beyond the assessment itself to tasks in the TLU domain in which decisions are to be made. To support these warrants, the test developer needs to identify and describe the relevant TLU domain, which she will do when she articulates Warrant C1 under Claim 3 about the generalizability of the interpretations about test takers' language ability. In the Design Statement, part 6, the test developer will provide an elaborated description of the TLU domain. This description of the TLU domain will provide as much detail as needed to guide assessment development, and will perform two functions. The first function is to clearly describe the domain beyond the assessment itself to which the test developer wants her assessment-based interpretations to generalize. This also defines the TLU domain for which the decisions will be relevant. Second, the description of the TLU domain tells her where to find TLU tasks that she can use as a basis for developing assessment tasks.

In many situations, identifying and describing the TLU domain for the purpose of developing and using a language assessment will be relatively straightforward.[4] However, in some assessment development situations there is essentially no specific TLU domain to start out with. This could be the case when an assessment is being developed for use with a wide variety of test takers whose TLU domains and needs are very different. This could also be the case when the TLU domains and needs of the test takers may be either non-existent or very vaguely defined in terms of some possible future need to use the language. In such situations, it may be difficult to specify any TLU domain with much precision and any attempt to select specific tasks as a basis for assessment tasks would not yield a manageable number of tasks.

One type of the "no specific TLU domain" situation is encountered in conducting some kinds of applied linguistics research in which the focus of the research is on the meaningfulness of interpretations, rather than on their generalizability, and the interpretations will not be used to make decisions about the test takers. In such situations, test takers might be selected as participants in the research because they represent a sample of some population of individuals in whom the researcher is interested. In addition, the assessment tasks that are used will be selected because of their potential for eliciting the language abilities in which the researcher is interested, rather than on characteristics that may be related to tasks in a particular TLU domain. (This situation is illustrated in Project 14 on the web).

Another "no specific TLU domain" situation is sometimes encountered in countries where students may be studying English in primary and secondary schools and in universities because of the perceived importance of this for the country's global economic development. Elementary school students may in fact be studying English so that they can pass an examination for entrance to secondary school. Secondary school students may be studying English in order to pass the university entrance examination. Finally, university students may be actually learning English in order to obtain jobs that will be rewarding financially as well as professionally.

It is not our place or intention to question the right of individual countries to pursue such a language policy, or to criticize such a policy. On the contrary, our point is simply that this situation makes it very difficult to identify a specific TLU domain for the purpose of developing language assessments. For example, in the secondary school and university entrance examinations, is the TLU domain the one in which the students have just been studying English, or the one that they will be entering? If it is the case, as it frequently is, that the students may in fact not use English at all outside of the English classroom, then the TLU domain for the assessments might reasonably be the English that is used in English classes. However, when we consider what the TLU domain might be for a university "exit" examination in English, we run into a problem. Is the TLU domain for this examination the content of the English classes they have attended? Or the English that they may have used in some of their academic courses? Or the TLU domain of their future job or profession?

In situations such as these, we would advise the test developer to attempt to define a TLU domain to which she wants to generalize, based on the attributes of the test takers and the construct to be assessed. Thus, in the previous situation, a test developer who is charged with developing the English section of the university entrance examination might think of language use situations and tasks that students who have completed secondary school might reasonably be expected to perform—given their age, academic interests, amount of English instruction, and that would engage the ability to be assessed. If the test developer does not define a reasonable TLU domain, then she will be faced with the problem of having to develop assessment tasks that may have no correspondence to language use outside of the assessment itself, and with not being able to justify generalizing beyond the assessment.

Relevant part of the Design Statement for the University example

The TLU domain in the University example is "readings in textbooks in introductory level academic courses."

Discussion of the example

The needs analysis helped the test developer arrive at a construct definition, and was also used to describe the TLU domain and to select TLU tasks as a basis for developing assessment tasks (described in section 7 below).

The three steps that were followed in the University example are:

1 Identifying the stakeholders who are familiar with the TLU domain [D]

The stakeholders that were identified are the same as those discussed above, in section 5, "Defining the construct to be assessed."

2 Developing procedures to be followed in describing the TLU domain and selecting TLU tasks for consideration as assessment tasks. [D]

The procedures to be followed in describing the TLU domain and selecting TLU tasks for consideration as assessment tasks were the same as those for the needs analysis discussed above, in section 5, "Defining the construct to be assessed."

3 Describing the relevant TLU domain [D]

In the University example, students who were exempted from any additional reading courses would need to cope with their reading needs primarily on their own, and not in the ESL reading class. Since their reading could be taking place in a variety of places, the development team initially defined the TLU domain as the "real life" domain in which students would be performing tasks that require reading.

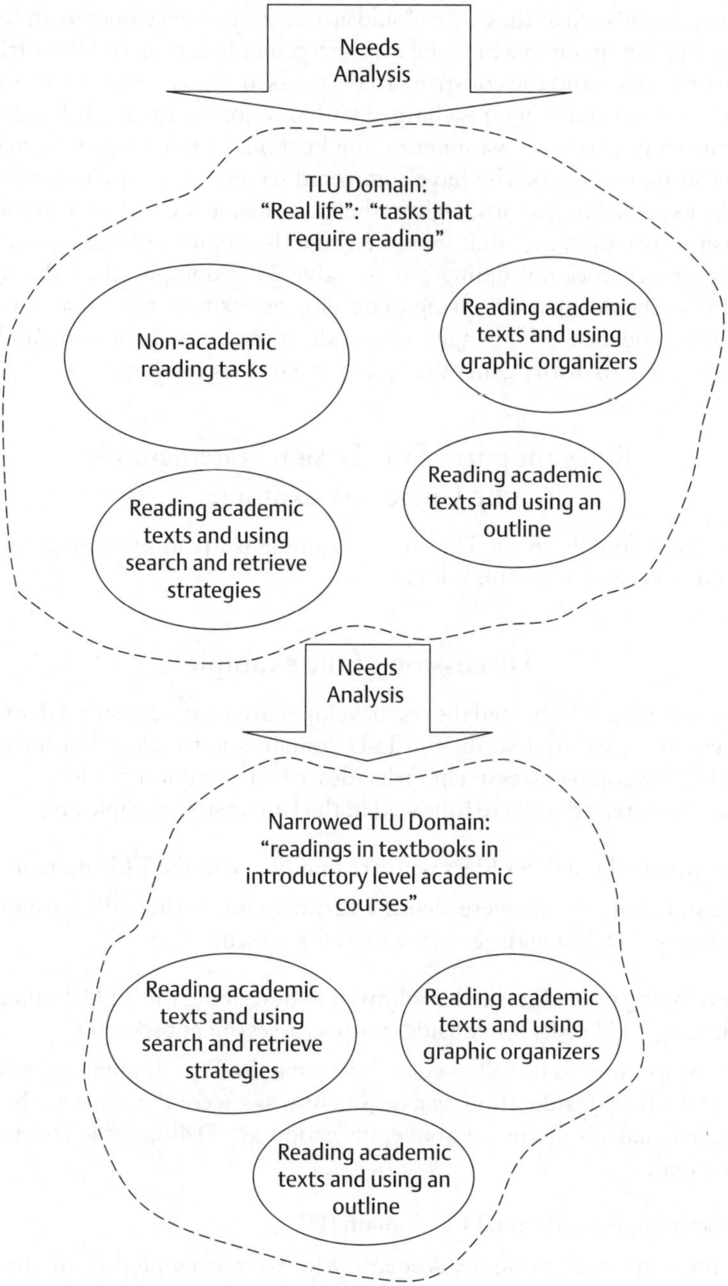

Needs Analysis

TLU Domain:
"Real life": "tasks that require reading"

Non-academic reading tasks

Reading academic texts and using graphic organizers

Reading academic texts and using an outline

Reading academic texts and using search and retrieve strategies

Needs Analysis

Narrowed TLU Domain:
"readings in textbooks in introductory level academic courses"

Reading academic texts and using search and retrieve strategies

Reading academic texts and using graphic organizers

Reading academic texts and using an outline

Figure 14.1 Defining and narrowing the TLU domain through needs analysis

The stakeholders then considered the possible sub-domains in the real life domain in which the test takers might need to perform reading tasks involving knowledge of rhetorical organization in written texts. They decided that performing such tasks in non-academic settings such as reading magazines, socially oriented email or text messages to friends, or web pages accessed for personal reasons were less important than performing reading tasks in academic settings. Therefore, the stakeholders narrowed the scope of the TLU domain to "academic reading in university classes."

They then surveyed the various kinds of university classes, including introductory level courses, advanced courses, courses specific to particular academic majors, and courses that would fulfill students' general education requirement. After analyzing the reading demands of all of these different kinds of courses, they decided to further narrow the scope of the TLU domain to "academic readings in introductory level courses," since these courses did not presuppose highly specialized topical knowledge. Finally, the test development team collected course descriptions and reading lists from a wide range of introductory level courses at the university and considered the various types of material students were required to read in these courses, including texts, journals, and material in the media. Since most of these courses had required textbooks and not all used journals or material from the media, the test development team decided to further narrow the scope of the domain to "academic readings in *textbooks* in introductory level courses."

This narrowing down of the TLU domain is illustrated in Figure 14.1.

7 SELECTING TLU TASKS AS A BASIS FOR DEVELOPING ASSESSMENT TASKS

General considerations

In most assessment situations it is not possible to include every task in the TLU domain as an assessment task. Therefore, the test developer will generally need to select those TLU tasks that he thinks might possibly serve as a basis for developing assessment tasks. In selecting such tasks, the test developer will consult with other members of the test development team, with the decision makers, and ideally with other stakeholders. Their decisions will be guided largely by considerations of the qualities of the claims in the AUA and by practicality.

Qualities of the claims in the AUA

The selection of TLU tasks as a basis for assessment tasks is highly subjective and is based on the best judgment of the test developer and the other stakeholders with whom she consults. It is for this reason that we recommend using the warrants in the AUA as a guide in this process. In considering which

TLU tasks have the most potential for satisfying the claimed qualities in the AUA, the test developer will consider all of the qualities, but will focus primarily on the intended beneficial consequences of using the assessment (Claim 1), on the qualities of assessment-based interpretations (Claim 3), and on the consistency of assessment records (Claim 4). Of particular importance in language instructional settings is the potential of the TLU task for promoting good instructional practice and effective learning, as stated in Warrant A5 under Claim 1. This warrant will lead the test developer to consider tasks for learning and instruction in the classroom as a basis for developing assessment tasks. With respect to the assessment-based interpretations, the test developer will focus particularly on meaningfulness, impartiality, and generalizability, as stated in the warrants under Claim 3 of the AUA. In considering the potential *meaningfulness* of interpretations based on performance on TLU tasks, the test developer will consider Warrants A3 and A4. Warrant A3 will guide the test developer to consider how an assessment record could be produced from performance on the TLU task. Continuing with the above example, in developing a test to measure "understanding of the content of academic lectures," even though "understanding" might be thought of as an internal process with no observable product, the test developers would want to select TLU tasks that have some sort of observable response that could be described or quantified to produce an assessment record. The above example illustrates one such type of response (the test takers select correct answers from among alternatives). Another TLU task with an observable response might involve students taking notes on a lecture. An assessment task based on this task could provide an observable response that could be rated or scored according to a scoring rubric.

Warrant A4 will lead the test developer to consider the extent to which the TLU task will actually engage the ability to be assessed, as defined in the construct definition. This will involve considering not only the input in the task that needs to be processed, but also the way in which language users respond to the tasks. In this regard, some TLU tasks may be inappropriate because they can be carried out with little use of the areas of language ability that the assessment is intended to measure. To illustrate this, consider the following example.

One of the authors was once involved in helping a large multinational company develop a test to assess the capacity of individuals for using Chinese and English accurately and appropriately to function effectively as a bilingual receptionist in one of their Asian offices. This test would be used as part of the selection procedure for hiring a new receptionist. In this situation, the client clearly wanted an individual who could use both languages accurately and appropriately, so both grammatical knowledge and sociolinguistic knowledge (essentially knowledge of appropriate registers and forms of address) were included in the construct definition. One of the task types in the TLU domain involved the employee's answering the phone and transferring the call to another employee. This particular task could be accomplished by means of a couple of short formulaic utterances, such as (in English) "Hello, this is B-P Enterprises. How may I direct your call?" and "Just a moment, please, and I'll transfer your call."

In this example, the client was interested in being able to make meaningful interpretations about the test takers' grammatical and sociolinguistic knowledge, and this task type would not be adequate for making interpretations about these areas of language knowledge since it might require little more than the knowledge of prefabricated patterns. That is, using this TLU task as a basis for developing a test task might limit the meaningfulness of the interpretations we want to make.

In considering the *impartiality* of the interpretations, the test developer will look at Warrants B1 and B2, to make sure that the responses to the TLU task will not favor or disfavor some test takers, and that the task does not include content that may be offensive or linguistically inappropriate for some test takers. Thus, some TLU tasks may not be appropriate for developing assessment tasks because they are not appropriate for all of the test takers. This may occur, for example, when the TLU domain is very broadly defined, such as in a situation where a language test is needed for use, along with other kinds of information, for making decisions involving selecting students for entrance into a university. The TLU domain in this case involves using English in a university setting, and includes a wide range of tasks that are likely to vary in a number of ways, including the areas and levels of specific topical knowledge required to perform them. The test takers will most likely be a diverse group with relatively general topical knowledge, who will eventually choose different majors. If the test developer included test tasks that correspond, in level and areas of topical content, to tasks in the TLU domain, tasks such as these could be considered unfair to test takers who do not already have the levels of specialized knowledge such tasks require and raise the likelihood of convincing rebuttals to the impartiality warrants. In this case, the test developer might attempt to minimize these problems by excluding the tasks that require more specialized topical knowledge and trying to include test tasks whose characteristics are common to the TLU tasks that all of the test takers will need to perform.

In considering the *generalizability* of the interpretations, the test developer will refer to Warrant C2. This warrant will lead the test developer to consider the extent to which an assessment record from performance on an assessment task that is based on the TLU task can be arrived at using criteria that are similar to those used by language users in assessing performance on the TLU task. For example, if we follow up on the example of a test to measure ability to make inferences about the content of academic lectures in students' L2, test developers might want to use criteria similar to those that teachers actually use in assessing students' performance on these tasks, such as responding to comprehension checks orally or in writing. An example of criteria for which it would be harder to argue would be required native-like pronunciation or grammatical accuracy in responses.

With respect to generalizability, the test developer will also need to consider the whole range of tasks in the TLU domain to assure that she does not miss any TLU tasks that might be essential for language users to be able to carry out in order to perform successfully in the TLU domain. Suppose, for example, that non-native English speaking immigrant midwives were applying to be licensed to work as midwives in the United States, and the licensing procedure included a test of their ability in English. Suppose that a needs analysis indicated that translating prescriptions verbatim from the language of immigrants into English was an essential task that midwives had to perform. In this case, because this TLU task is essential, we would want to make sure that it was selected as a basis for developing assessment tasks.

Finally, the test developer will consider the extent to which it will be possible to develop, on the basis of the TLU task, multiple assessment tasks that are consistent in their task characteristics (Warrant 1, Claim 4), that can be administered consistently (Warrant A2), and that will yield test takers' performance that can be scored consistently (Warrant A3).

Practicality

While the primary criteria for selecting TLU tasks as a basis for developing assessment tasks are based on the warrants in the AUA, the test developer's selection of tasks will also be subject to considerations of practicality. First, the test developer will need to consider the costs that will be involved in creating multiple assessment tasks that are like a given TLU task, and of administering and generating an assessment record for this. It may be that some TLU tasks that satisfy the relevant warrants in the AUA are practical to use as is, for assessment tasks. Others, however, may require extensive resources to replicate, administer, and score, and hence be impractical. Finally, some TLU tasks might be practical to use as assessment tasks, but fail to satisfy one or more of the relevant warrants in the AUA, as in the example above.

Trade-offs between the demands of AUA warrants and practicality

Considering the demands of the AUA warrants and practicality on the selection of TLU tasks as a basis for developing assessment tasks, there are four possible combinations, as illustrated in Table 14.5.

	Practical	**Not practical**
Satisfies AUA warrants	A Select and use as is as an assessment task	B Select; possibly modify to make practical
Does not satisfy AUA warrants	C Select; possibly modify to satisfy warrants in the AUA	D Do not select

Table 14.5 AUA and practicality in selecting TLU tasks

The test developer may select and use the TLU tasks in cell A as is as assessment tasks, while TLU tasks in cell D would generally not be considered for selection. TLU tasks in cells B and C, however, might be selected, but will require some modifications. Tasks in cell B will need to be modified so as to be practical, while still satisfying the warrants in the AUA. Tasks in cell C, on the other hand, will need to be modified to satisfy the warrants in the AUA, while still being practical. In either case, the test developer will need to consider the costs of modifying the TLU task so that it will be both practical and will satisfy the relevant warrants in the AUA as much as possible. Thus, in selecting such tasks as a basis for developing assessment tasks, there will almost always be trade-offs between satisfying the demands of the AUA and the limitations of practicality.

"Critical" TLU tasks

In some TLU domains either the stakeholders or a needs analysis may identify certain TLU tasks that are essential to the successful performance of the language user's duties or responsibilities. We will refer to such TLU tasks as **critical TLU tasks.** In the University example, the test development team identified "reading textbooks in introductory level academic courses" as a task that was essential, or critical, for students to succeed in their academic courses, since *all* students needed to take courses at this level and read texts such as these. In a business setting, the ability to make formal introductions in a way consistent with the culture of high-stakes business negotiations in a particular country might be considered to be a critical task. When critical TLU tasks occur and are identified in the TLU, the test developer must find a way to include them in the TLU tasks that are selected as a basis for assessment tasks.

Using a needs analysis as the basis for describing the TLU domain and considering the warrants in the AUA as criteria for selecting certain TLU tasks as a basis for developing assessment tasks is not aimed at yielding a set of TLU tasks that constitute a "representative sample" of that TLU domain in any statistical or quantitative sense. This is because, in the vast majority of situations, the tasks in the TLU domain are likely to include a wide variety of language use activities (i.e., listening, speaking, reading, and writing) aimed at performing a broad range of language functions (e.g., greeting, describing, explaining, persuading, assessing). In such domains the tasks are highly heterogeneous, so that it is seldom possible to arrive at a representative sample by selecting some of these tasks at random. Rather than being objective or "quantitative," the process of describing the TLU domain and selecting TLU tasks is a qualitative one, involving the best combined judgments of the test development team, based on information that is collected through a systematic procedure involving collaboration with all relevant stakeholders. It is through this systematic process that the test developer can arrive at a set of TLU tasks that he believes will engage the construct to be assessed, and from which assessment-based interpretations will generalize beyond the assessment itself to the TLU domain.

The selection process will yield a set of TLU tasks that the test developer believes are most likely to elicit performance from which an assessment record can be obtained, that will provide the basis for interpretations that are meaningful, impartial, and generalizable, and that will be practical for use as assessment tasks. In most situations, there will be some TLU tasks that satisfy some but not all of the warrants in the AUA. Some tasks, for example, might be very typical of the TLU domain, but may not elicit the ability in which the test developer is interested, while some that do elicit the ability to be assessed may not occur very often in the TLU domain. In our experience, we only rarely find TLU tasks that satisfy all of the relevant warrants in the AUA. It is for this reason that the test developer will almost always need to modify the selected TLU tasks in some way to make them appropriate as assessment tasks. (The process of modifying TLU tasks to develop assessment tasks is discussed in Chapter 15.)

The amount of time and effort expended in defining the TLU domain and selecting TLU tasks for consideration as assessment tasks will be influenced by the demands of the particular assessment situation. For example, when designing a high-stakes assessment for use with a wide variety of test takers, it might be important to conduct a very detailed needs analysis and prepare an extensive list of TLU tasks consistent with this analysis. On the other hand, when designing a low-stakes classroom assessment for use with a single group of students, the test developer may already have in mind some specific tasks to be used as the basis for developing assessment tasks, so the process might be much less involved.

Relevant part of the Design Statement for the University example

The TLU task that was selected as a basis for developing assessment tasks is "reading a passage from a textbook in an introductory level academic course and developing an outline of this."

Discussion of the example

In the University example, the stakeholders most familiar with the construct to be measured and tasks in the TLU domain were L2 students in introductory level courses who already had strategies for using their knowledge of rhetorical organization to make sense of texts they had read. The test development team met with these students in focus groups and they described three tasks they performed to help them understand the texts they read in their introductory general education courses:

1 Using graphic organizers, such as Chains, Diagrams, and Maps;
2 Outlining;
3 Using "search and retrieve" strategies such as finding the main idea in paragraphs and writing it down, and finding details about a specific main idea and writing these down.

The team then discussed which of these tasks would be the most appropriate for use as a basis for developing assessment tasks and ruled out two of them. They ruled out tasks involving completing graphic organizers because there were several different kinds of graphic organizers in use and no single one seemed to be equally familiar to or used by all the different students in the university. The test development team thus felt that interpretations based on this task would not be impartial (Warrant B1, under Claim 3). Furthermore, the test development team felt that a graphic organizer would not engage the knowledge of the multilevel rhetorical organization of written texts, and that interpretations based upon this would therefore not be meaningful (Warrant A4, under Claim 3). They also ruled out the "search and retrieve" tasks for essentially the same reasons.

The team selected the "reading and outlining" TLU task as a basis for developing assessment tasks for several reasons. A wide range of students reported using an outline as a tool for comprehending academic texts. Furthermore, the instructors in the academic courses reported that their students frequently used outlining, and that it is often provided as a pre-organizer in academic texts. In addition, the ESL reading instructors said that they taught this activity in the reading course.

Thus, it was expected that most of the students taking the test would already be familiar with this type of task. Instructors also felt that students who were not familiar with outlining would benefit from becoming familiar with this type of task, because outlining is usable with a wide variety of texts. Thus, the test included a short tutorial on outlining for these students. Finally, the outlining task could be adapted to a test task involving limited production responses that could be objectively scored using a scoring key. This was an important practical consideration because of the large number of students who would be taking the test and the need to use an economical scoring procedure and report scores quickly.

8 DESCRIBING THE CHARACTERISTICS OF SELECTED TLU TASKS

General considerations

After completing the needs analysis and selecting the TLU tasks that will provide the basis for the development of assessment tasks, the test developer then needs to describe the selected TLU tasks in terms of their task characteristics. In some cases the test developer may find the framework for describing task characteristics described in Chapter 3 satisfactory for describing TLU tasks. In other cases he may want to modify the framework. This may involve omitting certain characteristics which do not seem relevant or adding others. The main point is that some sort of task characteristics framework and systematic analysis is useful in bringing precision to the development of assessment tasks, and comparing the characteristics of these tasks with those of TLU tasks.

TLU task characteristics as templates for developing assessment tasks

When the test developer describes the selected TLU tasks in terms of their task characteristics, these tasks are no longer holistic entities, but become sets of task characteristics, as in the University example (Table 14.6). These sets of task characteristics provide "templates" that the test developer and task creators can use for developing assessment tasks. The relationship between TLU tasks and these templates is illustrated in Figure 14.2.

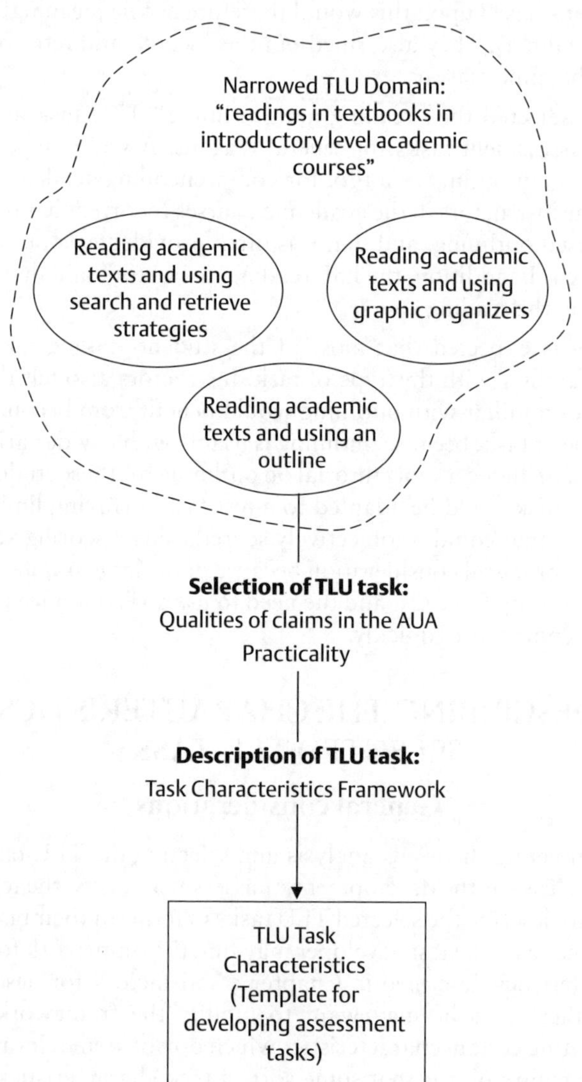

Figure 14.2 Selecting TLU tasks and describing their characteristics

Relevant part of the Design Statement for the University example

The task characteristics of the "outlining" TLU task for the University example are given in Table 14.6. We use a table to present these characteristics because when there are multiple TLU tasks selected as templates for developing assessment tasks, a table (with multiple "Characteristics" columns) provides a convenient way to compare the characteristics of the different TLU task templates.

	Characteristics of "outlining" TLU task
Setting	**Physical characteristics:** home, library, and classroom, computer, course text **Participants:** the student; possibly teacher and other students
Rubric (all implicit in the TLU task)	
Instructions	Target language, written, visual, or internally generated by the student; specification of procedures and tasks based upon students' prior instruction in and experience with outlining
Structure	**Number of parts:** one part (outline) per reading **Salience of parts and tasks:** salience of parts: not applicable, only one part; salience of tasks (entries associated with each level of the outline): highly salient **Sequence of tasks:** determined by sequence of information in reading **Relative importance of tasks:** tasks associated with main headings may be relatively more important than tasks associated with relatively minor details in sub-headings **Number of tasks**: depends upon length of reading passage, number of levels in outline, and number of entries under each level
Time allotment	Highly variable
Recording method	**Criteria for recording:** degree of association of organization of outline with organization of reading text; meaning of entries far more important than grammatical accuracy **Procedures for recording the response:** student's internally generated feedback based upon usefulness of the outline in helping the student interact with the material in the reading; possible written or spoken feedback from instructor **Explicitness of criteria and procedures for recording the response:** fairly explicit if student has been given formal instruction in outlining **Recorders:** variable (the student, other students, instructors)
Input	
Format	Input for interpretation, written, lengthy, English, unspeeded

Language characteristics	**Grammatical:** complex **Textual:** highly organized **Functions:** most frequently ideational, can also be manipulative (persuasive) **Genre:** introductory academic course text **Dialect:** academic **Register:** formal **Naturalness:** natural **Cultural references:** variable **Figures of speech:** variable
Topical characteristics	Variable: topics consistent with introductory general education course content
Expected response	
Format	Written, English, extended production, relatively unspeeded
Language characteristics	**Grammatical:** somewhat complex **Textual:** outline **Functions:** ideational **Genre:** outline **Dialect:** standard academic **Register:** formal **Naturalness:** natural **Cultural references:** variable, depending upon course content **Figures of speech:** variable
Topical characteristics	Variable: topics consistent with introductory general education course content
Relationship between input and expected response	
Type of external interactiveness	Non-reciprocal interaction between test taker, reading passage, incomplete outline as provided in test, and developing outline emerging as test taker completes the test
Scope	Narrow
Directness	Direct

Table 14.6 Example description of TLU task characteristics

9 DEVELOPING A PLAN FOR COLLECTING FEEDBACK AND BACKING

General considerations

This activity makes explicit how the test developer will go about collecting feedback to help him improve the assessment itself, and to provide the backing that will enable him to justify the intended uses (decisions, consequences) of test takers' assessment performance. The product of this activity is a plan that will guide the collection of feedback as part of the assessment production process, and backing as part of the assessment justification process.

Backing is likely to include a wide range of information. As discussed in earlier chapters, some of the backing will come from the assessment development process itself, and the documentation (Initial Plan, Design Statement, Blueprint) that grows out of this. Other backing may be qualitative, such as test developers' and test users' evaluations of the warrants in the AUA, observer's descriptions and verbal self-reports from students on the assessment taking process, as well as documents, such as regulations and laws, and educational and societal values, which may be documented, or may be collected through qualitative methods. Other evidence may be quantitative, such as test scores, scores on individual test tasks, and other measures of the abilities to be assessed. Finally, the plan will include procedures for analyzing the backing we have collected. This will include statistical analyses of scores and appropriate analyses of the qualitative data. This process of collecting backing is discussed in detail in Chapter 19. The plan for collecting backing, which will be based on the AUA, will include the following components:

A the specific claims and warrants for which backing will be provided,
B the evidence that will be collected as backing,
C activities that will be used to collect and analyze the backing,
D the stages in the assessment development process at which the backing will be collected,
E the specific individuals who will be responsible for either collecting the backing or analyzing it, or both.

The activities that are specified in the plan will be conducted at each stage during the process of assessment development and use. Because of possible changes in resources and stakeholders' needs, as discussed in Chapter 20, the process of collecting backing is likely to be iterative.

Relevant part of the Design Statement for the University example

A part of the plan for collecting backing for the University example is provided in Table 14.7 on p. 298. In the interest of brevity, we include only the plan for Stages 1 and 2. The backing collected during these stages will be in the form of documents and processes followed. (See Chapter 19 for a discussion of how backing can be collected during stages 3, 4, and 5.) Note that a plan for collecting backing will be organized chronologically, from Stage 1 through Stage 5, which will help the test developer to schedule these activities and then allocate the required resources. Note too, that one activity that is repeated at each stage is a documentation of the procedures that have been followed. This documentary narrative of the entire process of assessment development and use provides valuable backing to support the claims and warrants in the AUA.

Stage	Activities	Backing	Claim, Warrants supported	Person(s) responsible
I Pre-dev planning	1 Consulting documents 2 Consulting stakeholders 3 Documenting the procedures followed	Doc: Initial Plan Doc: Description of procedures followed	Claims 1 and 2	ESL Program Director, ESL Reading Course instructors
II Design	1 Identifying stakeholders 2 Documenting the procedures followed	Doc: DS, Pt 1, list of stakeholders Doc: Description of procedures followed	Claim 1 Claim 1	Project Director (the Visiting Professor), ESL Program Director, ESL Reading Course instructors
	3 Consulting with stakeholders: • ELL students at the university • ESL reading teachers • Academic course instructors 4 Documenting the procedures followed	Doc: DS, Pt 2, list of intended consequences and potential detrimental consequences Doc: DS, Pt 3, list of decisions to be made, who is responsible for making these, and who will be affected by these Doc: DS, Pt 4: description of relative seriousness of decision errors and performance standards for making classification decisions Doc: Description of procedures followed	Claim 1, W A1 Claim 2 Claim 2, W A2, A3a, A3b Claims 1 & 2	Project Director, ESL Program Director, ESL Reading Course instructors
	5 Conducting a needs analysis 6 Describing TLU task characteristics 7 Documenting the procedures followed • Documents consulted • Stakeholders consulted • TLU domain observed	Doc: DS, Pt 5, definition of construct Doc: DS, Pt 6, description of TLU domain Doc: DS, Pt 7, list of TLU tasks selected Doc: DS, Pt 8, description of TLU task (templates) Doc: Description of procedures followed	Claim 3, W A1 Claim 3, W C1, C2 Claim 3, W C1, C2 Claim 3, W C1, C2 Claim 3	Project Director, ESL Program Director, Ph.D. students in language testing, ESL Reading instructors, Academic course instructors

Table 14.7 Plan for collecting backing for the University example

In Table 14.7 we have provided more detail rather than less in order to illustrate the kinds of information that can go into such a table. The amount of information that test developers actually provide will depend upon the stakes of the test and the background of those individuals who will be using the table or referring to it during the assessment development process. Thus, the level of detail in this might be quite reasonable for a relatively high-stakes test to be administered to large numbers of test takers, while in a low-stakes setting much less detail would most likely be sufficient.

10 DEVELOPING A PLAN FOR OBTAINING, ALLOCATING, AND MANAGING RESOURCES

General considerations

In order to implement assessment production and justification activities, the test developer will first need to estimate the amounts of human and material resources and time that will be needed for these activities. This estimate will provide the basis for a plan for how the needed resources can be obtained, and for how these can be most effectively allocated and managed. Having a well-specified plan will help assure that the necessary resources are available and are used appropriately, effectively, and efficiently during subsequent stages of assessment development. This plan will evolve during the process of assessment development. This is for two reasons. First, as assessment development proceeds, more and more detailed information about the assessment itself and the justification process will become available, and more resources may be required than were estimated at the Design stage. During Stage 3, Operationalization, task specifications will be developed, and the kinds of tasks that will be included, how test takers are expected to respond to these, and the ways in which the responses will be recorded will have implications for the kinds of resources that will be required. For example, if the decision were made to deliver the assessment tasks via computers or the web, this would require additional expertise in computer/web programming, so that the test developer would need to obtain support to hire individuals with this expertise, and then work with them and the rest of the test development team to determine how best to allocate their expertise and time. During Stage 4, Trialing, it may turn out that some assessment tasks are not suitable, for a number of reasons, so that the test development team may need to go back and develop new tasks. This will require additional resources. Finally, during Stage 4, Assessment Use, the test developer may find that the backing that he intended to collect will not be sufficient for some stakeholders, so that he will need to provide additional backing, which will require more resources. Second, as discussed in Chapter 13, real world uncertainties can lead to changes in both the resources that will be needed and those that are available. This is particularly an issue for long-term assessment development and use projects, in which the costs of various resources can increase over time, members of the test development team may leave, and new people will need to be found to replace them, and the uses of the assessment itself may evolve, requiring additional resources for ongoing assessment justification. Thus, just as the AUA, the Design Statement, and the Blueprint must be flexible, so the plan for the allocation and management of resources needs to be adaptable to changing conditions in the real world.

Estimating required resources

Initial estimates of the resources that will be required and available will have already been made in the Initial Planning Stage, as discussed in Chapter 7. However, at the Design Stage, as more details of the assessment are specified, a more accurate and detailed estimate of required resources will be possible and needed. For example, at this stage, the test developer will have a much more specific definition of the construct to be measured and will know the characteristics of the TLU tasks that have been selected as a basis for developing assessment tasks. In addition, the test developer will have a plan for collecting backing for the AUA. This additional information may have implications for the kinds of resources that will be needed. Thus, the estimate of required resources at the Design stage will need to include more detailed estimates of resources for *both* assessment production *and* assessment justification, and will need to cover all stages of the assessment development process. Providing this additional detail and projecting resource needs for the entire assessment development process makes it much more feasible to develop a plan for obtaining and managing resources.

Relevant part of the Design Statement for the University example

Estimated needs of resources during the process of test development and use

An estimate of the resources needed during the process of test development and use is shown in Table 14.8.

Discussion of the example

In the Initial Planning stage, as discussed in Chapter 7, the ESL Program Director consulted with the ESL instructors about the resources that would be required to develop a placement/exemption test. The estimate of required resources at that stage was essentially a list of resources, with very little detail, and with no indication of how much of these would be required at different stages of assessment development. (See the University example in Chapter 7.) The plan that was developed during the Design Stage extended this initial estimate in two ways. First, it provided much greater detail, estimating the required personnel resources in terms of numbers of hours. Second, it

	STAGES				
RESOURCES	**1 Initial planning**	**2 Design**	**3 Operationalization**	**4 Trialing**	**5 Use**
Personnel					
Project Director (Visiting Professor)		40 hours week	40 hours week	40 hours/ week	40 hours/ week
ESL Program Director	40 hours	10 hours	10 hours	10 hours	10 hours
Development team	10 hours/ person	10 hours/ person/ week	10 hours/person/ week	10 hours/ person/ week	20 hours/ person/ term
Computer programmer		30 hours	50 hours	50 hours	10 hours/ term
Clerical support	2 hours	10 hours	30 hours	40 hours	20 hours/ term
Test administrators/ Scorers				20 hours	20 hours/ term
Space	Meeting room	Meeting room	Meeting room	Meeting room, rooms for adminis-tering the test	Meeting room, rooms for adminis-tering the test
Equipment	PCs	PCs	PCs	PCs	PCs

Table 14.8 Estimation of required resources for the University example at the Design stage

estimated the resources required for the different stages of the assessment development process.

Obtaining and managing resources

After identifying the resources that will be required, the assessment developer needs to develop a plan to obtain and manage these. This plan will include three parts: (1) a list of proposed or actual sources for obtaining the resources needed, (2) a proposal for allocating and managing these, and (3) a time line that specifies the various tasks involved in the test development and use process, the sequence in which they will be carried out, and the time by which each needs to be completed. In low-stakes situations, the developer will likely only consider developing an assessment for which she has sufficient resources on hand. In higher-stakes situations, the demands on resources may be much greater, so a systematic plan for obtaining, allocating, and managing them will be needed.

Relevant part of the Design Statement for the University example

List of resources that will be available

I Personnel

- A Project Director: Dr Shin has been hired full-time as Project Director.
- B Development team: Two ESL reading teachers will be available part-time, and three Ph.D. students in language assessment have been hired as part-time research assistants.
- C Computer programmers: One Ph.D. student in the Department with expertise in computer data bases has been hired as a part-time research assistant.
- D Clerical support: Department Chair will provide one person, part-time, or clerical support.
- E Test administrators: Teaching assistants (TAs) in the Department will be paid on an hourly basis to administer the test (check student IDs, seat students, supervise students taking the test, etc.) and to score the test.

II Space

- A Meeting rooms are available free of charge from the department.
- B Rooms for administering the test are available upon request from the campus Office of Space Management.

III Equipment

- A Use PCs currently owned by Project Director and members of development team.
- B A large PC will be purchased to keep all the records and databases for the project.

Allocation of available resources

To assure that these available resources will be allocated so as to be equal to or exceed the resources that will be required at every stage in assessment development, the test developer can add these resources to the list of required resources, as in Table 14.9. Resources that will be required are the top row in each category, while resources that will be available are in the bottom row in italics.

Time line

In developing a time line, the test developer will specify the various specific tasks to be accomplished in the assessment development process, the individual(s) responsible for carrying these out, the sequence in which they will be carried out, and the time by which each needs to be completed. Each task is put into a sequenced list, which specifies its temporal relationship to other tasks in the process. This time line can then provide the test developer and test

	STAGES				
RESOURCES	**1 Initial planning**	**2 Design**	**3 Operationalization**	**4 Trialing**	**5 Use**
Personnel					
Project director (Dr Shin)	40 hours	40 hours/week	40 hours/week	40 hours/week	40 hours/week
ESL Program Director		10 hours	10 hours	10 hours	10 hours
Development team	10 hours/person	10 hours/person/week	10 hours/person/week	10 hours/person/week	20 hours/person/term
2 ESL instructors	*10 hours/person*	*10 hours/person/week*	*10 hours/person/week*	*10 hours/person/week*	*10 hours/term*
1 academic course instructor		*10 hours/person/week*	*10 hours/person/week*	*10 hours/person/week*	*10 hours/person/week*
3 Ph.D. students		*10 hours/person/week*	*10 hours/person/week*	*10 hours/person/week*	*10 hours/person/week*
Computer programmers		30 hours	50 hours	50 hours	10 hours/term
1 Ph.D. student with expertise in computer programming		*10 hours/week*	*10 hours/week*	*10 hours/week*	*10 hours/week*
Clerical support	2 hours	10 hours	30 hours	40 hours	20 hours/term
From Dept. Chair	*2 hours*	*10 hours*	*30 hours*	*40 hours*	*20 hours/term*
Test administrators/ scorers				20 hours	20 hours/term
TAs in the Department				*20 hours*	*20 hours/term*
Space	Meeting room	Meeting room	Meeting room	Meeting room, computer labs with internet connections	Meeting room, computer labs with Internet connections
Department Office of Space Management	*2117 Rolfe*	*2117 Rolfe*	*2117 Rolfe*	*2117 Rolfe, large lecture rooms*	*2117 Rolfe, large lecture rooms*
Equipment	PCs	PCs	PCs	PCs	PCs
Personal PCs, Department of Applied Linguistics	*7 personal PCs*	*7 personal PCs*	*7 personal PCs, 1 large PC*	*7 personal PCs, 1 large PC*	*7 personal PCs, 1 large PC*

Table 14.9 Resources required and available for University example

development team a way to assure that the assessment production process is conducted in as efficient and timely manner as possible. The time line is the most detailed specification of the plan for managing resources. The time line for the University example is presented and discussed in Chapter 20.

Discussion of the example

By the beginning of the Design stage, the Department had used the funds available from the Dean to hire a recent Ph.D. graduate in language assessment as a full-time visiting assistant professor to oversee the test development, and four Ph.D. students in language assessment had been hired as research assistants to be on the test development team. One of these students had considerable experience in database design and management. At this stage the test development team thus included the following seven individuals: a visiting assistant professor as Project Director, two reading instructors in the ESL program, one instructor in an introductory academic course that satisfied the general education requirement, and three Ph.D. students in the Department who were specializing in language assessment. It was this team, in consultation with the ESL Program Director and other stakeholders, that developed the Design Statement, including this plan for obtaining, allocating, and managing resources.

EXERCISES

1 Think of an assessment that you need to develop. Create a Design Statement for the assessment. In the process, what issues did you find you needed to address that you had not considered prior to reading this chapter on Design Statements?
2 Look through the example projects. Find one that interests you for which a Design Statement is not provided. Create a Design Statement for the project. What did you learn from the process?
3 Imagine that you have been asked to critique a test for which no Design Statement exists. How would you structure such a critique? Given the absence of a Design Statement, what problems might you run into in critiquing the test?
4 Think of a test you might need to develop. Go through the process of conducting a needs analysis to develop a construct definition.
5 Think of a test you might need to develop. Go through the process of conducting a needs analysis to identify and describe the TLU domain. Then go through the process of selecting a TLU task from within this domain to be used as a basis for developing assessment tasks. Explain how you used the warrants in the AUA as a guide in this process. Then explain how you considered the demands of practicality on the selection of this TLU task.
6 Describe the characteristics of the critical TLU task you selected in Exercise 5 above.

SUGGESTED READINGS

Glatthorn, A., F. Boschee, and B. Whitehead. 2006. *Curriculum Leadership: Development and Implementation*. Beverly Hills, CA: Sage Publications, Chapter 5.

Graves, K. 2000. *Designing Language Courses: A Guide for Teachers*. Boston: Heinle & Heinle Publishers, Chapter 6.

Gupta, K., C. M. Sleezer, and D. F. Russ-Eft. 2007. *A Practical Guide to Needs Assessment*. San Francisco: Preiffer.

Long, M. 2006. *Second Language Needs Analysis*. Cambridge: Cambridge University Press.

Richards, J. C. 2001. *Curriculum Development in Language Teaching*. Cambridge: Cambridge University Press, Chapter 3.

Soriano, F. I. 1995. *Conducting Needs Assessments: A Multidisciplinary Approach*. Beverly Hills, CA: Sage Publications.

Witkin, B. R. and J. W. Altschuld. 1995. *Planning and Conducting Needs Assessments: A Practical Guide*. Beverly Hills, CA: Sage Publications.

NOTES

1 The term "level of minimum competency" is also sometimes used to refer to a performance standard.

2 We would note that vagueness, impression, and uncertainty are all part of the real world of language assessment.

3 There are a number of different epistemological perspectives and a multitude of methodological approaches to designing and conducting needs analysis, as well as a wide range of specific techniques and procedures for collecting relevant information. Discussions of these issues can be found in the references listed in the Suggested Readings at the end of this chapter.

4 We are frequently asked how to identify a TLU domain for the purpose of assessment development in an instructional setting in which characteristics of tasks in the language teaching domain may have little in common with characteristics of tasks from a real life language use domain in which the students are likely to use the language. We think that this is an important issue having to do with the interface between instructional design and assessment, but a discussion of this is beyond the scope of this book.

15

Developing assessment tasks

INTRODUCTION

Just as language use tasks can be viewed as the elemental activities and situations of language use, so the assessment task is the elemental unit of any language assessment. The central activity in the Operationalization stage, therefore, is the development of assessment tasks. Test developers can, and often do, come up with ideas for assessment tasks either off the top of their heads or based upon experience they have had either as test takers themselves or in developing assessment tasks in other situations, or because they may think it's important to be creative, or for no particular reason. However, such non-systematic approaches often lead them to develop assessment tasks that they cannot support with a convincing AUA. For example, tasks that are created this way may have little correspondence to TLU tasks, and hence be of questionable generalizability. Or they may not take into consideration the construct that is to be assessed, and hence they may provide little basis for justifying the meaningfulness of the intended interpretations. Thus, test developers often end up having to justify the tasks without any convincing argument or backing. Yet another problem is that creating tasks in this way may not take into consideration the resources that will be required, and hence create unanticipated and excessive demands on resources. In this case, the test developer is faced with hustling up additional resources needed to actually use these tasks after they are already, in a sense, stuck with them.

To minimize problems such as these, we propose a systematic process that draws upon the components in the Design Statement, the claims and warrants in the AUA, and that also takes into consideration real world constraints on resources such as those we discussed in Chapter 13. By drawing upon the Design Statement and the AUA, the developers assure that the use of the assessment tasks can be justified. By keeping real world considerations in mind, they assure that the tasks are practical.

As discussed in Chapter 14, one of the products of the Design Stage will be a set of TLU tasks that the test developer has selected for use as a basis for assessment tasks. The relationship between TLU tasks and assessment task types is illustrated in Figure 15.1 below.

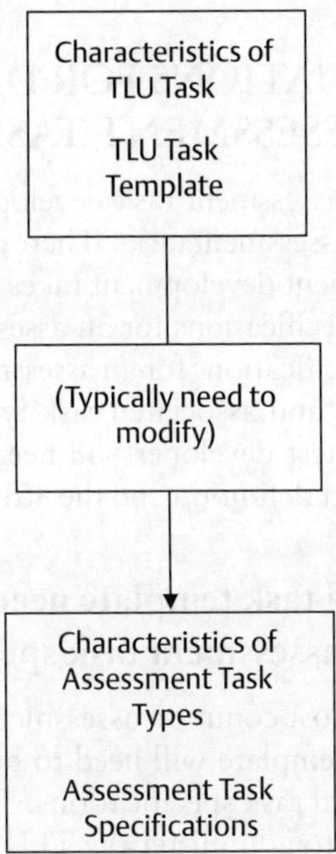

Figure 15.1 Relationship between TLU task template and assessment task type/specifications

Each TLU task that has been selected consists of a set of task characteristics that constitute a "template" for developing a type of assessment task. As discussed below, the test developer will typically need to modify the characteristics of the TLU task template to develop an assessment task type, because TLU tasks are rarely simply observed as is. (See discussions of Situations 1–3 below.) The assessment task type also consists of a set of characteristics, which constitute the assessment task specifications that will guide task writers in creating multiple assessment tasks.

In this chapter, we will describe a general process for developing assessment tasks on the basis of these TLU task templates. This process involves (1) determining which of three situations for developing assessment tasks the assessment developers are working with and (2) developing assessment task specifications in ways that are appropriate to the particular situation.

Although we describe these activities in this order, we would emphasize that they will not necessarily be implemented in a linear sequence, but are iterative. That is, just like the overall process of test development itself, developing assessment tasks is cyclical, with revisions typically occurring as the process proceeds.

We conclude the chapter by illustrating how these procedures were followed in developing test tasks for the University example.

THREE SITUATIONS FOR DEVELOPING ASSESSMENT TASKS

Different situations for assessment task development will require different approaches to developing assessment tasks. There are essentially three kinds of situations in which assessment development takes place: (1) a TLU task needs to be modified to create specifications for an assessment task type, (2) a TLU task can be used as is as specifications for an assessment task type, and (3) there is no specific TLU domain and associated task types from which to develop assessment tasks, and the test developer will need to create assessment task types based on the construct definition and the attributes of the test takers.

Situation 1: TLU task template needs to be modified for use as assessment task specifications

In our experience, the most common assessment development situation is one in which a TLU task template will need to be modified in some way to make it usable as assessment task specifications. This can be for two reasons: (1) it may not be practical to administer the TLU task as is as an assessment task, or (2) the task does not completely satisfy all of the relevant warrants in the AUA. In situations such as this, the test developer will need to modify the characteristics of the TLU task template to create specifications for an assessment task type that is as similar as possible to the TLU task. That is, the test developer will try to change only those characteristics of the TLU task that will make it usable as an assessment task. Here, again, we see that assessment is "the art of the possible".

In some situations, the test developer may be able to use the TLU task with very little modification other than the place at which it is performed, administering it as part of an assessment, rather than observing test takers' performance in the TLU domain. Suppose, for example, that a test developer wanted to use a test to assess a potential employee's control of professional vocabulary, rhetorical organization, and formal register in writing market reports. The test developer might observe the performance of employees in the company who were doing this, and then recreate this TLU task as an assessment task, administering it under controlled conditions. In this case the modification to the TLU template is minimal, involving only the characteristics of the setting. Everything else remains the same. However, it is important to keep in mind that as minimal as the modifications of the TLU template may be, the consequences of the test taker's performing the assessment task will not be the same as they would be if the task were performed on the job by someone already employed by the company rather than as a display of the test taker's language ability. Performing the task on the job will have consequences for a variety of stakeholders, including the employer and customers with whom the test taker interacts. Performing the task as part of an assessment will primarily have consequences for the test taker's ability to get hired for the job.

In other situations, the modifications that need to be made to the TLU task template may be more extensive. For example, suppose test developers wanted to develop a test to measure students' ability to use language to process topical information in academic lectures. Suppose further that a TLU task chosen as a template consisted of the students responding orally to "comprehension checks", which were *wh-* questions that the teacher used for formative assessment periodically during her lectures to see whether students were following what she was saying. In this TLU task, the input to the students consisted of the teachers' lectures and spoken *wh-* questions. The students' expected responses consisted of oral answers to the questions. Because of resource constraints and limitations on when the test needs to be administered, it is not possible to ask students to sit in on an actual lecture and observe their responses to the lecturer's comprehension questions. Therefore, in order to make this TLU task practical, the characteristics of the input of the TLU task template might be modified. This could be done by changing the live lecture and comprehension-check questions to a videotaped lecture and comprehension checks. If it is not practical to record students' oral responses, the characteristics of the expected response in the TLU task might be modified by changing the channel from oral responses to written responses. Finally, if it is not practical to score written responses, the expected response characteristics could be further modified by having students select one alternative in multiple-choice items, rather than writing short answers.

As can be seen from this example, modifying the TLU template task characteristics may result in an assessment task that is quite different from the TLU task upon which it is based. Thus, the test developer must always keep the warrants in the AUA in mind as she modifies the characteristics of the TLU task template. In the above example, the test takers' expected response—marking their selection on multiple-choice questions—is quite different from the oral responses that students perform in the class. Nevertheless, because the construct to be measured is the ability to use language to process topical information in academic lectures, the way test takers indicate their comprehension may not matter. What is important in this task, in terms of the warrants in the AUA, is that the characteristics of the input correspond to those in the TLU task template.

This process of modifying characteristics of a TLU task template is also illustrated in Project 4 on the web, in which we designed a test to measure the ability of potential employees in a company to perform a routine writing task: writing letters in response to customer complaints that had been taken over the phone by another employee. In this situation, the TLU domain contained a task that was obviously critical to the potential employee's ability to perform his job; however, it was not possible to observe the potential employee performing the task on the job, since the test taker was not yet employed. Nevertheless, we were able to reproduce almost all of the characteristics of the TLU task template in our test tasks. We supplied the test takers with comparable input, including an actual memo form from the phone company with the co-worker's notes about the complaint that a customer made over the phone. We also required the test takers to write a formal letter replying to the customer, dealing with the complaint, and an informal memo to the appropriate person in the phone company explaining the problem and asking the person to deal with it. In this test task, the characteristics of the input and response, as well as the major characteristics of the relationship between input and response for the test task, correspond very closely to those of the TLU task.

Finally, in some situations a TLU task might be practical to use as an assessment task, but it may need to be modified to create one that satisfies the relevant warrants in the AUA. For example, suppose that a test developer wanted to make inferences about test takers' knowledge of specific grammar points in tasks involving editing their academic writing. In the TLU task chosen as a template, the input would normally consist of writing that the test takers produced themselves. However, this writing might not contain instances of the grammar structures included in the definition of the construct to be tested. Therefore, the test developer might decide to use the writing of other students and modify the input to contain examples of these structures used incorrectly. The expected response, in which the test takers would have to correct the errors in order to demonstrate their knowledge of these grammatical structures, would remain unchanged. The TLU task modified in this way would support the meaningfulness warrants in the AUA.

Situation 2: TLU task is the assessment task

In other situations, the TLU task template may support the warrants in the AUA and may be practical, so that it can be used as is, without any changes, as an assessment task. This situation occurs when the test taker is observed performing a TLU task in the TLU domain, and some provision is made for producing an assessment record (score or description) of the observed performance. In this situation, the "test taker" is not "taking" an assessment in the ordinary sense of the word. He is simply doing what he normally does in the TLU situation, and the assessor observes and records his performance. Moreover, the consequences of the test taker's language use are the consequences *in the TLU domain*. For example, if a record is made of a test taker providing answers to technical questions as part of his job as a technical support provider for a computer software company, the consequences of his answers for the individual asking the question will be unaffected by the fact that a record is made of the test taker's performance. Note also that the term "test taker" here may be somewhat misleading in this situation since the computer support person is not "taking a test" in an ordinary sense. He's just doing his job.

This situation is typical in the context of classroom assessment, where teachers may decide to collect information for making decisions on the basis of their students' performance on instructional tasks. This assessment-based information may be used for a variety of decisions, such as modifying their own instructional practice, guiding their students' learning activities, or assigning grades. In the Kindergarten example, the performance objective for the lesson states that students will demonstrate their knowledge of letter formation, concepts of print, and oral language in one specific interactive writing activity. Thus, this specific language teaching TLU domain contains only one task (the interactive writing activity) and the procedures for developing the assessment task involve observing the students performing this TLU task and using an observational checklist to record their performance. Another example of this in an instructional setting would be the use of a portfolio, which includes samples of students' performance on various kinds of learning tasks.

It may be possible to use observations of performance on TLU tasks in other settings as well. In some cases, observing candidates' performance on a TLU task might be part of a certification assessment. One part of a certification examination for language teachers, for example, might include two examiners observing one or more lessons that a candidate teaches.

Situation 3: no specific TLU domain

A third assessment development situation is one in which there is essentially no specific TLU domain to start out with, as we discussed in Chapter 14. In such a situation, it may be difficult to specify any TLU domain with much precision and any attempt to select specific tasks as a basis for assessment tasks would not yield a manageable number of tasks.

Where there is no specific TLU domain, test developers will need to create specifications for original types of assessment tasks. In doing so, the developers still need to keep in mind the warrants in the AUA, particularly those related to meaningfulness and generalizability. Thus, the test developer should consider the attributes of the test takers and the construct definition, and then create a hypothetical TLU domain or domains and TLU tasks that would be appropriate for these test takers and that would engage them in language use that could be interpreted as an indicator of the construct.

In one such text development situation, we needed to develop an assessment of several areas of language knowledge as realized in an oral face-to-face interview to be used with a very diverse group of test takers with widely varying TLU needs. Because we were not dealing with a specific TLU domain in this project, we could not locate a single, specific, limited TLU task type that would serve as an appropriate starting point for developing test tasks. We therefore imagined some hypothetical situations in which the test takers might conceivably find themselves. We then imagined what kinds of tasks they might perform in these hypothetical situations and created assessment tasks that resembled these hypothetical TLU tasks to some extent. For example, we imagined that the test takers might find themselves in a situation in which they were being interviewed for some reason or other, so we developed an assessment task involving an interview-type role-play. We also imagined that they might have to introduce themselves in both relatively formal and relatively informal situations, so we created tasks involving formal and informal introductions. Because the attributes of the test takers differed widely, we created a variety of role-plays appropriate to the attributes of these test takers (such as an interview with a professor for students or an interview with a potential employer for an employee). However, each variant was designed to allow us to make interpretations about the constructs in which we were interested, such as range and accuracy of knowledge of grammar, knowledge of cohesion, and sensitivity to differences in register.

In all three situations for developing assessment tasks, in addition to keeping the warrants of the AUA in mind, the test developer will also need to pay particular attention to the attributes of the test takers to assure that the assessment tasks are appropriate for all of the potential test takers. If this is not done, the

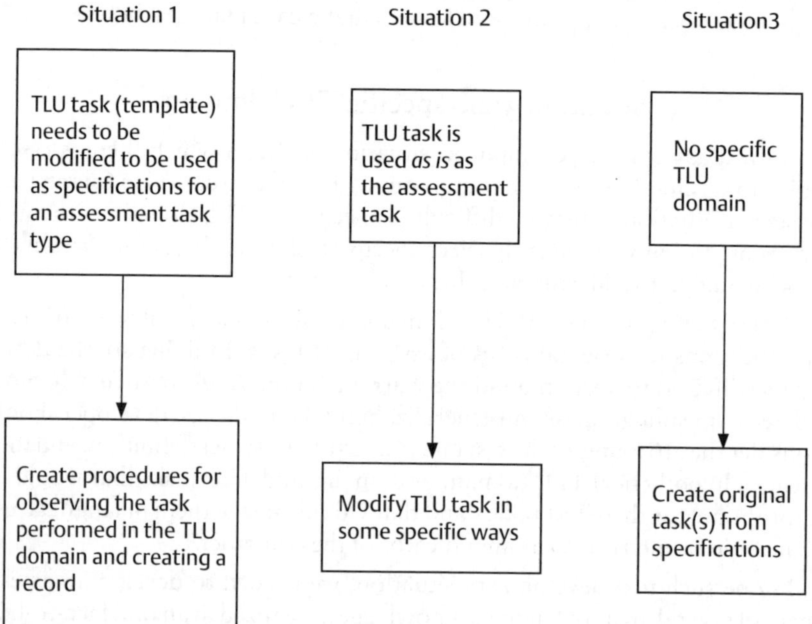

Figure 15.2 Situations for assessment task development

support for the warrants in the AUA will be weakened. For example, suppose an assessment task included non-language visual input such as pictures. The test developer would want to make sure that these pictures used in the assessment task are appropriate for the age of the test takers. In addition, the test developer would also need to take steps to make sure that the pictures are impartial to various sub groups of test takers such as males and females or test takers from different cultural backgrounds. Thus, for example, if the test task required test takers to respond to the content of pictures, the pictures should depict content to which all of the test takers can relate and easily respond. Figure 15.2 summarizes the three situations described above for developing assessment tasks.

DEVELOPING ASSESSMENT TASK SPECIFICATIONS

Assessment task specifications provide a detailed description of everything that individual task writers need know in order to write actual assessment tasks that will support the warrants in the AUA. Depending upon how experienced the task writers are, the stakes of the assessment, and the degree of complexity of the assessment task, the specifications may be written at different levels of detail. For the Kindergarten example, the specifications could be written with very little detail. For the University example, much more detail is needed. For any given type of assessment task, the assessment task specifications will include the parts described in this section.

The definition of the construct to be assessed

In many assessments, different constructs may be assessed in different sections of the assessment or by different assessment task types. Therefore, the definition of construct(s) to be assessed with a given assessment task is needed so that test writers will understand what a given assessment task is supposed to be assessing. This definition is also helpful for test users and other stakeholders, in interpreting the results of assessment.

The characteristics of the setting of the assessment task

The characteristics of the setting of the assessment task, including the time allotment for the task, may vary from one task type to another and needs to be specified here. (See Chapters 4 and 17 for more detailed discussion of the setting.)

Characteristics of input, response, and relationship between input and response

The characteristics of the input, expected response, and relationship between input and expected response of the specific test task type can be conveniently provided in a table, as illustrated in Chapter 4 or in outline form as illustrated below in task specifications for the University example.

Method for recording test takers' performance

Performance on different types of test tasks may be scored or, in the case of a qualitative record, described differently, so the recording method needs to be specified for each. (See Chapter 16 for a discussion of recording method.)

Instructions for responding to task

Instructions for responding to the test task need to be provided in enough detail to allow the test takers to perform at their best. (See Chapter 18 for a discussion of procedures for creating instructions for responding to assessment tasks.)

DEVELOPING MULTIPLE ASSESSMENT TASKS FROM ONE TASK SPECIFICATION

A single task specification may be used by task writers to create one or more assessment tasks. In the University example, the task writers needed to create multiple forms of the incomplete outline task (reading passage and incomplete outline) from the task specifications. To do this the task writers needed to find a different reading passage and develop an incomplete outline for each form of the test. Each of these tasks was written from the same set of specifications, thus generating forms of the test that were equivalent.

In other situations, a single test may contain multiple individual tasks based upon the specifications for a single task type. For example, the specifications for a single type of task used to test the meanings of vocabulary items might be used to generate multiple individual items (one per vocabulary item being tested. Figure 15.3 shows the relationship between assessment task specifications and multiple assessment task(s) written from these specifications.

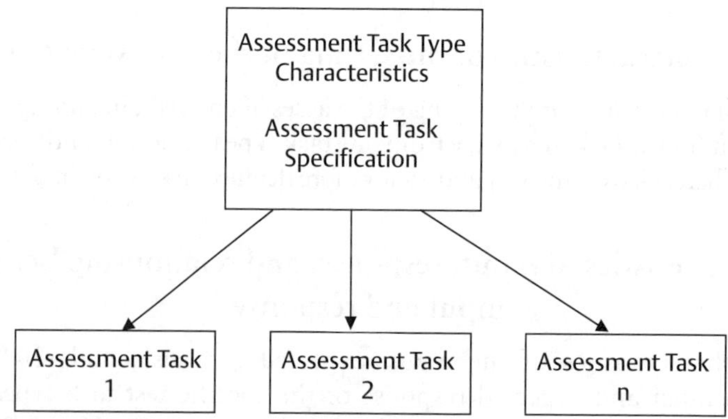

Figure 15.3 Creating multiple assessment tasks from a single task specification

University example

In this section we describe how the test developers went through this process for the University example. We first describe three possible test task specifications the developers derived from the TLU task template. We then discuss the process they went through in weighing the strengths and weaknesses of the alternatives and deciding upon one of them.

Three alternative versions of assessment tasks based upon TLU task template

Version 1

Version 1 of the assessment task illustrates the least degree of modification of the TLU task characteristics (template). The test takers are given a reading passage and they produce a response consisting of an outline of the passage. The test takers' responses (outlines of the reading passage) are rated using a rubric. (See Chapter 16 for a discussion of this scoring method.)

In this version, the assessment task characteristics are very similar to those of the TLU task. Only the source of the reading passage, which may not come from a text the test takers would actually need to read in one of their classes, and the location of the test, the testing center rather than the classroom or at home, differ. As in the TLU task template, the test takers provided an extended production response in the form of an outline.

Version 2

Version 2 of the assessment task is the one we have been working with throughout this book. It illustrates a somewhat greater degree of modification of the TLU task characteristics (template). The test takers are given a reading passage to outline. However, instead of creating their own complete outline as they would in the TLU situation, they complete portions of an incomplete outline. The test takers' responses are scored using a scoring key. (See Chapter 16 for the details.)

In this version, both the characteristics of the input and expected responses of the TLU task are modified to some extent. While the test takers are still provided with a complete reading passage to outline (as was the case in Version 1), the characteristics of the input are modified in that the test takers are also provided with input in the form of an incomplete outline. The characteristics of the expected response are also modified because instead of responding by creating a complete outline, the test takers provide limited constructed responses by filling in gaps in an incomplete outline. By modifying the characteristics of the input and expected response, the test developers were able to create a test task that could be scored by means of a computer algorithm. See discussion below for how the test developers weighed the strengths and weaknesses of this option, both in terms of the degree of support for the AUA and in terms of practicality considerations.

Version 3

Version 3 of the assessment task illustrates an even greater degree of modification of the TLU task characteristics. As was the case with Version 2, the test takers are provided with input in the form of a reading passage and an incomplete outline with gaps. However, unlike for Version 2, for each gap, additional input is provided in the form of three alternative responses, only one of which is correct. Characteristics of the expected response are also further modified in that instead of responding by creating limited production responses, the test takers respond by selecting the correct response among the alternatives provided. Thus, the expected response for this task type is non-language (a simple check mark). The test takers' responses are scored by means of a simple computer program. (See Project 2 in Part IV for the details.)

Considering alternative AUAs in choosing among alternatives

In deciding among alternative versions of assessment tasks, the test developers took into consideration both the strength of the various competing AUAs and real world considerations. Table 15.1 below summarizes some differences among the competing AUAs for the assessment tasks involving varying degrees of modification of the TLU task template.

AUA CONSIDERATIONS	DEGREE OF MODIFICATION OF TLU TASK TEMPLATE		
	to a lesser extent		**to a greater extent**
	Version 1 Read text and outline it.	**Version 2** Read text and complete portions of an incomplete outline.	**Version 3** Read text and selective alternatives for incomplete portions of an outline.
Warrants associated with outcomes of Claim 1: Consequences	No obvious differences among versions.	No obvious differences among versions.	No obvious differences among versions.
Warrants associated with outcomes of Claim 2: Decisions	No obvious difference among versions.	No obvious difference among versions.	No obvious difference among versions.
Warrants associated with outcomes of Claim 3: Interpretations	Strong support for meaningfulness Warrants A4, and A5. Strong support for generalizability Warrants C1 and C2.	Strong support for meaningfulness Warrants A4, and A5. Moderate support for generalizability Warrants C1 and C2.	Strong support for meaningfulness Warrants A4, and A5. Weaker support for generalizability Warrants C1 and C2.
Warrants associated with Claim 4: Records	Possibly lower consistency associated with ratings.	Possibly greater consistency associated with machine scoring.	Possibly greater consistency associated with machine scoring.

Table 15.1 Considerations of competing AUAs in selecting among alternative assessment tasks

As can be seen from the table, the main differences among the alternative assessment tasks lie in the degree of support for warrants about generalizability, with the strongest support provided by Version 1, the next strongest for Version 2, and the third strongest for Version 3. Differences might be found in the strength of support for consistency warrants, but these differences might only be discovered after trialing and collecting data on the consistency of the alternative scoring methods. (See Chapter 19 for a discussion of backing for consistency warrants.)

Real world considerations in choosing among alternatives

The development team also weighed real world considerations in choosing among the three versions of test tasks. These considerations included

REAL WORLD CONSIDERATIONS	DEGREE OF MODIFICATION OF THE CHARACTERISTICS OF THE TLU TASK TEMPLATE		
	to a lesser extent		**to a greater extent**
	Version 1 Read text and outline it.	**Version 2** Read text and complete portions of an incomplete outline.	**Version 3** Read text and select alternatives for incomplete portions of an outline.
Resource considerations	**Design and operationalization** • Relatively few resources	**Design and operationalization** • More resources to develop scoring key	**Design and operationalization** • More resources to develop alternative responses; few resources to develop scoring key
	Use • More resources for scoring/rating • More resources required to deal with disputes resulting from scoring disputes and test taker complaints	**Use** • Few resources for scoring.	**Use** • Few resources for scoring • Very low potential for scoring disputes requiring program administrator's time for resolution
Tolerance for uncertainty	**Associated with scoring** • More uncertainty and more resulting potential for complaints	**Associated with scoring** • Less uncertainty but potential for ongoing changes in scoring key	**Associated with scoring** • Essentially no uncertainty

Table 15.2 Real world considerations in selecting among alternative assessment tasks based upon a TLU task template

resources required during various stages of test development and use and tolerance for uncertainty. Table 15.2 on p. 317 summarizes some of these considerations for Versions 1–3 of the test tasks.

After weighing the strengths and weaknesses of the three versions, the test development team found the AUA for Version 2 most convincing, the demands on resources acceptable, and the amount of uncertainty associated with using this version tolerable. The test task specifications for the University example are presented below in Table 15.3.

Test task specifications for University example

I Definition of the ability to be assessed
  A Knowledge of multilevel rhetorical organization of written texts

II Chvaracteristics of the setting in which the tasks will be administered
  A Physical characteristics
    1 Computer lab on campus, quiet, comfortable
    2 Equipment
      a) Each test taker provided with a PC
      b) Internet connection
      c) Degree of familiarity with PC: all quite familiar with PC and Internet
  B Participants
    1 Test takers: incoming students who are non-native speakers of English
    2 Test administrator: trained and experienced in computer-based testing and having a positive attitude toward the test takers
  C Time of task: by appointment within a fixed time period during the day

III Characteristics of the input, response, and relationship between input and response
  A Input
    1 Format
      a) Channel: visual (written text on the computer)
      b) Form: language, but some passages may also contain non-language
      c) Language: English (target)
      d) Length
        (1) Passage: 1 long passage (450–500 words)
        (2) Incomplete outline: 1 page, based on the passage
      e) Vehicle: reproduced
      f) Degree of speededness: relatively unspeeded—generous time limit provided
      g) Type: input for interpretation
        (1) Text (passages),
        (2) Incomplete outline following the structure of the passage with a word/phrase/sentence for each heading
    2 Language of input
      a) Language characteristics
        (1) Organizational characteristics: as occurs in passages from textbooks/course readers/website assigned in the syllabus

(a) Grammatical
(i) Passages
(*a*) Morphology and syntax: wide range of organized structures
(*b*) Vocabulary: wide range of general and technical vocabulary
(*c*) Graphology: typewritten
(ii) Incomplete outline: grammar and vocabulary similar to that in passages, but in outline format
(b) Textual (cohesion and organization)
(i) Passages: wide range of cohesive devices and rhetorical organizational patterns, including narration, description, definition, classification, comparison and contrast, and argumentation
(ii) Incomplete outline: word/phrase/sentence level, all related to be an outline
b) Pragmatic characteristics: as occurs in authentic passages from textbooks/ course readers/website assigned in the syllabus
(1) Functional
(a) Passage: ideational, heuristic, and manipulative, possibly some imaginative
(b) Incomplete outline: ideational and heuristic
(2) Sociolinguistic (passage and incomplete outline): standard dialect, formal/informal register, natural, varied on cultural references and figurative language
3 Topical characteristics (passage and incomplete outline): academic, drawn from textbooks used in introductory level academic courses
B Expected response
1 Format
a) Channel: visual
b) Form: language
c) Language: English (target)
d) Length: 1–3 words/phrases per blank heading
e) Type: limited production
f) Degree of speededness: relatively unspeeded—generous time limit provided
2 Language characteristics
a) Organizational characteristics: vocabulary similar to that in texts and items; morphology and syntax standard English, but not scored; graphology: typewritten
b) Pragmatic characteristics: mostly same as passages and item stems, plus some need for appropriate register use; little need likely for manipulative functions
3 Topical characteristics: same as passages and item stems
C Relationship between input and expected response
1 Type of external interaction: Interrelatedness: nonreciprocal
2 Scope of relationship: both broad and narrow—narrow in that specific pieces of information must be provided, and broad in that those pieces' relationship to the text as a whole must be kept in mind by test takers
3 Directness of relationship: direct

IV Method for recording test takers' performance
  A Initially, during try-out: scored by single human rater according to objective scoring key containing all acceptable alternatives; initial list of acceptable answers and the number of points for each to be provided by item writer. Partial credit based on acceptability of content, not linguistic accuracy. Rater compiles list of variations on those answers for subsequent inclusion in the computer scoring key
  B During operational testing: scored by computer matching with list compiled by human raters
  C Explicitness of criteria and procedures: explicitly explained in general terms, with instructions
  D Scorers or raters (during tryout): instructor in ESL reading program assigned to test development team

V Instructions for responding to task
  A Directions: Complete the outline based on your reading of the passage. When you have completed the outline, click the "submit" button to send your answers to the Testing Center.

Table 15.3 Task characteristics for the University example

EXERCISES

1 Make a list of some tests you have developed or used. Which of the three situations for developing assessment task specifications do you think applied in each case?

2 Look over the Projects on the web. Find one that interests you that briefly describes assessment task type, but for which no specifications are provided. Create specifications for this task type following the format in Table 15.3.

3 Look through the examples of assessment task types in the Projects on the web (http://www.oup.com/LAIP). Then think about your own assessment needs. Locate a task type that seems like it might be appropriate for use in your assessment situation. How might this task type need to be modified for your purposes?

4 Think about a test you have developed or used for which a task type seems to have been clearly based upon a TLU task. Describe the characteristics of both the TLU task (template) and the test task. What are the similarities and differences between these two sets of characteristics?

16

Recording and interpreting assessment performance

INTRODUCTION

Test users and other stakeholders will use information from the assessment to interpret test takers' performance on an assessment as an indicator of the construct to be assessed. As discussed in Chapter 6, this information will come from two sources: the assessment record that is produced and the interpretive information that is provided by the test developer. However this information is presented, it will include information about the ability to be assessed, about the types of tasks that were presented to test takers, and about how assessment records were produced. This information can be directly linked, through the Blueprint and Design Statement, to the relevant warrants in the AUA, and will pertain to the meaningfulness and generalizability of the interpretation.

In this chapter we will first discuss some of the issues to be considered in different methods for recording test takers' responses. Because the results of language assessment are most often reported as numbers or scores, we will begin with a discussion of scoring. This will include all three types of responses: selected, limited production, and extended production. We will then provide an example of a method for producing an assessment record that consists of a description. Finally, we will discuss the process of interpreting assessment records as indicators of test taker's ability.

PRODUCING ASSESSMENT RECORDS

An assessment record provides part of the information that the test developer and other stakeholders will use to arrive at an interpretation of the test takers' language ability. This is often the primary, or most salient, information that stakeholders other than the test takers themselves and the individuals who administer the test will be provided. For this reason it is essential for test developers to use procedures to record test takers' performance that will support the warrants in the Assessment Use Argument (AUA), specifically the warrants under Claim 3, about interpretations, and Claim 4, about the assessment records themselves.

In Chapter 15 we described the process of developing task specifications for each assessment task type in the assessment. As described in Chapter 4, test takers' responses to assessment tasks can be of three types: selected responses, limited production responses, and extended production responses. As we might expect, the procedures used to produce an assessment record will be related to the type of response. Thus, there is a very close link between the assessment task specifications and the procedures that will be used to record test takers' responses to assessment tasks.

In determining the recording method to be used, the test developer needs to consider two products of the assessment development process discussed in the previous chapters: (1) the definition of the construct to be assessed, which is specified in the Design Statement (see Chapter 14), and (2) the assessment task specifications, which are part of the Blueprint (see Chapter 17). As discussed in Chapter 11, the way we define the construct for a particular assessment situation will determine which areas of language ability we need to include in our assessment record and whether test takers' topical knowledge will also be included in the record. The construct definition will also help determine the type of record, whether this is a profile of scores for different components of language ability, a single composite score, or a verbal description of the test taker's performance.

As with most decisions in designing and developing language assessments, the initial decisions about recording will be made during the Design and Operationalization stages, as discussed in Chapters 14 and 15. However, these initial decisions must be checked by actually giving the assessment and evaluating the assessment procedures and results in terms of the claims and warrants in the AUA. That is, until the test developer has administered the assessment, observed test takers, recorded their responses, and interpreted these results, the initial decisions about the recording method must be considered tentative. Thus, a critical step in the development of a recording method is to try out the assessment tasks with one or more groups of individuals who are representative of the intended test takers, record their responses, and analyze the results.

In this chapter we will discuss some of the issues to be considered in different methods for recording test takers' responses. Because the results of language assessment are most often reported as numbers or scores, we will begin with a discussion of scoring. This will include all three types of responses: selected, limited production, and extended production. We will then provide an example of a method for producing an assessment record that consists of a description. Finally, we will discuss the process of interpreting assessment records as indicators of test taker's ability.

Scores as assessment records

Because of the wide variety of uses made of language test scores, as well as the large number of different tasks used in language tests, many different specific scoring methods have been developed. However, all of these methods fall into two broad approaches. In one approach, the score is defined as the number of test tasks successfully completed, so that the number of correct responses is added up to obtain a total score for the test. This approach, which is sometimes characterized as "counting," is typically used with items that require selected or limited production responses.

The other general approach is to define several levels on one or more rating scales of language ability, and then to rate responses to test tasks in terms of these scales. This approach, which is sometimes characterized as "judging," is typically used with tasks in which the type of input is a prompt that requires test takers to produce an extended production response. In both approaches, the specification of a scoring method involves two steps:

1 specifying the criteria for correctness, or the criteria by which the quality of the response is to be evaluated, and
2 determining the procedures that will be used to produce a score.

In this part we will discuss these two general approaches to scoring, and various criteria for correctness and procedures for scoring within each. We first discuss scoring methods for items that elicit either selected or limited production responses. We then discuss the scoring of extended production responses.

Scoring as the number of tasks successfully completed

General considerations

Tasks that consist of items (see Chapter 4) can be used to measure specific areas of language knowledge, as well as the components of language ability that are required to perform receptive language use tasks, that is, listening and reading comprehension. In tests that consist of items, test takers are typically required either to select an answer from among several options (selected response) or to produce a limited sample of language in response to the task (limited production response). For both of these response types, the most commonly used approach to scoring is to add up the number of tasks successfully completed—the number of correct responses. Assuming that the task is sufficiently well defined by the way the item is designed and written, the main considerations for scoring are:

1 specifying the criteria for what constitutes a correct response to the task, and
2 determining procedures for scoring the responses, that is, deciding whether responses will be scored as right or wrong or in terms of degrees of correctness (partial credit scoring).

Specifying the criteria for correctness

Areas of language knowledge

A variety of criteria for correctness can be used with both selected and limited production responses, depending upon the areas of language knowledge to be assessed. In one approach to scoring that informs many language tests, it is considered essential to use a single criterion for correctness, in the attempt to achieve a "pure" measure of a specific area of language knowledge. Thus, for an item intended to measure only grammatical knowledge, for example, one might reasonably use grammatical accuracy as the sole criterion for correctness. This can be done quite easily with selected response items, by providing only one alternative that is grammatically correct, the "key," while all the other choices, or "distracters," are grammatically incorrect, even though they may be appropriate in terms of lexical choice, as in example (1).

(1) My neighbor asked me _____ away the tall weeds in my yard.
  (a) clear
  *(b) to clear
  (c) cleared
  (d) clearing
(* indicates the key, or correct response)

While the use of a single criterion may work reasonably well with selected responses, this may create problems with limited production responses. For example, using grammatical accuracy as the sole criterion for correctness may result in counting as correct some answers that are lexically inappropriate as in example (2).

(2) She turned the wheel quickly to <u>preserve</u> a tractor and her car went off the road.

In items designed to measure lexical knowledge, on the other hand, the test developer might not consider grammatical accuracy at all, but use meaningfulness as the sole criterion, as in the following example, which would be counted as a correct answer if grammatical accuracy were not considered.

(3) We mailed out several hundred <u>copy</u> of the advertisement to our customers this morning.

Examples (2) and (3) illustrate how the criteria for correctness need to be determined by the way we define the construct we want to measure. They also illustrate the kind of problem that can arise when we attempt to design test tasks involving limited production responses to measure a single area of language knowledge in isolation: we may end up giving credit for an answer that would be perceived as somehow incorrect or inappropriate in non-test language use settings.

Given our view of language use as an interactive process involving multiple areas of language knowledge, and our belief in the importance of being able to support warrants about the generalizability of assessment tasks, we would argue that, in order to make inferences about test takers' language ability on the basis of their responses to test tasks, multiple criteria for correctness will necessarily be involved in the scoring of these responses. In developing a scoring method, we would therefore employ multiple criteria for correctness, such as (but not limited to) grammatical accuracy, meaning, and appropriateness, as would be the case in non-test language use situations. If this combination of criteria were used, neither of the answers given in examples (2) and (3) would be counted as correct. However, "avoid" and "dodge" might both be considered correct responses for example (2) and "copies," "off-prints," and "duplicates" might all be acceptable responses to example (3). (See the discussion of partial credit scoring for multiple criteria below.)

Topical content and topical knowledge

In tests intended to measure language use in receptive tasks, such as listening or reading comprehension, the criteria for correctness may be based on topical content in the input for interpretation. The following item, for example, focuses primarily on the comprehension of content in a reading passage, rather than on a particular area of language knowledge.

(4) According to the passage, the most effective way to avoid procrastination is to _____.

In scoring items such as this, we face a problem that has been discussed throughout this book: whether to try to distinguish language ability from topical knowledge, and if so, how. We have argued that our primary interest in language testing is to make inferences about test takers' language ability and not about their knowledge of a particular discipline or topic. Thus, if we wanted to try to make "pure" inferences about test takers' ability to perform reading tasks, the criteria for correctness for items such as item (4) could be limited to the specific information that is included in the input for interpretation. However, test takers' topical knowledge will almost always affect their performance on such tasks to some degree, just as their topical knowledge plays a vital role in their non-test language use. If test takers already happen to know specific information that is supplied in the input for interpretation and correctly answer questions on the basis of this knowledge, rather than from reading the passage, how are we to know? It may therefore not be possible to completely isolate language ability from topical knowledge in some test tasks, no matter how we score test takers' responses. (See the discussion of how to deal with topical knowledge in the construct definition, in Chapter 11.) Furthermore, not to consider test takers' use of topical knowledge in scoring such items would appear to reduce their potential for meaningfulness and generalizability. If we only accept as correct the information that is contained in the reading passage, we are, in effect, denying test takers the possibility of answering the questions on the basis of whatever relevant real world knowledge they may already have.

Thus, there would appear to be somewhat of a trade-off in the scoring of tasks aimed primarily at testing comprehension. We can include in our criteria for correctness only information that is provided in the item input by adding a phrase such as "according to the reading passage" in each item, in the hope that this will enable us to make meaningful inferences about language ability, but we do so at the risk of somewhat reducing the ability to support generalizability warrants. Or, we can accept as correct any accurate information the test takers may provide from their own topical knowledge, in the hope that this will increase the generalizability of the task, but do so at the risk of making it more difficult to make meaningful inferences about language ability. Which way to go in this trade-off should be decided with respect to the Table of Specifications: the purpose of the test, the nature of the TLU environment, and the definition of the construct. In making this decision, however, the test developer must recognize that the focus chosen will be relative, and that the inferences that can be made are most likely to vary somewhat from one test taker to another. That is, the reality of language testing is that a given test task will involve varying degrees of language ability and topical knowledge for different test takers. Similarly, a test task is likely to be perceived as relatively similar to tasks within TLU domains and meaningful by some test takers and as relatively dissimilar to tasks within their TLU domains and unmeaningful by others.

There remains the problem of quantifying the content. That is, how do we count the information in the test takers' responses? It might appear quite obvious simply to count up the pieces of accurate information included in the response. But what counts as a "piece"? How many pieces of information, for example, are in the following possible response to example item (4): "break your project up into smaller tasks and then work on these one at a time"? Assuming that we can determine what to count as a piece of information, will we count all pieces as equally important? (See the University example below, for a description of one approach to dealing with this issue.) In attempting to address these issues in developing criteria for scoring, the test developer may be able to refer to specific materials and guidelines in a teaching syllabus, or to research in reading and listening that pertains to identifying information units.[1]

It is not our intention, in this discussion of topical content and topical knowledge, to discourage language testers from attempting to measure test takers' ability to comprehend the information in the input. The ability to interpret discourse is at the heart of language use, and is one that we must, in many situations, try to measure. Nevertheless, we hope this discussion will lead to a greater appreciation of the complexities and uncertainties involved in scoring responses to test tasks that are aimed at enabling us to make inferences about cognitive processes and representations of meaning that are essentially internal and therefore not directly observable.

Determining procedures for scoring the responses

Both selected and limited production responses can be scored in one of two ways: right/wrong or partial credit. With right/wrong scoring, a response receives a score of "0" if it is wrong and "1" if it is correct, or "right." With partial credit scoring, responses can be scored on several levels, ranging from no credit ("0") to full credit, with several levels of partial credit in between.[2] In the past, many language testers tended to favor right/wrong scoring for selected and limited production responses, largely because the techniques that were available for statistically analyzing the characteristics of test items—difficulty and discrimination—were designed to work best if responses were scored according to a single criterion for correctness (such as grammatical accuracy or meaning), and if scores on test items were dichotomous, that is, having only two possible values ("0" for wrong and "1" for right). With the development of more sophisticated statistical procedures, however, it is becoming increasingly common to see selected and limited production responses scored using partial credit. (See the Suggested Readings for information on these statistical procedures.)

Right/wrong scoring

Right/wrong scoring works reasonably well if we only want to measure a single area of language knowledge, and thus decide to score responses in terms of a single criterion for correctness. However, if we are interested in assessing responses as instances of language use, several areas of language knowledge are likely to be involved, so that responses may be scored according to several criteria for correctness, either implicitly or explicitly. In example (2), test takers might give a number of different answers, some of which are grammatically accurate, some of which are semantically appropriate, and some of which meet both of these criteria for correctness. When we have multiple criteria for correctness and use right/wrong scoring, the score of a wrong response fails to reflect the specific area(s) of language knowledge in which the test taker is deficient. Thus, with right/wrong scoring, the following answers to example (2) above would all receive a score of "0": "hitted," "avoided," and "preserve," even though they are wrong for different reasons. "Hitted" is wrong according to both grammatical and semantic criteria; "avoided" is grammatically inaccurate but semantically appropriate, and "preserve" is grammatically accurate but semantically inappropriate.

In order to capture information about which criteria for correctness the response failed to satisfy, there are essentially two options: give multiple right/wrong scores for each item, or use partial credit scoring. Using the former approach for example (2), each of the example answers would receive two scores, one for grammar and one for meaning, as in Table 16.1 on p. 328.

Thus, "hitted" would receive a "0" for grammar and a "0" for meaning, while "preserve" would receive a "1" for grammar and a "0" for meaning, and "avoid" would receive a "1" for both grammar and meaning.

Response/criterion	Grammar score	Meaning score
"hitted"	0	0
"avoided"	0	1
"preserve"	1	0
"avoid"	1	1

Table 16.1 Multiple right/wrong scores for responses to a single item

Partial credit scoring

With partial credit scoring we apply multiple criteria for correctness to produce a single score for each item: we give full credit for a response that satisfies all criteria for correctness, partial credit for responses that satisfy some of the criteria, and no credit for answers that satisfy none of the criteria. The way we assign the scores will depend on how, if at all, we prioritize the areas of language ability to be measured. Assuming that grammar and meaning are to be given equal priority in scoring, using partial credit scoring for example (2), the answers would receive the scores shown in Table 16.2.

Response/criterion	Grammar score	Meaning score	Single score for both
"hitted"	0	0	0
"avoided"	0	1	1
"preserve"	1	0	1
"avoid"	1	1	2

Table 16.2 Single partial credit scores for responses to a single item

In this approach, "hitted" would receive a single score of "0," while "preserve" would receive a single score of "1," and "avoid" would receive a single score of "2."

There are two advantages with either of these approaches—multiple scores or partial credit scoring. First, they offer the test user the potential for capturing more information about responses, and hence more information about test takers' areas of strength and weakness, than does giving a single right/wrong score. With the multiple-score approach it is possible to report separate scores for the different areas of language ability that are tested. In the above example, assuming that there are many items in the test, the grammar scores for all the items could be added up to yield a total score for grammar, and similarly for meaning. Reporting separate scores like this may be particularly useful where tests are to be used for diagnostic purposes, that is, for providing feedback to students on their areas of strength and weakness and to teachers on which areas of the syllabus appear to be working effectively to promote learning and which areas need improvement.

In order to realize this potential advantage, however, the decision to use either approach—assigning multiple right/wrong scores or partial credit scoring—needs to be based on a clear specification of the areas of language knowledge required for correct responses, and the criteria for correctness, which must themselves derive from the definition of the construct to be measured. This requirement is a second advantage of these scoring approaches, since it strengthens the link between the scores we produce and the interpretations we want to make about test takers' areas of language knowledge. For this reason, neither multiple marks nor partial credit scoring should be used simply to resolve uncertainties about the relative correctness of specific responses. Rather, it should be implemented in a principled way, deriving from the specifications of the assessment tasks.

The disadvantage of both these approaches is that they require more resources than giving single right/wrong scores, in terms of both the actual scoring and creating the items. If test takers' responses will be scored by human scorers, the scoring will be more time consuming. If they will be scored by a computer algorithm (see discussion below), it will require more time to develop instructions that the computer can follow without error.

In general we recommend using either multiple scores or partial credit scoring with items in which multiple criteria for correctness are used, and where the primary use of the test is to make inferences about profiles of language ability, such as in diagnostic or achievement testing. In such situations, if the construct to be tested includes several areas of language knowledge (e.g., grammar and pragmatics, grammar and pronunciation), partial credit scoring would be preferred. We suggest that single right/wrong scores should be used only where there is a single, clearly defined construct, and where a single criterion for correctness can be justified.

Selected responses

Specifying the criteria for correctness

Test tasks that require a selected response are of two types, in terms of the criteria of correctness of the options from which the test taker must select a response. One type is the "best answer" type, in which the test taker is expected to choose the best answer *from among the choices given*. In a multiple-choice test of vocabulary, for example, test takers may be asked to choose, from among several alternatives, the word that is closest in meaning to an underlined word or phrase in the stem of the item. This is a best answer type, since it is possible that there is another word, not given in the choices, that is as close a synonym as any of the choices given. This is because the meaning of any lexical item involves more than a single aspect, so that different words may be synonymous with the underlined word or phrase in different ways.

Thus, before selecting one word from among those given, the test taker must first determine the basis of the synonymy. For an item such as the following, this may be quite simple:

(5) All professors at the university *ceased* their teaching because of the large pay raises given to top administrators while faculty salaries were frozen.
(a) began
(b) changed
*(c) stopped
(d) increased

This item would be considerably more difficult with the following options, which are much closer in meaning, so that the differences in synonymy are much more subtle:

(a) terminated
(b) finished
*(c) discontinued
(d) completed

Another example of a best answer task is when test takers are asked to choose the best title for a reading passage, meaning "best" from among the choices given, even though the test taker may be able to think of a better title than any of the choices provided.

The other type of selected response task is the "correct answer" type, which implies that there is only one correct answer in the world, and that this answer is among the choices provided. Multiple-choice tests of grammar, for example, are typically correct answer types, since there is (presumably) only one answer that is grammatically acceptable in the particular variety and register of the target language of the test. The following item illustrates this task type:

(6) If I had gone to school instead of staying home, I _____ able to attend Prof. Schumann's lecture.
(a) will have been
*(b) would have been
(c) will have gone
(d) would have gone

One variation of the selected response task that is sometimes used is an editing task, in which the test taker is asked to identify something in the input that is actually incorrect or inappropriate according to some specified criterion. Consider the following example, in which test takers are asked to indicate which of the italicized words or phrases is stylistically inappropriate:

(7) One way to *determine* the *appropriateness* of the *method*
a b c
is by *shooting the breeze* with *individual practitioners*.
d e

This item may be intended to measure sensitivity to register. The correct answer is "d," because the phrase "shooting the breeze" is very informal and does not go with the rest of the sentence, which is relatively formal.

Editing tasks can also require the processing of larger texts, either with specific words and phrases underlined to focus the task for test takers, or a more open-ended task, with no indication of which words or phrases are potentially incorrect. In any of these tasks, either the best (worst) or correct (incorrect) answer criterion can be used.

Whether the test developer designs a question to be a best answer type or a correct answer type will be determined primarily by the component of language ability that is being tested, and by the domain of possible options within that area. If the construct to be measured requires fine discriminations and involves multiple components of language ability, then the best answer type will be the most appropriate. Suppose, for example, we were interested in assessing students' ability to make inferences from a reading passage. Such a task is likely to involve many, if not all, of the components of language ability. In this case, for a selected response task type the best answer type would be the most appropriate. If, on the other hand, the construct is defined in terms of a single area of language knowledge, then the correct answer type may suffice.

Determining procedures for scoring the responses

Tasks that require a selected response have traditionally been scored according to a single criterion, so that right/wrong scoring is generally used with this task type.

This is not to say, however, that partial credit scoring cannot be used with selected task types. Indeed, it is our view that best answer tasks, as discussed above, lend themselves particularly well to partial credit scoring. Consider a typical type of reading comprehension question, the "main idea" question. The test developer typically presents test takers with several choices, each of which might have some elements of the main idea, but only one of which adequately captures the entire main idea. Differing amounts of partial credit could be given for the choices that contain only some elements of the main idea. Having said this, we would add the caution that writing selected response items with partially correct responses is extremely difficult to do and, as with all test items, should never be used without pre-testing.

For selected response type items with a specific number of choices, there is some possibility that test takers will be able to select the correct response by guessing.[3] With this type of item the test taker is presented with a small number of options from which to choose, so that the probability of chance success can be calculated, and procedures for "correcting" for chance guessing are available. Because of this, test users sometimes want to employ a correction for guessing when selected response type items are used.

In deciding whether or not to do so, several issues must be considered. First, we need to realize that the tendency to guess is affected by a number of different personality characteristics and varies greatly from one individual test taker to the next. The "cautious" type of test taker will typically omit most, if not all, responses to items of which they are unsure, while the "risk taker" may not omit any responses at all. The intention of correction procedures is to remove any advantage the risk taker may gain, by guessing at random, over the cautious test taker. However, we only know which items test takers omit, and not why they omit them, so corrections for guessing actually correct for differential omissions and not for guessing itself. Furthermore, many other factors, including the test taker's level of ability and the nature of the test task itself, affect guessing. Finally, there is a difference between random guessing and informed guessing, in which test takers are able to narrow down the number of possible correct responses on the basis of partial knowledge. Corrections for guessing fail to take this into account, since they are based on the probability of random guessing. If a test taker is able to respond correctly through partial knowledge, we feel that this should be rewarded, preferably through partial credit scoring, and that correction for guessing would be inappropriate.

In summary, it is our view that correction for guessing with selected responses is virtually never useful in language tests. Our recommendation is to include in the test design provisions for eliminating or reducing the potential causes of random guessing, rather than correcting for it after the fact. First, we need to provide ample time for the majority of test takers to complete all the tasks in the test. Second, we need to match the difficulty of items with ability levels of test takers. Both of these provisions can be checked empirically by trialing the tests, observing test takers' patterns of response, analyzing their responses, and collecting self-reports from test takers on their reasons for choosing specific options. Finally, we recommend encouraging test takers to make informed guesses on the basis of partial knowledge. One way to accomplish this is to instruct them to answer every item, and, for items where they are not completely sure of the correct answer, to eliminate as many incorrect choices as they can, and then guess from among those remaining.

While we make these recommendations in the context of equalizing the effects of differential guessing or omissions, we believe that they are all consistent with the principles outlined in this book. With respect to adequate time and appropriate difficulty of test tasks, we believe that this reflects non-test language use, in which participants in a speech event have numerous means at their disposal for controlling or accommodating the speed and complexity of the discourse they must process. And even where we get lost because of either the speed or the complexity of the discourse, we virtually never make a totally random guess at meaning; rather, we use the means at our disposal—language knowledge, topical knowledge, and metacognitive strategies—to arrive at a possible understanding of the meaning. Finally, these recommendations are in accord with our emphasis on the importance of planning and test design as the crucial step in producing useful language tests.

Limited production responses

Unlike tasks aimed at eliciting a selected response, in which the range of possible responses is generally quite small and fixed, in limited production tasks the range of possible responses is very large, if not infinite. Even in tasks that require only a single word to complete a sentence, the domain of options from which the test taker can choose may be quite large, depending on her level of ability in the area being measured and the size of her domain in that area. Consider again example (5), which could be revised and presented as a limited production task, as follows:

(8) All professors at the university _____ their teaching because of the large pay raises given to top administrators while faculty salaries were frozen.

For test takers toward the low end of the ability range, the domain of possibly correct responses might be limited to those verbs having the general meaning of modifying an activity (teaching, in this case), so that verbs such as "stopped," "started," "began," "changed," "hated," "disliked," "increased," and "decreased" might appear equally correct. For test takers at the high end of this ability range, on the other hand, the domain of possible lexical choices might be further constrained to include only verbs that have to do with *the interruption or termination* of an activity. Their choice may be from among a fairly large set of options, such as "ceased," "stopped," "halted," "delayed," "terminated," "finished," "discontinued," "concluded," "suspended," and "quit," depending on the test takers' lexical knowledge. Not only is the range of possible responses very large, but in many limited production tasks there are likely to be several acceptable answers. Thus, in the example above, "ceased," "stopped," "halted," "terminated," "discontinued," "suspended," and "quit" might all be considered correct responses.

The size and range of both possible and acceptable responses is even greater for limited production tasks that require the test taker to produce more than a single word or phrase. Consider, for example, the range of acceptable responses to the following item:

(9) All professors at the university ceased their teaching because of the _____ given to top administrators while faculty salaries were _____.

The potentially large range of acceptable responses that limited production tasks are likely to elicit has two implications for scoring. First, assuring that the criteria for correctness correspond to the construct definition is more complicated, since responses that are identified as being acceptable may not all fit the specified criteria for correctness. That is, even though the test developer may specify criteria for correctness that reflect the way the construct to be measured is defined, some of the actual responses that are identified as acceptable, through trying out the test items with various groups of individuals, may not satisfy the specified criteria for correctness. Consider, for example, the following item from a gap-filling test:

(10) The teaching staff wants to use the _____ to improve presentations and teaching methods of the course.

The words "results," "study," and "evaluation" occur elsewhere in the passage, and if the test developer intends for this blank to measure test takers' sensitivity to lexical cohesion, all of these responses may be considered acceptable. However, a number of other possibly acceptable responses, such as "outcomes," "research," and "materials," which do not occur elsewhere in the passage, might be produced by test takers. In this case, the test developer is faced with three choices. One is to stay with the original criteria for correctness and count as incorrect any words that do not have cohesive ties with other words in the text. However, this would mean using criteria for correctness that do not correspond to use in the TLU domain, in which responses such as "outcomes," "research," and "materials" would be acceptable. In addition, test takers might perceive this criterion as overly strict and unfair. The second choice would be to expand the original list of acceptable answers, and respecify the criteria for correctness. This would mean that this item now measures something different from the original construct, sensitivity to lexical cohesion, which may present a problem for the meaningfulness of the interpretation. The third choice would be to decide that this item is not suitable, since there are acceptable responses to it that do not depend on knowledge of lexical cohesion, in which case the test developer would not delete this word, but would select another word for deletion.

Thus, with limited production tasks, determining if the criteria for correctness correspond to the way in which the construct is defined will depend on the different types of acceptable responses that are identified in the trialing of the items. But rather than considering this complication a disadvantage, we would argue that it is an advantage, since it leads the test developer to constantly consider the relationship between construct definitions and criteria for correctness. Furthermore, it strengthens the tryout and revision cycle that is part of the evaluation of usefulness in the test development process.

A second scoring implication of limited production tasks is that the test developer will need to develop a scoring key which lists those responses that will be considered acceptable, and, if partial credit scoring is used, how much credit each of these responses will be given. This is necessary in order to avoid introducing inconsistencies in the way scorers apply criteria of correctness. If a scoring key is not provided, the individuals who score the responses will need to exercise their own judgment in assigning scores. While there is nothing inherently wrong with such subjective scoring, it does introduce another potential source of inconsistency, which we will need to investigate empirically, in order to estimate how great it is and its effects on test scores.

(See Bachman 2004b for a discussion of procedures for estimating inter- and intra-scorer consistency; see the University example below for a discussion of empirically deriving a scoring key for partial credit scoring of limited production responses.)

Specifying the criteria for correctness

As with selected response tasks, test tasks intended to elicit limited production responses can be used to measure specific areas of language knowledge, as well as comprehension in receptive language use tasks. Essentially the same considerations in specifying criteria for correctness that have been discussed under Discussion apply. Unlike selected response tasks, however, where the range of options is limited to a small finite set, with limited production tasks test takers actually construct their own responses, so that the range of response options is virtually unlimited. For this reason, limited production tasks are by definition the best answer type.

Determining procedures for scoring the responses

Given the greater complexity and variety of responses that are possible with limited production tasks, we believe that our arguments in favor of partial credit scoring are even stronger with this type of test task. Since the probability of guessing the correct answer by chance is essentially nil for limited production tasks, correction for guessing is not generally a consideration.

Real world example

Developing a key for scoring limited production responses in the real world can often be more challenging than one might initially anticipate. The following example describes the process one group of test developers went through in developing a test and scoring key and what they learned from the process. The test developers were a group of teachers developing a final exam for use in a course in editing grammar and punctuation errors in writing. These teachers developed a test task in which the test takers were given a writing sample containing a number of grammar errors corresponding to the teaching points in the course for which the test was being developed. The test task was patterned after exercises the students did in class, so they were very familiar with how to do it.

For each line in the writing sample, the number of errors to be corrected (from zero to two) is indicated next to the line. The purpose of indicating the number of errors to be corrected was to help the test takers focus their attention on problems, and not spend time and energy searching for problems everywhere and worrying about whether they had found them all. The test takers were instructed to correct the errors by crossing out incorrect material and writing in corrections above the line. Figure 16.1 shows an example of a portion of the test as it was presented to the test takers.[4]

EXAMPLE PASSAGE	
After finished her undergraduate studies, Maria decided to take year off and travel. She visited several	**2**
countries in Europe, spending most of her times in Austria and Switzerland. She truly enjoy this	**2**
experience. Not only she was using her German, but she also got the opportunity to learn how to be	**1**
independent. Having improved her German, she decided to go back to school and get her MA degree in	
German. She has now took three semesters as a graduate student. In addition, she got a job as a TA	**1**
and this means that she is getting teaching experience as well as her education. Soon, she will graduate	**1**
and will have to make another decision.	

Figure 16.1 Example of a portion of a grammar editing test

In Figure 16.2, an example is provided of how one test taker attempted to correct the errors. The number of points awarded for the responses in each line of the paragraph is indicated in column A.

ACTUAL TEST TAKER RESPONSES AND POINTS AWARDED (SEE COLUMN A)	A
a	
After finished her undergraduate studies, Maria decided to take / year off and travel. She visited several	**1**
time es	
countries in Europe, spending most of her time/s in Austria and Switzerland. She truly enjoy / this	**1**
was she	
experience. Not only / ~~she was~~ using her German, but she also got the opportunity to learn how to be	**1**
independent. Having improved her German, she decided to go back to school and get her MA degree in	
taken	
German. She has now/ ~~took~~ three semesters as a graduate student. In addition, she got a job as a TA	**1**
and this means that she is getting teaching experience as well as her education. Soon, she will graduate	**0**
and will have to make another decision.	

Figure 16.2 Example actual answers to a portion of a grammar-editing test

Figure 16.3 provides an example of the feedback that would be given to the student.

The teachers initially assumed that developing a scoring key would be a relatively simple matter. They started by developing a key containing the very small number of ways they thought the test takers might correct the grammar errors that immediately came to mind, assuming that this would "work fine"

EXAMPLE OF FEEDBACK TO STUDENT	**A**
having a	
After /finished her undergraduate studies, Maria decided to take / year off and travel. She visited several	**1**
time **ed**	
countries in Europe, spending most of her time /s in Austria and Switzerland. She truly enjoy/ this	**1**
was she	
experience. Not only / ~~she was~~ using her German, but she also got the opportunity to learn how to be	**1**
independent. Having improved her German, she decided to go back to school and get her MA degree in	
taken	
German. She has now/ ~~took~~ three semesters as a graduate student. In addition, she got a job as a TA	**1**
, which	
/~~and this~~ means that she is getting teaching experience as well as her education. Soon, she will graduate	**0**
and will have to make another decision.	

Figure 16.3 Example feedback to a student for a portion of a grammar-editing test

in scoring the test takers' responses. However, when they trialed the test on a number of test takers, the first time they used their key to score the tests, they found that the test takers came up with a much larger number of correct alternatives than they had anticipated. Further, the teachers found that different scorers had different opinions of what answers should be considered to be correct. They realized that in order to deal with these problems they would need to score some of the tests multiple times to take into account the changes in the key that seemed to be taking place each time it was used. As a consequence, the teachers then developed a more complicated version of the scoring key, a portion of which is reproduced below in Figure 16.4.

1 Line 1

Item 1: one point for any of the following:
- After finishing
- After having finished
- After she finished

2 Line 2

Item 1: one point for the following:
- time

Item 2: one point for the following:
- enjoyed

3 Line 3

Item 1: one point for any of the following:
- Not only was she
- Besides/Along with/In addition to using her German + deleted 'but"
- She not only used her German, but also…

4 etc.

Figure 16.4 Example of a portion of a grammar editing test

However, when the teachers tried to use this revised key, a number of problems came up that they did not anticipate, some of which they did not notice for quite some time.

- Different levels of correctness, such as correct words but misspelled.
- Test taker fixes something that wasn't wrong, but change is also correct.
- Test taker fixes one problem but in doing so creates another problem.
- Different raters see additional correct answers or wrong answers (key never stops changing).

For example, after the teachers had been using the key for months, one test taker responded to the first item by correcting it as follows: "After Maria finished her undergraduate studies, Maria decided..." Some of the teachers thought this should be scored as correct, while others said that the correction introduced another problem, namely that one would not normally repeat the proper name, but use a pronoun in the second occurrence, as follows: "After Maria finished her undergraduate studies, she decided..."

The purpose of this example is to illustrate some of the real world problems associated with developing scoring procedures. In using the test in the preceding example, the teachers had to come to grips with unanticipated demands on resources involved with keeping up with a key that seemed never to stop changing. They also had to deal with the uncertainty associated with sometimes conflicting opinions of criteria for scoring individual items as correct or incorrect, and if they were to use partial credit scoring, how much partial credit should they assign. (For an extended example of developing a key for scoring limited production responses by computer, see University Reading example on pp. 449 et seq.)

Scoring as levels of language ability

There are many situations, most commonly when the test developer wants to test the use of language in tasks that involve speaking or writing, in which test takers are presented with tasks aimed at eliciting extended production responses. In contrast to selected and limited production responses, extended production responses constitute instances of discourse or situated language use, and identifying individual tasks or responses to score is extremely difficult, if not impossible. Therefore, we judge the quality of the response in terms of levels of ability demonstrated in completing the test task, using rating scales defined and developed for this purpose. In this section we present an approach to developing rating scales that incorporates the notion that language ability consists of multiple components, and that involves separate *analytic* ratings for each of the specific components in the construct definition. Before describing this approach, however, we feel it is important to point out some of the problems associated with a more widely used approach which uses global, rather than analytic, scales. (For more detailed discussions of approaches to rating extended production responses to assessment tasks, see the Suggested Readings at the end of this chapter.)

Global scales of language ability

One traditional approach to developing rating scales of language proficiency is based on the view that language ability is a single unitary ability, and yields a single score, called a "global," or "holistic," rating. Many such scales, however, contain multiple "hidden" components of language ability. Here are two examples of global scales of language ability. The first is an example of a portion of a global scale of oral proficiency developed by the United States Foreign Service Institute (FSI), which is a US government institution that trains American foreign service officers. This scale is used to rate the "oral proficiency" of test takers based on their performance in a face-to-face oral interview.

(11) Global Scale 1

Speaking 2 (Limited Working Proficiency)

Able to satisfy routine social demands and limited work requirements. Can handle routine work-related interactions that are limited in scope. In more complex and sophisticated work-related tasks, language usage generally disturbs the native speaker. Can handle with confidence, but not with facility, most normal, high-frequency social conversational situations including extensive, but casual conversations about current events, as well as work, family, and autobiographical information. The individual can get the gist of most everyday conversations but has some difficulty understanding native speakers in situations that require specialized or sophisticated knowledge. The individual's utterances are minimally cohesive. Linguistic structure is usually not very elaborate and not thoroughly controlled; errors are frequent. Vocabulary use is appropriate for high-frequency utterances, but unusual or imprecise elsewhere. (Interagency Language Roundtable, 2008)

Here is a portion of another global scale:

(12) Global Scale 2

80–90 These people can write English fairly well, but they are not good enough to carry a full-time academic load. They make frequent errors, more basic errors, and they use less complex grammatical structures. These compositions should be understandable, but the authors clearly need special attention and consideration in their written work.

There are three major types of problems with global scales: problems of interpretation, difficulties in assigning levels, and differential weighting of components.

The problems of interpretation

The use of global or holistic scales makes it difficult to know what a score reflects: multiple areas of language knowledge, topical knowledge, or multiple language use situations. In (11) a Speaking-2 rating on Global Scale 1, for example, refers to multiple areas of language knowledge (language usage, cohesion, vocabulary, linguistic structure), multiple areas of topical knowledge (current events, work, family, autobiographical information), and multiple TLU domains (work-related tasks, everyday conversations, situations that require specialized or sophisticated knowledge). Global Scale 2 in (12) also refers to multiple components: the TLU domain (carry a full-time academic load), language ability (basic errors, less complex grammatical sentence structure), the composition reader (understandable), and instructional treatment (authors clearly need special attention and consideration in their written work).

Problems of meaningfulness

Because of this confounding of multiple aspects of language use, it is difficult to know what interpretations based on either of these scales mean. Does a rating on Global Scale 1 indicate that the test taker has limited control of areas of language knowledge, and if so, which ones? Does it tell us about test takers' knowledge of current events, their familiarity with their workplace? Or all of the above? Does the score from Global Scale 1 reflect the test takers' capacity to function in the TLU domain, their accuracy of language use, how effectively they communicate, or the amount of further instruction in writing that they need? What it appears to reflect is a profile of a particular type of test taker, including a description of some aspects of language ability (errors), prediction of future performance (not good enough to carry a full-time academic load), and a prescription for treatment.

Problems of generalizability

When global scales refer to multiple TLU domains, or multiple TLU tasks, it is difficult to know to which TLU domain or tasks the interpretations of language ability generalize. With Global Scale 1, for example, if the oral examiner doesn't happen to ask the candidate about current events, can we infer that the interpretation does not generalize to this domain?

Difficulty in assigning levels

A second problem with global scales, related to the problem of interpretation, is that with such scales raters frequently have difficulty in assigning levels. Consider, for example, Global Scale 2, which includes reference to language, task, and reader. If all of these criteria are not satisfied at the same time (and this is often the case), the rater will have to determine which takes precedence. What if the composition uses highly complex grammatical structures with frequent errors? What if the composition does not contain frequent, basic errors (in grammar) but for other reasons (such as organizational problems), it is difficult to understand? What if other factors, such as the writer's academic preparation, control of topical knowledge, or study habits, would tend to qualify her for full-time academic work? Furthermore, how are raters to assign specific scores within this band of 80–90?

Differential weighting of components

With global scales, there is always the possibility that different raters (or the same rater on different occasions) may either consciously or unconsciously weigh the hidden components differently in arriving at their single rating. This is also a potential problem with analytic scales. However, with these, the components to be included and how each is to be rated are made explicit, so that we are in a position to control the weighting of the different components, either through rater training, or through statistical procedures.

In summary, many rating scales that are called "global" or "holistic" include multiple components, with little or no indication as to how these different components are to be considered either in arriving at a single rating or in interpreting it. We recognize that much of the information included in global scales should be considered in the ultimate decision about the individual test taker. At the same time, we would point out that the test developer must carefully consider how much of this can be derived from the test score. That is, test developers need to be able to distinguish between everything that might be of interest in making a particular decision and the specific information that is needed to make the decision, and the extent to which the test score can provide this.

Analytic scales of language ability

Our approach to developing rating scales adheres to two principles. First, the scales are defined according to the way we have defined the specific construct to be measured. This construct definition may be based on a course syllabus, a needs analysis of tasks in a TLU domain, a general theory of language, or all three, as discussed in Chapter 11. Second, the scale levels are criterion referenced to specified levels in different areas of language ability, with the lowest level on our rating scales defined as "no evidence of" the ability and the highest level as "evidence of mastery of" the ability.

Ability-based scales

We have consistently argued that the design and development of language tests must be based upon a clear definition of language ability, and our approach to defining rating scales also follows this principle. In designing rating scales, we start with construct definitions that include multiple components of language ability and create *analytic* scales, which require the rater to provide separate ratings for the different components of language ability in the construct definition. In developing analytic rating scales we will have the same number of separate scales as there are distinct components in the construct definition.

In situations where it might be useful to provide a single score, we recommend producing this by combining scores which are arrived at by the use of analytic rating scales, rather than developing a single global rating scale.

This is because of the problems involved with the use of global scales that are discussed above.

The use of analytic scales has two practical advantages. First, it allows the test developer to provide a "profile" of the areas of language ability that are rated. In most language teaching and testing situations, the test users will want to differentiate among areas of relative strength and weakness. For example, the test developer might want to provide interpretations such as "Organizes writing very well, but doesn't have much control of register in formal writing; writes a formal business letter as if it were a conversation with a friend" or "Has a large vocabulary but continually makes grammar mistakes when speaking about chemistry."

A second advantage is that analytic scales tend to reflect what raters actually do when rating samples of language use. For example, even when expert raters are asked to sort writing samples into levels on the basis of *overall* quality, they report that they take into consideration specific areas of language ability (such as grammar, vocabulary, content) when they do so.[5]

Criterion-referenced scales of language ability

Our second principle is to define scales in terms of criterion levels of ability. The primary advantage of criterion-referenced scales is that they allow test users to make inferences about how much language ability a test taker has, and not merely how well she performs relative to other individuals, including native speakers. We define the lowest level of our scales in terms of no evidence of knowledge or ability and the highest level in terms of mastery, or complete knowledge or ability. We will thus always have zero and mastery levels in our scales, irrespective of whether there are any test takers at these levels.

The main question that remains is how many levels to have between zero and mastery. This depends primarily upon the specific warrants in the AUA. Suppose, for example, that the director of a writing program wanted to measure test takers' writing ability in order to place them into four different levels in this program. Suppose further that she decides to administer a writing test and then rate test takers' performance on this. How will she decide how many levels she should have in her rating scales? To support warrants about *consistency*, she will need to consider the number of distinctions raters can reasonably be expected to make consistently. It would be easy to create rating scales with, say, ten ability levels, but it is unlikely that raters could make so many distinctions with any kind of consistency. The Program Director will also need to consider the *meaningfulness* of the scales, in terms of the degree to which they correspond to levels of ability that are assumed for the different levels of course. Finally, she will need to consider the number of classification decision levels that will be required on the basis of the interpretations. For example, in order to place a wide range of students into four levels of the writing program, a minimum of four scale levels is needed. This minimum number of levels assumes, of course, that ratings are absolutely consistent and correspond perfectly to levels in the course. Since this is virtually never the case, test developers will generally need more scale levels than there are decision levels. If the number of decision levels required exceeds the number of levels that raters can consistently distinguish, then it may be possible to use a composite score by combining the ratings of the separate analytic scales to obtain a score with a larger number of levels. (Composite scores are discussed below, on pp. 355–7.) A final consideration is practicality, as the number of levels decided upon will have implications for both the selection and training of raters and the amount of time required to do the ratings.

Scale definitions

In our approach, the construct definitions from which rating scales can be developed refer only to areas of language ability, independent of any considerations of the characteristics of the specific testing situation and prompt with which they might be used. For example, we define grammatical knowledge to include rules of syntax and phonology/graphology without reference to language use situations such as "conversation with an employer in an office environment."

The *scale definition* includes two parts:

1 the specific features of the language sample to be rated with the scale, and
2 the definition of scale levels in terms of the degree of mastery of these features.

It is these specific features of language use that should be kept in mind when carrying out ratings, and the amount of detail and how this is communicated in the scale definition will depend upon a number of factors.

How are we going to use the ratings?

Does the test developer intend the inferences about language knowledge to generalize to a broadly defined or to a highly specific TLU situation? For example, in order to generalize to mastery of a specific body of course material, as in achievement testing, it is necessary to provide enough detail to relate the construct definition to instructional content. When rating writing samples in a composition course, for example, the test developer might want to add to the construct "knowledge of rhetorical organization" details such as "knowledge of introduction, thesis statement, topic sentences, and topic headings."

Who are the intended audiences of the rating scales?

Alderson (1991) described three different purposes, or functions, that rating scales can serve in terms of the different groups of stakeholders for whom they may be designed. One purpose, which he called "user-oriented," serves the purpose of providing meaningful information to test users. Such scales tend to describe test takers' performance in terms of "typical or likely behaviours of candidates at any given level" (Alderson 1991: 72). A second purpose is to guide the raters in the process of administering the assessment and assigning ratings, and he called scales such as these "assessor-oriented." Such scales provide guidance not only on how to rate the performance, but also on what kinds of tasks to present to candidates in order to elicit performance that can be rated. The third function, which he described as "constructor-oriented," is to guide the construction of the test itself at the different levels needed. Alderson's distinctions suggest that while a single construct definition may underlie all three kinds of scales, and while each scale may have the same number of levels, the amount and kinds of information that are included in the descriptions of the scale levels are likely to vary from one function or audience to another.

How much detail do the raters need in order to provide ratings that can be justified?

This will be influenced by the characteristics of the raters. For example, if trained English composition teachers were rating punctuation, a construct definition that included a detailed list and usage notes for all of the punctuation marks in English might not be unnecessary. On the other hand, if native speakers of English who were not trained either as language teachers or language testers were rating a construct such as "sociolinguistic knowledge," a fairly detailed definition of this construct would probably be required in order to familiarize them with what to look for. This is because they would most likely not be familiar with the term "sociolinguistic knowledge," and would not know how this is realized by language users as they interact orally.

Examples of criterion-referenced ability-based analytic scales

The following two scales illustrate ratings derived from ability-based construct definitions. These scales might be used for placing students into a multilevel conversation course in which knowledge of both syntax and register is used to make placement decisions. These examples are intended to be illustrative, and although they may be appropriate for use in actual testing situations, this would need to be determined by the test developer, after constructing an AUA and providing backing to justify their use.

The scale shown in Figure 16.5 could be used to rate knowledge of syntax.

Construct definition	Knowledge of syntax
Performance criterion	Evidence of accurate use of a variety of syntactic structures as demonstrated in a structured face-to-face oral interview with two examiners, one of the specific tasks (as specified in the task specifications) that have been presented, and as rated on the following scale:

Levels of knowledge/mastery	**Description**
0 None	*No evidence of knowledge* of syntax Range: zero Accuracy: not relevant
1 Limited	Evidence of *Limited knowledge* of syntax Range: small Accuracy: poor, moderate, or good accuracy. If test taker only attempts a very few structures, accuracy may be good
2 Moderate	Evidence of *Moderate knowledge* of syntax Range: medium Accuracy: moderate to good accuracy within range. If test taker attempts structures outside of the controlled range, accuracy may be poor
3 Extensive	Evidence of *Extensive knowledge* of syntax Range: large, few limitations Accuracy: good accuracy, few errors
4 Complete	Evidence of *Complete knowledge* of syntax Range: no evidence of restrictions in range Accuracy: evidence of complete control except for slips of the tongue

Figure 16.5 Example scale for rating knowledge of syntax

The next scale (Figure 16.6 on p. 346) could be used to rate knowledge of register.

Each of these scales includes both the numbers and short labels for the levels as well as descriptions of the levels. Each scale also includes an explicit distinction between **range** or variety in the use of the particular component (for example, syntactic structures, markers of register) and **accuracy** or **appropriateness** in using those components. It has been our experience over the years that this distinction is very useful for developing rating scales for a wide variety of components of language ability.

Construct definition	Knowledge of the appropriate register for a particular purpose and audience
Levels of knowledge/mastery	**Description**
0 Zero	*No evidence of knowledge* of register Range: zero Appropriateness: not relevant
1 Limited	Evidence of *Limited knowledge* of only one register Range: evidence of only one register in formulaic expressions and substantive discourse Appropriateness: poor
2 Moderate	Evidence of *Moderate knowledge* of two registers Range: evidence of two registers in formulaic expressions and substantive discourse Appropriateness: good for one register, poor for another
3 Extensive	Evidence of *Extensive knowledge* of two registers Range: evidence of two registers in formulaic expressions and substantive discourse Appropriateness: good for two registers, few errors
4 Complete	Evidence of *Complete knowledge* of two registers Range: evidence of two registers in formulaic expressions and substantive discourse Appropriateness: completely appropriate use of two registers, no errors

Figure 16.6 Example scale for rating knowledge of register

The next example (Figure 16.7 on p. 347) illustrates a layout for a rubric used to rate students' control of elements in a specific genre, a multi-paragraph cause–effect academic essay, and provide them with feedback on their performance. In this rubric, range is implicit in the number of performance criteria that are included in the essay being rated and accuracy is implicit in the degree to which these criteria are controlled.

When teachers use this rubric, they read a composition and look for the performance criteria for each part of the construct. If a performance criterion is met consistently for one of the construct, the teacher puts a check ("✓" in Figure 16.8 on p. 348) on the line preceding the criterion. If not, the teacher leaves it unchecked. The teacher then looks at all the checks for criteria, or lack thereof, and uses these to produce a rating for the level of effectiveness for that part of the construct. The teacher can then return the rubric to the students,

PARTS OF THE ESSAY AND PERFORMANCE CRITERIA FOR EACH	**LEVEL** (0–4)	**LEVELS OF EFFECTIVENESS**				
		4 Complete *All* characteristics present	**3 Extensive** *Most* characteristics present	**2 Moderate** *Some* characteristics present	**1 Limited** *Few* characteristics present	**0 Zero** *No* characteristics present
		COMMENTS (Teacher's comments for additional feedback to students.)				
1 Hook _ Inviting hook _ Suitable hook						
2 Background information _ Provides relevant background information _ Provides sufficient background information						
3 Thesis statement _ Restricted topic _One, limited central idea _ Appropriate						
4 Topic sentences _ At the beginning of each paragraph _ Restricted aspect of main topic _ Specific, relevant controlling idea						
5 Organizing principle: cause–effects _ Causes and effects logically related _ Causes/effects are significant						
6 Overall unity & support _ All details are relevant _ Specific, well-developed examples _ Logical organization of examples						
7 Overall coherence _ Use of transitional expressions within each paragraph _ Use of transitional expressions between paragraphs _ Variety of transitional expressions _ Logical arrangement of sentences						
8 Conclusion _ Restates thesis in an interesting manner _ No new information _ Puts a logical end to the essay						
9 Sources _ All sources are appropriately cited						
	TOTAL 30 max.					

Figure 16.7 Example scale for rating control of elements in a specific genre (Christison and Palmer 2005, p. 102)

who can use it as feedback on particular areas of mastery or non-mastery. The teacher can also write comments for each part of the construct to help explain her rating.

Figure 16.8 on p. 348 provides an example assessment record that includes quantitative information in the form of ratings on parts of the essay and non-compensatory sum of ratings. In addition, it includes qualitative descriptive information of two types. One type consists of the checked and unchecked characteristics of each component of the construct. The other

PARTS OF THE ESSAY AND PERFORMANCE CRITERIA FOR EACH	LEVEL (0–4)	LEVELS OF EFFECTIVENESS 4 **Complete** *All* characteristics present | 3 **Extensive** *Most* characteristics present | 2 **Moderate** *Some* characteristics present | 1 **Limited** *Few* characteristics present | 0 **Zero** *No* characteristics present **COMMENTS (Teacher's comments for additional feedback to students.)**
1 Hook _ Inviting hook ✓ Suitable hook	3	Your hook is on topic, but you might find a way to make it more inviting. Perhaps personalizing it might help.
2 Background information ✓ Provides relevant background information ✓ Provides sufficient background information	4	
3 Thesis statement ✓ Restricted topic ✓ One, limited central idea ✓ Appropriate	4	
4 Topic sentences _ At the beginning of each paragraph ✓ Restricted aspect of main topic ✓ Specific, relevant controlling idea	2	In paragraphs 3-4, your topics sentences were buried in the middle of the paragraphs. They would be easier to identify if they were placed at the beginning. This could be done without changing the way in which they are worded. By putting topic sentences at the beginning, you give the reader advanced information about what the paragraph is about, which can make it easier to read quickly.
5 Organizing principle: cause-effects ✓ Causes and effects logically related ✓ Causes/effects are significant	4	
6 Overall unity & support _ All details are relevant ✓ Specific, well-developed examples _ Logical organization of examples	3	In the third paragraph, the details you provide in the second and third examples are not completely relevant to what you lead the reader to expect in your topic sentence. The same is true for the first example in the fourth paragraph.
7 Overall coherence ✓ Use of transitional expressions within each paragraph _ Use of transitional expressions between paragraphs ✓ Variety of transitional expressions _ Logical arrangement of sentences	2	In paragraphs 2 and 4, you could provide transitional expressions to link these paragraphs to the preceding ones. Also, work on providing a greater variety of transitional expressions. You tend to repeat the same conjunctive adverbs: "first", "second", "third". Try also using "moreover", "on the other hand", "in addition", and so on. In addition, try using more subordinating conjunctions, such as "since", "because", and "although". Finally, in paragraph 3, the examples you provide could be given in temporal order, since this ordering would be obvious to the reader. The reader might wonder why they are not ordered in this way in the paragraph.
8 Conclusion ✓ Restates thesis in an interesting manner ✓ No new information	4	
9 Sources ✓ All sources are appropriately cited	4	
	TOTAL 30	

Figure 16.8 Example report of control of elements of a specific genre containing both quantitative and fairly extensive descriptive information

type consists of explanatory comments when some characteristics were not checked.

Note that there is *not* a one-to-one relationship between the number of characteristics checked and the rating assigned for the component of the construct. In other words, the rating is *not* arrived at by adding up the number of characteristics checked. Moreover, the users of this rubric were not able to devise a system for doing this that made sense to them. This relationship between number of criteria checked and rating level assigned is a judgment call.

If the teacher needed to report students' achievement to other stakeholders, such as other teachers who might be interested in knowing students' areas of strength and weakness, she might provide just the level and descriptive labels on the different parts of the essay, as in Figure 16.9.

PARTS OF THE ESSAY	LEVEL (0–4)	LEVELS OF EFFECTIVENESS
1 Hook	3	Extensive control
2 Background information	4	Complete control
3 Thesis statement	4	Complete control
4 Topic sentences	2	Moderate control
5 Organizing principle	4	Complete control
6 Overall unity & support	3	Extensive control
7 Overall coherence	2	Moderate control
8 Conclusion	4	Complete control
9 Sources	4	Complete control
	TOTAL 30	

Figure 16.9 Another version of a report of control of elements of a specific genre

If a teacher needed to use the record as part of the students' grade for course, she might simply provide the total—in this case a non-compensatory composite rating of 30.

Topical knowledge

In some situations we may want to make generalizations from test scores about the test takers' topical knowledge to be included in the construct definition. (See the discussion in Chapter 11.) The way topical knowledge is handled in our approach is that the area of specific topical knowledge is defined operationally as an additional component of the construct and a separate rating scale is developed for this, so as to obtain distinct ratings for topical knowledge. This is quite different from the global approach, in which topical knowledge is generally hidden in the scale definitions, and thus cannot be distinguished from language ability. For example, suppose that for their final course exam, students completing a sheltered subject matter course in botany were asked to write a short essay describing the process of photosynthesis in plants. Suppose that a global or holistic rating scale were used, and that this scale mentioned control of grammar and technical vocabulary, as well as accuracy of content. Suppose that some students used grammar and technical vocabulary correctly, but incorrectly described the process of photosynthesis. They might know what the words "oxygen," "carbon dioxide," and "chloroplast" mean and use these words accurately, but if they don't describe the process correctly their topical knowledge is incorrect. Or suppose some students accurately described the process, but used only very general vocabulary. In this case, their grammar and topical knowledge may be high, but their knowledge of technical vocabulary would be low. In either of these cases, how would we produce a global rating of their essays? If we used separate analytic scales for grammar, vocabulary, and topical knowledge, this would not be a problem.

Figure 16.10 is an example of a scale for rating topical knowledge.

Construct definition:	Knowledge of relevant topical information
Levels of knowledge/mastery	Description
0 Zero	*No evidence of knowledge* of relevant topical information Range: zero, test taker demonstrates no knowledge of assigned topic Accuracy: not relevant
1 Limited	Evidence of *Limited knowledge* of relevant topical information Range: small, test taker deals only with a small portion of assigned topic Accuracy: poor, moderate, or good accuracy within range
2 Moderate	Evidence of *Moderate knowledge* of relevant topical information Range: medium Accuracy: moderate to good accuracy of knowledge within range
3 Extensive	Evidence of *Extensive knowledge* of relevant topical information Range: wide, few limitations Accuracy: good accuracy throughout range
4 Complete	Evidence of *Complete knowledge* of relevant topical information Range: evidence of unlimited range of relevant topical information Accuracy: evidence of complete accuracy throughout range

Figure 16.10 Example rating scale for topical knowledge

Ratable samples

In order for ratings of extended production responses to support the warrants in an AUA, the language produced has to constitute what is called a "ratable sample" of language. One characteristic of a ratable sample of language is that there is opportunity for the full range of components that are to be rated to occur. A second characteristic is that a ratable sample provides evidence of the test taker's highest level of ability on these components. What constitutes a ratable sample, therefore, depends directly upon the components of language ability to be rated, while the extent to which ratable samples can be obtained in a given language test depends on the characteristics of the test tasks. Consider, for example, the kinds of tasks that might be used to elicit a sample of spoken language that could be rated using "knowledge of register." Several test tasks that the test developer believes will engage the areas of language ability to be tested, and that correspond to tasks in the TLU domain, would be set up, in the expectation that these will provide opportunities for the full range of appropriate markers of register to occur, and will enable test takers to perform at their highest levels of ability. In an oral interview, for example, several role-plays might be set up. In some the interviewer could play a role such as a close friend or sibling, where it would be appropriate for the test taker to use an informal or intimate register, while in others the interviewer could take a role where a more formal register would be appropriate, such as an older relative, a teacher, or a prospective employer. Tasks to elicit different registers in formulaic language, such as introductions, greetings, and leave-takings, would be included, as well as tasks to elicit appropriate register in extended discourse, such as a job interview or short presentation.

By providing a test task that engages the components of language ability we want to measure and that corresponds to TLU tasks, the test developer tries to assure that there is an adequate sample of language to rate. If this approach is not followed, the task can easily become a discrete-point approach in which it is necessary to prepare a list of the specific elements of language to be measured and then specify test tasks that will elicit these elements. This can lead to the use of tasks that do not correspond to speaking tasks in the TLU domain. While there may be components of language ability which can be assessed efficiently with discrete items, we believe that any gain in efficiency would need to be balanced against the potential loss in meaningfulness and generalizability.

Using rating scales

Rating scales have often been seen as inefficient, inconsistent ways of scoring language tests, and it is partly for this reason that the use of objective procedures—items with selected responses that can be scored efficiently by either untrained personnel or machines—has become so widespread in language testing. While inefficiency and inconsistency are potential problems, they are by no means insurmountable. With sufficient planning and development, rating procedures can be highly consistent and relatively efficient.

Anticipating problems

Demand on resources

Ratings might appear to be the least efficient way of scoring language tests. After all, ratings involve subjective judgments in the scoring process, which is not the case for objectively scored tests. It is true that, relative to machine scoring, ratings are more demanding in terms of human resources. However, ratings can provide information that is very difficult to obtain from objective scoring, such as profiles of areas of language knowledge in tests that require test takers to actually produce samples of language. Ratings can also put human beings in contact with the test method in ways that objective scoring procedures may not. Raters are constantly in contact with responses and often, as in the case of oral interview procedures, in contact with input as well. Thus, ratings provide greater opportunity for assessing the effectiveness of the test task, as well as its impact on test takers. For such reasons, we believe that ratings are well worth their relatively high cost in human resources.

The use of rating scales places two kinds of demands on human resources:

1 the amount of time involved, and
2 the number of people involved.

Rating samples of language production always requires time to listen to or read them, and the longer the samples, the more time is required. Moreover, the total amount of rating time increases as the number of ratings increases, but using multiple ratings and averaging them is one way to increase their consistency. Therefore, this demand on human resources must be recognized as an unavoidable cost of obtaining the kinds of information that ratings can provide. In terms of supporting warrants in an AUA, we believe that the potential gains in meaningfulness and generalizability more than offset any potential loss in practicality.

Inconsistency

Another potential problem with ratings is inconsistency, which can be attributed to three causes: different interpretations of scales, different standards of severity, and reaction to elements not relevant to scales.

Different interpretations of a given rating scale, both by different raters and by the same rater on different occasions, can lead to inconsistent scoring. One reason raters may interpret scales differently is that the scales may be inadequately specified. For example, if raters who are not sophisticated in linguistics are asked to rate an oral interview on "knowledge of register" without being given a clear definition of what is meant by "register," some raters might interpret register as something entirely different, such as the use of a different regional variety. (See discussion above, of "assessor-oriented" scales.) This can be a particular problem with global or holistic ratings of language production, in which raters may tend to develop their own internal analytic rating criteria, which differ from rater to rater and within a single rater on different occasions.

Another problem of inconsistency stems from lack of agreement on the meanings of the different levels of ability within a scale. For example, two raters may agree on the definition of sociolinguistic knowledge for the purposes of rating, but they may disagree on how well test takers must perform in order to reach the different levels on the scale. Thus, one rater may rate a test taker a "2" in sociolinguistic knowledge while another may rate the same test taker a "3." Or one rater may rate more severely during one rating session than another.

Another problem of inconsistency stems from reaction to elements not relevant to scales. Since ratings are subjective, and since the language sample is likely to include content or features not directly relevant to particular scale definitions, ratings may be influenced by this irrelevant material. For example, although raters may be instructed to rate compositions only on textual and functional knowledge, they may nonetheless be influenced by features such as the test takers' handwriting and knowledge of the topic, as well as by the positions they take on the issues. In addition, if raters know the test takers, they may find themselves influenced by prior knowledge of the test takers' performance.

Dealing with problems

While the use of rating scales brings with it a number of potential problems, there are several ways in which the test developer can deal with these to reduce their impact. (See the Suggested Readings at the end of this chapter for more detailed discussions of these.)

Preparing raters

One of the most effective ways of dealing with inconsistency is through the proper selection and training of raters. One primary consideration in the selection of raters is the required level of language ability. For some rating tasks, we might want to select only raters whose language ability is at the level of complete mastery of the components of language ability on which they are rating test takers' performance. This would certainly be the case if they were required to rate a full range of language ability. However, for rating performance that is at the levels of only limited to moderate ability, raters with less than complete mastery might be selected.

Regardless of the backgrounds of the raters selected, it is important to provide them with adequate training. Here are six steps in a general procedure for training raters:

1 Read and discuss scales together.
2 Review language samples which have been previously rated by expert raters and discuss the ratings given.

3 Practice rating a different set of language samples. Then compare the ratings with those of experienced raters. Discuss the ratings and how the criteria were applied.
4 Rate additional language samples and discuss.
5 Each trainee rates the same set of samples. Check for the amount of time taken to rate and for consistency.
6 Select raters who are able to provide reliable and efficient ratings.

Obtaining a sufficient number of ratings

A second way to deal with inconsistency is to make sure a sufficient number of ratings is obtained. All other things being equal, the more ratings that are obtained, the more stable their average becomes. So while any single rater can have a "bad day," or be overly lenient or severe in his ratings, it is unlikely that this will occur with two or three raters at the same time or in the same ways. Thus, it is good practice always to obtain at least two ratings per sample. A typical procedure is to have all samples rated by two raters and to have a third rater rate those samples on which the first two raters differ by more than one scale level. Then the score can be produced by averaging the three ratings.

Estimating the consistency (reliability) of the ratings

An important step in developing a test is the statistical analysis of quantitative information obtained in trialing, and this includes estimating the degree of consistency, or reliability, of the ratings. This information will allow the test developer to make decisions about how effectively inconsistency has been controlled, and if the results are unsatisfactory, what additional steps can be taken to increase consistency. For ratings, the primary concerns are in estimating the consistency between different raters (inter-rater consistency) and, within the same rater, across occasions of rating (intra-rater consistency), although procedures for estimating the extent to which different raters rate different kinds of language samples differently are also available. (See Bachman 2004b, as well as the references listed in Chapter 19 of this book for discussions of appropriate procedures for estimating inconsistencies in ratings.)

COMPUTER SCORING OF WRITING

A large number of automated essay scoring (AES) systems have been developed in the past forty years. The first ones, such as Project Essay Grade (Page 1968), relied solely on a statistical procedure to predict the essay score on the basis of surface features of written texts such as average sentence length, number of subordinating conjunctions, number of relative pronouns, and punctuation. The AES systems that are currently available are more sophisticated, and most incorporate, in one way or another, Latent Semantic Analysis (LSA). LSA is a method for computer modeling and simulation of the meaning of words and passages by analysis of representative corpora of natural text (Landauer and Dumais, http://www.scholarpedia.org/article/Latent_semantic_analysis). In applying LSA to the analysis of written essays, a writing teacher could use a computer program to analyze the content of a number of sample student essays that were written in response to a particular learning activity. The computer program generates a "model" of the essay that includes information about the semantic similarity of words and text, and this model can then provide feedback to the teacher and his students about the qualities of their essays. In using LSA for scoring responses to essay tests, the test developer uses the computer program to analyze essays written by test takers in response to a particular writing prompt, and that have already been scored by human raters according to a rating scale. The computer program then generates a model of these essays, along with the specific linguistic and content features that are characteristic of each score on the rating scale. This model is then used to analyze essays written by other test takers in response to the same prompt, and to assign scores to these on the basis of their linguistic and content characteristics.

Many of these AES systems are commercially available and can be purchased for use by classroom teachers or schools, for a wide range of applications, from writing instruction, to formative assessment, to large-scale high-stakes assessments of writing. A review of these systems is far beyond the scope of this book. Suffice it to say that most of these systems have been developed on the basis of extensive research addressing many of the same issues—consistency of ratings, meaningfulness of interpretations—that are of concern with human raters. Interested readers will find references to specific AES programs in Valenti et al. (2003), Jamieson (2005), and Douglas and Hegelheimer (2007), as well as in the Suggested Readings at the end of this chapter.

PRODUCING TOTAL TEST SCORES FROM THE SCORES OF PARTS

Profile scores for parts of the test

In many cases the test developer may want to report a profile of scores corresponding to the different areas of language ability measured. With items that elicit either selected or limited production responses, the scores for the individual items in each part of the test that measures a particular area of language ability can be added up and the total score for that part reported. The use of analytic rating scales also allows profiles of levels of ability on different constructs included in the rating scales to be reported. Indeed, if the rating procedures advocated in this book are followed and only analytic scales used, all scoring will include profiles of the areas of language ability measured.

Composite scores

There are sometimes situations in which it will be useful to report a single score, in which case a composite score can be produced. A **composite score** is one that is arrived at by considering *all* the different parts of a test, or different analytic rating scales. There are two approaches for producing a composite score from part scores: compensatory and non-compensatory.

Compensatory composite scores

In some situations the test developer or test user may assume that individuals with high levels in some of the areas of language ability to be tested can use these high levels of ability to compensate for low levels of ability in other areas. In such situations a **compensatory composite score** can be produced by summing or averaging the separate scores. This is because when the scores from the different parts of the test or different analytic rating scales are added up or averaged, the composite score arrived at balances out high scores and low scores. Suppose, for example, that it was necessary to select the top few candidates from among a large number of applicants for a language teaching position, and that language ability was one of the qualifications for the job. Assuming that this particular teaching position will require the teacher to use language in tasks that involve writing, reading, speaking, and listening, the test developer could design a test that includes tasks that engage test takers in all of these language use activities, and design separate scoring methods and produce scores for these different types of tasks. These scores, if reported individually, would provide a profile of applicants' language ability across different types of language use tasks. In addition, in order to more easily rank applicants in terms of their language ability, a single score of their ability to use language in all of these types of tasks could be obtained by adding their scores on the different parts of the test, and this might be reported in addition to the profile of scores on the various parts of the test. Or suppose it was necessary to produce a single rating for performance on speaking tasks from separate analytic ratings of organizational, textual, and sociolinguistic knowledge. These three ratings for each test taker might be added up and averaged.

It is important for test developers to understand that when the scores from different parts of a test, or the ratings from different analytic scales, are added to produce a non-compensatory composite score, the relative importance of the part scores in this composite score will be a function of the statistical properties of the part scores. Because of this the sum or average of the part scores may not reflect the relative importance of the parts that the test developer intends. In some situations, the test developer may consider all the parts of the test, or areas of language ability that are rated, to be equally important. In other situations the test developer may have good reasons for wanting some scores to carry more weight than others. In the former situation, simply adding or averaging the scores may not result in equal weighting of the part scores. In the latter situation, simply multiplying the more important part scores by some number, say 2 or 3, will not necessarily result in these parts being two or three times as important in the composite score. In both cases, the test developer should follow the appropriate procedures to derive weights for the part scores that will assure that the relative importance of these in the composite score reflects the test developers' intentions. (See Bachman 2004b:

Chapter 11, for a complete discussion of procedures for weighting the parts of composite scores.)

Non-compensatory composite scores

In some situations the test developer or test user may feel that individuals must demonstrate a minimum level of ability in every area of language ability tested, and that high levels of ability in some areas cannot compensate for low levels in others. For example, teachers in a given language course may feel that students must demonstrate a minimum level of mastery on each component of the course in order to be placed or advanced into a given level. Or an employer may require that new employees have a minimum level of mastery in several areas of language ability. In such situations it might be appropriate to calculate and report a **non-compensatory composite score**, which is the lowest score achieved in any of the parts of the test. In the example above, if a certain minimum level of language ability were considered essential for language teachers, candidates' composite scores would be based on the lowest score received on any of the four parts. Or suppose a test taker's ratings, based on a writing sample, were "2" for knowledge of vocabulary, "3" for knowledge of rhetorical organization, and "3" for knowledge of register. This test taker would receive a non-compensatory composite score of "2." (The fact that the test taker received "3s" on two of the scales does not compensate for the "2" that he received on the other.)

DESCRIPTIONS AS ASSESSMENT RECORDS

The variety of different ways of providing information about test takers' performance in forms other than, or in addition to, scores is virtually limitless, and ranges from rich descriptions that are part of or elaborations of rating scales, to descriptions based on the analysis of the language features in test takers' performance, to audio and video recordings of their performance. Indeed, we would suggest that the possibilities for finding new ways of recording test takers' responses are limited only by the creativity of the test developer and the test development team, as well as the usual real world constraints on resources. Thus, our discussion of these will necessarily be illustrative, rather than exhaustive. Furthermore, because of the limitations of the medium of print, we will only be able to describe, but not illustrate, the use of audio and video records.

Descriptions from rating scales

As discussed above under rating scales, the test developer may provide relatively rich descriptions of the different scale levels, whether these are holistic or analytic. This is one way to provide qualitative descriptions as part of the assessment record. The most extensive work in this area is in the assessment of speaking and writing, and so the examples we provide are from this.

The first example is taken from the American Council for the Teaching of Foreign Languages (ACTFL) Proficiency guidelines, which are used for rating test takers' performance on the ACTFL oral proficiency interview (Breiner-Sanders et al. 2000). This test involves a face-to-face oral interaction between an examiner and a test taker. Test takers' performance is scored on a scale with four main levels: Novice, Intermediate, Advanced, and Superior. Each of these levels is subdivided into sublevels of low, mid, and high. This scale was developed for use in foreign language programs in the United States as a means for assessing students' speaking, and also for promoting positive impact on instruction, specifically, more emphasis on learning to speak a language. The example we provide is the descriptor for the Advanced–Low level in speaking.

> Speakers at the Advanced-Low level are able to handle a variety of communicative tasks, although somewhat haltingly at times. They participate actively in most informal and a limited number of formal conversations on activities related to school, home, and leisure activities and, to a lesser degree, those related to events of work, current, public, and personal interest or individual relevance.
>
> Advanced-Low speakers demonstrate the ability to narrate and describe in all major time frames (past, present, and future) in paragraph length discourse, but control of aspect may be lacking at times. They can handle appropriately the linguistic challenges presented by a complication or unexpected turn of events that occurs within the context of a routine situation or communicative task with which they are otherwise familiar, though at times their discourse may be minimal for the level and strained. Communicative strategies such as rephrasing and circumlocution may be employed in such instances. In their narrations and descriptions, they combine and link sentences into connected discourse of paragraph length. When pressed for a fuller account, they tend to grope and rely on minimal discourse. Their utterances are typically not longer than a single paragraph. Structure of the dominant language is still evident in the use of false cognates, literal translations, or the oral paragraph structure of the speaker's own language rather than that of the target language.
>
> While the language of Advanced-Low speakers may be marked by substantial, albeit irregular flow, it is typically somewhat strained and tentative, with noticeable self-correction and a certain "grammatical roughness." The vocabulary of Advanced-Low speakers is primarily generic in nature.
>
> Advanced-Low speakers contribute to the conversation with sufficient accuracy, clarity, and precision to convey their intended message without misrepresentation or confusion, and it can be understood by native speakers unaccustomed to dealing with non-natives, even though this may be achieved through repetition and restatement. When attempting to perform functions or handle topics associated with the Superior level, the linguistic quality and quantity of their speech will deteriorate significantly. (From Breiner-Sanders et al. 2000: 15–16)

The ACTFL Oral Proficiency Interview is not linked to any particular language course or any particular language use domain. The construct that is assessed is very broad, and its primary uses are for assessing the amount of improvement students make during a course of study, evaluating the effectiveness of a foreign language program, or for predicting their capability of using the language in a future job.

The second example consists of a scoring rubric and a feedback form that is used in a pre-academic intensive ESL writing course intended to prepare students for academic writing in their undergraduate courses (Weigle 2002: 190–1; Weigle and Nelson 2001). In the scoring rubric, there are two constructs, "Content/Organization" and "Language Use." The scoring rubric is provided in Figure 16.11.

Content/Organization	**Language Use** The essay:
9–10	9–10
• The treatment of the assignment completely fulfills the task expectations and the topic is addressed thoroughly. • The introduction orients the reader effectively to the topic and to the author's thesis (purpose, plan, and focus). • The conclusion effectively reinforces and comments on the thesis, providing closure to the essay. • Fully developed e.vidence for generalizations and supporting ideas/arguments is provided in a relevant and credible way. • Paragraphs are separate and logical units, fully developed, clearly related to the thesis and effectively connected to each other by appropriate, well-chosen, and varied transitions. • Sentences within paragraphs form a well-connected series, using appropriate transition words and other cohesion devices.	• is clearly written with few errors; errors do not interfere with comprehension. • includes accurate and diverse academic vocabulary. • includes accurate word forms and verb tenses. • uses a variety of sentence types accurately. • incorporates ideas from assigned readings and/or outside sources without plagiarism; sources are cited correctly and paraphrased using a variety of techniques.
7–8	7–8
• The treatment of the assignment fulfills the task expectations competently and the topic is addressed clearly. • The introduction orients the reader sufficiently to the topic and to the author's thesis. • The conclusion competently reinforces and comments on the thesis. • Strong evidence for generalizations and supporting ideas/arguments is provided in a relevant and credible way. • Paragraphs are separate and logical units, well developed, clearly related to the thesis and well connected to each other by appropriate and varied transitions. • Sentences within paragraphs form a well-connected series, using appropriate transition words and other cohesion devices.	• is clearly written with few errors; errors do not interfere with comprehension. • includes academic vocabulary that is rarely inaccurate or repetitive. • may include inaccurate word forms and verb tenses. • uses a variety of sentence types. • incorporates ideas from assigned readings and/or outside sources without plagiarism; most sources are cited correctly and paraphrased using a variety of techniques.
5–6	5–6
• The treatment of the assignment adequately fulfills the task expectations and the topic is addressed clearly. • The introduction orients the reader sufficiently to the topic and to the author's thesis, though it may be brief and/or undeveloped. • The conclusion reinforces and comments on the thesis.	• is generally clearly written with few errors; at most a few errors interfere with comprehension. • demonstrates occasional problems with word choice. • includes some inaccurate word forms and verb tenses.

Figure 16.11 Scoring rubric for pre-university writing course (Weigle 2002: 193)

Unlike the previous example of the ACTFL speaking rubric, this scoring rubric is tailored to the specific learning objectives of this course, so that the construct to be assessed is very focused. Another difference is that this scoring rubric is designed to provide feedback to help students improve their writing. In addition to the scoring rubric, teachers in the course also provide students feedback through a feedback form, given in Figure 16.12.

Descriptions from analyses of test takers' performance

Another way in which assessment records as verbal descriptions can be produced is by analyzing the features of test takers' performances. This was the approach taken in an assessment that was intended to test the foreign language ability of undergraduate students at a large university in the United States (Bachman et al. 1992). The purpose of the assessment was to place students into one of two different programs in a study abroad program. The lowest level consisted of summer courses overseas to help students improve their language. The next level consisted of "sheltered" academic courses at universities abroad. These were academic courses that were designed specifically for English speaking students, and included special support in the language, such as TAs who were trained language teachers, glossaries, and lectures that were delivered in simplified language.

The test was delivered via videotape and consisted of two modules, Module 1: Listening, Note-taking, and Speaking, and Module 2: Reading and Writing. For Module 1, which students took first, they listened to an academic lecture and took notes. Then they answered a number of open-ended questions to test their comprehension. They were given two oral prompts to which they responded, recording their speech on tape. For the reading and writing module, which we will use as an example, students read a passage from an academic textbook and took notes on this. They then answered a number of open-ended questions to test their comprehension. Finally, they were given a writing prompt that required them to write an essay that brought together the content of both the lecture and the reading passage. The prompt specifically asked them to choose an example, from their own experience, of a key concept that was discussed in either the lecture or the reading passage, describe this example, and then analyze it in terms of how this illustrated the concept.

Students' essays were rated on analytic scales for vocabulary, cohesion, organization, grammar, and content. For the purposes of analyzing the language features of the speaking samples and essays, a total score was also calculated, which was the average of the five analytic ratings. In order to provide rich feedback to students who took this test, the test development team analyzed both the speech samples and essays of all the students who took the test. For the essays, the team arranged all the essays according to their ratings on the different analytic scales. For example, they arranged the papers according to the ratings for cohesion, from those that received the top rating (5) to those that received the lowest (1). Members of the team then

ESL 0640/0650 Writing Feedback Form

Name: ____________________

Assignment: ____________

Total: _____/20 Revision/Editing: _____ Grade: _____

❏ First Draft ❏ Final Draft

<table>
<tr><th>CONTENT/ORGANIZATION _____/10
(See Scoring Rubric for Descriptions of Point Values)</th><th>LANGUAGE USE _____/10
(See Scoring Rubric for Descriptions of Point Values)</th><th>REVISION/EDITING
(Final Version Only)
E VG G F P</th></tr>
<tr><td>— Your paper addresses the content of all parts of the task with little or no off-topic material.
— Your introduction effectively orients the reader to the topic and your thesis.
— Evidence to support main idea (examples, illustration, details) is well chosen, clearly explained, and sufficient enough to support the main idea.
— Your conclusion provides effective closure to the paper.
— Each paragraph has one main idea, developed logically and completely through examples and details.
— A variety of transitions (words, phrases, or entire sentences) is used effectively to connect sentences and paragraphs.
— You reached the following special goals for this assignment:
____
____
____________</td><td>— Your paper is clearly written with few errors.
— Your paper includes accurate and diverse academic vocabulary.
— You use a variety of sentence types accurately.
— Ideas from assigned readings and/or outside sources are cited correctly and paraphrased using a variety of techniques.
Your paper has a pattern of errors in the following areas:
— fragments
— verbs
— agreement
— run-on/comma splice
— word order
— word choice
— word form
— assignment specific goals:
____________</td><td>— You have incorporated feedback from your instructor and/or classmates to improve the content of your paper.
— You have incorporated feedback from your instructor and/or classmates to improve the organization of your paper.
— Your paper has been edited carefully for the language features that have been discussed in class.
— Your paper is formatted appropriately (margins, double spaced, indented paragraphs, headings, references, title page).
— Your paper has been edited carefully for spelling, punctuation, and capitalization.
****
— Few revisions were necessary because your first draft was outstanding.
____
E = Excellent
VG = Very Good
G = Good
F = Fair
P = Poor</td></tr>
</table>

Figure 16.12 Example feedback form for pre-university writing course (Weigle 2002: 195)

analyzed the papers in each score group in terms of that construct. From this they were able to produce descriptions of the specific features for each construct at each level. This procedure was also followed to arrive at overall descriptions, using the total scores as levels.

An example of the descriptions of the vocabulary at different levels in the essays that was included as part of the assessment record, along with the students' scores is given below.

This category includes range and accuracy of vocabulary and their effect on communicating ideas. It also reflects the effectiveness of your use of the vocabulary in the original documents: the reading passage, and the lectures.

5: complete control of the necessary vocabulary to address this task; large range of vocabulary; often sophisticated vocabulary; adequate choice of synonyms to avoid repetitiveness; absence of false cognates; original language from reading passage/lecture(s) used appropriately: more paraphrasing/embedding than quoting.

4: large range of vocabulary; sometimes sophisticated vocabulary; very few errors; original language from reading passage and/or lecture(s) used appropriately, either paraphrased or embedded in candidate's own writing, or quoted appropriately.

3: not a large range of vocabulary, but an adequate enough range to discuss the topic; appropriate and accurate use of vocabulary in most cases; original language from reading passage and/or lecture(s) paraphrased appropriately or used within candidate's own construction, not just copied verbatim.

2: somewhat limited range of vocabulary with frequent repetition; marked interference of English in the form of false cognates, borrowed words, or actual English words in quotation marks; original language from reading passage and/or lecture(s) copied verbatim rather than incorporated into candidate's own writing.

1: not enough language produced to be able to judge candidate's vocabulary ability, OR the essay consisted primarily of material copied verbatim from the reading passage, OR candidate did not address essay topic at all.

TRIALING

As with most aspects of test development, the development of a scoring method is iterative and cyclical, involving:

1 initial specification,
2 tryout,
3 analysis, and
4 revision.

In developing a scoring method for items for eliciting selected responses, for example, the test task writer will typically include in each item several choices from which test takers are to select, one of which is intended to be the "correct" or "best" answer. The items are then tried out with groups of test takers, and feedback on their performance collected, both qualitatively and quantitatively. Finally, based on these analyses, the items may be revised, including the choice intended to be the correct one. Items for eliciting limited production responses are often tried out with test takers in order to identify the expected range of responses, and to make an initial scoring key. If partial credit scoring is to be used, an initial specification will be provided of the number of points to be given for each response. Then the items are tried out and, on the basis of the analyses of the responses, the items may be revised and the scoring method refined. A very similar procedure is followed with rating scales. We begin with initial scale definitions, including the number of levels, for each of the areas of language ability to be rated. Then, based on feedback collected as part of the trialing of the rating scales, the construct definitions may need to be refined, and the number of scale levels either expanded or reduced. Thus, the development of a scoring method is not simply a matter of deciding on criteria for correctness and determining procedures for scoring responses during test specification and incorporating these in the Blueprint. This is because it is only through trying out the method empirically and analyzing the results that a full range of backing for the AUA can be provided. (A detailed discussion of procedures for trying out test tasks and scoring methods and analyzing the results is provided in Chapter 19.)

INTERPRETING ASSESSMENT RECORDS

As mentioned at the beginning of this chapter, test users and other stakeholders use information from the assessment to make interpretations about the construct to be assessed. The assessment record, discussed in the previous section, provides some of this information. The record, however, needs to be supplemented by interpretive information that describes the construct to be assessed, the kinds of assessment tasks that were presented to test takers, and how the assessment record was produced. So the question is "Where does this information come from?" In some cases the assessment record and interpretive information will be provided separately, while in other situations, this information may be combined in the form of an assessment report.

Interpretive information

As discussed in Chapter 6, during the process of assessment development and use the test developer assembles information that will be provided to test users and other stakeholders in terms and in a format that will be easily accessible and useful for them. This interpretive information will include a description of the construct to be assessed, along with a description of the assessment tasks that were presented to test takers and how the assessment records were produced. By providing a description of the construct to be assessed, the test developer provides backing for Warrant A5 about meaningfulness, while the description of the assessment tasks and how the assessment records are produced provides backing for Warrants B1 and B2, respectively, about generalizability under Claim 3.

Interpretive information can be provided by test developers in a number of ways. Perhaps the most common is in the form of a manual that provides a rich source of information about the assessment, including information about the intended uses of the assessment, a description of the construct to be assessed, often accompanied by a discussion of the research and theory or curriculum upon which this is based, a description of the assessment itself, often including examples of the different types of tasks included in the assessment, and a description of the assessment records and how these are produced. In addition, many users' manuals will include information about backing that has been collected during trialing and operational use of the assessment, such as quantitative studies into the consistency of scores and backing to support the meaningfulness of interpretations. Users' manuals for large-scale assessments are now most commonly available on-line from the test developer's web page. In some cases, the interpretive information will be provided via an interactive web page.

Assessment reports

As discussed in Chapter 5, an assessment report will include the assessment record plus an interpretation of the record, in terms of the ability to be assessed. Many large-scale assessments of English as a foreign language, for example, provide both scores and verbal descriptions of the level of language ability associated with those scores. In some cases the assessment report may also include the decision that is made. The specific content of this assessment report will vary, depending upon the situation in which the assessment is used. What needs to be included in reports will depend upon what test users and other stakeholders require in order to interpret the assessment performance as an indicator of the ability to be assessed.

In using the information provided by the test developer, the test user and other stakeholders will need to access as much information as needed to make the interpretation. If the assessment provides only an assessment record, then the test user will need to read the information provided in the test users' manual or access the test developer's web page to obtain the relevant interpretive information.

SUMMARY

Recording and interpreting test takers' performance involves using both an assessment record and interpretive information provided by the test developer. Developing a recording method involves first deciding what type of assessment record (score, description) will be produced. If the record is a score, the criteria for correctness need to be specified. For both scores and descriptions, the procedures for producing an assessment record need to be specified. Scores can be produced in two ways, counting and adding up the number of tasks successfully completed, and defining several levels on one or more rating scales of language ability, and then rating responses to test tasks in terms of these scales. Both kinds of scores—based on number correct or ratings—need to be accompanied by verbal descriptions of the construct to be assessed and the kinds of tasks that were presented to test takers.

In order to interpret assessment records as indicators of the ability to be assessed, test users and other stakeholders will also need to use interpretive information describing the ability to be assessed, types of the assessment tasks that test takers are presented, and the method by which assessment records are produced.

As with most aspects of assessment development, the development of a recording method and interpretive information is iterative and cyclical, involving

1 initial specification (Design Statement)
2 assessment task specification (Blueprint)
3 tryout, and analysis of results, during Trialing and Assessment Use
4 revision.

By collecting information on test takers' performance during Trialing and Assessment Use and analyzing the results we can provide backing support about the meaningfulness and generalizability of interpretations.

EXERCISES

1 Think of a situation for assessment use that you face that involves the use of rating scales. Then go through the examples of rating scales in this chapter and in the example Projects. Do the scales in any of these examples appear to be relevant to your needs? If so, what modifications to the scales might be necessary?
2 Think of a situation in which you have had to use rating scales. How well did the scales work for you? Did you have any problems using the scales? If so, can you articulate the nature of the problems using the language of the warrants in the AUA?
3 Find an example of a short, well-organized example of academic writing that could be easily outlined. Outline it to three levels; then delete portions of the outline at each of the three levels. Create four selected response alternatives for each of the gaps in the outline. Do your best to provide distracters that, while incorrect, are still attractive. Try the test out and obtain feedback from the test takers on the responses. Would you make any changes in the alternatives on the basis of this information?
4 Obtain a copy of a test involving either selected or limited production responses. Determine how the responses are supposed to be scored. Is provision already made for partial credit scoring? If not, can you tell from the test specifications why not? If so, can you tell how partial credit scoring strengthens the link between the scores and the constructs they are intended to measure?
5 Obtain a copy of a test involving either selected or limited production responses with single right/wrong scores. Examine the test specifications,

and determine whether partial credit scoring might be used to strengthen the link between the construct to be measured and the test scores. Then develop a partial credit scoring procedure to establish this link.

6 Obtain a test involving selected response tasks. Determine whether the test takers are told to choose the "best" response or the "correct" answer. Are the instructions consistent with the actual criteria that the test takers use to select the responses? Why or why not?

7 Obtain a foreign language textbook. Develop a set of test tasks involving limited production responses to test several grammar points from the text. Determine how the construct to be measured might be defined. Then have a number of test takers complete the test tasks. From the responses, develop a partial credit answer key for scoring the responses.

8 Obtain a language test involving the use of "global" rating scales. How do the scales address or deal with the problem of inference, difficulty in assigning levels, and differential weighting of components? How might the scales be revised to deal with difficulties that you foresee?

9 Obtain a language test involving the use of analytic scales. Are these scales based upon a clear definition of language ability or not? What components of language ability are measured by means of these scales? Are the scales criterion-referenced, or are they referenced to the abilities of a particular kind of language user? How many levels are defined? Can you figure out the rationale for the number of levels included in the scales?

10 Are you faced with a testing situation for which it would be appropriate to use test tasks scored by means of analytic, criterion-referenced scales? If so, develop a set of specifications for a test, a preliminary description of one or more test tasks, and scales for scoring the responses.

11 Obtain a language test with tasks involving written responses scored by means of rating scales. Either administer the test or obtain copies of responses to the test tasks. Have several people score the responses using the rating scales. Then compare the scoring. If raters disagreed, have them explain the basis for their ratings in order to determine why they disagreed. Would it be possible to design a training program for raters that would reduce the amount of disagreement? What might such a training program look like?

12 Obtain a language test involving either written or spoken responses scored by means of rating scales. Examine the rating scales and the characteristics of the expected responses. Do the expected responses provide a ratable sample, one in which there is opportunity for a full range of components that are to be rated to occur? If not, how might the characteristics of the test task(s) be modified to provide a ratable sample?

13 Obtain a language test in which a single, composite score is produced from a profile of scores. Are the composite scores obtained through compensatory or non-compensatory procedures? Can you determine the rationale for the particular procedures? How do the procedures either enhance or limit the usefulness of the test?

SUGGESTED READINGS

Bachman, L. F. 2004. *Statistical Analyses for Language Assessment*. Cambridge: Cambridge University Press, Chapter 4.

Chapelle, C. A. and **D. Douglas.** 2006. *Assessing Language Ability by Computer*. Cambridge: Cambridge University Press, Chapter 3.

Fulcher, G. 2003. *Testing Second Language Speaking*. London: Pearson Longman, Chapters 4 and 6.

Luoma, S. 2004. *Assessing Speaking*. Cambridge: Cambridge University Press, Chapters 3 and 7.

Weigle, S. C. 2002. *Assessing Writing*. Cambridge: Cambridge University Press, Chapters 6 and 8.

NOTES

1 See Davison and Green (1988), the papers in Zakalak and Samuels (1988), and the chapters in Hughes (1999) for discussions of these issues.

2 Partial credit scoring generally takes one of two forms: partial points or marks (for example, 0, 1/4, 1/2, 3/4, 1) or multiple points or marks (for example, 0, 1, 2, 3, 4). Since these two forms yield identical results with respect to statistical characteristics, choosing between them is largely a matter of whether one wants to deal with fractions or decimals, as in the case of partial points, or whole numbers, as in the case of multiple points.

3 When test takers are presented with a selected response task, the probability of getting the correct answer by chance alone depends on the number of options from which they have to choose. Thus, with a true/false question, the probability of getting the correct answer by chance is one out of two, or 50%, while with a four-choice multiple-choice item the probability is one out of four, or 25%. Thus, the probability of getting a selected response question correct by chance is 1/n, where "n" is the number of options. From this it can be seen that by increasing the number of options, we decrease the probability of test takers getting the correct answer by chance. Procedures for correcting for guessing typically involve deducting a certain number of points from each test taker's score. Such procedures are discussed in most standard measurement texts.

4 We'd like to credit Mara Haslam and Zuzana Tomas for coming up with this specific example passage.

5 See, for example, Vaughan (1991).

17 Blueprints

INTRODUCTION

A Blueprint, sometimes also called a "table of specifications" is the primary document that guides the test developer or test development team in the process of creating assessment tasks and assessments. A Blueprint includes a description of the overall structure of the assessment, the specifications for each type of task to be included in the assessment, the procedures for setting cut scores, the procedures and formats for reporting assessment records, and the procedures to be followed in administering the assessment.

In this chapter, first we discuss the purposes of a Blueprint. Next, we describe the various components of the Blueprint, how they relate to either warrants in the AUA or parts of the Design Statement, and how they are used. We conclude by illustrating these components and their functions with a Blueprint for the University example.

PURPOSES OF BLUEPRINTS

As discussed in previous chapters, the Blueprint plays an essential role in both the processes of assessment production and assessment justification. In the process of assessment production, the Blueprint helps to assure that the test developer's intentions, as specified in the AUA and the Design Statement, are actually implemented in the creation of assessments. In the process of assessment justification, the Blueprint provides documentary evidence as backing for various warrants in the AUA. Finally, as with the AUA and the Design Statement, the Blueprint provides additional interpretive information for test users and other stakeholders.

Assessment production

The Blueprint is the link between the Design stage and the assessment itself. To put it another way, the Blueprint provides the specifications for operationalizing support for the warrants in the AUA and parts of the Design Statement in the production of assessment tasks and assessments. Assessment task specifications, discussed in Chapter 15, are part of the Blueprint and prescribe the kinds of assessment tasks that task writers will create. In many assessments, the Blueprint will require many individual assessment tasks for any given assessment task type. In addition, in many situations, the test developer will need to develop multiple forms of the assessment, and this can be accomplished by following the Blueprint for each form of the assessment that is developed. One way to develop comparable forms of an assessment is to use the task specifications to generate a task bank, which is a set of assessment tasks developed from the same task specifications.[1] Tasks from this task bank can then be used, following the Blueprint, to construct whole assessments. Thus, the Blueprint provides the basis for the test developer and task writers to create assessment tasks and forms of the assessment that are comparable.

In addition to guiding the creation of assessment tasks and assessments, the Blueprint provides a way for the test developer to compare the equivalence of different assessment tasks and forms of the assessment. In this function, the Blueprint provides a basis for quality control during the production of the assessment. Thus, by continuously monitoring the creation of different assessment tasks and different forms of the assessment, the test developer and the test development team can correct any discrepancies they find between the specifications in the Blueprint and the characteristics of the assessment tasks and different forms of the assessment.

Assessment justification

As will be seen from the discussion below of individual components of the Blueprint, each of these implements one or more warrants in the AUA, as well as the relevant part of the Design Statement. This close correspondence between the AUA, the Design Statement, and the specifications in the Blueprint provides documentary backing for the warrants in the AUA. For example, generalizability Warrant C1 under Claim 3 states that the characteristics of the assessment tasks correspond closely to those of TLU tasks. Since the Blueprint provides a detailed description of the assessment task characteristics, these can be compared with the TLU task characteristics that are specified in Part 8 of the Design Statement to provide backing for this warrant.

In addition, as mentioned above, the Blueprint provides a basis for ongoing quality control in the process of assessment production. By documenting this process of monitoring the assessment production process, the test developer also provides backing for the warrants in the AUA.

COMPONENTS OF A BLUEPRINT

The components of the Blueprint are listed in Figure 17.1 on p. 370. For ease of reference, we will number the headings in this chapter as in Figure 17.1, in the discussion below.

Blueprint

1 Assessment specifications

(a) Number of parts

(b) Number of tasks per part

(c) Sequence of parts and tasks

(d) Relative importance of parts and tasks

(e) Time allotment: for each part and overall

(f) Instructions

2 Task specifications (for each task type)

(a) Construct to be assessed

(b) Characteristics of the setting

(c) Characteristics of input, expected response, and relationship between input and response

(d) Recording method

(e) Instructions for responding to the assessment task

3 Procedures for setting cut scores and making decisions

4 Procedures and formats for reporting assessment records, interpretations, and decisions.

5 Procedures for administering the assessment

Figure 17.1 Components of a Blueprint

The components included in Figure 17.1 are for assessments with multiple tasks, which is most typically the case in language assessments. The first two components of the Blueprint, Assessment specifications and Task specifications, are derived largely from the Task Characteristics described in Chapter 4. When there are multiple tasks in an assessment, the characteristics of the "Rubric" are divided between these two components. This is because components 1a through 1e, which are characteristics of the Rubric, specify the structure of the assessment as a whole, while components 2b through 2d will be unique to each assessment task type. There may also be separate instructions for the assessment as a whole and for each part, depending on the specific assessment task types that are included. For an assessment consisting of a single task, there would be no "Assessment specifications," and the time allotment would be included in the Task specifications.

1 Assessment specifications

The assessment specifications consist of characteristics that prescribe the structure, or organization, of the assessment as a whole. These specifications serve two purposes. First, they assure that the relevant warrants in the AUA and parts of the Design Statement are actually implemented in the assessment. They also help assure that different forms of the assessment are comparable. In addition, the assessment structure, as realized in the actual assessment itself, will help guide test takers through the process of taking the assessment. Many assessments will include multiple parts, and each part will include multiple tasks. In assessments such as these, it is important for test takers to be able to identify these different parts, particularly if they differ in their task characteristics or in the areas of language ability they are intended to assess. For example, including both selected response and limited production response task types in the same part of the assessment may be confusing to some test takers, because these require very different kinds of responses. Or suppose that a test developer or user treats a task that may appear as a single task to the test takers as consisting of distinct tasks, each of which is scored separately. This may be a source of bias because test takers do not realize that they will be assessed on these different tasks. For example, an assessment might require the test takers to make an oral presentation, which they perceive as a single task. However, the test user might treat the presentation as a sequence of parts, such as the introduction, body, and conclusion, and rate the test takers' performance on each part separately.

By clearly indicating the numbers of parts and tasks in the assessment and how these are sequenced, the test developer helps to assure that these different parts and tasks will be *salient* to the test takers, and hence give them a better opportunity to perform at their best on the assessment.

(a) Number of parts

When we create an assessment, we need to specify how many parts will be included in the assessment. Some assessments may consist of a single task, which thus constitutes a single part. In the University example, the assessment consists of a single task: reading a passage from an academic text and completing an incomplete outline that is based in this passage. Other assessments can contain a single part but multiple tasks. For example, an assessment designed to measure knowledge of punctuation might consist of a single paragraph with multiple punctuation errors to be corrected, each of which would be treated as a separate task.

Other assessments may contain multiple parts, and this may be for a variety of reasons. Parts may need to be distinguished because different instructions are needed for different types of assessment tasks. Thus, tasks that require the same kinds of responses, such as limited production, might be included in the same part, while selected response tasks might be included in a different part. Parts may need to be distinguished because they may need to be administered at different times or with different times allotted to each. For example, it might not be feasible to administer tasks that require test takers to listen to short recorded conversations and respond in the same part as tasks that require them to read written passages and respond to these. In other situations, parts may need to be distinguished because they involve the use of different types of materials. An assessment task that requires test takers to write a composition, for example, would typically be administered in a separate part from, say, an oral interview, which might be a separate part of the assessment.

(b) Number of tasks per part

The number of tasks per part needs to be specified so that assessment developers can keep the lengths of different forms comparable. In many assessments, the number of tasks per part may be stated as a range, with a minimum and maximum number of tasks, rather than an exact number, so as to allow the test developer some flexibility to use the results of feedback from trialing to decide on how many tasks there may be in a part for any given form of the assessment.

(c) Sequence of parts and tasks

Because the parts and tasks in an assessment will be presented to test takers in real time, the sequence of parts and tasks needs to be specified in order to assure that different forms of the assessment are comparable. This sequence can be important if the assessment developer wants to order the tasks from easier to more difficult, or if the developer wants to be sure that material in one part of the assessment does not give away the answers to material in another part.

(d) Relative importance of parts and tasks

The relative importance of parts and tasks needs to be specified for a variety of reasons. It needs to be specified so that the assessment developer will know how much weight to give to records of performance on the different parts of the assessment. It must also be included in the instructions, since knowing the relative importance of parts may influence how test takers perform. Failure to do so may weaken the support for Warrant B1 about impartiality under Claim 3.

(e) Time allotment: for each part and overall

For most assessments, the time allotted for each part and overall must be indicated. In some assessment situations, particularly "speeded" assessments, the allotted time may need to be carefully controlled.[2] In most language assessments, however, sufficient time is provided to permit each test taker to at least attempt to respond to each task. This provides backing for Warrant A3 (meaningfulness) under Claim 3. Even if an assessment is not "speeded", the time for each part and overall must be specified and adhered to in order to provide backing for Warrant B1 about impartiality under Claim 3.

(f) **Instructions**

Instructions for an assessment tell the test takers how they are to proceed in taking the assessment, the types of tasks they are going to encounter, the ways in which they are expected to respond to these tasks, and how their responses are going to be scored or described. For assessments that consist of multiple task types and multiple parts, there may be separate instructions for each task type. (See Chapter 18 for a discussion of preparing instructions.)

2 Task specifications

We discussed the assessment task specifications in Chapter 15, and so will only list them here.

(a) The definition of the construct to be assessed
(b) The characteristics of the setting in which the tasks will be administered
(c) The characteristics of the input, expected response, and relationship between input and response
(d) Recording method
(e) Instructions for responding to the assessment task

3 Procedures for setting cut scores

In order to set a cut score for making decisions on the basis of an assessment, the performance standard that is defined in the Design Statement needs to be implemented as a specific score on the assessment. In other words, the test developer needs to determine what score on the assessment corresponds to the level on the performance standard that is specified in the Design Statement. In determining what score(s) from the assessment to use as the cut score(s), several considerations need to be addressed:

1 the relative seriousness of decision classification errors,
2 the performance standard, or level on the ability to be assessed, that will be used to categorize test takers into groups,
3 the specific standard-setting procedures that will be used to set the cut score, and
4 the dependability, or agreement of classification decisions at the cut score.

Seriousness of classification decision errors

The relative seriousness of the classification errors is articulated in Warrant A2 about the values sensitivity of decisions under Claim 2, in the AUA, and in part 4 of the Design Statement. As discussed in Chapter 9, the consequences of false positive and false negative errors can be quite different and not equally serious. The *number* of false positive and negative classification errors will depend in part upon where the cut score is set. For example, if a cut score is set relatively high, there will be relatively fewer false positives and relatively more false negatives. If a cut score is set relatively low, there will be relatively fewer false negatives and relatively more false positives. In addition, as discussed below, the relative number of classification errors in general will depend on the dependability of the cut score, with respect to classification agreement. Thus, the rationale for setting cut scores needs to be based on consideration of the relative seriousness of decision classification errors and be carefully thought through and described for each assessment development project.

In the University example, false positive classification decisions are considered to be relatively more serious than false negative classification errors.

Performance standard

The performance standard defines a minimum level of the ability to be assessed that will be acceptable to be classified as a "master," "proficient," or "certified," depending on the specific situation. The performance standard will be specified in part 4 of the Design Statement, and is typically in the form of a verbal description. In the University example, the performance standard is as follows: Students must demonstrate that they have sufficient knowledge of multilevel rhetorical organization of introductory academic texts to enable them to successfully participate in introductory level academic courses.

Standard-setting procedures

The process of determining what score from the test corresponds to the performance standard is referred to as "standard setting". This process is followed to determine the "cut score" for making classification decisions. There is an extensive body of research on standard setting and setting cut scores in the educational measurement literature, and a large number of methods for standard setting have been developed. (See, for example, Cizek 1996, 2001; Hambleton and Pitoniak 2006.) We will thus not discuss these in detail here. Suffice it to say that some of these methods involve asking experts to classify individual test tasks in terms of how test takers who are "masters" and "non-masters" would perform. Other procedures involve trying the test out with contrasting groups, or individuals who are comparable to the intended test taker in most of their attributes, but who are known to be different, contrasting levels on the ability to be assessed. It is also important to note that most of the research in this area strongly supports the use of more than one standard-setting procedure.

For an example of standard-setting procedures see the University Reading example (Project 2) on p. 449.

Dependability of classification decisions at the cut score

Another consideration in setting cut scores is the dependability, or agreement, of classification decisions at the cut score. The cut score is an actual score that will be obtained by some test takers, and as such it will be, to some extent, affected by measurement error. This, in turn, will affect the probability of decision classification errors: the larger the measurement error at the cut score, the more likely it is that the decision maker will make classification errors. What the test developer would like to be able to estimate, therefore, is the probability of making classification errors at any particular score she might select as the cut score. To put it another way, the test developer would like to be able to estimate the percentage of correct classifications she is likely to make if she were to use a particular score as the cut score. A statistical estimate of this is referred to as an "agreement index." (There are a number of ways for estimating agreement indices, and we would refer readers to Brown and Hudson (2002) for a detailed discussion of these.)

In relatively low-stakes settings, the test developer may not have the resources (time, expertise, access to test data) to use a formal standard-setting procedure for setting cut scores. In situations such as these, the test developer and other stakeholders may be able to collaboratively use their knowledge of the test takers and the level or performance that is expected to set the cut scores on the test. For example, in an end-of-course test that will be used, in part, to assign grades, teachers in the course may collaborate on developing the test. In writing the test tasks, they may also specify a cut score, based on their knowledge of the content of the test and the level of ability that they believe is needed in order to achieve different grades.

Regardless of the specific assessment setting, whether this is relatively low stakes or high stakes, we would strongly advise the test developer to either consult with an assessment specialist or do some reading on his or her own about what might be the most appropriate approach to standard setting for his or her specific needs. In addition, the test developer should understand that the cut score that is initially determined may need to be adjusted, or adjustments may need to be made to the assessment itself, based on feedback from trialing. This is discussed in Chapter 19.

For an example of estimating the dependability of classification decisions see the University Reading example on p. 449.

4 Procedures and formats for reporting assessment records

Once assessment records (scores, descriptions) have been obtained the test developers need to determine the optimal procedures and format for reporting these to test takers and other relevant stakeholders. These procedures will need to take into consideration the needs and levels of expertise, with respect to knowledge of language ability and measurement, of the different stakeholders to whom assessment records will be reported. Thus, some stakeholders may be familiar with standardized scores, such as percentile ranks, while others may find the simple raw score more meaningful. (A full discussion of different ways of reporting test scores is beyond the scope of this book. For a detailed discussion see Bachman (2004b).

5 Procedures for administering the assessment

Assessment administration, which takes place in Stage 4, Trialing and Stage 5, Assessment Use, involves a variety of activities in actually giving an assessment to test takers. The test developer administers the assessment for three purposes: (1) to collect feedback to improve the assessment itself, (2) to collect backing to support the warrants in the AUA, and (3) to make interpretations about test takers' language ability, and to make decisions that will affect stakeholders. Using information from assessment administrations for the first two of these purposes is discussed in Chapter 19. Using this information responsibly to make interpretations and decisions is discussed in Chapter 21.

In order to accomplish these purposes, the test developer will need to specify procedures for administering the assessment. Recall, from Chapter 2, that one quality of an assessment is that it is done systematically:

> assessments ... are designed and carried out according to clearly defined procedures that are methodical and open to scrutiny by other test developers and researchers, as well as by stake holders in the assessment. This means that an assessment conducted by one person at one time could potentially be replicated by another person at another time.

Thus, one reason for specifying procedures for administering the assessment is to assure that the assessment is administered systematically, that is, in a way that is consistent from one group of test takers to another, and from one time to another. This will help assure that differences in the way the assessment is administered will not affect the way test takers perform, and will provide backing for Warrant B4, about impartiality, under Claim 3, as well as for Warrant 2 about consistency, under Claim 4. Another equally important reason is that these procedures will guide test takers through the process of taking the assessment, so as to enable them perform at their highest level of ability.

The audience for the procedures for administering the assessment includes anyone who will be involved in this activity. In a classroom assessment, this may be a single teacher, while in a large-scale assessment, this may involve a large number of individuals, including site supervisors and coordinators, head proctors for individual rooms, and sometimes several proctors for each room. In some situations, such as a classroom assessment, the procedures for administration may be specified relatively informally, while in large-scale high-stakes assessments, the procedures will need to be very specific and detailed. Whether the procedures for administering the assessment are relatively informal, or whether they are specified in detail in a document for use by individuals who will be involved in administering the assessment, they will need to specify how the following activities will be conducted:

(a) preparing the assessment setting
(b) identifying test takers and monitoring their performance
(c) establishing and maintaining a supportive testing environment
(d) communicating the instructions
(e) making the materials and equipment that will be used in administering the assessment accessible to test takers
(f) collecting the materials and equipment that has been used in administering the assessment
(g) dealing with irregularities.

Preparing the assessment setting

The first activity in assessment administration is preparing the assessment setting to be consistent with the specifications for the setting in each assessment task type in the Blueprint. This involves arranging the *place* and *physical conditions* where the assessment will be administered, the *materials and equipment* to be used, the *personnel* who will oversee the administration of the assessment, and the *time* at which the assessment will be administered.

For example, in one test developed by the authors that required speaking, the test specifications required a place large enough to allow us to create two separate testing areas, with different characteristics, one suitable for a formal role-play and one suitable for an informal role-play. Materials and equipment included, among other things, two different kinds of desks, one designed to create a highly formal atmosphere and another to create a very informal atmosphere, recording equipment, two telephones, test booklets with different colored covers, and a set of prompt materials for the interviewers (Bachman and Palmer 1982, 1983).

The personnel characteristics of the interviewers were closely controlled prior to and during the test administration. For example, as interviewers, we took the roles that best suited our personalities. Thus, one of us dressed informally, in shorts, a T-shirt, and zoris while the other dressed formally, in a suit and tie. We also practiced administering our test a number of times and made some specification changes on the basis of our experience.

The time chosen for testing was influenced primarily by considerations of consistency and practicality. We administered the test during the day since we then had the best access to test takers, the majority of whom were students who were near the campus testing site during class hours. We scheduled the test at 40-minute intervals to allow sufficient time for debriefing following each test. We also scheduled longer breaks at regular intervals to avoid fatigue and loss of concentration, which could have adversely affected test takers' performance.

A contrasting situation is that of large-scale group administrations of written tests, in which test takers need to have adequate writing equipment, which might include sharpened pencils, erasers, paper for writing notes, or computers and word processors; in other words, whatever they need to do their best work. In addition, test takers will obviously need an environment in which they will not be distracted by other test takers.

Identifying the test takers and monitoring their performance

In any assessment, it is essential that the test user be able to assure that the performance upon which assessment records and interpretations are based can be attributed to specific individual test takers. It is thus essential that the administration procedures include the means for uniquely identifying each test taker. In large-scale assessments, for example, where the test administrators may not know the individual test takers personally, they could be asked to show the test administrator official photo identification cards.

In addition to uniquely identifying individual test takers, it is also essential to assure that all test takers perform under the same conditions. In many assessments, the test developer expects test takers to perform the assessment tasks independently, so that steps need to be taken to prevent test takers from exchanging information during the assessment administration. In addition, the test developer will need to specify whether any aids, such as dictionaries, textbooks, or information on the web, will be permitted during the administration. In large-scale, high-stakes assessments, it is typical for test takers to be seated and monitored so as to prevent the exchange of information or the use of aids that are not permitted. It is important for both the test takers and the test administrators to understand that the intention behind these procedures is not to focus attention on "preventing cheating," but rather on maximizing the qualities of the assessment records and interpretations that are based on test takers' performance.

While the need to identify and monitor test takers' performance during the assessment administration is quite obvious for large-scale assessments, this is also important for low-stakes classroom assessments. This is because in a classroom assessment the teacher who administers the assessment will use the results of the assessment to make instructional decisions, such as suggesting particular learning activities, that may affect individual students differently.

Establishing and maintaining a supportive testing environment

As mentioned above, one reason for specifying administrative procedures is to facilitate test takers' performance. Thus, it is essential for the test administrator to maintain a supportive environment throughout the administration of the assessment. This can be accomplished in a number of ways, for example avoiding distractions such as uncomfortably low or high temperature, noise, or excessive movement. In large-scale assessments, test takers are frequently required to remain in their seats until the end of the assessment administration to avoid movement and noise that might be distracting to other test takers. Thus, assuring that the test takers are situated comfortably is a major responsibility of the test administrators. Probably the single most important factor in maintaining a supportive environment is the attitude that is displayed by assessment administrators. Thus, proctors should be trained to view the purpose of monitoring of the test takers as facilitative, and conducive to enabling them to perform at their best, rather than as "policing" to enforce the administrative procedures.

Before administering an assessment, test developers need to think through what kind of assistance they want the proctors to provide during the administration of the assessment. Traditionally, much of the focus of attention on the assessment environment has been on controlling variability in order to increase consistency. While consistency is obviously an important quality of assessment records, we feel that qualities of other claims are equally important. For example, to what extent might an attempt to create a highly stable assessment environment limit the generalizability of the interpretations to a TLU domain in which tasks may occur in a wide variety of contexts? Or to what extent might attempts to enforce the assessment procedures too rigorously intimidate test takers and cause them to underperform, and hence limit the meaningfulness of assessment-based interpretations?

Communicating the instructions

Another factor in facilitating test takers' performance on the assessment is to assure that the instructions are communicated in such a way that they will be understood by all test takers. The preparation of effective instructions as well as the components of instructions are discussed in Chapter 18. When administering an assessment it is essential that the test takers receive the full benefit of the instructions. This includes the obvious steps of providing suitable conditions (time, lighting, lack of distraction) for reading written instructions, as well as for listening to oral instructions. In addition, some selection and/or training of personnel in administering instructions orally may be needed.

Making the materials and equipment that will be used in administering the assessment accessible to the test takers

Another activity that needs to be specified in the administration procedures is how the materials and equipment to be used in the administration will be made accessible to test takers. In large-scale assessments that are administered in a paper and pencil format, test administrators will need to distribute these materials in a way that assures that all test takers will have the same amount of time to complete the assessment. For example, in order to assure that test takers who are the first to receive the assessment materials do not begin before all the test takers have received the materials, the test administrator may instruct all test takers not to begin until they are told to do so. Or, proctors may require test takers to keep the materials face down on their desks until they are instructed to begin. In assessments that are administered via computer or on the web, test takers will need to follow specific procedures to log on to the assessment site, which may be programmed to pace their completion of the assessment.

Collecting the materials and equipment that has been used in administering the assessment

The final activity in assessment administration is collecting the materials and equipment that have been used in administering the assessment. In large-scale assessments that are administered in a paper and pencil format, one set of materials that will need to be collected, of course, is the sheets on which test takers have indicated their answers. In addition, in many such situations, other assessment materials will also need to be collected in order to assure the security and integrity of the assessment. In assessments that are administered via computer or on the web, all the relevant information may be provided entirely electronically, and test takers will indicate their responses electronically as well, so that there will be no materials to collect. However, in computer- or web-based assessment administrations, it will typically be necessary for test takers to follow specific procedures to log off the computer so as to save their answers or transmit them to the computer database.

Dealing with irregularities

No matter how well prepared the assessment setting and the administrators are, and no matter how well specified the administrative procedures are, there is always a possibility that something unexpected will occur that may adversely affect test takers' performance and hence the meaningfulness of the assessment-based interpretations. For example, a number of years ago, one of the authors was responsible for administering a large-scale international test of English as a foreign language at a large test center in a city in Asia. One part of this test was aimed at testing test takers' listening comprehension. This particular test center was a large university, and test takers were seated in many different rooms, ranging from a large auditorium with an array of audio-speakers, to small classrooms, also with speakers, to language laboratories. The tape recording for the input for the listening comprehension test was played from a central station in the university language laboratory and transmitted to all the rooms in which the test was being administered. About fifteen minutes into the listening test, the tape broke, so that rather than hearing someone speaking, all the test takers heard a loud hiss or white noise. Since this was a high-stakes test, used for making admission decisions at universities in many English speaking countries, the test takers were quite upset. Fortunately, the administrator's manual for this test provided specific instructions about how such an eventuality should be handled, and that this would be taken into consideration in scoring test takers' answers. The administrator was able to explain this over the public address system to the test takers, and then proceed with the rest of the test. In addition, the test administrator completed a detailed report on this irregularity and returned this, along with the test materials, to the testing agency.

(For an example of a complete Blueprint, see the University example on p. 467.)

FROM BLUEPRINTS TO ASSESSMENTS

Once the Blueprint, including the specifications for each assessment task type, has been developed, this provides the basis for generating actual assessment tasks and compiling these into either a single assessment or several comparable forms of the assessment. In many cases the purpose of an assessment development project is to produce a single assessment. For example, a teacher might need to produce a classroom quiz to determine whether a group of students is ready to go on to the next lesson. Or, in another situation, a decision maker might need to produce a single assessment to be used to place students who are transferring from another college or university into upper division university language courses. In other cases, it may be necessary or desirable to produce several comparable forms of the assessment. For example, a Program Director might want to develop an assessment to measure progress at various stages in a course of instruction, and need several forms of this, either for security, or to minimize the practice effect of students taking the same form several times. We cannot be sure that multiple forms of an assessment will provide parallel, or equivalent, measures of test takers' abilities until we have tried them out and analyzed their results.[3] However, if the test developer develops these assessments from the same Blueprint, following the procedures we have described, she can be reasonably sure that these assessments will be comparable in terms of their content, structure, and the tasks they require of test takers. Furthermore, the Blueprint provides a basis for investigating and demonstrating the comparability of the different forms, and it is our view that without comparability of constructs and task characteristics, any demonstration of statistical equivalence will be meaningless.

While we include a complete set of characteristics in the specifications for each different assessment task type, it may be the case, for a given assessment, that there will be some overlap between characteristics of different assessment task specifications, so that these may need to be included only once in the actual assessment. For example, it may be that even though a given assessment includes several different assessment task types, these may be similar enough in their formats to permit them to be grouped together with one set of instructions.

In Part IV, we provide a number of examples of assessment development projects that illustrate the process of using components of the Design statement to develop assessment Blueprints and actual assessment tasks.

EXERCISES

1 Think of an assessment that you developed or are familiar with that started with writing tasks without the existence of a Blueprint. Did you or the assessment developers or users run into any problems, either immediately or later when the test was used, that might have been avoided had the tasks

been developed from a Blueprint? How might these problems have been avoided if there had been a Blueprint to work with?

2 Have you ever developed multiple forms of a test? How did you go about doing so? What role did a Blueprint play in the process? Given what you know about Blueprints now, how would you go about the process differently?

3 Go through the Projects on the web (http://www.oup.com/LAIP). Find one that interests you for which no Blueprint is provided. Create a Blueprint for that project containing the components in Table 17.1. Look at Blueprints in other Projects to find language that may be helpful in creating the Blueprint you are working on.

4 Think of an experience you have had administering or taking a test. What procedures were followed? In what ways did these procedures seem to provide backing for warrants in the AUA? In what ways could the procedures have been improved?

5 Think of an experience you have had taking a test in which the way the test was administered seemed particularly conducive for your performing at your best. What characteristics of the procedures for administering the test seemed particularly helpful in this regard?

NOTES

1 In this book, we will use the term "comparable" to refer to assessments that have the same assessment specifications. This is not to be confused with the terms "equivalent" and "parallel" which have a technical meaning in measurement. "Parallel" in measurement theory means that different forms of a test have statistical properties (e.g., means and standard deviations) that are the same. "Equivalent" is also sometimes used with this same meaning.

2 A "speeded" test is one in which all the tasks are of about equal difficulty, and test takers are not expected to complete all of them. Thus, in a speeded test, speed of processing is part of the construct definition. A "power" test, on the other hand, is one in which the tasks are ordered from easiest to most difficult, and sufficient time is allowed to permit most of the test takers to at least attempt all the tasks. In power tests, speed of processing is not part of the construct definition.

3 There are certain statistical characteristics that the scores from different forms of a test must satisfy in order for these scores to be considered equivalent, or "parallel." These are discussed at length in Bachman 1990: Chapter 6 and in Bachman 2004b: Chapter 5, as well as in the statistical and measurement references provided in the Suggested Readings for Chapter 19.

18

Preparing effective instructions

INTRODUCTION

As discussed in Chapter 4, the way test takers perform on language assessments is affected to some extent by the characteristics of the assessments themselves. In keeping with the maxim that we want to make it possible for test takers to perform their best (Warrant A3, about meaningfulness under Claim 3), it is essential that they clearly understand how they are to proceed in taking the assessment, the types of tasks they are going to encounter, the ways in which they are expected to respond to these tasks, and how their responses are going to be scored or described. The assessment instructions are particularly important because it is through these that the test developer informs test takers how they are expected to approach and attempt the assessment tasks.

The instructions provide backing for several warrants in the AUA, specifically those under Claim 3 about meaningfulness and impartiality. The instructions will also reflect the considerations that we have included in the Design Statement (discussed in Chapter 14) and will thus communicate to the test takers the intentions of the test developers. These include the decisions that will be made on the basis of the assessment, the language abilities to be assessed, and the structure, or organization of the assessment, as discussed in Chapter 17. The test developer conveys the instructions explicitly by what we include in them and the way we present them. In this chapter we will discuss ways in which instructions can be most effectively specified to promote the best assessment performance in a given group of test takers. We will discuss general principles and what we believe are the essential components of instructions, along with suggestions on how these can be effectively written and presented to test takers.

PURPOSE OF INSTRUCTIONS

The instructions are typically the first part of the assessment that test takers encounter. It is the instructions, therefore, that bear much of the responsibility for setting the test takers' expectations and appropriately motivating them to do their best on the assessment. The primary purpose of the assessment instructions is thus to assure that the test takers understand the exact nature of the assessment procedure and of the assessment tasks, how they are to respond to these tasks, and how their responses will be evaluated. The instructions thus provide backing for Warrants A3 and A7 about meaningfulness, and B3 about impartiality under Claim 3 in the AUA. To the extent that the instructions function effectively to help standardize the administration of the assessment, they also provide backing for Warrant A1 about consistence under Claim 4. The essential components of the assessment instructions, therefore, are:

1 statement of the purpose(s) for which the assessment is intended,
2 statement of the language abilities that the assessment is intended to assess,
3 specification of the procedures and tasks, and
4 specification of the criteria for correctness.

Assessment instructions also serve as an important affective goal: motivating students to do their best. Effectively presented assessment instructions can go a long way toward assuring test takers that the assessment is fair and does not make unreasonable expectations.

The different components of instructions can be presented at different times and at different levels in the assessment. With published assessments, general instructions are often available to test takers well before the assessment is taken, and are usually repeated in greater detail at the time of the assessment administration. In most situations, however, general instructions covering all parts of an assessment are presented either orally by the person who administers the assessment, or in writing in the first part of the assessment itself. In addition, specific instructions may be given for different parts of the assessment. Irrespective of when or at what level instructions are provided, their overall purpose is to facilitate the assessment taking process and to encourage students to perform at their highest level.

MAKING INSTRUCTIONS UNDERSTANDABLE

If instructions are to accomplish their purposes, then we must do whatever is necessary to assure that they can be understood by the test takers. They should *not* be considered part of the assessment itself, since they are not part of the input to which test takers are expected to respond directly. In deciding how best to make the instructions understandable, we need to consider:

1 the language and
2 the channel through which the instructions are presented,
3 the need for providing examples, and
4 the need to try out the instructions with test takers.

Language of presentation

Instructions may be presented in either the test takers' native language or, depending on their level of ability, in the target language (the language being assessed). Where test takers share a common native language, if there is any doubt that test takers might misunderstand it is best to present the instructions in the native language. Often, however, test takers come from many different first language backgrounds, so that the instructions must be presented in the target language. In such situations, care should be taken that the level of difficulty of the language of the instructions is not greater than that of the assessment questions themselves. In situations where the assessment is delivered via computer, it is possible to allow individual test takers to choose the language in which they would like to receive the instructions.

Channel of presentation

Understandability can also be facilitated by presenting the instructions in a channel that is most appropriate to the purpose and abilities being assessed, and that test takers are most likely to find easy. In assessments whose input is presented in the visual channel (written), instructions are also typically presented in this way. Instructions for completing an assessment with tasks that require reading, for example, would typically be presented in writing, as would instructions for composition assessments. However, in assessments with listening or speaking activities, which typically involve input in the aural channel, instructions would also be presented in this channel. Thus, if the assessment were presented "live" by the person administering the assessment, the instructions would be read aloud to the test takers, and if the assessment were presented via an audio or video tape player, the instructions would be presented on the tape. Some test takers may be able to perform one type of language use activity better than another, in which case it may be helpful if instructions are presented both orally and in writing. If students are relatively good at reading and weak at listening, for example, they could be given a set of written instructions for the tasks that involve listening and asked to follow these as they are presented orally, either by the assessment administrator or on a tape player. If, on the other hand, they are more able at listening than at reading, the assessment administrator might read the written instructions aloud while test takers read them silently. The purpose of presenting the instructions both orally and in writing is to assure that students understand. However it is possible that some students will find this distracting, and that it interferes with comprehension of the instructions. Since different test takers vary as to whether both oral and written instructions will facilitate or interfere with understanding, the test developer must base the decision on a thorough understanding of the personal characteristics of the particular test takers, and, if possible, on the feedback obtained from pre-testing.

Providing example tasks

Providing example tasks can also facilitate assessment taking, particularly when test takers may not be familiar with the specific task type, or with complex question types. Consider the following assessment task, for example:

> Instructions: Make the necessary changes and additions to the following sets of words and phrases to produce a complete sentence for each. Write the sentence in the space provided.
>
> I just finish/six-week data processing course/local college.
>
> ____

Even with fairly detailed instructions, it may not be entirely clear to all test takers just what their response is supposed to be. An example task such as the following could help:

> *Example*: I be quite happy/receive/letter/you yesterday.
> *Answer*: I was quite happy to receive a letter from you yesterday.

While we generally recommend providing examples as a means for assuring that test takers understand assessment tasks, there are two types of costs involved. First, providing good examples can be as difficult as writing good assessment tasks. Second, reading through examples requires additional time on the part of the test takers. However, if the test developer feels that a new type of assessment task is particularly useful, or if the ability cannot be easily assessed in another more familiar way, example tasks need to be provided. The burden of writing example tasks can be alleviated to some degree by using assessment tasks that have been discarded after pre-testing as too easy for the assessment. This has the added benefit that the example tasks will be easier and hence more understandable than the tasks in the assessment.

COMPONENTS OF INSTRUCTIONS

Many language assessments are aimed at measuring more than one aspect of language ability, or employ more than one method of assessing, and thus include more than one part. With such assessments, it is useful to provide, at the beginning of the assessment, a set of *general instructions* that apply to all parts of the assessment. In addition, if the different parts include different task types, require different procedures, or use different criteria for correctness, then these need to be made explicit in *specific instructions* for each part. Thus, assessments with multiple parts may include both general and specific instructions. In assessments with only one part, on the other hand, there need be only one set of instructions. In either case, instructions need to include descriptions of the following:

- Assessment purpose
- Language abilities to be assessed

- Parts of the assessment and their relative importance
- Procedures to be followed for all parts of the assessment
- Scoring method.

Assessment purpose

The purpose of the assessment is its intended use, and we have discussed a variety of uses in Chapters 5 and 9. How will the information obtained from the assessment be used? What inferences or decisions are to be made on the basis of the assessment records? These will all be specified during the assessment development process, as part of the assessment specifications. If the assessment is designed to serve several purposes, then the instructions should be specific to each given purpose. Furthermore, if the assessment is used for some purpose other than that stated in the specifications, then this may constitute a misuse of the assessment. The reason we want test takers to know what the assessment will be used for is twofold. First, it provides a justification for giving an assessment. If there is no legitimate use for the assessment results, then test takers may well question why they should take the assessment at all. Second, as a matter of fundamental fairness, we believe that test takers are entitled to know how their assessment scores will be used. If test takers understand that there is a fair and legitimate use for a given assessment, they will be more likely to take the assessment seriously and to attempt to do their best. Furthermore, an explicit statement of intended assessment use helps assure that both the test developer and potential test users are accountable to test takers for how the results of the assessment are used.

In most classroom assessment, the purpose of a given assessment will be obvious to students, particularly if certain uses of assessments, such as diagnosis, progress, and grading, are an integral part of the instructional program. Even so, decisions of varying importance may be made on the basis of students' assessment performance, so that it is essential that students clearly understand the particular use of each assessment. Thus, while we want our students to attempt to do their best on all assessments, high motivation and effort are probably more important for an assessment that will be used to assign course grades than for a daily quiz that may be used primarily for diagnostic feedback. In classroom assessment, the purpose can be provided as part of the orientation to the instructional program. In a writing class, for example, the teacher may inform the students at the beginning of the course that short daily writing tasks will be used to diagnose their writing problems and to provide feedback for correction, a weekly in-class essay will be given to assess their progress and provide feedback, and two longer essay exams, to be given at specified times, will be used to assign course grades. If assessment is not a routine part of the instructional program, then the classroom teacher will need to inform students of the purpose of the assessment, either before the assessment itself, or as part of the assessment administration.

In large-scale testing programs, the purpose of the assessment is usually known to test takers by virtue of their having chosen or been required to take it. Students who have taken a foreign language in secondary school, for example, may either choose or be required to take a language assessment to determine which level of college or university foreign language course is appropriate for them, or to determine if credit can be given for having achieved a specified level of ability in the foreign language. Another example is that of non-native English speaking students who take a standardized assessment of English as part of the requirements for admission to institutions of higher learning in countries where English is the medium of instruction.

Language abilities to be assessed

The rationale for informing students of the language abilities we intend to measure is essentially the same as that for informing them of the assessment's purpose. In addition, providing a statement of the abilities to be assessed gives test takers the means for assessing the relevance of these abilities. This provides backing for Warrants A3 about meaningfulness and Warrant D about relevance under Claim 3:

1 to the assessment's intended purpose,
2 to a particular course of instruction, either already completed or about to be entered,
3 to their TLU tasks, and
4 to the types of assessment tasks used.

As with stating the purpose of the assessment, we believe that an explicit statement of the abilities to be measured will help motivate students to do their best and will also help assure accountability of assessment use. In multi-part assessments that assess different aspects of language ability, statements of the abilities to be assessed should be given in the specific instructions to the different parts.

Since very few individuals who take language assessments are either language teachers or trained linguists, it is important that our descriptions of the language abilities to be assessed should be stated in non-technical language. In classroom assessment, a "label"—a word or phrase—may be sufficiently clear for assessments that are directly related to learning objectives and activities. In large-scale assessment, however, where test takers may come from a wide variety of learning backgrounds, labels are seldom sufficient, in that even an apparently obvious label, such as "reading comprehension," for example, may have different connotations for different test takers and test users. For such situations we would recommend that the instructions include more than a label, and that a brief description of the areas of language ability being measured should be provided. Since terms such as "proficiency," "competence," "comprehension," and "communicate" are ambiguous even to language teachers, it is not likely that they will be clear to test takers. We would therefore recommend that the abilities to be measured should be described in terms of specific language use activities, since it is these that are more likely to be understood by test takers. Thus, rather than a statement such as "This assessment is a measure of your listening comprehension," for example, we would prefer a statement such as "This is an assessment of how well you can understand spoken English in lectures and classroom discussions."

Parts of the assessment and their relative importance

With assessments that consist of several different parts, it is important for test takers to understand:

1 how many parts there are,
2 how many tasks there are in each part,
3 the relative importance of each part, and task, often stated in terms of a maximum score per part or task, and
4 how much time will be allocated to each.

For most assessments, the time allotted for each part and overall needs to be indicated again, so that test takers will be able to pace themselves so as to perform at their best. In some assessment situations, particularly speeded assessments, the allotted time may need to be carefully controlled. In other high-stakes assessment, even if an assessment is not speeded, the time for each part and overall must be specified and adhered to in order to provide backing for the Claim 3, Warrant 2 (Impartiality).

The general instructions should thus include descriptions of the different parts of the assessment, including the types and numbers of tasks in each, and how much time test takers will be given to complete each part. Depending on the number of different parts and how distinct they are, it may also be helpful to provide a summary table, as in Table 18.1.

Part	Task Type	Number of Tasks	Time Allowed
I Listening Tasks	Short answer questions	20 questions/items	10 mins
II Reading Tasks	Reading passage followed by short answer questions	two passages; 15 questions	20 mins
III Writing Tasks	Prompt requiring an extended written answer	two prompts	30 mins
Total			60 mins

Table 18.1 Example description of assessment parts

Different types of assessment tasks may be appropriate for different areas of language ability for a given assessment purpose or group of test takers, and these tasks may vary in their efficiency in terms of adequately measuring the specific area in a given amount of time. For this reason there is not necessarily a one-to-one relationship between the relative importance of the parts of a given test, the number of tasks in the different parts, or the amounts of time allowed for the different parts. Test takers thus may not be able to determine the relative importance of the different parts from either the number of tasks or the times allowed, and we therefore believe it is important to provide an explicit statement of the relative importance of each part. In the example above, although the listening and reading parts are equally important (30 per cent each), there are more tasks in the former. This may reflect the test developer's perception that reading tasks are relatively more difficult for the intended test takers. Furthermore, although there are more listening than reading tasks, more time is allowed for the latter. This difference may also reflect the test developer's perception of the difference in difficulty. The test developer may also know that the test takers for whom this assessment is intended typically require more time for reading than for listening tasks.

Procedures to be followed

For many assessments that consist of several parts, there will be general procedures for test takers to follow with regard to how to proceed from one part to the next, and how and where to indicate their responses. It is often desirable, for standardization in large-scale assessments, to make sure that test takers complete the parts in the order presented, and that they adhere to the time allocations for the different parts. In such situations, the instructions need to state explicitly that test takers must stop at the end of each part and wait to begin the next part until they are told to do so.

On the other hand, in less formal assessment situations, such as in a class progress assessment, it may not matter whether test takers complete the parts in the order presented, or that they rigorously adhere to the times allowed for each part. In this case, the instructions should indicate those parts of the assessment that may be completed in any order, that the times indicated in the instructions are suggested times, and that test takers may, if they choose, spend more or less time on the various parts than indicated by these suggested times. In the example above, it is likely that the listening part would be presented aurally first, and would be timed by the test administrator, so that there would be no flexibility with either the order or timing. However, the test developer might want to give test takers the flexibility of completing either the reading or the writing next, as long as they complete both parts within the total time allowed. In this way, the test developer provides the opportunity for test takers to set their own goals and plans for how to respond to the different parts of the assessment.

Test takers also need to understand exactly how and where they are to indicate their responses to the assessment questions. If all the parts of the assessment follow the same question format, directions can be given in the general instructions. Otherwise, separate directions need to be provided in the specific instructions for each part of the assessment. In paper and pencil assessments, responses can be written either on the assessment itself or on a separate answer sheet. In either case, the instructions should explicitly state how test takers are to indicate their responses. For selected responses, the instructions should state how and where test takers are to indicate their response (for example, circle or check the letter of their choice), while for limited and extended production responses they should be told where to write their response (for example, in the space provided). If machine-scannable answer sheets are used, the general instructions must explain how students are to mark their choices so that they will be clearly legible to the machine. If a separate answer sheet is used, test takers need to be told in the general instructions to mark their answers on the answer sheet and not in their assessment booklets (particularly if the assessment booklets are to be reused). For assessments administered by means of a computer, specialized instructions on how to use the computer may be necessary, depending upon the personal characteristics of the test takers.

In other types of assessments, in which either the input or the response or both are in the audio channel, the order in which test takers answer questions and indicate their responses may be controlled as part of the administration. In an assessment with tape-mediated speaking tasks, for example, in which test takers listen to aural input from a tape player and record their spoken responses on a tape recorder, the order in which they answer the different parts or tasks is controlled by the tape that presents the input. Similarly, the type and length of each spoken response will be controlled by the type of tasks posed and amount of time allowed on the tape.

Procedures for recording test takers' responses

In order for test takers to understand what they are expected to do, and hence to perform at their best, they need to know how their responses are going to be evaluated. If the assessment includes several parts that will be scored in the same way, the criteria for correctness can be stated in the general instructions. If different parts will be scored differently, then these criteria should be given in the specific instructions for each part.

For selected responses, there are generally two considerations that need to be made explicit. First, the test taker needs to understand whether the item is a "correct answer" type (there is only one correct answer and this is provided among the choices) or a "best answer" type (there may be many possible answers, and the test taker must choose the best one from among those provided in the choices). Second, will the test taker's score be corrected for guessing? Although corrections for guessing are not widely used in language tests, some test takers may come from countries or educational systems in which this is routine for multiple-choice tests. Such individuals may be reluctant to guess on the basis of partial knowledge (i.e., they can rule out one or two incorrect choices), and thus may perform differently from other test takers who are willing to do so. (These considerations are discussed more extensively in Chapter 16 above.)

For tasks that require a limited or extended production response, the test takers' understanding of the criteria for correctness may affect the way they approach the given assessment task and hence the way they perform. For example, test takers are likely to approach a writing task differently if they believe that the primary criterion for correctness is grammatical accuracy than if they know that it will be scored primarily on its content. Since test takers are likely to have preconceptions about what criteria of correctness will be applied to their answers, and since these are likely to influence the way in which they construct their responses, we believe that it is crucial for the instructions to state explicitly what criteria will be used in evaluation.

HOW EXTENSIVE SHOULD INSTRUCTIONS BE?

From the discussion so far, it may appear that instructions need to be long, complex, and extremely detailed. This need not be the case. Efficient, effective assessment instructions have three qualities:

1 they are simple enough for test takers to understand,
2 they are short enough not to take up too much of the assessment administration time, and
3 they are sufficiently detailed for test takers to know exactly what they are expected to do.

The best basis for writing understandable instructions and for knowing how much of the assessment administration time they will take is a thorough knowledge of the personal attributes of the test takers for whom the assessment is intended, combined with actual tryouts of the instructions with test takers. For classroom assessments, in addition to trialing the instructions, a very effective way to assure that assessment instructions are appropriate for the students is to ask them to write the assessment instructions as a learning activity.

The amount of detail required in the instructions will depend on two factors:

1 how familiar test takers are with the assessment tasks, and
2 the number and variety of task types used in the assessment.

Assessments that consist of multiple parts and employ a variety of relatively unfamiliar assessment tasks are likely to require complex instructions.

Thus, while there may be legitimate reasons for using a variety of task types in a given assessment, such as promoting generalizability and beneficial consequences for instruction, there is no particular virtue in proliferating different task types simply for the sake of variety or novelty.

EXERCISES

1 Look through the example Projects. Find one or more in which instructions for the test taker are provided. Evaluate them according to the criteria in this chapter.
2 Look through the example Projects. Find one for which instructions are not supplied. Create a complete set of instructions for this Project.
3 Obtain a language assessment. Do the instructions provide a statement of the purpose(s) for which the assessment is intended, a statement of the language abilities that the assessment is intended to measure, a specification of the procedures and tasks, and a specification of the criteria for correctness? How might you revise the instructions to provide any missing information?
4 Recall a language assessment you have taken. What kind of instructions were provided? How did you react to them? What changes do you wish had been made in the instructions?
5 Obtain a published assessment. Compare the information provided in the general instructions with the information provided in the specific instructions for each part. Does the division of information seem appropriate for this assessment? Why or why not?
6 Obtain a language assessment that consists of several parts. Do the instructions indicate how many parts there are, the relative importance of each, what each part is like, and how much time will be allocated to each? If not, how might the instructions be improved to provide this information?
7 Prepare a set of instructions for an assessment that you are developing. Explain how your decisions with respect to the instructions helped you maximize the usefulness of the assessment.
8 Obtain a test. Delete the written instructions. Then locate two individuals: one who has no language teaching experience and one who has. Explain orally what the test requires the test takers to do. Have each individual write instructions for the test. Compare the language of the instructions in terms of the degree to which it shows sensitivity to the language abilities of the test takers (i.e., to what degree are the instructions written in effective "teacher talk." To what degree does the simplification of the grammar and vocabulary differ between the two instruction writers?

19

Collecting feedback and backing

INTRODUCTION

In the preceding chapters, we have described the first three stages in assessment development: Initial Planning, Design, and Operationalization, during which the test developers create a Design Statement, a Blueprint, and a preliminary version of the assessment. The test developers will use these documents and the reasoning process they went through in creating them to start to provide backing for the warrants in the AUA. Backing from these sources has been discussed in Chapters 9 through 12. But backing from the assessment development process itself will not be sufficient in many assessment situations to convince stakeholders that the intended uses of the assessment are justified. This is particularly the case in high-stakes assessments, where stakeholders may require backing that can only be obtained by trialing the assessment with test takers. In addition to providing backing for warrants in the AUA, information collected during Trialing and Assessment Use can provide feedback to the test developer to help improve the assessment itself.

During Trialing and Assessment Use, test developers collect additional information of two types: feedback and backing. **Feedback** is information from administering the assessment that the test developer can use to confirm or revise the original Design Statement and Blueprint and to make changes in the assessment tasks themselves. Some of this information will be about how the assessment achieves the purpose for which it was intended, and some will be about real world considerations, especially the use of resources. Backing, as discussed throughout this book, is collected as part of the process of justification and provides support for the warrants in the AUA.

In this chapter we turn to gathering information for assessment development during the final two stages in assessment development: Trialing and Assessment Use. While Trialing is obviously a part of assessment development, we also consider Assessment Use (also referred to as "operational use," see Chapter 6) to be part of development because in many assessment development situations, especially higher-stakes situations, the process of improving an assessment continues while the assessment is actually being used to make decisions.

STAGES OF ASSESSMENT DEVELOPMENT DURING WHICH FEEDBACK IS OBTAINED

In much language assessment practice, it is fairly common to end the process of collecting feedback after the assessment has been used the first time, as is often the case with a classroom test used as an end-of-course examination. This can also happen, although probably not as frequently, in the development of high-stakes assessments, if no more improvements are made to the assessment after the initial trialing and it is only used to make records of performance and make decisions. It is our belief, however, that this practice of collecting feedback only the first time an assessment is used is generally counterproductive. We take the view that the more care is taken to develop an assessment and the more feedback obtained, the more beneficial the consequences of assessment use and the decisions made will be. Furthermore, we would argue that the process of obtaining feedback for improving the assessment should continue as long as the assessment continues to be used. For example, if we were developing a comprehensive oral interview for use in evaluating the success of an entire undergraduate foreign language program, feedback might continue to be obtained over its entire life span, perhaps by periodically debriefing examiners and assessment takers and making appropriate modifications to the assessment itself. In such a situation, the process of collecting feedback for improving the assessment might be considered to be an ongoing activity that is a part of every assessment administration.

Feedback collected during the Trialing stage

Trialing, often called "pre-testing," precedes assessment use in time, and its sole purpose is to collect feedback rather than to make decisions.[1] The amount and kind of data collected during trialing will vary, depending on the stakes and scale of the assessment. Generally, the larger the scale of the assessment and the numbers of stakeholders involved, the more rigorous and extensive the trialing.

The amounts and types of revisions made on the basis of feedback collected during trialing will also vary from minor editing of single assessment tasks to major revisions involving making major changes in the Design Statement and Blueprint. In large-scale testing efforts, tests or test tasks are almost always tried out before use and extensive changes are frequently made, including revisions to many of the tasks and elimination of tasks that do not perform as expected. In classroom assessment trialing is often omitted, although giving the assessment to selected students or fellow teachers in advance is always a good idea, since this can provide useful information for improving the assessment and assessment tasks.

Early trialing

When developing an assessment, much of the early trialing is done more or less informally with individuals and small groups, and involves collecting mostly qualitative feedback. After working out potential problems with specific tasks, instructions, and administrative procedures at this level, test developers generally move to larger groups, with which more quantitative feedback can also be collected.

Late trialing

Late trialing is usually a field trial, in which the assessment is administered under operational conditions, that is, following the exact administrative procedures that will be used when the assessment is given for its intended purpose. The purpose of a field trial, however, is still to collect backing for warrants in the AUA and to make final changes in the assessment itself, and *not* to make the decisions for which the assessment was designed.

Feedback collected during the Assessment Use stage

During the Assessment Use stage, the assessment is administered to make interpretations about the test takers' language ability and to use these interpretations to make decisions in the TLU domain. However, during the Assessment Use stage, it is also important to continue to collect backing for warrants in the AUA, as well as information for use in making future modifications to the assessment.

SOME MAJOR USES OF FEEDBACK

Determining the adequacy/efficiency of administrative procedures

Try as we may to anticipate potential problems in the assessment environment and with the procedures for administering the test, and to develop administrative procedures that avoid these, it is impossible to know how problem-free the administrative procedures are without trying them out. Feedback about the administrative procedures includes information on circumstances and events taking place during the test administration. This may pertain either to activities of the test takers or to circumstances or activities surrounding the test takers. This kind of information is useful in evaluating the degree to which the assessment environment supports the test takers in doing their best work.

Discovering problems with the assessment environment

Problems with the assessment environment may be due to unexpected conditions with the physical setting, the participants, the time of the assessment, or to a combination of these. One type of problem stems from distracting noise at the assessment site, for example, noise from activities in adjacent rooms, noisy heating or air conditioning systems, test takers leaving a test early, and so on. In one instance, when developing a listening test involving the use of recorded material and a test booklet we did not anticipate the possibility that the noise of turning pages might interfere with test takers hearing the recorded material. Early trialing of the materials with a few test takers did not reveal the problem. In fact, only a field trial with a large number of test takers at the actual testing site did so. Our solution was to allocate more time between those questions that occurred across page breaks in the test booklet.

Discovering problems with the procedures for giving the assessment

Feedback about the procedures for giving the assessment itself includes information on circumstances and events taking place during the assessment administration. This may pertain either to activities of the test takers or to circumstances or activities surrounding the test takers. This kind of information is useful in evaluating the degree to which the assessment environment supports the test takers in doing their best work. For example, problems with procedures may come from the test supervisors themselves. They may have insufficient training in answering procedural questions, may not be sufficiently supportive of test takers, may be unable to speak the test takers' native language, and so on. Some obvious solutions to these problems would include providing supervisors with more background information, providing simulated training sessions in which supervisors are given feedback on their non-verbal communication, providing debriefing sessions following operational test use, and so on.

Determining appropriate time allocations

Trialing can also be used to determine whether time allocations are appropriate and allow test takers to perform at their best. For example, suppose a test developer was trialing a test with two separately timed sections. During trialing, the test developer might discover that the amount of time test takers needed to complete tasks in the second section varied widely, whereas they required essentially the same amount of time to complete tasks in the first section. One solution would be to change the order of the tasks so that the faster test takers did not need to wait for the slower ones during the first part of the test. Alternatively, test takers might be permitted to leave as soon as they had completed the test.

Another common problem with time allocation is failure to anticipate how much time is required for test takers to read and understand instructions or examples, so that the actual amount of usable time for carrying out the test task varies. This may result in interpretations of test takers' language ability being less meaningful for some test takers than for others. One solution would be to provide a separately timed period for test takers to read the instructions and ask questions. Other possible solutions would be to make the language of the instructions easier, to reduce the length of the instructions, to rely more on simple examples, or to provide instructions in the test takers' native language.

Identifying problems in task specification and clarity of instructions

A third purpose of trialing is to identify problems in task specification and instructions. For example, for a writing task that included a prompt for an essay, the test developer would want to be sure that the prompt adequately specified the nature of the required writing sample, so that the characteristics of the expected response might match, to as great an extent as possible, the characteristics of the TLU tasks. In the operationalization stage of test development, the developer could go through all of the characteristics of the test task and try to determine what needed to be said about each set of characteristics (organizational and pragmatic) in order to adequately describe the task to the test takers. In the trialing stage, the developer could identify any remaining problems and make modifications to procedures and instructions.

Discovering how test takers respond to the test tasks

Trialing is also used to obtain preliminary information on how test takers respond to the test tasks in two areas: their test-taking processes and their perceptions of test tasks. To obtain these types of information, test developers will typically rely upon qualitative assessment procedures. (See the discussion of these below.) Feedback on test-taking processes typically includes observations of test takers as they take the test and various kinds of self-reports. Feedback on how test takers perceive a test and react to it typically comes from self-reports of perceptions of the relevance of the test, its difficulty, the appropriateness of the time allocation and administration procedures, and so forth.

SOME MAJOR SOURCES OF FEEDBACK

During test administration feedback can be obtained from a variety of stakeholders, such as test takers, test administrators, and test users. Test takers can provide feedback on their perceptions of and attitudes toward the assessment and assessment tasks, and on their performance. Assessment administrators/proctors can provide feedback on the degree to which the administration procedures are conducive to the test takers' performing at their best. Assessment users can provide feedback on the consequences of the decisions based upon the interpretations of test takers' language ability with respect to their particular needs.

The decision as to where to get feedback depends upon the use to be made of it. If the focus is on tailoring an assessment to the abilities of a specific group of test takers, they would be the primary source of feedback. For example, to determine if the test was appropriate for a given group of test takers, the test could be administered and it could be determined what proportion of the test takers performed well (or poorly) on the test. Or the test takers could be asked for their reactions to the instructions, clarity of the task, appropriateness of the task, and so forth.

If the purpose of collecting feedback were to determine whether or not the test was practical for the people administering and scoring it, it would be obtained from these individuals. For example, feedback from oral interview test administrators might be obtained using a questionnaire about their perception of the clarity of the test tasks, the amount of time they had to complete the tasks, the understandability of the rating scales, and so forth.

If feedback on the use of test scores were required, it would be natural to go directly to the users for this information. For example, an assessment used to make placement decisions might be given to a sample of students with whom the teachers affected by placement decisions are familiar, the students placed using the preliminary version of the test, and the teachers provided with placement levels, and then asked whether they thought the levels were appropriate.

AMOUNTS OF RESOURCES INVOLVED IN OBTAINING FEEDBACK

In order to decide how and what kind of feedback to obtain, the usefulness of the feedback must be balanced against the cost (in terms of resources) of obtaining it. For example, given funding to develop a battery of tests used to make placement decisions for use in a large intensive English program, one might feel justified in using a portion of the funds to pay individuals to take the test and go through a lengthy debriefing process prior to the first operational use of the test. On the other hand, if developing a midterm examination for use in a current course, one might feel less justified in taking time from instruction to put students through an involved trialing process. Instead, more feedback might be collected before, during, and following each operational use of the test. Economical procedures such as short questionnaires attached to the end of the test or selective debriefing of a few of the test takers might also be used to obtain feedback. Ultimately, what is important is to balance the intended use of the test with the resources available.

The issue of using resources to obtain feedback also applies to the development of teacher-made tests for classroom use. We feel that such tests will be much more useful if extra resources are allocated to designing them, collecting feedback, and revising them, rather than "reinventing the wheel" each time a similar test is required. In this regard, it should be kept in mind that although collecting feedback is essential, it need not necessarily be elaborate or cumbersome. Adopting our approach to assessment development thus implies that the test developer will be much less likely to develop a test and use it only once.

SOME METHODS FOR OBTAINING FEEDBACK

A variety of methods are available for obtaining feedback. Some of these include questionnaires, verbal protocols, observations and descriptions, interviews, and statistical analyses of assessment records.

Questionnaires

Questionnaires ask the test takers to respond to specific queries about various aspects of their test-taking experience. Three commonly used formats for questionnaires are multiple-choice (selected response) questions, rating scales, and open-ended questions.

Multiple-choice questions

Multiple-choice questionnaires can be used to obtain quantitative feedback when test developers have in mind a number of specific test-taking strategies about which they want feedback from test takers. For example, Nevo (1989) describes a procedure in which test takers are provided with a list of test-taking strategies, each appearing with a brief description designed to prompt rapid processing of the checklist. The test takers are asked to indicate which of the strategies they used in responding to each item. In effect, in this procedure the test takers answered a sixteen-alternative multiple-choice question following each test item.

Example (1) illustrates how such strategies might be used:

(1) After you answer each item, check which of the following strategies you used to answer the item:
[Item 1]
Strategies
( ) Background knowledge: general knowledge outside the text called up by the reader in order to cope with written material.
( ) Guessing: blind guessing not based on any particular rationale.
( ) Returning to the passage: returning to the text to look for the correct answer, after reading the questions and the multiple-choice alternatives.
Etc.

The multiple-choice format can be modified in several ways. One modification would be to define each strategy only once at the beginning of the feedback form and list only the names of the strategies after each item. Another modification would be to name and define the strategies once at the beginning of the item and have the respondent simply list the numbers of the strategies used after each item. A strength of the multiple-choice format is that it allows the feedback collector to focus and limit responses to particular kinds of feedback. A weakness is that stakeholders may use strategies outside of the range of alternatives provided in the checklist, and these strategies may thus be missed by the person collecting the feedback.

Rating scales

Rating scales can also be used to obtain feedback from stakeholders on the strength and direction of their feelings about specific test-related issues. Several questions using rating scales (Sternfeld 1989, 1992) are illustrated in (2)–(7).

(2) How well does this test measure the ability *to write extemporaneously in German on a familiar topic*?

very poorly ... very well
1 2 3 4 5

(3) How well prepared did you feel for this kind of test?

not at all ... very well
1 2 3 4 5

(4) How clear were the instructions?

not at all ... very clear
1 2 3 4 5

(5) How well do you think you did in absolute terms?

0% ... 100%
1 2 3 4 5

(6) How well did you do relative to your hypothetical "peak performance"?

worst performance ... best performance
1 2 3 4 5

(7) How useful was this test *to you* for learning about your German-language skills?

not at all useful ... very useful
1 2 3 4 5

A strength of rating scales is that they elicit responses to specific questions in the form of scaled, quantifiable data that can then be subjected to powerful statistical analyses. A weakness is that they restrict the range and content of stakeholders' responses.

Open-ended questions

Open-ended questions provide a third format for a questionnaire. In this format, the test taker is simply asked to provide feedback by means of a free response to a question. Nevo (1989: 215) combines this method with multiple-choice questions by including the option "other strategy" along with a space to describe it.

A strength of the open-ended questionnaire format is that it elicits responses that might not be anticipated. A weakness is that it does not assure that the respondent has considered specific responses that are of interest.

Verbal protocols

A second general method for obtaining feedback is by means of verbal protocols. **Think-aloud** protocols are accounts given by the test takers of the processes they go through while actually taking the test. They provide an opportunity for test takers to describe their test-taking processes while actually using them. Such protocols can be provided orally and in writing, as illustrated in (1) and (2).

(1) In the following test of reading comprehension, as you take the test, describe whatever you are doing as you are doing it. Record your description by speaking into the microphone provided.

(2) In the following test of writing ability, as you write your composition, briefly write down the process you are using.

A strength of the think-aloud protocol is that it is the most immediate of those methods described. Feedback is obtained on the test-taking process as it is being carried out (at least in the oral format). In the written format, responses may be slightly delayed. A weakness is the relative lack of control of the content of the feedback and the practical difficulty of obtaining immediate feedback for tests of listening and speaking in which the test taker is highly involved.

For such tests **stimulated recall** protocols can be useful. (3) is an example of a stimulated recall protocol that a test taker provided on her experience of taking an experimental videotaped lecture listening comprehension test.

(3) Watch the video of yourself taking the listening comprehension test and describe your thoughts and feelings as you took the test.

"The Instructions were too fast for me. I couldn't get my sheets out in time, and gave up. Speech style for lecture was not ordinary spoken language. I got lost in the questions and couldn't figure out which question I was supposed to be on. I spent time searching the questions (written in German) for what I was supposed to be listening for and got upset, which interfered with my listening. I tuned out the last three-quarters of the test."

Observation and description

A third general method of obtaining feedback from a test administration is to have an outside observer monitor the test-taking process and describe what was observed. This can be done either in an open-ended format in which the observer simply notes whatever she happens to notice, or it can be done by providing the observer with directives or checklists which define specific categories of behaviors to be observed.

Interviews

A fourth method of obtaining feedback is by providing "debriefing" interviews for test takers after the test-taking process. Test takers can be invited to meet with test developers and talk about their test-taking experience. This can be used either as an opportunity for test takers to talk about whatever they want or for the interviewer to ask questions focusing on specific kinds of information.

The following is an example of notes from a relatively unstructured interview designed primarily to allow the test takers to express their feelings about a set of experimental tests.

(1) Student "A": Felt quite negative toward exams, no personal benefit. Thought she had done well in 5th quarter German, but felt like a failure on tests, which weren't representative of what she can do. Main gripes: too little time, no human content, tests not predictive of success in country with human contact. Thought other students felt the same, that tests were a total waste of time. Resented extra learning assignments in class along with testing. Varied reactions to the different tests. Felt tests were an imposition, "I was forced to do it." She tried to do her best, but felt discouraged because it was her worst performance. She only relaxed because she knew she'd get credit for the course.

(2) Student "B": Didn't resent the tests, liked that they were different, but wondered how useful they were. What was in it for him? Disliked missing three and a half days of class time. Liked some tests, not others. Said some tests (such as writing) were mostly irrelevant for him. Liked to be able to be debriefed. Said tests were well organized and liked the researcher's comments on the difficulty of various listening tests. Generally positive comments.

As these two summaries indicate, one strength of a debriefing interview is that it provides test takers an opportunity to interact personally with test developers. This lets them know that they have been heard and may contribute to positive impact. A weakness is that the format is costly in terms of time and may be less efficient if a large amount of feedback on specific issues is required.

Statistical analyses of assessment records

A fifth method of obtaining feedback is through the statistical analysis of assessment records and item performance. A discussion of the specific statistical procedures appropriate for use in collecting backing for the warrants in the AUA lies outside the scope of this book. (See the references provided in the Suggested Readings at the end of this chapter.)

PLAN FOR COLLECTING BACKING

Before starting to collect feedback, it is important to develop a plan for its collection. This plan will assure that the types of feedback needed to provide backing for warrants in the AUA and data for evaluating the practicality of the assessment are thought through systematically. Without a plan, the test developer may easily forget to gather important feedback or may embark on feedback collection without taking into consideration the cost of obtaining it and whether sufficient resources are available.

Form of plan

One way to organize a plan for collecting feedback is by means of a table. In Chapter 14, we provided a table organized first in terms of the stages in assessment development during which the feedback is gathered (column 1), and then the activities used to collect the feedback, the types of evidence collected, the Claims and Warrants supported by the feedback, and the person(s) responsible for collecting it. Once the feedback has been collected and entered into the cells in the table, it can be incorporated in a time line for managing the resources, including time needed to collect the feedback. (See Chapter 20.)

Kindergarten example

Plan for collecting feedback and backing for warrants

The kindergarten teacher most likely won't prepare a formal plan for collecting backing during his administration and use of the assessment. However, he will implement some informal means for collecting backing to support the warrants in the AUA. He will conduct and observe an interactive writing activity, noting how effective the observation procedures and checklist are for providing the information he needs. He will also keep track of the reactions of his students as he gives them feedback.

University example

Plan for collecting feedback and backing for warrants

A plan for collecting feedback for the University example (which was presented in abbreviated version in Chapter 13) is organized chronologically, from Stage I through Stage V. The entire plan is presented in Table 19.1 on pp. 405–8. This plan will help the test developer to schedule these activities in the plan and to allocate the required resources. Note, too, that one activity that is repeated at each stage is a documentation of the procedures that have been followed. This documentary narrative of the entire process of assessment development and use provides valuable backing to support the claims and warrants in the AUA.

Stage	Activities	Evidence (Documentation)	Claim, Warrants supported	Person(s) responsible
I Pre-dev. planning	1 Consulting documents 2 Consulting stakeholders	Initial Plan Description of procedures followed	Claims 1 and 2	ESL Program Director ESL reading course instructors
	3 Documenting the procedures followed			
II Design	4 Identifying stakeholders	DS, Pt 1, list of stakeholders	Claim 1	ESL Program Director ESL reading course instructors
	5 Documenting the procedures followed	AUA: description of procedures followed in creating list of stakeholders	Claim 1	
	6 Consulting with stakeholders • ELL students at the university • ESL reading teachers • Academic course instructors	DS, Pt 2, list of intended consequences and potential detrimental consequences	Claim 1, W A1	
		DS, Pt 3, list of decisions to be made, who is responsible for making these, and who will be affected by these	Claim 2	
		DS, Pt 4, description of relative seriousness of decision errors and performance standards for making classification decisions	Claim 2, W A2, A3a, A3b	

Stage	Activities	Evidence (Documentation)	Claim, Warrants supported	Person(s) responsible
	7 Documenting the procedures followed	AUA: description of procedures followed		
	8 Conducting a needs analysis	DS, Pt 5, definition of construct	Claim 3, W A1	
		DS, Pt 6, description of TLU domain	Claim 3, W C1	
		DS, Pt 7, List of TLU tasks selected	Claim 3, W C1, C2	
	9 Describing TLU task characteristics	DS, Pt 8, description of TLU task (templates)	Claim 3, W C1, C2	
	10 Documenting the procedures followed • Documents consulted • Stakeholders consulted • TLU domain observed	AUA: description of procedures followed	Claims 1, 2, and 3	
III Operation-alization	11 Consulting documents created during development stage	BP, Pt 1, assessment task specifications	Claim 3, W A2, C1, C2	ESL Program Director
		BP, Pt 3, procedures for setting cut scores and making decisions	Claim 2, WA3 Claim 1, W A3, A4; Claim 4, W 2 Claim 3, W A3	ESL reading course instructor Ph.D. students in language testing
		BP, Pt 4, procedures and formats for reporting assessment records		
		BP, Pt 5, procedures for administering the assessment		

Stage	Activities	Evidence (Documentation)	Claim, Warrants supported	Person(s) responsible
	12 Documenting the procedures followed	AUA: description of procedures followed	Claims 1, 2, and 3	
IV Trialing	13 Consulting stakeholders	Report: summary of results of test-taker questionnaire	Claim 1, W A1	ESL Program Director
	14 Pre-testing	Report: summary of results of pre-testing	Claims 2, 3, and 4	Ph.D. students in language testing
	15 Statistical analysis of test scores			
	16 Documenting the procedures followed	Report: summary of results of pre-testing	Claims 2, 3, and 4	
V Use	17 Consulting stakeholders	Report: results of questionnaire (given to test takers, ESL reading teachers, and academic instructors in courses into which test takers were placed) on accuracy (?) of placement/ exemption decisions	Claim 2, W A3; B1, Claim 3, W E	ESL Program Director Ph.D. students in language testing
		Report: results of questionnaire (given to test takers) on administration procedures followed	Claim 1, W A2, A3, A4	

Stage	Activities	Evidence (Documentation)	Claim, Warrants supported	Person(s) responsible
		Report from Program Director on placement procedures followed	Claim 2, W B1, B2,	
	18 Statistical analysis of test scores	Report: statistical analysis of test scores	Claim 4, W, 5, 6, 7, 8, 9, 10	

Table 19.1 Plan for collecting backing and feedback for the University example

In this chapter we've described two uses of information that is collected during the Trialing and Assessment Use stages of assessment development: improving the assessment itself (feedback), and supporting the warrants in the AUA (backing). A variety of procedures can be used for collecting this information, some of which will be used only for improving the assessment, some for supporting the warrants in the AUA, and some for both purposes. Collecting feedback to improve the assessment and backing to support the warrants in the AUA are essential activities in responsible assessment use, to which we turn in the final chapter of the book.

EXERCISES

1 Consider the problems with the assessment environment discussed on p. 396. How might different types of problems with the assessment environment affect the backing for the warrants in the AUA? Do different types of problems affect the different warrants in the same way?

2 Consider the problems with the procedures for giving the assessment discussed on p. 397. How might different types of problems with the assessment environment affect the backing for the warrants in the AUA? Do different types of problems affect the different warrants in the same way?

3 Recall an assessment you have developed in the past. Describe the process you used to pre-test and administer the assessment. Which of the procedures described in this chapter did you follow? Why? How might you change the procedures if you developed the assessment again?

4 Think of an assessment that you might develop. Prepare a list of pre-testing and administration procedures for this assessment.

5 Recall an assessment you took. To what extent did the administration procedures help you do your best work? To what extent did they get in the way? What changes would you suggest?
6 Recall an assessment you have used. What kinds of feedback on usefulness from stakeholders did you obtain? What kinds of feedback might you now want to obtain if you used the test again? What procedures might you use to obtain this feedback?
7 Recall a time when you developed an assessment for classroom use and then used it only once. What kinds of resources went into developing this assessment? What other opportunities may have existed for using this assessment test again? How might you have allocated available resources toward developing a more useful test to be administered on multiple occasions?
8 If you are a teacher who regularly needs to develop classroom assessments, think of ways in which you might reorganize your current assessment program in order to channel available resources into improving your assessments, rather than reinventing them.
9 How have you traditionally given assessments? What kinds of impressions do you think your procedures have made on the test takers? Do you think these impressions have contributed positively to the usefulness of your assessments? If not, what changes might you make in your assessment giving procedures?
10 Do some library research on recent controversies in educational measurement (not necessarily language assessment). Try to find instances where assessments "made the news" due to administrative issues, such as a cheating scandal that was later solved by an administrative change, or a lawsuit brought by an examinee who detected some questionable practice. These are examples of feedback of a very critical nature. What does it mean to a test developer or test user when his or her assessment gets in the news? What kind of feedback is that, and how can it affect later assessment practice?

SUGGESTED READINGS

Measurement and statistical analysis

Bachman, L. F. 2004. *Statistical Analyses for Language Assessment*. Cambridge: Cambridge University Press.

Glass, G. V. and **K. D. Hopkins.** 2008. *Statistical Methods in Education and Psychology* (3rd edn.). New York: Prentice-Hall, Inc.

Kubiszyn, T. and **G. D. Borich.** 2009. *Educational Testing and Measurement: Classroom Application and Practice* (9th edn.). New York: Wiley.

Miller, M. D., N. E. Gronlund, and **R. L. Linn.** 2008. *Measurement and Assessment in Teaching* (10th edn.). Westport, CT: Prentice-Hall, Inc.

Popham, W. J. 1999. *Modern Educational Measurement: Practical Guidelines for Educational Leaders* (3rd edn.). White Plains, NY: Allyn & Bacon.

Research methods

Creswell, J. W. 2008. *Research Design: Qualitative, Quantitative, and Mixed Methods Approaches*. Beverly Hills, CA: Sage Publications.

Patton, M. Q. 2001. *Qualitative Research and Evaluation Methods* (3rd edn.). Beverly Hills, CA: Sage Publications.

Research methods for applied linguistics, language testing, and language teaching

Brown, J. D. 2001. *Using Surveys in Language Teaching*. Cambridge: Cambridge University Press.

——and **T. S. Rodgers.** 2003. *Doing Second Language Research*. Oxford: Oxford University Press.

Dörnyei, Z. (2007). *Research Methods in Applied Linguistics*. Oxford: Oxford University Press.

Gass, S. M. and **A. Mackey.** 2000. *Stimulated Recall Methodology in Second Language Research*. Hillsdale, NJ: Lawrence Erlbaum Associates.

Green, A. 1998. *Verbal Protocol Analysis in Language Testing Research: A Handbook*. Cambridge: Cambridge University Press.

Hatch, E. and **A. Lazaraton.** 1991. *The Research Manual: Design and Statistics for Applied Linguistics*. New York: Newbury House Publishers.

Johnson, D. 1992. *Approaches to Research in Second Language Learning*. London: Longman.

Lazaraton, A. 2002. *A Qualitative Approach to the Validation of Oral Language Tests*. Cambridge: Cambridge University Press.

Nunan, D. 1992. *Research Methods in Language Learning*. Cambridge: Cambridge University Press.

Perry, F. L. 2005. *Research in Applied Linguistics: Becoming a Discerning Consumer*. Hillsdale, NJ: Lawrence Erlbaum.

NOTE

1 The term “pre-test” can be used to refer to the procedure itself, as well as to the activity, so that “pre-test” is commonly used as either a noun or a verb. Other terms that are commonly used more or less synonymously with “pre-test” include “pilot,” “trial,” and “tryout.”

20

Identifying, allocating, and managing resources

INTRODUCTION

One of the most important parts of any assessment development process is to take stock of the available resources and estimate the resources required. The amount of resources required will differ from situation to situation, depending upon the stakes of the assessment and the scope of the project. For some low-stakes assessments, relatively few resources may be required. For example, suppose you were teaching a course and wanted to prepare a short vocabulary quiz whose use was to provide students with feedback on what they had mastered and not mastered so that they could decide to complete additional practice material accordingly. You might be able to produce your test rather quickly because at the outset you would probably have a fairly clear idea of the consequences of assessment use, the decisions that need to be made, the construct to be measured, the TLU domain and tasks, the attributes of the test takers, as well as how you will go about creating an AUA. Moreover, you would probably write all of the assessment tasks, administer and analyze the results, and archive these yourself.

High-stakes assessments will typically require many more resources. For example, suppose you were responsible for developing a final exam for a multi-section course. This is very common practice in many language-teaching programs, and we have participated in a number of projects like this, in several different countries. Since these tests are frequently given to hundreds or thousands of students, and whether students pass or fail depends heavily upon the results of the test, a lot of resources go into the planning, including time spent by the Department chairperson, the director of the testing program, a testing committee, and the instructors teaching the courses for which the test is being developed. In situations such as this, a team of teachers often spends a great deal of time typically preparing an initial pool of test items. These items are then revised by a smaller team of teachers with skills and experience in test development, and these items are then submitted for final review to the Project Director. A secretarial pool prepares the final version of the test and reproduces the test booklets from this. Another team scores the test, prepares grade reports, and makes recommendations to the developer regarding score criteria for assigning grades and making decisions.

Classroom teachers may find the demands on resources to lie somewhere between the two extremes described above. In developing a midterm test covering several chapters in a textbook, a teacher might need to spend some time planning and producing the test, and creating an AUA and collecting backing, to score those parts of the test employing subjective scoring procedures, and so on. However, regardless of the stakes and scope of the assessment development project, without taking steps to be realistic about resources, a test developer may take on a project that will either be impossible to complete or will drain the developer's energy to do so.

In this chapter we first discuss how resources can be used in the different stages of assessment development. Next, we describe the various kinds of resources that can be used. We then show how to prepare a table of tasks and resources. We follow this up by showing how to prepare a time line to organize the implementation of activities in assessment development. We then discuss the various strengths and weaknesses of the use of resources in individual and team efforts. Finally, we revisit the trade-offs resulting from limitations on resources.

STAGES OF ASSESSMENT DEVELOPMENT DURING WHICH RESOURCES ARE USED

Initial planning

As we have noted in Chapter 7, the amount of resources needed for initial planning will depend upon the stakes of the assessment. In low-stakes projects, initial planning may be relatively informal and require only a few resources. In high-stakes projects, initial planning will involve a considerable amount of resources. If, as a result of initial planning, the decision maker determines that an assessment needs to be developed, the final step in planning will be to make an inventory of the types of resources needed and whether these resources are already available or can be obtained.

Justification: AUA and backing

Demonstrating to stakeholders that the intended uses of an assessment are justified, which informs all remaining stages of assessment development, will also require resources. The question of the resources that will be required to develop an AUA and provide the backing to support this is an important one.

In this regard, there are three **resourcing considerations** that we need to take into account: specificity, focus, and cost-effectiveness.

Specificity

One consideration in the development of an AUA is that of **specificity**. The test developer needs to develop an AUA *for each specific use* for which an assessment is intended. This is because each specific language assessment situation is virtually unique. The intended use may be a fairly common one, or the test developer may intend to assess an aspect of language ability that others have assessed, or she may be using assessment tasks that are very similar to those used in other language assessments, or the stakeholders may be very similar to those in other assessment situations. Nevertheless, despite elements in common with other assessment situations, each assessment situation is most likely a unique *combination* of intended use, areas of language ability to be assessed, tasks to be used, and particular values and interests of the particular stakeholders. This is not to say that the test developer cannot draw on the AUAs of another language assessment as she develops her assessment. However, it is highly unlikely that the AUA for another assessment will be completely adequate or appropriate for a different specific intended use.

Focus

A second consideration is that of **focus**. The test developer needs to focus his resources on those warrants of the AUA that are most likely to require the most support and most extensive backing. He will also need to focus on those rebuttals that are the most problematic or likely and that thus will require the most extensive data to either reject or weaken. In the example above, of the midterm test, students who think the test is unfair may not be at all interested in how consistently their responses were scored; they need to be convinced that the test content matches the content of the syllabus. In order to anticipate the possibility that students will complain that the test included material that was not taught (rebuttal to Warrant B3 about equitability under Claim 2), the teacher could make a list of which specific part of the course content each test task was related to. It will be less important for the teacher to spend resources to collect backing in support of the Warrants about consistency under Claim 4, such as conducting statistical analyses to estimate the consistency (reliability) of the test scores. However, if a parent complained that he felt his child's test performance was not scored accurately, then he would need to be convinced that the scoring was reliable. Furthermore, the teacher may not need to collect backing to support Warrants A1, 2 and 4 about impartiality under Claim 3 *unless* some of the students or other stakeholders complain that the test was biased against a particular group of students.

The allocation of resources can also change as the demands of stakeholders change. For many years, developers of large-scale, high-stakes tests in the US focused their resources on providing evidence for the consistency (reliability) of test scores and the meaningfulness (validity) of interpretations. However, after a series of high-profile court cases in which members of different ethnic groups successfully argued that these tests were biased, the test developers now expend considerable resources providing backing for Warrant B3 about equitability under Claim 2, and Warrants A1–5 about impartiality under Claim 3. This backing consists of both "bias reviews" by experts and extensive statistical analyses of test results.

Thus, different stakeholders may be concerned about different parts of the AUA, and hence need to be convinced by different kinds of backing. The credibility of an AUA and its supporting backing depends on providing coherent warrants and relevant backing at every link in the chain of argumentation from assessment performance. Therefore, the test developer needs to try to anticipate what the potential weaknesses in his AUA might be and what the likely concerns of the various stakeholders are. He then needs to focus on making the argument as strong as possible at those points, and be prepared to provide backing in support of the warrants that will be convincing to these stakeholders. By concentrating on these areas, the test developer can optimize his resources. Since assessment development efforts are typically short of resources, the AUA can provide a valuable guide for identifying the kinds of backing that are the most important, so that the test developer can allocate adequate resources to providing these.

Cost-effectiveness

A third consideration is that of **cost-effectiveness**. Here, the test developer compares the cost, in terms of resources, of articulating an AUA and collecting the relevant backing, with the potential impact on or consequences for stakeholders. The more important the decision(s) to be made and the intended consequences are, the more resources the test developer needs to allocate to developing an AUA and providing backing in support of his warrants and claims. The intended uses of an assessment will differ in terms of how they affect the lives of stakeholders. For example, in a classroom quiz that is used to identify areas that need to be reviewed and worked on, the decision will have a relatively small effect on the students and the teacher. In a **low-stakes use** such as this, the teacher may articulate a very general AUA and may be able to provide adequate backing from documents such as course syllabi, curriculum guides, and textbooks, and may not need to collect any empirical backing. With a national university entrance examination, on the other hand, the decision to admit or not to admit students into a university will have a major impact on the lives of test takers, their families, and the universities to which they are admitted, and potentially the secondary schools from which they graduate. In a **high-stakes use** such as this, the test developer would need to allocate substantial resources to developing a detailed AUA, providing documentation, and collecting extensive empirical evidence to support the warrants and claims in the AUA.

Assessment production: design, operationalization, and trialing

Design

Creating a design statement

The process of creating a Design Statement can consume different amounts of resources depending upon the complexity of the document. A complex, detailed Design Statement needed for a high-stakes assessment may require a lot of time and highly trained personnel to create and revise, while a Design Statement for a low-stakes test might be created with relatively few resources. (See the University Project on p. 449 for an example in which considerable resources were needed to define the multiple constructs.)

Consequences of Design Statement for demands on resources in later stages of assessment development

In addition to the resources used during the process of creating a Design Statement, the content of the statement can have major consequences for the demands on resources during later stages of assessment development. With respect to the definition of the construct(s), if multiple constructs are defined, multiple TLU task types may be needed in the Design Statement to allow the needed interpretations to be made, and it is often the case that developing multiple assessment task types will require more resources than a single assessment task type. In addition, if multiple TLU tasks are selected because they are needed to make a convincing argument for generalizability, this may also make heavier demands on resources than if a single task is selected.

The presence of certain characteristics in a TLU task template may also make heavy demands on resources in the Operationalization, Trialing, and Assessment Use stages of assessment development. For example, if a template contains a characteristic of the setting "multiple participants of a particular type," creating assessment tasks in which these multiple participants are present may be an expensive proposition. Thus, in creating a Design Statement, the test developer needs to take into consideration the implications for demands on resources during assessment task development and use.

Operationalization

The way the assessment developers go about operationalizing the Design Statement as a Blueprint for one or more assessments will have obvious consequences for demands on resources.

Creating a Blueprint

The process of creating a Blueprint can consume different amounts of resources depending upon the complexity of the assessment and the need to document the process of Operationalization. An assessment with multiple parts and multiple task types will require a more complex Blueprint than will one with only one or two parts and few different task types. A high-stakes assessment will require a detailed Blueprint, requiring a lot of time and highly trained personnel to create and revise, while a Blueprint for a low-stakes test might be created with relatively few resources.

Implications of Blueprint for demands on resources in later stages of assessment development

As with the Design Statement, the content of the Blueprint can have major consequences for the demands on resources during later stages of assessment development. For example, a Blueprint that specifies a large number of test tasks with selected responses (multiple-choice items) will require test writers with the expertise to come up with such tasks, an experienced editor to review them, and resources to pre-test and revise them. Such expertise and resources often do not come cheaply, so the test developer might think twice before developing a Blueprint with these types of task specifications.

Creating one or more assessments

Clearly different assessment task types will require different amounts of resources to actually create. For example, producing an assessment consisting only of a short prompt and rubric for assigning ratings may make relatively few demands on human resources (the item writer), whereas writing a script for a lengthy, scripted oral interview test may make very heavy demands on time resources needed for personnel to write and revise the script.

Trialing

The way that assessment developers choose to trial the assessment will also have consequences for demands on resources. Trialing can be conducted on a limited or very large scale. It can make heavy or relatively few demands on personnel. It can require the involvement of highly trained personnel and associated heavy payments or personnel with less training who can be involved at fairly low cost. For example, when trialing high-stakes standardized tests, large numbers of test takers may need to be paid to take the test, and highly trained assessment specialists may need to be paid to review the qualitative and quantitative feedback from the trialing, and highly paid editors may need to be paid to make necessary revisions.

Assessment use

The way an assessment is used will also influence the demands on resources. An assessment whose use involves trained examiners and raters can be relatively costly to administer. For example, an oral interview used for making high-stakes decisions would need to be administered and rated by two individuals with a considerable amount of training. If this test were to be used for making relatively low-stakes decisions, as in a classroom summative assessment, the rating criteria and procedures could to be modified to reduce demands on resources to an acceptable level.

TYPES OF RESOURCES

One way for the developer to get a better sense of the kinds of resource that will be needed is to list the major stages in assessment development and ask what kinds of resources will be involved in carrying out each step. The developer can then create a list of available resources for each of the steps. The following is a discussion of some of the resources typically required for assessment development. This discussion draws on and expands on the discussion of resources in Chapter 13.

Human resources

A critical resource in assessment development consists of the individuals who carry it out. Human resources can best be thought of in terms of roles or functions that individuals perform in the assessment development process. In some situations, individuals will have very clearly defined roles and functions, while in other cases the individuals involved may change roles and functions as assessment development proceeds. In most projects several roles will be filled by the same person, so that there need not necessarily be one person per role.

Test developer

One role or function that we have referred to frequently is that of the test developer. The test developer supervises the assessment development from beginning to end. In some projects, such as developing a small classroom quiz, the teacher is the most likely person to serve in this role, and this person will perform all roles in test development. In other projects, a director with extensive training and experience in assessment will supervise a large test development team, including task writers.

Task writers

The task writers (sometimes referred to as item writers) are key personnel in the assessment development process. (We use the term "task writers" in a general sense to refer not only to writing *per se* but also to other assessment development tasks such as collecting material already written, editing, and recording.) The qualifications of task writers and the amount of time they will need to put in on the project will vary according to its nature. For example, suppose one person "writes" a short gap-filling test in which "gaps" in the passage are created by deleting words at random. The test takers respond by trying to fill in the gaps with the original, deleted words. Preparing this kind of test may involve very little "task writing" expertise and time, although collecting the backing to *justify* the use of such a test would require both expertise and time. On the other hand, developing a script for a lengthy oral interview test may be very demanding. In any case, it is important to think in terms of the abilities of task writers to write different kinds of assessment tasks and consider assigning writers to tasks accordingly.

Assessment administrators

Assessment administrators carry out the process of giving the assessment. For some assessments, such as group-administered paper and pencil assessments, relatively little training may be required to administer the assessments, although administrators will still need to be coached on how to interact with the test takers. For others, such as face-to-face oral interview tests, much more training may be necessary.

Individuals who produce assessment records

Individuals who produce assessment records, such as assessment raters and scorers, also play an important role in assessment, development and use. In tests such as face-to-face oral interviews, for example, the raters/scorers either need to be on hand during each test administration or have access to digital recordings. Raters and scorers can also provide valuable input into the scoring procedures of the test. Depending on the particular scoring method used, raters may need to be highly proficient in the language being tested.

Clerical support

Many assessment development projects require rather extensive clerical support, including word processing, data entry, photocopying, record keeping, etc., and this needs to be taken into consideration in advance. In one large overseas project, we did not know until we were well into the project that we would have to type all of the original test copy ourselves, not only for the pre-test but also for the final version. Since the complete pre-test was over fifty pages long, this turned out to be a huge and unexpected job. Moreover, it took a lot of our energy away from writing and editing.

Material resources

In Chapter 13 we introduced the discussion of various types of materials used in assessment development, and in Chapter 17 we discussed the role of materials in administering the assessment. We now discuss these types of material in more detail.

Space

Space is almost always an important consideration. In one of our research projects, sixty students had to take eight subtests in a single day, and each subtest had to be administered in a different room. This required that a number of the instructors' offices be used, as well as the computer laboratory. Space can be particularly critical and requires careful planning and management in assessments that involve a variety of task types requiring different types of space, such as an examination that includes paper and pencil parts, listening tasks that need to be administered to smaller groups, and a one-on-one oral interview.

Equipment

Equipment also plays an important role in assessment development and production. The list is long, and includes, for example, computers, data projectors, audio recorders, video recorders, photocopiers, computer laboratories, and machine scoring devices. While it may seem obvious that the test developer needs to plan for needed equipment from the beginning, the developer sometimes finds herself in situations where equipment that she generally assumes will be available is simply not to be found.

Assessment materials

Assessment materials include whatever the assessment itself is made of and whatever may be used in the process of taking the assessment. This may include pencils, assessment booklets, answer sheets, flash memory devices, videotapes, audio tapes, computers, etc.

Time

Time is a critical resource that needs to be considered with respect to each of the other kinds of resources. There are two aspects to this resource: (1) development time and (2) the time required to complete the parts of each stage of the assessment development process. It is important to estimate the total amount of time that will be needed and available from personnel and, possibly, from equipment such as computers and language laboratories.

PREPARING A TABLE OF TASKS AND RESOURCES

To allocate resources, the test developer will need to prepare a table of the resources that will be needed to complete each stage of assessment development. These resources will be specified in terms of the most convenient and appropriate units. For example, when allocating personnel to a specific task, the developer might want to specify their time in terms of numbers of hours or days, and may also want to specify salary figures. When allocating space to a task, the developer would probably enter a value for the area required (e.g., square feet or meters or the number of usable seats).

Table 20.1 on p. 420 is an estimation of required resources for the University example during the various stages of assessment development.

RESOURCES	STAGES 1 Initial planning	2 Design	3 Operationalization	4 Trialing	5 Use
Personnel					
Project Director	40 hours	20 hours/ term	30 hours/ term	20 hours/ term	10 hours/ term
Development team	10 hours/ person	10 hours/ person/ week	10 hours/ person/ week	10 hours/ person/ week	2 hours/ person/ term
Computer programmer		30 hours	50 hours	50 hours	10 hours/ term
Clerical support	2 hours	10 hours	30 hours	40 hours	20 hours/ term
Test administrators/ Scorers				20 hours	20 hours/ term
Space	Meeting room	Meeting room	Meeting room	Meeting room, rooms for administering the test	Meeting room, rooms for administering the test
Equipment	PCs	PCs	PCs	PCs	PCs

Table 20.1 Estimation of required resources for the University example

DETERMINING TOTAL COST OF ASSESSMENT DEVELOPMENT AND USE PREPARING A BUDGET

In order to estimate the total cost of the project, the test developers add up the estimated costs of the various types of resources. In many teacher-directed projects, the total cost is much less of a concern than determining the practicality (required resources vs. available resources) at each stage of assessment development. (See Chapter 13 for a discussion of practicality.) If the project is not practical at one stage, the test developer may need to shift resources from another stage or delay starting the next phase. For example, if the developer discovers that the operationalization stage is requiring more human resources for writing than she anticipated, she may need to ask for more released time for task writers or delay the start of the assessment use stage. In larger projects, it is almost always necessary to prepare a budget, including an estimate of the project's total cost.

Typically included in a budget will be the following:

1 The estimated monetary cost of human resources, including salaries of people such as assessment designers, item writers, scorers, administrators, and clerical staff,
2 The estimated monetary cost of physical resources, including equipment, space rental, printing, computer time, etc.,
3 The estimated monetary cost of taking the assessment for the test takers (if they are charged for taking the test).

Table 20.2 is an example of a budget for a project funded by a grant that required a detailed account of the cost of all resources in US dollars.

Personnel	**Total cost**
Project Director: 60 hrs. @ $75/hour	$ 4,500
Task writers: 25 hrs. @ $25/hour	$ 625
Editors: 20 hrs. @ $25/hour	$ 500
Raters: 30 hrs. @ $25/hour	$ 750
Administrators: 10 hrs. @ $20/hour	$ 200
Clerical support: 30 hrs. @ $30/hour	$ 900
Subtotal	$ 7,475
Space	
Design: 225 sq. ft. for 55 hours @ $.025/sq. ft./hour	$ 309
Operationalization: 225 sq. ft. for 45 hours @ $.025/sq. ft./hour	$ 253
Giving the test: 900 sq. ft. for 15 hours @ $.025/sq. ft./hour	$ 338
Scoring: 225 sq. ft. for 35 hours @ $.025/sq. ft./hour	$ 197
Analyses of information 225 sq. ft. for 25 hours @ $.025/sq. ft./hour	$ 141
Subtotal	$ 1,238
Equipment	
Computer and monitor	NC
Recording studio	$ 1,500
Subtotal	$ 1,500
TOTAL BUDGET	$ 10,213

Table 20.2 Example budget

PREPARING A TIME LINE

A **time line** is a document specifying the tasks involved in the assessment development process, the sequence in which they will be carried out, and the time by which each task needs to be completed. Each task is put into a sequenced list, which specifies its temporal relationship to the other tasks in the project. The following are the steps in developing a time line:

1 Write down your objectives. Specify what you want to accomplish and when you want to accomplish it.
2 Break your objectives down into major steps or activities.
3 Organize the activities in a logical order.

OBJECTIVE: Develop a set of three fully scripted oral interview tests and videotaped tests of listening comprehension to be administered at the end of the first-, second-, and third-year Spanish courses. To be completed by 4/30/2009.

1 Start-up
(6/1/08)
Appoint Project Director from within Department
Complete initial planning and initial drafts of AUA and Design Statement, including estimation of required resources
2 Secure resources
(7/1/08)
Consult with Departmental chairperson
Consult with Dean
Secure final approval of budget
3 Assemble development team
(7/30/08)
4 Revise Design Statement, as needed, with the development team
(8/15/08)
5 Complete operationalization (including all scripts and video recordings)
(12/1/08)
6 Trialing
(2/1/09)
Train test administrators
Obtain space for trialing
Obtain subjects for trialing
Arrange payment for subjects for trialing
7 Try out the test
(2/30/09)
8 Analyze and interpret results
(3/30/09)
9 Revise Design Statement, Blueprint, and tests
(5/30/09)

Table 20.3 Example time line for large test development project

4 Estimate how long each major activity will take to complete, and assign a calendar date to each major activity.
5 Break down each major activity into minor activities and add these to the time line.

Table 20.3 is an example of a time line for a large test development project.

INDIVIDUAL AND TEAM EFFORTS

Over more years than we care to reveal, we have been involved with a variety of assessment development efforts, and in doing so we have become increasingly impressed by the effectiveness of team, as opposed to individual, assessment development efforts. Many years ago, one of us was involved in an individual test development effort when he first went overseas to work. The first job he took involved working for a small, private company writing pseudo-TOEFL tests so that students could take them as practice for the TOEFL. In this project, the developer worked entirely alone. He was given some examples of the test items and then had to write, revise, and edit two forms of the entire test. All of the responsibility for the success of the project rested on his shoulders, and he soon realized that he could not do all parts of the project equally well. He also noticed how little he enjoyed the process, having previously always been part of a highly cohesive development team. He had no one to talk with, no one to bounce ideas off, and no one to get feedback from. There was no opportunity for humor, which is often a much-needed characteristic of the real world that frequently keeps projects going long after the developers have begun to go nuts.

Right after completing the individual effort, he was hired to direct a different project aimed at developing a test for selection and placement of all entering students in English courses at a major university. He started by working closely with the Department chairperson and her main assistant. They discussed the purposes of the test and reviewed past test development efforts. In the early planning stages, he had the opportunity to discuss ideas and proposals with these colleagues before investing any effort into putting them into action. Many unsatisfactory proposals were reviewed and rejected at this stage without creating any problems. Once they had a general plan for the test, they took it to all of the teachers in the Department. They got immediate feedback as to the strengths and weaknesses of the proposal from these stakeholders and were able to make appropriate revisions. When they had finished the plan, they knew that the procedures for test development and use had the approval of the great majority of the stakeholders who would have to live with the results. In addition to being involved with the test planning, the teachers were also involved with most of the remaining steps in the test development process. Procedures were developed by which teachers would help produce the initial pool of items. Then certain particularly skillful teachers assisted in the editing. All of the teachers were present at the tryout and helped with the tabulations needed for the analysis of results and revision. As a result, they knew just how much work went into developing the test, and they went to great pains to make sure that the test was properly administered and kept secure.

The developer's experience in this second project was entirely different from what he had experienced just months before. He felt supported instead of isolated. He felt acknowledged for his work, rather than merely paid for it. He felt confident that the test would make a difference because he knew the teachers (and students) and knew how much the test was needed. He knew the test had passed before many eyes and that they were not likely to suddenly discover glaring mistakes or gaps after the project was finished. For this developer, the team effort was much more rewarding both in terms of the process and the product. The process was more rewarding because of the interaction and cooperation. It offered more opportunities to share successes and provided the team members with more support during "down" times. The product of the team effort was certainly better, both because of the increased numbers of points of view incorporated in the planning process and the greater diversity of creative thought that went into the items themselves. In retrospect, we now see that one reason this project was so successful is that it involved a wide range of stakeholders interacting throughout the entire test development project.

Finally, while we personally find team efforts particularly rewarding, we also acknowledge that there is a place for one-person efforts. For example tests developed for use in language testing research projects frequently seem to be the result of one person's creative thinking, though tests designed for use as research tools, e.g., in applied linguistics, are generally much more effective if feedback on them has been invited from fellow students or research colleagues during the development phase. Moreover, we realize that for many classroom assessments limitations on resources may require the individual teacher to create the assessment on his own. However, as we have noted many times, we believe that most assessment development projects will involve interaction among a variety of stakeholders and that high-stakes projects will require the involvement of a team.

Being realistic about resources

Being realistic about resources is an important part of developing assessments in the real world, and one important facet of this is being realistic about the amount of support the developer will have from other people. This is particularly important if the developer is in a situation in which he is perceived to be the lone "expert" in assessment and the person everyone runs to whenever anything having to do with testing has to be done. Some language testers tend to take on too many projects because the excitement of a new project may overwhelm the rationality of adding more work to an already busy schedule, or they may take on too many projects because they have difficulty saying "no."

If either of these scenarios sounds uncomfortably familiar to you, here are some suggestions. First, get absolutely clear on what support you do and do not have. Who can you count on to support and work with you, and who can you not count on? How reliable (really) are the others who might help out? How much energy can you expect them to provide? How much work will you have to do yourself in the worst-case scenario, when everyone else bails out on you? Then ask yourself whether you are willing to take on the project knowing that you may wind up with little support. If you are really willing to do the project alone, then go for it. If not, turn it down. If you take on the project without an appropriate amount of support, you will be upset with the extra work you end up doing, and you will be upset with yourself for not having taken the time to get clear on the situation in advance. And you're likely to beat yourself up with "Why do I keep doing this?" In any case, a test development project taken on when it is not really feasible is not likely to produce a test whose uses can be justified, so it is always best to get clear in advance on what is expected and what resources will be made available.

Finally, in some situations a test developer may find herself in a position in which she knows that there are insufficient resources to complete a quality project but wants to look for an alternative to turning it down completely. One strategy is to use the AUA to organize her thinking about the types of justification she can provide with varying degrees of effort and support. In one case in which one of our colleagues worked with very little official support, she mobilized volunteers to get what she called "quick fixes" done to a really bad test. Her doing that drew attention from potential support givers, and put her in a position to argue for official support. So, even though the "quick fixes" were not the project that she wanted, that approach acted as a first step.

TRADE-OFFS TO REDUCE DEMANDS ON RESOURCES

Because almost all assessment development projects are carried out with limited resources, the test developer will always have to make choices, and these involve trade-offs. As we noted in Chapter 13, a trade-off involves reducing the importance of one or more qualities of a claim in order to maintain or increase the qualities of another claim, either in response to competing values of different stakeholders, or in order to make the assessment practical. In Chapter 13, we described an example test development situation in which two versions of a test, a multiple-choice test and a composition exam, were being considered to measure students' ability to write effective academic papers. In Table 20.4 on p. 426, we show some of the trade-offs the test developers made in order to reduce the demands on resources in this example test development situation.

Alternative uses of resources	TRADE-OFFS IN TERMS OF QUALITIES OF CLAIMS			
	Claim 1 Consequences	**Claim 2 Decisions**	**Claim 3 Interpretations**	**Claim 4 Records**
Multiple-choice test: more human resources into task writing	Possibly reduced support for beneficial consequences of using the test: teachers may reduce amount of composition writing students do in class	No obvious trade-offs in support for values sensitivity and equitability warrants	Less support for generaliz-ability warrants	Possibly greater support for consistency warrants
Composition exam rated by instructors: more human resources into scoring	Possibly reduced support for beneficial consequences of using the test: teachers may reduce amount of composition writing students do in class	No obvious trade-offs in support for values sensitivity and equitability warrants	Greater support for generaliz-ability warrants	Possibly some-what less support for generaliz-ability warrants

Table 20.4 Trade-offs in terms of support for warrants and qualities of claims as a result of different allocation of resources

SUMMARY

Resource allocation and management is one of the most important activities in the assessment development process, for it allows the test developer to determine whether or not assessment development is feasible. Resources include human resources (the Project Director, assessment writers, scorers, assessment administrators, and clerical support), material resources (space, equipment, assessment materials), and time. Resources can be prioritized and allocated by means of a table of tasks and resources. Tasks can then be sequenced by means of a time line, which specifies for each one their temporal relationship to other tasks in the process. How complex these processes are depends upon the size of the project. For high-stakes assessments, the resource allocation and management may require a great deal of effort.

Assessment development can be carried out either individually or by a team. While individual efforts may be appropriate for the development of low-stakes classroom assessments or for individuals who really prefer working alone, interactive team efforts offer many benefits. The process is frequently more enjoyable and the product is often better thought out. Finally, whenever taking on the development of assessment with wide-ranging consequences, it is important to determine at the outset how much support exists for the project and to decide whether or not one is willing to work with that level of support, or perhaps modify the project.

EXERCISES

1 Recall a test you developed or helped develop. Prepare a table of tasks and resources for your project. Compare your table with those of other classmates.

2 Think of a test you are planning to develop. Prepare a table of tasks and resources for your future project. Discuss possible areas in which anticipated resources may exceed available resources.

3 Prepare a time line for specifying the test development tasks in Exercise 2 above.

4 Think of an assessment you might create for which you can imagine using two different types of test tasks. Briefly, compare the two types of tasks in terms of the trade-offs in terms of qualities of claims, and demands on resources.

5 Recall a time when you developed a test in cooperation with other individuals. What was your experience of working on a team? What were the rewards? What were the problems? How might you avoid such problems in future team efforts?

6 Invite someone who has prepared a "high-stakes" test to tell the class about the process she went through and how resources were allocated to each step in the process. Ask her how she might allocate resources differently if she had another chance to develop the same test.

7 Think of an assessment development process that you were involved in that turned out to be way more resource intensive than you imagined. Explain where your advance thinking went awry, what problems this created for you, how upset you were with yourself, and what you'll do to be sure it never happens again.

21

Using language assessments responsibly

INTRODUCTION

In this book we have presented an approach to the development and use of language assessments that we believe provides a principled basis for enabling test developers and users to deal with the uncertainties in the real world of assessment use. But, as we pointed out in Chapter 13, not everything goes as planned in the real world. When things do go wrong, the questions that arise are, "Where and how did it go wrong?," and "Who is responsible for correcting this, or for getting it right in the first place?" One of the questions we have been asked literally hundreds of time all over the world is some version of the following quote from a recent workshop we conducted for language teachers:

> We are ESL teachers. We have years of experience with our students, their language use needs, and we have created the curriculum to meet these needs. But we are told we have to use tests created by a central authority to make the high-stakes decisions. On the basis of these tests, we have to make high-stakes decisions about whether our students pass or fail. Also, these tests are used by the central authority to make decisions about the effectiveness of our program and funding for our school.
>
> The problem is that these tests are completely out of touch with our curriculum. The students hate the tests and feel like they are unfair. We teachers hate the test too. We feel like we've been put in a situation in which we have to choose between two bad alternatives. Do we teach to the test and abandon the curriculum and types of instruction with which we have years of experience and expertise? Or do we teach our curriculum, have our students perform poorly on the test, and suffer the consequences? We don't have anything to do with test development. The central authority never consults us. And we know that many of the people that wrote these tests have never even been teachers!

This is, in our view, a legitimate complaint that vividly illustrates the strength of emotion that stakeholders can feel when things go wrong with a language assessment.

So, who's responsible for making sure things go right in the development and use of language assessments? Concerns for fairness imbue our entire approach to the process of assessment development and use, and we believe that it is clearly the responsibility of the test developer to provide warrants and backing to stakeholders to demonstrate this for any given assessment. However, if the test developer does this, will he have fully exercised his responsibilities? That is, if he develops an assessment and is able to convince stakeholders that the intended uses are justified, is he finished? Can he consider himself to be a "responsible" test developer? Does his responsibility end with the development of the assessment?

What about assessment use? Who is responsible for assuring that the same considerations of fairness that have informed assessment *development* also inform assessment *use*? In Chapter 10 we discussed the decisions that need to be made in order to promote the intended beneficial consequences. There we discussed the different kinds of decisions that are made, but also the individuals who are responsible for making these, that is, the decision makers, or test users. These are the individuals who are actually using the assessment-based interpretations to make decisions that will have consequences. Therefore, we might well ask what responsibility they have for assuring that these decisions are values sensitive and equitable. What is their responsibility for justifying assessment use, and when, if ever, does this end?

The two key roles in assessment use are those of the test developer and the decision maker. Sometimes these roles are performed by the same person or group of persons. In many situations, particularly in large-scale assessments, the two roles are played by entirely different individuals or groups of individuals. In either situation, questions about who is responsible for what constantly arise. How does the test developer respond when test users complain about the assessment? How do test users respond when the test developer feels that the assessment is not being used appropriately? Where does the responsibility for assessment development end and for assessment use begin? Or can we even draw a clear distinction between these two?

In this chapter we attempt to address the issues involved in using assessments responsibly. These issues arise because language assessments, once they are used to make decisions that have consequences, become part of that real world we discussed in Chapter 13. As long as the assessment is still in development, or even during trialing, when the test developer tinkers with it to improve it, he is able, by and large, to control it. However, once the assessment-based interpretations are actually used for the purpose for which they are intended, the assessment can develop a life of its own. It may be lured out of the well-described domain where the test developer intended it to reside, and other test users may co-opt it for uses beyond those for which it was developed. We begin by reviewing the processes of assessment production and justification, and point out the difficulty of trying to clearly separate these from assessment use. We then use the framework of an AUA to help us think about the responsibilities of test developers and decision makers in the development and use of language assessments. We then discuss the ways in which the different stakeholders interact in the development and use of language assessments in the real world. We provide some actual examples of issues that we've encountered or have been asked about as we've ventured beyond the haven of our ivory tower and the safety of the psychometric test tube to toil in the fields of language assessment practice. Finally, we conclude with a few thoughts that will hopefully lead us onward.

ASSESSMENT DEVELOPMENT AND USE

In Chapter 6, we described the process of assessment development and use as a series of activities that result in decisions and consequences that can be justified to stakeholders. We also described this process as consisting of several stages, with assessment *development* occurring largely in Stages 1–4, and assessment *use* in Stage 5. Assessment *development* consists of two parallel processes that serve two purposes. The assessment justification process, which includes the articulation of an AUA and the collection of backing, is aimed at justifying the assessment for its intended uses. The assessment production process, which proceeds through the stages of planning, design, operationalization, and trialing, is aimed at producing an assessment. These two processes yield two "products" that enable the decision maker to use the assessment for its intended purposes. One product is the assessment itself, which will be used to collect information from test takers that can be used to make interpretations and decisions. The other product is the AUA and its supporting backing, which enables the test users to justify the use of the assessment so as to be accountable to stakeholders.

We have described assessment *use*, on the other hand, as making decisions on the basis of assessment-based interpretations, and the consequences of using the assessment and of the decisions that are made. However, we have also described the entire process of assessment development and use as iterative, with the possibility of making changes in the warrants in the AUA, the Design Statement, the Blueprint, and the assessment itself, at any stage. Thus, information that is collected during assessment use will also be used to provide backing for warrants and to improve the assessment itself. This information is also likely to present the test developer and user with evidence that may weaken some of the warrants of the AUA, so that they will need to go back and reconsider these, make changes in them, or make changes in the Blueprint and the assessment. Consider, for example, an assessment of academic achievement that is intended for making decisions about whether students will pass a course or need to repeat it, but is also intended to have a positive impact on teachers' instruction and students' study habits. If the test developer or test user collects information following the use of the assessment that indicates that neither the teachers nor the students have been affected in the way they teach and study, then they would have to either reconsider this warrant, or make changes to the assessment or the way it is used, such as providing richer feedback to students and teachers that will help them better understand how they can improve their teaching and learning. So is this activity part of assessment development or assessment use? Or consider the typical practice of trialing an assessment with test takers who are similar to those for whom the assessment is intended. The very act of administering the assessment and thus putting it "out there" to other stakeholders besides the test developer will have consequences. Trialing an end-of-course achievement test, for example, might jeopardize the security of the test, so that potential test takers or teachers might focus their learning on the content of the test. Even the trialing of individual test items in operational administrations of computer-delivered tests, as is common practice with many high-stakes assessments, has consequences for test takers. So are these practices part of assessment development or assessment use?

RESPONSIBILITY FOR THE DEVELOPMENT AND USE OF ASSESSMENTS

There are probably lots of ways in which one could conceptualize the responsibilities of test developers and test users in the development and use of language assessments. We believe that our approach provides two different, complementary ways of doing this. One way is to think of the activities that occur in the different stages of assessment development use and consider which of these are the responsibility of the test developer or test user. Another way is to consider their responsibility in articulating the claims and warrants in an AUA to build a "case" that the intended uses of the assessment are justified.

Responsibilities for activities in stages of assessment development and use

One way of thinking about the responsibilities of the test developer and decision maker is to consider the activities in which they engage in assessment development and use, and what these activities entail. Looking at responsibility this way, it might appear that their responsibilities are quite clear: the test developer is responsible for assessment development, while the test user is responsible for assessment use, with some overlap of responsibilities during Stages 1 and 4. This division of responsibilities for the different activities of assessment development and use are illustrated in Figure 21.1 on p. 432.

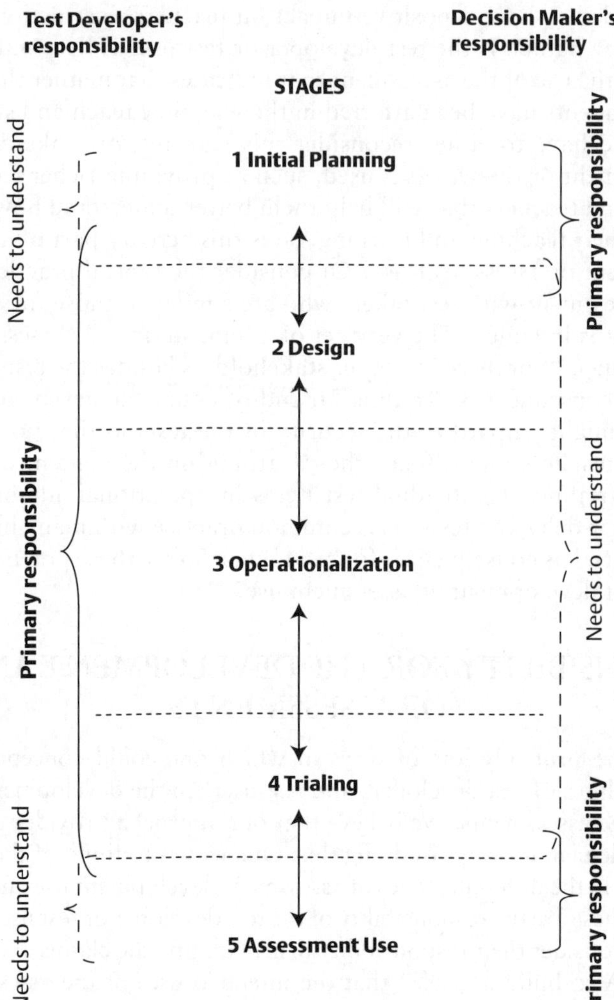

Figure 21.1 Responsibilities of test developer and decision maker at different stages of assessment development and use

This way of viewing the test developer's and test user's responsibilities may appear to be quite reasonable and logical, in that it associates these with what is more or less the temporal flow of activities in assessment development and use. Thus, it could be very useful in providing a starting point for determining areas of responsibility in a given assessment situation. However, this view is limited in that it ignores the responsibilities of the test developer and test user for justification, or for making a "case" that the intended uses of the assessment are justified. That is, this view of responsibility for activities suggests that the test developer really isn't responsible for assessment use, when we've argued throughout the book that the intended uses drive both the articulation of the AUA and the production of the assessment. This "neat" division of labor would also suggest that the decision maker doesn't need to be concerned about kinds and degrees of uncertainty that are inherent in the AUA and its backing, and in the assessment itself. So are the test developer and decision maker both responsible for both assessment development and assessment use? The short answer to this question is, of course, "yes." The long answer, however, is a bit more complicated, because what parts of the AUA the test developer and user are responsible for and the degree to which they are responsible will also vary as a function of the claims and warrants in the AUA, as well as the inevitable uncertainties of interacting with each other and other stakeholders in the real world.

Responsibilities for claims and warrants in the AUA

We've argued that those who are responsible for developing and using an assessment must be able to be held accountable to the stakeholders who will be affected by the assessment and the decisions that are made. We've identified two stakeholders—the test developer and the test user, or decision maker—as being responsible for developing and using an assessment.

We've also argued that a principled basis for being held accountable is the process of justification, which includes an AUA and its supporting backing. The AUA and the evidence that supports it constitute, in effect, the "case" that the test developer and user build to convince themselves and other stakeholders that the intended uses of the assessment are justified.

In our view, building the "case" for assessment development and use is the *shared* responsibility of the test developer and the decision maker. The test developer must understand and be aware of decisions to be made and the intended consequences of assessment use. His primary responsibility, however, is to convince the decision maker that the assessment records are consistent and that the assessment-based interpretations are meaningful, impartial, generalizable, relevant, and sufficient. In addition, he should make a systematic attempt to convince other stakeholders, as well. Convincing these individuals can be accomplished in a number of ways, such as involving them in the process, presenting them with the AUA and its backing, the Design Statement, and perhaps the Blueprint and pointing out the uncertainties in all of these, and soliciting their input. The decision maker, on the other hand, needs to be aware of the uncertainties involved in the AUA, the assessment records and the interpretations. Her primary responsibility, however, is to convince the other stakeholders that the decisions are values sensitive and equitable and that the consequences are beneficial. These areas of responsibility are illustrated in Figure 21.2 on p. 434.

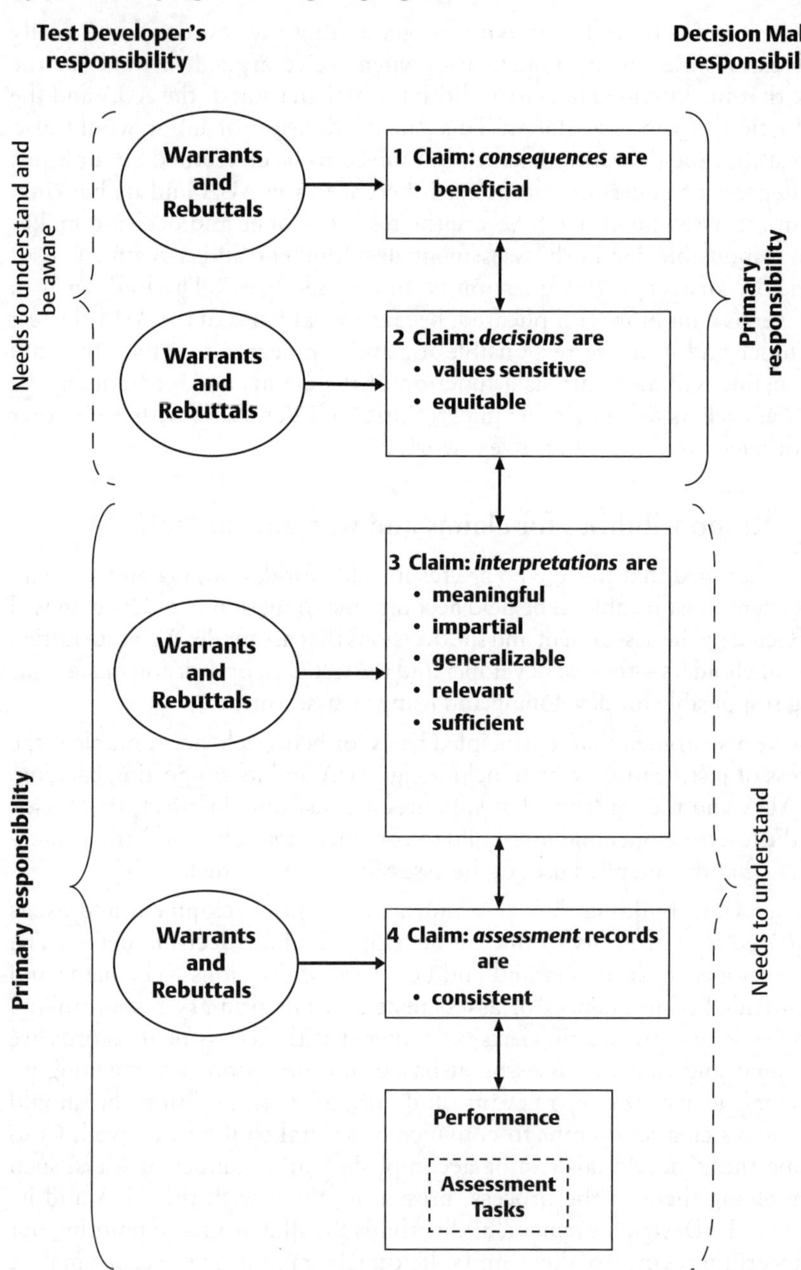

Figure 21.2 Responsibilities of test developer and decision maker in terms of the claims and warrants in an AUA

INTERACTIONS AMONG THE TEST DEVELOPER, TEST USER, AND OTHER STAKEHOLDERS IN THE REAL WORLD

As we've suggested above, the responsibilities of the test developer and decision maker can be described *conceptually* in terms of activities performed at the different stages of assessment development and use, or in terms of their areas of shared responsibility with respect to articulating claims and warrants in an AUA. However, given the ways in which test developers, test users, and other stakeholders can vary in the real world, and the many different ways in which these stakeholders may interact with each other, the specific areas of shared responsibility will most likely vary from one assessment situation to another. Thus, while our conceptualizations of responsibility—stages or AUA—provide a framework for thinking about responsibilities, how these are determined in any given assessment situation in the real world will involve interaction and negotiation among these three stakeholder groups. The extent to which any given assessment results in uses that are justified will depend on the nature and degree of the interactions among the test developer, test user, and other stakeholders. In an ideal world, all three would work closely together in articulating the AUA, in developing the assessment, and in monitoring its use. In the real world, however, as with true love, the course of language assessment development and use does not always run smoothly.

In interacting with the decision maker, the test developer needs to be sensitive to, try to understand, and respond appropriately to the test user's comfort zone and to the amount of information she may want or need. As discussed in Chapters 5 and 13, decision makers will vary in their tolerance for classification decision errors, or what we have called their "comfort zone." This will vary from one decision maker to another in part as a function of different personality characteristics. This will also vary as a function of the decision maker's particular situation, in terms of the resources (e.g., jobs, admission places, or promotions) she has to offer, the kinds of competing demands she has for her time, and the pressures she may be under from managers or supervisors. Finally, the decision maker's comfort zone may vary from time to time, as the availability of resources changes, or as demands on her time and pressures from supervisors change.

The responsible test developer will work with and come to an understanding with the decision maker about which kind of decision errors (false negative or false positive) she considers most serious, and her degree of tolerance for classification errors. He will then work with her to define a performance standard that she is comfortable with. He will also take this into consideration in the way he goes about setting cut scores for assessment-based decisions, asking the decision maker for input and feedback along the way.

Decision makers will also vary in the amount of information about the assessment they either want or need, so that the test developer will need to gauge this in order to make sure that the information he provides to the decision maker will be appropriate for her needs. However, there is a bit of a dilemma here, in terms of how much information to provide. Some decision makers are willing to use the assessment-based interpretations with very little evidence from the test developer. They may be satisfied with a simple list of scores and associated decision recommendations. Is it the responsibility of the test developer to "educate" these individuals about the need for them to be fully informed about the assessment, its areas of and amounts of uncertainty, and the appropriate uses of the assessment-based interpretations? Other decision makers, on the other hand, when given some information, will ask for more, and will want to use this to help them better understand the uncertainties involved in using the assessment to make decisions.

Consider, for example, college admissions officers who may use scores from a standardized test of academic achievement or aptitude to make decisions about which applicants to admit. Many such individuals will take the time and effort to read the technical manuals that describe the procedures used to develop the test, along with information of reliability, validity, and the appropriate uses of these scores. Some may even recognize the need for them to set local standards and cut scores for admissions decisions. On the other hand, there may be some admissions officers who simply want a list of test scores with associated recommendations, such as "Students below this score are likely to have serious difficulty in taking academic classes taught in English," and neither want nor are able to use more detailed information about the assessment or the uncertainties in using it to make admissions decisions.

In interacting with other stakeholders, both the test developer and the test user need to be sensitive to and try to understand stakeholders' different perceptions of and responses to the decisions that are made and the use of an assessment. These differing perceptions may reflect differing sets of values, or they may be idiosyncratic to individuals or individual stakeholder groups. Some stakeholders may question whether a decision should be made at all, or whether this should be made on the basis of an assessment. Some will challenge the decision, while others will accept it. Stakeholders may also differ in their levels of tolerance for uncertainty. Thus some stakeholders may be convinced by the evidence presented by the test developer, while others may need more or different kinds of evidence to be convinced. Stakeholders will also differ in their levels of knowledge of and interest in the assessment. Some stakeholders will be very well informed about and interested in the uses of assessments in general, and may be able to evaluate the AUA and its backing to judge for themselves the degree to which they believe the use of the assessment is justified. Other stakeholders may not be as knowledgeable, but may want to become better informed. And then there will always be some stakeholders who will be uninformed and not interested in becoming more knowledgeable about the assessment. Finally, stakeholders' perceptions of the assessment not only vary, but they can change over time, for better or worse.

There is also the issue of what stakeholders will need in order to be convinced that the intended use of the assessment is justified. In order to determine this, the test developer and decision maker will need to ask the question "How much evidence is needed to convince the relevant stakeholders?" Again, different stakeholders are likely to be convinced by different kinds and amounts of information. Some, as with decision makers, will accept virtually any assessment and decision virtually without question, while others may take serious action, such as suing the test developer and decision maker in a court of law. Thus, the responsible test developer or decision maker will make every effort to solicit stakeholders' input and feedback throughout the entire process of assessment development and use. If the test developer and test user involve the other stakeholders in assessment development, it is less likely that there will be problems when the assessment is used.

The quotation from the ESL teacher at the beginning of this chapter provides an example of a situation in which the test developer or decision maker has not interacted sufficiently with stakeholders. We think that these teachers have accurately identified the source of the problem: the test developers have not consulted with major stakeholders affected by the consequences of test use and the decisions made on the basis of test scores. Unfortunately, we do not see an easy "solution" to the problem, one that would allow the continued use of the tests "as is." The only solution we can suggest in situations like this is to do one's best to come up with a strategy for increasing communication between the test developers and major stakeholders. The specifics of how one goes about doing this will depend upon the ways in which the culture deals with problematic situations, but we think that the focus of the solution should be on creating a climate for more communication between test developers and stakeholders.

Given these differing situations and differing needs of stakeholders, we might well ask how much information is sufficient. Is it sufficient for the test developer to fully inform stakeholders of the claims and warrants in the AUA, along with the attendant uncertainties, so as to convince them that the intended uses of the assessment are justified? What about the stakeholders we've mentioned above who will accept the uses of the assessment without question, or on the basis of very little evidence? Is it the test developer's responsibility to "educate" these stakeholders to be better informed and more discerning in their acceptance of the assessment? Is it his responsibility to motivate stakeholders to become better informed and involved in the uses of the assessment?

ONWARD

In this book we have presented what we think is a principled approach to developing and using language assessments. The primary motivation behind this approach is the axiom that test developers and test users need to be accountable to stakeholders. We also recognize that language assessment development and use take place in a real world that is full of uncertainties and conflicts, and that is constantly changing. Thus, we have discussed ways in which our approach can help test developers and test users, if not to resolve the problems that the real world throws at them, at least to think about these in a systematic way.

We have offered no solutions to specific assessment issues, no recipes, and no concrete answers. Rather, we believe that we have provided an approach to assessment development and use that individual test developers and test users can systematically tailor to their own specific assessment situations. Assessment development and use, and the process of justification, are necessarily local. Each AUA and the backing that is collected to support it will be unique to a particular assessment situation. Thus, what we have presented is not a "theory" of test development and use, but rather an approach that enables test developers and test users to articulate "local theories," if you will, to guide their own development and use.

We believe that our approach also offers a way of thinking about broader issues in language assessment. However, we have only begun to address questions such as "What does it mean to be a 'responsible assessment user'?," "What constitutes 'responsible assessment use'?," "Who is responsible for 'responsible assessment use?'," and "Is there a limit to this responsibility?" These are questions that are of considerable interest to the field of language testing in general, and ones that language testers have been grappling with for several years. Indeed these concerns have been articulated in the Codes of Ethics and Guidelines for Practice of the International Language Testing Association (ILTA),[1] as well as in those of regional language testing associations[2] and language testing organizations.[3]

An equally pertinent question is "What does it mean to be assessment literate?" In the real world, many stakeholders, especially decision makers, often have little or no knowledge and understanding about language assessment, or no "assessment literacy," which can be a major reason why assessment development and use can go wrong (Taylor 2009). As Taylor has pointed out, this is another area in which increasing professionalism in the field of language testing, along with greater dissemination of codes of practice to decision makers and other consumers of language assessments, can improve the general quality of language assessment use in the real world.

Related to this is the question we address in the very first chapter of this book, "What does it mean to be competent in language assessment?" We pointed out that many individuals who are, in fact, helping schools and institutions develop and use language assessments do not have adequate "competence in language assessment" to be performing this function professionally. In that chapter we stated that being "competent in language assessment" means being able to demonstrate to stakeholders that the intended uses of their assessments are justified.

These are all important and pressing issues. These questions will also, no doubt, continue to be asked far into the future. It is our hope that our approach may point some directions for specific research and may help the field address some of these questions. More importantly, in our view, these issues and questions are relevant to the development, use, and justification of any particular assessment, because they force us, as test developers and users, to confront the uncertainties of the real world with what little certainty we believe we have found in the process of justifying that assessment.

EXERCISES

1 Recall an assessment use situation with which you are familiar. What role(s) did you play? Test developer? Decision maker? Both? How did you exercise your responsibilities in either or both of the roles? Now that you are older and wiser, how might your actions be different?

2 Look over Project 12 (conflicting AUAs at http://www.oup.com/LAIP). Have you ever found yourself in such a situation, or do you know someone who has? What do you think would be responsible behaviour on the part of the assessment developers and users? In the cosmic scheme of things, how likely do you think this is to happen?

3 Recall a situation in which you have developed or used a test in which there was insufficient interaction among the test developers, the test users, and other stakeholders in the real world and the test ended up not being used responsibly. What were the negative consequences of this? What might have been done to elicit more interaction from the beginning that might have led to more responsible use?

4 Recall how you thought about language assessment before you picked up this book. Think about the long, Zen-like path you have followed as you worked your way through its chapters. How has your internal world changed? In what ways are you a better person as a result? Or, are you ready to find another occupation?

5 OK! So now you've stroked your way through the smooth waters of LAIP, and you're ready to take the plunge into the unpredictable waters of the Real World. How will you navigate the rapids? What will you do when you encounter a whirlpool? How will you handle the tsunamis that threaten to pound you to the bottom? How might the pearls of wisdom in this book help you navigate the waters from whence they came? Do you think the writers have gone off the deep end? If so, will they find more pearls or will they have rapture of the deep and reach enlightenment?

NOTES

1 The ILTA *Code of Ethics* and *Guidelines for Practice* can be found at: http://www.iltaonline.com/index.php?option=com_content&view=article&id=57&Item id=47 and http://www.iltaonline.com/index.php?option=com_content&view= article&id=122&Itemid=133

2 Codes of practice for other language assessment associations and language testing organizations can be found at the following web pages: www.alte.org/cop/index.php (ALTE, The Association of Language Testers in Europe); www.ealta.eu.org/guidelines.htm (EALTA, The European Association for Language Testing and Assessment); www.avis.ne.jp/~youichi/COP.html (JLTA, the Japan Language Testing Association).

3 See, for example, Educational Testing Service 2002, 2003; Cambridge ESOL and Fairness, http://www.cambridge-efl.org/.

Project 1

Kindergarten ELL speaking and writing assessment in support of instruction and learning

(Adapted from Frey and Fisher 2003)

SETTING

The setting for this Project is several kindergarten classes in a large urban elementary school with about 1,500 students who come from a wide variety of cultures and backgrounds; most are English Language Learners (ELLs) with a wide variety of first languages. The teacher of these classes would like to collect information about students' performance that will help guide his instructional practice, that is, to help him set the pace of instruction for these students, and to help him improve his instruction for the future. He believes that continuous assessment as part of regular learning activities will provide the best opportunity for him to collect the information he needs. In addition, such assessment will not be intrusive, and will not require additional time. In this example, the classroom teacher is both the test developer and test user, or decision maker.

INITIAL PLANNING QUESTIONS AND ANSWERS

1 What beneficial consequences does the teacher want to happen? Who are the stakeholders? Who will be directly affected by the use of this assessment?

(a) Who are the intended test takers, and how will they be affected?

The test takers are the kindergarten students, who are English Language Learners with varied native languages and cultures and of beginning level ESL proficiency. Students will be positively motivated by the feedback the teacher provides.

(b) Who else will be affected, and how will they be affected?

(i) *The kindergarten teacher; his instruction may become more effective.*

(ii) *Possibly other kindergarten teachers, who may adopt the teacher's assessment and teaching methods.*

(iii) *Possibly the First Grade teachers, who will teach his students the following year.*

2 What specific decisions does the teacher need to make to help promote the intended consequences?
Formative decisions: The teacher will use the results of the assessment to pace his own instruction with this class of students, as well as to make adjustments in the way he conducts this instructional activity in the future.

3 What does the teacher need to know about students' language ability in order to make the intended decisions?
The teacher needs to collect information about how well students can perform on a particular set of speaking and writing activities that are related to learning objectives that are specified in the syllabus.

4 What sources does he have for obtaining this information?
(a) *Implicit (continuous, on-going, dynamic) assessments.* (See Chapter 2 for a discussion of this.)
(b) *Explicit assessments.* (See Chapter 2 for a discussion of this.)

5 Does he need to use an assessment to obtain this information? *Yes, an informal assessment.*

6 Is an existing assessment available?
(a) *Is an existing assessment available that provides the information the teacher needs for the decisions he needs to make? No*
(Questions 6b–6d are not relevant, because the answer to 6a is "no".)

7 Does the teacher need to develop his own assessment? *Yes*
(a) How will the teacher assure that the intended uses (i.e., decisions and consequences) of the assessment can be justified with an AUA and backing?
The teacher is familiar with justification procedures and will construct an AUA and collect backing at a level of detail suitable for this low-stakes assessment. The teacher will observe an interactive writing activity that is widely known and used; the observation procedure will be followed consistently for all test taker groups, and from one class to the next; only the specific content will vary from lesson to lesson. The teacher will make every effort to follow the same observation procedures for all occasions, and for all his classes. An observation checklist will include well-specified categories and areas to be assessed, and the teacher is very familiar with these.
(b) What resources will he need for the development and use of the assessment (including justifying the intended uses of the assessment)?
The teacher's own time and efforts in developing the observation checklist, which can be developed as part of his lesson planning. No additional class time will be needed for the observation and assessment.

(c) What resources does the teacher have? *His own time and effort; class time, in addition to his own experience and knowledge of the syllabus and the test-takers.*

As a result of this initial planning, the teacher decides to develop his own classroom assessment in the form of assessment activities and an observation checklist (see below).

ASSESSMENT USE ARGUMENT

Consequences

Claim 1: The consequences of using the observation checklist and of the formative decisions that the teacher makes to improve his instruction are beneficial to the students (test takers), the kindergarten teacher, and other teachers who will teach these students in first grade.

Stakeholders

i ELL students in the kindergarten class
ii the kindergarten teacher
iii other teachers who will teach these students.

Warrants, consequences of using the checklist

A1 The consequences of using the observation checklist that are specific to the students (test takers), the kindergarten teacher, and other teachers who will teach these.

A2 The checklist that the teacher completes for each student is kept confidential.

A3 The information in the checklist that may help the students in their learning is presented in ways that are clear and understandable to his students.

A4 Not needed, because the teacher does not distribute his checklists to anyone else, including the students.

A5 The use of the checklist will help the teacher improve his instructional practice and will facilitate effective learning by his students.

Warrants, consequences of the decisions that are made

B1 The consequences of the kindergarten teacher's changes in his instructional practice will be beneficial to the teacher.

B2 The consequences of the kindergarten teacher's changes in his instructional practice will be beneficial for his students.

B3 The consequences of the teacher's changes in his instructional practice, and of the students learning pre-literacy skills, will be beneficial for the teachers in first grade, who will teach these students to read.

Rebuttal: None. Students are not classified on the basis of test results. The only decisions made are to modify instruction on the basis of feedback from formative assessment.

Decisions

Claim 2: The formative decisions that are made in support of instruction and learning take into consideration existing educational and societal values and relevant legal requirements and school regulations and are equitable for the kindergarten students. These decisions will be made by the classroom teacher.

Warrants: values sensitivity

A1 Relevant educational values of the kindergarten teacher and his colleagues, and school regulations are carefully considered in the decisions to modify instruction as needed.

A2 Since students are not classified on the basis of this assessment, this warrant is not needed.

A3 Since students are not classified on the basis of this assessment, and the information the teacher obtains from the assessment is not in the form of scores, this warrant is not needed.

Warrants: equitability

B1 The primary decisions to be made are instructional ones, by the teacher, and students are not classified into groups, so this warrant does not apply.

B2 Because decisions are made only about the learning and teaching tasks the instructor uses, and not about specific students, this warrant is not needed.

B3 No decisions are made involving achievement and certification. The decisions are only formative decisions that are made in support of instruction and learning. Therefore, this warrant is not needed.

Interpretations

Claim 3: The interpretations about the students' knowledge of letter formation and concepts of print, and their oral language, are **meaningful** with respect to the teaching syllabus and the teaching/learning activities in the class, **generalizable** to subsequent learning activities in the class, and **relevant** to and **sufficient** for the formative decisions that are to be made.

Warrants: meaningfulness

A1 The constructs to be assessed include (a) letter formation, (b) concepts of print, and (c) oral language. These construct definitions are based on the teaching syllabus and clearly distinguish the constructs from other related constructs, such as knowledge of numbers.

A2 The assessment task specifications clearly specify that the instructor will observe performance of selected students during the interactive writing activity, and will record this in a checklist, from which the instructor can make interpretations about letter formation, concepts of print, and oral language.

A3 Not needed, because the assessment is not administered. Performance on an instructional task is simply observed.

A4 The observation checklist and procedures for using it focus on letter formation, concepts of print, and oral language. These aspects of the performance are identical to the knowledge component of the learning objectives for this lesson in the syllabus.

A5 The assessment tasks engage the abilities "knowledge of (a) letter formation, (b) concepts of print, and (c) oral language."

A6 The instructor's notes on student performance on instructional tasks are interpreted as indicators of "knowledge of (a) letter formation, (b) concepts of print, and (c) oral language."

A7 The teacher provides informal verbal feedback to students in terms they will understand.

Warrants: impartiality

B1 The interactive writing activity is a task that the teacher uses for instruction, and does not include response formats or content that may either favor or disfavor some kindergarten students.

B2 The interactive writing activity does not include content that may be offensive to some kindergarten students.

B3 This warrant is not needed because the assessment record is not made available to the test takers.

B4 Kindergarten students are treated impartially while the teacher observes their performance on the interactive writing activity.

a–c Not needed. Only minimal documentation is required for this very low-stakes assessment, and the teacher's reputation for fair concern for his students and fair play will suffice.

B5 Interpretations of the test takers' "knowledge of (a) letter formation, (b) concepts of print, and their oral language" are equally meaningful across students from different linguistic/ethnic groups.

Warrants: generalizability

C1 The assessment tasks are the same as the TLU tasks, i.e., the instructional tasks.

C2 The way the assessment record is obtained is the same for the assessment tasks and instructional tasks.

Warrant: relevance

D Interpretations about (a) letter formation, (b) concepts of print, and (c) oral language provide information that is relevant to the teacher's decisions about instruction.

Warrant: sufficiency

E Interpretations about (a) letter formation, (b) concepts of print, and (c) oral language provide enough information for the teacher to make decisions about instruction.

Assessment records

Claim 4: The teacher's notes in his observation checklist are consistent across different lessons and different students, and across different classes of students.

Warrants: consistency

1 The teacher elicits students' performance consistently across different administrations of the interactive writing task, across different sections of the class, for all students.
2 Procedures for recording students' performances in the checklist are well specified and are adhered to.

Since the teacher does not assign scores, and since he is the only person who produces assessment reports, Warrants 3–9 are not relevant in the Kindergarten example.

10 The teacher's notes on his observation sheet and checklist are consistent across different groups of students and across different classes.

BACKING FROM PROCEDURES AND DOCUMENTATION

Since these are discussed in detail in the relevant Chapters 9–12 in the book, these are not repeated here.

DESIGN STATEMENT

1 Description of the test takers and other stakeholders: kindergarten students in teacher's class.
2 Intended beneficial consequences: teacher will modify instruction and students will learn more effectively as a result.
3 Descriptions of the decisions to be made and of the decision makers (Claim 2): teacher makes a variety of formative decisions to modify instruction.
4 The relative seriousness of classification errors, policy-level decisions about standards, the standards themselves (Claim 2, Warrants A2 and A3): no classification decisions are made.

5 Definitions of the constructs: knowledge of letter formation and concepts of print, oral language ability.
6 Tasks selected as a basis for developing assessment tasks: instructional activities that require students to communicate orally and write words and phrases on board.
7 Description of the characteristics of TLU tasks that have been selected as a basis for assessment tasks: see instructions for instructional activities.
8 Plan for collecting feedback and backing: teacher observes student performance on instructional activity to determine how the activity might be modified in the future to increase its effectiveness as an instructional/assessment task.
9 Plan for acquiring, allocating, and managing resources: not needed. Teacher knows how much time it will take to carry out the instructional/assessment activity. The only materials needed are the rubric sheets.

Blueprint

1 Assessment specifications
  (a) Number of parts: 2
    (i) Students discuss questions about new classroom aquarium among themselves.
    (ii) Students write key words and phrases for questions on the board.
  (b) Number of tasks per part: 1
  (c) Sequence of parts and tasks: as indicated above
  (d) Relative importance of parts and tasks: not specified in advance. Teacher uses his judgment to decide how to use the information from each part of the assessment to modify instruction
  (e) Time allotment for each part and overall: sufficient for students to complete instructional activities that are observed in this assessment
  (f) Instructions: teacher explains what students need to know about the activity (as described below) in appropriate teacher talk
    (i) The teacher begins by saying that a surprise visitor will be coming to class the next day to answer questions about the new classroom aquarium. Students discuss this among themselves, coming up with questions they would like to ask the visitor. The teacher has a chart on the board, and calls on individual students to write key words and phrases for questions on the board. Each student in the class has an individual white board on which they write the key words and phrases as they are written on the board at the front of the room.
2 Task specifications
  (a) Constructs to be assessed: knowledge of letter formation and concepts of print, oral language ability
  (b) Characteristics of the setting: kindergarten classroom
  (c) Characteristics of input, expected response, and relationship between input and responses: see instructions above

(d) Procedures for recording test takers' performance: check level of performance on observation checklist
(e) Instructions for responding to the assessment tasks: see instructions above.

3 Procedures for setting cut scores and making decisions
(a) No decisions are made about students
(b) Teacher uses information on rubric to help him improve instruction

4 Procedures and formats for reporting assessment records, interpretations and decisions
(a) Assessment records are not reported.

5 Procedures for administering the assessment
(a) See instructions above.

EXAMPLE ASSESSMENT TASK

Assessment activities: The assessment takes place as part of an interactive group writing activity in a "Writing Corner" of the classroom. The teacher begins by saying that a surprise visitor will be coming to class the next day to answer questions about the new classroom aquarium. Students discuss this among themselves, coming up with questions they would like to ask the visitor. The teacher has a chart on the board, and calls on individual students to write key words and phrases for questions on the board. Each student in the class has an individual white board on which they write the key words and phrases as they are written on the board at the front of the room.

Evaluation procedures: The teacher identifies several students to observe each day for the purpose of assessing their progress in the three areas above (letter formation, concepts of print, and oral language). The teacher observes the activities of several students during each class period, recording their performance in the observation checklist (below) to assess their performance.

The areas of ability to be assessed are listed in the first column in the observation checklist. (Table P1.1 on p. 448) The four categories of assessment are defined as follows:

Only in the most general of ways. "Proficient" means that. "Attempted" means that the child used the language, but it was not free from error (either syntactically or semantically). "Not evidenced" means that. "Not available" means that.

- Proficient: the language used is syntactically and semantically correct.
- Attempted: the child used the language, but it was not free from error (either syntactically or semantically).
- Not evidenced: there were opportunities to use the language, but the child did not use it.
- Not available: no opportunity presented for the child to use the language.

Student Name: ______ **Date:** ______ **Writing Topic:** ______				
	Proficient	*Attempted*	*Not Evidenced*	*Not Available*
Letter Formations (Record letters)				
Concepts of Print				
Spelling				
Directionality				
Capitals				
Oral Language				
Uses language to represent ideas				
Grammatically correct				
Predicts and recalls				
Uses accurate vocabulary				
Interacts with peers				
On topic				
Inquires				

Table P1.1 Observation checklist (Frey and Fisher 2003: 65)

COLLECTION OF BACKING FROM TRIAL AND USE

In a low-stakes assessment such as this, the primary user of the AUA is the teacher himself. He will observe how well the assessment seems to be helping make the decisions to modify instruction but will not need to collect systematic backing for an AUA. However, his understanding of the claims and warrants in the AUA will inform the notes he makes during assessment use. For example, he may note that the concepts of print in the observation checklist might need to be expanded to provide the information he feels are necessary to make decisions to modify instruction. If so, this information would be relevant backing for Claim 3, Sufficiency Warrant E. However, systematically collecting backing for every warrant in the AUA would be overkill and make excessive demands on the teacher's time for a low-stakes assessment of this type.

Frey, N. and **D. Fisher.** 2003. 'Linking assessments with instruction in a multilingual elementary school' in C. A. Coombe and N. J. Hubley (eds.). *Assessment Practices* (pp. 63–74). Alexandria, VA: Teachers of English to Speakers of Other Languages.

Project 2
University ESL reading test for making placement/exemption decisions

SETTING

The director of an ESL program at a large research university in which English is the medium of instruction needs to collect information to make decisions about placing non-native English speaking students who have been admitted to the university into an ESL reading course, or exempting them from study in these courses. For the past several years, she has been using a fairly traditional multiple-choice reading test, administered in a paper and pencil format, for collecting this information. However, the costs of producing copies of the test, of administering it to large groups of students, and of producing test reports and sending these to the students and university administrators have escalated at a time when the university is facing a budget crisis. She is thus under pressure from the administration to find a way to cut the costs of administering this test. In addition, the teachers in the ESL reading course have become increasingly dissatisfied with the test itself. They feel that the test items do not reflect what students actually do in their academic reading courses, and they believe the test does not really measure what students need in order to successfully complete these courses.

Based on their many years of experience, the ESL director, the ESL reading teachers, and the academic course teachers agree that placing students who need developmental instruction in English academic reading into an ESL reading course greatly facilitates their academic coursework and reduces their time to degree. They also know that exempting students who do not need additional instruction will conserve resources for both teachers and students. Finally, they all agree that the most effective way to obtain the information they need is to give students a placement test. Thus, the decision is not to eliminate the use of a test, but whether to adapt an existing one or develop a new one.

Since the decisions the ESL Program Director needs to make are relatively high stakes, she is willing to allocate considerable resources for assessment development, if it is determined that this is needed. As in the previous Project, the "test developer" consists of a team of individuals. In this example, the team includes the ESL Program Director and ESL instructors, with all members of the team assuming a collective responsibility for the test development, use, and justification. While the ESL Program Director is the decision maker, the ESL instructors and academic course instructors can also be considered to be test users.

INITIAL PLANNING QUESTIONS AND ANSWERS

1 What beneficial consequences does the ESL Program Director want to happen? Who are the stakeholders? Who will be directly affected by the use of the assessment?

(a) Who are the intended test takers? How will they be affected?

Intended test takers: non-native English speaking students. ESL reading instruction will be appropriate to students' level of reading and, therefore, more effective and less frustrating; students who take the ESL reading course will have improved chances of succeeding in their academic courses.

(b) Who else will be affected? How will they be affected?

(i) *ESL course instructors: more knowledge of students' reading ability will enable instructors to better tailor their instruction appropriately; their teaching will be more effective and they will feel more rewarded when they teach classes with students at about the same level of ability.*

(ii) *ESL Program Director: fewer student complaints about inappropriate instruction or about their to inability to pass reading courses; fewer complaints from ESL teachers about difficulty in teaching to students of widely varying abilities.*

(iii) *Instructors in academic courses: L2 students will be better able to handle the reading demands of academic courses.*

2 What specific decisions does the ESL Program Director need to make to help promote the intended consequences?

Decisions to place non-native English speaking students into ESL reading classes or exempt them from these classes.

3 What do we need to know about the test takers' language ability in order to make the intended decisions?

The Program Director needs to collect information about students' reading ability relevant to making the decisions listed above. Consultation with the teachers in the program indicates the specific information needed is the ability to recognize the rhetorical structure of academic reading passages.

4 What sources could the ESL Program Director use or are available for obtaining this information?

(a) *Student self-placements into or exemptions from the program.*

(b) *Existing scores from the standardized tests of EFL that the university requires international students applying for admission to the university to provide.*

(c) *Develop her own assessment.*

5 Does the ESL Program Director need to use an assessment to obtain this information?

Yes. Years of experience on the part of the ESL Program Director and the teachers in the program indicate that self-assessments are not likely to provide the needed information. Some students may over-report their language ability in order to avoid having to take ESL classes. Others may under-report it in order to take courses they don't need, in order to raise their Grade Point Averages (GPAs).

6 Is an existing assessment available?

Yes. The Test of English as a Foreign Language (TOEFL) or the International English Language Testing System (IELTS), either of which is required of all international students applying to the university. (The ESL Program Director searched the information available on the web pages for these two tests. She also consulted with the University Admissions Office to see if this information would be available for all students.)

(a) Does either of these tests provide the information needed for the decisions the ESL Program Director needs to make?

No. Although both the TOEFL and IELTS include sections that test reading, neither of these tests focuses on the specific area of language ability that the stakeholders have identified.

(b) Are the assessments appropriate for the intended test takers? *Yes.*

(c) Do the assessment tasks correspond to TLU tasks?

Not closely. Tasks on these tests do not involve the same language use activities, such as outlining, as do tasks in the TLU domain.

(d) Do the test developers provide evidence justifying our intended uses of the assessments?

No. These tests are intended primarily for making admissions decisions and not placement decisions.

(e) Can we afford it?

Yes. Most L2 speakers of English will already have taken one of these tests.

7 Does the program need to develop its own assessment? *Yes.*

(a) How will the ESL Program Director assure that the intended uses (i.e., decisions and consequences) of the assessment can be justified with an AUA and backing?

The ESL Program Director will assign this task to the Visiting Assistant Professor with expertise in language assessment, who will, in turn, assign the task of producing portions of the AUA and backing to Ph.D. students on the test development committee and will oversee their work. The Visiting Assistant Professor will put a template on line in which members of the committee can enter their justification and review material entered by other members of the committee. Thus, an evolving document will be continually available to all members of the committee.

(b) What resources will the Program Director need for the development and use of the assessment (including justifying the intended uses of the assessment)?

(i) *Human: (Administrator to direct and monitor the progress of the test development effort, people with expertise in reading to provide input into the selection of reading passages, creation of test tasks, the creation and implementation of the scoring procedures; someone with expertise in language assessment to provide guidance in the development of the speaking tasks and scoring procedures, and with analyses of the test results; project staff; support staff).*

(ii) *Material: (e.g., copies of academic reading texts, paper, personal computers, statistical analysis software, space for administering the reading test).*

(iii) *Time: Two years for the development of the test; one hour per student for administering the test, several hours for scoring the test and reporting the results to test takers and relevant university officials; one month for analyzing data and improving the test.*

(c) What resources does the program have or is able to obtain?

(i) *Human: The instructors in the ESL program will serve as members of the test development team. The ESL Director will use funds from the Dean to hire a full-time Visiting Assistant Professor with expertise in language assessment to oversee the development of the test, as well as several Ph.D. students in language testing as part-time Research Assistants.*

(ii) *Material: Some will be made available from the ESL program, and some will be purchased from the grant from the Dean. The Department of Applied Linguistics will provide space for the test development team to meet, and space for administering the test can be scheduled regularly with the campus Office of Space Management.*

(iii) *Time: The ESL Director has received a grant from the Dean for two years for developing and administering this placement test. The Chair of the Department of Applied Linguistics has also made a commitment of clerical support and space for an indefinite period of time.*

Discussion

Because of the cost of personnel for administering the placement test, including proctors for the large lecture rooms in which it is administered, the ESL Program Director is looking for ways to reduce this expense. In addition, she needs to find a way to cut the costs of reproducing copies of the test and of printing test reports. During the initial planning it thus becomes clear to the ESL director and instructors that administering the placement test in a paper and pencil format to large groups of test takers will no longer be feasible, given the increased costs of this and the reduced resources that are available. One way that is suggested to make the test feasible is to administer it via computers. Therefore, as a result of this planning, the Program Director decides to develop a new computer-administered placement test for the program.

Having decided to go ahead with assessment development, the test developers now need to continue the process of articulating an AUA.

ASSESSMENT USE ARGUMENT

Consequences

Claim 1: The consequences of using the reading assessment and of the placement/exemption decisions that are made are beneficial to the test takers, teachers in the ESL reading courses, the ESL Program Director, and instructors in academic courses at the university who will encounter ESL students in their classes.

Warrants, consequences of using the ESL reading test

A1 The consequences of using the outline reading test that are specific to the test takers, teachers in the ESL reading courses, the ESL Program Director, and instructors in academic courses at the university who will encounter ESL students in their classes will be beneficial.

A2 Assessment reports, which include (1) the scores from the outline reading test and (2) the placement decisions made on the basis of them, are treated confidentially.

A3 Assessment reports, which include (1) the scores from the outline reading test and (2) the placement decisions made on the basis of them are presented in ways that are clear and understandable to all the test takers.

A4 The ESL Program Director distributes the assessment reports to test takers and authorized university faculty and officials in time for them to be used for the intended decisions.

A5 Use of the outline reading test helps promote good instructional practice and effective learning by linking the assessment task specifications to one of the performance objectives in the ESL reading course into which students are placed.

Warrants, consequences of the decisions that are made

B1 The consequences of the placement and exemption decisions that are made will be beneficial for the students.

B2 The consequences of the placement and exemption decisions that are made will be beneficial for the teachers in the ESL reading course.

B3 The consequences of the placement and exemption decisions that are made will be beneficial for the teachers in academic university courses.

B4 The consequences of the placement and exemption decisions that are made will be beneficial for the ESL program administrator.

Rebuttal: The consequences of false positive and false negative classification errors will be different, as follows:

1 *False positive classification errors.* Exempting students from the ESL reading course who actually need the course will have detrimental consequences for students because they will feel overwhelmed, frustrated, may get low grades in their academic courses, and may even be dropped from the university. Furthermore, even though these students may have to struggle in their academic courses, they may not report this, and so there is little chance of helping them. Instructors in academic courses may also feel frustrated because their students are not able to keep up with the reading assignments. These instructors may complain to the ESL program administrator who will have to deal with complaints. In this example, therefore, false positive classification errors are regarded as very serious.
2 *False negative classification errors.* Placing students in the ESL reading course who do not need it will have detrimental consequences for students. Students may feel bored with the coursework and resent what they may perceive as time and money wasted for the course. They may also suffer because taking an ESL class prevents them from taking an additional academic course, which may delay their progress toward their degree. In this example, therefore, false negative classification errors are regarded as moderately serious.

Possible ways of mitigating the detrimental consequences of decision classification errors if they occur

1 *False positive classification errors.* Teachers in regular university courses will be notified of the existence of the ESL reading courses and asked to be alert for students who seem to be struggling with the reading assignments. They will be asked to advise students to consider taking the ESL reading course even though they were exempted from it on the basis of the ESL reading test.
2 *False negative classification errors.* ESL reading teachers will be alerted to be on the lookout for misplaced students, to collect additional information about the students' reading ability during the first week of class, and to make recommendations to the Program Director for exempting those students who they feel do not need the class.

Decisions

Claim 2: The decisions to place or exempt students from the ESL reading course reflect relevant existing educational and societal values and relevant university regulations and are equitable for those students who are placed or exempted. These decisions will be made by the ESL Program Director. The decisions she makes are whether new international students need to take an ESL reading course or can be exempted from this. The individuals affected by these decisions include the test takers, teachers in the ESL reading course, teachers in regular academic university courses in which the test takers are students, and the ESL program administrator.

The decisions, stakeholders affected by decisions, and individuals responsible for making the decisions are provided in Table P2.1 below.

Decision	Stakeholders who will be affected by the decision	Individuals(s) responsible for making the decision
Place students in ESL reading course	Students, instructors in ESL reading course, teachers in students' academic courses	ESL Program Director
Exempt students from ESL reading course	Students, instructors in ESL reading course, teachers in students' academic courses	ESL Program Director
Adjust instruction in ESL reading course	Instructors in ESL reading course, students in ESL reading course	Instructors in ESL reading course

Table P2.1 The decisions, stakeholders affected by decisions, and individuals responsible for making the decisions

Warrants: values sensitivity

A1 Relevant educational values of the university community and legal requirements of the university itself as an institution are carefully considered in the placement and exemption decisions that are made.

A2 Existing educational values of the ESL teachers and academic instructors, as well as relevant university regulations, are carefully considered in determining the relative seriousness of false positive and false negative classification errors.

A3 Cut scores are set relatively high so as to minimize the most serious classification errors, that is, false positives.

(a) *Relative seriousness of classification decision errors*: False positive classification errors are more serious than false negative ones.

(b) *Policy-level procedures for setting standards*: The standard for exemption from the ESL reading course was set by the ESL Course Director in consultation with ESL reading course instructors and academic course instructors.

(c) *Standard for exemption from the ESL reading course*: Students must demonstrate that they have sufficient knowledge of multilevel rhetorical organization of introductory academic texts to enable them to successfully participate in introductory level academic courses.

Warrants: equitability

B1 The same cut score is used to classify all students taking the ESL Outline Reading Test, and no other considerations are used.

B2 Test takers, ESL reading teachers, and other individuals within the university community are fully informed about how the decision will be made and whether decisions are actually made in the way described to them.

B2 No decisions are made involving achievement or certification. The only decisions made are "placed" or "exempt." Therefore, this warrant is not needed.

Interpretations

Claim 3: The interpretations about the students' "knowledge of multilevel rhetorical organization of written texts" are **meaningful** in terms of an analysis of texts used in introductory level academic university courses, **impartial** to all groups of test takers, **generalizable** to readings tasks in texts used in introductory level university courses, and **relevant** to and **sufficient** for the placement decisions that are to be made.

Warrants: meaningfulness

A1 The interpretations about the students' "knowledge of multilevel rhetorical organization of written texts" are meaningful with respect to introductory level academic university courses, generalizable to introductory level academic university courses, and relevant to and sufficient for the placement decisions that are to be made.

- The definition of the construct is "knowledge of multilevel rhetorical organization of written texts."
- This definition is based on a needs analysis that included input from instructors in introductory level academic university courses, students who had completed these courses, and teachers in the ESL courses. It clearly distinguishes the construct from other related constructs, such as ability to draw inferences, ability to read critically, or knowledge of figures of speech.

A2 The assessment task specifications clearly specify that the test takers will read a passage taken from an introductory academic text and then complete an incomplete outline that represents the rhetorical organization of this passage.

A3 The procedures for administering the incomplete outline test enable the test takers to perform at their highest level on the ability "knowledge of multilevel rhetorical organization of written texts."

A4 The scoring key and procedures for using the key focus on elements of multilevel outline structure that, in essence, define the construct "knowledge of multilevel rhetorical organization of written texts."

A5 The incomplete outline task engages the ability "knowledge of multi-level rhetorical organization of written texts."

A6 Scores on the incomplete outline test are interpreted as "knowledge of multi-level rhetorical organization of written texts."

A7 The ESL Program Director communicates the definition of the construct in non-technical language via the instructions for the outline completion task and examples of multilevel outlines. The construct definition is also included in non-technical language in the assessment report for test takers and other stakeholders.

Warrants: impartiality

B1 The outline completion task does not include response formats or content that may either favor or disfavor some test takers.

B2 The outline completion task does not include not include content that may be offensive to some test takers.

B3 The procedures for producing an assessment record for the incomplete outline test are clearly described in terms that are understandable to all test takers.

B4 Test takers are treated impartially during all aspects of the administration of the assessment.

(a) Test takers have equal access to information about of the assessment content and assessment procedures.

(b) Test takers have equal access to the assessment, in terms of cost, location, and familiarity with conditions and equipment.

(c) Test takers have equal opportunity to demonstrate their knowledge of multilevel rhetorical organization of introductory university academic reading passages.

(d) Not needed, since the test is administered by computer over the internet.

B5 Interpretations of the test takers' "knowledge of multilevel rhetorical organization of written texts" are equally meaningful across students from different first language backgrounds and academic disciplines."

Warrants: generalizability

C1 The characteristics of the outline completion task correspond closely to those of tasks of reading introductory academic texts both in the academic domain (non-ESL introductory-level university courses) as well as in the language teaching domain (the ESL reading course).

C2 The criteria and procedures for evaluating the responses to the outline completion task correspond closely to those that are typically used by teachers in assessing performance in reading introductory academic texts.

Warrant: relevance

D The interpretation "knowledge of rhetorical organization of written texts" provides the information that is relevant to the ESL program director's decisions about placement or exemption.

Warrant: sufficiency

E The assessment-based interpretation of "knowledge of multilevel rhetorical organization of written texts" provides sufficient information to make the placement/exemption decisions.

Assessment records

> **Claim 4:** The scores from the incomplete outline test are consistent across different forms and administrations of the test, across students from different academic disciplines, and across different groups of international students entering the university.

Warrants: consistency

1 The incomplete outline test is administered in a standard way every time it is offered.
2 The scoring criteria and procedures for the computer scoring algorithm are well specified and are adhered to.
3 The computer scoring algorithm was developed through extensive trialing and comparison with multiple human ratings.
4 The computer scoring algorithm was developed through trialing with several different groups of test takers.
5 Scores on different items in the incomplete outline test are internally consistent.
6 Not needed, since performance is not rated.
7 Not needed, since performance is not rated.
8 Scores from different forms of the incomplete outline test are consistent.
9 Scores from different administrations of the incomplete outline test are consistent.
10 Scores on incomplete outline test are consistent across different groups of students.

BACKING FROM PROCEDURES AND DOCUMENTATION

Since these are discussed in the relevant chapters in the book, these are not repeated here.

DESIGN STATEMENT

University example

1 Description of the test takers and other stakeholders (Table P2.2)

Stakeholders	Attributes
1 Test takers	English Language Learners (ELLs); varied languages and cultures; upper level ESL proficiency, adults (ages mostly in upper teens and early 20s, with some older students)
2 ESL reading teachers	TAs in MA and Ph.D. Applied Linguistics Program, many with several years' experience teaching in university ESL program, some with many years of experience teaching ESL prior to involvement in the graduate program in Applied Linguistics
3 Teachers in university academic classes	Regular faculty teaching introductory general education courses
4 ESL Program Director	Professor of Linguistics, 25 years' experience directing the ESL program in a large US university; extensive experience in language test design and development

Table P2.2 Attributes of stakeholders and individuals responsible for making the decisions

2 Intended beneficial consequences (Table P2.3)

Stakeholders	Intended beneficial consequences	
	Of using the assessment	**Of the decisions that are made**
1 **Test takers:**	Test takers placed in the ESL reading class will realize that the test tasks are similar to instructional tasks, and thus relevant to their target language use needs. Test takers placed in the ESL reading class will benefit from using the test by being tested in a way that is consistent with ways in which their performance in the ESL reading course is being evaluated.	Test takers who are exempted from the ESL reading course will benefit from not having to take a course they don't need. Test takers who are placed in the ESL reading course will benefit from being placed in a course they do need.
2 **ESL reading teachers:**	ESL reading teachers will benefit from using a test in which the criteria for making placement decisions are similar to those used in making decisions about the effectiveness of their instruction.	ESL reading teachers will benefit from being able to focus their instruction on a group of students who are relatively homogeneous in their reading ability.

3 Teachers in regular university academic classes:	Teachers in regular academic courses will be aware of the fact that students placed in their class, by virtue of their having taken the test, will have been sensitized to the need to pay attention to the rhetorical organization of material they read.	Teachers in regular university courses will benefit from having students in their classes who are prepared to read and understand the rhetorical structure of introductory texts.
4 ESL program administrator:	The ESL program administrator will benefit from using a test whose scoring criteria are consistent with the performance objectives for the course they supervise.	The ESL program administrator will have to deal with fewer complaints from bored or frustrated students and frustrated teachers.

Table P2.3 Intended beneficial consequences

3 Descriptions of the decisions to be made and of the decision makers (Claim 2)

The decisions, stakeholders affected by decisions, and individuals responsible for making the decisions are provided below (Table P2.4).

Decision	Stakeholders who will be affected by the decision	Individuals(s) responsible for making the decision
Place students in ESL reading course	Students, instructors in ESL reading course, teachers in students' academic courses	ESL Program Director
Exempt students from ESL reading course	Students, instructors in ESL reading course, teachers in students' academic courses	ESL Program
Adjust instruction in ESL reading course	Instructors in ESL reading course	Instructors in ESL reading course

Table P2.4 The decisions, stakeholders affected by the decisions, and individuals responsible for making the decisions

4 The relative seriousness of classification errors, policy-level decisions about standards, the standards themselves (Claim 2, Warrants A2 and A3)

- *Relative seriousness of classification errors*: False positive classification decisions are relatively more serious than false negative classification decisions.
- *Policy-level procedures for setting standards*: The standard for exemption from the ESL reading course was set by the ESL Course Director in consultation with ESL reading course instructors and academic course instructors.

- *Standard for exemption from the ESL reading course*: Students must demonstrate that they have sufficient knowledge of multilevel rhetorical organization of introductory academic texts to enable them to successfully participate in introductory level academic courses.

5 Definition of the construct(s) (Claim 3, Warrant A1)

The definition of the construct for the University example is "knowledge of multilevel rhetorical organization written texts."

This definition of the construct to be assessed is based upon a needs analysis of reading tasks in courses fulfilling students' general education requirement, and this is the domain within which the construct is meaningful.

6 Description of the TLU domain (Claim 3, Warrant C1)

The TLU domain in the University example is "academic readings in textbooks in introductory courses."

7 Tasks selected as a basis for developing assessment tasks

The TLU task that was selected as a basis for developing assessment tasks is "reading a passage from a text in an introductory academic course and developing an outline of this."

8 Description of the characteristics of TLU tasks that have been selected as a basis for assessment tasks (Table P2.5)

	Characteristics of "outlining" TLU task
Setting	**Physical characteristics**: home, library, and classroom, computer, course text **Participants**: the student; possibly teacher and other students
Rubric (all implicit in the TLU task)	
Instructions	**Target language**: written, visual, or internally generated by the student; specification of procedures and tasks based upon students' prior instruction in and experience with outlining
Structure	**Number of parts:** one part (outline) per reading **Salience of parts & tasks:** the student used the language, but it was not free from error (either syntactically or semantically) **Sequence of tasks:** determined by sequence of information in reading **Relative importance of tasks:** tasks associated with main headings may be relatively more important than tasks associated with relatively minor details in sub-headings **Number of tasks**: depends upon length of reading passage, number of levels in outline, and number of entries under each level
Time allotment	Highly variable

Recording method	**Criteria for recording**: degree of association of organization of outline with organization of reading text; meaning of entries far more important than grammatical accuracy **Procedures for recording the response:** student's internally generated feedback based upon usefulness of the outline in helping the student interact with the material in the reading; possible written or spoken feedback from instructor **Explicitness of criteria and procedures for recording the response:** fairly explicit if student has been given formal instruction in outlining **Recorders:** variable (the student, other students, instructors)
Input	
Format	Input for interpretation, written, lengthy, English, unspeeded
Language characteristics	**Grammatical**: complex **Textual:** highly organized **Functions:** most frequently ideational, can also be manipulative (persuasive) **Genre:** introductory academic course text **Dialect:** academic **Register:** formal **Naturalness**: natural **Cultural references**: variable **Figures of speech:** variable
Topical characteristics	**Variable:** topics consistent with introductory general education course content
Expected response	
Format	Written, English, extended production, relatively unspeeded
Language characteristics	**Grammatical:** somewhat complex **Textual:** outline **Functions:** ideational **Genre:** outline **Dialect:** standard academic **Register:** formal **Naturalness**: natural **Cultural references**: variable, depending upon course content **Figures of speech**: variable
Topical characteristics	**Variable**: topics consistent with introductory general education course content
Relationship between input and expected response	
Type of external interactiveness	Non-reciprocal interaction between test taker, reading passage, incomplete outline as provided in test, and developing outline emerging as test taker completes the test
Scope	**Narrow**
Directness	**Direct**

Table P2.5 Characteristics of the selected TLU task

9 Plan for collecting backing and feedback (Table P2.6)

Stage	Activities	Evidence (Documentation)	Claim, Warrants supported	Person(s) responsible
I Pre-dev planning	1 Consulting documents	Initial Plan	Claims 1 and 2	ESL Program Director, ESL Reading Course instructors
	2 Consulting stakeholders	Description of procedures followed		
	3 Documenting the procedures followed			
II Design	4 Identifying stakeholders	DS, Pt 1, list of stakeholders	Claim 1	ESL Program Director, ESL Reading Course instructors
	5 Documenting the procedures followed	AUA: Description of procedures followed in creating list of stakeholders	Claim 1	
	6 Consulting with stakeholders • ELL students at the university • ESL reading teachers • Academic course instructors	DS, Pt 2, list of intended consequences and potential detrimental consequences	Claim 1, W A1	
		DS, Pt 3, list of decisions to be made, who is responsible for making these, and who will be affected by these	Claim 2	
		DS, Pt 4: description of relative seriousness of decision errors and performance standards for making classification decisions	Claim 2, W A2, A3a, A3b	

	7 Documenting the procedures followed	AUA: Description of procedures followed		
	8 Conducting a needs analysis	DS, Pt 5, definition of construct	Claims 1 & 2	
		DS, Pt 6, description of TLU domain	Claim 3, W A1	
		DS, Pt 7, list of TLU tasks selected	Claim 3, W C1, C2	
			Claim 3, W C1, C2	
	9 Describing TLU task characteristics		Claim 3, W C1, C2	
		DS, Pt 8, description of TLU task (templates)	Claim 3	
	10 Documenting the procedures followed • Documents consulted • Stakeholders consulted • TLU domain observed	AUA: Description of procedures followed		
III Operation-alization	11 Consulting documents created during development stage	BP, Pt 1, assessment task specifications	Claim 3, W A2, C1, C2	ESL Program Director, ESL Reading Course instructor
			Claim 2, WA3	
		BP, Pt 3, procedures for setting cut scores and making decisions	Claim 4, W A1, A2	Ph.D. students in language testing
		BP, Pt 4, procedures and formats for reporting assessment records	Claim 2, W A3	
			Claim 3, W A3	
		BP, Pt 5, procedures for administering the assessment		

	12 Documenting the procedures followed	AUA		
IV Trialing	13 Consulting stakeholders 14 Pre-testing	Report: summary of results of test taker questionnaire	Claim 1, W A1	ESL Program Director, Ph.D. students in language testing
	15 Statistical analysis of test scores	Report: summary of results of pre-testing		
	16 Documenting the procedures followed	AUA		
V Use	17 Consulting stakeholders	Report: results of questionnaire (given to test takers, ESL reading teachers, and academic instructors in courses into which test takers were placed) on accuracy (?) of placement/ exemption decisions	Claim 1, W A1 Claim 1, W A2, A3, A4	ESL Program Director Ph.D. students in language testing
		Report: results of questionnaire (given to test takers) on administration procedures followed Report from Program Director on placement procedures followed	Claim 2, W B3	
	18 Statistical analysis of test scores	Report: statistical analysis of test scores	Claim 4, W, 10, 11, 12	

Table P2.6 Plan for collecting backing and feedback

10 Plan for acquiring, allocating, and managing resources (Tables P2.7 and P2.8)

	STAGES				
RESOURCES	**1 Initial planning**	**2 Design**	**3 Operation-alization**	**4 Trialing**	**5 Use**
Personnel					
Project Director (Visiting Professor)		40 hours/ week	40 hours/ week	40 hours/ week	40 hours/ week
ESL Program Director	40 hours	10 hours	10 hours	10 hours	10 hours
Development team	10 hours/ person	10 hours/ person/ week	10 hours/ person/week	10 hours/ person/week	20 hours/ person/term
Computer programmer		30 hours	50 hours	50 hours	10 hours/term
Clerical support	2 hours	10 hours	30 hours	40 hours	20 hours/term
Test administrators/ scorers				20 hours	20 hours/term
Space	Meeting room	Meeting room	Meeting room	Meeting room, rooms for administering the test	Meeting room, rooms for administering the test
Equipment	PCs	PCs	PCs	PCs	PCs

Table P2.7 Estimates of required resources

	STAGES				
RESOURCES	**1 Initial planning**	**2 Design**	**3 Operation-alization**	**4 Trialing**	**5 Use**
Personnel					
Project director (Dr. Shin)		40 hours/ week	40 hours/ week	40 hours/ week	40 hours/week
ESL Program Director	*40 hours*	*40 hours*	*40 hours*	*40 hours*	*40 hours*
Development team	10 hours/ person	10 hours/ person/ week	10 hours/ person/week	10 hours/ person/week	20 hours/ person/term
2 ESL instructors	*10 hours/ person*	*10 hours/ person/ week*	*10 hours/ person/week*	*10 hours/ person/week*	*10 hours/term*

1 academic course instructor		*10 hours/ person/ week*	*10 hours/ person/week*	*10 hours/ person/week*	*10 hours/ person/week*
3 Ph.D. students		*10 hours/ person/ week*	*10 hours/ person/week*	*10 hours/ person/week*	*10 hours/ person/week*
Computer programmers		30 hours	50 hours	50 hours	10 hours/term
1 Ph.D. student with expertise in computer programming		*10 hours/ week*	*10 hours/week*	*10 hours/week*	*10 hours/week*
Clerical support	2 hours	10 hours	30 hours	40 hours	20 hours/term
From Dept. Chair	*2 hours*	*10 hours*	*30 hours*	*40 hours*	*20 hours/term*
Test administrators/ scorers				20 hours	20 hours/term
TAs in the Department				*20 hours*	*20 hours/term*
Space	Meeting room	Meeting room	Meeting room	Meeting room, Computer labs with internet connections	Meeting room, Computer labs with internet connections
Department Office of Space Management	*2117 Rolfe*	*2117 Rolfe*	*2117 Rolfe*	*2117 Rolfe, Large lecture rooms*	*2117 Rolfe, Large lecture rooms*
Equipment	PCs	PCs	PCs	PCs	PCs
Personal PCs, Department of Applied Linguistics	*7 personal PCs*	*7 personal PCs*	*7 personal PCs, 1 large PC*	*7 personal PCs, 1 large PC*	*7 personal PCs, 1 large PC*

Table P2.8 Resources required and available

(Resources that will be required are the top row in each category, while resources that will be available are in the bottom row in italics).

BLUEPRINT

I Assessment specifications

A Number of parts: One, consisting of one written passage and one incomplete outline

B Number of tasks per part: Approximately 10–15 blanks in the outline per reading passage. These blanks include: At least 1 blank at highest level of information, at least 4 blanks at the second level of information, at least 3 blanks at the third level of information.

C Sequence of parts/tasks: Reading passage was presented first, then the incomplete outline could be viewed alongside the reading passage in a separate column.

D Relative importance of parts/tasks: All parts of same importance

E Time allotment: Generous time limit

F Instructions: General and for each part

1 General

a See example tutorial below.

b Complete the outline based on your reading of the passage. (See example tutorial below.)

c When you have completed the outline, click the "submit" button to send your answers to the testing center and continue the test.

2 For each part: Instructions are the same for each part.

II Task specifications

A Definition of ability to be assessed: Knowledge of multilevel rhetorical organization

B Setting

1 Physical characteristics: Computer lab on campus, quiet, comfortable

2 Equipment: Each test taker seated at a PC with headphones

3 Attributes of participants

a Test takers: Incoming students who are non-native speakers of English

b Degree of familiarity with PC: All quite familiar with PC

c Test administrator: Trained and experienced in computer-based testing and having a positive attitude toward the test takers

4 Time of task: By appointment within a fixed time period during the day

C Characteristics of the input, expected response, and relationship between input and response

1 Input

a Format

1) Channel: visual (written text on the computer)

2) Form: language, but some passages may also contain non-language

3) Language: English (target)

4) Length

a) Passage: 1 long passage (approximately 450–500 words)

b) Incomplete outline: 1 page, based on the passage

5) Vehicle: reproduced

6) Degree of speededness: relatively unspeeded—generous time limit provided

b Type: input for interpretation
 1) Text: passages
 2) Incomplete outline following the structure of the passage with a word/phrase/sentence for each level of information

c Language of input
 1) Organizational characteristics: as occurs in passages from textbooks/course readers/website assigned in the syllabus
  (a) Grammatical
   (1) Passages
    (a) Morphology and syntax: wide range of organized structures
    (b) Vocabulary: wide range of general and technical vocabulary
    (c) Graphology: typewritten
   (2) Incomplete outline: grammar and vocabulary similar to that in passages, but in outline format
  (b) Textual (cohesion and organization)
   (1) Passages: wide range of cohesive devices and rhetorical organizational patterns, including narration, description, definition, classification, comparison and contrast, and argumentation
   (2) Incomplete outline: word/phrase/sentence level, all related to be an outline
 2) Pragmatic characteristics: as occurs in actual passages from textbooks/course readers/website assigned in the syllabus
  (a) Functional
   (1) Passage: ideational, heuristic, and manipulative, possibly some imaginative
   (2) Incomplete outline: ideational and heuristic
  (b) Sociolinguistic (passage and incomplete outline): standard dialect, formal/informal register, natural, varied on cultural references and figurative language

d Topical characteristics (passage and incomplete outline): academic, drawn from textbooks from introductory courses meeting students' General Education requirement

2 Characteristics of the expected response
 a Format
  1) Channel: visual
  2) Form: language
  3) Language: English (target)
  4) Length: 1–3 words/phrases per blank in the incomplete outline
  5) Type: limited production
  6) Degree of speededness: relatively unspeeded—generous time limit provided

b Language characteristics
1) Organizational characteristics: vocabulary similar to that in texts and items; morphology and syntax standard English, but not scored; graphology: typewritten
2) Pragmatic characteristics: mostly same as passages and item stems, plus some need for appropriate register use; little need likely for manipulative functions

c Topical characteristics: same as passages and item stems

3 Relationship between input and expected response and type of interaction
a Type of external interactiveness: non-reciprocal
b Scope of relationship: both broad and narrow—narrow in that specific pieces of information must be provided, and broad in that those pieces' relationship to the text as a whole must be kept in mind by test takers
c Directness of relationship: direct, aside from ability to organize and categorize rhetorically

D Procedures for recording test takers' performance (Scoring method)
1 Criteria for correctness: partial credit based on acceptability of content, not linguistic accuracy. These criteria were applied to each individual item as described below.
2 Scoring procedures: scored by computer matching regular expressions with list of acceptable answers compiled by human raters. (See example scoring algorithm below.)

Discussion

One of the motivations for developing a web-based assessment was to use this technology to develop assessment tasks whose characteristics would correspond more closely to reading tasks in the students' academic courses than was possible in the paper and pencil format. In other words, the test developers wanted to improve the generalizability of the test-based interpretations to the TLU domain. The test development team thus made a decision early on to include only test tasks that would require test takers to produce some language, rather than having them respond simply by choosing among several alternatives. Once this decision had been made, the feasibility of scoring these constructed responses became an issue. Because of the quick turn-around time for reporting results to the test takers and relevant individuals in the university, and the limited availability of human scorers, the decision was made to explore the possibility of scoring the students' responses by computer. The computer programmers working on the project were able to develop the software for scoring the open-ended responses by computers, using regular expressions as the keys. (In computing, **regular expressions** provide a concise and flexible means for identifying strings of text of interest, such as particular characters, words, or patterns of characters.)[1]

In order to implement the computer scoring, the test development team had to determine what the acceptable answers for each blank in the incomplete outline would be and then translate these into regular expressions that the computer could understand. This was done in several stages. First, for each test, a scoring key containing the acceptable responses and the number of points for each was provided by the item writer. The list of acceptable answers and number of points was then reviewed and discussed by the entire development team, and the scoring key was revised, as needed. (See example scoring procedure below.) Second, during the trialing stage, test takers' responses were scored by several human raters according to the scoring key. During this process, a list of additional acceptable answers was compiled and added to the scoring key for subsequent inclusion in the computer scoring algorithm. Finally, using the acceptable answers in the scoring key, a set of regular expressions was written to guide the machine scoring. (See example below.)

3 Explicitness of criteria and procedures: criteria explicitly explained, scoring procedure described in general terms, with instructions
4 Scorers or raters (during tryout): instructors and research assistants (RAs) in ESL reading program assigned to test development team. Computer scoring algorithm (during operational use)

E Instructions for responding to the assessment task (See example test task below.)

III Procedures for setting cut scores

According to the Design Statement, false positive classification errors were considered to be more serious than false negative errors. Therefore, standard-setting procedures were aimed at setting the cut score so as to minimize false positive classification errors while maximizing the consistency of classification decisions at the cut score. These standard-setting procedures were followed separately for each form of the test. The performance standard was defined as "sufficient knowledge of multilevel rhetorical organization of introductory academic texts to enable them to successfully participate in introductory level academic courses."

Three different standard-setting methods were used: the Modified Angoff method, Borderline-Group method, and Cluster Analysis. Each of these methods yields a tentative cut score. In the Modified Angoff method, several experts, in this case the ESL reading instructors and the academic course instructors, were asked to look at items from the test and to judge whether students who had "sufficient knowledge of multilevel rhetorical organization of introductory academic texts to enable them to successfully participate in introductory level academic courses" would get the item correct. In the Borderline-Group method, these same experts were asked to estimate the probability (between 0 and 100%) that a student who was on the borderline between insufficient and "sufficient knowledge of multilevel rhetorical organization of introductory academic texts to enable them to successfully participate in introductory level academic courses" would get the item correct. Cluster Analysis was used to determine the extent to which test takers' performance on the test, i.e., their total scores, clustered into the two groups identified by the Borderline-Group method. In this case, a cluster solution corresponded to the grouping of the Borderline-Group analysis, and the median score for the minimally competent group provided a tentative cut score.

Next, threshold-loss agreement indices were calculated for each of the three cut scores from the three different standard-setting methods, along with the percentages of students classified as "exempt." Using this information, a cut score was set that maximized the dependability of classification decisions and minimized false positive classification errors. Again, these indices were calculated for each subsequent form of the test.

After the first round of placing students into ESL reading or exempting them, both the ESL reading instructors and the academic course instructors were asked to identify students whom they felt were misplaced. This procedure was followed as subsequent forms of the test were developed. This feedback indicated very few misplacements, and most of these were false negatives, that is, students who were placed in the ESL reading course but who should have been exempt. Since the ESL teachers had the opportunity to recommend students for exemption within the first week of classes, the detrimental consequences of false negative decisions could be mitigated. Thus, for each form, the test developer decided to continue using the original cut score. Because the different forms of the test included slightly differing numbers of items, raw scores were converted to a common standard scale, a linear T, and the cut score on this scale was 78.[2]

IV Procedures and formats for reporting assessment records

A Procedures

1 Assessment reports are e-mailed to test takers' secure university e-mail addresses within 24 hours after they have taken the test.

2 Assessment reports are reported on a secure website accessible only by university administrators, with password only.

B Formats

1 Exempt/non-exempt decision

2 For those students who were not exempted from the ESL reading course, the report included the URL for a webpage that provided a complete description of the course, along with procedures for registering, and procedures for challenging or appealing the decision.

Discussion

With the previous paper and pencil test format, students were sent written reports that included their score, the placement decision, and a description of the ESL reading course. The assessment reports from the web-based test, on the other hand, include only the exempt/non-exempt decision.

EXAMPLE ASSESSMENT TASK

The incomplete outline task was presented via the web in secure computer labs on the university campus. Each test taker sat at a computer terminal and viewed the instructions and the task on-screen. The instructions for completing the tasks were given in two parts. First a general introduction to the types of blanks test takers would be asked to complete was provided, as in Figure P2.1 below.

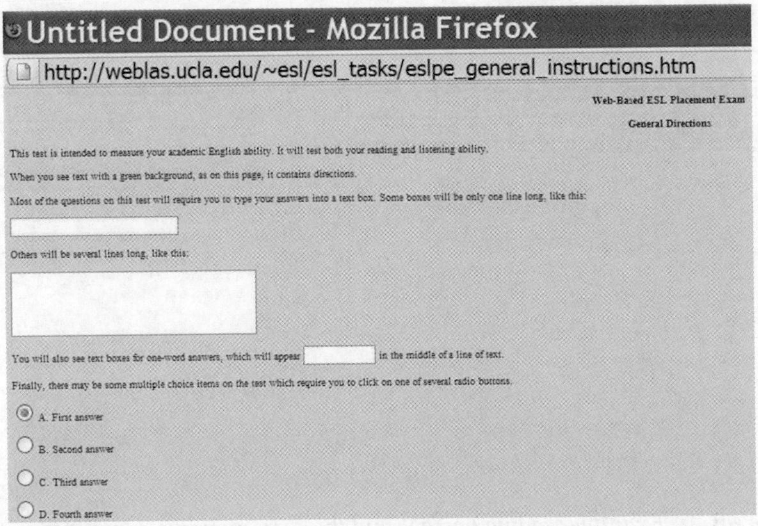

Untitled Document - Mozilla Firefox

http://weblas.ucla.edu/~esl/esl_tasks/eslpe_general_instructions.htm

Web-Based ESL Placement Exam

General Directions

This test is intended to measure your academic English ability. It will test both your reading and listening ability.

When you see text with a green background, as on this page, it contains directions.

Most of the questions on this test will require you to type your answers into a text box. Some boxes will be only one line long, like this:

Others will be several lines long, like this:

You will also see text boxes for one-word answers, which will appear in the middle of a line of text.

Finally, there may be some multiple choice items on the test which require you to click on one of several radio buttons.

A. First answer

B. Second answer

C. Third answer

D. Fourth answer

Figure P2.1 Initial instructions for the ESL incomplete outline task

This was followed by a short tutorial, which included first an example of what the headings in an outline look like, as in Figure P2.2 below.

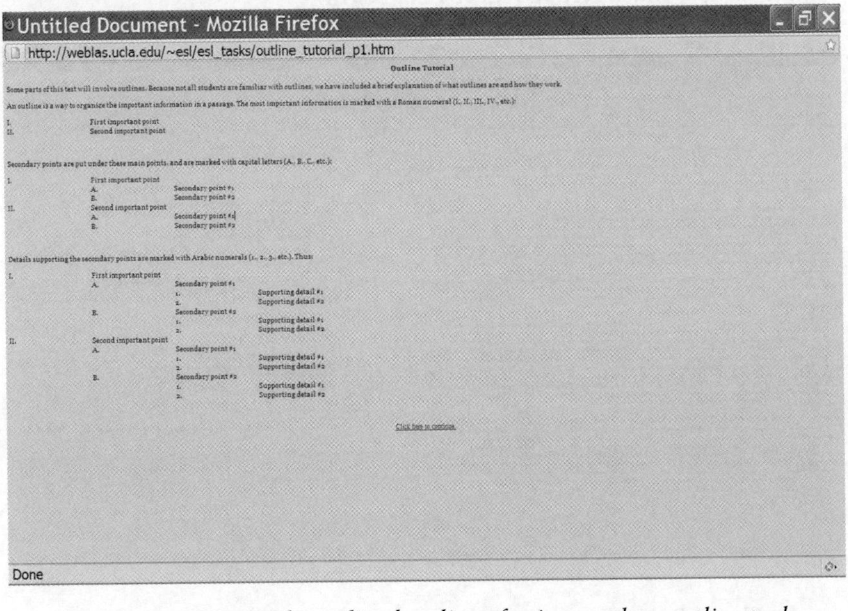

Untitled Document - Mozilla Firefox

http://weblas.ucla.edu/~esl/esl_tasks/outline_tutorial_p1.htm

Outline Tutorial

Some parts of this test will involve outlines. Because not all students are familiar with outlines, we have included a brief explanation of what outlines are and how they work.

An outline is a way to organize the important information in a passage. The most important information is marked with a Roman numeral (I., II., III., IV., etc.):

I. First important point
II. Second important point

Secondary points are put under these main points, and are marked with capital letters (A., B., C., etc.):

I. First important point
A. Secondary point #1
B. Secondary point #2
II. Second important point
A. Secondary point #1
B. Secondary point #2

Details supporting the secondary points are marked with Arabic numerals (1., 2., 3., etc.). Thus:

I. First important point
A. Secondary point #1
1. Supporting detail #1
2. Supporting detail #2
B. Secondary point #2
1. Supporting detail #1
2. Supporting detail #2
II. Second important point
A. Secondary point #1
1. Supporting detail #1
2. Supporting detail #2
B. Secondary point #2
1. Supporting detail #1
2. Supporting detail #2

Click here to continue.

Done

Figure P2.2 Example outline headings for incomplete outline task

This was followed by a short passage and the corresponding completed outline, as illustrated in Figure P2.3 below.

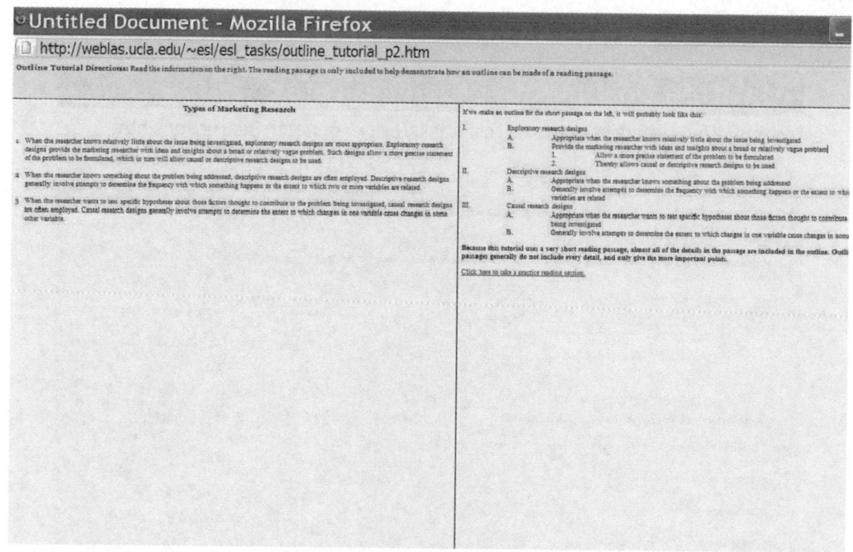

Untitled Document - Mozilla Firefox

http://weblas.ucla.edu/~esl/esl_tasks/outline_tutorial_p2.htm

Outline Tutorial Directions: Read the information on the right. The reading passage is only included to help demonstrate how an outline can be made of a reading passage.

Types of Marketing Research

1 When the researcher knows relatively little about the issue being investigated, exploratory research designs are most appropriate. Exploratory research designs provide the marketing researcher with ideas and insights about a broad or relatively vague problem. Such designs allow a more precise statement of the problem to be formulated, which in turn will allow causal or descriptive research designs to be used.

2 When the researcher knows something about the problem being addressed, descriptive research designs are often employed. Descriptive research designs generally involve attempts to determine the frequency with which something happens or the extent to which two or more variables are related.

3 When the researcher wants to test specific hypotheses about those factors thought to contribute to the problem being investigated, causal research designs are often employed. Causal research designs generally involve attempts to determine the extent to which changes in one variable cause changes in some other variable.

If we make an outline for the short passage on the left, it will probably look like this:

I. Exploratory research designs
  A. Appropriate when the researcher knows relatively little about the issue being investigated
  B. Provide the marketing researcher with ideas and insights about a broad or relatively vague problem
    1. Allow a more precise statement of the problem to be formulated
    2. Thereby allows causal or descriptive research designs to be used
II. Descriptive research designs
  A. Appropriate when the researcher knows something about the problem being addressed
  B. Generally involve attempts to determine the frequency with which something happens or the extent to whi variables are related
III. Causal research designs
  A. Appropriate when the researcher wants to test specific hypotheses about those factors thought to contribute being investigated
  B. Generally involve attempts to determine the extent to which changes in one variable cause changes in som

Because this tutorial uses a very short reading passage, almost all of the details in the passage are included in the outline. Outli passages generally do not include every detail, and only give the more important points.

Click here to take a practice reading section.

Figure P2.3 Example reading passage and the corresponding completed outline

The last screen in the tutorial presented test takers with a short passage and an incomplete outline, which they could complete, but their answers were not recorded. After the tutorial, test takers were presented with an incomplete outline task, as illustrated in Figure P2.4 below.

Untitled Document - Mozilla Firefox

http://weblas.ucla.edu/~esl/esl_tasks/demo_read_out_mrkting1.htm

Timer here...

Directions: Complete the outline based on your reading of the passage. When you have completed the outline, click the "submit" button to send your answers to the testing center and continue the test.

TTCs

Marketing Research in a Marketing Environment

1 Problem formulation [in marketing research] is important because it determines the information that will be needed. Information needs determine the objectives of the research and, in large measure, what kind of research design is most appropriate. The way the problem is formulated with respect to the research objective and accompanying research questions places certain demands on the research design.

2 In certain instances, the research problem to be solved is rather broad or vague. In such cases, the research designs must be flexible to permit the researcher to exercise judgment concerning possible areas and tactics of investigation. For example, although the Campbell Soup Company has tried to convince consumers that "soup is good food," increasing numbers of consumers have been ***shunning*** canned soup because of its high sodium content. More frustrating, however, is the fact that Campbell has had a low-sodium line on the market for years, but consumers have been unmoved. In addressing the problem of why low-sodium soups have not had greater market penetration, the marketing researcher will probably have to conduct research that will give some ideas about and insights into the problem. One way to proceed is to interview small groups of soup consumers to find out about their experiences with, and reactions to, low-sodium soups. When the researcher knows relatively little about the issue being investigated, *exploratory research designs* are most appropriate. Exploratory research designs provide the marketing researcher with ideas and insights about a broad or relatively vague problem. Such designs allow a more precise statement of the problem to be formulated, which in turn will allow causal or descriptive research designs to be used.

3 In certain instances, the research problem to be solved is more specific in the sense that the marketing researcher and client/decision maker are aware of those factors that may be contributing to the problem. In such instances, the research design must allow the researcher to focus on specific aspects of the product or on the relationship between those factors thought to be contributing to the problem. For example, having ***determined*** that soup consumers believe low-sodium soups are not much different from soups having normal sodium content, Campbell might initiate a study to develop demographic and lifestyle profiles of those people who are currently buying low-sodium and health conscious products and their perceptions of the benefits offered by such products with particular emphasis on why a low-sodium appeal is more believable in certain product categories. When the researcher knows something about the problem being addressed, *descriptive research designs* are often employed. Descriptive research designs generally involve attempts to determine the frequency with which something happens or the extent to which two or more variables are related.

4 Finally, in certain instances, the research problem to be solved is clearly and specifically identified. In such instances, the research design must allow the researcher to assess the exact relationship between factors thought to contribute to the problem. For example, having determined that soup consumers are confused about what low sodium actually means, Campbell might ***initiate*** a study to determine which of two advertisements produce greater change in consumers' understanding of the benefits of specific levels of sodium and their perceptions of products with different sodium levels. The purpose of this study is to test the informational effect of the two advertisements with a view toward determining which advertisement is superior. When the researcher wants to test specific hypotheses about those factors thought to contribute to the problem being investigated, *causal research designs* are often employed. Causal research designs generally involve attempts to determine the extent to which changes in one variable cause changes in some other variable.

I. Problem formulation is important
  A. It determines the information that will be needed
  B. Information needs determine:
    1.
    2.
  C. The way the problem is formulated places certain demands on the research design
II. Research designs that are used when the research problem is rather broad or vague
  A. The research design must be flexible to permit the researcher to exercise judgment regarding:
    1. Possible areas of investigation
    2. Possible tactics of investigation
  B. These designs may involve interviewing small groups of consumers
  C.
    1.
    2.
    3. Their results allow other types of research designs to be used subsequently
III. Research designs that are used when the research problem is more specific, in that the factors that may contribute to the problem are known
  A.
    1. Specific aspects of the problem
    2.
  B. These designs may involve studying:
    1.
    2. Perceptions of consumers
  C. Such designs are called descriptive research designs
  D. They usually involve attempts to determine:
    1.
    2.
IV.
  A. The research design must allow the researcher to assess the exact relationship between factors thought to contribute to the problem
  B.
  C. These research designs usually involve attempts to determine the extent to which changes in one variable cause changes in some other variable

Click the "Submit" button below when you are finished.

Submit

Done

Figure P2.4 Example reading passage and incomplete outline

In order to complete the incomplete outline tasks, students were able to size their own computer screen to their desired size, and to scroll either the reading passage or the incomplete outline up and down while filling in the blanks. When they hit the "submit" button, they were shown the following message:

> If you wish to go back and check your answers, click the "Go back" button. If you want to submit your answers and go on to the next part of the test, click the "Submit" button. You will not be able to go back to this part of the test once you submit your answers.

EXAMPLE SCORING ALGORITHM

For the example assessment above, the regular expressions for scoring items II.C and II.C.1 and 2 using the computer scoring algorithm were developed in several steps. First, the test developers provided complete answers for these three items, as follows. (Note that test takers could simply copy the relevant parts of the second paragraph into the blanks. However, the fact that they could select these specific parts and put them into the correct level in the incomplete outline was viewed as evidence of knowledge of rhetorical organization.)

II.C When the researcher knows relatively little about the issue being investigated, exploratory designs are most appropriate.

1 Provide the marketing researcher with ideas and insights about a broad or relatively vague problem.

2 Such designs allow a more precise statement of the problem to be formulated.

Next, the development team needed to pare down these answers to what they believed to be the minimal information required to indicate comprehension. This was necessary because the criterion for correctness was accuracy of the content with respect to the reading passage, and not linguistic accuracy. This led to the following shortened answers:

II.C exploratory designs; appropriate.

All the other information in the "complete" answer was regarded as redundant ("knows relatively little about the issue being investigated" essentially repeats what is given in "research problem is rather broad or vague").

1 provide ideas and insights
(The phrases "the marketing researcher" and "about a broad or relatively vague problem" were also redundant with other information in the passage.)

2 allow precise statement of the problem to be formulated.
(The phrase "such designs" repeats what is in II.C)

The next step was to determine the exact words that would be considered correct, and how many points to count for each answer. This led to the following final scoring key:

II.C exploratory (1), designs (1), appropriate (1) Maximum: 3 points
1 provide ideas (1), provide insights (1), provide ideas insights (2) Maximum 2 points
2 allow precise statement problem (1point)

In order to accommodate a whole range of possibly correct answers, the development team then created the regular expressions below.

Since responses were not scored according to grammatical accuracy, these regular expressions allow both singular and plural forms as an acceptable answer. For example, "design" and "designs" both will be scored as acceptable answers.

Item number	Regex	Points
II.C	[Ee]xploratory\b	1
II.C	[Dd]esign\b|[Dd]esigns\b	1
II.C	[Aa]ppropriate\b	1
1	([Pp]rovide).*((idea\b)|(ideas\b))	1
1	([Pp]rovide).*((insight\b)|(insights\b))	1
2	([Aa]llow).*(precise).*(statement).*((problem\b)|(problems\b))	1

COLLECTION OF BACKING FROM TRIALING AND USE

The plan for collecting feedback and backing that is described above was followed during the trialing of the test and operational use.

REFERENCE

Bachman, L. F. 2004. *Statistical Analyses for Language Assessment*. Cambridge: Cambridge University Press.

NOTES

1 http://en.wikipedia.org/wiki/Regular_expression.
2 See Bachman 2004, for a discussion of the linear T transformation.

Project 3

University Elementary Modern Chinese speaking assessment

(Adapted from materials supplied by Michelle Fu and Hongyin Tao)

SETTING

Native English speaking students at a large US university are studying Elementary Modern Chinese. There are multiple sections of this course, and multiple TAs as instructors. The instructors in the course are native Chinese speaking graduate students. The course supervisor is a native speaker of Modern Chinese, an experienced language teacher and supervisor, and has a Ph.D. in Chinese linguistics. She would like the instructors to test their students' ability to speak Chinese in order to assign course grades and provide feedback to students on their achievement of course objectives.

The supervisor believes that a formal speaking test administered on a program-wide basis several times each term will provide the program a way to obtain this information systematically in all sections of the course. She also believes that such assessments will have a positive impact on the way instructors teach and students study. She thus needs to decide how best to obtain this information for these purposes. In this example, the "test developer" consists of a team of individuals including the Chinese course supervisor and the classroom instructors, with all members of the team assuming a collective responsibility for the test development, use, and justification. For the formative decisions at the level of the classroom, the students and course instructors are the decision makers. For the summative decisions about students' grades, course instructors are the decision makers. For decisions about curriculum and staffing, the Course Coordinator is the decision maker.

INITIAL PLANNING QUESTIONS AND ANSWERS

1 What beneficial consequences does the supervisor want to happen? Who are the stakeholders? Who will be directly affected by the assessment?

a The intended test takers, students in Elementary Modern Chinese classes, will take the course's learning objectives in speaking seriously and organize their study accordingly, so as to optimize the time and effort spent learning to speak Chinese.

b Instructors will use the experience of giving the mini-speech test and the students' performance on this to make adjustments in their teaching, and hence make this more effective.

c The course supervisor will use scores and descriptions from the mini-speech tests to collect feedback on the effectiveness of instructors and the instructional program, to make decisions about retaining and hiring of instructors, and about changes in the syllabus that will improve the course as a whole.

2 What specific decisions do the stakeholders need to make to help promote the intended consequences?

a Students in Elementary Modern Chinese classes will make formative decisions about how to best focus their study time and effort.

b Instructors: summative decisions: assign course grades (A–E); formative decisions: decide how to improve their teaching.

c Course supervisor: alterations in the course syllabus; retention (or not) and hiring of new instructors.

3 What do the instructors and the course supervisor need to know about students' language ability in order to make the intended decisions?

a The instructors need to collect information about students' achievement in speaking Chinese.

b The course supervisor needs to collect information on the effectiveness of the instruction.

4 What sources could the course supervisor and instructors use for obtaining this information?

a Observing students' classroom performance.

b A formal assessment.

c An informal assessment.

5 Do the course supervisor and instructors need to use an assessment to obtain this information?

Yes. Instructors need to provide evidence of students' speaking ability on the basis of performance on a controlled task in order to justify decisions made on the basis of this evidence. Without a formal test, students may argue that they have not had equal opportunities to demonstrate their ability to speak Chinese. Also, for the supervisor to evaluate the effectiveness of the instruction, she needs to have consistent information about students' achievement in all sections.

6 Is an existing assessment available?

a Is an existing assessment available that provides the information that is needed for the decisions we need to make?

Yes. Several standardized tests of Modern Chinese are available.

Scores on incomplete outline test are consistent across different groups of students. *Both are intended for beginning to intermediate learners of Modern Chinese.*

b Do the assessment tasks correspond to TLU tasks?
No. The tasks in the assessments are typical of a very general TLU domain, while the content of the course is focused more on a specific set of rhetorical functions that are performed in speaking.

c Does either of these tests provide the information needed for the decisions the course supervisor and instructors need to make?
Possibly. Two of the tests include a section that assesses speaking.

d Does either assessment assess the areas of speaking in which the course supervisor and instructors are interested?
No. Both assessments provide only a single global score, and the course instructors need more detailed scores for formative purposes.

7 Scores on incomplete outline test are consistent across different groups of students. Does the supervisor need to develop her own assessment for the course? *Yes.*

a How will the program assure that the intended uses (i.e., decisions and consequences) of the assessment can be justified?
An Assessment Use Argument will be used to guide design and development, including warrants for meaningfulness, relevance, and consistency. Appropriate procedures for estimating the consistency of scores, and the meaningfulness and relevance of the interpretations will be put into place and followed during the development of the test. Students will perform a standard task under controlled conditions about which they will be informed in advance. The content of the tasks and the expected responses will be based on the kinds of speaking tasks students have practiced in class. Instructors will use the same rubric to rate all students' performances, and will be trained in the use of the rubric.

b What resources will the supervisor and instructors need for the development and use of the assessment (including justifying the intended uses of the assessment)?

i *Human: (Administrator to direct and monitor the progress of the test development effort; people with expertise in Chinese speaking to provide input into the creation of the speaking tasks and scoring procedures; someone with expertise in language assessment to provide guidance in the development of the speaking tasks, scoring and rater training procedures, and with analyses of the test results; support staff).*

ii *Material: (e.g., copies of speaking tasks used in the course, paper, personal computers, statistical analysis software; rooms for administering the test).*

iii *Time: 20 minutes for administering each test; 10 minutes for scoring each test.*

c What resources do the supervisor and instructors have or can they obtain?
The course supervisor's own time and expertise; the time and expertise of the instructors who will develop and administer and score the assessment. A Ph.D. student who is studying language assessment is willing to work on the project, as he may be able to base a Qualifying Paper on this. Each instructor will be able to administer his assessments within one hour and score them within one additional hour. The head of the department will allocate 25% of one of the support staff's time to this project.

As a result of this planning, the course supervisor decides to develop her own assessment of speaking.

ASSESSMENT USE ARGUMENT

Consequences

Claim 1: The consequences of using the mini-speech tests and of the decisions that are made based on them will be beneficial for students, the instructors, and the course supervisor.

Stakeholders

i Native English speaking students at a large US university who are studying Elementary Modern Chinese
ii Instructors in the course, who are native Chinese speaking graduate students in the Departments of Asian Languages and Literatures and Applied Linguistics
iii The course supervisor, who is a native speaker of Modern Chinese, an experienced language teacher and supervisor, and has a Ph.D. in Chinese linguistics.

Warrants, consequences of using the checklist

A1 The consequences of using the assessment that are specific to each stakeholder group will be beneficial. Specifically, the consequences for each stakeholder group will be as follows:
  i Students: The Chinese speaking of students in Elementary Modern Chinese classes will improve.
  ii Instructors: The classroom teaching of the instructors will improve.
  iii Course supervisor: The overall effectiveness of the course will improve.

A2 The scores from the mini-speech tests and the course grades of individual students are treated confidentially.

A3 The scores from the mini-speech tests and the course grades are reported in ways that are clear and understandable to students, teachers, and the course supervisor.

A4 Scores from the mini-speech tests and the course grades are reported in a timely manner.

A5 The mini-speech test helps promote good instructional practice and effective learning, and the use of this is thus beneficial to students, instructors, the course supervisor, and the program. Because the mini-speech test requires students to speak Chinese,

i *students* will take the course's learning objectives in speaking seriously and organize their study accordingly, so as to optimize the time and effort spent learning to speak Chinese;

ii *instructors* will devote more time to activities that engage students in speaking Chinese. Instructors will use the experience of giving the mini-speech test and the students' performance on this to make adjustments in their teaching, and hence make this more effective;

iii the *course supervisor* will observe greater attention to speaking in the classes. The course supervisor will use scores to make decisions about retaining and hiring of instructors, and about changes in the syllabus that will improve the course as a whole.

Warrants, consequences of the decisions that are made

B1 The consequences of using scores from the mini-speech test to make progress/not progress decisions about students in the course are beneficial to students, instructors, and the course supervisor.

i Because the scores from the mini-speech test will be used to determine whether students pass to the next higher course, students will take the learning objectives of the course seriously and organize their study accordingly, so as to optimize the time and effort spent studying Chinese, and hence mastering the course objectives and improving their spoken Chinese.

ii Because the scores from the mini-speech test will be used to determine whether students pass to the next higher course, and because these will be part of their evaluation, instructors will make adjustments in their teaching, and hence make this more effective.

iii Because the scores from the mini-speech test will be used to determine whether students pass to the next higher course, and because these will be part of the instructors' evaluations, the course supervisor will observe greater attention to speaking in the classes.

Rebuttal: The consequences of making progress/not progress decisions about students will be detrimental for students who are erroneously assigned the incorrect grade.

i False *positives* (allowing students who should not progress to progress) can result in students receiving unrealistic feedback on their abilities; students may move on to courses for which they are unprepared.

ii False *negatives* (not letting students progress who should progress) can result in students feeling demotivated.

1 Possible remedies for false *positives*:
   - Use additional information, such as class participation, and other speaking assignments, to assign grades.
   - Provide additional tutoring or small group work to help students practice their speaking.

2 Possible remedies for false *negatives*:
   - Use additional information, such as class participation and other speaking assignments, to assign grades.

Decisions

> **Claim 2:** The decisions to be made reflect the university's regulations and values, and the common practice and values of the academic community, including students, teachers, and administrators, and are equitable to all students in the course.

The specific decisions to be made, the stakeholders who will be affected by these, and the individuals responsible for making these decisions are given in Table P3.1 below:

Decision	Individual(s) responsible for making the decision	Stakeholders who will be affected by the decision
Decide which students progress to the next course partly on the basis of scores on the mini-speech test	1 Instructors 2 Course supervisor	Students
Adjust individual learning activities to focus on speaking	1 Students 2 Instructors	Students, instructors
Adjust teaching style, focus, and activities	Classroom instructors	Instructors, students
Revise curriculum	1 Course supervisor 2 Instructors	Instructors, students
Maintain or change instructional staff	Course supervisor	Course supervisor, instructors, students

Table P3.1 Decisions, decision-makers, and affected stakeholders

Warrants: values sensitivity

A1 University and departmental regulations, "customary practice" among the faculty in the Department, and the opinions of students were carefully and critically considered in the kinds of decisions that are to be made.

A2 University and departmental regulations, "customary practice" among the faculty in the Department, and the opinions of students were carefully and critically considered in determining the relative seriousness of false positive and false negative classification errors.

A3 Because the scores on the mini-speech tests comprise just one part of students' course grades, no cut scores are needed.

Warrants: equitability

B1 Decisions about which students will progress to the next course are awarded only according to the procedures that have been established, and not on the basis of other considerations.

B2 Students and instructors are fully informed of the procedures for making decisions about which students will progress to the next course whether these procedures are actually followed making these decisions.

B3 Students have equal opportunities to learn or acquire speaking ability in Modern Chinese.

Interpretations

> **Claim 3:** The interpretations about language ability in Modern Chinese are **meaningful** with respect to the course syllabus, **impartial** to the students in the course, **generalizable** to tasks in the language instructional domain, **relevant** to the different kinds of decisions to be made, and **sufficient** for the different kinds of decisions to be made.

Warrants: meaningfulness

A1 The definition of the construct includes (1) freedom from grammatical and pronunciation errors, (2) organization, (3) spontaneity, creativity, and fluency, (4) vocabulary and sentence patterns used, and (5) ability to stay within allotted time. These abilities differ from other possible construct definitions, such as knowledge of the Chinese writing system. This definition of the construct is based on the course syllabus.

A2 The test task specifications clearly specify the mini-speech test procedure that will elicit speaking performance from which we can make inferences about (1) freedom from grammatical and pronunciation errors, (2) organization, (3) spontaneity, creativity, and fluency, (4) vocabulary and sentence patterns used, and (5) ability to stay within allotted time.

A3 The procedures for administering the mini-speech test are followed consistently across classes and different occasions.

A4 The rating scales that are used to score the students' performance on the mini-speech test reflect the five parts of the definition of language ability in Chinese articulated in Warrant A2.

A5 The mini-speech test tasks engage the students in speaking Chinese.

A6 The scores from the mini-speech test can be interpreted as indicators of the students' language ability in Chinese.

A7 The instructors communicate the definition of language ability in Chinese articulated in Warrant A2 in terms that are clearly understandable to the students.

Warrants: impartiality

B1 The mini-speech test tasks do not include response formats or content that may either favor or disfavor some students.

B2 The assessment tasks do not include content that may be offensive (topically, culturally or linguistically inappropriate) to some test takers.

B3 Students are treated impartially during all aspects of the administration of the mini-speech tests.

B4a Students have equal access to information about the test content and procedures, and have equal opportunity to prepare for the mini-speech test.

B4b Students have equal access to the test. It is given as part of the course at no extra cost, in the Chinese classrooms, under conditions with which the students are familiar.

B4c Students have equal opportunity to demonstrate their Chinese speaking.

B5 Interpretations of language ability in Chinese based on the mini-speech tests are equally meaningful across different classes in the Modern Chinese course.

Warrants: generalizability

C1 The characteristics (e.g., input, expected response, type of external interaction) of the mini-speech test tasks correspond closely to those of instructional tasks.

C2 The criteria and procedures for evaluating the responses to the mini-speech test tasks correspond closely to those that instructors have identified as important for assessing performance in other speaking tasks in the instructional setting.

Warrant: relevance

D The interpretations of speaking based on the mini-speech tests provide information that is needed by the course director, instructors, and students to make the decisions articulated in Table 8.3 in Chapter 8.

Warrant: sufficiency

E The interpretation of language ability in Chinese based on the mini-speech test scores is *not* sufficient to make the decisions listed in Table 8.3 in Chapter 8. That is, this interpretation needs to be supplemented with other information gathered by the class instructors.

Assessment records

Claim 4: Scores obtained from students' performance on the mini-speech tests are consistent across different tasks, administrations, instructors/raters, and classes of students.

Warrants: consistency

1 Administrative procedures are followed consistently across different occasions, and for all classes and students.
2 The criteria and procedures for rating students' performance on the mini-speech task are well specified and adhered to.
3 Instructors undergo training at the beginning of each school term.
4 Instructors are trained to avoid bias for or against different groups of students.
5 (Not relevant to this test, since the mini-speech test is essentially a single task.)
6 Ratings of different instructors are consistent.
7 Different ratings by the same instructor are consistent.
8 Scores from different forms of the mini-speech test are consistent.
9 Scores from different administrations of the test are consistent.
10 Ratings of students' performance on the mini-speech test are of comparable consistency across different classes and subgroups of students in the elementary Modern Chinese course.

Bibliography

Alderson, J. C. 1991. 'Bands and scores' in J. C. Alderson and B. North (eds.): *Language Testing in the 1990s: The Communicative Legacy* (pp. 71–86). London: Macmillan Publishers Limited.

——and **L. F. Bachman** (eds.). 2000–6. Cambridge Language Assessment Series. Cambridge: Cambridge University Press.

——**C. Clapham** and **D. Wall.** 1995. *Language Test Construction and Evaluation.* Cambridge: Cambridge University Press.

——and **A. H. Urquhart.** 1985. 'The effect of students' academic discipline on their performance on ESP reading tests.' *Language Testing* 2 (2): 192–204.

——and **D. Wall.** 1993. 'Does washback exist?' *Applied Linguistics*, 14: 115–129.

——1996. Special Issue: 'Washback'. *Language Testing* 13 (3).

American Council on the Teaching of Foreign Languages. 1983. *ACTFL Proficiency Guidelines.* Hastings-on-Hudson, NY: Author.

American Educational Research Association, American Psychological Association, and National Council on Measurement in Education. 1999. *Standards for Educational and Psychological Testing.* Washington, DC: Author.

Archibald, D. A. and **F. M. Newman.** 1988. *Beyond Standardized Testing: Assessing Authentic Academic Achievement in the Secondary School.* Reston, VA: National Association of Secondary School Principals.

Aschbacher, P. R. 1991. 'Performance assessment: state activity, interest, and concerns'. *Applied Measurement in Education* 4: 275–88.

Association of Language Testers in Europe. 1993. 'Principles of good practice for ALTE examinations.' www.alte.org/about_alte/index.cfm: The Association of Language Testers in Europe.

Bachman, L. F. 1990. *Fundamental Considerations in Language Testing.* Oxford: Oxford University Press.

——1991. 'What does language testing have to offer?' *TESOL Quarterly* 25 (4): 671–704.

——2002. 'Alternative interpretations of alternative assessments: some validity issues in educational performance assessments.' *Educational Measurement: Issues and Practice* 21 (3): 5–18.

——2004a. 'Linking observations to interpretations and uses in TESOL research.' *TESOL Quarterly* 38 (4): 723–8.

——2004b. *Statistical Analyses for Language Assessment.* Cambridge: Cambridge University Press.

——2005. 'Building and supporting a case for test use.' *Language Assessment Quarterly* 2 (1): 1–34.

——2006a. 'Generalizability: a journey into the nature of empirical research in applied linguistics' in M. Chalhoub-Deville, C. Chapelle, and P. Duff (eds.): *Inference and Generalizability in Applied Linguistics: Multiple Perspectives* (pp. 165–207). Dordrecht: John Benjamins.

——2006b. 'Linking interpretation and use in educational assessments.' Paper presented at the National Council for Measurement in Education, San Francisco, April.

——2009. 'Generalizability and research use arguments' in K. Ercikan and W.-M. Roth (eds.). *Generalizing from Educational Research: Beyond the Quantitative–Qualitative Opposition.* Mahwah, NJ: Lawrence Erlbaum.

——, **B. K. Lynch,** and **M. Mason.** 1995. 'Investigating variability in tasks and rater judgments in a performance test of foreign language speaking.' *Language Testing* 12: 238–57.

——and **M. Egbert.** 1992. *Education Abroad Program language ability assessment system: Year 1 interim report.* Los Angeles Department of Applied Linguistics & TESL: University of California, Los Angeles.

Bachman, L. F. and **A. S. Palmer.** 1980. 'The construct validation of oral proficiency tests. *TESL Studies* 3, 1–20.

——1981. The construct validation of the FSI oral interview. *Language Learning* 31(1) 67–86.

Bachman, L. F. and **A. S. Palmer.** 1982. 'The construct validation of some components of communicative proficiency.' *TESOL Quarterly* 16 (4): 449–65.

——1983. *Oral Interview Test of Communicative Proficiency in English.* Los Angeles: Authors.

——1996. *Language Testing in Practice: Designing and Developing Useful Language Tests.* Oxford: Oxford University Press.

Baker, E. L., H. F. O'Neil, and **R. L. Linn.** 1993. 'Policy and validity prospects for performance-based assessment.' *American Psychologist* 48 (12): 1210–18.

Bialystok, E. 1990. *Communication Strategies.* Cambridge, MA: Basil Blackwell.

Bond, L. 1995. 'Unintended consequences of performance assessment: issues of bias and fairness.' *Educational Measurement: Issues and Practice* 14 (4): 21–4.

Breiner-Sanders, K. E., J. Pardee Lowe, J. Miles, and **E. Swender.** 2000. 'ACTFL proficiency guidelines—speaking': revised 1999. *Foreign Language Annals* 33: 13–18.

Brown, G. and **G. Yule.** 1983. *Discourse Analysis.* Cambridge: Cambridge University Press.

Brown, H. D. 2000. *Principles of Language Learning and Teaching* (4th edn.). New York: Pearson Education.

Brown, J. D. 1989. 'Improving ESL placement tests using two perspectives.' *TESOL Quarterly* 23: 65–83.

——(ed.) 1998. *New Ways of Classroom Assessment.* Alexandria, VA: TESOL.

——2001. *Using Surveys in Language Teaching.* Cambridge: Cambridge University Press.

——and **Hudson, T.** 2002. *Criterion-referenced Language Testing.* Cambridge: Cambridge University Press.

——, **J. M. Norris,** and **W. J. Bonk.** 2002. *An Investigation of Second Language Task-based Performance Assessments* (Vol. SLTCC Technical Report 24). Honolulu: Second Language Teaching & Curriculum Center: University of Hawai'i at Manoa.

——and **T. S. Rodgers.** 2003. *Doing Second Language Research.* Oxford: Oxford University Press.

Bygate, M., P. Skehan, and **M. Swain.** (eds.) 2001. *Researching Pedagogic Tasks: Second Language Learning, Teaching and Testing.* Harlow: Longman.

Canale, M. 1983. 'On some dimensions of language proficiency' in J. W. Oller (ed.). *Issues in Language Testing Research.* Rowley, MA: Newbury House.

——1988. 'The measurement of communicative competence.' *Annual Review of Applied Linguistics* 8: 67–84.

——and **M. Swain.** 1980. 'Theoretical bases of communicative approaches to second language teaching and testing.' *Applied Linguistics* 1 (1): 1–47.

Carroll, J. B. 1961. 'Fundamental considerations in testing English proficiency of foreign students' in *Testing the English Proficiency of Foreign Students* (pp. 30–40). Washington, DC: Center for Applied Linguistics.

——1968. 'The psychology of language testing' in A. Davies (ed.). *Language Testing Symposium: A Psycholinguistic Approach* (pp. 46–69). London: Oxford University Press.

——1993. *Human Cognitive Abilities: A Survey of Factor-analytic Studies.* Cambridge: Cambridge University Press.

Chalhoub-Deville, M. 1999. *Issues in Computer-Adaptive Testing of Reading Proficiency.* Cambridge: University of Cambridge Local Examinations Syndicate and Cambridge University Press.

Chapelle, C. A. and **D. Douglas.** 2006. *Assessing Language Ability by Computer.* Cambridge: Cambridge University Press.

Cheng, L. 1999. 'Changing assessment: washback on teacher perceptions and actions.' *Teaching and Teacher Education* 15: 253–71.

——, **Y. Watanabe,** and **A. Curtis.** (eds.) 2004. *Washback in Language Testing: Research Contexts and Methods*. Mahwah, NJ: Lawrence Erlbaum Associates.

Christison, M. A. and **A. S. Palmer.** 2005. Teaching assistants' handbook. Department of Linguistics: University of Utah.

Cizek, G. J. 1996. 'Standard-setting guidelines.' *Educational Measurement: Issues and Practice* 15 (1): 13–21.

——(ed.). 2001. *Setting Performance Standards*. Mahwah, NJ: Lawrence Erlbaum Associates.

Clark, J. L. D. 1979. 'Direct vs. semi-direct tests of speaking ability' in E. Brière and F. B. Hinofotis (eds.): *Concepts in Language Testing: Some Recent Studies*. Washington, DC: TESOL.

Cohen, A. D. 1984. 'On taking tests: what the students report.' *Language Testing* 1 (1): 70–81.

——1994. *Assessing Language Ability in the Classroom* (2nd edn.). Boston: Heinle & Heinle.

——1998. *Strategies in Learning and Using a Second Language*. New York: Addison-Wesley.

Coombe, C. A. and **N. J. Hubley.** (eds.). 2003. *Assessment practices*. Arlington, VA: Teachers of English to Speakers of Other Languages.

——(eds.). 2003b. *Teachers of English to Speakers of Other Languages*. Alexandria, VA: TESOL.

Creswell, J. W. 2008. *Research Design: Qualitative, Quantitative, and Mixed Methods approaches*. Beverly Hills, CA: Sage Publications.

Crookes, G. V. and **S. Gass.** 1993a. *Tasks and Language Learning: Integrating Theory and Practice*. Clevedon: Multilingual Matters.

——1993b. *Tasks in a Pedagogical Context: Integrating Theory and Practice*. Clevedon: Multilingual Matters.

Darling-Hammond, L., J. Ancess, and **B. Falk.** 1995. *Authentic Assessment in an Era of Restructuring*. Alexandria, VA: Association for Supervision and Curriculum Development.

Davies, A. 1997. Special Issue: 'Ethics in language testing.' *Language Testing* 14 (3).

Davison, A. and **G. Green.** (eds.). 1988. *Linguistic Complexity and Text Comprehension: Readability Issues Reconsidered*. Mahwah, NJ: Lawrence Erlbaum Associates.

Denzin, N. K. and **Y. S. Lincoln.** (eds.). 2005. *The Sage Handbook of Qualitative Research* (3rd edn.). Newbury Park, CA: Sage Publications.

Dörnyei, Z. 2007. *Research Methods in Applied Linguistics*. Oxford: Oxford University Press.

Douglas, D. 2000. *Assessing Language for Specific Purposes: Theory and Practice*. Cambridge: Cambridge University Press.

——and **V. Hegelheimer.** 2007. 'Assessing language using computer technlogy.' *Annual Review of Applied Linguistics*: 27: 115–32.

Doye, P. 1991. 'Authenticity in foreign language testing' in S. Anivan (ed.): *Current Developments in Language Testing* (pp. 103–10). Singapore: SEAMEO Regional Language Centre.

Dunbar, S. B., D. Koretz, and **H. D. Hoover.** 1991. 'Quality control in the development and use of performance assessments.' *Applied Measurement in Education* 4: 289–304.

Eckert, P. and **J. Rickford.** 2001. *Style and Sociolinguistic Variation*. Cambridge: Cambridge University Press.

Educational Testing Service. 2000. *ETS Standards for Quality and Fairness*. Princeton: Author.

——2002. *ETS Standards for Quality and Fairness*. Princeton: Author.

——2003. *Educational Testing Service Fairness Review Guidelines*. Princeton: Author.

Elder, C. 1997. 'What does test bias have to do with fairness?' *Language Testing* 14 (3): 261–77.

——, **Brown, A., E. Grove, K. Hill, N. Iwashita, T. Lumley, T. McNamara,** and **K. O'Loughlin.** (eds.). 2001. *Experimenting with Uncertainty: Essays in Honour of Alan Davies*. Cambridge: Cambridge University Press.

Freedman, A. and **P. Medway** (eds.). 1994. *Genre and the New Rhetoric*. London: Taylor & Francis.

Frey, N. and **D. Fisher.** 2003. 'Linking assessments with instruction in a multilingual elementary school' in C. A. Coombe and N. J. Hubley (eds.): *Assessment Practices* (pp. 63–74). Alexandria, VA: Teachers of English to Speakers of Other Languages.

Fulcher, G. 2003. *Testing Second Language Speaking*. London: Pearson Longman.

Gass, S. M. and **A. Mackey.** 2000. *Stimulated Recall Methodology in Second Language Research*. Hillsdale, NJ: Lawrence Erlbaum Associates.

Glass, G. V. and **K. D. Hopkins.** 2008. *Statistical Methods in Education and Psychology* (3rd edn.). New York: Prentice-Hall, Inc.

Glatthorn, A., F. Boschee, and **B. Whitehead.** 2006. *Curriculum Leadership: Development and Implementation*. Beverly Hills, CA: Sage Publications, Chapter 5.

Goodwin, C. and **M. H. Goodwin.** 1992. 'Assessments and the construction of context' in A. Duranti and C. Goodwin (eds.): *Rethinking Context: Language as an Interactive Phenomenon* (pp. 147–89). Cambridge: Cambridge University Press.

Graves, K. 2000. *Designing Language Courses: A Guide for Teachers*. Boston: Heinle & Heinle Publishers, Chapter 6.

Green, A. 1998. *Verbal Protocol Analysis in Language Testing Research: A Handbook*. Cambridge: Cambridge University Press.

Gupta, K., C. M. Sleezer, and **D. F. Russ-Eft.** 2007. *A Practical Guide to Needs Assessment*. San Francisco: Preiffer.

Hambleton, R. K. and **M. J. Pitoniak.** 2006. 'Setting performance standards' in R. L. Brennan (ed.): *Educational Measurement* (4th edn.). American Council on Education: Praeger.

Hamp-Lyons, L. 1997. 'Ethics in language testing' in C. Clapham and D. Corson (eds.): *Encyclopedia of Language and Education* (Vol. vii: *Language Testing and Assessment* (pp. 323–33). Dordrecht: Kluwer Academic Publishers.

——and **Davies, A.** 2008. 'The Englishes of English tests: bias revisited.' *World Englishes* 27 (1): 26–39.

Hatch, E. and **A. Lazaraton.** 1991. *The Research Manual: Design and Statistics for Applied Linguistics*. New York: Newbury House Publishers.

Hawkey, R. 2006. *Impact Theory and Practice*. Cambridge: Cambridge University Press.

Heider, K. G. 1988. 'The Rashomon effect: when ethnographers disagree.' *American Anthropologist* 90 (1): 73–81.

Hoejke, B. and **K. Linnell.** 1994. '"Authenticity" in language testing: Evaluating spoken language tests for international teaching assistants.' *TESOL Quarterly* 28 (1): 103–26.

Hsiao, T.-Y. and **Oxford, R. L.** 2002. 'Comparing theories of language learning strategies: a confirmatory factor analysis.' *Modern Language Journal* 86 (3): 368–83.

Hudson, T. and **J. D. Brown** (eds.). 2001. *A Focus on Language Test Development*. Honolulu: Second Language Teaching & Curriculum Center, University of Hawai'i at Manoa.

Hughes, A. 2003. *Testing for Language Teachers* (2nd edn.). Cambridge: Cambridge University Press.

Hughes, R. E. (ed.). 1999. *What is Literacy?* Washington, DC: International Reading Association.

Hymes, D. H. 1972. 'On communicative competence' in J. B. Pride and J. Holmes (eds.): *Sociolinguistics* (pp. 269–93). Harmondsworth: Penguin.

Interagency Language Roundtable. Interagency Language Roundtable Language Skill Level Descriptions: Speaking. Retrieved 8 August, 2008, from http://www.govtilr.org/Skills/ILRscale2.htm#2.

International Language Testing Association. 2000. ILTA Code of Ethics: *Language Testing Update* 27: 14–22. http://www.iltaonline.com/code.pdf.

——2005. ILTA Code of Practice. Retrieved May 24, 2008, from http://www.iltaonline.com/ILTA-COP-ver3-21Jun2006.pdf.

Jacoby, S. and **T. F. McNamara.** 1999. 'Locating competence.' *English for Specific Purposes* 18 (3): 213–41.

Jamieson, J. 2005. 'Trends in computer-based second language assessment.' *Annual Review of Applied Linguistics*, 25: 228–42.

Johnson, D. 1992. *Approaches to Research in Second Language Learning*. London: Longman.

Kane, M. 2002. 'Validating high-stakes testing programs.' *Educational Measurement: Issues and Practice* 21 (1): 31–41.

Kane, M. 2006. 'Validation' in R. L. Brennan (ed.): *Educational Measurement* (4th edn.). New York: American Council on Education and Praeger Publishers.

——, **T. Crooks,** and **A. Cohen.** 1999. 'Validating measures of performance.' *Educational Measurement: Issues and Practice* 18 (2): 5–17.

Kirk, J. and **M. L. Miller.** 1999. *Reliability and Validity in Qualitative Research*. Newbury Park, CA: Sage Publications.

Koenig, J. A. (ed.). 2002. *Reporting Test Results for Students with Disabilities and English-Language Learners*. Washington, DC: National Academy Press.

—— and **L. F. Bachman.** (eds.) 2004. *Keeping Score for All: The Effects of Inclusion and Accommodation Policies on Large-scale Educational Assessment*. Washington, DC: National Research Council, National Academies Press.

Kohonen, V. 1997. 'Authentic assessment as an integration of language learning, teaching, evaluation and the teacher's professional growth' in A. Huhta, V. Kohonen, L. Kurki-Suonio, and S. Luoma (eds.): *Current Developments and Alternatives in Language Assessment: Proceedings of LTRC* 96 (pp. 7–22). Jyvaskyla: University of Jyvaskyla.

Kubiszyn, T. and **G. D. Borich.** 2009. *Educational Testing and Measurement: Classroom Application and Practice* (9th edn.). New York: Wiley.

Kunnan, A. J. 2000a. 'Fairness and justice for all' in A. J. Kunnan (ed.): *Fairness and Validation in Language Assessment* (pp. 1–14). Cambridge: Cambridge University Press.

—— (ed.) 2000b. Fairness and validation in language assessment: selected papers from the 19th Language Testing Research Colloquium, Orlando. Cambridge: Cambridge University Press.

—— 2004. 'Test fairness' in M. Milanovic and C. Weir (eds.): *European Language Testing in a Global Context* (pp. 27–48). Cambridge: Cambridge University Press.

Lado, R. 1961. *Language Testing*. New York: McGraw-Hill.

Language Testing. 1985. Special issue on Authenticity. *Language Testing* 2 (1).

Lazaraton, A. 2002. *A Qualitative Approach to the Validation of Oral Language Tests*. Cambridge: Cambridge University Press.

Lewkowicz, J. A. 2000. 'Authenticity in language testing: some outstanding questions.' *Language Testing* 17 (1): 43–64.

Linn, R. L. 1994. 'Performance assessment: policy promises and technical measurement standards.' *Educational Researcher* 23 (9): 4–14.

——, **Baker, E. L.,** and **S. B. Dunbar.** 1991. 'Complex, performance-based assessment: expectations and validation criteria.' *Educational Researcher* 20 (8): 15–21.

—— and **E. Burton.** 1994. 'Performance-based assessment: implications of task specificity.' *Educational Measurement: Issues and Practice* 13 (1): 5–8, 15.

Long, M. 2006. *Second Language Needs Analysis*. Cambridge: Cambridge University Press.

Lowe, P. Jr. 1988. 'The unassimilated history' in P. Lowe, Jr. and C. W. Stansfield (eds.): *Second Language Proficiency: Current Issues* (pp. 11–51). Englewood Cliffs, NJ: Prentice-Hall Regents.

Luoma, S. 2004a. *Assessing Speaking*. Cambridge: Cambridge University Press.

—— 2004b. *Statistical Analyses for Language Assessment*. Cambridge: Cambridge University Press.

McKay, P. 2006. *Assessing Young Learners*. Cambridge: Cambridge University Press.

McNamara, T. F. 1996. *Measuring Second Language Performance*. London: Longman.

—— and **K. Roever.** 2006. *Language Testing: The Social Dimension*. Malden, MA: Blackwell.

Messick, S. 1989. 'Validity' in R. L. Linn (ed.): *Educational Measurement* (3rd edn., pp. 13–103). New York: American Council on Education and Macmillan Publishing Company.

—— 1994a. 'Alternative modes of assessment, uniform standards of validity.' Paper presented at the Conference on Evaluating Alternatives to Traditional Testing for Selection, Bowling Green State University, October 25–6.

—— 1994b. 'The interplay of evidence and consequences in the validation of performance assessments.' *Educational Researcher* 23 (2): 13–23.

—— 1995. 'Standards of validity and the validity of standards in performance assessment.' *Educational Measurement: Issues and Practice* 14 (4): 5–8.

Miller, M. D., N. E. Gronlund, and **R. L. Linn.** 2008. *Measurement and Assessment in Teaching* (10th edn.). Westport, CT: Prentice-Hall, Inc.

Mislevy, R. J., L. S. Steinberg, and **R. G. Almond.** 2003. 'On the structure of educational assessments.' *Measurement: Interdisciplinary Research and Perspectives* 1 (1): 3–62.

Morrow, K. 1986. 'The evaluation of tests of communicative performance' in M. Portal (ed.): *Innovations in Language Testing* (pp. 1–13). Windsor: NFER-Nelson.

Moss, P. A. 1992. 'Shifting conceptions of validity in educational measurement: implications for performance assessment.' *Review of Educational Research* 62: 229–58.

Nevo, N. 1989. 'Test-taking strategies on a multiple-choice test of reading comprehension.' *Language Testing*, 6(2): 199–215.

Norris, J. M., J. D. Brown, T. Hudson. and **J. Yoshioka.** 1998. *Designing Second Language Performance Assessments* (Vol. SLTCC Technical Report #18). Honolulu: Second Language Teaching & Curriculum Center, University of Hawai'i at Manoa.

Norton, B. and **P. Stein.** 1998. 'Why the "Monkeys Passage" bombed: tests, genres and teaching' in A. J. Kunnan (ed.): *Validation in Language Assessment* (pp. 231–52). Mahwah, NJ: Lawrence Erlbaum Associates.

Nunan, D. 1992. *Research Methods in Language Learning*. Cambridge: Cambridge University Press.

Oller, J. W. (ed.). 1983. *Issues in Language Testing Research*. Rowley, MA: Newbury House.

O'Malley, J. M. and **L. V. Pierce.** 1996. *Authentic Assessment for English Language Learners*. New York: Addison-Wesley.

Orlikowski, W. J. and **J. Yates.** 1994. 'Genre repertoire: the structuring of communicative practices in organizations.' *Administrative Science Quarterly* 39 (4): 541–74.

Oxford, R. 1996. *Language Learning Strategies Around the World: Cross-cultural Perspectives*. Honolulu: University of Hawai'i Press.

Page, E. B. 1968. 'The use of the computer in analyzing student essays.' International Review of Education / Internationale Zeitschrift für Erziehungswissenschaft / Revue Internationale de l'Éducation, 14(2): 210–25.

Palmer, A. S. 1972. 'Testing communication.' *International Review of Applied Linguistics and Language Teaching* 10: 35–45.

—— 1981. 'Measurements of reliability and validity in two picture-description tests of oral communication' in A. S. Palmer, P. J. M. Groot, and G. A. Trosper (eds.): *The Construct Validation of Tests of Communicative Competence* (pp. 127–39). Washington, DC: TESOL.

——**, P. J. Groot,** and **G. A. Trosper** (eds.): 1981. 'The construct validation of tests of communicative competence.' Washington, DC: TESOL.

Patton, M. Q. 2001. *Qualitative Research and Evaluation Methods* (3rd edn.). Beverly Hills, CA: Sage Publications.

Pawley, A. and **F. H. Syder.** 1983. 'Two puzzles for linguistic theory: nativelike selection and nativelike fluency' in J. C. Richards and R. W. Schmidt (eds.): *Language and Communication* (pp. 191–226). New York: Longman.

Perry, F. L. 2005. *Research in Applied Linguistics: Becoming a Discerning Consumer*. Hillsdale, NJ: Lawrence Erlbaum.

Popham, W. J. 1999. *Modern Educational Measurement: Practical Guidelines for Educational Leaders* (3rd edn.). White Plains, NY: Allyn & Bacon.

Purpura, J. E. 1999. *Modeling the Relationships Between Test Takers' Reported Cognitive and Metacognitive Strategy Use and Performance on Language Tests*. Cambridge: University of Cambridge Local Examinations Syndicate and Cambridge University Press.

Richards, J. C. 2001. *Curriculum Development in Language Teaching*. Cambridge: Cambridge University Press, Chapter 3.

Savignon, S. J. 1972. *Communicative Competence: An Experiment in Foreign Language Teaching*. Philadelphia: Center for Curriculum Development.

——1983. *Communicative Competence: Theory and Classroom Practice*. Reading, MA: Addison-Wesley.

Schumann, J. H. 1997. *The Neurobiology of Affect In Language*. Malden, MA: Blackwell.

Shavelson, R. J., G. P. Baxter, and **J. Pine.** 1992. 'Performance assessments: political rhetoric and measurement reality.' *Educational Researcher* 21 (4): 22–7.

Shohamy, E. 1984. 'Does the testing method make a difference? The case of reading comprehension.' *Language Testing* 1 (2): 147–70.

——2001. *The Power of Tests: A Critical Perspective on the Uses of Language Tests*. London: Pearson.

——and **Reves, T.** 1985. 'Authentic language tests: where from and where to?' *Language Testing* 2 (1): 48–59.

Skehan, P. 1989. *Individual Differences in Second-language Learning*. London: Edward Arnold.

——1998. *A Cognitive Approach to Language Learning*. Oxford: Oxford University Press.

Soriano, F. I. 1995. *Conducting Needs Assessments: A Multidisciplinary Approach*. Beverly Hills, CA: Sage Publications.

Spolsky, B. 1985. 'The limits of authenticity in language testing.' *Language Testing* 2 (1): 31–40.

Sternberg, R. J. 1985. *Beyond IQ: A Triarchic Theory of Human Intelligence*. New York: Cambridge University Press.

——1988. *The Triarchic Mind: A New Theory of Human Intelligence*. New York: Viking.

Sternfeld, S. 1989. Test Packet for the University of Utah's Immersion/Multiliteracy Program. Photocopied materials.

——1992. 'An experiment in foreign language education: the University of Utah's immersion/multiliteracy program.' in R. J. Courchêne, J. I. Glidden, J. St. John, and C. Thérien (eds.): *Comprehension-based Language Teaching/L'enseignement des langues secondes axé sur la compréhension* (pp. 407–32). Ottawa: University of Ottawa Press.

Stevenson, D. K. 1985. 'Authenticity, validity and a tea party.' *Language Testing* 2 (1): 41–7.

Swain, M. 1985. 'Large-scale communicative language testing: a case study' in Y. P. Lee, A. C. Y. Fok, R. Lord, and G. Low (eds.): *New Directions in Language Testing*. Oxford: Pergamon.

Swales, J. M. 1990. *Genre Analysis: English in Academic and Research Settings*. Cambridge: Cambridge University Press.

——2004. *Research Genres: Explorations and Applications*: Cambridge University Press.

Taylor, C., I. Kirsch, D, Eignor, and **J. Jamieson.** 1999. 'Examining the relationship between computer familiarity and performance on computer-based language tasks.' *Language Learning* 49 (2): 219–74.

Taylor, L. 2009. 'Developing assessment literacy.' *Annual Review of Applied Linguistics*, 29: 21–36.

Terwilliger, J. 1997. Semantics, psychometrics and assessment reform: a close look at "authentic" assessments. *Educational Researcher* 26 (8): 24–7.

Toulmin, S. E. 2003. *The Uses of Argument* (updated edn.). Cambridge: Cambridge University Press.

Valenti, S., F. Neri, and **A. Cucchiarelli.** 2003. 'An overview of current research on automated essay scoring.' *Journal of Information Technology Education*, 2: 319–30.

van Dijk, T. A. 1977. *Text and Context: Explorations in the Semantics and Pragmatics of Discourse*. London: Longman.

Vaughan, C. 1991. 'Holistic assessment: what goes on in the raters' minds?' in L. Hamp-Lyons (ed.): *Assessing Second Language Writing in Academic Contexts*. Norwood, NJ: Ablex.

Wall, D. 1996. 'Introducing new tests into traditional systems: insights from general education and from innovation theory.' *Language Testing* 13 (3): 334–54.

——1997. 'Impact and washback in language testing' in C. Clapham and D. Corson (eds.): *Encyclopedia of Language and Education* (Vol. vii: *Language Testing and Assessment*, pp. 291–302). Dordrecht: Kluwer Academic Publishers.

——and **J. C. Alderson.** 1993. 'Examining washback: the Sri Lankan impact study.' *Language Testing* 10 (1): 41–69.

Wang, Z. 2008. Exploring the role of overt articulation in L2 output practice: a comparison between task repetition and strategic planning. Paper presented at the Annual Meeting of the American Association for Applied Linguistics, April.

Weigle, S. C. 2002. *Assessing Writing*. Cambridge: Cambridge University Press.

Weigle, S. C. and **G. Nelson.** 2001. 'Academic writing for university examinations' in I. Leki (ed.): *Academic Writing Programs* (pp. 12–135). Alexandria, VA: TESOL.

Weir, C. J. 1990. *Communicative Language Testing*. New York: Prentice Hall.

Widdowson, H. G. 1978. *Teaching Language as Communication*. Oxford: Oxford University Press.

——1983. *Learning Purpose and Language Use*. Oxford: Oxford University Press.

——2001. 'Communicative language testing: the art of the possible' in C. Elder, A. Brown, E. Grove, K. Hill, N. Iwashita, T. Lumley, T. McNamara, and K. O'Loughlin (eds.): *Experimenting with Uncertainty: Essays in Honour of Alan Davies* (pp. 12–21). Cambridge: Cambridge University Press.

Wiggins, G. 1989. 'A true test: toward more authentic and equitable assessment.' *Phi Delta Kappan*, 1989 (May): 703–13.

——1993. 'Assessment: authenticity, context and validity.' *Phi Delta Kappan*, 1993 (November): 200–14.

Witkin, B. R. and **J. W. Altschuld.** 1995. *Planning and Conducting Needs Assessments: A Practical Guide*. Beverly Hills, CA: Sage Publications.

Zukalak, B. L. and **J. S. Samuels.** (eds.): 1988. *Readability: Its Past, Present, and Future*. Newark, DE: International Reading Association.

Index

Note : The end of Chapter exercises are not indexed